GOSPEL WITNESS
THROUGH THE AGES

GOSPEL WITNESS THROUGH THE AGES

a history of evangelism

David M. Gustafson

William B. Eerdmans Publishing Company
Grand Rapids, Michigan

Wm. B. Eerdmans Publishing Co.
4035 Park East Court SE, Grand Rapids, Michigan 49546
www.eerdmans.com

Published 2022
Printed in the United States of America

28 27 26 25 24 23 22 1 2 3 4 5 6 7

ISBN 978-0-8028-7728-4

Library of Congress Cataloging-in-Publication Data

Names: Gustafson, David M., 1959– author.
Title: Gospel witness through the ages : a history of evangelism / David M. Gustafson.
Description: Grand Rapids, Michigan : William B. Eerdmans Publishing Company, [2022] | Includes bibliographical references and index. | Summary: "A definitive history of Christian evangelism that introduces readers to noteworthy persons, movements, and methods from over two thousand years of church history"—Provided by publisher.
Identifiers: LCCN 2021038219 | ISBN 9780802877284
Subjects: LCSH: Evangelistic work—History. | BISAC: RELIGION / Christian Ministry / Evangelism | RELIGION / Christian Church / History
Classification: LCC BV3770 .G87 2022 | DDC 269/.2—dc23
LC record available at https://lccn.loc.gov/2021038219

Contents

Preface

Our perception of evangelism is shaped by models we have seen. For the past two thousand years, Christians have practiced a variety of means for communicating the good news of Jesus Christ. I have written this book to expand readers' perceptions of the evangelistic task that Jesus has given to his church, to appreciate and learn from the contributions of earlier generations of Christians, and to shape our identity as gospel witnesses today. The history of evangelism should lead us to caution too, alerting us to the mistakes and abuses of the past that we would do well to avoid.

The history of evangelism has become an important area of study recently. The increased interest has come as the church faces the challenges of religious pluralism, persecution, and defending the gospel. The cultural shift in the West toward post-Christendom has meant that the church no longer has the advantage of general acceptance that it once did. Increasingly, Christians must proclaim the gospel with little or no support, except from God, one another, and the message of the gospel itself. In some regions of the world, governments and societies are even hostile to the church and our message. For these reasons, we find ourselves identifying with Christians of earlier centuries, especially those of the pre-Constantinian era.

I was introduced to the history of evangelism when I was a student at Trinity Evangelical Divinity School (TEDS). Professor John D. Woodbridge opened up to me the history of evangelism through his lectures about the martyrs and apologists of the early church. Then as a doctoral student at Fuller Theological Seminary, C. Peter Wagner assigned readings that included *Evangelism in the Early Church* by Michael Green and *Christianizing the Roman Empire* by Ramsey MacMullen, further opening the subject to me.

My doctoral studies in church history at Linköpings universitet with professor Kjell O. Lejon gave me the opportunity to write a dissertation on the American evangelist D. L. Moody. Subsequently I have taught courses in church history and the history of preaching. While at the University of Houston, I taught a course titled Bible in Western Culture, which expanded my understanding of the diverse and creative ways that Christians have communicated the gospel during the past twenty centuries.

At TEDS, in addition to other courses, I teach History of Evangelism. I am grateful to my former dean, Graham Cole, for this opportunity and to my colleagues Craig Ott, Alice Ott, Harold A. Netland, Tite Tiénou, and Manuel Rauchholz for their support. I am grateful for my students who have read drafts of this book and contributed to writing the discussion questions. In particular, I wish to thank Chris Hatch, William Green, Sharon Gustafson, and Taylor Bradman for proofreading the manuscript. I thank my colleagues Mark Teasdale at Garrett-Evangelical Theological Seminary and Mary Lederleitner at Wheaton College, as well as Paul Barger at Cru City Austin, for proofreading sections of the book. Finally, I wish to thank James Starr and Lars-Göran Sundberg, who hosted me at Johannelunds teologiska högskola in Uppsala, Sweden, during my writing sabbatical.

Much of the source material for this book has come from textbooks that I have used to teach on the subject. I have made generous use of footnotes not simply to give authors proper credit but to direct readers to additional resources. I am grateful to Eerdmans acquiring editor David Bratt and to Ryan Davis, copyeditor, for their expertise during the publishing process. I sincerely hope that this book will be a resource for seminary students, Christian leaders, pastors, evangelists, and church staff. As you become better acquainted with the Christians and movements described in this book, I hope you will grow in your gospel identity and take a larger role in Jesus's commission to preach the gospel to all creation.

David M. Gustafson
Deerfield, Illinois

Abbreviations

ANF	*The Ante-Nicene Fathers*. Edited by Alexander Roberts, James Donaldson, and A. C. Coxe. 10 vols. Buffalo: Christian Literature, 1885–1887.
HCC	*History of the Christian Church*. By Philip Schaff and David S. Schaff. 8 vols. New York: Charles Scribner's Sons, 1882–1910.
NPNF[1]	*Nicene and Post-Nicene Fathers*, Series 1. Edited by Philip Schaff. 14 vols. 1886–1889. Reprint, Peabody, MA: Hendrickson, 1994.
NPNF[2]	*The Nicene and Post-Nicene Fathers*, Series 2. Edited by Philip Schaff and Henry Wace. 14 vols. 1890–1900. Reprint, Peabody, MA: Hendrickson, 1994.

Introduction

Foundations to the History of Evangelism

> My prayer is not that you [Father] take them [my disciples] out of the world but that you protect them from the evil one. They are not of the world, even as I am not of it. Sanctify them by the truth; your word is truth. As you sent me into the world, I have sent them into the world. For them I sanctify myself, that they too may be truly sanctified. My prayer is not for them alone. I pray also for those who will believe in me through their message.
>
> —Jesus Christ[1]

The church began and has existed as God's people redeemed by Jesus Christ and empowered by the Holy Spirit to worship and serve the triune God. Jesus intended Christian evangelism to be a defining mark of the church ever since he told his disciples, "The Messiah will suffer and rise from the dead on the third day, and repentance for the forgiveness of sins will be preached in his name to all nations, beginning at Jerusalem. You are witnesses of these things" (Luke 24:46–48).

The church is inextricably tied to the history of evangelism. The history of the church cannot be understood apart from its evangelistic witness.[2] To reflect on the history of evangelism is to reflect on the church because

1. John 17:15–20.

2. Richard R. Cook, "The Great Commission in Asia," in *The Great Commission: Evangelicals and the History of World Missions*, ed. Martin I. Klauber and Scott M. Manetsch (Nashville: B&H, 2008), 150.

evangelism is not accidental, coincidental, or additional but essential to the church's nature. There is no church apart from the events of Jesus's incarnation, crucifixion, and resurrection, and no church apart from the proclamation of these events. In other words, there is no church without witness to the gospel of Jesus Christ.[3]

Evangelism is the activity of announcing good news.[4] The Greek word *euangelizomai* means "to evangelize" or to proclaim the evangel (*euangelion*), "the good news that Jesus is the Messiah," and "the good news of peace through Jesus Christ, who is Lord of all" (Acts 5:42; 10:36).[5] It is communication of the message "that Christ died for our sins according to the Scriptures, that he was buried, that he was raised on the third day" (1 Cor. 15:3–4). It is the verbal proclamation of his person and life, communicated in words that are meaningful to listeners.[6] The Lausanne Covenant defines evangelism as "spread[ing] the good news that Jesus Christ died for our sins and was raised from the dead according to the Scriptures, and that as the reigning Lord he now offers the forgiveness of sins and the liberating gift of the Spirit to all who repent and believe."[7]

In the history of the church, the word *evangelize* and its cognate *evangelization* have taken a further meaning. These words have been used to describe a positive response to the gospel, meaning the "conversion" of peoples; the good news is not only announced but accepted. A definition of evangelism in this sense was given in 1918 by the Anglican Archbishops' Committee of In-

3. David M. Gustafson, "Missionality of Apostolicity," *Theofilos* 9, no. 1 (2017): 95.

4. The English word *evangelism*, according to the Oxford English Dictionary, dates back to the mid-seventeenth century when Francis Bacon wrote in his book titled *New Atlantis* that England was "saved from infidelitie . . . through the Apostolicall and Miraculous Evangelisme of S. Bartholomew." David Male and Paul Weston, *The Word's Out: Principles and Strategies for Effective Evangelism Today* (Abingdon, UK: Bible Reading Fellowship, 2019), 46–47.

5. G. Friedrich, "*Euangelizomai*," in *Theological Dictionary of the New Testament: Abridged in One Volume*, ed. Gerhard Kittel and Gerhard Friedrich, trans. Geoffrey W. Bromiley (Grand Rapids: Eerdmans, 1985), 267.

6. Several Greek words describe activities related to evangelism in reference to the gospel. These include *laleō*, "to speak" (Acts 4:1), *didaskō*, "to teach" (Acts 4:2), *kērussō*, "to proclaim" (Acts 8:5), *katangellō*, "to announce publicly" (Acts 17:3), *diamartyromai*, "to testify solemnly or bear witness" (Acts 10:42; 18:5), and *dialegomai*, "to reason" (Acts 18:4). David M. Gustafson, "Church Growth by Conversion: Creating Strategies That Observe the Principles of Evangelism" (DMin diss., Fuller Theological Seminary, 1995), 9n14.

7. Timothy P. Weber, "Evangelism," in *Evangelical Dictionary of Theology*, 2nd ed., ed. Walter A. Elwell (Grand Rapids: Baker Academic, 2001), 410.

quiry into the Evangelistic Work of the Church, which stated, "To evangelize is so to present Christ Jesus in the power of the Holy Spirit, that men [and women] *shall come to put their trust* in God through Him, to accept Him as their Savior, and serve Him as their King in the fellowship of His Church."[8] In other words, evangelism is "to win souls"—not simply to proclaim the gospel but to persuade people to become Christians.

The difference of these definitions lies between the essence of evangelism, which is the faithful proclamation of the good news, and the goal of evangelism, which is for people to accept Jesus Christ as King and Savior.[9] Since the Bible's use of *evangelize* refers to its essence rather than its goal, that is the normative meaning in this book.[10] However, certain sources and citations speak of the "evangelization" of peoples, meaning their conversion to Christian faith.

The word *evangelize* also has been used in a broad sense to encompass activities that positively affect the church's witness to Jesus Christ and its credible presence in the world. The gospel may be embodied in charitable deeds that are catalytic to the church's verbal witness. These activities must be tied to the verbal proclamation of the gospel for them to be considered evangelistic.

The Old Testament and Gospel Witness

There is no Christian church and no New Testament apart from Israel and the Hebrew Scriptures, the Old Testament. So, one may speak of "pre-Christian evangelism" that happened prior to the incarnation of Jesus Christ. Of course, this raises questions about the relationship between Israel and the church, and about their continuity and discontinuity.[11] While this book

8. Darrell L. Guder, "Incarnation and the Church's Evangelistic Mission," in *The Study of Evangelism: Exploring a Missional Practice of the Church*, ed. Paul W. Chilcote and Laceye C. Warner (Grand Rapids: Eerdmans, 2008), 177 (emphasis mine).

9. William J. Abraham, *The Logic of Evangelism* (Grand Rapids: Eerdmans, 1989), 40; John R. W. Stott, *Christian Mission in the Modern World* (Downers Grove, IL: InterVarsity Press, 2008), 62.

10. J. I. Packer, *Evangelism and the Sovereignty of God* (Downers Grove, IL: InterVarsity Press, 1975), 40. While the Bible shows a correlation between the proclamation of the gospel and positive results, it also describes the proclamation of the gospel with no correlation to results. The conclusion is that evangelization is not contingent on results (see Acts 8:25, 40; 10:36; 14:7; Rom. 15:19–20).

11. See John S. Feinberg, ed., *Continuity and Discontinuity: Perspectives on the Relationship Between the Old and New Testaments* (Westchester, IL: Crossway, 1988).

examines the history of Christian evangelism, we begin by examining briefly the background of Israel's evangelism, particularly the examples of certain patriarchs and prophets of Israel who foreshadowed or pointed to the gospel and Christian evangelism.[12]

The Great Commission that Jesus gave to his disciples certainly required more detail about him and his work of redemption than pre-Christian evangelism (Matt. 28:18–20; Mark 16:15; Luke 24:46–48). Furthermore, Jesus sent his disciples outward, making the church's witness centrifugal, moving from Jerusalem to the nations and to the ends of the earth (Matt. 24:14; Acts 1:8). In contrast, the witness of Israel was centripetal, moving gentile nations to the center, inviting gentiles to Jerusalem to worship Yahweh, the God of Israel. In other words, Israel was to be a "kingdom of priests" and a "light for the Gentiles" in order to draw them to God (Exod. 19:4–6; Isa. 42:6; 49:6; cf. Ps. 96:3–10).[13] While the church today is also a "royal priesthood" and the "light of the world" (1 Pet. 2:9; Matt. 5:14), Jesus sends it outward with the gospel to the nations, requiring it to cross geographical and cultural boundaries, going to "the farthest parts of the earth" (Acts 1:8 NET). While there have been points of continuity with Israel, Jesus's Great Commission to the church is unique.[14]

Promises and Prophecies

Evangelism is the act of announcing the good news of Jesus Christ, who is Israel's Messiah. Israel received from God promises and prophecies—written in the Hebrew Scriptures—that pointed to the gospel of Jesus and Christian evangelism.[15] The apostle Paul spoke of Israel's embryonic form of evangelism when he said, "But God has helped me to this very day; so I stand here and testify to small and great alike. I am saying nothing beyond what the prophets and Moses said would happen—that the Messiah would suffer and, as the first to rise from the dead, would bring the message of light to his own

12. As will be described, passages such as Isaiah 40:9–11 and 52:7 would be "good news" to Israel, but they did not constitute an explicit, formulated kerygma or universal gospel that is revealed in Jesus Christ.

13. Robert G. Tuttle, *The Story of Evangelism: A History of the Witness to the Gospel* (Nashville: Abingdon, 2006), 59.

14. Michael W. Goheen, *A Light to the Nations: The Missional Church and the Biblical Story* (Grand Rapids: Baker Academic, 2011), 197.

15. Walter C. Kaiser Jr., *Mission in the Old Testament: Israel as a Light to the Nations*, 2nd ed. (Grand Rapids: Baker Academic, 2012), 82.

people and to the Gentiles" (Acts 26:22–23). The promises and prophecies given to Israel were signposts of what would come fully in Jesus and the church's witness to him.

Abraham of Ur of the Chaldeans

Abraham (ca. 2000–1825 BCE) was a patriarch of Israel and witness to the gospel. He was called by God to leave his country in Ur, and his father's household, and go to the land that the Lord would show him. God promised Abraham that he would make him into a great nation, that he would bless him, and that all the peoples of earth would be blessed through him (Gen. 12:1–3; 22:17–18).

Two thousand years later, Jesus said to a group of Jews, "Your father Abraham rejoiced at the thought of seeing my day; he saw it and was glad" (John 8:56). The apostle Paul commented, "Scripture foresaw that God would justify the Gentiles by faith, and announced the gospel in advance to Abraham: 'All nations will be blessed through you'" (Gal. 3:8). This promise was fulfilled at the birth of the Messiah, who came to redeem humans from their sin "in order that the blessing given to Abraham might come to the Gentiles through Christ Jesus" (Gal. 3:14).

Moreover, Abraham obeyed God by faith. He left his homeland and traveled to Canaan, "even though he did not know where he was going" (Heb. 11:8). In the Valley of Shaveh, he encountered Melchizedek, the "king of Salem and priest of God Most High . . . [who] blessed him" (Heb. 7:1–2).[16] Abraham also obeyed when God told him, "Take your son, your only son, whom you love—Isaac—and go to the region of Moriah. Sacrifice him there as a burnt offering on a mountain I will show you" (Gen. 22:2; cf. Rom. 4:1–25). This act foreshadowed God's sacrifice of his only Son—Jesus Christ (John 3:16; Rom. 8:32; Heb. 11:17–19). Both the promise given to Abraham and his life of faithful obedience pointed to the gospel of Jesus Christ and Christian evangelism.

Moses of Egypt

While the account of Abraham is written in the books of Moses known as the Torah, Moses the person (ca. 1395–1275 BCE) was a witness to the gospel as well. God called Moses to redeem the children of Israel from slavery

16. Cf. Gen. 14; Ps. 110:4; Heb. 5:6–10; 7:1–21.

in Egypt. Although God was ultimately the one to "rescue them from the hand of the Egyptians," he said to Moses, "So now, go. I am sending you to Pharaoh to bring my people the Israelites out of Egypt" (Exod. 3:8, 10). In this commission, the Lord performed signs and wonders through Moses, including leading the people through the Red Sea to a new and redeemed life in the promised land.[17]

In the years that followed, Moses experienced God's provision of bread from heaven (Exod. 16:4–32), led the construction of the tabernacle (Exod. 25:1–37:17), and, in an act to save Israelites, lifted up the serpent on a pole in the wilderness (Num. 21:4–9). All these events pointed to the person and work of Jesus Christ (John 1:14; 3:14–15; 6:22–59; Heb. 10:10–22).[18] The gospel writer Luke says that "beginning with Moses and all the Prophets," Jesus explained "what was said in all the Scriptures concerning himself" (Luke 24:27). Moses was a witness to the gospel.

King David of Jerusalem

King David (ca. 1035–970 BCE) was also a witness to the gospel. The gospel writer Matthew uses the title "Son of David" to emphasize Jesus's fulfillment of the promise to David through Nathan the prophet (Matt. 1:1; 9:27; 12:23). The Lord said to David, "I will raise up your offspring to succeed you, your own flesh and blood, and I will establish his kingdom. He is the one who will build a house for my Name, and I will establish the throne of his kingdom forever" (2 Sam. 7:12–13; cf. Isa. 11:1–10). While these words appeared immediately to refer to Solomon, they pointed to David's ultimate son, the Messiah.

Centuries later, on the day of Pentecost, Peter spoke to his fellow Israelites in Jerusalem about Jesus's death, burial, and resurrection and about forgiveness in his name. Regarding the resurrection, Peter referred to David's words from Psalm 16:9–10, "my body also will rest in hope, because you will not abandon me to the realm of the dead, you will not let your holy one see decay" (Acts 2:26–27). Peter continued: "Fellow Israelites, I can tell you confidently that the patriarch David died and was buried, and his tomb is here to this day. But he was a prophet and knew that God had promised him on oath that he would place one of his descendants on his throne. Seeing what was to come, he spoke of the resurrection of the Messiah, that he was not abandoned to the realm of the dead, nor did his body see decay. God has raised this Jesus to life, and we are all witnesses of it" (Acts 2:29–32).

17. Tuttle, *Story of Evangelism*, 44.
18. D. A. Carson, *The Gospel according to John* (Grand Rapids: Eerdmans, 1991), 98.

David's prophecy about the Messiah's resurrection was a type of evangelistic witness. In his psalms, David referred also to Jesus's divine and human natures,[19] his crucifixion,[20] and his kingly rule over the whole earth.[21] Moreover, David pointed to the church's evangelistic task when he expressed his own desire to witness to others, saying, "I will praise you, Lord, among the nations" (Ps. 18:49).

Jonah the Prophet of Israel

Jonah (ca. 835–765 BCE) was a prophet of the northern kingdom of Israel who pointed to the gospel and Christian evangelism.[22] Unique among the prophets, Jonah was called by God to travel to the city of Nineveh, crossing geographical and cultural boundaries in order to warn the residents of this Assyrian city about God's impending judgment because of their sin. Reluctant to carry out his mission, Jonah boarded a ship headed to Tarshish, traveling in the opposite direction of Nineveh. During a violent storm, when the ship's crew learned of his disobedience to his God, they threw Jonah overboard. He was swallowed by a great fish, vomited onto shore three days later, and finally made his way toward Nineveh.

While Jonah was not the ideal prophet to deliver a message from God, Jesus made references to him when scribes and Pharisees asked for a miraculous sign. Jesus said, "For as Jonah was three days and three nights in the belly of a huge fish, so the Son of Man will be three days and three nights in the heart of the earth. The men of Nineveh will stand up at the judgment with this generation and condemn it; for they repented at the preaching of Jonah, and now something greater than Jonah is here" (Matt. 12:40–41). Jonah's revived life after three dark days inside the great fish foreshadowed Jesus's resurrection. Jonah's life pointed to the gospel and Christian evangelism.

Isaiah the Prophet of Judah

Finally, another prophet who pointed to the gospel and Christian evangelism is Isaiah, son of Amoz (ca. 795–715 BCE). In 740, Isaiah had a vision of the Lord, high and exalted, seated on a throne. In response to this vision, Isaiah cried, "Woe to me! . . . I am ruined! For I am a man of unclean lips, and I live

19. Ps. 2:7–9; cf. Matt. 3:17; 17:5; John 10:30–33.
20. Ps. 22:1–31; cf. Matt. 26:38; Luke 18:32–33; 22:34, 44; 23:35; John 19:22–24, 28.
21. Ps. 2:8–10; 110:2, 6; cf. Matt. 28:18; Eph. 1:20–21; Rev. 17:14; 19:11–21.
22. Kaiser, *Mission in the Old Testament*, 65–73.

among a people of unclean lips, and my eyes have seen the King, the Lord Almighty" (Isa. 6:5). After Isaiah's guilt was removed and his sin atoned for, the voice of the Lord said, "Whom shall I send? And who will go for us?" Isaiah responded, "Here am I. Send me!" (Isa. 6:8).

Early church fathers described the book of Isaiah as the "fifth Gospel."[23] Jerome said of Isaiah, "He was more of an evangelist than a prophet, because he described all of the mysteries of the Church of Christ so vividly that you would assume he was not prophesying about the future, but rather was composing a history of past events."[24] Gregory of Nyssa believed that Isaiah "[knew] more perfectly than all others the mystery of the religion of the Gospel."[25]

The book of Isaiah speaks of the coming king (Isa. 9–11) and servant who would suffer in order to bring redemption to the people (Isa. 40–55) and tells of the new heavens and new earth (Isa. 56–66). Isaiah is quoted by authors of the New Testament many times, describing how the suffering servant would die to save the people from their sins (Isa. 53:10–12). Isaiah also described how the suffering servant would be buried in the tomb of a rich man (Isa. 53:9). The prophecies were fulfilled in the person of Jesus Christ.[26]

Gospel in the Septuagint

The second section of the book of Isaiah announces the good news of God's reign for Israel (Isa. 41:27). At God's initiative, a messenger would arrive in Jerusalem bearing good news of peace. Isaiah writes,

> How beautiful on the mountains
> are the feet of those who bring good news,
> who proclaim peace,
> who bring good tidings,
> who proclaim salvation,
> who say to Zion,
> "Your God reigns!" (Isa. 52:7)

23. John F. A. Sawyer, *The Fifth Gospel: Isaiah in the History of Christianity* (New York: Cambridge University Press, 1996), 44.

24. Jerome, *Dogmatic and Polemical Works*, trans. by John N. Hritzu, The Fathers of the Church 53 (Washington, DC: Catholic University of America, 1965), 156–57.

25. Gregory of Nyssa, *Against Eunomius* 5.1 (*NPNF*^{2} 5:173).

26. Walter C. Kaiser Jr., "The Identity and Mission of the 'Servant of the Lord,'" in *The Gospel according to Isaiah 53: Encountering the Suffering Servant in Jewish and Christian Theology*, ed. Darrell L. Bock and Mitch Glaser (Grand Rapids: Kregel Academic, 2012), 87–107.

With this good news, God comforted and redeemed his people (Isa. 52:8–12). Thus, the apostle Peter writes, "Concerning this salvation, the prophets, who spoke of the grace that was to come to you [Christians], searched intently and with the greatest care, trying to find out the time and circumstances to which the Spirit of Christ in them was pointing when he predicted the sufferings of the Messiah and the glories that would follow" (1 Pet. 1:10–11).

The Septuagint (LXX) is the collection of Greek translations of the Hebrew Scriptures produced by numerous scribes over several decades. This translation of the Old Testament shaped the choices of words used by authors of the New Testament. The Greek word *euangelion* derived its meaning, in part, from the Septuagint.[27] This meaning came particularly from the verb *euangelizō*, meaning "to announce good news," used in the Septuagint. In Isaiah, the participle *euangelizomenos* was used to translate the Hebrew word *mebasseret* as "you who bring good news" (Isa. 40:9), "a messenger of good news" (41:27), and "those who bring good news" (52:7). The middle form of the verb was used to translate the Hebrew verb *basar* when Isaiah writes,

> The Spirit of the Sovereign LORD is on me,
> because the Lord has anointed me
> to proclaim good news [*euangelisasthai*] to the poor.
> He has sent me to bind up the brokenhearted,
> to proclaim freedom for the captives
> and release from darkness for the prisoners,
> to proclaim the year of the LORD's favor. (Isa. 61:1–2)[28]

Both Matthew and Luke use the same verb when they quote this text, following the Hebrew idea that connected Jesus's proclamation of the good news and the coming reign of God (Matt. 11:5; Luke 4:18). On a Sabbath day, Jesus read these words from Isaiah in the synagogue of Nazareth. When he finished reading the words, he rolled up the scroll, and with all eyes fixed on him, he said, "Today this scripture is fulfilled in your hearing" (Luke 4:21).

27. Timothy M. Law, *When God Spoke Greek: The Septuagint and the Making of the Christian Bible* (New York: Oxford University Press, 2013), 95–96; Priscilla Pope-Levison, *Models of Evangelism* (Grand Rapids: Baker Academic, 2020), 6–7, 119.

28. Ralph P. Martin and Carl N. Toney, *New Testament Foundations: An Introduction for Students* (Eugene, OR: Cascade, 2018), 156.

Patriarchs and prophets of Israel pointed to the gospel and Christian evangelism through their words and actions. God's promises and prophecies in the Old Testament were realized in Jesus Christ, the evangelist of God's messianic kingdom. The good tidings arrived in him.[29]

Historiography

This book examines persons, movements, and methods that have been used in the history of the church to communicate the gospel. It presents biographical sketches and contributions of persons as well as examples of their messages whenever possible. It describes the non-Christian peoples with whom they spoke, and provides reports of evangelism including the good, the bad, and the ugly. As will be shown, the history of evangelism is filled with both positive and negative examples, giving insights as to what is beneficial to the church's witness and what has been unfruitful or even harmful.

This book builds on the foundation of the evangelist-historian Luke. In Acts of the Apostles, the sequel to Luke's Gospel, he tells about the spread of the Jesus movement that is led by the apostles beginning in Jerusalem, moving westward across the Aegean region to the capital city of Rome. In his account, Luke provides specific examples of evangelism. He tells about Peter preaching the gospel in Jerusalem on Pentecost (Acts 2:37–40), Stephen explaining the person of Jesus within God's redemptive history (7:2–53), Peter sharing the good news with Cornelius in his home with family and friends (10:27–43), Paul debating Epicurean and Stoic philosophers in Athens (17:16–34), and Paul testifying about Jesus before King Herod Agrippa II (26:4–29).

The present book depends also on other historians like Eusebius of Caesarea (ca. 263–339 CE). Eusebius provides one of the most detailed accounts of apostles, evangelists, and pastors of the second and third centuries. For example, he writes,

> And there were many others besides these [Christian leaders] who were known in those days, and who occupied the first place among the successors of the apostles. And they also, being illustrious disciples of such great men, built up the foundations of the churches which had been laid by the apostles in every place, and preached the Gospel more and

29. Mortimer Arias, *Announcing the Reign of God: Evangelization and the Subversive Memory of Jesus* (Eugene, OR: Wipf & Stock, 2001), 15.

> more widely and scattered the saving seeds of the kingdom of heaven far and near throughout the whole world. For indeed most of the disciples of that time, animated by the divine word with a more ardent love for philosophy, had already fulfilled the command of the Saviour, and had distributed their goods to the needy. Then starting out upon long journeys they performed the office of evangelists, being filled with the desire to preach Christ to those who had not yet heard the word of faith, and to deliver to them the divine Gospels.[30]

The scope of this book is the entire Christian era, from Jesus and the apostles until today. A wholly exhaustive or comprehensive account, of course, would require a description of every Christian who during the past two thousand years verbally communicated the gospel to a non-Christian person. Such a massive undertaking would be overwhelming to readers and impossible for the author. Therefore, this book follows a more practical approach with particular limits.

Sources

All historians are limited to the source materials that have survived. Consider, for instance, cases of the early church when an evangelist arrived at a remote village or town and met with others to tell them the gospel but left no record, or the record was destroyed. Historians are limited to the extant texts that are available. The historian Eusebius spoke of this: "For a great many wonderful works were done through them [Christian leaders] by the power of the divine Spirit, so that at the first hearing whole multitudes of men [and women] eagerly embraced the religion of the Creator of the universe. But since it is impossible for us to enumerate the names of all that became shepherds or evangelists in the churches throughout the world in the age immediately succeeding the apostles, we have recorded, as was fitting, the names of those only who have transmitted the apostolic doctrine to us in writings still extant."[31]

Moreover, consider the missionary monks of the medieval period, for example, who entered frontier regions, perhaps areas hostile to the gospel, where accounts of their evangelism were not written, or perhaps were destroyed along with the missionaries themselves as they faced martyrs'

30. Eusebius, *Ecclesiastical History* 3.37.2–3 (*NPNF*^{2} 1:169).
31. Eusebius, *Ecclesiastical History* 3.37.2–3 (*NPNF*^{2} 1:169).

deaths. Consider, too, that Christian slaves were brought to regions where they shared the gospel prior to the arrival of missionaries but left no record of their evangelistic work.[32]

In other cases, there are reams of source materials. Over the past two centuries, for example, stories of evangelism by missionaries, pastors, and evangelists are contained in missionary newsletters, Christian biographies, denominational periodicals, filmstrips, webpages, and blogs. In cases where there are large volumes of sources, historians must select the people, movements, and stories to be included and described, and those that will not. Thousands of missionaries, evangelists, and pastors have proclaimed the gospel, representing hundreds of Protestant denominations and the Roman Catholic and Eastern Orthodox churches, but cannot be mentioned in this book because of space limitations. This does not imply that they were unimportant or did not contribute to the practice of evangelism.

Therefore, limitations are a reality because of the number of extant sources and the need for selection. The evangelists, missionaries, laypeople, and pastors included in this volume are representative of their period of history. They are innovative or creative examples of gospel witness within their historical and cultural contexts, while holding to orthodox Christian faith. The vital dates of birth and death are given only for those who are deceased.

Practical Application

This book is written as a resource for present and future pastors, evangelists, missionaries, church staffs, and Christian leaders. For this reason, an additional criterion for selection has been practicality, leading to several questions. What will be helpful or formative to the readers? What examples from church history provide a broader view of the evangelistic task? What people and movements brought new insights to the theology and practice of evangelism? Which Christians have represented the church in its diversity, comprising people of "every tribe and language and people and nation" (Rev. 5:9)?

32. For example, findings at Varnhem, Sweden, indicate that Christianity may have arrived there, likely from slaves or travelers, before the missionary Ansgar. Maria Vretemark, "Aristocratic Farms and Private Churches: The Varnhem Case Study," in *The Buildings of Medieval Reykholt: The Wider Context*, ed. Guðrún Sveinbjarnardóttir and Bergur Þorgeirsson (Reykjavik: Snorrastofa and University of Iceland Press, 2017), 143–57.

As readers will observe, models and means of evangelism have not been so rigid in form and style that evangelists were unable to adapt them to the changing environments and contexts in which they lived. In the early church, the gospel flowed into "every nook and cranny of Roman life."[33] The church father Tertullian said, "We [Christians] are but of yesterday, and we have filled every place among you [pagans]—cities, islands, fortresses, towns, market-places, the very camp, tribes, companies, palace, senate, forum—we have left nothing to you but the temples of your gods."[34] While the church's models and means of evangelism have changed to the environment, the core of the gospel of Christ's incarnation, crucifixion, resurrection, and forgiveness in his name, in most cases, has remained constant.

Historical Interpretation and Discussion Questions

This volume provides historical interpretation of people and events, though in some cases interpretation is left to the reader. The discussion questions at the end of each chapter are not simply for group discussion, though this is highly recommended. The questions provide a way for readers to consider the historical significance of the people and their contributions to evangelism.[35] In some cases, discussion questions connect ideas and examples from earlier periods mentioned in other chapters.

Historical and Theological Bias

The matter of historical and theological bias in sources and in the writing of history is inevitable. Historians do not write in a vacuum but bring their interests and biases to the task. For example, Eusebius of Caesarea was known to hold certain assumptions and then buttress them with arguments and supporting facts.[36] All historians, whether researching or writing, op-

33. Glenn K. Fluegge, "The Dual Nature of Evangelism in the Early Church," *Concordia Journal* 42, no. 4 (Fall 2016): 318.

34. Tertullian, *Apology* 37 (*ANF* 3:45).

35. It is recognized that historical interpretation is "enormously difficult given that the connections between the traces [or sources] are the points at which meaning is inferred—whether it is meaning for us or meaning for whatever happened in the past." James E. Bradley and Richard A. Muller, *Church History: An Introduction to Research, Reference Works and Methods* (Grand Rapids: Eerdmans, 1995), 34–35.

36. Arieh Kofsky, *Eusebius of Caesarea against Paganism* (Boston: Brill Academic, 2002), 243–50.

erate from certain historical backgrounds and theological bents that shape how they look at historical events and persons. For example, Martin Luther may be viewed by some historians as a heretic and others as a saint. To this point, Carter Lindberg says, "What is observed is influenced by the observer."[37] Even with the best intentions, bias can do violence to objectivity. Stanley N. Gundry describes the problem of bias:

> The eulogistic biographers tend to touch up their portraits to eliminate the warts and blemishes. Another class of historians, the "debunkers," does its level best to discredit its subjects and to portray them as anything but what they claimed or appeared to be. The institutions founded or shaped by these individuals want to be viewed as their legitimate successors, but in supporting those claims they often ignore certain uncomfortable facts about their founders, or worse yet they engage in revisionist history. And as for the rest of us—well, it is only natural that we would like to have our heroes support those beliefs and practices that we hold dear.[38]

So what is the solution to theological and historical bias? Is it possible for historians to attain objectivity, and if so, how? To this question, James E. Bradley and Richard A. Muller respond,

> The goal . . . is to pursue balance and objectivity without abdicating one's personality or losing entirely one's sense of involvement in and with the events of history. It is, after all, involvement with past events that engenders continued historical interest. Objectivity in historical study does not, and cannot, exist if it is defined as an absence of involvement with or opinion about the materials. Instead, historical objectivity results from a methodological control of the evidence, of the various levels of interpretation both inherent in and related to the evidence, and of one's own biases and opinions concerning the evidence and the various known interpretations.[39]

37. Carter Lindberg, *The European Reformations* (Cambridge, MA: Blackwell, 1996), 4.

38. Stanley N. Gundry, "Demythologizing Moody," in *Mr Moody and the Evangelical Tradition*, ed. Timothy George (London: T&T Clark, 2005), 14.

39. Bradley and Muller, *Church History*, 49.

The goal of this volume is to pursue reasonable objectivity by a methodological control of the evidence. This includes acknowledging my own background and interests.

Author's Background and Interests

I am Protestant in the Pietist-revivalist tradition and hold to the evangelical conviction to proclaim the gospel to the whole world. The word *evangelical* refers to "people of the *euangelion*" and is rooted in the Scriptures, as mentioned above.[40] *Evangelical* was used historically to describe Martin Luther and Philip Melanchthon of the *Evangelische* Reformation, and George Whitefield and John Wesley of Britain's Evangelical Revival. More recently, the Lausanne Movement, organized by Billy Graham and John R. W. Stott, is thoroughly evangelical, holding to the exclusive claims of Jesus Christ and the need for personal conversion to faith in him.[41]

For many Christians today, especially those of the evangelical Protestant tradition, the idea of evangelism may conjure up thoughts of Billy Graham preaching to thousands of listeners at an evangelistic crusade, or someone sharing Bill Bright's Four Spiritual Laws. These methods have shaped the perception of evangelism for many Christians today.[42] However, a study of the history of evangelism that describes how the gospel has been communicated in different times and places can broaden the reader's perspective. Several excerpts from primary sources are included in order to give readers access to the writings of selected evangelists and gospel preachers.

This book follows the tradition of orthodox Christianity, and evangelical Protestantism within it, and provides examples of evangelism from around the world, including Africa, India, Japan, and South America. Several accounts describe women who have played important roles in the history of evangelism. Thus, the book includes well-known figures like Perpetua of

40. Kevin J. Vanhoozer, "Scripture and Hermeneutics," in *The Oxford Handbook of Evangelical Theology*, ed. Gerald R. McDermott (New York: Oxford University Press, 2013), 35.

41. John Stott, ed., *Making Christ Known: Historic Mission Documents from the Lausanne Movement, 1974–1989* (Grand Rapids: Eerdmans, 1997). For additional definitions of *evangelical*, see Tite Tiénou, "The Great Commission in Africa," in *The Great Commission: Evangelicals and the History of World Missions*, ed. Martin I. Klauber, Scott M. Manetsch, and Kwame Bediako (Nashville: B&H, 2008), 164–65.

42. Male and Weston, *Word's Out*, 19–20.

Carthage and lesser-known figures such as Consuella York of Chicago. By including a variety of people and approaches from history, the hope is to expand the readers' understanding of evangelism.[43]

At the same time, the hope is to demonstrate the centrality and unity of the gospel among followers of Christ mentioned in these pages. This book neither intends to overlook differences between Christians nor assumes that everyone was essentially a modern-day evangelical Protestant; they were not. I hope that readers will share with the good examples that follow—despite different historical periods, ecclesial traditions, and cultural contexts—a gospel identity as people who announce the *euangelion*.

43. David M. Gustafson, "Creating and Critiquing Evangelism Strategies," *Journal of the Academy for Evangelism in Theological Education* 12 (1996–1997): 69–76.

1

The Beginning of Christian Evangelism

Now, Lord, consider their threats and enable your servants to speak your word with great boldness. Stretch out your hand to heal and perform signs and wonders through the name of your holy servant Jesus.

—Disciples of Jesus, AD 32[1]

Jesus of Nazareth said to his disciples, "You will receive power when the Holy Spirit comes on you; and you will be my witnesses in Jerusalem, and in all Judea and Samaria, and to the ends of the earth" (Acts 1:8). The book of Acts describes the early spread of the gospel of Jesus Christ, beginning with his small circle of disciples. The followers of Jesus took the message of his birth, life, death, and resurrection across the Roman Empire.

Little is known about the specific endeavors of their evangelistic work. Eusebius of Caesarea records an account of the disciples being dispersed throughout the world: "Parthia, according to tradition, was allotted to Thomas as his field of labor, Scythia to Andrew, and Asia to John, who after he had lived some time there, died at Ephesus. Peter appears to have preached in Pontus, Galatia, and Bithynia, Cappadocia and Asia to the Jews of the dispersion. And at last, having come to Rome, he was crucified upside down."[2] Another early record says that Thomas went to India. While it may be difficult to assess the historical accuracy of such early church tradi-

1. Acts 4:29–30.
2. Eusebius, *Ecclesiastical History* 3.1.1 (*NPNF*^{2} 1:132).

tions, they clearly describe the function of Jesus's apostles; they established churches in new territories by proclaiming the gospel.[3]

Like the word *evangel* mentioned in the introduction, the English word *evangelism* comes from the Greek word *euangelion*, meaning "good news."[4] Christian evangelism is the act of telling the good news of Jesus Christ. The English word *gospel* is a synonym of *evangel* and comes from the Old English *gōdspel*, which combined *gōd* (good) and *spel* (news).[5] Christian evangelism began in the first century with the birth announcement of Jesus of Nazareth. At the beginning of Luke's Gospel, the Virgin Mary testifies to the great things God has done for her and his people (Luke 1:46–55). Then an angel of the Lord announces to shepherds in the field near Bethlehem, "Do not be afraid. I bring you good news that will cause great joy for all the people. Today in the town of David a Savior has been born to you; he is the Messiah, the Lord" (Luke 2:10–11). Shortly after the birth of Jesus, Simeon and Anna—two pious Jews—testify to his messiahship (Luke 2:25–38).[6]

The announcement that Jesus is the Messiah continued with the public ministry of John the Baptist. In John's Gospel, when he sees Jesus walking toward him, John the Baptist says, "Look, the Lamb of God, who takes away the sin of the world!" (John 1:29). The next day, when Andrew hears John say, "Look, the Lamb of God," he follows after Jesus (John 1:35–37). He finds his brother Simon Peter and says, "We have found the Messiah" (John 1:41). In each of these instances, the good news of Jesus is communicated to others.

Jesus of Nazareth came announcing the gospel himself. In the prologue to Mark's Gospel, we read, "Jesus went into Galilee, proclaiming the good news of God. 'The time has come,' he said. 'The kingdom of God has come near. Repent and believe the good news!'" (Mark 1:14–15). In a commentary on the Gospel of John, Origen of Alexandria (184–253) describes how Jesus is the gospel himself, saying the "good things . . . are simply Jesus."[7] Certainly, Jesus's announcement of the good news was a self-declaration that he is the Messiah, the anointed King of Israel.[8]

3. See Bryan M. Litfin, *After Acts: Exploring the Lives and Legends of the Apostles* (Chicago: Moody, 2015), 13–25.

4. Michael Green, *Evangelism in the Early Church* (Grand Rapids: Eerdmans, 1970), 48–57.

5. Roland H. Bainton, *Christianity* (Boston: Houghton Mifflin, 2001), 48.

6. Walter L. Liefeld, "Women and Evangelism in the Early Church," *Missiology* 15, no. 3 (July 1987): 292.

7. Origen, *Commentary on John* 1.10 (*ANF* 10:302).

8. Everett Ferguson, *Church History*, vol. 1, *From Christ to Pre-Reformation* (Grand Rapids: Zondervan, 2005), 33.

With time, Jesus's messiahship became apparent to his disciples. When Jesus asked Peter, "But what about you? . . . Who do you say I am?" Peter replied, "You are the Messiah, the Son of the living God." Jesus replied, "Blessed are you, Simon [Peter] son of Jonah, for this was not revealed to you by flesh and blood, but by my Father in heaven" (Matt. 16:15–17).

When Jesus was crucified on the hill outside Jerusalem, a Roman centurion exclaimed, "Surely he was the Son of God!" (Matt. 27:54). After Jesus was buried in the tomb belonging to Joseph of Arimathea, an angel appeared to the women who had come there to visit on the third day. The angel said to them, "Why do you look for the living among the dead? He is not here; he has risen! Remember how he told you, while he was still with you in Galilee: 'The Son of Man must be delivered over to the hands of sinners, be crucified and on the third day be raised again'" (Luke 24:5–7). The women, including Mary Magdalene, Joanna, and Mary the mother of James, left the tomb and "told all these things to the Eleven [apostles] and to all the others" (Luke 24:9).

The New Testament contains not merely the evangel of Jesus and examples of those who proclaimed it but also statements that this message will be proclaimed in future generations. When Jesus appeared to his disciples after his resurrection, he said to them, "This is what is written: The Messiah will suffer and rise from the dead on the third day, and repentance for the forgiveness of sins will be preached in his name to all nations, beginning at Jerusalem. You are witnesses of these things" (Luke 24:46–48). Jesus told his disciples that they were witnesses of his messiahship, of his death and resurrection, and of forgiveness of sins in him.[9]

The task of the disciples was to announce this message. The book of Acts records them carrying out the task. They "preached the word wherever they went" (Acts 8:4). We read that on one occasion, Simon Peter entered the house of Cornelius in Caesarea and declared,

> You know the message God sent to the people of Israel, announcing the good news [*euangelizomenos*] of peace through Jesus Christ, who is Lord of all. . . . We are witnesses of everything he did in the country of the Jews and in Jerusalem. They killed him by hanging him on a cross, but God raised him from the dead on the third day and caused him to be seen. He was not seen by all the people, but by witnesses whom God had already chosen—by us who ate and drank with him after he rose

9. M. Green, *Evangelism in the Early Church*, 71.

> from the dead. He commanded us to preach to the people and to testify that he is the one whom God appointed as judge of the living and the dead. All the prophets testify about him that everyone who believes in him receives forgiveness of sins through his name. (Acts 10:36, 39–43)

In this account, Peter announces the gospel, participating in the task that Jesus has given to his disciples.

Praeparatio Evangelica

The message of God's acts in Jesus Christ intersected human history, as followers of Jesus, beginning in Jerusalem, testified about him. This message spread as Jesus's disciples announced it further and further outside Jerusalem. In the following decades and centuries, his disciples continued this gospel-sharing activity, and human history has never been the same.

When Jesus ascended from the Mount of Olives in Jerusalem to heaven, the disciples numbered about 120 men and women (Acts 1:15). A few days later, on the Jewish holiday of Pentecost, the number increased to three thousand, and another two thousand were added shortly afterward (Acts 2:41; 4:4). In the first century, this movement of Jesus's followers—known by such names as The Way, Nazarenes, Christians, and Galileans—was a very small group in the Roman Empire.[10] However, the movement grew exponentially as the disciples announced the evangel, taking it to the ends of the earth (Acts 1:8). They did this despite social opposition, political pressure, and physical persecution.[11]

It was clear that every Christian was called to be a witness to Christ, "not only by life but by lip."[12] Each had the responsibility to spread the good news by every means possible. Everyone was to be an apologist, at least to the extent of being ready to give an account of the hope of the gospel within them (1 Pet. 3:15). This sense of personal responsibility to share the gospel was simply one of many factors that facilitated the spread of the evangel throughout the Roman Empire.[13]

10. Tacitus, *Roman Annals* 15.44, cited in F. F. Bruce, *Jesus and Christian Origins outside the New Testament* (Grand Rapids: Eerdmans, 1974), 22. It is estimated that by 70 CE the world population was 0.1 percent Christian. Robert G. Tuttle, *The Story of Evangelism: A History of the Witness to the Gospel* (Nashville: Abingdon, 2006), 82.

11. M. Green, *Evangelism in the Early Church*, 40.

12. M. Green, *Evangelism in the Early Church*, 175.

13. Bainton, *Christianity*, 51.

Greek Logic

Clement of Alexandria (ca. 150–215) viewed Greek philosophy as a preparation for proclaiming the gospel (*praeparatio evangelica*). He held that Greek logic provided a philosophical foundation to formulate and communicate truths in Christian writings, as well as in apologetic works to the people of the day.

The Greek word *logos*, meaning "reason" or "word," was a widely used philosophical term. Aristotle tied the concept closely to the divine. Moreover, Stoics understood *logos* as the divine element through which all things were created and controlled, and part of every human being. Thus, the concept of *logos* served as a bridge between Greek philosophy and the Christian gospel. The writings of the apostle John, as well as early church fathers, used *logos* in reference to Jesus Christ, the Word (*logos*) who became flesh (John 1:1, 14).[14]

Religious Pluralism

Greco-Roman cults and religions were another element of *praeparatio evangelica*. The religious world of the first century was polytheistic and pluralistic, with multiple religions and a pantheon of gods. The Roman Empire kept "the old gods by whose favor the [Roman] legions had conquered the world," as well as the "new gods" from territories that the legions conquered and annexed.[15] Generally speaking, attitudes toward different gods and religions were lenient as long as any single religion did not force itself above the others, encourage sedition against the empire, or interrupt social and public order.[16]

The religious pluralism of Athens, for instance, gave the apostle Paul the opportunity to engage in discourse at the Areopagus. He said, "People of Athens! I see that in every way you are very religious. For as I walked around and looked carefully at your objects of worship, I even found an altar with this inscription: to an unknown god. So you are ignorant of the very thing you worship—and this is what I am going to proclaim to you" (Acts 17:22–23). At this time ancient polytheistic religions with their "capricious and malicious deities" were losing credibility from the impact of rational

14. Milton L. Rudnick, *Speaking the Gospel through the Ages: A History of Evangelism* (St. Louis: Concordia, 1984), 14–15.

15. Henry Chadwick, *The Early Church* (London: Penguin, 1993), 25.

16. Chadwick, *Early Church*, 25.

Greek philosophy.[17] Greco-Roman culture was moving toward moralistic monotheism, which aligned with Christian teaching at points.[18]

Judaism

Judaism also aided the spread of the gospel. The Jewish religion was accepted as a legal or legitimate religion (*religio licita*) by the Roman state.[19] This acceptance occurred after Judea was conquered by the Roman general Pompey in 63 BCE. By the first century CE, Jews were a sizable minority within the empire, comprising 7–10 percent of the population.[20] Synagogues were established in major centers of the Jewish diaspora around the Mediterranean basin.

To some extent, Jews introduced conversion—or more accurately proselytism—to their monotheistic religion.[21] Some gentiles integrated into Judaism by way of circumcision and their acceptance of the dietary and ceremonial laws. Others accepted Judaism's doctrinal and moral standards, worshiped in synagogues, and associated with Jewish communities informally. In many cases, these God-fearing gentiles were ready to respond to the gospel of Jesus Christ.[22]

Pax Romana

Another element of *praeparatio evangelica* was the *pax Romana*, the political "peace of Rome."[23] Caesar Augustus ushered in this period, which lasted about two hundred years, beginning in 30 BCE.[24] For two centuries, the Mediterranean basin was under the control of the Roman Empire, and order was maintained by the Roman military stationed around its borders. With its frontiers firmly garrisoned, Roman citizens could "sleep in peace."[25] In the view of Melito, bishop of Sardis (ca. 160–170 CE), the establishment of

17. Ruth A. Tucker, *From Jerusalem to Irian Jaya: A Biographical History of Christian Missions* (Grand Rapids: Zondervan, 2004), 22.

18. Rudnick, *Speaking the Gospel*, 14.

19. Alvin J. Schmidt, *How Christianity Changed the World* (Grand Rapids: Zondervan, 2009), 26; Bainton, *Christianity*, 56.

20. Rudnick, *Speaking the Gospel*, 15.

21. M. Green, *Evangelism in the Early Church*, 26.

22. Chadwick, *Early Church*, 13; Ferguson, *Church History*, 1:35–36.

23. Bainton, *Christianity*, 51.

24. M. Green, *Evangelism in the Early Church*, 13.

25. M. Green, *Evangelism in the Early Church*, 15.

political peace under Caesar Augustus was "a providential part of the divine preparation of the gospel."[26]

In addition, Rome built, maintained, and policed its system of roads known as the *curia viarum* and guarded its sea lanes on the Mediterranean against pirates. This allowed Roman citizens to travel freely, traders to conduct business, and Roman military troops to move swiftly from one end of the empire to the other. The road system facilitated the transmission of news through the Roman postal system, the *cursus publicus*.[27] With this infrastructure, followers of Jesus traveled freely with relative safety to major cities of the empire, sometimes carrying letters and, in subsequent decades, copies of the Gospels and New Testament epistles.[28]

Greek Language

The *praeparatio evangelica* was attributed also to the Greek language. The common (*koinē*) Greek language was nearly universal within the Greco-Roman world as a result of the earlier Grecian conquests by Alexander the Great (356–323 BCE).[29] Only Spain and areas near the capital of Rome remained Latin-speaking. The common Greek language served as the medium not only of learning but also of trade. This meant that people of different nationalities and languages could communicate easily with one another. In addition, manuscripts written in Greek were compiled into a book. This form of bound manuscript was highly portable and could transmit not merely philosophical concepts but also theological writings and eventually the Bible with the Old and New Testaments.

Motivations for Evangelism

Despite the religious pluralism of the first century, the Christian gospel made exclusive claims on those who believed in and followed after Jesus Christ.[30] Before a person could say yes to Christ, she would need to say no to idols and other gods. Christians belonged exclusively to Jesus Christ as Lord (*kyrios*) and master (*despotēs*).[31] The gospel summoned a response that

26. Chadwick, *Early Church*, 71.

27. M. Green, *Evangelism in the Early Church*, 15, 256–57.

28. Dana L. Robert, *Christian Mission: How Christianity Became a World Religion* (Malden, MA: Wiley-Blackwell, 2009), 10.

29. M. Green, *Evangelism in the Early Church*, 16.

30. M. Green, *Evangelism in the Early Church*, 146.

31. M. Green, *Evangelism in the Early Church*, 146–47.

was costly. Jesus said, "And whoever does not carry their cross and follow me cannot be my disciple. . . . Those of you who do not give up everything you have cannot be my disciples" (Luke 14:27, 33).

Christians were called to acknowledge no other king, master, or lord, whether pagan deity or Roman emperor. This became an increasing challenge for Christians, especially with the rise of the imperial cult that required all Roman citizens to worship the emperor as a god. Historian Michael Green says,

> In July 44 B.C., four months after [Julius] Caesar's murder, during the very celebration of the games in honour of his victory, an unexpected comet appeared in the sky. It was a prodigy, accepted by the populace as evidence—even before the expertise of the priests had been consulted—that Julius Caesar was now in heaven, a god, *divus Julius*. . . . With such a pedigree, [Caesar] Augustus could look forward to divinization at his death and such, in fact, was accorded to him, and most of his successors. . . . Christians, accordingly, appeared most dangerous people; they would not share in this basic pledge of loyalty to the state. . . . Of course, on their principles, they could not. Jesus had laid the foundation of the distinction between the realm of God and Caesar in his answer about the tribute money, and his followers pursued this line of demarcation. Caesar should be honored, not worshipped. They would not bow the knee or sprinkle incense to Caesar. How could they? They belonged to another *divi filius* [divine Son]; they owed allegiance to another *imperator*; they were securely related to God through another *pontific maximus* [high priest]. . . . A Christian could not consistently say, "Caesar is Lord" if he professed, "Jesus is Lord."[32]

With such exclusive commitment to Jesus Christ, Christians (while viewed initially as a sect of Judaism) soon became a threat to the Roman Empire. The Roman authorities were tolerant of all religions and cults as long as adherents paid token allegiance to the emperor as a deity. Christians, however, were not willing to do this. For them, there was only one *divus*—not Caesar in Rome but the Lord Christ in heaven.[33] Their unwillingness to

32. M. Green, *Evangelism in the Early Church*, 42–43.

33. Timothy George, "The Challenge of Evangelism in the History of the Church," in *Evangelism in the Twenty-First Century*, ed. Thom Rainer (Wheaton, IL: Shaw, 1989), 10.

compromise the claims of the evangel led them to face persecution and even death.

In ancient Roman religious practices, whether people turned to philosophy or magic, to astrology or gnosis, or to the rites of Osiris or Mithras was immaterial because every one of these practices was understood to supplement and not supplant ancestral religion.[34] But the Christian claim that "Jesus is the Christ" required that all other religions be displaced. The apostle Peter declared to his fellow Israelites, "God has made this Jesus, whom you crucified, both Lord and Messiah" (Acts 2:36). When questioned about healing a lame beggar, Peter replied, "It is by the name of Jesus Christ of Nazareth, whom you crucified but whom God raised from the dead, that this man stands before you healed. . . . Salvation is found in no one else, for there is no other name under heaven given to mankind by which we must be saved" (Acts 4:10, 12). This conviction about the person and work of Christ alone for salvation, and the call to live under his kingship, prompted first-century Christians to proclaim the gospel with boldness despite any harm or hardship they would face.

Transformed Lives

Because Christians experienced the saving power of Christ, they wished for others to experience it too. Thus, they testified to the power of the gospel, as well as to the power of God to raise Jesus from the dead. They had "found the treasure" of the resurrected Christ and wished to share him and his message with others.[35]

In some cases, the preaching of the gospel was accompanied by miracles. People were delivered from sickness and the influence of demons. The acts of deliverance and miracles of healing by God advanced the proclamation and reception of the good news.[36] These acts authenticated the message and demonstrated that the reign of God had come in Jesus Christ (Luke 5:15; John 6:2; 10:38; 12:9–11).

34. M. Green, *Evangelism in the Early Church*, 146.

35. M. Green, *Evangelism in the Early Church*, 243–44.

36. Chrysostom held that Jesus performed miracles to prove himself "credible and draw men to him." Rowan A. Greer, *The Fear of Freedom: A Study of Miracles in the Roman Imperial Church* (University Park, PA: Penn State University Press, 1990), 49, 52, 55; M. Green, *Evangelism in the Early Church*, 110, 123, 188. Miracles without (and sometimes with) the preaching of the gospel led to misunderstandings (John 6:26–30, 60–66; Acts 14:3–6, 8–18; 19:11–16).

Second Coming

After Jesus's ascension to heaven, Christians looked expectantly toward his promised return, prompting them to share the evangel with Jews and gentiles alike (Matt. 16:28; 24:34; Mark 9:1; 13:30, Luke 9:27; 21:32). Jesus's disciples believed that he would fulfill the Jewish prophecies that the Messiah would return in glory and establish his reign on earth. His second coming was tied to their message, for Jesus said, "And this gospel of the kingdom will be preached in the whole world as a testimony to all nations, and then the end will come" (Matt. 24:14).

First Methods of Evangelism

Several early sources, including the New Testament, the Apostolic Fathers, ancient church traditions, and early church histories, provide information about evangelism in the first century.[37] It appears that several methods were practiced and varied according to the context.

Public Evangelism

Jesus's ministry was one of "proclaiming the good news of God" (Mark 1:14), and in turn, he trained his disciples and sent them to preach this message. In some instances, they went two by two and preached in the home of a "person of peace" who welcomed and offered them hospitality (Luke 10:5–7). At other times, they preached in a public, open-air venue where people would gather to hear them, such as in the temple courts in Jerusalem and at marketplaces, schools, city wells, seashores, and synagogues (Acts 17:1–3, 22).

Although the words *preach* and *preacher* are often associated with a clergyman or clergywoman standing behind a pulpit and delivering a sermon from a text of Scripture, this was not the setting of the New Testament era. After the apostle Paul quotes from Joel 2:32, which says, "Everyone who calls on the name of the Lord will be saved," he asks, "How, then, can they call on the one they have not believed in? And how can they believe in the one of whom they have not heard? And how can they hear without someone preaching to them [*kēryssontos*]? And how can anyone preach unless they are sent? As it is written: 'How beautiful are the feet of those who bring good news!'" (Rom. 10:13–15).

37. Robert, *Christian Mission*, 10.

In Paul's words, "someone preaching" (*kēryssontos*) or "a preacher" refers to a Christian who announces the gospel to people who do not yet believe. These "preachers" may be apostles, evangelists, prophets, pastor-teachers, or anyone else who believes in and follows after Jesus Christ—including men, women, and children. "Someone preaching" or "a preacher" is a broader category than someone gifted by God as a pastor-teacher, for example, serving a local congregation as an elder (*presbyteros*) or overseer (*episkopos*). All Christian disciples, laymen and laywomen, young and old, were called to be "preachers" of the evangel. Of course, the settings could range from open-air preaching in a public arena to speaking quietly at the city well.

Person-to-Person Evangelism

From the beginning, Christians assumed responsibility to preach the gospel in their respective places of influence to the best of their God-given abilities (Matt. 28:18–20; Luke 24:44–48; Acts 1:8). They were called to give testimony to Christ, whether to family, friends, or even strangers (Acts 2:42–47; 8:4–6). For example, Philip says to Nathanael, "We have found the one Moses wrote about in the Law, and about whom the prophets also wrote—Jesus of Nazareth, the son of Joseph" (John 1:45).

The story of Philip and the Ethiopian (Acts 8:26–40)—an official in charge of the treasury of the queen of the Ethiopians—illustrates the early practice of one-on-one evangelism. Prompted by the Spirit, Philip approaches the Ethiopian official, who is sitting in a chariot reading the words of Isaiah 53:7–8. Philip asks him, "Do you understand what you are reading?" "How can I," the official asks, "unless someone explains it to me?" The man then invites Philip to sit with him and says, "Tell me, please, who is the prophet talking about, himself or someone else?" So "Philip [begins] with that very passage of Scripture and [tells] him the good news about Jesus." In this instance, evangelism was person-to-person.[38]

Household Evangelism

The book of Acts says that the apostles taught and proclaimed "the good news that Jesus is the Messiah" in "the temple courts and from house to

38. Rodney Stark, *The Rise of Christianity: How the Obscure, Marginal Jesus Movement Became the Dominant Religious Force in the Western World in a Few Centuries* (San Francisco: HarperSanFrancisco, 1997), 208.

house" (Acts 5:42). Decades later, the apostle Paul said to the elders of the church at Ephesus, "You know that I have not hesitated to preach anything that would be helpful to you but have taught you publicly and from house to house. I have declared to both Jews and Greeks that they must turn to God in repentance and have faith in our Lord Jesus" (Acts 20:20–21).

In the first century, the house provided an informal and hospitable environment that made it a natural setting for evangelism.[39] Acts records an account of three men who come to the apostle Peter:

> "We have come from Cornelius the centurion. He is a righteous and God-fearing man, who is respected by all the Jewish people. A holy angel told him to ask you to come to his house so that he could hear what you have to say." Then Peter invited the men into the house to be his guests. The next day Peter started out with them, and some of the believers from Joppa went along. The following day he arrived in Caesarea. Cornelius was expecting them and had called together his relatives and close friends. (Acts 10:22–24)

A household (*oikos*) in the ancient Near East consisted of relatives and close friends.[40] This was the fundamental unit of society for both Roman and Israelite cultures.[41] In addition to kin, the *oikos* included household slaves and freedmen who sometimes took the family name and remained connected to it, although loosely. Added to kin or *familia* was the kith or *amici*, the trusted friends.[42] This was the position of Manaen, who was brought up in the household of Herod the tetrarch (Acts 13:1).

Whenever a person turned to God in repentance and placed their faith in the Lord Jesus, whether a father, wife, child, slave, or household worker, they generally shared the gospel along relational lines of family and friends, from household to household, and along social networks formed by impersonal attachments.[43]

39. M. Green, *Evangelism in the Early Church*, 207–8, 322.

40. Roger W. Gehring, *House Church and Mission: The Importance of Household Structures in Early Christianity* (Peabody, MA: Hendrickson, 2004), 8.

41. M. Green, *Evangelism in the Early Church*, 209.

42. M. Green, *Evangelism in the Early Church*, 210; Tuttle, *Story of Evangelism*, 98.

43. Gehring, *House Church and Mission*, 54; Stark, *Rise of Christianity*, 18, 20–21; David M. Gustafson, *Gospel Witness: Evangelism in Word and Deed* (Grand Rapids: Eerdmans, 2019), 180–83.

When the head of a household converted to faith and others in the household followed, this basic unit of society—the *oikos*—became a Christian community through which the gospel spread to other households.[44] The house was the meeting place for the new Christian community, or "house church" (Rom. 16:5; Col. 4:15). When Lydia of Thyatira responded to the apostle Paul's message, "she and the members of her household [*oikos*] were baptized" (Acts 16:14–15). When the Philippian jailer believed the word of the Lord that Paul and Silas preached, "he was baptized at once, he and all his family. . . . And he rejoiced along with his entire household that he had believed in God" (Acts 16:33–34 ESV). Thus, in the first century, homes were used for predetermined evangelistic meetings (Acts 10:22), for spontaneous evangelistic gatherings (16:32), and for spiritual conversations with seekers (18:26).

As more and more households began to meet regularly as basic Christian communities, the church at large within a city was decentralized in neighborhoods. The multiplication of house churches led to more and more believers having conversations with their nonbelieving neighbors, friends, and acquaintances, whether at the village well, across a fence, or at the market stands.[45]

Evangelism by Women

Women played a prominent role in evangelism in the first century.[46] In John 4, the woman at the well of Sychar testified to Jesus Christ, and as a result "many of the Samaritans from that town believed in him because of the woman's testimony" (John 4:39). Several women accompanied Jesus on his missionary travels and supported him financially (Luke 8:1–3). Martha testified prior to Jesus's act of raising Lazarus from the dead, saying, "I believe that you are the Messiah, the Son of God" (John 11:27). Mary Magdalene, Mary the mother of James, and Salome—despite their initial fears—gave the first testimony to Jesus's resurrection (Mark 16:1; Matt. 27:56). Luke says, "When they came back from the tomb, they told all these things to the Eleven and to all the others" (Luke 24:9). These women were not merely witnesses of the

44. Gehring, *House Church and Mission*, 17.

45. M. Green, *Evangelism in the Early Church*, 243.

46. William C. Weinrich, "Evangelism in the Early Church," *Concordia Theological Quarterly* 45, nos. 1–2 (January–April 1981): 67–68; Tuttle, *Story of Evangelism*, 98.

Figure 1.1. Christ and the Samaritan woman at the well of Sychar, fresco, ca. 320, Catacomb Via Latina, Rome. *(Scala/Art Resource, NY)*

facts and receivers of the message, but "they were the first proclaimers of it by the direct command of the angels and of Christ himself."[47]

Women such as Dorcas, Lydia, Priscilla, and the four prophesying daughters of Philip played significant roles in spreading the gospel.[48] Paul mentions Euodia and Syntyche who worked with him, saying, "Help these women since they have contended at my side in the cause of the gospel, along with Clement and the rest of my co-workers, whose names are in the book of life" (Phil. 4:2–3). Priscilla and her husband, Aquila, are mentioned together as Paul's "co-workers in Christ Jesus" who "risked their lives" for Paul (Rom. 16:3–4). They shared the gospel and made generous use of their homes for this purpose (Acts 18:2; Rom. 16:3).[49]

Paul mentions Tryphena, Tryphosa, and Persis, who "worked very hard in the Lord" (Rom. 16:12). Although he does not mention precisely what all these women did, their activity contributed to announcing the evangel of the kingdom. Since churches normally met in larger homes, Christian women

47. Mary J. Evans, *Woman in the Bible* (Downers Grove, IL: InterVarsity Press, 1983), 54, cited in Ruth A. Tucker and Walter Liefeld, *Daughters of the Church: Women and Ministry from New Testament Times to the Present* (Grand Rapids: Zondervan, 1987), 40.

48. M. Green, *Evangelism in the Early Church*, 175–76.

49. M. Green, *Evangelism in the Early Church*, 118.

had considerable influence among friends, family, servants, and neighbors.[50] Moreover, they exercised their various spiritual gifts to reach unbelievers who attended house meetings (1 Cor. 14:23–25).[51]

Itinerant Evangelism

The gospel spread by apostles, prophets, evangelists, and pastor-teachers (Eph. 2:20; 4:11). Some examples are the prophet Agabus (Acts 11:27–28; 19:6; 21:4, 10–12), Philip the evangelist, and Philip's four prophesying daughters (Acts 6:5; 21:8–9). They and others responded to Jesus's mandate to "preach the gospel to all creation" (Mark 16:15). Some early Christians functioned as wandering missionaries and prophets who evangelized unreached areas, built up new believers, and equipped newly formed churches (1 Cor. 14:26; cf. 1 Thess. 5:20).[52]

The first-century church depended on Spirit-led Christians at a time when much of the Christian life dealt with spreading the gospel. The apostolic father known as Hermas writes, "When, then, a man who has the divine Spirit enters a gathering of righteous men who have faith in God's Spirit, and this assembly of men offers up prayer to God, then the angel of the prophetic Spirit, who is destined for him, fills the man, and the man being filled with the Holy Spirit, speaks to the multitude as the Lord wishes. Thus, then, will the Spirit of divinity become manifest."[53] Irenaeus of Lyons similarly says, "In likely manner we also hear many brethren in the church, who profess prophetic gifts. . . . Only those to whom God sends His grace from above possess the divinely bestowed power of prophesying, and then they speak where and when God pleases."[54]

A number of wandering prophets and traveling evangelists were active between 70 and 135 CE. They ministered to the sick and demonized, and announced the gospel while depending on persons of peace and Christian communities to provide for their daily needs (Luke 10:3–9). The Didache, written around 70–110, mentions that itinerant "apostles and prophets"

50. Robert Banks and Julia Banks, *The Church Comes Home* (Peabody, MA: Hendrickson, 1998), 29. It was necessary to use private homes or rented rooms for these purposes because burgeoning local churches did not yet have their own common properties.

51. Liefeld, "Women and Evangelism," 295.

52. M. Green, *Evangelism in the Early Church*, 167–68.

53. Shepherd of Hermas, Mandates 11 (43.9) (*ANF* 2:27–28).

54. Irenaeus, *Against Heresies* 13.4 (*ANF* 1:335).

needed to be shown hospitality.[55] They moved from village to village, staying for a brief time in each location, continuing in the pattern established by Jesus (Mark 1:38).

Generally, these itinerant preachers acted independently, traveling long distances within the Roman Empire to announce the evangel.[56] Historian Adolf von Harnack emphasizes the importance of these devout Christians: "The most numerous and successful missionaries of the Christian religion were not the regular teachers but Christians themselves, in virtue of their loyalty and courage. . . . We cannot hesitate to believe that the great mission of Christianity was in reality accomplished by means of informal missionaries."[57]

It is likely that some of these informal missionaries came to faith in Christ shortly after Peter delivered his sermon on Pentecost in the year 30. It appears that their independence, in some cases, led to problems such as the "super" or "most eminent" apostles that Paul faced at Corinth (2 Cor. 11:5). Perhaps for this reason, the Didache advised Christians to honor certain "apostles" but warned against abuses and provided guidelines to detect false prophets.[58]

Church Planting

The book of Acts was not written as an exhaustive account of evangelism in the first century. The apostles Peter, Paul, and Barnabas and the evangelists Philip and Mark were only five of the hundreds of apostles, prophets, and evangelists who traveled throughout the Roman Empire and beyond, announcing the evangel of Jesus Christ.[59] In Acts, churches are mentioned at Rome and Antioch without a description of any apostle or evangelist previously working in these cities or areas.[60] It is likely that the churches

55. Didache 11.3, in *Documents of the Christian Church*, ed. Henry Bettenson and Chris Maunder (New York: Oxford University Press, 2011), 69.

56. M. Green, *Evangelism in the Early Church*, 21, 243.

57. Adolf von Harnack, *The Mission and Expansion of Christianity in the First Three Centuries* (New York: Harper, 1961), 366–68, cited in James Montgomery Boice, *Foundations of the Christian Faith: A Comprehensive and Readable Overview of Christian Beliefs* (Downers Grove, IL: InterVarsity Press, 1986), 651. Cf. Stephen Neill, *A History of Christian Missions* (London: Penguin, 1986), 21–23, 26.

58. Didache 12, in Bettenson and Maunder, *Documents of the Christian Church*, 69.

59. Glenn K. Fluegge, "The Dual Nature of Evangelism in the Early Church," *Concordia Journal* 42, no. 4 (Fall 2016): 313.

60. Neill, *Christian Missions*, 22.

were the result of new converts who returned home from Jerusalem after Pentecost, or were scattered when the persecution of Christians broke out a few years later (Acts 2:9–11; 8:1).[61] Luke writes, "Those who had been scattered preached the word wherever they went" (Acts 8:4).

Similarly, churches surfaced in Cyprus and Cyrene apart from the work of any known apostle (Acts 11:19–21). The historian Stephen Neill points out that the origin of the church at Alexandria, Egypt, has remained "conspicuously silent."[62] In these instances where churches appeared without documented origins, they may have been planted by Christian merchants, traders, soldiers, or slaves who traveled throughout the empire.[63] Christians in these places formed basic Christian communities or house churches while working behind the scenes with no extant source to describe their work.[64]

For the capital city of Rome, it is clear that Andronicus and Junias were converted to Christ before the apostle Paul, who encountered Christ around 33–35 CE (Rom. 16:7). During Claudius's reign (41–54), the emperor ordered all Jews to leave Rome; that included Priscilla and Aquila (Acts 18:2). In all likelihood, a number of gentile Christians remained and led the house churches there. After Claudius's death in 54, Jews were allowed to return to Rome. The theologian Ambrosiaster later spoke of the church of Rome: "It is established that there were Jews living in Rome in the times of the Apostles, and that those Jews who had believed [in Christ] passed on to the Romans the tradition that they ought to profess Christ but keep the law [Torah]. . . . One ought not to condemn the Romans, but to praise their faith, because without seeing any signs or miracles and without seeing any of the apostles, they nevertheless accepted faith in Christ, although according to a Jewish rite."[65]

Like Christians in other parts of the empire, those in Rome gathered regularly for worship, teaching, and fellowship with an elder (presbyter-

61. Robert H. Gundry, *A Survey of the New Testament* (Grand Rapids: Zondervan, 2003), 392–93.

62. Neill, *Christian Missions*, 22.

63. It is estimated that during the first part of the first century, there were thirty-three million people living in the Roman Empire, of which half were slaves. Tuttle, *Story of Evangelism*, 75.

64. M. Green, *Evangelism in the Early Church*, 172.

65. Ambrosiaster, *Commentary on Romans*, in Corpus Scriptorum Ecclesiasticorum Latinorum 81.1, 5–6, cited in A. J. M. Wedderburn, *The Reasons for Romans* (New York: T&T Clark International, 2004), 51. By the time of Nero's reign (54–68), the gospel had penetrated noble families of the capital city, even those who belonged to Caesar's household (Phil. 4:22). In Emperor Domitian's reign (81–96), there is evidence that his cousin and wife were Christians.

pastor) presiding over each congregation.[66] When Paul wrote his Epistle to the Romans (ca. 55–58), there was a network of multiple house churches, each with their respective leaders and no centralized administration (Rom. 16:3–15).

Congregation-Based Evangelism

Jesus instituted the gathering of his disciples and promised that he would build his church, signifying all who believed in and followed after him (Mark 3:14; Matt. 16:18; Eph. 1:22–23). In Jerusalem, after worshiping at the temple courts, his disciples gathered in homes throughout the city (Acts 2:46). Their meeting together was vital to their Christian lives and witness (Acts 2:42; Heb. 10:23–25).

Congregational evangelism happened whenever the church gathered for the worship of the triune God and the edification of Christian disciples. House churches welcomed both Jews and gentiles, who were united together in Christ (Eph. 2:14). There was fellowship between the Roman citizen and the slave, men and women, poor and rich, Greek and Jew, because all were baptized into Christ Jesus (1 Cor. 12:13; Gal. 3:26–28; 1 Pet. 3:7; 1 John 1:3). This fellowship stood in stark contrast to the broader Roman society that was hierarchical, with wealthy male citizens on the highest stratum, slaves on the lowest, and women, children, noncitizens, and the poor in between.

The church displayed a unity that transcended the social barriers of nationality, race, gender, income, and class.[67] Congregations of diverse Christians were a testimony to the reconciling power of the gospel in Christ. As Christians in house churches gathered for worship and ate with one another at the same table, their pagan neighbors and family members saw a unity that no ancestral religion or ancient philosophy had ever produced.[68]

The English word *pagan* comes from the Latin *paganus*, which referred to a person from the countryside or rural area.[69] With the growth of Christianity, especially in cities, *paganus* and its plural, *paganii*, came to mean

66. Peter Lampe, *Christians in Rome in the First Two Centuries: From Paul to Valentinus* (London: Continuum, 2006), 373–80, 431–32.

67. Robert J. Banks, *Paul's Idea of Community: Spirit and Culture in Early House Churches* (Grand Rapids: Baker Academic, 2020), 95–101; Chadwick, *Early Church*, 58–60; Neill, *Christian Missions*, 37.

68. M. Green, *Evangelism in the Early Church*, 27.

69. Bainton, *Christianity*, 61.

"non-Christians."[70] Generally speaking, people living in the country held on to their traditional, ancestral beliefs and were slower to accept the gospel. Thus, by the fourth century, the designation "pagan" referred simply to unbelievers or those outside the church.

Whenever pagans came to faith, it was important to gather them as new Christians and appoint leaders from among them to instruct and build up others in the Christian faith. This is why the apostle Paul said to Titus, "The reason I left you in Crete was that you might put in order what was left unfinished and appoint elders in every town, as I directed you" (Titus 1:5). It was necessary to identify qualified Christians as leaders to oversee the spiritual life of the newly formed Christians and their house churches (1 Tim. 3:1–7; Titus 1:6–9). These gatherings of believers were both the result of evangelism and the base from which the gospel would spread further geographically.[71] In addition, the formation of churches would extend the witness of the gospel to future generations.[72]

The spiritual leader of a house church was the elder (*presbyteros*), known also as an overseer (*episkopos*; Acts 14:21–23), who had the responsibility to shepherd or pastor the people.[73] Paul told the elders at Ephesus, "Keep watch over yourselves and all the flock of which the Holy Spirit has made you overseers. Be shepherds [or pastors; *poimainein*] of the church of God, which he bought with his own blood" (Acts 20:28).

In the Pastoral Epistles, Paul gives his protégé, Timothy, the charge to "preach the word" and to "correct, rebuke and encourage—with great patience and careful instruction" (2 Tim. 4:2). In addition, he tells Timothy to "do the work of an evangelist" (2 Tim. 4:5). While these roles were not exclusive to the elder/overseer/pastor, it was apparent that Jesus Christ gave his followers certain abilities to carry out his work, giving "the apostles, the prophets, the evangelists, the pastors and teachers, to equip his people for works of service" (Eph. 4:11–12). With these God-given aptitudes and abilities, Christians were able to lead in ways that benefited both believers inside the church and unbelievers outside the church.

70. Stark, *Rise of Christianity*, 10; Ramsay MacMullen, *Christianizing the Roman Empire: A.D. 100–400* (New Haven: Yale University Press, 1984), 83.

71. Robert, *Christian Mission*, 11.

72. Michael W. Goheen, *The Church and Its Vocation: Lesslie Newbigin's Missionary Ecclesiology* (Grand Rapids: Baker Academic, 2018), 5–7.

73. Gehring, *House Church and Mission*, 25–26. The Greek word *poimēn* (shepherd) was equivalent to the Latin word *pastor*.

An example is Philip, the evangelist. In Jerusalem, he was one of the seven people chosen to serve the needs of widows by "waiting on tables," a ministry of distributing food (Acts 6:2, 5). Later, Philip "went down to a city in Samaria and proclaimed the Messiah there" (Acts 8:5). On his way to Gaza, he met an Ethiopian man, referred to earlier. After Philip "told him the good news about Jesus" (Acts 8:35), he baptized the Ethiopian man. According to church tradition, this conversion marked the beginning of the Ethiopian church. Years later, Irenaeus of Lyons wrote, "This man [Simeon Bachos, the Eunuch] was also sent into the regions of Ethiopia, to preach what he had himself believed, that there was one God preached by the prophets, but that the Son of this [God] had already made [his] appearance in human flesh, and had been led as a sheep to the slaughter; and all the other statements which the prophets made regarding Him."[74]

After this evangelistic encounter with the Ethiopian eunuch, Philip went about "preaching the gospel in all the towns until he reached Caesarea" (Acts 8:40). He lived at Caesarea Maritima where he, along with his four daughters, was active in the church (Acts 21:8–9). Although Philip was a servant, he became known as an evangelist because of his God-given ability and aptitude for evangelical witness.

Another example of God-given abilities can be seen at the church in Antioch, where "there were prophets and teachers: Barnabas, Simeon called Niger, Lucius of Cyrene, Manaen (who had been brought up with Herod the tetrarch) and Saul" (Acts 13:1). The book of Acts records, "While they were worshiping the Lord and fasting, the Holy Spirit said, 'Set apart for me Barnabas and Saul for the work to which I have called them.' So after they had fasted and prayed, they placed their hands on them and sent them off" (Acts 13:2–3). In this example of congregation-based evangelism, Barnabas and Saul (Paul), who were among the "prophets and teachers," were commissioned as apostles and sent on a missionary journey to preach the gospel, to make disciples, and to plant new churches.[75]

In addition to preaching the evangel, the rite of baptism played a role in congregation-based evangelism linked to Christ's commission to make disciples (Matt. 28:19; Acts 2:38; 8:36).[76] As a public act, baptism of new

74. Irenaeus, *Against Heresies* 3.12.8 (*ANF* 1:433).

75. Ferguson, *Church History*, 1:36.

76. The rite of the Lord's Supper was not associated with evangelism in the early church. It was exclusive, and nonbaptized visitors were dismissed before the "love feast." Justo L. González, *The Story of Christianity: The Early Church to the Present Day* (Peabody, MA: Prince, 1999), 1:49–50, 99. *Contra* Tuttle, *Story of Evangelism*, 99.

believers in water was a symbol of their spiritual baptism and union with Jesus in his death, burial, and resurrection (Rom. 6:3–10). It was a visible demonstration of new birth in Christ and the Christian's willingness to respond to the gospel in repentance and faith.[77] Nonetheless, for pagans who witnessed this public act, baptism was a means of gospel proclamation.[78]

Commissioned Evangelism

In addition to the spontaneous and Spirit-led Christians of the first century who traveled long distances to proclaim the gospel, missionaries were sent out from churches. As mentioned above, Paul and Barnabas were sent and then reported back to the church at Antioch about their mission, showing the close connection between a congregation and its commissioned apostles (Acts 13:1–14:26). Later, Paul sought to be commissioned by the church at Rome for his missionary journey to Spain (Rom. 15:23–24). In these cases, Christians were recognized in the local church as spiritually and theologically qualified, as well as possessing abilities and gifts to pioneer in places where the gospel had not been heard. Thus, congregations of Christians could enter into mission activity by sending their own apostles to unreached areas. These missionaries were supported by members of churches or a network of house churches and were accountable to them.

The Latin word *mitto* and the Greek word *apostellō* both mean "send."[79] The Latin-based English word *mission* came into popular usage centuries later.[80] In the early church, the Greek word *apostolos*, as well as the related Latin word *apostolus*, was commonly used to speak of a missionary.[81] This word was used in the New Testament of the Twelve who were sent to spread the good news of Jesus. The Gospel of Mark says, "He [Jesus] went up on the mountain and called to him those whom he desired, and they came to him. And he appointed twelve (whom he also named apostles [*apostolous*])

77. M. Green, *Evangelism in the Early Church*, 152–53.

78. Millard J. Erickson, *Christian Theology*, 3 vols. (Grand Rapids: Baker, 1983–1985), 1101.

79. J. Herbert Kane, *Understanding Christian Missions* (Grand Rapids: Baker, 1987), 27.

80. Craig Ott and Stephen J. Strauss, *Encountering Theology of Mission: Biblical Foundations, Historical Developments, and Contemporary Issues* (Grand Rapids: Baker Academic, 2010), xiv.

81. Kevin DeYoung and Greg Gilbert, *What Is the Mission of the Church? Making Sense of Social Justice, Shalom, and the Great Commission* (Wheaton, IL: Crossway, 2011), 62–63.

so that they might be with him and he might send them out [*hina apostellē autous*] to preach and have authority to cast out demons" (Mark 3:13–15 ESV; cf. Luke 6:13).

While Luke gives little attention in the book of Acts to the twelve apostles of Jesus, it appears that most of them carried out their mission among fellow Jews in Jerusalem, Judea, and Samaria.[82] Church tradition further records that Matthew went later to Persia and Ethiopia.[83] Peter went to Pontus, Cappadocia, Galatia, Betania, and Italy. A noncanonical record titled the Acts of Peter tells of Peter's eventful ministry in Rome and concludes with the account of his crucifixion head-down.[84] Andrew preached to the Thracians and Scythians along the shore of the Black Sea.[85] Thomas traveled east and preached to the Parthians, Medes, Persians, Bactrians, Hyrcanians, and Margians, dying in India.[86] Philip preached in Phrygia and was crucified in Hierapolis, modern-day Turkey.

Thaddaeus preached in Edessa, Mesopotamia, Berytus (Beirut), and Armenia, dying in Ararat. Eusebius records that when Thaddaeus preached in Edessa, the apostle said, "Since I was sent to preach the word, summon for me tomorrow an assembly of all your citizens, and I will preach before them and sow in them the word of life."[87]

Bartholomew (Nathanael) preached in India with Thomas and then went to Armenia. James, son of Alpheus, ministered in Syria and Egypt.[88] Simon the Zealot went to Persia. Matthias, who replaced Judas, traveled to Syria, and then to Cappadocia, in modern-day Turkey.[89] John ministered in Asia Minor and was exiled on the island of Patmos.[90] From historical records and archaeological evidence of churches established in these regions, the apostles and their disciples carried out their missionary roles of proclaiming the gospel, making Christian disciples, and planting churches.

82. Late in the second century, churches in every important city began to claim apostolic origins. For caution regarding these traditions, see González, *Story of Christianity*, 1:29–30.

83. David M. Gustafson, "Missionality of Apostolicity," *Theofilos* 9, no. 1 (2017): 83–104.

84. Ferguson, *Church History*, 1:39.

85. Eusebius, *Ecclesiastical History* 3.1 (*NPNF*² 1:132).

86. Ferguson, *Church History*, 1:42; Tuttle, *Story of Evangelism*, 74–75.

87. Eusebius, *Ecclesiastical History* 2.1 (*NPNF*² 1:103–5).

88. Tuttle, *Story of Evangelism*, 102.

89. In order to reach those living in the Tigris/Euphrates Valley, evangelists learned Syriac. Tuttle, *Story of Evangelism*, 100, 107.

90. Schmidt, *How Christianity Changed the World*, 19.

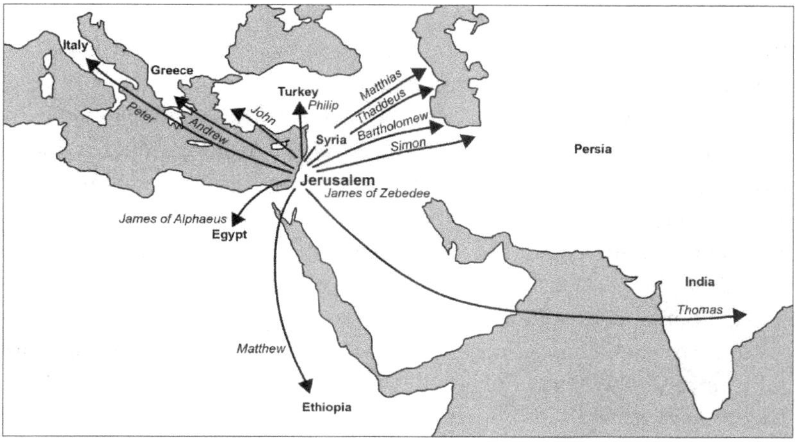

Figure 1.2. **Missionary tradition of the twelve apostles.** *(Paul D. Gustafson, 2020. Courtesy of Yellow Slide Media, North Carolina)*

Although the original apostles of Jesus were foundational, the New Testament mentions additional apostles. Paul and James, the half-brother of Jesus, are two examples. Paul asks of himself, saying, "Am I not an apostle? Have I not seen Jesus our Lord? Are not you my workmanship in the Lord? If to others I am not an apostle, at least I am to you, for you are the seal of my apostleship in the Lord" (1 Cor. 9:1–2). As for James, the brother of Jesus, Paul says, "But I saw none of the other apostles except James the Lord's brother" (Gal. 1:19 ESV).[91] Paul and James each rose to prominence in their respective spheres of leadership among the Twelve. Paul was named the "apostle to the Gentiles" (Rom. 1:1, 5; 11:13). James, the brother of Jesus, became the leader of the church in Jerusalem and was a principal author of the Apostolic Decree (Acts 15). Moreover, both are mentioned as eyewitnesses of the risen Lord. Paul himself writes, "[Jesus] appeared to Cephas [Peter], then to the twelve. Then he appeared to more than five hundred brothers at one time, most of whom are still alive, though some have fallen asleep. Then he appeared to James, then to all the apostles. Last of all, as to one untimely born, he appeared also to me. For I am the least of the apostles, unworthy to be called an apostle, because I persecuted the church of God" (1 Cor. 15:5–9 ESV).

91. Some question whether James, the half brother of Jesus, was an apostle, since in Gal. 1:19 the *ei mē* is ambiguous. Colin Brown, *New International Dictionary of New Testament Theology* (Grand Rapids: Zondervan, 1986), 1:130.

While Luke usually limits his use of *apostolos* to the Twelve, he refers to "the apostles Barnabas and Paul" (Acts 14:14; cf. 14:4).[92] Barnabas collaborated with Paul and was commissioned with him by the Holy Spirit to Seleucia and Cyprus (Acts 13:2–4). Like Paul, Barnabas worked to fulfill the apostolic ministries of proclaiming the gospel and planting churches. Moreover, there were Apollos, Silas, and Timothy. Paul referred to himself and Apollos as apostles (1 Cor. 4:6–9; cf. 1 Cor. 1:12; Acts 18:28), and to himself, Silas, and Timothy as apostles (1 Thess. 1:1; 2:6). He even asked, "Don't we have the right to take a believing wife along with us, as do the other apostles and the Lord's brothers and Cephas?" (1 Cor. 9:5).

In turn, Paul alludes to the apostolic activity of others, speaking with reluctance to "build on someone else's foundation" (Rom. 15:20 ESV).[93] Clearly, as with Paul and notably with James, the apostolate or apostles referred to a group larger than the Twelve. All other apostles of the church built on the foundation of Jesus and the Twelve, and in no way supplanted or altered their apostleship. They traveled to regions of the Roman Empire and beyond, proclaiming the gospel and baptizing those who believed in Christ. They engaged in public, household, and person-to-person evangelism, taught new believers the word of God and obedience to Jesus's teachings, and formed new churches that served as a basis for further evangelistic witness.[94]

Literary Evangelism

The apostle Paul was a model missionary of the first century. He was known by Christians from the early days not simply because he traveled thousands of miles but because of his letters to churches. His epistles were the earliest documents of the New Testament and provided a Christian theology of the teachings of Jesus in contexts where the gospel spread.[95] The four Gospels, the Epistles, and other New Testament writings were the beginning of literary evangelism.[96] The teachings of Jesus and the apostles, with both brief and longer explanations of the good news, were written, circulated, read publicly, copied, and proclaimed widely.

92. Cf. Acts 13:50–14:4; Kane, *Understanding Christian Missions*, 28.
93. Fluegge, "Dual Nature of Evangelism," 311–12.
94. George, "Challenge of Evangelism," 10.
95. Robert, *Christian Mission*, 12.
96. M. Green, *Evangelism in the Early Church*, 229–35.

Prayer-Filled Evangelism

Christians of the first century prayed. Following his resurrection, Jesus appeared to his disciples and reminded them of the Holy Spirit, whom the Father would send to empower them to be his "witnesses in Jerusalem, and in all Judea and Samaria, and to the ends of the earth" (Acts 1:8). When Jesus ascended to heaven, the apostles returned to the room in Jerusalem where they were staying and "joined together constantly in prayer, along with the women" (Acts 1:14). After nine days, the Spirit descended on them with the sound of a great wind and what seemed like tongues of fire.

When Peter preached the gospel on Pentecost, three thousand people believed and were baptized. After this, they continually "devoted themselves to the apostles' teaching and to fellowship, to the breaking of bread and to prayer" (Acts 2:42). The disciples praised God and enjoyed the favor of all people, and "the Lord added to their number daily those who were being saved" (Acts 2:47).

When the apostles heard that Samaritans had accepted the word of God, they sent Peter and John to visit them. The two apostles prayed for the Samaritans "that they might receive the Holy Spirit" (Acts 8:14–15). Peter and John then set out for Jerusalem, and along the way they preached the gospel in "many Samaritan villages" (Acts 8:25). When Peter traveled later to Lydda, he was called to nearby Joppa where a disciple named Tabitha (Dorcas) had died (Acts 9:37). Despite this, Peter went to the room where her dead body lay, "got down on his knees and prayed" (Acts 9:40). Tabitha was raised to life, and news of this miracle spread all over and "many people believed in the Lord" (Acts 9:42).

When the Holy Spirit said to the church at Antioch, "Set apart for me Barnabas and Saul for the work to which I have called them," the leaders "fasted and prayed" (Acts 13:2–3). When Paul and Barnabas returned from the mission, they gathered the church together and "reported all that God had done through them and how he had opened a door of faith to the Gentiles" (Acts 14:27).

The apostle Paul exhorted Christians to pray, saying, "I urge, then, first of all, that petitions, prayers, intercession and thanksgiving be made for all people—for kings and all those in authority, that we may live peaceful and quiet lives in all godliness and holiness. This is good, and pleases God our Savior, who wants all people to be saved and to come to a knowledge of the truth" (1 Tim. 2:1–4). Besides praying for kings and those in authority, Paul prayed for his fellow Jews that "they might be saved" (Rom. 10:1). He requested prayer for himself as well, saying, "Pray for us, too, that God may open a door for our message, so that we may proclaim the mystery of Christ. . . . Pray that I may proclaim it clearly, as I should" (Col. 4:3–4).

The practice of prayer-filled evangelism continued. The Didache, an early Christian text, for example, instructs Christians to pray the Our Father (Matt. 6:9–13) three times a day. Jesus had taught his disciples this prayer, asking for God's kingdom to come on earth, which includes his reign and rule coming to people, a vital element in disciple making (Matt. 28:19).[97] Christians in the first century knew that evangelism depended on prayer. It was as dependent on the knees that pray as on the feet that walk, the hands that serve, and the voices that speak.

Discussion Questions

1. In the first century, a number of conditions within the Roman Empire facilitated the spread of the gospel. What means are available to us today to spread the gospel?
2. In Acts 10:36–43, the apostle Peter announced the gospel. Compare his telling of the gospel here with his message in Acts 2:22–39 and two descriptions of the gospel by the apostle Paul (Rom. 1:2–5; 1 Cor. 15:1–6). In less than two hundred words, how would you summarize the gospel? Use a basic outline.
3. What are the advantages to a local congregation when all Christians witness to the gospel and not merely the pastor-elder? What are the advantages when laypeople explain the gospel to nonbelievers? What are the advantages when pastors explain the gospel?
4. Although house churches were popular in the first century, should they be reinstituted so that their benefits can be felt once more, or are they less than ideal? Were they a necessity in the first century rather than simply effective?
5. In what ways does living in a pluralistic society present challenges and opportunities for the church? What can we learn from Christians of the first century as we navigate our pluralistic contexts today?

97. Geoffrey Wainwright and Karen B. Westerfield Tucker, *The Oxford History of Christian Worship* (New York: Oxford University Press, 2005), 60.

2

Early Church Evangelism

> We pray and we entreat God, whom those men [our persecutors] do not cease to provoke and exasperate, that they may soften their hearts, that they may return to health of mind when this madness has been put aside, that their hearts, filled with the darkness of sin, may recognize the light of repentance, and that they may rather seek that the intercession and prayers of the bishop be poured out for themselves than that they themselves shed the blood of the bishop.
>
> —Cyprian, bishop of Carthage (210–258)[1]

At the beginning of the second century, the ministries of apostles, evangelists, and prophets continued on the pattern of those of the first century, traveling from place to place without staying long in any single location. These Christians lived simply and were dependent on the hospitality of others.[2] Many ventured out on their own, sensing their commission from God to preach the gospel to everyone they met. At the time, the Christian movement was composed of networks of house churches but began moving toward more formalized structures.

1. Cyprian, *St. Cyprian: Letters 1–81*, trans. Rose Bernard Donna, The Fathers of the Church 51 (Washington, DC: Catholic University of America, 2010), 191.

2. Michael Green, *Evangelism in the Early Church* (Grand Rapids: Eerdmans, 1970), 167–70.

Spirit-Led Spontaneity to Structure

As mentioned in the previous chapter, a house church was overseen by an elder-presbyter who carried out the role of pastor-teacher. In the second century there came a distinction between elder (*presbyteros*) and overseer (*episkopos*, also described in English as bishop).[3] The new threefold ecclesial structure consisted of (1) an overseer/bishop (*episkopos*) who superintended several house churches, (2) an elder-presbyter (*presbyteros*) who served as the pastor-teacher of a house church, and (3) a deacon (*diakonos*), or multiple deacons, who carried out particular ministries within the house church.[4] The second century also witnessed a shift from more gift-based or itinerant leadership toward settled leadership with the threefold offices.[5] Thus, the growth of the church at large was not merely geographical and numerical but organizational. The apostles, prophets, and evangelists served increasingly outside the churches rather than at the center of congregational life as practiced earlier.[6]

There were exceptions, however. Some apostles in the second century worked with bishops who superintended house churches. The Shepherd of Hermas (ca. 100–160) mentions those who were called by God as "apostles and bishops and teachers and deacons."[7] Irenaeus (ca. 130–202) explains roles more specifically: "Polycarp also was not only instructed by apostles, and conversed with many who had seen Christ, but was also, by apostles in Asia, appointed bishop of the Church in Smyrna."[8]

Although the designation of apostles, prophets, and evangelists remained alongside bishops, elders (pastors-teachers), and deacons, the former increasingly moved into frontier areas. Nevertheless, some of these Spirit-gifted leaders exercised their abilities locally as they filled the offices of

3. The English word *bishopric* comes from the Old English *biscop* and *rice*, meaning "realm." Later, the Celtic Christians followed this pattern; the Celtic bishop was the prime evangelist. John Finney, *Recovering the Past* (London: Darton, Longman & Todd, 2011), 55.

4. Everett Ferguson, *Church History*, vol. 1, *From Christ to Pre-Reformation* (Grand Rapids: Zondervan, 2005), 107.

5. Robert J. Scudieri, *The Apostolic Church: One, Holy, Catholic and Missionary* (St. Louis: Mission Nation, 2016), 18. Guder posits that the term "office" to describe the positions of elder and deacon was a construct of ecclesial tradition adopted to describe church leadership. Darrell L. Guder, *Called to Witness: Doing Missional Theology* (Grand Rapids: Eerdmans, 2015), 144.

6. Ferguson, *Church History*, 1:101; M. Green, *Evangelism in the Early Church*, 168.

7. Shepherd of Hermas, Visions 3.5 (13.1) (*ANF* 2:14).

8. Irenaeus, *Against Heresies* 3.3.4 (*ANF* 1:416).

bishop, elder, and deacon. In fact, some bishops led the evangelistic charge, preaching the gospel to the surrounding area while they watched over house churches under their care. Moreover, these evangelist-bishops appointed elders to oversee newly gathered disciples who formed new churches.

Irenaeus is an example of an evangelist-bishop. He actively evangelized pagan tribes that lived outside the city of Lyons in Gaul, modern-day France. In order to reach these barbaric inhabitants—namely, Celts—Irenaeus learned their language and presented the gospel to them.[9] He commented later that he had become so accustomed to using their "barbarous dialect" that he forgot how to communicate in proper Greek.[10]

Melito (ca. 120–180) served as bishop of Sardis in Asia Minor, modern-day Turkey, during the latter part of the second century. As we learn from his writings, he was also an evangelist-bishop. A fragment exists of a discourse that he delivered before Emperor Antoninus Pius. In his message, Melito exhorted the emperor to acquaint himself with God, and then proceeded to show him the "Way of Truth." Melito also wrote an *Apology* (Greek and Latin *apologia*) in which he argued for the "True Philosophy" and dedicated the work to Emperor Marcus Aurelius (Verus).[11]

On another occasion, in a message titled *On the Passover* (*Peri Pascha*), Melito told the story of the Jewish Passover as fulfilled in Jesus Christ, the Paschal Lamb.[12] The message was based on Exodus 12 and was delivered on Passover in 165 to Christians of a house church. Given the practice at the time, Melito most likely sat in a chair while he delivered the sermon.[13] Melito proclaimed that salvation comes through Jesus Christ, who was prefigured in the Passover, and explained that the "paschal mystery" was a unified event that included Christ's incarnation, crucifixion, resurrection, and ascension.[14]

9. William C. Weinrich, "Evangelism in the Early Church," *Concordia Theological Quarterly* 45, nos. 1–2 (January–April 1981): 66.

10. Irenaeus, *Against Heresies* 1.pref.3 (*ANF* 1:316).

11. Eusebius, *Ecclesiastical History* 4.13.8 (*NPNF*[2] 1:186).

12. Lynn Cohick, "Melito of Sardis's 'Peri Pascha' and Its 'Israel,'" *Harvard Theological Review* 91, no. 4 (October 1998): 351–72.

13. O. C. Edwards, *A History of Preaching* (Nashville: Abingdon, 2004), 17–18. Melito belonged to the Quartodeciman party of Christians that celebrated the Passover on the fourteenth of the first month, Aviv (Nisan). Rome instituted the festival of Easter in place of Passover around 165.

14. Edwards, *History of Preaching*, 18. At the end of the homily, Melito turns to Christian prophecy in which Christ speaks through him in the first person. M. Green, *Evangelism in the Early Church*, 201.

Excerpts from *On the Passover (Peri Pascha)* by Melito

(47b) When "God in the beginning had made the heaven and the earth" [Gen. 1:1] and everything in them by the Logos, he molded the human being out of earth and shared breath with the form [he had made]. Then he set him in paradise, toward the East, in Eden, to live there in contentment. By a commandment he gave this law: "Eat of every tree in paradise for nourishment, but do not eat of the tree of the knowledge of good and evil. On the day that you eat of it you shall die" [Gen. 2:16–17].

(48) But the human being, being naturally receptive to both good and evil, just as a parcel of soil is receptive to seed from either direction, took evil and deceptive counsel; he touched the tree, he transgressed the commandment, and he disobeyed God. Therefore, he was thrown out into this world as into a prison camp for the condemned.

(49) When he had become fruitful and very aged and had returned to the earth [in death] on account of his eating from the tree, he left an inheritance for his children. He left his children, as an inheritance, not chastity but adultery, not incorruption but corruption, not honor but dishonor, not liberty but slavery, not kingly rule but tyranny, not life but death, not salvation but destruction.

(50–52a) The perdition of human beings on earth was an unheard-of and frightening thing. Look what happened to them: They were carried off by sin, their oppressor, and led into the world of lusts, where they were drowned by insatiable pleasures—adultery, fornication, impudence, lust, love of money, murders, blood-sheddings, the tyranny of evil, the tyranny of lawlessness. For father drew sword against son; and son lifted hand against father and, irreverent struck his mother's breasts; and brother slew brother; and the host wronged his guest, and the friend murdered friend; and human being slit the throat of his fellow with tyrannical hand. . . .

(54) At this, sin was happy. Co-worker with death that she is, sin made her way first into people's souls and got the bodies of the dead ready for death to feed on. Sin left her mark in every soul, and those in whom she left it were those who had to come to an end.

(55–56) So all flesh fell under sin, and each body fell under death, and each soul was removed from its fleshly home, and what had been taken from earth was resolved into earth, and what had been given by God was locked up into Hades, and the happy union was dissolved and the beautiful body was broken up into parts. Humanity was being cut in parts by death, for a new kind of misfortune and captivity held it. It was carried away captive under the shadow of death. The image of the Father was left desolate. This, then is the reason why the mystery of the Passover has been completed in the body of the Lord. . . .

(66) He [Christ] arrived on earth from the heavens for the sake of the sinner who suffered. He clothed himself in the sufferer by means of a virgin's womb and came forth as a human being. He took to himself the sufferings of the sufferer by means of a body capable of suffering, and he destroyed the sufferings of the flesh. By a Spirit incapable of death he killed off death, the homicide.

(67) This is the one who like a lamb was carried off and like a sheep was sacrificed. He redeemed us from slavery to the cosmos as from the land of Egypt and loosed us from slavery to the devil as from the hand of Pharaoh. And he sealed our souls with his own Spirit and the limbs of our body with his own blood.

(68) This is the one who covered death with shame and made a mourner of the devil, just as Moses did Pharaoh. This is the one who struck lawlessness a blow and made injustice childless, as Moses did Egypt. This is the one who rescued us from slavery into liberty, from darkness into light, from death into life, from a tyranny into an eternal kingdom (and made us a new priesthood and a peculiar, eternal people).

(69) He is the Passover of our salvation. He is the one who in many folk bore many things. He is the one who was murdered in the person of Abel, bound in the person of Isaac, exiled in the person of Jacob, sold in the person of Joseph, exposed in the person of Moses, sacrificed in the person of the lamb, persecuted in the person of David, dishonored in the person of the prophets.

(70) This is the one who was made flesh in a virgin, hanged upon the wood, entombed in the earth, raised from the dead, lifted up to the heights of the heavens. He is the speechless lamb.

(71–72) He is the lamb who was slaughtered. He is the one born of Mary the beautiful ewe. He is the one who was taken from the flock and dragged to slaughter and killed at evening and buried at night, who was not crushed on the cross, was not dissolved into the earth, who rose from the dead and raised humanity from the grave below. This man was killed. And where was he killed? In the middle of Jerusalem. . . .

(103) So come, all families of human beings who are defiled by sins, and receive remission of sins. For I am your forgiveness, I am the Passover of salvation. I am the Lamb sacrificed for your sake. I am your ransom. I am your life. I am your resurrection. I am your light. I am your salvation. I am

your King. I lead you toward the heights of heaven. I will show you the eternal Father. I will raise you up with my right hand.

(104) This is he who made the heavens and the earth, and formed humanity in the beginning, who is announced by the Law and the Prophets, who was enfleshed in a Virgin, who was hanged on the Tree, who was buried in the earth, who was raised from the dead and went up into the heights of heaven, who is sitting on the right hand of the Father, who has the authority to judge and save all things, through whom the Father made the things which exist, from the beginning to all the ages.

(105) This one is "the Alpha and the Omega," this one is "the beginning and the end"—the beginning which cannot be explained and the end which cannot be grasped. This one is the Christ. This one is the King. This one is Jesus. This one is the Leader. This one is the Lord. This one is he who has risen from the dead. This one is he who sits on the right hand of the Father. He bears the Father and is borne by the Father. "To him be the glory and the power to the ends of the ages. Amen." (O. C. Edwards, *A History of Preaching* [Nashville: Abingdon, 2004], 2:6–18)

Martyrs as Witnesses

As mentioned earlier, Christians were recognized originally as a sect of Judaism and thus were tolerated by the Roman state. This recognition provided protection since Judaism was a legal religion (*religio licita*).[15] However, the distinction between Jews and Christians became greater as the church grew with gentile converts. The result was that Roman authorities no longer viewed Christianity as a sect within Judaism but as a completely different religion, and thus an illegal religion (*religio illicita*) not tolerated by the state.[16] For this reason Christians came increasingly under pressure from Roman authorities and subject to persecution, even death.

The first persecution at the hands of the Roman government took place in 64 CE under Emperor Nero, who unfairly accused Christians of setting a fire in the capital city of Rome. The historian Tacitus writes, "Before killing the Christians, Nero used them to amuse the people. Some were

15. Justo L. González, *The Story of Christianity: The Early Church to the Present Day* (Peabody, MA: Prince, 1999), 1:32.

16. M. Green, *Evangelism in the Early Church*, 35–36.

dressed in furs, to be killed by the dogs. Others were crucified. Still others were set on fire early in the night, so that they might illumine it."[17] Nero's persecution set a precedent that magistrates could kill Christians simply because they were Christians.[18] According to tradition, during this time the apostle Paul was beheaded and the apostle Peter was crucified upside down.[19]

In the year 91, Emperor Domitian expanded persecution against Christians beyond the city of Rome. Domitian may have had a personal vendetta against them, or he viewed them as subversive because they rejected the Roman gods and civic traditions.[20] Under Domitian's reign, the apostle John was exiled to the island of Patmos.

In 112, Emperor Trajan set a policy that remained in force for more than a century. In a letter sent to Pliny the Younger, governor of Bithynia, Trajan wrote, "Christians are not to be sought out. Do not go looking for them. But if someone denounces someone as a Christian, then bring that person in and question them. And if that person refuses to recant and worship our gods, then they should be punished."[21]

Martyrdom as a form of Christian witness began earlier with John the Baptist, Jesus, Stephen, and Jesus's apostles. For this reason, the Greek word for "witness" (*martyria*) took on the meaning of "martyr" because Christians witnessed to the gospel by their deaths.[22] To die as a martyr was one way for a Christ follower to testify to their faith in the gospel. Moreover, their martyrdom was a visible symbol of their union with Christ. The apostle Paul writes, "I want to know Christ—yes, to know the power of his resurrection and participation in his sufferings, becoming like him in his death, and so, somehow, attaining to the resurrection from the dead" (Phil. 3:10–11). Martyrdom as a form of gospel witness played an important role in the growth of the early church (Rev. 3:11).[23]

17. González, *Story of Christianity*, 1:35.

18. Henry Chadwick, *The Early Church* (London: Penguin, 1993), 26.

19. Bernard Green, *Christianity in Ancient Rome: The First Three Centuries* (London: T&T Clark, 2010), 46–48.

20. Ferguson, *Church History*, 1:65.

21. *Epistles* 10.96, in Ferguson, *Church History*, 1:65. Cf. Milton L. Rudnick, *Speaking the Gospel through the Ages: A History of Evangelism* (St. Louis: Concordia, 1984), 21.

22. Ferguson, *Church History*, 1:82–83, 154.

23. Rodney Stark, *The Rise of Christianity: How the Obscure, Marginal Jesus Movement Became the Dominant Religious Force in the Western World in a Few Centuries* (San Francisco: HarperSanFrancisco, 1997), 174.

Ignatius of Antioch

In 107, Ignatius of Antioch (ca. 35–108), a student of the apostle John, refused to offer incense to the Roman imperial cult and was condemned to death.[24] On his way to the city of Rome, he learned that Christians were seeking his release. Ignatius resisted any such attempt, saying that he was ready to testify about Jesus with his own blood.[25] He viewed the well-meaning efforts of his Christian brothers and sisters in Rome as an obstacle to imitate the suffering and death of Jesus. Ignatius held that the sacrifice of martyrdom makes discipleship complete (Matt. 16:24).[26] As he faced death, he wished only that his fellow Christians would pray for him to have the strength to face the trial.[27] He died as a martyr shortly after arriving in Rome, likely being fed to lions at the Colosseum.

Polycarp of Smyrna

Ignatius's friend Polycarp of Smyrna (ca. 69–156) was also a disciple of the apostle John. Both Ignatius and Polycarp became bishops with oversight of house churches in Asia Minor. Before his death, Ignatius wrote to Polycarp, exhorting him to press on in the faith and encouraging him to "pray for all men that they may be saved."[28]

Heeding his friend's advice, when Polycarp was required to offer sacrifices to the Roman imperial cult, he refused. He was brought before the Roman authorities and given the chance to recant and worship the imperial gods, or be put to death.[29] As he came forward, the assembled crowd cried out against him, saying, "This is the teacher of Asia, the father of the Christians, the over-thrower of our gods; he who has been teaching many not to sacrifice, or to worship the gods."[30]

An eyewitness of the account wrote that the Roman governor asked Polycarp to identify himself, saying whether or not he was indeed Polycarp, the

24. The date of Ignatius's death is disputed. Timothy Barnes suggests as late as the 140s. Timothy D. Barnes, "The Date of Ignatius," *Expository Times* 120, no. 3 (December 2008): 119–30.

25. Ferguson, *Church History*, 1:55.

26. Stark, *Rise of Christianity*, 180–81.

27. González, *Story of Christianity*, 1:43.

28. Ignatius, *Epistle to Polycarp* 1 (Syrian) (*ANF* 1:99).

29. Roland H. Bainton, *Christianity* (Boston: Houghton Mifflin, 2000), 65.

30. *Martyrdom of Polycarp* 12 (*ANF* 1:41).

bishop of Smyrna.[31] After hearing that he was indeed Polycarp, the governor tried to dissuade him, saying, "Have respect for your old age; swear by the fortune of Caesar; repent and say, 'Down with the Atheists!'"[32] By this the governor meant "Down with the Christians," who were viewed by Roman polytheists as atheists because they did not worship the Roman gods.[33] Despite the governor's appeal, Polycarp turned the gesture in the opposite direction and waved his hand in the air, pointing toward the pagans in the arena, and said, "Down with the Atheists!" because *they* did not believe in Jesus, the divine Son of God. Again, the governor urged Polycarp, "Renounce Christ and I will set you free." Polycarp responded, "Eighty and six years have I served Him, and He never did me any wrong; how then can I blaspheme my King and my Saviour?"[34] With his refusal to recant, Polycarp was tied to the stake and the wood around him was lit on fire. In the midst of flames, he looked up and prayed for others to hear:

> O Lord God Almighty, the Father of your beloved and blessed Son Jesus Christ, by whom we have received the knowledge of you, the God of angels and powers and of every creature, and of the whole race of the righteous who live before thee, I give you thanks that you have counted me worthy of this day and this hour, that I should have a part in the number of your martyrs, in the cup of thy Christ, to the resurrection of eternal life, both of soul and body, through the incorruption [imparted] by the Holy Spirit. Among whom may I be accepted this day before you as a holy and acceptable sacrifice, according as you, the ever truthful God, have pre-ordained, have revealed beforehand to me, and now have fulfilled. Therefore, I praise you for all things, I bless you, I glorify you, along with the everlasting and heavenly Jesus Christ, your beloved Son, with whom to you, and the Holy Spirit, be glory now and to all coming ages. Amen.[35]

With these final words, Polycarp died as a witness to the gospel before hundreds of spectators in the arena.[36]

31. Ferguson, *Church History*, 1:80.

32. *Martydom of Polycarp* 9 (*ANF* 1:41).

33. Ferguson says, "An atheist was someone who did not observe the traditional religious practices, regardless of the faith he professed." *Church History*, 1:67.

34. *Martyrdom of Polycarp* 9 (*ANF* 1:41).

35. *Martyrdom of Polycarp* 14 (*ANF* 1:42).

36. Although the account of Polycarp's death appears sensational, without doubt

Although persecution against Christians such as this was sporadic and local rather than empire-wide, it was directed mostly toward leaders or highly visible Christians like Polycarp. Seasons of relative peace gave Christians opportunities to evangelize more freely.[37] But when they faced the choice of denying Christ, they refused and received torture or death, simply stating, "I am a Christian."[38]

In several instances, Roman officials who assisted in the execution became Christians themselves. This was the case with Basilides, an officer of the court in Egypt, after a Christian woman named Potamiaena was threatened with being handed over to gladiators if she refused to renounce her faith.[39] Following her refusal and subsequent torture, Basilides led her, along with her mother, Marcela, to execution. When the multitude closed in around Potamiaena, chanting taunts against her, he kept the people at a distance, treating her with consideration and dignity.[40] Not long after her death, Basilides was required by his fellow soldiers to take an oath, but he explained that he would not because he had become a Christian. At first they thought he was joking, but seeing that he was serious, they denounced him. Basilides was condemned to death by beheading.

In 161, Emperor Marcus Aurelius ordered that Christians be persecuted, blaming them for "bringing the wrath of the gods upon the empire."[41] For Aurelius, refusal to worship at the imperial cult was political disloyalty. He viewed Christians as subversive and thus as enemies of the state. It is true that Christians not only abstained from practicing the imperial religion but also encouraged others to do so. They denounced the Roman gods as nonexistent, or even as demons.[42] The Roman authorities merely wished for Christians to renounce their claim that Christ is Lord in an effort for the empire to regain the favor of the gods. The Romans believed this favor had been lost because of recent natural disasters and military defeats, which they attributed to the subversive actions of the "Atheists."

In 177, forty-eight Christians were put to death at Lyons, including a

---

he died as a martyr at Smyrna. He was known to speak with language saturated with the Scriptures. Ferguson, *Church History*, 1:57.

37. González, *Story of Christianity*, 1:82.

38. Rudnick, *Speaking the Gospel*, 35.

39. Eusebius, *Ecclesiastical History* 2.5 (*NPNF*^{2} 1:253).

40. Arthur James Mason, *The Historic Martyrs of the Primitive Church* (New York: Longmans, Green, 1905), 86.

41. Ferguson, *Church History*, 1:66, 69; González, *Story of Christianity*, 1:45–48.

42. Rudnick, *Speaking the Gospel*, 21.

ninety-year-old bishop named Potheinos.[43] Melito of Sardis suffered martyrdom too, most likely at the hands of Commodus, son of and co-emperor with Aurelius. Another martyr was Blandina, who was tied to a stake and offered as prey to wild beasts. In her final moments, she encouraged onlookers to live and suffer for the glory of Christ.[44]

In 193, Septimius Severus became emperor and, at first, did not oppose Christians, but by the turn of the century he changed his view. At a time when he sought to build up the Roman army, leaders of the church were raising questions about whether it was right for a Christian to serve in the military.[45] Thus, in 202, Severus issued an edict that prohibited Christians from making converts in his attempt to eliminate any relative freedom for them.[46] Moreover, his intention was to bring all Roman subjects, religions, and philosophies under the worship of *Sol Invictus*—the Unconquered Sun.[47] The persecution against Christians that followed was empire-wide, and particularly harsh in North Africa.

Perpetua and Felicitas

Among the well-known martyrs of the third century were Vibia Perpetua (ca. 182–203) and Felicitas (ca. 182–203).[48] Perpetua was born into a wealthy family in Carthage of North Africa, a city in the Roman Empire that was considered second in importance only to Rome. She converted to faith in Christ through the witness of Saturas, a deacon who taught catechetical classes to new converts. When this was discovered in 203, Perpetua and her slave named Felicitas, along with Saturus and two other men, Revocatus and Secundulus, were taken captive.[49] All five were charged with conversion to the Christian faith and stood in violation of the emperor's edict.

43. Eusebius, *Ecclesiastical History* 5.1.29–31 (*NPNF*[2] 1:214–15).

44. Eusebius, *Ecclesiastical History* 5.17–56 (*NPNF*[2] 1:213–17).

45. A Roman soldier who refused to wear a victory garland on his head because of its pagan associations and because he was a Christian was discharged and sentenced to die as a martyr. Tertullian, *The Crown* 1 (*ANF* 3:93).

46. Ferguson, *Church History*, 1:160.

47. González, *Story of Christianity*, 1:83.

48. Ruth A. Tucker and Walter L. Liefeld, *Daughters of the Church: Women and Ministry from New Testament Times to the Present* (Grand Rapids: Zondervan, 1987), 100–102. See also Bryan M. Litfin, *Early Christian Martyr Stories: An Evangelical Introduction with New Translations* (Grand Rapids: Baker Academic, 2014), 91–109.

49. González, *Story of Christianity*, 1:83–84; M. Green, *Evangelism in the Early Church*, 177.

The governor of Carthage enforced the edict and took them prisoner. Perpetua's father tried to convince her to yield and renounce her conversion in order to save her life because she had an infant son at home. At the same time, the slave girl Felicitas was eight months pregnant and gave birth to her child while in prison.[50] Perpetua and Felicitas died as martyrs in the amphitheater along with the three men at Carthage.

Excerpts from *The Passion of Perpetua and Felicitas*

[Perpetua said:] "Father, do you see, let us say, this vessel lying here to be a little pitcher, or something else?" And he said, "I see it to be so." And I replied to him, "Can it be called by any other name than what it is?" And he said, "No." "Neither can I call myself anything else than what I am, a Christian." Then my father, provoked at this saying, threw himself upon me, as if he would tear my eyes out. But he only distressed me, and went away overcome by the devil's arguments. . . . In that same interval of a few days we were baptized, and to me the Spirit prescribed that in the water of baptism nothing else was to be sought for bodily endurance. After a few days we were taken into the dungeon, and I was very much afraid, because I had never felt such darkness. . . .

And Hilarianus the procurator, who had just received the power of life and death in the place of the proconsul Minucius Timinianus, who was deceased, said, "Spare the grey hairs of your father, spare the infancy of your boy, offer sacrifice for the well-being of the emperors." And I replied, "I will not do so." Hilarianus said, "Are you a Christian?" And I replied, "I am a Christian." And as my father stood there to cast me down from the faith, he was ordered by Hilarianus to be thrown down, and was beaten with rods. And my father's misfortune grieved me as if I myself had been beaten, I so grieved for his wretched old age. The procurator then delivered judgment on all of us, and condemned us to the wild beasts, and we went down cheerfully to the dungeon. . . .

Again, after a few days, Pudens, a soldier, an assistant overseer of the prison, who began to regard us in great esteem, perceiving that the great power of God was in us, admitted many brethren to see us, that both we and they might be mutually refreshed. . . .

50. Ruth A. Tucker, *From Jerusalem to Irian Jaya: A Biographical History of Christian Missions* (Grand Rapids: Zondervan, 2004), 34.

But respecting Felicitas (for to her also the Lord's favor approached in the same way), when she had already gone eight months with child (for she had been pregnant when she was apprehended), as the day of the exhibition was drawing near, she was in great grief lest on account of her pregnancy she should be delayed [execution]—because pregnant women are not allowed to be publicly punished. . . . Moreover, also, her fellow martyrs were painfully saddened lest they should leave so excellent a friend, and as it were companion, alone in the path of the same hope. Therefore, joining together their united cry, they poured forth their prayer to the Lord three days before the exhibition. Immediately after their prayer her pains came upon her, and when, with the difficulty natural to an eight-month delivery, in the labor of bringing forth she was sorrowing, some one of the servants of the *Cataractarii* said to her, "You who are in such suffering now, what will you do when you are thrown to the beasts, which you despised when you refused to sacrifice?" And she replied, "Now it is I that suffer what I suffer; but then there will be another in me [Christ], who will suffer for me, because I also am about to suffer for Him." Thus she brought forth a little girl, which a certain sister brought up as her daughter. . . .

The day of their victory shone forth, and they proceeded from the prison into the amphitheater, as if to an assembly, joyous and of brilliant countenances; if perchance shrinking, it was with joy, and not with fear. Perpetua followed with a serene look, and with step and gait as a matron of Christ, beloved of God; casting down the luster of her eyes from the gaze of all. Moreover, Felicitas, rejoicing that she had safely brought forth, so that she might fight with the wild beasts; from the blood and from the midwife to the gladiator, to wash after childbirth with a second baptism [of martyr's blood]. And when they were brought to the gate, and were constrained to put on the clothing—the men, that of the priests of Saturn, and the women, that of those who were consecrated to Ceres—that noble-minded woman [Perpetua] resisted even to the end with constancy. For she said, "We have come thus far of our own accord, for this reason, that our liberty might not be restrained. For this reason, we have yielded our minds that we might not do any such thing as this: we have agreed on this with you." Injustice acknowledged the justice; the tribune yielded to their being brought as simply as they were. Perpetua sang psalms, already treading underfoot the head of the Egyptian; Revocatus, and Saturninus, and Saturus uttered threatenings against the gazing people about this martyrdom. When they came within sight of Hilarianus, by gesture and nod, they began to say to Hilarianus, "You judge

> us, but God will judge you." At this the people, exasperated, demanded that they should be tormented with scourges as they passed along the rank of the *venatores* [Roman gladiators who specialized in hunting wild animals]. And they indeed rejoiced that they should have incurred any one of their Lord's passions. (*Passion of Perpetua and Felicity* [ANF 3:699–706])

Christian Apologetics

In the second century, Christian scholars produced various writings to argue for the Christian faith, presenting reasoned defenses (*apologiai*) for the attacks against the teachings of Jesus, as well as for the unfair treatment of Christians. In most cases, these Christian apologists hoped that readers would consider reasons for the gospel and believe in Jesus as the Christ.[51] They defended and commended the gospel.[52]

Writers such as Melito, Tertullian, Clement of Alexandria, and Justin Martyr presented their messages in the language, literary styles, and philosophical systems of the time. Their works proved effective as members of the nobility, intellectual elites, and pagan students turned to the gospel.[53]

Tertullian

The theologian Tertullian (ca. 160–235) came from Carthage. His father was the captain of a Roman legion and provided his son with education to become a lawyer. When Tertullian was about forty years old, he converted to faith in Christ, embracing the gospel fully. He used his legal training and skill to defend Christianity and to articulate its teachings.

Tertullian wrote his work titled *Apology* to the provincial governor as a defense of the Christian faith and as a plea for religious toleration of Christians. He argued that the Roman government should protect its Christian citizens, not persecute them. He described how emperors blamed Christians for everything that went wrong: "If the Tiber [River] rises as high as the

51. M. Green, *Evangelism in the Early Church*, 160.

52. M. Green, *Evangelism in the Early Church*, 172.

53. Timothy George, "The Challenge of Evangelism in the History of the Church," in *Evangelism in the 21st Century: The Critical Issues*, ed. Thom S. Rainer (Wheaton, IL: Shaw, 1989), 12.

city walls, if the Nile does not send its waters up over the fields, if the heavens give no rain, if there is an earthquake, if there is famine or pestilence, straightway the cry is, 'Away with the Christians to the lion!'"[54]

Tertullian also claimed that putting Christians to death did not dissuade them; it only gave them additional opportunities to spread their beliefs. "The more often we are mown down by you, the more in number we grow; the blood of Christians is seed."[55] Writing to Scapula, governor of Carthage, Tertullian explained, "For all who witness the noble patience of its [the gospel's] martyrs, as struck with misgivings, [they] are inflamed with desire to examine into the matter in question; and as soon as they come to know the truth, they straightaway enroll themselves [as] its disciples."[56] Tertullian's observation was that persecution of Christians gave them a public witness that did not destroy the Christian movement but expanded it. Certainly, martyrdom provided an indelible witness to the gospel.[57]

Tertullian made his point not merely to Roman authorities but also to his fellow Christians. He claimed that persecution did not happen without God allowing it. He held that persecution was fitting, or even necessary at times for God's judgment, explaining, "This is that fan which even now cleanses the Lord's threshing floor—the church, I mean—winnowing the mixed heap of believers, and separating the grain of the martyrs from the chaff of deniers."[58]

Clement of Alexandria

Clement of Alexandria (ca. 160–215) wrote an apologetic work titled *Exhortation to the Heathen* in order to expose and discredit pagan philosophies and religions, and to plead with readers to accept Christ as the superior alternative.[59] His message was not limited to biblical words but directed to his context, inviting his listeners to embrace Christ. In his work, Clement pleads with heathen, for instance, who follow the mythic Teiresias, a blind prophet of Apollo in Thebes, writing, "Come you also, O aged man, leaving Thebes, and casting away from you both divination and Bacchic frenzy, allow yourself to be led to the truth. I give you the staff [of the cross] on

54. Tertullian, *Apology* 40 (*ANF* 3:47).
55. Tertullian, *Apology* 50 (*ANF* 3:55).
56. Tertullian, *To Scapula* 5.4 (*ANF* 3:108).
57. Liefield, "Women and Evangelism in the Early Church," 296.
58. Tertullian, *Flight in Persecution* 1 (*ANF* 4:116).
59. Rudnick, *Speaking the Gospel*, 40–41; Ferguson, *Church History*, 1:130–31.

which to lean. Haste, Tiresias; believe, and you will see. Christ, by whom the eyes of the blind recover sight, will shed on you a light brighter than the sun; night will flee from you, fire will fear, death will be gone; you, old man, who saw not Thebes, shall see the heavens."[60]

Justin Martyr

At a time when wandering philosophers were as common as wandering prophets, the philosopher-theologian Justin Martyr (ca. 100–165) wandered from town to town presenting his evangelistic lectures in public venues. In particular, he used the concept of the divine *logos* as a means of evangelism, utilizing Jewish thought as well as Stoic, Epicurean, and Platonic philosophies to appeal to intellectuals of society.[61] He posited that any truth in the Greek philosophies was the Word (Logos) of God reaching out to sinful humans.[62]

Justin, born Flavius Justinus of Samaria, came to faith after an encounter with an elderly Christian philosopher on a beach near Ephesus. The older man struck up a conversation with Justin, drew out his philosophical views, gently challenged his assumptions and conclusions, and offered him Christ as the superior alternative.[63]

Similarly, Justin wrote his work titled *Dialogue* in the form of a discussion with a Jewish man named Trypho.[64] At the conclusion, Trypho says to Justin, "And if we could do this more frequently, we should be much helped in the searching of the Scriptures themselves."[65] Justin replies, "I exhort you to give all diligence in this very great struggle for your own salvation, and to be earnest in setting a higher value on the Christ of the Almighty God than on your own teachers." After this, Justin, praying with Trypho, says, "I can wish no better thing for you . . . than this, that, recognizing in this way that intelligence is given to every man, you may be of the same opinion as ourselves, and believe that Jesus is the Christ of God."[66]

60. Clement, *Exhortation to the Heathen* 12 (*ANF* 2:205).

61. Glenn K. Fluegge, "The Dual Nature of Evangelism in the Early Church," *Concordia Journal* 42, no. 4 (Fall 2016): 307.

62. Ferguson, *Church History*, 1:75–77.

63. Justin Martyr, *Dialogue with Trypho* 3–8 (*ANF* 1:195–99).

64. Ferguson, *Church History*, 1:73–75, 78.

65. Justin Martyr, *Dialogue with Trypho* 142 (*ANF* 1:270).

66. Justin Martyr, *Dialogue with Trypho* 142 (*ANF* 1:270). Justin's evangelism to Jews was important because during the early church they continued to be an important source of converts to the Christian faith. Stark, *Rise of Christianity*, 49.

In addition, Justin wrote his *Apology* to Emperor Antoninus Pius in an appeal for justice for Christians. His *Second Apology*, addressed to a Cynic philosopher named Crescens, stated his intention that readers would convert to Christ.[67] It was reported that during the time when he stayed at the house of Martinus in Rome, Justin imparted words of truth to all who would listen. After presumably defeating Crescens in a public debate, the Cynic philosopher brought Justin and six of his students to the attention of the Roman prefect, Rusticus. When they refused to make sacrifices to the Roman gods as the imperial edict required, they were condemned and beheaded. Therefore, Justin received the honored title "Martyr." Despite Justin's martyrdom, his disciple, Tatian of Syria, continued the same pattern of ministry, as did Rhodo, the disciple of Tatian.[68]

Catechetical Schools

Another apologist during this time was Pantaenus (ca. 120–216), a Stoic philosopher who converted to Christ and traveled as far as India, preaching the gospel before he founded a catechetical school in Alexandria, Egypt.[69] Not only did this school instruct new converts, but it became a center for Christian higher education. Curious and interested pagan students came to hear the teachers expound their philosophical views from a Christian perspective.[70] In this way the teachers evangelized them. In addition, they took it upon themselves to preach the gospel to the surrounding neighborhood.[71]

Origen

Christian teachers such as Pantaenus and his student Origen of Alexandria (ca. 184–253) became so well known that they were criticized by Celsus, a Greek philosopher and opponent of Christianity, who accused them of taking advantage of "ignorant, common folk in the marketplace."[72] In re-

67. Weinrich, "Evangelism in the Early Church," 66.
68. Eusebius, *Ecclesiastical History* 5.13 (*NPNF*² 1:227).
69. Alvin J. Schmidt, *How Christianity Changed the World* (Grand Rapids: Zondervan, 2009), 26; Gerald R. McDermott and Harold A. Netland, *A Trinitarian Theology of Religions: An Evangelical Proposal* (New York: Oxford University Press, 2014), 116–17.
70. Eusebius, *Ecclesiastical History* 5.10 (*NPNF*² 1:224–25).
71. M. Green, *Evangelism in the Early Church*, 204.
72. Origen, *Against Celsus* 3.50–58 (*ANF* 4:484–87).

sponse, Origen defended the practice by calling attention to the Cynics, who employed the same methods of recruiting and educating students.

In his work titled *Against Celsus*, Origen provided arguments about Jesus fulfilling Old Testament prophecy, and developed a moral argument that Jesus and his followers, unlike magicians of the time, did not receive any earthly rewards or gain for their deeds but brought benefits to others.[73]

Origen's teaching at the catechetical school in Alexandria became so well known that Julia Mamaea, the mother of Emperor Alexander Severus, visited Origen to hear him present the tenets of Christian faith.[74] Eusebius writes that when Mamaea was at Antioch, "she sent a detail of soldiers to fetch him [Origen]. He stayed with her for some time, revealing to her many things to the glory of the Lord and of the virtue of the divine message."[75]

Gregory Thaumaturgus

Gregory Thaumaturgus (ca. 210–265) was a student who converted to faith in Christ under Origen.[76] When Gregory was eighteen, he and his brother, both pagans in Neo-Caesarea in Pontus, were traveling to study law at Berytus, modern-day Beirut.[77] When they came to Caesarea in Palestine, they met Origen, who persuaded them to stay and offered tutoring in the history of philosophy. In his approach, Origen combined principles of philosophy and Christian doctrine, showing the two brothers how Jesus Christ could change their lives in both personal and practical ways.

Gregory remained a student of Origen for seven years.[78] Sometime later, in a treatise that he wrote in Origen's honor, Gregory described his teacher's methods of leading students to faith. He said that Origen blended persuasive candor with outbursts of temper, and then he would present a theological argument quickly and cleverly, drawing on his persuasive skills, sincerity, and deep conviction.[79]

73. Edward L. Smither, *Mission in the Early Church: Themes and Reflections* (Eugene, OR: Cascade, 2014), 81.

74. Ferguson, *Church History*, 1:133, 135; M. Green, *Evangelism in the Early Church*, 262.

75. Eusebius, *Ecclesiastical History* 6.21 (*NPNF*² 1:268–69).

76. M. Green, *Evangelism in the Early Church*, 226.

77. Ferguson, *Church History*, 1:174.

78. M. Green, *Evangelism in the Early Church*, 342–44.

79. Gregory Thaumaturgus, *Oration and Panegyric Addressed to Origen* 13–15 (*ANF* 6:33–36).

Gregory went on to become an evangelist-bishop. After his years of instruction under Origen, he longed for the time when he could demonstrate to common people that the gospel was "the only true and good philosophy."[80] Gregory's preaching was so powerful that most citizens of Pontus in Asia Minor were converted to Christ. It was said that while there were only seventeen Christians in Pontus when Gregory arrived, thirty years later there were only seventeen pagans left.[81]

Clearly, catechetical schools proved to be an effective means of evangelism.[82] While those at Alexandria, Antioch, Caesarea of Palestine, and other places were established to educate teachers, they soon developed into training schools for pastor-teachers, missionaries, and evangelists. Like local churches, these schools extended their witness for generations beyond that of the founders.

Miracles and Healing

The activity of evangelism was not limited to intellectual development of the Christian faith, although this was vitally important. Evangelism depended on the powerful work of God to dissuade pagans from their worship of false gods and to persuade them to believe the gospel.[83] Moreover, the activity of evangelism depended on the work of the Holy Spirit to empower Christ followers to perform miracles and healings (John 14:12).

Eusebius notes that early Christians were evangelizing with God's grace, "for a great many wonderful works were done through them by the power of the divine Spirit."[84] Hippolytus highlights the role of miracles, saying, "These gifts were first bestowed upon us, the apostles, when we were about to preach the gospel . . . for the conviction of unbelievers, that those who the Word did not persuade, the power of signs might put to shame; for signs are not for us who believe, but for the unbelievers, both for the Jews

80. Charles G. Herbermann, Edward A. Pace, and Thomas J. Shahan, eds., *The Catholic Encyclopedia: An International Work of Reference on the Constitution, Doctrine, Discipline and History of the Catholic Church* (New York: Robert Appleton, 1910), 7:15.

81. S. D. F. Salmond, "Introductory Note to Gregory Thaumaturgus" (*ANF* 6:6). Gregory combined exorcising demons and evangelism. Ramsey MacMullen, *Christianizing the Roman Empire: A.D. 100–400* (New Haven: Yale University Press, 1984), 60–64.

82. Eusebius, *Ecclesiastical History* 6.3–4 (*NPNF*^{2} 1:251–52).

83. Stark, *Rise of Christianity*, 90–91.

84. Eusebius, *Ecclesiastical History* 3.37.3 (*NPNF*^{2} 1:169).

and Gentiles."[85] Gregory, discussed above, not only exposed pagan miracles as frauds, but by the power of God he performed wonders himself. Thus, Gregory became known as *Thaumatourgos* (Latinized as *Thaumaturgus*), meaning "wonder worker."[86]

Historian Ramsey MacMullen concludes that a major reason for the rapid growth of Christianity in the early church was the "persuasive influence of miracles, particularly exorcisms and healings," which validated the gospel.[87] Michael Green writes, "It is an interesting fact arising from all this evidence that exorcisms were done in an evangelistic context. They were so clearly designed to back up the claims of the preached word."[88]

Christian *Caritas*

Whereas MacMullen and Green conclude that a major reason for the growth of the Christian movement was miracles, historian Henry Chadwick attributes the growth to the "practical application of charity."[89] Similarly, Adolf von Harnack posits that a major reason the church was attractive to the common people was its social message.[90] Harnack lists several acts of charity practiced by the early church, including feeding the hungry; caring for the poor; caring for slaves, orphans, widows, prisoners, and the sick and infirm; aiding travelers; and contributing to the needs of Christians facing poverty and peril.[91]

It was expected within the early church that a portion of every congregation's offerings would go to aid the poor, widows, and orphans.[92] In 251, the church at Rome supported fifteen hundred widows and persons in need. The church provided burials for the poor, showed hospitality to traveling evangelists, visited prisoners, and cared for the elderly. These and other acts of charity soon caught the attention of pagans. Tertullian writes,

85. M. Green, *Evangelism in the Early Church*, 192.

86. Stephen Neill, *A History of Christian Missions* (London: Penguin, 1986), 34.

87. MacMullen, *Christianizing the Roman Empire*, 35, 40. Cf. Rowan A. Greer, *The Fear of Freedom: A Study of Miracles in the Roman Imperial Church* (University Park, PA: Penn State University Press, 1990), 49, 52.

88. M. Green, *Evangelism in the Early Church*, 191.

89. Chadwick, *Early Church*, 56. Cf. Stark, *Rise of Christianity*, 74.

90. Adolf von Harnack, *The Expansion of Christianity in the First Three Centuries*, trans. and ed. James Moffatt (London: Williams and Norgate, 1904–1905; repr., Eugene, OR: Wipf & Stock, 1998), 1:184–85.

91. Harnack, *Expansion of Christianity*, 153–54.

92. Ferguson, *Church History*, 1:156.

> Though we have our treasure chest, it is not made up of purchase-money, as of a religion that has its price. On the monthly day, if he likes, each puts in a small donation, but only if it be his pleasure, and only if he be able, for there is no compulsion; all is voluntary. These gifts are, as it were, piety's deposit fund. For they are not taken and spent on feasts and drinking bouts and eating-houses, but to support and bury poor people, to supply the wants of boys and girls destitute of means and parents, and of old persons confined now to the house; such, too, as have suffered shipwreck; and if there happen to be any in the mines, or banished to the islands, or shut up in the prisons, for nothing but their fidelity to the cause of God's Church, they become the nurslings of their confession. But it is mainly the deeds of a love so noble that lead many to put a brand upon us. "See," they say, "how they love one another."[93]

Churches in the second and third centuries emphasized helping the poor and destitute so much that a theological question arose concerning whether a wealthy person could be saved.[94] Despite the debate, the Scriptures led Christians to build refuges for the disabled, construct dispensaries for the poor, and rescue orphans from drowning and exposure. Christian charity was symbolized in sculptures of Caritas (Latin, meaning "love") that portrayed a wet nurse who cared for orphaned and abandoned children by nursing them to health.[95]

Christians built hospitals, hospices, and hostels to nurse the sick and to provide shelter for travelers. These acts of Christian charity, along with the wholesome conduct of Christians, gave unbelieving outsiders a favorable view and impression of Christ and the church.[96]

Symbols of the Christian Faith

The word *symbol* comes from the Latin *symbolum* (from Greek *symbolon*), meaning "mark" or "token." Symbols are verbal; they are composed of words.

93. Tertullian, *Apology* 39 (*ANF* 3:46).

94. There were apparently a sufficient number of rich people among the Christians of Alexandria for this to become a pastoral dilemma. Some of the well-to-do listeners of Clement of Alexandria became concerned that wealth itself was a hindrance to entering heaven. Clement wrote a homily on Mark 10:17–31 titled *Who Is the Rich Man That Shall Be Saved?* in response to this concern. Clement, *Salvation of the Rich* 1–41 (*ANF* 2:591–604).

95. Schmidt, *How Christianity Changed the World*, 126–28.

96. Justin Martyr, *Apology* 1.16 (*ANF* 1:168).

Figure 2.1. Caritas (Charity), ca. 1321, by Tino da Camaino (1285–1337), Museo Bardini, Florence. *(© Alinari Archives/Art Resource, NY)*

They are also visual; they represent something. The Latin word *symbolum* originally denoted the Apostles' Creed, a statement that defines the core belief of a follower of Christ.

The Apostles' Creed

The Apostles' Creed (Latin *symbolum apostolorum*) represented the gospel from "the apostles' teaching" of the New Testament (Acts 2:42).[97] The creed, known originally in Greek as "the symbol of faith" (*symbolon tēs pisteōs*), was written about 150 CE, most likely in Rome, and was used as a baptismal formula to ask questions of the baptismal candidate.[98] An example of the questions is preserved in the *Apostolic Tradition* that describes baptism in the early church:

> "Do you believe in God the Father Almighty?" And the one being baptized shall answer, "I believe." . . . Then he [the presbyter-pastor] shall ask, "Do you believe in Jesus Christ, the Son of God, who was born of the Holy Spirit and the Virgin Mary, who was crucified under Pontius Pilate, and died, and rose on the third day living from the dead, and ascended into heaven, and sat down at the right hand of the Father, the one coming to judge the living and the dead?" . . . Then he shall ask, "Do you believe in the Holy Spirit and the Holy Church and the resurrection of the flesh?" Then each being baptized shall answer, "I believe."[99]

In its confessional form, this symbol was the "mark of a Christian," the core belief of a Christian.

While each of the four Gospels gives a full account of the gospel, the New Testament contains summaries and creedal statements, mentioned in the previous chapter (Acts 2:22–39; 10:36–43; Rom. 1:2–5; 1 Cor. 15:1–6).[100] These passages summarize the Gospels, speaking of the work of God in Jesus Christ to reconcile human beings to himself. Such summaries provided the

97. The Apostles' Creed was an early rule of faith. The statements of the rule of faith focused on "the historical acts of God's saving work in Jesus Christ: his virgin birth, ministry, death, resurrection, and coming again in judgment." Ferguson, *Church History*, 1:110–11.

98. Henry Bettenson and Chris Maunder, eds., *Documents of the Christian Church* (New York: Oxford University Press, 2011), 25–26; J. N. D. Kelly, *Early Christian Creeds* (Oxfordshire, UK: Taylor & Francis, 2017), 101.

99. Hippolytus, *Apostolic Tradition* 21.12–18; Gregory Dix and Henry Chadwick, eds., *The Treatise on the Apostolic Tradition of St. Hippolytus of Rome, Bishop and Martyr* (London: Curzon, 1992), 36–38.

100. Kelly, *Early Christian Creeds*, 13.

substance of the Apostles' Creed and other ancient Christian symbols, giving Christians easy-to-use means in order to share the gospel with others.[101]

ΙΧΘΥΣ

The gospel was communicated also through visual symbols. For example, an acronym whose letters spell the Greek word for "fish" (*ichthys*) was adopted as a symbol by early Christians. The acronym consists of the initial letters in the phrase "Jesus [the] Messiah, God's Son, Savior."[102]

Jesus made multiple references to fish. He said to his disciples, "Come, follow me, . . . and I will send you out to fish for people" (Matt. 4:19). He told them a parable of drawing in the fishing net in which the fisherman keeps the good fish and throws away the bad (Matt. 13:47–49).

Figure 2.2. ΙΧΘΥΣ, funerary stele of Licinia Amias, early third century, near the Vatican Necropolis, Rome. *(Former Kircherian Collection, Baths of Diocletian, National Roman Museum)*

The symbol of the *ichthys* was not merely a means to describe Jesus Christ but also a means for Christian disciples to explain him to others. The letters of the acronym could be recalled easily, explained simply, and retold by new believers immediately after their conversion to faith. These verbal and visual symbols were means to communicate the gospel during the second and third centuries and appealed to people at large.[103] They were used not simply by bishops,

101. Scot McKnight, *The King Jesus Gospel: The Original Good News* (Grand Rapids: Zondervan, 2016), 63–70.

102. Ferguson, *Church History*, 1:169; Schmidt, *How Christianity Changed the World*, 293. Iota (Ι) is the first letter of *Iēsous* (Ἰησοῦς), Greek for "Jesus." The second letter, chi (Χ), is the first letter of *Christos* (Χριστός), meaning "anointed" or "messiah." Theta (Θ) is the first letter of *Theou* (Θεοῦ), meaning "of God," the genitive case of *Theos* (Θεός), meaning "God." Upsilon (Υ) is the first letter of *Yios* (Ὑἱός), meaning "Son." Sigma (Σ) is the first letter of *Sōtēr* (Σωτήρ), meaning "Savior." T. Rasimus, "Revisiting the Ichthys: A Suggestion Concerning the Origins of Christological Fish Symbolism," in *Mystery and Secrecy in the Nag Hammadi Collection and Other Ancient Literature: Ideas and Practices*, ed. Christian H. Bull, Liv Ingeborg Lied, and John D. Turner (Leiden: Brill, 2012), 327–48.

103. Ferguson, *Church History*, 1:171.

elders, and missionaries but also by lay Christians who gave testimony to "Jesus the Christ, the Son of God, the Savior" whether in cobbler shops, in mines, on merchant ships, at schools, and in laundries. Symbols of the gospel prepared them to speak about Jesus with their family, neighbors, and even strangers.[104]

The Gospel in the Letter to Diognetus

In the second century, the author of the *Letter to Diognetus* presented the message of Jesus. The unknown author—sometimes referred to as Mathetes (Greek *mathētēs*, meaning "disciple")—explained that God disclosed his truth through his Son, through whom all things were made and ordered. God sent his Son because humans were incapable of delivering themselves from sin and its consequences, and thus unable to enter God's presence and kingdom. In a mysterious and marvelous transaction, God provided the means through the sacrifice of his Son in order that humans might receive his righteousness.[105]

Excerpts from *The Letter to Diognetus*

But truly the Almighty Creator of the Universe, the Invisible God Himself from heaven planted among men the truth and the holy teaching which surpasseth the wit of man, and fixed it firmly in their hearts, not as any man might imagine, by sending (to mankind) a subaltern, or angel, or ruler, or one of those that direct the affairs of earth, or one of those who have been entrusted with the dispensations in heaven, but the very Artificer and Creator of the Universe Himself, by Whom He made the heavens, by Whom He enclosed the sea in its proper bounds. . . .

Was He sent, think you, as any man might suppose, to establish a sovereignty, to inspire fear and terror? Not so. But in gentleness [and] meekness has He sent Him, as a king might send his son who is a king. He sent Him, as sending God; He sent Him, as [a man] unto men; He sent Him, as Saviour, as using persuasion, not force: for force is no attribute of God. He sent Him, as summoning, not as persecuting; He sent Him, as loving, not as judging. . . .

Having thus planned everything already in His mind with His Son, He permitted us during the former time to be borne along by disorderly impulses

104. Rudnick, *Speaking the Gospel*, 37.
105. *Epistle to Diognetus* 7–9 (*ANF* 1:27–28).

as we desired, led astray by pleasures and lusts, not at all because He took delight in our sins, but because He bore with us, not because He approved of the past season of iniquity, but because He was creating the present season of righteousness, that, being convicted in the past time by our own deeds as unworthy of life, we might now be made deserving by the goodness of God, and having made clear our inability to enter into the kingdom of God of ourselves, might be enabled by the ability of God.

And when our iniquity had been fully accomplished, and it had been made perfectly manifest that punishment and death were expected as its recompense, and the season came which God had ordained, when henceforth He should manifest His goodness and power (O the exceeding great kindness and love of God), He hated us not, neither rejected us, nor bore us malice, but was long-suffering and patient, and in pity for us took upon Himself our sins, and Himself parted with His own Son as a ransom for us, the holy for the lawless, the guileless for the evil, the just for the unjust, the incorruptible for the corruptible, the immortal for the mortal.

For what else but His righteousness would have covered our sins? In whom was it possible for us lawless and ungodly men to have been justified, save only in the Son of God? O the sweet exchange, O the inscrutable creation, O the unexpected benefits; that the iniquity of many should be concealed in One Righteous Man, and the righteousness of One should justify many that are iniquitous! Having then in the former time demonstrated the inability of our nature to obtain life, and having now revealed a Saviour able to save even creatures which have no ability, He willed that for both reasons we should believe in His goodness and should regard Him as nurse, father, teacher, counsellor, physician, mind, light, honour, glory, strength and life. (*Epistle of Mathetes to Diognetus* 7–9 [*ANF* 1:27–28])

Disciple-Making in *The Apostolic Tradition*

Within the early church, a pattern or order of disciple-making in house churches emerged as described in *The Apostolic Tradition*, commonly attributed to Hippolytus (ca. 170–236).[106] This disciple-making pattern achieved widespread acceptance from Alexandria, Egypt, to the capital city of Rome.

106. Priscilla Pope-Levison, *Models of Evangelism* (Grand Rapids: Baker Academic, 2020), 75–78. Ferguson says, "The apparently successful reconstruction in the twentieth

The disciple-making process began with pagans who inquired about the gospel as a result of attending a meeting at a house church, listening to an evangelistic message, or hearing a Christian's testimony of faith. The pagan *inquirers* or seekers were welcomed to attend the worship service of the house church where they heard the teachings of Jesus, messages from the Epistles, and perhaps a spontaneous, Spirit-led prophecy. After the first part of the service, they were dismissed before the Eucharist and agape feast took place, reserved for only catechized and baptized Christians, known also as *the faithful.*

All inquirers who became prospective converts were invited to meet with the presbyter-pastor of the house church to be questioned privately about matters of the gospel.[107] The purpose of the meeting was for the pastor to set forth Jesus's call to "follow me" (Mark 1:17; 10:21). The seeker was asked to turn from all other religions to Christ as Lord, embracing his way of life. The decision to follow Christ was ratified later by a rite of welcome that signaled the new convert's beginning of discipleship. The rite included walking before the congregation during a service of the house church, renouncing false religions and paganism, receiving the sign of the cross, and taking a seat among the congregation as a sign of entrance into the church, the local body of believers.

In the next phase of disciple-making, the new convert was considered a *hearer* or catechumen, meaning "one who is instructed." Along with inquirers, the hearers at a worship service were dismissed after the sermon and before the Eucharist.[108] During this phase the catechumens received instruction in Christian doctrine, Christian disciplines, and development of Christian character. Generally, converts were hearers for one to three years before their baptism.[109] Nonetheless, they were considered Christians and tentative members of the congregation.[110]

The shift to postpone baptism occurred early in the second century.[111] This allowed for a period of instruction, as well as observation and evalua-

---

century of the influential Apostolic Tradition of Hippolytus is now being called into question." *Church History*, 1:136.

107. Paul F. Bradshaw, Maxwell E. Johnson, and L. Edward Phillips, *The Apostolic Tradition: A Commentary* (Minneapolis: Fortress, 2002), 84.

108. Ferguson, *Church History*, 1:244–45.

109. Bradshaw, *Apostolic Tradition*, 84.

110. From Acts 2 and 9 it appears that baptism was administered shortly after a profession of faith. However, there developed a delay in baptism, probably due to some people falling away from the faith (Acts 8:9–25; Heb. 5:11–14).

111. Rudnick, *Speaking the Gospel*, 39–40.

tion of the convert's life before baptism. When the catechumen was judged to be sufficiently informed, sincere, and walking in a manner worthy of the gospel, she could enroll for baptism. This was marked publicly when she declared her intent to be baptized.

During the next several weeks, the convert entered a time of purification that concluded with the rite of baptism, generally at sunrise on Easter Sunday.[112] The convert was described during this phase of purification as a *kneeler*. This was a time of self-examination, fasting, and prayer to prepare for the rite of baptism.[113] During the weeks leading up to Easter Sunday, it was acknowledged that the kneeler needed to confront doubts and temptations from carnal, worldly, and demonic sources. Yet the kneelers were reminded that although Satan is a powerful being, he was defeated by Christ on the cross and is restrained in power by the Holy Spirit. During this time, kneelers were brought forward during the worship services. Members of the faithful laid hands on them and prayed for them, asking God to protect them from evil and to form within them the character of disciples who live in the victory of Christ.[114]

At sunrise on Easter Sunday, the house church gathered for the baptism service. Before entering the water, each kneeler was asked again to renounce the world, the flesh, and the devil, and to confess faith in Jesus Christ, reciting creedal statements or answering questions of the baptismal rite (Apostles' Creed) that expressed the gospel of Christ, as noted above.[115]

Then the convert was baptized in the name of the triune God, symbolizing death and burial with Christ, and raised up from the water, symbolizing the second birth to resurrection and union with him (Rom. 6:4–8). The leader anointed each person with the oil of thanksgiving.[116] Then the newly baptized persons dried off, put on clothes, and entered the assembly where they were embraced and welcomed by the faithful.[117] The newly baptized

112. Ferguson, *Church History*, 1:149; Smither, *Mission in the Early Church*, 159–60.

113. John H. Westerhoff, "Evangelism, Evangelization, and Catechesis," in *The Study of Evangelism: Exploring a Missional Practice of the Church*, ed. Paul Wesley Chilcote and Laceye C. Warner (Grand Rapids: Eerdmans, 2008), 240–41.

114. Robert E. Webber, *Ancient-Future Evangelism: Making Your Church a Faith-Forming Community* (Grand Rapids: Baker Books, 2003), 45; Bradshaw, *Apostolic Tradition*, 102.

115. Bettenson and Maunder, *Documents of the Christian Church*, 25–26.

116. Ferguson, *Church History*, 1:149.

117. Millard J. Erickson, *Christian Theology*, 3 vols. (Grand Rapids: Baker, 1983–1985), 1089.

convert then participated fully in the life of the church and the full worship service, partaking of the Eucharist and agape feast. During the weeks following Easter, they were led in reflection on the mystery of faith and the meaning of baptism and the Eucharist. They were also taught to care for the needy and poor as important steps of Christian discipleship.

The Apostolic Tradition describes the rite of ordination for members of the faithful who were gifted and prepared for leadership as presbyter-pastors and as deacons. For presbyter-pastors, they were to show evidence of the Spirit-filled life, and their primary function was to bear witness to the truth. They ministered in Word and sacrament publicly in worship services and at exorcisms and baptisms along with deacons, who had specific responsibilities in these tasks.

This disciple-making pattern was shaped by the teachings of Jesus and the apostles, as well as the context of the early church. As long as Christianity was considered a *religio illicita* by imperial authorities, leaders and members of the faithful faced persecution and martyrdom. They also faced the reality of apostasy by those who lapsed in their Christian faith and renounced Christ as Lord.

The Decian Persecution

Emperor Decius, who reigned from 249 to 251, was considered, politically speaking, one of the better emperors of the Roman Empire. However, he did not tolerate Christianity. During his reign, "the empire declared war on the church with an effort at systemic oppression."[118] Decius's main goal was to restore the empire to its ancient glory with its ancestral religion. Therefore, in 250, he decreed that Roman citizens must publicly worship the state's gods by offering sacrifices to the gods and burning incense before a statue of Decius. While Jews were exempt, Christians were not. All citizens of the empire, including women and children, who were willing to offer the required sacrifices were given a *libellus*, or certificate.[119] Those who refused were persecuted and possibly put to death.

The Decian persecution had a distressing impact on the church, and many apostatized, falling away from Christ and the church.[120] When a black market arose to sell bogus *libelli*, some Christians bought the counterfeit

118. Ferguson, *Church History*, 1:161.
119. Bainton, *Christianity*, 81–82.
120. Rudnick, *Speaking the Gospel*, 21–22.

certificates, which raised questions about them denying the faith. Other Christians resisted initially, but when brought before the Roman authorities, they offered the required sacrifices and lapsed in their devotion to Christ. Other Christians resolved to stand firm and refused to obey the edict, even in the face of threats, torture, and death.

This persecution ended suddenly in 251, when Decius was killed fighting the Goths along the Danube River. After this, the church faced questions about how to handle those who lapsed. They were reminded of Tertullian's words that described persecution as the "winnowing fan which even now cleanses the Lord's threshing floor, his church."[121]

Exponential Growth

Despite persecution and apostasy, the number of converts to Christ grew throughout the Roman Empire and beyond. During the second and third centuries, the gospel spread as evangelists and missionaries carried the message of Jesus Christ along the empire's roads, rivers, and sea lanes. Christian merchants evangelized as they traveled, and converted Roman soldiers witnessed to the gospel wherever they were stationed.

Historian Timothy George describes the effort of Christians to advance the gospel: "They went everywhere—into the arena, the academies of learning, the marketplace, to faraway lands such as India and Ethiopia, into every nook and cranny of the Roman Empire. But they targeted especially the great urban centers of the Mediterranean world. . . . By the year 200 there were flourishing Christian communities in Antioch and Alexandria, Ephesus and Corinth, Carthage and Caesarea, and, of course, in Rome itself."[122] From these centers, Christians traveled with the good news eastward to Arabia and Persia, westward through Alexandria and along the coast of North Africa, northward to Pontus and Armenia, and eventually westward to Gaul and Britain.[123]

The first translation of the New Testament was in the Syriac language in the East, as was the first Christian hymnbook, *The Odes of Solomon*.[124] The

121. Tertullian, *Flight in Persecution* 1 (*ANF* 4:116).

122. George, "Challenge of Evangelism," 10.

123. Herbert Kane, *A Global View of Missions* (Grand Rapids: Baker, 1975), 10; John Mark Terry, *Evangelism: A Concise History* (Nashville: B&H, 2014), 30; Ferguson, *Church History*, 1:353.

124. Samuel H. Moffett, *A History of Christianity in Asia* (Maryknoll, NY: Orbis, 1998).

first known building to be used specifically for a Christian congregation was at Edessa in Dura Europos, in modern-day Syria. From Edessa, Christianity spread to Arbela, across the Tigris near ancient Nineveh. By the end of the second century there were churches as far east as Persia and modern-day northern Afghanistan. By the year 225 there were twenty bishoprics in Persia alone.[125]

In North Africa, Christianity moved from Egypt south to Numidia and west to Carthage, where gatherings of Christians were the first Latin-speaking churches.[126] By the second century, the Greek texts of the Gospels and Epistles were translated into Latin.[127] The gospel also spread to Germania and Gaul, where the Rhone Valley became a center of Christian activity. Moreover, the church grew in Britain as a result of Roman soldiers who converted to Christian faith. The government offered retiring soldiers plots of land in this newly acquired territory.[128]

By the end of the second century, Christians were 2.4 percent of the world's population.[129] By the end of the third century, the number of Christians reached an estimated 10 percent, with 5 to 7.5 million people within the Roman Empire.[130] The expansion of the church was itself testimony to the fact that evangelism was the privilege and responsibility of every Christian.

In a refutation of Celsus, Origen spoke of the desire of Christians to take the gospel to places without a gospel witness: "Christians do not neglect, as far as in them lies, to take measures to disseminate their doctrine throughout the whole world. Some of them, accordingly, have made it their business to itinerate not only through cities, but even villages and country houses, that they might make converts to God."[131] Similarly, Tertullian said, "We are but of yesterday, and we have filled every place among you—cities, islands, fortresses, towns, market-places, the very camp, tribes, companies, palace, senate, forum,—we have left nothing to you but the temples of your gods."[132]

125. Tuttle, *Story of Evangelism*, 114–15.

126. Neill, *History of Missions*, 36; cited in Terry, *Evangelism*, 31.

127. Dana Robert, *Christian Mission: How Christianity Became a World Religion* (Oxford: Wiley-Blackwell, 2009), 10.

128. W. O. Carver, *The Course of Christian Missions* (New York: Revell, 1932), 51.

129. Tuttle, *Story of Evangelism*, 116.

130. Stark, *Rise of Christianity*, 6–7, 93.

131. Origen, *Against Celsus* 3.9 (*ANF* 4:468).

132. Tertullian, *Apology* 37 (*ANF* 3:45).

Discussion Questions

1. Perpetua sought to identify with Christ in his death by dying as a martyr. Should we have the same attitude about martyrdom? If martyrdom is identification with Jesus, how can we identify with him in life and not just in death? Is it wrong to resist martyrdom?
2. Should churches today follow *The Apostolic Tradition* in delaying baptism in order to see obedience and fruit in the life of the new believer? What are pros and cons of delaying baptism?
3. In what ways can Christians bring back the practices of *caritas* of the early church and care better for the poor, orphaned, and widowed? How can you do this as a member of a local church?
4. Compare the excerpts of Melito's *On the Passover* and the *Letter to Diognetus*. How does each describe the gospel? What elements do they share? How are they different from what you discovered when comparing Peter's and Paul's descriptions of the gospel?
5. The Greek term *logos* is used by the apostle John to describe Jesus Christ, as well as by Justin Martyr. When is it appropriate to use a philosophical term or religious concept to convey some aspect of the gospel? For example, in Chinese culture, the term *dao* means the "way" or "word." Should it be used? What other words in your cultural context might be useful?

3

Christendom and Monastic Evangelism

You are Jesus, the Son of the Father, he who commands the Cherubim and Seraphim. You have existed always with the Father in truth. You are the power of the Heavens, the crown of the Martyrs, the deep counsel of the Saints. In you is the counsel of the Father hidden. You are the mouth of the Prophets, the tongue of the Angels. You are Jesus, my Life, the object and boast of the world, Yea, Amen.

—Athanasius of Alexandria (ca. 297–373)[1]

A respite of more than forty years separated the persecution of Christians under Decius and the great persecution that began in 303 at the instigation of Emperor Galerius, with the support of Emperor Diocletian.[2] Diocletian's goal, like other emperors, was to restore the glory and greatness of the Roman Empire under the old pagan tradition. To do this, he eliminated Christians from the armed forces and government positions and ordered authorities to seize church buildings and to confiscate copies of the

1. Adapted from "The Dying Prayer of St. Athanasius, Archbishop of Alexandria," in A. W. T. Budge, *Coptic Homilies in the Dialect of Upper Egypt* (New York: AMS), 1012–20, cited in George D. Dragas, *Saint Athanasius of Alexandria: Original Research and New Perspectives* (Rollinsford, NH: Orthodox Research Institute, 2005), 92.

2. Everett Ferguson, *Church History*, vol. 1, *From Christ to Pre-Reformation* (Grand Rapids: Zondervan, 2005), 179.

Scriptures for burning.[3] All citizens, including church leaders, were required to sacrifice to the gods or suffer torture, death, or a life of forced labor.[4]

Thousands of Christians died horrific deaths rather than deny Jesus Christ as Lord. Others confessed their faith despite extreme forms of torture. For example, at the hands of persecutors, the right eye of Potamon, bishop of Heraklea, was gouged out.[5] Persecution continued intermittently under Diocletian's successors. Emperor Licinius, for example, had the bishop of Neo-Caesarea, Paul, tortured with a red-hot iron and his hands crippled.

Naturally, the fear of persecution discouraged many Roman citizens from considering the gospel and conversion to Christ. However, others were deeply affected by the devotion of Christian confessors who were willing to die because of their faith. Even Diocletian's wife, Prisca, and daughter, Valeria, were favorable to Christianity, if not persuaded by the witness of Christians to become Christ followers themselves, straining family relations either way.[6]

Legalization of Christianity

In 311, persecution came to an end in the eastern half of the empire when the ailing Emperor Galerius issued an edict granting amnesty to Christians.[7] He issued the Edict of Toleration, not because of his sympathy for them, but because pagans pressed him about the unwarranted brutal treatment of Christians.[8]

In the first two decades of the fourth century, the empire experienced waves of political conflict as Roman emperors competed with one another. This conflict came mainly from a bad decision made earlier by Diocletian to separate the empire into a tetrarchy, dividing it into eastern and western parts, with two caesars and two augustuses in each.[9] This led to battles between the four Roman leaders, who each tried to extend their rule in the empire.

3. Roland H. Bainton, *Christianity* (Boston: Houghton Mifflin, 2001), 87.

4. Milton L. Rudnick, *Speaking the Gospel through the Ages: A History of Evangelism* (St. Louis: Concordia, 1984), 22.

5. *HCC* 3:626, 873.

6. *HCC* 2:174.

7. Ferguson, *Church History*, 1:181; Rudnick, *Speaking the Gospel*, 22; Bainton, *Christianity*, 89.

8. Henry Bettenson and Chris Maunder, eds., *Documents of the Christian Church* (New York: Oxford University Press, 2011), 16–17.

9. Peter J. Leithart, *Defending Constantine: The Twilight of an Empire and the Dawn of Christendom* (Downers Grove, IL: IVP Academic, 2010), 44–45, 59.

In 312, Constantine's quest to become the single emperor of the western half of the empire led him to advance troops toward Rome to face Maxentius. On the eve of the battle, Constantine reportedly looked up toward the sun and saw a cross of light above it. The sign appeared as the Greek letters X (*chi*) and P (*rho*), with one letter superimposed on the other. This vision led him to believe that he was fighting under the protection of the Christian God, since X (*chi*) and P (*rho*) are the first two letters of the name Christ (Χριστός).[10] As Constantine saw the vision, he purportedly heard a divine voice say, "In this [sign] conquer," which he interpreted as an omen that he would be successful in battle.[11] Therefore, he placed the *chi-rho* (☧) symbol on the shields of his soldiers and went on to defeat Maxentius's troops in battle at Milvian Bridge near Rome.[12] With this victory and the death of Maxentius, Constantine became the sole emperor of the west.[13] The experience of the vision also marked his "conversion" to faith in the Christian God.[14] The sincerity of his conversion would be questioned by devout Christians for years to come.[15] Minimally, he sought the aid of the Christian God to accomplish his political goals.[16]

In 313, Constantine met with Licinius, who succeeded Galerius as emperor in the east. The two emperors, Constantine in the west and Licinius in the east, agreed to end the persecution of Christians by signing the Edict of Milan.[17] With this act, Christianity received legal status from the Roman state, making it a legal religion (*religio licita*). The edict said, "It was right that Christians and all others should have freedom to follow the kind of religion they favored. . . . Christians . . . are to be permitted to continue . . . without any let or hindrance, and are not to be in any way troubled or molested."[18]

By 324, Constantine won control of the east too, making him sole emperor of the empire.[19] Then he moved the capital from Rome to the ancient

10. Ferguson, *Church History*, 1:182–83.

11. Eusebius, *Life of Constantine* 1.28–38 (*NPNF*² 1:490–93).

12. Leithart, *Defending Constantine*, 71, 76.

13. Bainton, *Christianity*, 89; Leithart, *Defending Constantine*, 106.

14. Ramsey MacMullen, *Christianizing the Roman Empire A.D. 100–400* (New Haven: Yale University Press, 1984), 43–44; Leithart, *Defending Constantine*, 79–81.

15. Ferguson says, "Constantine was a 'prudential Christian' whose primary concern was to hold the empire together. He never clearly distinguished between 'worship of the Sun and the Son.'" *Church History*, 1:181.

16. Ferguson, *Church History*, 1:185.

17. Bettenson, *Documents of the Christian Church*, 17; Bainton, *Christianity*, 89.

18. Bettenson, *Documents of the Christian Church*, 17.

19. Ferguson, *Church History*, 1:182–83.

city of Byzantium in the east and renamed it for himself, Constantinople, modern-day Istanbul, Turkey. In the following years, Christianity was not only legalized but favored by him as he enacted legislation to benefit the church.[20] Despite his questionable conversion, he tried to understand the church's teachings and promoted it with his political power.[21] This introduced a new era of the church—the Constantinian era—which brought significant changes to the relationship between the church and state.[22]

Christians benefited from their new legal status in several ways. Earlier they had gathered for worship in houses or clandestine places out of fear of being discovered by Roman authorities, but after the Edict of Milan they were free to worship publicly and to build edifices for worship that included basilicas able to accommodate hundreds of people.[23] The new buildings for churches were patterned after the imperial basilicas used for audiences, reception halls, and governmental affairs.[24]

Constantine made the first day of the week, Sunday, in respect to the sun God (*Sol Invictus*), an official holiday, allowing people the freedom to worship, which meant that Christians could freely worship the triune God.[25] In addition, Constantine gave gifts to the church, such as the Lateran Palace in Rome as a place of worship. He granted bishops and elders/presbyters exemption from property taxes and worked to free Christian slaves.[26] Moreover, the new legal status gave Christians opportunities to discuss and debate theology publicly. When Eusebius of Caesarea observed all the positive changes taking place, he viewed Constantine favorably as God's vice-regent on earth.[27]

Nevertheless, the changes brought negative consequences and dangers to the church. As Christianity became favored by the Roman state, vast numbers of people streamed into the Christian congregations. In 313, at the signing of the Edict of Milan, approximately 10 percent of the population of the empire was composed of Christians; by the end of the century, the

20. Eusebius, *Life of Constantine* 1.41–44 (*NPNF*[2] 1:494–95).

21. Leithart, *Defending Constantine*, 28.

22. Bainton, *Christianity*, 90–91.

23. Ferguson, *Church History*, 1:172, 185, 253.

24. Rodney Stark, *The Triumph of Christianity* (New York: HarperOne, 2011), 173.

25. Ferguson, *Church History*, 1:184.

26. Eusebius, *Life of Constantine* 2.22–47 (*NPNF*[2] 1:505–11).

27. Glen L. Thompson, "From Sinner to Saint? Seeking a Consistent Constantine," in *Rethinking Constantine: History, Theology, and Legacy*, ed. Edward L. Smither (Eugene, OR: Pickwick, 2014), 20. Cf. Eusebius, *Life of Constantine* 3.10 (*NPNF*[2] 1:522).

Christian population rose to 66 percent. As could be expected, many people identified as Christians because of the civil, social, and political advantages of being a "Christian," and not for spiritual or convictional reasons.[28]

During the pre-Constantinian era it had been costly to follow Christ, but during the Constantinian era this changed.[29] There was no longer persecution as a "winnowing fan" to separate the "wheat of the martyrs from the chaff of the deniers."[30] In many cases, the church's new status fostered *nominal Christianity*, in which people became Christians in name only, showing little or no evidence of personal devotion to Christ.[31] In some cases, instruction in ritual and custom replaced the catechesis that emphasized Christian character and spiritual disciplines.

The sudden growth of local congregations brought increased challenge for presbyters and bishops to oversee their churches, prompting a more structured ecclesial hierarchy. In addition, as the church adapted to its Roman imperial context, its forms increasingly reflected that of the state and civil government. Historian Justo L. González has noted that while there was a Christianization of the Roman Empire, there was also a Romanization of the church as Christian worship was influenced by imperial protocol.[32] This and other significant changes posed a threat that the church might lose its character as a people led by the Spirit under the lordship of Christ.

Christendom

The Roman Empire and the Christian faith were moving toward *corpus Christianum*, or Christendom, the joining of church and society, religion and civil government, the "alliance of throne and altar."[33] This alliance would become official in 391 under Emperor Theodosius, when he issued an edict

28. Rudnick, *Speaking the Gospel*, 16.

29. Ferguson, *Church History*, 1:186.

30. Tertullian, *Flight in Persecution* 1 (*ANF* 4:116).

31. Ferguson, *Church History*, 1:241.

32. Justo L. González, *The Story of Christianity: The Early Church to the Present Day* (Peabody, MA: Prince, 1999), 1:125. Historian Stephen Neill says, "With a new freedom, the church was able to go out into the world; at the same time, in a new and dangerous fashion, the world entered into the church." *A History of Christian Missions* (London: Penguin, 1986), 41.

33. James A. Patterson, "Politics," in *Evangelical Dictionary of World Missions*, ed. A. Scott Moreau (Grand Rapids: Baker Books, 2000), 765; Ferguson, *Church History*, 1:182, 197. Cf. Philip Jenkins, *The Next Christendom: The Coming of Global Christianity* (New York: Oxford University Press, 2011), 13–14.

mandating Christianity as the authorized religion of the empire.[34] He prohibited all other religions, as well as heresies, and ordered the destruction of pagan idols and temples.

In the meantime, Emperor Constantine did not make Christianity the single, authorized religion of the empire but favored it above many other religions. In 325, Constantine convened the Council of Nicaea because of his concerns for the unity of the empire.[35] He considered any form of disunity, even within the church, to be a threat to the Roman state. At the time, many of the bishops and presbyters of churches did not question or challenge his intervention in the church's theological disputes, but welcomed it.[36]

In calling for a council, Constantine summoned bishops or their representatives to Nicaea, near Constantinople, by issuing an edict and paying all travel costs and expenses out of the public treasury.[37] An estimated three hundred bishops and elders-presbyters attended, including Potamon of Heraklea and Paul of Neo-Caesarea, mentioned above, who still bore the scars of Diocletian's persecution. At the center of debate at the council was the nature of Jesus Christ in relation to God the Father. The outcome of the deliberations was the Nicene Creed, which affirmed core tenets of the gospel, including the nature of Jesus Christ being fully divine and fully human.[38]

Following the death of Constantine, the next decades were tumultuous, as successive emperors had varying opinions toward Christianity. Nevertheless, the Nicene Christian faith continued to displace the old Roman religion, as well as heretical views. At the same time, numbers of nominal Christians increased in the churches. This brought new challenges to the nature and task of evangelism.[39]

Evangelism became not merely a matter of preaching the gospel to those who were ignorant of the person and work of Jesus Christ but a matter of

34. Ferguson, *Church History*, 1:239–40. For Augustine's view, see Bainton, *Christianity*, 122–23. The church was to direct the state, and the state was to uphold the church. Dana Robert, *Christian Mission* (Malden, MA: Wiley-Blackwell 2009), 18.

35. Ferguson, *Church History*, 1:193–94; Leithart, *Defending Constantine*, 87.

36. Timothy Dowley, *Introduction to the History of Christianity* (Minneapolis: Fortress, 2002), 144. Ferguson says, "Nicaea served as a symbol of imperial involvement in church affairs. It was different from previous councils because of the personal presence of a formidable new factor, the emperor Constantine. . . . The age of persecution was over and the age of Christendom—Christianity as a religion favored by government—had begun." *Church History*, 1:197.

37. *HCC* 3:335.

38. Bettenson and Maunder, *Documents of the Christian Church*, 27–28.

39. Ferguson, *Church History*, 1:187.

convincing nominal Christians that they needed to be converted to Christ. Often the latter proved more difficult than the former, especially as Christianity became increasingly identified with the Roman Empire, Christian rulers, and majority-Roman culture.[40]

Monasticism

The reaction of some devout Christians to the influx of nominal Christians into the church was to flee from the church and Roman society altogether.[41] As devout Christians saw insincerity, lack of spiritual devotion, and in some cases blatant worldliness or secularization in their local congregations, they concluded that the church was becoming apostate.[42] Although they were critical of what they observed and did not want to break fellowship with the broader church, they did so for a life of prayer, meditation, and self-denial.[43]

Some who left the church for the monastic life simply wanted to follow Christ and to "know the power of his resurrection and participation in his sufferings, becoming like him in his death" (Phil. 3:10–11). Without persecution at the hands of the state, the act of discipleship to become like Christ in his death was no longer possible. Thus, monasticism became a means to participate in Jesus's sufferings—a "white martyrdom" or life of self-deprivation, in contrast to "red martyrdom," persecution and death at the hands of the state.[44]

A life of self-denial had been practiced earlier by Christians, largely by individuals who spent time in prayer and fasting and perhaps practiced celibacy for a season.[45] By the end of the third century, the ascetic life became distinct as a number of Christians withdrew from society to solitary places in uninhab-

40. Alan Kreider and Eleanor Kreider, *Worship and Mission after Christendom* (Scottdale, PA: Herald, 2011), 15.

41. Rudnick, *Speaking the Gospel*, 47, 49–50.

42. John Mark Terry, *Evangelism: A Concise History* (Nashville: B&H, 2014), 41; Bainton, *Christianity*, 100–101.

43. Mark Sheridan, "Early Egyptian Monasticism: Ideals and Reality, or: The Shaping of the Monastic Ideal," *Journal for the Canadian Society of Coptic Studies* 7 (2015): 15.

44. Timothy George, "The Challenge of Evangelism in the History of the Church," in *Evangelism in the Twenty-First Century*, ed. Thom Rainer (Wheaton, IL: Shaw, 1989), 12; Rodney Stark, *The Rise of Christianity: How the Obscure, Marginal Jesus Movement Became the Dominant Religious Force in the Western World in a Few Centuries* (San Francisco: HarperSanFrancisco, 1997), 183.

45. Matt. 6:16–18; 19:12; Luke 12:33; Acts 13:2–3; Rom. 8:13; 1 Cor. 7:3–5; 1 John 2:15–16.

ited regions.[46] By the fourth century, the monastic movement became widely popular, both as an element of protest against the secularization of the church and as a countercultural witness to Christ and a life of following after him.[47]

Those who sought the simple, ascetic life were called monks. The word *monk*, from the Greek word *monachos*, meant "solitary" and referred to a devout Christian who lived alone.[48] A monk's daily routine centered on prayer, intercession, and meditation while abstaining from worldly pleasures. The renunciation of human relationships was regarded as part of the cost of discipleship and liberated the Christian to concentrate exclusively on his or her relationship with God (Luke 14:26).

As the number of monks increased in solitary regions, they began to cloister into small communities or "monasteries." Pachomius (290–346) wrote a set of rules for monastic communal life that contained three main vows: celibacy, poverty, and obedience to the abbot, the spiritual father of the monastery.[49] With time, monastic communities turned outward to preach the gospel. With this outward direction, monks became the leading evangelistic force of the church. Basil of Caesarea in the eastern part of the Roman Empire and Martin of Tours in the western part led this development.[50] Others, such as Patrick, promoted the movement in Ireland. Proponents of monasticism did not view it as a special form of the Christian life, as it came to be considered later, but as the call of every Christian.[51] After all, Jesus said to everyone, "Whoever wants to be my disciple must deny themselves and take up their cross daily and follow me" (Luke 9:23).

Basil of Caesarea

Basil (330–379) established a monastery in Pontus of Cappadocia, modern-day Turkey. While he embraced the communal life of Pachomius, his rule for monks turned their lives outward in gospel witness and service to their

46. Ferguson, *Church History*, 1:228–29. Anthony of Egypt (ca. 251–356), known as the father of monasticism, lived in the Egyptian desert where he prayed, meditated, and "wrestled with the devil." Henry Chadwick, *The Early Church* (London: Penguin, 1993), 177.

47. For a sociological perspective of costly demands of religious groups to mitigate "free-rider" problems that lead to lower levels of member commitment and participation, see Stark, *Rise of Christianity*, 177.

48. Bainton, *Christianity*, 101.

49. Rudnick, *Speaking the Gospel*, 50.

50. Robert, *Christian Mission*, 25.

51. Ferguson, *Church History*, 1:229–33.

neighbor.[52] For Basil, the ascetic life of a monk should not be self-serving but should include gospel witness in word and deed to the community.

In order to practice this, Basil established a complex of buildings on the outskirts of Caesarea. The complex, known as the Basileias, contained a home for the poor, a hospital, a workshop where the poor developed job skills, a storehouse with food supplies, and a hospitality house for travelers.[53] Basil often challenged the rich to remember their obligation to give to the poor and thereby show gratitude to God for all that he had given them.[54]

Basil was well known as a defender of Nicene theology and preached twice a day, expounding the gospel of the Nicene Creed. While he was burdened for the poor and sick, he regarded preaching the gospel as the central task of his ministry.[55] He praised the earlier work of Gregory Thaumaturgus for bringing the gospel to Cappadocia.[56] Moreover, Basil knew the importance of instructing the faithful in the gospel and sending preachers who would reach pagans with the good news. He writes,

> That the faithful should be instructed in all the precepts of the Lord in the Gospel and also those transmitted to us through the Apostles as well as all that are to be inferred therefrom. . . . That the preacher of the Word should visit all the towns and cities in his charge. . . . That all should be summoned to the hearing of the Gospel, that the Word must be preached with all candor, that the truth must be upheld even at the cost of opposition and persecution of whatever sort, unto death. . . . That we should not preach the Gospel in a spirit of strife or envy, or rivalry with anyone. . . . That one who is entrusted with the preaching of the Gospel should possess nothing more than is strictly necessary for him. . . . That we should instruct our adversaries in forbearance and mildness in the hope of their conversion until the full measure of kindness has been exercised toward them. . . . That we should depart from those who through obstinacy do not receive the Gospel, not allowing ourselves to accept even corporeal necessities from them.[57]

52. Chadwick, *Early Church*, 178–79.

53. Edward L. Smither, *Mission in the Early Church: Themes and Reflections* (Eugene, OR: Cascade, 2014), 132–39.

54. Philip Rousseau, *Basil of Caesarea* (Berkeley: University of California Press, 2008), 136–40. Cf. Tom Holland, *Dominion: How the Christian Revolution Remade the World* (New York: Basic Books, 2019), 140–43.

55. Smither, *Mission in the Early Church*, 139.

56. Basil, *On the Holy Spirit* 29.34; see also Stark, *Rise of Christianity*, 37.

57. Basil, *Morals* 70.5, 11, 12, 24, 27, 31, 33, in *Ascetical Works*, trans. M. Monica

The gospel witness that Basil and his community practiced did not go unnoticed. Emperor Julian, known as "the apostate" (361–363), testified to the charitable acts of Christians.[58] In the spirit of Decius and Diocletian, Julian had tried to restore the popularity of Roman paganism.[59] In doing so, however, he recognized that the greatest challenge was the sacrificial love demonstrated by Christians. In a letter to Arsacius, Julian wrote, "Why then do we [pagans] think that this is sufficient and do not observe how the kindness of Christians to strangers, their care for the burial of their dead, and the sobriety of their lifestyle has done the most to advance their cause? Each of these things, I think, ought really to be practiced by us. For it is disgraceful when . . . the impious Galileans [Christians] support our poor in addition to their own."[60]

Basil's pioneering work to establish Christian benevolent institutions, such as homes for the poor, hostels for travelers, and hospitals for the sick, was combined with verbal witness to the gospel and became a common evangelistic practice for centuries.[61]

Macrina the Younger

Macrina (324–379), named for her grandmother, was the older sister of Basil of Caesarea and his brothers, Gregory of Nyssa and Peter of Sebaste.[62] Macrina's father had arranged for her to marry, but when her fiancé died before the wedding, she decided not to be betrothed to another man but to seek Christ as her bridegroom. She devoted herself to a chaste and humble life, studied the Scriptures, and taught her younger brothers the way of Christ.

Her influence on her family was profound. As a result of Macrina's life and teaching, Gregory says in his biography of her that she influenced Basil toward Christian ministry.[63] After Basil had acquired rhetorical skills and

---

Wagner, The Fathers of the Church 9 (Washington, DC: Catholic University of America, 1962), 166–82.

58. Bainton, *Christianity*, 100.

59. Bettensen, *Documents of the Christian Church*, 22.

60. John Dickson, *The Best Kept Secret of Christian Mission* (Grand Rapids: Zondervan, 2010), 94. Cf. Stark, *Rise of Christianity*, 83–84, 189.

61. Ferguson, *Church History*, 1:214.

62. Gregory of Nyssa, *The Life of Saint Macrina*, trans. Kevin Corrigan (Eugene, OR: Wipf & Stock, 2005), 6–7, 30.

63. Ruth A. Tucker and Walter Liefeld, *Daughters of the Church: Women and Ministry from New Testament Times to the Present* (Grand Rapids: Zondervan, 1987), 120.

earned a name for himself, he became "puffed up with arrogance" until Macrina persuaded him toward "the ideal of philosophy" so that "he renounced worldly appearance."[64] Basil pursued a life of theology, Christian community, preaching, and gospel witness. In turn, Macrina founded a convent, a monastery for women, on the family estate in Pontus near the monastery that Basil had founded for men.[65] She and others helped rescue abandoned infants. When she died, a number of those in the convent wept and grieved for her as their own mother because she had rescued them from the roadsides and nurtured them to become holy women and servants of Christ.[66]

Martin of Tours

Martin of Tours (ca. 316–397) brought monasticism to the western part of the Roman Empire, where in 360 he established the first monastery in Gaul, of modern-day France. He attracted a group of new disciples from among the pagans, a phenomenon observed by all the pagans of the area. Ten years later, Martin became the bishop of Tours and oversaw the churches in the area. His monastery became a center for evangelism to reach other districts. He traveled widely throughout Gaul as a bishop-evangelist and won thousands of people to Christ by preaching the gospel and performing miracles.[67] It was reported that a whole village converted to Christian faith after witnessing the miracle of a boy restored to life.

Patrick of Ireland

Patrick is the most respected evangelist of this era. Numerous historical sources, including his own *Confessions* (*Confessio*), give details of his life, mission, and theology.

Before the gospel arrived in Ireland, Celtic islanders were known for their Druid culture that revolved around nature, dreams, and spirits. Druid priests lived in huts or caverns in the forest and professed to know the secrets of astrology, medicine, and arts of divination.[68] Celts were known to

64. Gregory of Nyssa, *Life of Saint Macrina*, 26.
65. Tucker and Liefield, *Daughters of the Church*, 120.
66. Holland, *Dominion*, 143–44.
67. Sulpitius Severus, *Dialogues* 2.4 (*NPNF*^{2} 11:40).
68. *HCC* 4:22–23.

practice human sacrifice and to decapitate their conquered enemies.[69] For these reasons, Romans categorized them as barbarians.[70]

The Christian faith came first to Ireland by Palladius, who in 431 was appointed bishop of Ireland by Celestine, the bishop of Rome.[71] Palladius's charge from Celestine was not to evangelize the pagan natives but to minister to Roman Christians who were working in the coastal trading villages. The ministry of Patrick was different.

Patrick (ca. 389–461) was an Englishman born on the western coast of England in the Romano-British town of Banneventa. His father was a deacon in the local church from the pre-Constantinian tradition, and his grandfather had served as the church's presbyter-pastor.[72] When Patrick was sixteen years old, he was captured by Celtic marauders and transported by boat to Ireland. He was sold as a slave to a man named Miliucc at Connaught, near the woods of Foclut. Patrick worked there as a shepherd for six years.

During this time Patrick prayed a hundred prayers a day. According to his writings, he did not value his catechetical training from his youth, admitting that he "cared nothing for religion" and that he was "an atheist from childhood."[73] Nonetheless, his years in captivity changed his views. He became a devoted follower of Jesus Christ while living as a slave in Ireland.

Patrick escaped from his master and traveled to the European continent on a boat carrying Irish hounds.[74] When he returned to England, he hoped never to see Ireland again. However, in a dream, an Irishman named Victoricus came to him with letters from the Irish people. As Patrick read one of the letters, he heard a voice like that of the people of Foclut begging him: "Come and walk among us once more."[75] Patrick tried to forget the dream but, when unable to, concluded that God was calling him to return to the land of his captivity in order to bring them the gospel.[76]

69. George G. Hunter III, *The Celtic Way of Evangelism: How Christianity Can Reach the West Again* (Nashville: Abingdon, 2000), 19.

70. Hunter, *Celtic Way of Evangelism*, 17. The Romans also categorized Goths, Visigoths, Vandals, Franks, Frisians, and Huns as barbarians.

71. Thomas O'Loughlin, *Discovering Saint Patrick* (London: Darton, Longman & Todd, 2005), 38.

72. O'Loughlin, *Discovering Saint Patrick*, 43.

73. Phillip Freeman, *St. Patrick of Ireland* (New York: Simon & Schuster, 2004), 13; O'Loughlin, *Discovering Saint Patrick*, 53.

74. Bainton, *Christianity*, 128.

75. Patrick, *Confession* 23, in *The Works of St. Patrick, St. Secundinus Hymn on St. Patrick*, ed. and trans. Ludwig Bieler (New York: Paulist, 1953), 28.

76. Caroline T. Marshall, "Patrick: Missionary to the Irish," in *Great Leaders of the Christian Church*, ed. John D. Woodbridge (Chicago: Moody, 1988), 96.

Figure 3.1. St. Patrick lighting the paschal fire, mosaic by Boris Anrep in the Chapel of St. Patrick, Cathedral of Christ the King, Mullingar, Ireland. *(© Fr. Robert McCabe by kind permission of Fr. Derek Darby, Adm., Cathedral of Christ the King, Mullingar, County Westmeath)*

Patrick prepared for his mission, receiving theological training in Britain and likely in Gaul because of his ties with the monasteries of Martin of Tours.[77] After his studies, Patrick was ordained as a presbyter-pastor.

In 432, he returned to Ireland with his "apostolic team," a band of twelve that included priests, seminarians, women, and a brewmaster.[78] Although Patrick knew the language and culture of Ireland, he viewed himself as an alien and sojourner among the barbarians.[79]

Patrick and his disciples held open-air meetings where they engaged the Celtic people in discourse around the gospel, using poetry, story, song, and symbols.[80] He told of a deity greater than those of the Druids. He preached the good news of the "God of the three faces," in reference to the triune God. He preached about this God who provided the sacrifice for the sins of people through his divine Son, in contrast to an angry Celtic god that demanded human sacrifices. Patrick effectively spoke of revered objects of nature, such as trees, fire, and mountains, to explain the God of the Scriptures. He summarized the gospel this way:

> Because there is no other God, nor ever was, nor will be, than God the Father unbegotten, without beginning, from whom is all beginning, the Lord of the universe, as we have been taught; and His Son Jesus Christ, whom we declare to have always been with the Father, spiritually and ineffably begotten by the Father before the beginning of the world, before all beginning; and by Him are made all things visible and invisible. He was made man, and, having defeated death, was received into heaven by the Father; and He hath given Him all power over all names in heaven, on earth, and under the earth, and every tongue shall confess to Him that Jesus Christ is Lord and God, in whom we believe, and whose advent we expect soon to be, judge of the living and of the dead, who will render to every man according to his deeds; and He has poured forth upon us abundantly the Holy Spirit, the gift and pledge of

77. Bainton, *Christianity*, 128. John Finney says, "It is generally thought that Irish monasticism was imported via Martin of Tours." *Recovering the Past: Celtic and Roman Mission* (London: Darton, Longman & Todd, 2011), 54.

78. Hunter, *Celtic Way of Evangelism*, 21; Stephan Mansfield, *The Search for God and Guinness* (Nashville: Thomas Nelson, 2009), 21.

79. Patrick, *Epistola militbus Corotici*, cited in O'Loughlin, *Discovering Saint Patrick*, 173.

80. Hunter, *Celtic Way of Evangelism*, 21, 73–74.

> immortality, who makes those who believe and obey sons of God and joint heirs with Christ, and Him do we confess and adore, one God in the Trinity of the Holy Name.[81]

In addition to preaching the gospel, Patrick never hesitated to call on the triune God to prove himself to the pagan Druids. He believed that the gospel must interact with their world and redeem the Celts through Christ at several levels.[82]

When entering a new area, Patrick engaged first with the tribal chief. He knew that if the chief were to convert to Christ, the rest of the tribe would follow en masse. As pagans converted to faith, Patrick and his band of disciples baptized them. Then Patrick would ask the chief or local leader for a plot of land in order to establish a monastery where converts would be taught Christian doctrine.[83] He and his disciples placed the converts in charge of the monastery while they moved to an area where the gospel had not been preached. Following this pattern, the Christians of Ireland were organized around monasteries.[84] The monastic communities were centers of evangelism, education, and copying books, particularly the Scriptures and writings of the church fathers.[85]

The monasteries were composed of monks or nuns, known commonly as regular clergy because they followed a rule—in Latin, *regula*. In contrast, secular clergy were the presbyters-pastors (priests) and deacons who served the everyday needs of the people in the broader, secular world (from the Latin *saeculum*).[86]

Celtic Christians were characterized by evangelistic zeal. Like Patrick and his evangelistic band, they believed that every Christian should communicate the gospel to others.[87] One peculiarity of the Celtic monastics was the *peregrinati*, meaning "wanderers," who traveled far and wide.[88] Their zeal

81. Patrick, *Confession* 4, in Bieler, *Works of St. Patrick*, 22.

82. J. Finney, *Recovering the Past*, 87; David M. Gustafson, *Gospel Witness: Evangelism in Word and Deed* (Grand Rapids: Eerdmans, 2019), 166–68. Some legends of Patrick in the Celtic church tradition appear embellished.

83. Bainton, *Christianity*, 128.

84. Ferguson, *Church History*, 1:354; J. Finney, *Recovering the Past*, 28.

85. *HCC* 4:52; Ruth Tucker, *From Jerusalem to Irian Jaya* (Grand Rapids: Zondervan, 2004), 41.

86. Bainton, *Christianity*, 146.

87. Ferguson, *Church History*, 1:354.

88. J. Finney, *Recovering the Past*, 56–57; Robert G. Tuttle, *The Story of Evangelism: A History of the Witness to the Gospel* (Nashville: Abingdon, 2006), 171.

led them to function like itinerant evangelists and wandering prophets of the second century.

The ancient document titled *Annals of the Four Masters* reported that Patrick's mission planted around seven hundred churches, ordained about a thousand clergy (both regular and secular), and saw the conversion of thirty to forty of Ireland's 150 tribes.[89]

Celtic Monastic Mission

The Irish sent missionaries to England, Scotland, and continental Europe. Earlier, Scotland had been partially evangelized by Ninian (ca. 360–432), a British missionary trained in Rome who worked among the Picts of southern Scotland.[90] After Ninian, the gospel came through the preaching of Columba (521–597), a disciple of Patrick, who was exiled from Ireland to the Scottish island of Iona.[91] In 565, at Iona, Columba built a monastery, from where he and his disciples went further into Scotland to reach the Picts.

From Iona, the Celtic mission pushed to reach northern Anglo-Saxons of Northumbria. In 634, Aidan, a missionary from Iona, founded the monastery at Lindisfarne, or "Holy Isle," known for the colorfully produced Lindisfarne Gospels. Meanwhile, the first wave of Irish, Scottish, and English monks left their homelands to cross the English Channel to preach the gospel in continental Europe.[92] Columbanus (543–615) and other Irish missionaries went as far as Switzerland and northern Italy, leaving their mark with the Iona Cross that was unique to Celtic Christians.[93]

The Irish monks brought with them their practices such as tonsure, referring to their bobbed hair with a bald spot on top, and their date to celebrate Easter. Although the Irish and their northern Anglo-Saxon disciples were not against the bishop of Rome, whose influence as the "pope" (from the Greek *pappas*, meaning "father") was increasing, they were not tied directly to the Roman Church leaders.[94] Moreover, the Irish form of Christianity of Patrick and his followers followed the old British-Roman form, in contrast to the new imperial Roman form of Constantine and the emerging papacy of the Roman Church.[95]

89. Hunter, *Celtic Way of Evangelism*, 23.
90. Ferguson, *Church History*, 1:353.
91. *HCC* 4:69; Hunter, *Celtic Way of Evangelism*, 36–37.
92. Ferguson, *Church History*, 1:355; J. Finney, *Recovering the Past*, 31.
93. J. Finney, *Recovering the Past*, 58; Hunter, *Celtic Way of Evangelism*, 39.
94. Joseph Lynch, *The Medieval Church: A Brief History* (London: Routledge, 2014), 52.
95. *HCC* 4:47.

North African Evangelism

Christianity in Africa began in Egypt and spread south and west. With the increasing influence of the bishop of Alexandria, this church leader was also referred to as the "pope," or "father."[96] Eusebius writes that Mark the Evangelist, a companion of the apostle Peter, founded the church at Alexandria and served as its first overseer.[97] In addition, the church in Africa produced the leading apologists Origen and Tertullian, the martyrs Perpetua and Felicitas, and the theologians Athanasius and Augustine of Hippo.[98]

Athanasius of Alexandria

Athanasius of Alexandria (ca. 293–373) stood as a staunch defender of Nicene theology. He wrote a volume with two parts, titled *Against the Pagans* and *On the Incarnation*, in which the first part addresses pagan beliefs and practices and the second part argues that the central tenet of the Christian faith, as well as all human history, is the incarnation of God in Jesus Christ. His work constituted the first classic treatment of orthodox, Nicene theology. He set forth in reference to John 1:1–4 that the Son of God—the eternal Word (Logos) through whom God created the world—entered the world as a human being in order to lead sinners back to a relationship with God.[99]

Athanasius was described as a dark-skinned and short man. He came originally from a village on the shore of the Nile River in Egypt. He spoke the Coptic language as well as Greek. At the Council of Nicaea in 325, which sought to resolve the Arian controversy, he served as assistant to Alexander, the bishop of Alexandria, and later took up the mantle as a champion of Nicene orthodoxy along with Basil of Caesarea.[100]

After the council, the Arians, who had denied that Jesus was of the same divine substance as God the Father, continued to resist the orthodox teaching of the wider church.[101] Therefore, Athanasius presented from the Scriptures a clear and compelling argument that Jesus Christ, the Son of God, is

96. For example, Dionysius referred to Heraclas, the bishop of Alexandria, as "our blessed father." Eusebius, *Ecclesiastical History* 7.7.4 (*NPNF*[2] 1:296).

97. Eusebius, *Ecclesiastical History* 2.24 (*NPNF*[2] 1:130–31).

98. Thomas C. Oden, *How Africa Shaped the Christian Mind: Rediscovering the African Seedbed of Western Christianity* (Downers Grove, IL: InterVarsity Press, 2010), 106, 128–30.

99. Athanasius, *On the Incarnation* 41 (*NPNF*[2] 4:58).

100. Ferguson, *Church History*, 1:205.

101. Bettenson, *Documents of the Christian Church*, 46.

of the same substance of the Father, God of God, and that he became human. With importance to evangelism, González states, "The Arian controversy was not a matter of theological subtleties with little or no relevance. In it, the very core of the Christian message was at stake."[102] Athanasius knew that central to the task of evangelism is a right understanding of the evangel, which speaks of Jesus's incarnation, death, and resurrection.[103]

With the Arian controversy, all Christians were pressed to study the Scriptures and to articulate the gospel with greater clarity. The church emerged from this controversy with renewed confidence in its core message.[104] Athanasius modeled this, presenting his case that the gospel from the Scriptures is integral to evangelism. With time he and other Nicene theologians persuaded the large majority of people so that Nicene teaching was retained at the Council of Constantinople, which convened in 381 under Emperor Theodosius.[105]

Excerpts from *On the Incarnation* (*De incarnatione*) by Athanasius

For this purpose, then, the incorporeal and incorruptible and immaterial Word of God comes to our realm, howbeit he was not far from us before. For no part of Creation is left void of Him: He has filled all things everywhere, remaining present with His own Father. But He comes by descending to show loving-kindness upon us, and to visit us.

And seeing the race of rational creatures in the way to perish, and death reigning over them by corruption; seeing, too, that the threat against transgression gave a firm hold to the corruption which was upon us, and that it was monstrous that before the law was fulfilled it should fall through: seeing, once more, the unseemliness of what had come to pass: that the things whereof He Himself was Designer were passing away: seeing, further, the exceeding wickedness of men, and how little by little they had increased it to an intolerable pitch against themselves: and seeing, lastly, how all men were under penalty of death: He took pity on our race, and had mercy on our infirmity, and descended to our corruption, and, unable to bear that death should have the mastery—lest the creature should perish, and His Father's handiwork in men be spent for naught—He takes unto Himself a body, and that of no different sort from ours.

102. González, *Story of Christianity*, 1:175. Cf. Bainton, *Christianity*, 95–97.
103. Ferguson, *Church History*, 1:205.
104. Rudnick, *Speaking the Gospel*, 23–24.
105. Bainton, *Christianity*, 100.

For He did not simply will to become embodied, or will merely to appear. For if He willed merely to appear, He was able to effect His divine appearance by some other and higher means as well. But He takes a body of our kind, and not merely so, but from a spotless and stainless virgin, knowing not a man, a body clean and in very truth pure from intercourse of men. For being Himself mighty, and Designer of everything, He prepares the body in the Virgin as a temple unto Himself, and makes it His very own as an instrument, in it manifested, and in it dwelling.

And thus taking from our bodies one of like nature, because all were under penalty of the corruption of death He gave it over to death in the stead of all, and offered it to the Father—doing this, moreover, of His loving-kindness, to the end that, firstly, all being held to have died in Him, the law involving the ruin of men might be undone . . . and that, secondly, whereas men had turned toward corruption, He might turn them again toward incorruption, and quicken them from death by the appropriation of His body and by the grace of the Resurrection, banishing death from them like straw from the fire. . . .

We have, then, now stated in part, as far as it was possible, and as ourselves had been able to understand, the reason of His bodily appearing; that it was in the power of none other to turn the corruptible to incorruption, except the Saviour Himself, that had at the beginning also made all things out of naught and that none other could create anew the likeness of God's image for men, save the Image of the Father; and that none other could render the mortal immortal, save our Lord Jesus Christ, Who is the Very Life; and that none other could teach men of the Father, and destroy the worship of idols, save the Word, that orders all things and is alone the true Only-begotten Son of the Father.

But since it was necessary also that the debt owing from all should be paid again: for, as I have already said, it was owing that all should die, for which special cause, indeed, He came among us: to this intent, after the proofs of His Godhead from His works, He next offered up His sacrifice also on behalf of all, yielding His Temple to death in the stead of all, in order firstly to make men quit and free of their old trespass, and further to show Himself more powerful even than death, displaying His own body incorruptible, as first-fruits of the resurrection of all. . . .

Again, if the Lord's death is the ransom of all, and by His death the middle wall of partition is broken down, and the calling of the nations is brought about, how would He have called us to Him, had He not been crucified? For it is only on the cross that a man dies with his hands spread out. Whence it was fitting for the Lord to bear this also and to spread out His hands, that with the one He might draw the ancient people, and with the other those from the Gentiles, and unite both in Himself. For this is what He Himself has said, signifying by what manner of death He was to ransom all: I, when I am lifted up, He says, shall draw all men unto Me. (Athanasius, *On the Incarnation* 8, 20, 25 [*NPNF*^{2} 4:40–49])

Frumentius and Aedessius

Around the year 340, Frumentius and Aedessius—two young brothers who were Christians from Tyre, modern-day Lebanon—accompanied their uncle on a voyage. Their ship was attacked by marauders, who killed the crew but spared the boys.[106] The brothers were captured and taken as slaves to Aksum of Abyssinia, present-day Ethiopia, where the king made them civil servants of his household. In their witness to the gospel through words and actions, the king converted to faith in Christ.[107] Shortly before his death, he set them free.

Frumentius and Aedessius joined the queen's court as royal administrators and tutors of the crown prince, Ezana. Frumentius was given authority to grant religious freedom to visiting Christian merchants of the Roman Empire and was allowed the privilege to evangelize. Therefore, he encouraged visiting Christians to practice their faith openly, and secured places "where they could come together for prayer according to the Roman Rite."[108] Frumentius and Aedessius invited local Abyssinians to attend the meetings as well and saw a number of them accept Jesus Christ as Lord.

When the crown prince became an adult, Aedessius decided to return to Tyre.[109] Frumentius chose to remain, hoping to see the conversion of the Abyssinian people. However, Frumentius accompanied his brother as far as Alexandria. While there, Frumentius visited Athanasius and reported to him all the activities in Aksum, asking him if he would send a bishop and missionaries to Abyssinia. When Athanasius heard Frumentius's request, he

106. Elizabeth Isichei, *A History of Christianity in Africa: From Antiquity to the Present* (Grand Rapids: Eerdmans, 1995), 32–33.

107. Ferguson, *Church History*, 1:237.

108. Saheed A. Adejumobi, *The History of Ethiopia* (Westport, CT: Greenwood, 2007), 171.

109. Terry, *Evangelism*, 42.

asked, "Who better than [you] yourself can scatter the mists of ignorance and introduce among this people the light of divine preaching?"[110]

Athanasius believed that Frumentius was the person best suited for the role and set him apart to oversee the church there, commissioning him to initiate translation of the Bible and other writings into the Abyssinia language.[111] Frumentius returned to Aksum, where he baptized King Ezana, and together they worked to spread the gospel and establish churches. Ezana made Christianity the official religion of the Aksumite kingdom.

Frumentius organized the Aksumite church around Nicene theology and became known within the church as Abba Salama, "Father of Peace." This is an early example of a ruler who received the gospel from captives and insisted that the message be proclaimed throughout his kingdom.

Persia

Syriac-speaking Christians carried the gospel to Mesopotamia and Persia. By the end of the second century, missionary expansion advanced the church as far east as Bactria, in modern-day Afghanistan. In 224, when the Sassanid dynasty overthrew the Parthians, there were several local churches in Persia.[112] The Sassanians made Zoroastrianism the state religion but offered religious toleration to Christians at a time when Christians in the Roman Empire were being persecuted.

In 324, Constantine misguidedly wrote to Shapur II, the Persian emperor and political enemy, on behalf of Christians because their political loyalty in Persia had become suspect. Constantine urged the Persian emperor to protect the Christians.[113] However, since they belonged to the religion now favored by Constantine, they appeared as allies of Rome. Persecution of the Persian Christians began in force in 339 and lasted forty years. The Christian historian Sozomen (ca. 400–450) claimed that sixteen thousand Christians faced the martyr's death. It is estimated that more Christians were martyred there than in the Roman Empire during the previous three centuries.[114]

110. Theodoret of Cyprus, *Ecclesiastical History* 1.22 (*NPNF*[2] 3:58).
111. Terry, *Evangelism*, 43.
112. Ferguson, *Church History*, 1:235. See Acts 2:9.
113. Eusebius, *Life of Constantine* 4.8–13 (*NPNF*[2] 1:542–44).
114. Ferguson, *Church History*, 1:235.

Armenia and Georgia

In 301, Armenia became the first nation to make Christianity the state religion.[115] According to tradition, Christianity was introduced there by the apostles Bartholomew and Thaddaeus. Christianity became the state religion when Gregory the Illuminator, also known as the Baptizer, proclaimed the gospel to Tiridates III, king of Armenia, and persuaded him to become a Christian.[116] As in other places, Christianity spread from the king to the nation's subjects.

The Caucasus region, including Georgia, was evangelized by Armenian Christians, in addition to the apostle Andrew, who, according to tradition, arrived there in the first century.[117] Following the example of Armenia, Georgia became a Christian nation.[118] The conversion of Georgia was attributed to the witness and miracles of Nino (ca. 330), a Christian slave girl from Cappadocia. After Nino's gift of healing was brought to the attention of Queen Nana of Georgia, she healed the queen in the name of Christ from a serious illness. The queen's conversion was followed by that of King Mirian.[119]

Gospel Preaching within Christendom

With Christianity legalized and favored within the Roman Empire, the effects on public preaching were soon noticeable. Christian preaching within Christendom took place in buildings erected for large crowds of worshipers. A number of preachers, such as John Chrysostom, Ambrose of Milan, and Augustine of Hippo, were successful in attracting listeners, including pagans, to the larger facilities. At the worship services people heard the gospel from clergy trained in Greek and Roman rhetoric. In contrast to the pre-Constantinian era, when a presbyter-pastor of a house church sat in a chair to deliver a message, in the new era the preacher stood before the assembly and delivered the sermon with oratorical skill.

115. Ferguson, *Church History*, 1:235–36.

116. Lois Farag, "The Middle East," in *Christianities in Asia*, ed. Peter C. Phan (Malden, MA: Wiley-Blackwell, 2011), 249.

117. Eleanor H. Tejirian and Reeva Spector Simon, *Conflict, Conquest, and Conversion: Two Thousand Years of Christian Missions* (New York: Columbia University Press, 2014), 2.

118. Ferguson, *Church History*, 1:236–37.

119. Everett Ferguson, "Women in the Post-Apostolic Church," in *Essays on Women in Earliest Christianity*, ed. Carroll D. Osburn (Joplin, MO: College Press, 1993; repr., Wipf & Stock, 2007), 1:507.

John Chrysostom

John Chrysostom (ca. 347–407) was one of the most eloquent preachers of the time. *Chrysostomos* means "golden-mouthed," a title given to him because of his fluent preaching.[120] When John was young, he converted to faith from the influence of his mother.[121] He studied philosophy and rhetoric, and soon people recognized his gift of speaking, which in the ancient world was considered the ultimate talent.

Chrysostom was drawn to the ascetic life and dedicated himself to serve Christ and the church. For several years he lived as a hermit in the hills outside Antioch, but he returned to the city in 381 for health reasons.[122] He was ordained as a deacon while serving with Flavian, the bishop of Antioch, and five years later was consecrated as a presbyter-priest and appointed to be a preacher-evangelist.[123]

In 397, he was selected against his will to become bishop of Constantinople and was set apart for this office the following year.[124] He deplored the imperial-court protocol that gave him the same privileges as the highest state officials. Moreover, he saw the blatant need for reform among secular clergy who served the congregations, as well as among the regular clergy who labored as monks and nuns. The corruption had come earlier under his predecessor, Nectarius, who had made the bishop's palace a place of extravagant hospitality for the upper class of Constantinople as well as the clergy. Thus, Chrysostom enacted reforms, selling some of the palace's precious items and using the money to build a hospital and minister to the poor.[125]

Chrysostom's rejection of the lifestyle of a court bishop made him popular with common Christians, but his prophetic zeal and denunciation of extravagances made him an enemy of Empress Aelia Eudoxia, the wife of Arcadius, the Eastern Roman emperor.[126] Chrysostom spoke harshly against her, making references to her as Herod's wife, saying, "Once more Herodias de-

120. Chrysostom was born in Antioch (Syria) sometime between 344 and 354. David F. Wright, "John Chrysostom: Master Preacher," in *Great Leaders of the Christian Church*, ed. John D. Woodbridge (Chicago: Moody, 1988), 82.

121. González, *Story of Christianity*, 1:194–95.

122. Ferguson, *Church History*, 1:218.

123. Tuttle, *Story of Evangelism*, 136.

124. González, *Story of Christianity*, 1:196.

125. In addition, some priests who had taken a vow of celibacy lived with "spiritual sisters," but this was merely a scandalous arrangement. González, *Story of Christianity*, 1:196.

126. Ferguson, *Church History*, 1:218.

mands the head of John [the Baptist] on a platter."[127] As a result, Chrysostom was banished from the capital city of Constantinople to a remote village in the Caucasus in Armenia, where he lived the rest of his days.[128]

Ambrose of Milan

Ambrose (ca. 340–397) was the son of a Roman prefect in Trier and became governor of northern Italy with his office in Milan. He was a catechumen enrolled in instruction when the church at Milan experienced turmoil over a dispute between Nicene Christians and Arians. Amid the turmoil, Ambrose worked out a peaceful solution. Not long afterward, a child shouted the words "Ambrose for bishop," which led others to join in the refrain.[129]

The idea of Ambrose becoming bishop seemed premature, as he was still a catechumen. Nevertheless, provisions were made for him, and within eight days he was baptized, ordained, and consecrated bishop of Milan, starting this position in 374. He had been trained in rhetoric and soon attracted listeners, gaining a reputation as an eloquent preacher.

In 391, after Emperor Theodosius had made Christianity the official religion of the empire, Ambrose found himself on the two sides of Christendom—namely, on the side of the throne and the side of the altar.[130] When there was a resurgence of paganism following Theodosius's edict in 391, which mandated destruction of pagan idols and temples, Ambrose preached against paganism and asserted the truths of Christianity.[131] However, he also defended the autonomy of the church against the control of the state and its interference in the church's affairs. In one instance, Theodosius tricked the citizens of Thessalonica after they had been forgiven for a riot in the city. The emperor asked them to gather at the city amphitheater. When the crowd of seven thousand entered the large facility, he had them slaughtered.[132] Ambrose was incensed and condemned the actions of the emperor, asserting the church's independence from imperial control.

As bishop of Milan, Ambrose encouraged the evangelization of people living farther north in the Alps. In 390, Fritigil, queen of the Marcomanni, a Germanic people in the region, corresponded with him by means of a

127. Ferguson, *Church History*, 1:218.
128. González, *Story of Christianity*, 1:199; Ferguson, *Church History*, 1:219.
129. González, *Story of Christianity*, 1:189.
130. Ferguson, *Church History*, 1:239.
131. Ferguson, *Church History*, 1:240.
132. González, *Story of Christianity*, 1:192–93.

slave about the conversion of her people to Christian faith. This region was considered "heathendom," meaning the people who lived outside the realm of Christendom and its social influence. In response, Ambrose launched an evangelistic campaign, carried out mostly by slaves and soldiers who preached the gospel to the Marcomanni and other barbarian tribes to the north. These Christians gathered their new converts into communities and then churches.[133]

Augustine of Hippo

Augustine (354–430) is considered by many to be the greatest theological influence on the church since the apostle Paul. While Augustine was certainly among the finest theologians of the church, it is important to remember that he served equally as a pastor, evangelist, bishop, and teacher.

Augustine was born in Tagaste in North Africa, in modern-day Algeria. His mother, Monica, was a devout Christian but his father, Patricius, was not. At seventeen years of age, Augustine went to Carthage, where he studied rhetoric. In regard to faith, he was a Christian in name only. He quit his catechetical training as a young man in order to live with a woman, and together they had a son named Adeodatus.[134]

During his studies, Augustine read ancient works of rhetoric, including those of Cicero, the famous orator of Rome. While reading this rhetorician, he concluded that proper speech and style were not enough, but "one must seek after truth."[135] In his search for truth, he joined the Manichees for nine years, attracted to the sect by their view that matter is evil.[136] Then he turned to Neoplatonism, but this did not satisfy him either.

Augustine moved to Rome against his mother's wishes and while there became disillusioned to find the city no better than Carthage. Despite this, his mother urged him to travel north to Milan to hear Ambrose preach. After hearing him, Augustine was greatly impressed, not only by his sermons, which rivaled the Roman orators, but by his conviction in the gospel.

As a result, Augustine resumed his education as a catechumen and converted to faith in 386. He was baptized by Ambrose the following year on

133. Tuttle, *Story of Evangelism*, 136.

134. Bainton, *Christianity*, 116.

135. González, *Story of Christianity*, 1:208.

136. Some religions, such as Gnosticism and Manichaeism, taught that matter, including the human body, is hostile to God. Rudnick, *Speaking the Gospel*, 48.

Easter morning at sunrise, along with his son, Adeodatus. Augustine later summarized his spiritual journey: "I sought a way to obtain the strength which would be capable of enjoying Thee. I did not find it until I embraced the Mediator between God and man, the man Christ Jesus, who is above all things, God blessed forever who calls out and says: 'I am the Way, the Truth, and the Life.'"[137]

Augustine returned to Thagaste, where he and his colleagues examined other philosophies. In the end they studied the Bible, particularly the writings of the apostle Paul. Then, in 391, as Augustine was passing through Hippo Regius, he was ordained and became bishop of the city for the next five years. He turned his residence into a monastery where he lived with other clergy and friends. They developed a rule to guide their communal life and ministry, which became the basis for future Augustinian monks. Their residence was described as a "veritable nursery, ordaining priests and baptizing followers for monasteries that spread Christianity through the land."[138]

As a preacher, Augustine proclaimed the word of God and cared for the poor. Like his mentor Ambrose's, his sermons were biblical in content and delivered with rhetorical skill. As a pastor, he preached the gospel with urgency. In 397, Augustine delivered a message from the text, Mark 1:15: "The times are fulfilled and the kingdom of God has drawn near: repent and believe the gospel."[139] Augustine was clear that Christ came to offer mercy, but judgment was waiting the obstinate. Therefore, he exhorted his listeners to "renounce [sin] and be converted."[140] He spoke with urgency, calling to his listeners, "Do not delay being converted to the Lord." Historian Robert G. Tuttle writes, "As an evangelist, [Augustine] was constantly among the people, enforcing the word of God. Above all, he was the defender of truth and the shepherd of souls. As for message, he was forever revealing the intimate details of his conversion. He easily shared the arguments that convinced him—the life and conquests of the apostles—and his progress in the faith while studying Saint Paul. He was known for delightful, but heady, conversations with friends discussing the divinity of Jesus Christ and the transformation worked in his soul by faith."[141]

137. Augustine, *Confessions* 7.18.24, trans. Vernon J. Bourke (New York: Fathers of the Church, 1953), 188.

138. Tuttle, *Story of Evangelism*, 136.

139. Paul Sanchez, "Have You Met Augustine the Evangelist?," The Gospel Coalition, August 4, 2016, https://www.thegospelcoalition.org/article/have-you-met-augustine-the-evangelist/.

140. Sanchez, "Have You Met Augustine the Evangelist?"

141. Tuttle, *Story of Evangelism*, 136. Cf. Holland, *Dominion*, 202.

For readers of his time, Augustine's autobiographical work, *Confessions*, served as a written testimony that told of his journey to faith in Christ, weaving themes of the gospel throughout the book.[142] This work begins with his well-known statement, "Thou has made us for Thee and our heart is unquiet until it finds its rest in Thee."[143] Augustine provided stories of his struggles with sin, even stealing pears from a neighbor. As a storyteller, he helped readers understand sin, as well as sinful motives and guilt, providing his concluding confession, "Look at my heart. . . . It was filthy and I loved it."[144] Augustine further reflected on the cross of Jesus Christ as the means of forgiveness from sin:

> How you have loved us, O good Father, "who has not spared even your only Son" but have handed him over for us wicked men! How you hast loved us, for whom he "thought it not robbery to be equal with you and became obedient unto death on the Cross." He alone was "free among the dead," possessing the power to lay down his life and possessing the power to take it up again. He was for us both a Victor and a Victim unto you—a Victor because a Victim—for us a Sacrificer and a Sacrifice—a Sacrificer because a Sacrifice—making us change from servants into sons unto you, by his being born of you and by becoming our servant.[145]

In *Confessions*, Augustine also highlighted the role of intercessory prayer for those outside faith in Christ. He told how his own life turned around because of the prayers of his mother. He recalled, "And you [Lord] did put forth your hand from on high and drew forth my soul from this deep darkness of mind, while my mother, one of your faithful, wept for me before you, far more than do mothers who weep at bodily deaths. She saw my death in the spirit of faith and the spirit which she had received from you, and you heard her, O Lord."[146] He told of the numerous times in which she and other devout Christians tried to talk with him about the gospel but without apparent success. He recalled his own opportunities also to share his testimony of faith with others after his conversion.

Augustine's work titled *Catechizing the Uninstructed* was written as a guide for any Christian to instruct an inquirer about the Christian faith.

142. Ferguson, *Church History*, 1:268.
143. Augustine, *Confessions* 1.1 (Bourke, 4).
144. Augustine, *Confessions* 2.4.9 (Bourke, 41).
145. Augustine, *Confessions* 10.43.69 (Bourke, 324).
146. Augustine, *Confessions* 3.11.19 (Bourke, 68).

He wrote this disciple-making resource for a "brother" named Deogratias, a deacon in Carthage. The book provides both long and short forms that survey biblical history and allow the disciple-maker to explain points and answer questions that the seeker may have along the way.[147]

Excerpts from *Catechizing the Uninstructed (De catechizandis rudibus)* by Augustine of Hippo

The Bible's narrative is complete when each person is catechized in the first instance from what is written in the text, "In the beginning God created the heaven and the earth," on to the present times of the Church. This does not imply, however, that we ought to repeat from memory the entire Pentateuch, and the entire Books of Judges, and Kings, and Esdras, and the entire Gospel and Acts of the Apostles. . . . For neither does time admit that, nor does any necessity demand it. But what we ought to do is this: to give a comprehensive statement of all things, summarily and generally, so that certain of the more wonderful facts may be selected which are listened to with great satisfaction, and which have been ranked importantly among the major turning-points (of the history). . . .

However that may be, let us suppose that someone comes to us who desires to become a Christian, and who belongs indeed to the order of private persons, and yet not to the class of rustics, but to that of the city-born, such as those whom you cannot fail to come across in numbers in Carthage. Let us also suppose that, on being asked whether the reason leading him to become a Christian is any advantage in the present life, or hoped for after this life, he answers that his incentive has been the rest that is yet to come.

Then perhaps we should instruct this person in some manner of address as: "Thanks be to God, my brother; cordially do I wish you joy, and I am glad on your account that, amid all the storms of this world, which are at once so great and dangerous, you have thought yourself of some true and certain security. For even in this life men go in quest of rest and security at the cost of heavy labors, but they fail to find such in consequence of their wicked lusts. For their thought is to find rest in things which do not fulfill, and which do not endure. . . ."

If this discourse . . . appears to you to be too long, you are at liberty to expound these matters with greater brevity. . . . At the same time, much depends on what the case itself, as it goes on, may render advisable, and

147. Ferguson, *Church History*, 271–72.

what the person can bear and desires. . . . Then all that remains to be said to him should be put together in the following manner:

"All visible things pass away, and all the pomp, and pleasure, and solicitude of this world will perish, and (even now) they drag those who love them along with them downward to destruction. The merciful God, willing to deliver men from this destruction, that is to say, from everlasting pains . . . sent His only-begotten Son, that is to say, His Word, equal with himself, by whom he made all things. And he, while abiding indeed in his divinity, and neither receding from the Father nor being changed in anything, did at the same time, by taking on himself human nature, and appearing to men in mortal flesh, come unto men; in order that, just as death entered among the human race by one man, the first that was made, that is to say, Adam, because he consented unto his wife when she was seduced by the devil to the effect that they (both) transgressed the commandment of God; even so by one man, Jesus Christ, who is also God, the Son of God, all those who believe in him might have all their past sins done away with, and enter into eternal life." (Augustine, *On the Catechizing of the Uninstructed* 3.5–26.52 [*NPNF*[1] 3:285–313])

Faltonia Betitia Proba

In addition to theological, apologetic, and educational works, other types of writings were employed as means of evangelism during the fourth century. After her conversion to Christ, Faltonia Betitia Proba (ca. 322–370) arranged a type of Latin poem called a *cento* in which she drew from poems of Virgil such as the *Aeneid* and the *Georgics*.[148] Proba's work titled *Concerning the Glory of Christ* (*De laudibus Christi*) selectively used excerpts from Virgil's writings to tell the story of Christ within the Bible's narrative, beginning at creation. In this work, she imbued "the Christ with heroic virtues" akin to the Virgilian hero.[149]

In a creative and contextual manner, Proba described the events that led to the fall of Eve on the basis of the story of Dido from book 4 of the

148. Josephine Balmer, *Classical Women Poets* (Newcastle upon Tyne, UK: Bloodaxe, 1996), 111.

149. Elizabeth Clark and Diane Hatch, "Jesus as Hero in the Vergilian 'Cento' of Faltonia Betitia Proba," *Vergilius* 27 (1981): 36.

Aeneid.[150] Proba employed lines from book 2 of the same work, specifically about Laocoön's death, in order to describe the words of the serpent in the Garden of Eden. In telling about the birth and crucifixion of Jesus, she selected lines that related originally to Dido and Venus.[151] She wrote, "Because your Son descended from the high heaven and time brought to us with our hopes at last succor and the coming of God whom for the first time a woman bearing the guises and habit of a virgin—marvelous to say—brought forth a child not of our race of blood . . . one with God, the very image of his beloved Sire."[152]

The final section of her poem focuses on Christ's ascension and return in glory. Again Proba conveyed elements of the gospel from words that originally described the god Mercury and the prophecy in the Oracle of Delos, both taken from book 3 of the *Aeneid.*[153] She stated her purpose for the *cento*, saying, "But baptised, like the blest, in the Castalian font—I, who in my thirst have drunk libations of the Light—now begin my song: be at my side, Lord, set my thoughts straight, as I tell how Virgil sang the offices of Christ."[154]

Conversion and Christianization

After Christianity "triumphed" in the Roman Empire and Christendom was born, paganism by no means disappeared, especially in the rural areas. At this time, evangelists and missionaries started to shift their emphasis from conversion to Christianization. In other words, their goal was to enculturate people with Christian principles and lifestyle without emphasizing conversion to faith in Christ.

"Christianization" of pagans had the goal of making Christians of others; but without an emphasis on conversion, nominalism followed, along with syncretism, the mixing of Christian and pagan views. In many cases, people were satisfied initially and superficially to relate to Christ and the church, but in the long run Christianity had little transformational effect.

As the Roman Empire declined in power, pagan tribes moved into territories previously controlled by the Romans. The tribes eventually defeated

150. Sigrid Schottenius Cullhed, *Proba the Prophet*, Mnemosyne, Supplements 378 (Leiden: Brill, 2015), 142, 145.

151. Cullhed, *Proba the Prophet*, 176–83.

152. Walter L. Liefeld, "Women and Evangelism in the Early Church," in *The Study of Evangelism: Exploring a Missional Practice of the Church*, ed. Paul W. Chilcote and Laceye C. Warner (Grand Rapids: Eerdmans, 2008), 99.

153. Cullhed, *Proba the Prophet*, 185–86.

154. J. Balmer, *Classical Women Poets*, 113.

the Roman military, overthrew the government, and formed six kingdoms of their own. At the local level, they seized whatever land and property they wanted. Although their intention was not to destroy the Roman Empire, their actions did just that. The military and economy were dealt devastating blows.[155] Thus, the church faced the daunting challenge of evangelizing these tribes of pagans—their political enemies—and establishing churches among them.[156]

Discussion Questions

1. Constantine's political rule was a double-edged sword. In one sense, it provided an environment for Christianity to clarify its teaching and develop its leaders, but in another sense, it opened the door for nominal Christianity. How do we effectively share the gospel with people who claim to be Christians but do not show any evidence of conversion to Christ?
2. Why were the early monastic communities of Basil and Patrick effective at evangelism? What elements of their evangelism might be useful today? How can we preach the gospel in creative ways while maintaining the integrity of the message? How does Patrick's explanation of the gospel compare with Peter's and Paul's summaries examined earlier?
3. Why was Athanasius's argument about Christ's incarnation important to evangelism? How did he understand Christ's death in regard to reconciliation with God and with one another?
4. As with Frumentius and Aedessius, how has God used difficult circumstances in your life to prepare you for the sake of the gospel and Christian witness?
5. How does Augustine's explanation of the gospel in *Catechizing the Uninstructed* compare with Athanasius's view? What do they share in common? Why does Augustine frame the gospel within creation and Israel's history? What advice does he provide to the evangelist/disciple-maker that you can use?

155. Rudnick, *Speaking the Gospel*, 43.
156. Terry, *Evangelism*, 39.

4

Medieval Evangelism

We adore you, most holy Lord Jesus Christ, here, and in all your churches throughout all the world; and we bless you, because, by your holy cross, you have redeemed the world.

—Francis of Assisi (1182–1226)[1]

During the medieval period, which began in the fifth century, numerous people became Christians or at least were "Christianized" at a nominal or superficial level. At times, entire tribes or nations were baptized and declared Christians, having little personal or collective choice in the matter. In some cases, they were forced to become Christians against their will.[2]

Political rulers were motivated to impose demands of conversion on their subjects for several reasons. Many had a genuine concern for their spiritual well-being. The rulers themselves had become Christians after hearing the gospel and wished the same assurance of forgiveness and eternal life for their people. Moreover, the rulers concluded that Christianity was superior to pagan beliefs and ancestral traditions, and that the people's conversion to Christianity, even if requiring force, was for the best of the nation.[3] The social values and cultural expressions of Christian nations were deemed superior.

Historian Carl A. Volz describes the nature of pagan religions as "polytheistic, with a hierarchy of gods including elves, spirits, departed souls,

1. Helen Julian, *Francis and Clare: A Gospel Story* (Ijamsville, MD: Word Among Us, 2005), 45.

2. Roland H. Bainton, *Christianity* (Boston: Houghton Mifflin, 2001), 138–39.

3. Milton L. Rudnick, *Speaking the Gospel through the Ages: A History of Evangelism* (St. Louis: Concordia, 1984), 66.

witches, and demons as lower intermediaries."[4] Pagan traditions were based often on fear, "aimed at placating the anger of the gods, who determined the entire course of human affairs."[5] Rather than mortality and eternal life, pagans mostly sought tangible rewards from daily life; success in farming, hunting, and trade; and the welfare of their family or tribe.

By establishing Christianity as the official or authorized religion, a ruler was able to consolidate his or her power, provide a religious center for national life, and pave the way for improved relations with neighboring Christian nations.[6] Thus, rulers invited missionaries to evangelize their people, baptize en masse, teach the Scriptures, and conduct worship services.

Generally, a higher value was placed on the act of baptism than personal faith in the gospel, operating on the notion that pagans were made Christians by baptism. As a result, newly established churches were composed of both genuine converts to faith and those that were not. The established churches were a mixture of "wheat" and "tares" (Matt. 13:24–30).

Whenever the gospel did not supplant the former paganism, a syncretism of Christian and pagan practices operated together. The two produced a mere form or caricature of Christianity rather than people transformed by the gospel and power of the Holy Spirit. In many cases, Christianity became little more than a veneer over the old ancestral religion and its superstitions.[7]

Medieval Monasticism in the West

At the same time, efforts were made to convert "Christianized" people. This work of evangelism was carried out by thousands of monks and nuns who lived in monastic communities. After the political rulers, by edict, imposed Christianity on their subjects and on those whom they conquered,

4. Carl A. Volz, *The Medieval Church: From the Dawn of the Middle Ages to the Eve of the Reformation* (Nashville: Abingdon, 1997), 46.

5. Volz, *Medieval Church*, 46.

6. Dana L. Robert notes that monarchs were considered "the most powerful laymen." *Christian Mission: How Christianity Became a World Religion* (Oxford: Wiley & Sons, 2009), 27.

7. John M. Terry, *Evangelism: A Concise History* (Nashville: B&H, 2014), 50, 55. An example of syncretism is Helgi the Lean, who settled in Eyjafjordur Bay (ca. 890) in Iceland. He converted to Christianity and maintained his beliefs in Nordic paganism. *Landnámabók* chronicled that he "believed in Christ, but invoked Thor in matters of seafaring and dire necessity." Johannes Brønsted, *The Vikings* (Baltimore: Penguin, 1965), 306, cited in Rodney Stark, *The Triumph of Christianity* (New York: HarperOne, 2011), 196.

they often provided land to monks for monasteries with the understanding that the gospel would be taught and that this in turn would transform the people.[8] Certainly, the preaching, hospitality, teaching, and charity of monastic communities were instrumental in converting many people to Christian faith.[9]

By the fifth century, monastic life was regarded as the highest form of Christian life and service. It was considered the primary means for a Christ follower to give herself completely to God, flee temptations, devote attention to the worship of God, subjugate the will, compensate for sins, and earn eternal rewards, if not salvation itself.[10] Thus, evangelism was carried out by bands of monks who lived together under their rule, and their monasteries were linked together to provide resources to advance the gospel, along with the cultural benefits of Christianity.

Benedict of Nursia

If Basil of Caesarea was the foremost leader of monasticism in the East, the most influential leader in the West was Benedict of Nursia (ca. 480–540). Benedict was born in Rome, and at age fourteen he renounced the world and its pleasures. He moved to the Italian village of Monte Cassino, where in 529 he founded the monastery at St. Andrews.[11] At Monte Cassino, he wrote a monastic rule of seventy-three chapters based on the Rule of Basil.[12] Benedict's rule also prescribed life in community and service, balancing discipline and compassion, and living in obedience to the abbot.[13]

Benedict and his monks, known as Benedictines, built enclosed monasteries from which they cultivated the surrounding land, copied the Bible and sacred books, and developed a life of prayer, study, and work. This form of monastic life was described as *stabilitas loci*, or stability of place.[14] In this

8. Rudnick *Speaking the Gospel*, 67–68.

9. Rudnick, *Speaking the Gospel*, 44.

10. Rudnick, *Speaking the Gospel*, 47.

11. Everett Ferguson, *Church History*, vol. 1, *From Christ to Pre-Reformation* (Grand Rapids: Zondervan, 2005), 317.

12. Henry Bettenson and Chris Maunder, eds., *Documents of the Christian Church* (New York: Oxford University Press, 2011), 127–41.

13. Ferguson, *Church History*, 1:318.

14. John Finney, *Recovering the Past: Celtic and Roman Mission* (London: Darton, Longman & Todd, 2011), 65.

way, monks located a site and built a monastery as a center for evangelism to the surrounding area. They established a scriptorium, where the regional language was written and introduced to the local population.[15] They welcomed guests to the monastic house, offered hospitality, and evangelized the region by preaching and teaching the gospel. As local residents were baptized, monks would teach them—generally the children and youth—skills of reading and writing. For students who showed exceptional promise, they were invited to enter the communal life of the monastery as novices, where they began to receive theological training.

Each of the monks of a monastery or abbey worked daily, supporting the community economically, developing the land, and winning the favor of the people from the surrounding area. Over time, the monasteries became centers of learning and leadership that positively impacted the local society. The abbot would then commission a band of monks to enter an unreached area to establish a new monastery there and repeat the process.

The monastic strategy of *stabilitas loci* was dependent on befriending and welcoming the stranger or wayfarer. Benedict wrote,

> All guests who present themselves are to be welcomed as Christ, for he himself will say: "I was a stranger and you welcomed me" (Matt. 25:35). Proper honor must be shown to all, especially to those who share our faith (Gal. 6:10) and to pilgrims. Once a guest has been announced, the superior [abbot] and the brothers are to meet him with all the courtesy of love. First of all, they are to pray together and thus be united in peace, but prayer must always precede the kiss of peace because of the delusions of the devil. All humility should be shown in addressing a guest on arrival or departure. By a bow of the head or by a complete prostration of the body, Christ is to be adored because he is indeed welcomed in them. After the guests have been received, they should be invited to pray; then the superior or an appointed brother will sit with them. The divine law [Bible] is read to the guest for his instruction, and after that every kindness is shown to him. The superior may break his fast for the sake of a guest, unless it is a day of special fast which cannot be broken. The brothers, however, observe the usual fast. The abbot shall pour water on the hands of the guests, and the abbot with the entire community shall wash their feet. After the washing they will recite this

15. Jonathan Hill, *What Has Christianity Ever Done for Us? How It Shaped the Modern World* (Downers Grove, IL: InterVarsity Press, 2005), 88.

> verse: "God, we have received your mercy in the midst of your temple" (Ps 47[48]:10). Great care and concern are to be shown in receiving poor people and pilgrims, because in them more particularly Christ is received; our very awe of the rich guarantees them special respect.[16]

In his rule, Benedict instructed monks to honor all guests—Christian and non-Christian—to pray with them, read from the Scriptures for their instruction, and sit with them at the meal. The Rule of Benedict became the most popular monastic rule in the West and, by the ninth century, superseded all other rules, forming the basis of new orders such as the Cluniacs and Cistercians.[17] The rule was popularized especially by Gregory the Great.

Gregory the Great

Gregory (ca. 540–604) was a monk who became the bishop of Rome—the Latin pope—and well known for launching the first major mission to convert the pagan Anglo-Saxons of England to Christianity.[18] More often in the West than the East, monks of the regular (*regula*) orders who served in monastic communities also became presbyters, more commonly referred to as "priests" with secular (*secula*) orders to serve local congregations. In some cases, such as Gregory's, they became a bishop of a region, known commonly as a diocese. The Roman Church of the West, in contrast to churches in the East, progressively centralized ecclesial power under the pope.

When Gregory became pope, he convinced others of the need to evangelize the Anglo-Saxons, as well as Arian Germans, and thus he launched his great Gregorian mission.[19] The first wave of Roman monks was sent out in 597, even though they had little or no inclination toward ascetic pilgrimages and missions to far-off peoples. The monks departed Rome with fear and trepidation of the warlike heathens they would encounter to the north.[20]

16. Benedict, *Rule of Benedict* 53, in Bettenson and Maunder, *Documents of the Christian Church*, 131.

17. Kevin Madigan, *Medieval Christianity: A New History* (New Haven: Yale University Press, 2015), 123; Volz, *Medieval Church*, 87–93.

18. Madigan, *Medieval Christianity*, 61–63; J. Finney, *Recovering the Past*, 21–24.

19. Ferguson, *Church History*, 1:355.

20. Rudnick, *Speaking the Gospel*, 68.

Augustine of Canterbury

Among the monks that Gregory commissioned was Augustine of Canterbury (d. 604), not to be confused with the theologian, Augustine of Hippo. The Augustine sent by Gregory traveled from Rome to England, where, to his surprise, the pagan king Ethelbert received him and his companions cordially.[21] This was in part because the king's wife, Bertha, was a Christian. Augustine and his companions found favor with Ethelbert and were granted permission to build a church and monastery at Canterbury. For this reason, Augustine became known as Augustine of Canterbury.

In this context, Augustine and his band of missionaries carried out their monastic way of life. Using their monastery as a base, they traveled about the countryside preaching in the open air and, when appropriate, gathering people for baptism.[22] In 601, King Ethelbert converted to faith, and within a few years the Roman Church's mission had a small but secure base of operation.[23]

Gregory advised his monks to use the evangelistic principle of accommodation, or to contextualize Christian doctrine and practice in forms that were easily understood by the pagan peoples.[24] He recommended that heathen temples should not be destroyed and that festivals and other pagan practices need not be eliminated from the lives of the new Christians. Rather, these practices should be adapted for the worship of the triune God. The monks were instructed to remove only those things that were idolatrous and demonic, and substitute them with biblical meaning and Christian functions.[25] Gregory contended that this principle would aid in the transition from paganism to Christianity. He acknowledged that conversion to Christ takes time and that the monks as evangelists must be patient in the process.[26]

At the time, two forms of Christianity existed in England—the old Romano-British form of Patrick of Ireland and the new Romano-imperial

21. Bainton, *Christianity*, 135.

22. J. Finney, *Recovering the Past*, 2.

23. Joseph Lynch, *The Medieval Church: A Brief History* (London: Routledge, 2014), 51.

24. David J. Bosch, *Transforming Mission: Paradigm Shifts in Theology of Mission* (Maryknoll, NY: Orbis, 2011), 240.

25. Gregory practiced what has been described as "functional substitution." Gerald A. Arbuckle, *Earthing the Gospel* (Eugene, OR: Wipf & Stock, 2001), 11.

26. Edward L. Smither, *Mission in the Early Church: Themes and Reflections* (Eugene, OR: Cascade, 2014), 115.

form established by Augustine of Canterbury.[27] These two forms operated alongside each other in England until the Synod of Whitby in 664, when it was ruled that English Christians should conform to the customs of Rome rather than the indigenous customs of earlier Christians in Britain and the Celtic missionaries.[28]

Boniface of Germany

From England, some of the monks in the Romano-imperial tradition of Augustine of Canterbury ventured out, seeking contact with local leaders, assuming that if they responded, masses of people would follow. Since the Anglo missionaries were related ethnically and linguistically to the Germanic tribes, they discovered a level of success in reaching them with the gospel.[29]

Among the English missionaries was Willibrord (658–739), who went to the Frisians of Frisia, a large part of the modern-day Netherlands and parts of northern Germany.[30] The most famous English evangelist was Willibrord's disciple known by the Roman name Boniface (673–754).[31] Boniface was from Kirton in Wessex, and for forty-one years he taught poetry and grammar at a monastic school.[32]

Boniface began his evangelistic ministry among the pagans by assisting Willibrord. When they met resistance from the pagan king Radbod, Boniface traveled to Rome to secure backing from the church. At Rome, he was welcomed by Pope Gregory II and in 718 received a general commission to Christianize and Romanize central Europe. After Radbod died, evangelizing the region became less difficult, allowing Boniface to travel south to the German region of Hesse. In 722, Gregory II called Boniface back to Rome and appointed him as regional bishop of the Germanic peoples.[33]

When Boniface returned to Hesse, he engaged in a dramatic confrontation with pagans. In an encounter, he chopped down the sacred Oak of

27. J. Finney, *Recovering the Past*, 2–3.

28. Madigan, *Medieval Christianity*, 66–67.

29. Rudnick, *Speaking the Gospel*, 70.

30. Ferguson, *Church History*, 1:360–61.

31. Volz, *Medieval Church*, 41.

32. Winfrith received the name Boniface by Gregory II. Madigan, *Medieval Christianity*, 68. His Latin name symbolized his new Roman connection. Volz, *Medieval Church*, 42.

33. Boniface was named *episcopus regionarius*. *HCC* 4:93.

Donar at Geismar and took its wood to build a church at nearby Fritzlar. With this successful act, he traveled eastward to evangelize the people of Bavaria and Thuringia. In these areas he preached the gospel, destroyed idols, established monasteries, recruited missionaries, and planted churches. Volz describes Boniface's strategy:

> Christian missionaries almost always addressed crowds rather than individuals. . . . Preaching, in village after village, was the primary means of reaching people with basic Christian teachings. It was clearly imperative, therefore, to find preachers who could communicate with the pagans in their native tongue. . . . The contents of missionary preaching attempted to inform the pagans about the origins of the universe and of humankind, the fall into sin, the deluge, and the coming of Christ as Redeemer. The Bible played an important role in their work. At different times Boniface wrote to England for more copies of the Bible, and Pope Gregory II advised him to use both testaments to convert the pagans. Missionaries also pointed to the superiority of their god over all others, to his omnipotence, justice and mercy.[34]

In 732, Boniface was appointed archbishop of the ancient city of Mainz along the Rhine River. With political support, he improved order and discipline among the clergy and made significant contributions to reform the churches of the Franks. At first, most of the Frankish clergy resisted his efforts to enlist them in reform measures and evangelism. In fact, Boniface—who was loyal to the Roman pope—found that nearly everywhere he visited, especially in Bavaria and Thuringia, the missionaries and clergy functioned independently of the pope. Thus, Boniface's objective became not merely to convert pagans but to Romanize earlier forms of Christianity. In this task, he aided the family of Charles Martel in "reducing the Gallic clergy to obedience, exterminating the Celtic element, and consolidating the union with Rome."[35]

In 738, Boniface made a final pilgrimage to Rome along with several German converts and received authority to call a synod of bishops of Bavaria and Allemania. With this authority, he began to replace the Celtic missionary form of Christianity with that of the Romano-imperial church.

34. Volz, *Medieval Church*, 46. Cf. Tom Holland, *Dominion: How the Christian Revolution Remade the World* (New York: Basic Books, 2019), 201–5.

35. *HCC* 4:95.

In a struggle that ensued over centralizing the church under Rome, two men—Aldebert and Clemens—opposed Boniface and, in doing so, were "excommunicated as heretics and seducers of the people by a provincial Synod of Soissons in 744, and again in a Synod at Rome in 745 by Pope Zacharius."[36]

At a political level, Boniface aided Pepin, the son of Charles Martel, to secure the pope's recognition as king of the Franks. This act began a long relationship between the papacy of Rome and the emperors of the burgeoning Holy Roman Empire that began with Pepin's son, Charlemagne.[37]

At age seventy-eight, Boniface decided to return to evangelistic work among the Frisians, accompanied by a number of devoted companions. Despite his earlier work in Frisia, paganism had revived. When Boniface gathered a group of recently baptized converts on the banks of the Borne River near Dockum, he and his companions were attacked by armed pagans.[38] Although Boniface's companions took up arms, he prohibited them from using their weapons, urging them to accept joyfully the crown of martyrdom.[39] They died at the hands of their attackers.[40]

During his ministry, Boniface made alliances with the Roman papacy and the Frankish kings, leveraging their ecclesial and political authority to advance the preaching of the gospel. Before his death, he reported that 100,000 Germans had been baptized under his ministry, earning for himself the title "the apostle of Germany."[41]

The Carolingians

By force of arms, the Carolingian kings Pepin and Charlemagne doubled the size of their kingdom within four decades, conquering Saxony, Bavaria, the Lombard kingdom in Italy, the Aquitaine in northern Spain, and Brittany, the northwest region of modern-day France.[42] While the Latin-speaking West was stabilized under the Carolingian dynasty, it was divided nonetheless by regional languages and cultures, especially between the civilized Roman South and the barbaric German North.

36. *HCC* 4:91–92.
37. Bainton, *Christianity*, 148.
38. Holland, *Dominion*, 206–7.
39. *HCC* 4:95–96.
40. Ferguson, *Church History*, 1:363.
41. Rudnick, *Speaking the Gospel*, 70–71.
42. Lynch, *Medieval Church*, 66; Ferguson, *Church History*, 1:365–66.

The Carolingian intellectuals who shaped the Latin-speaking West were composed mostly of churchmen who thought in hierarchical terms. They believed that God had created human society with distinct ranks or *ordos*. They insisted on the proper order of the church and made the study of theological and ecclesial history and law important areas of research, setting the religious life of Europe on the course that included its ordered, hierarchical society. A result of this was the growing prestige and authority of the Roman papacy, as well as a sharper distinction between professional clergy of presbyters-priests and the laity. The lay Christians were expected merely to receive the sacraments of baptism and the Eucharist, pay tithes to the church, and conform to the standards of Christian moral behavior. Those who sought a more devout Christian life were encouraged to pursue a vocation of regular or secular clergy.

In 768, Charlemagne (742–814) became ruler of the Frankish kingdom. While there is a question over the nature of his devotion to Christ, he was clearly devoted to the church and the expansion of Christianity.[43] The church was virtually a department of state in his kingdom, and Charlemagne took an active role in summoning councils and interfering with their decisions.[44] Moreover, he promoted a revival of "classic Christian culture."

He sent missionaries to evangelize all areas of his kingdom but soon discovered that not everyone was receptive to the gospel. The Saxon tribes that lived along the northern border of his kingdom were particularly resistant to missionaries and continued to raid and ravage Frankish lands near the border. Therefore, with support from the clergy and approval from political officials, Charlemagne took military action, viewing his military policy as part of Christian missions, and vice versa.[45] In 772, he invaded Saxon territory, destroyed the pagan idols, and took Saxons hostage in order to ensure the safety of missionaries who accompanied his military expedition.[46] In this manner, the sword prepared the path for the gospel, and conversion by force became the rule. Charlemagne hoped that by hearing the gospel after their defeat, the fierce Saxons would become peaceful.

The initial successes were soon reversed by a revolt led by the Saxon chief Widukind.[47] The Carolingian forces undertook repeated campaigns

43. The question stems from his slaughtering more than four thousand Saxons and forcing survivors to convert to Christianity. Yet he was a regular worshiper at his church. Madigan, *Medieval Christianity*, 73–74.

44. Bainton, *Christianity*, 149.

45. Holland, *Dominion*, 208–14.

46. Ferguson, *Church History*, 1:366.

47. In 782, Charlemagne executed 4,500 Saxons in one day for resisting the faith. Rob-

to suppress the Saxons. The price of defeat for the Saxons would be not merely political submission but also Christian baptism and submission to the authority of the church.[48] A legislative act made obligatory the baptism of infants under one year of age. Any parent who hid a child would face the death penalty.[49]

The demand for all conquered subjects to be baptized caused massive resistance. Despite such pressure, in 785 Widukind surrendered and was baptized at his own request. Charlemagne announced to the others again that refusal to accept baptism or disrespect for Christianity were crimes punishable by death.[50] As one contemporary observed, "Charlemagne preached with the iron tongue."[51] As hostilities ceased, the policy of forced conversion was relaxed and more peaceful relations were established in which people received baptism as the means of Christianization.

Charlemagne's motives for forcing Saxons to conform to Christianity were not entirely imperialistic or defensive. As a ruler, he wanted to subdue and annex the Saxons, and from his point of view, their conversion would be authentic, even under duress.[52] He desired for them to become Christians like the other subjects of his kingdom. Certainly, such forceful means, as historian Philip Schaff says, were a "radical departure of the apostolic method."[53] Despite this unorthodox pattern of Christianization, many of the children and grandchildren of Saxons become devout followers of Jesus Christ.

Holy Roman Empire

In 800, Pope Leo III crowned Charlemagne as emperor of what later became known as the Holy Roman Empire.[54] This act clearly set his empire of the West apart from the old Roman or Byzantine Empire of the East with its ties

---

ert G. Tuttle, *The Story of Evangelism: A History of the Witness to the Gospel* (Nashville: Abingdon, 2006), 171.

48. Rudnick, *Speaking the Gospel*, 60. Volz writes, "In all of these efforts at spreading the faith, the primary goal of Christian missionaries was winning the consent of the pagans to receive baptism." *Medieval Church*, 45.

49. Ferguson, *Church History*, 1:366.

50. Rudnick, *Speaking the Gospel*, 59–60.

51. Ferguson, *Church History*, 1:366.

52. Rudnick, *Speaking the Gospel*, 59–60.

53. *HCC* 4:104.

54. Madigan, *Medieval Christianity*, 74–75. The coronation of Charlemagne is often described as the beginning of the Holy Roman Empire, but the designation is techni-

to other ancient orthodox churches. Thus, this political act of coronation further separated Christians in the Latin-speaking West from those of the Greek-speaking East. The new Holy Roman Empire began to rival the older Roman/Byzantine Empire.

The new empire in the West continued to follow the pattern of Christendom with an alliance between state and church, specifically an alliance of the Carolingian kings and the Roman pope. Historian Everett Ferguson notes, "As for Charlemagne, he evidently saw himself as a new Constantine."[55] Like the Roman emperor, Charlemagne was ruthless in expanding his domain while funding monasteries and promoting the church.[56]

Alcuin of York

Alcuin (ca. 735–804) was an educational and religious adviser to Charlemagne, and being the head of the emperor's court school, he was charged with teaching young Franks to read, write, and speak Latin.[57] Despite this, Alcuin deplored the emperor's measures of forced conversion of the Saxons. Instead, he advocated winsome persuasion to the gospel and voluntary baptism.

Alcuin's vision for the land of the Franks was for it to become "a new Athens enriched by the sevenfold fullness of the Holy Spirit."[58] Thus, he set out to revive the ancient disciplines of grammar, rhetoric, and dialectic as tools of the teacher, viewing teachers, not soldiers in arms, as the best propagators of the Christian faith. In protest against Charlemagne's imposition of baptism by force, Alcuin said to the king, "Give these conquered peoples teachers who shall feed them with the milk of babes. . . . And remember the teaching of Saint Augustine [of Hippo]: First, let a man be taught and brought to faith. Then, and only then, shall he be baptized."[59] However, Alcuin's words had little effect, as he later disclosed to a friend: "And so the wretched Saxons have

---

cally anachronistic, only used centuries later to describe what was emerging. Ferguson, *Church History*, 1:373–74. Cf. Volz, *Medieval Church*, 54–55.

55. Ferguson, *Church History*, 1:374.

56. Ruth A. Tucker, *Parade of Faith: A Biographical History of the Christian Church* (Grand Rapids: Zondervan, 2015), 146.

57. Lynch, *Medieval Church*, 87–88.

58. Bainton, *Christianity*, 150.

59. Eleanor Shipley Duckett, *Alcuin, Friend of Charlemagne: His World and His Work* (New York: Macmillan, 1951), 131–32. Charlemagne "delighted in Augustine's *De Civitate Dei* which became the primary source for his political and social policy." Tuttle, *Story of Evangelism*, 171.

so often lost the grace of baptism because they never had the foundation of faith in their hearts. What avails baptism without faith? A man can be driven to baptism, but not to belief."[60] Charlemagne admired his trusted adviser but did not always heed his counsel regarding military force. Nonetheless, Charlemagne established a policy to educate Saxon children.

Louis the Pious and the Heliand

Despite Charlemagne's forceful approach, his son Louis the Pious commissioned a poet-monk to write a poem titled *Heliand*, meaning "Savior."[61] The poem was composed in the old Saxon language and became known as the "Saxon Gospel," drawing from a harmony of the Gospels, written in epic poetry, and using terms and concepts familiar to Saxons.[62]

The poem tells of Jesus as a Germanic king and his disciples as his faithful warriors, and it highlights the virtue of loyalty to the king. The Saxon imagery of Christ's death on the cross carried special meaning to the Saxons, who were accustomed to seeing criminals and prisoners of war hung from trees sacred to the god Woden and then offered as sacrifices.[63] In this poem, Jesus is buried in a German earthen grave covered by a stone but raised by the resurrection from the dead. The *Heliand* was recited and sung by itinerant poets and singing monks.[64]

Heliand, Excerpts from Chapter 66, on the Crucifixion

Then they set up the gallows on the sandy ground,
High on the field, the folk of the Jews:
The beam on the hillside; and God's Bairn [Child] was tormented
Thereon, on the cross. They struck cold iron
Now in their eagerness, nails sharp and new,
Hard with their hammers, through His hands and His feet:
Bitter bonds were they. His blood ran to earth,
The gore of our Good Lord. . . .

60. Duckett, *Alcuin, Friend of Charlemagne*, 132.

61. Ferguson translates *Heliand* as "The Healing One." Ferguson, *Church History*, 1:366.

62. Douglas Hayward, "Contextualizing the Gospel among the Saxons: An Example from the Ninth Century of the Cultural Adaptation of the Gospel as Found in *The Heliand*," *Missiology* 22, no. 4 (October 1, 1994): 452–53.

63. G. Ronald Murphy, *The Heliand: The Saxon Gospel; A Translation and Commentary* (New York: Oxford University Press, 1992), 182.

64. Hayward, "Contextualizing the Gospel," 443.

Then the war-men dealt out the weeds of the Lord. . . .
His fair, rich robes. But the men could not rightly
Agree together about the same tunic . . .
The most winsome of weeds. The world-folk's herdsman,
The duke himself, hight that over the head
Of Christ on the cross there be writ
That this be the true king of Jews,
Jesus of Nazareth-burg, who stood there nailed
On the new gallows because of grim hatred—
On the beam of the rood. Then the folk bade him
To change that word, quoth that He Himself had so said as He wished . . .
Then spake the other man
Hanging there who stood held in his fetters,
Suffering great pain; "Wherefore wilt thou speak such a word,
Greetest thou Him with such scorn?
Thou standest here held to the gallows,
Broken on the beam. We both suffer sorely;
Because of our sin: our own deeds themselves,
Have brought us our pain. But He standeth there;
Faultless and free of all sin; for He Himself
Hath committed no crime; but for the hate of the crowd
He willingly endureth dire pain in this world.
(*Heliand*, trans. Mariana Scott, http://www.hieronymus.us.com/latinweb/Mediaevum/Heliand.htm)

Rabanus Maurus

Rabanus Maurus (ca. 784–856), a student of Alcuin, was born at the height of the Carolingian dynasty and its renaissance. Maurus was educated as a boy at the Benedictine monastery of Boniface at Fulda in Hesse.[65] The renaissance emphasized church reform as inspired by Boniface, promoted by Pepin, and written into policy by Charlemagne. The renewed interest in learning was exemplified by the emperor's mandate written to Baugulf, the abbot at Fulda, urging him to promote education in the region surrounding the monastery.[66]

65. Volz, *Medieval Church*, 41.
66. Madigan, *Medieval Christianity*, 75–76; Holland, *Dominion*, 212–13.

Rabanus was a remarkable student and thus sent to study under Alcuin. When Rabanus returned to Fulda, he became headmaster and worked to enact Charlemagne's legislation to educate children and youth.[67] He served as the abbot at Fulda from 822 until 842, when he became archbishop of Mainz.

The monastery at Fulda served as an educational center of the Carolingian renaissance and a theological center to evangelize Germany.[68] Rabanus's most complete theological work was an illustrated book titled *In Praise of the Holy Cross*, which featured thirty poems with woodcuts.[69] One illustration of Jesus Christ appeared to have random letters superimposed on the page. However, the letters within the image spell out a poem. In this way, Rabanus combined visual and verbal elements, presenting the gospel in a creative manner.[70] The lines within the image read, "This is the image of our Savior who, by the position of his limbs, made holy the life-giving and most sweet and most beloved form of the cross so that, believing in his name and obeying his commandments, we might obtain eternal life thanks to his passion. Therefore, every time we gaze on the cross, let us remember him who suffered for us in order to snatch us from the power of darkness, accepting death so that we might be heirs of eternal life."[71]

Rabanus's work titled *Church Disciplines* provided instruction for teachers to explain to ordinary people—children, youth, and adults—the fundamentals of the Christian faith, following closely Augustine's catechetical method.[72] In this way, the children and grandchildren of conquered Saxons became followers of Jesus Christ, and many entered the monastic work of evangelism.

Rabanus taught Latin and Greek and wrote commentaries on most books of the Bible.[73] He also wrote *On Clerical Formation*, a three-volume collec-

67. Hill, *What Has Christianity Ever Done for Us?*, 94.

68. Nearly eight thousand books copied during this period still survive. For each copy of works by Cicero, there were multiple copies of works by church fathers. Volz, *Medieval Church*, 56–57.

69. Linda Archibald, "Latin Verse," in *German Literature of the Early Middle Ages*, ed. Brian Murdoch (Rochester, NY: Camden House, 2004), 92.

70. Hill, *What Has Christianity Ever Done for Us?*, 34.

71. "On Rabanus Maurus: A Truly Extraordinary Personality of the Latin West," Zenit, June 3, 2009, https://zenit.org/articles/on-rabanus-maurus/.

72. Rudolph G. Bandas, *Contents and Methods of Catechization: For the Use of Lay Teachers of Religion, Sisters, Seminarians, and Priests* (Eugene, OR: Wipf & Stock, 2009), 14.

73. John M. Riddle, *A History of the Middle Ages, 300–1500* (Lanham, MD: Rowman & Littlefield, 2016), 195.

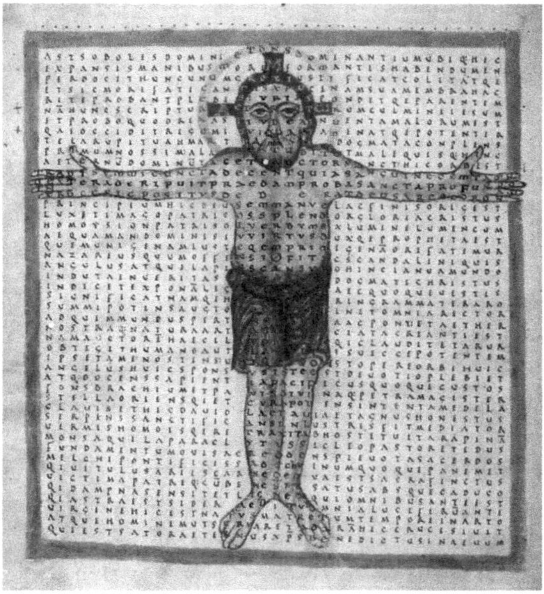

Figure 4.1. De laudibus Sanctae Crucis (In Praise of the Holy Cross), ca. 810, by Rabanus Maurus, Abbey of Saint-Denis in France 845–847, now in the Bibliothèque nationale de France.

tion of recommendations for the training of clergy, who, in his opinion, needed to take courses in all branches of knowledge in addition to theological training.[74] The writing, book copying, artistic work, and scholarship of Rabanus and his students furthered the Carolingian renaissance. He unquestionably deserved the title "the teacher of Germany."[75]

Cyril and Methodius

Cyril (827–869) and Methodius (815–885), missionary evangelists among the Slavic people, employed a simple form of evangelism that led to the conversion of King Bogoris of Bulgaria. When Bogoris asked Methodius to paint a scene on a wall of his palace, he painted a graphic picture of the rewards of heaven and the torments of hell. When the painting was unveiled, the king

74. Hill, *What Has Christianity Ever Done for Us?*, 94.

75. *Praeceptor Germaniae*; Ferguson, *Church History*, 1:379–80; Lynch, *Medieval Church*, 89.

and many of his court officials were reported to have accepted the invitation to Christian baptism immediately.[76]

Cyril and Methodius began their missionary work in Crimea.[77] Then, in 862, a letter arrived to the bishop of Constantinople from King Rostislav of Moravia, asking him to send missionaries to teach them the "whole truth."[78] The two brothers were commissioned at that time to work in Moravia.

Cyril devised a way to write Slavonic using letters that became known as the Cyrillic alphabet, which is still used today in some Slavic languages. With this alphabet, Cyril translated the Bible and other writings.[79] However, the brothers soon faced opposition from German missionaries who claimed that the only proper languages of the church were Latin, Greek, and Hebrew. In an effort to resolve the conflict, Cyril and Methodius traveled to Rome to meet with the pope, who decided in their favor. The only stipulation was that they come under his papal jurisdiction and authority.[80]

While in Rome, Cyril died. His last request was for his brother to return to work among the Slavs. By the time of Methodius's death, he had successfully evangelized Czechs, Croats, Serbs, and Bulgars.[81] As a result of their pioneering work, Cyril and Methodius became known as the "apostles to the Slavs."[82]

Reverse Conversion of Vikings

The Norsemen were Germanic peoples of Scandinavia. They were traders, warriors, mercenaries, and colonists, pagans who in some instances threatened the civilization kindled by the Carolingian renaissance.[83] The Norsemen invaded Ireland and the Northumbrian monasteries of England in the eighth century and extended their voyages to North Africa, Russia, and Constantinople in the centuries that followed.[84] Under an arrangement

76. Like other rulers who converted to Christian faith, Bogoris ordered his subjects to accept baptism or be killed. Terry, *Evangelism*, 51.

77. Ferguson, *Church History*, 1:348–49.

78. Volz, *Medieval Church*, 44.

79. Tuttle, *Story of Evangelism*, 173.

80. Justo L. González, *The Story of Christianity: The Early Church to the Present Day* (Peabody, MA: Prince, 1999), 1:263.

81. Tuttle, *Story of Evangelism*, 174.

82. David M. Gustafson, "Missionality of Apostolicity," *Theofilos* 9, no. 1 (2017): 91.

83. Madigan, *Medieval Christianity*, 78.

84. Holland, *Dominion*, 217.

with Charles the Simple, in 911 the Norse chieftain Rollo settled his people in the region of France that became known as Normandy.[85]

While the typical pattern of evangelism was for Christians to go and preach the gospel to pagans, in this case the pagans came to the Christians. After the Norsemen established their Norman colonies, they became interested in Christianity. For them, the Christian faith posed neither a political threat nor a mark of defeat and submission, but was regarded as superior to Nordic paganism. Their voluntary conversion to Christian faith provided further reason to evangelize Scandinavia.[86]

Rise of Islam

According to the book of Acts, there were Parthians, Medes, Elamites, and residents of Mesopotamia among the first converts to Christ at Pentecost (Acts 2:9). They visited Jerusalem from the lands east of Judea where their Jewish ancestors centuries earlier had been exiled but nonetheless chose to remain despite the Persian royal decrees allowing them to return.[87] These converts at Pentecost, as well as apostles and evangelists of the early church, especially Aramaic-speaking Christians, carried the gospel eastward (Acts 2:11). Included among these was the apostle Paul, who traveled to Arabia (Gal. 1:17). While ancient Christianity was strong in areas of southern Arabia with Najran as the center, Nestorian Christianity became a dominant sect in eastern Arabia.[88]

In 266, Lakhmids formed as a group of Arabian Christians who lived in south-central Iraq and made the city al-Hirah their capital, just south of modern-day al-Kūfah. The founder of the dynasty was ʿAmr, whose son Imruʾ al-Qais converted to faith in Christ, and after him the whole city converted to Christian faith.

In 523, when an uprising took place among the Himyarites at Najran, two hundred Christians died as martyrs.[89] The bishops of Najran were known to visit the great fairs of Minā and ʿUkāz, preaching the gospel while seated

85. F. Donald Logan, *A History of the Church in the Middle Ages* (London: Routledge, 2002), 82–85.

86. Ferguson, *Church History*, 1:383–84.

87. F. F. Bruce, *Commentary on the Book of Acts* (Grand Rapids: Eerdmans, 1986), 61–62.

88. William Tabbernee, ed., *Early Christianity in Contexts: An Exploration across Cultures and Continents* (Grand Rapids: Baker Academic, 2014), 47–60.

89. Volz, *Medieval Church*, 48.

on their camels.[90] Despite the influence of Christianity, the new religion of Islam emerged in the seventh century.

Islam originated from the life and work of Muhammad (ca. 570–632), who, at the age of forty, had a vision of the angel Gabriel and as a result began to proclaim an uncompromising monotheism, specifically a belief in and submission to the will of Allah. Islam identified as an Abrahamic faith and drew heavily from both Judaism and Christianity. Those who submitted to the will of Allah were called Muslims.[91] Earlier, many of the Arab peoples were pagan with indigenous polytheistic beliefs, others were Christians or Jews, and others adhered to Zoroastrianism. Muhammad, however, set about to convert everyone to submit to the will of Allah as described in a new revelation called the Qur'an (Koran).[92]

In 630, after Muhammad attacked the caravans of Mecca, the city accepted his religious reforms. When he died in 632, his followers chose Abu Bakr as "caliph," Muhammad's successor.[93] Under the direction of the new leader, Islamic forces swept the Middle East. Within two decades, the forces of the first three caliphs overran Judea, Syria, Mesopotamia, Persia, Egypt, and much of North Africa.[94] In 638, Muslims conquered Jerusalem. From North Africa, Islam spread by force into Spain and France, where it was stopped in 732 at the Battle of Tours, led by Charles Martel, grandfather of Charlemagne.[95] In the centuries that followed, Islam threatened the Byzantine capital of Constantinople. The capture of Jerusalem, Antioch, Alexandria, and Carthage left only Constantinople and Rome to stand for Christianity, free from the political and religious pressure of Muslims.

90. Cyril Glassé, *The Concise Encyclopaedia of Islam* (London: Stacey, 2008), 389.

91. Volz, *Medieval Church*, 48.

92. Islam held to the five pillars: (1) recite the creed ("There is no god but Allah, and Muhammad is his Prophet"), (2) daily prayers, (3) fasting, (4) almsgiving, and (5) pilgrimage to Mecca.

93. The Shi'ites and Sunnis divided over the question of leadership and authority. The division happened when Muslims faced the pressing question of who should succeed Muhammad. Shi'ites saw authority as vested in divinely appointed leaders, whereas the Sunni theory of the caliphate required that the leader meet certain qualifications but that the community would decide. Daniel Brown, *A New Introduction to Islam* (Hoboken: Wiley & Sons, 2017), 10.

94. Madigan, *Medieval Christianity*, 103.

95. Rodney Stark, *God's Battalions: The Case for the Crusades* (New York: HarperOne, 2009), 41–44. Ferguson, *Church History*, 1:334; Holland, *Dominion*, 193–96.

John of Damascus, Apologist

John (ca. 675–749) was a Byzantine Christian monk and priest who was born and raised in Damascus, Syria. He was educated with competencies in law, philosophy, theology, and music. He worked as an administrator for the Muslim caliph of Damascus prior to becoming a regular and secular clergyman.[96] John composed hymns and wrote books that expounded the Christian faith, not least *The Fount of Knowledge*, which included a chapter on the "heresy of the Ishmaelites," an apologetic refutation of Islam.[97] In this treatise, he described Muhammad as a false prophet and an anti-Christ. Following a critique of Islam, John summarized the Christian faith according to writings of the early church fathers. As a Christian writer, he was considered an evangelist in word and pen.

Excerpts from Writings of John of Damascus

There is also the superstition of the Ishmaelites which to this day prevails and keeps people in error, being a forerunner of the Antichrist. They are descended from Ishmael, [who] was born to Abraham of Agar, and for this reason they are called both *Agarenes* and *Ishmaelites*. They are also called *Saracens*. . . . A false prophet named Mohammed has appeared. . . .

This man, after having chanced upon the Old and New Testaments and likewise, it seems, having conversed with an Arian monk, devised his own heresy. Then, having insinuated himself into the good graces of the people by a show of seeming piety, he gave out that a certain book [Qur'an] had been sent down to him from heaven. He had set down some ridiculous compositions in this book of his and he gave it to them as an object of veneration. . . .

And he says this, that when the Christ had ascended into heaven God asked Him: "O Jesus, didst thou say: 'I am the Son of God and God'?" And Jesus, he says, answered: "Be merciful to me, Lord. You know that I did not say this and that I did not scorn to be thy servant. But sinful men have written that I made this statement, and they have lied about me and have fallen into error." And God answered and said to Him: "I know that thou didst not say

96. David R. Thomas, *Syrian Christians under Islam: The First Thousand Years* (Leiden: Brill, 2001), 19.

97. Madigan, *Medieval Christianity*, 116; Tuttle, *Story of Evangelism*, 173.

> this word." There are many other extraordinary and quite ridiculous things in this book which he boasts was sent down to him from God. But when we ask: "And who is there to testify that God gave him the book? And which of the prophets foretold that such a prophet would rise up?"—they are at a loss. (John of Damascus, *On Heresies* 101 [The Ishmaelites], in *Saint John of Damascus: Writings*, trans. Frederic H. Chase Jr. [New York: Fathers of the Church, 1958], 153–54)

> Every action, therefore, and performance of miracles by Christ are most great and divine and marvelous: but the most marvelous of all is His precious Cross. For no other thing has subdued death, expiated the sin of the first parents, despoiled Hades, bestowed the resurrection, granted the power to us of contemning the present and even death itself, prepared the return to our former blessedness, opened the gates of Paradise, given our nature a seat at the right hand of God, and made us the children and heirs of God, except the Cross of our Lord Jesus Christ. For by the Cross all things have been made right. "So many of us," the apostle says, "as were baptized into Christ, were baptized into His death, and as many of you as have been baptized into Christ, have put on Christ." (John of Damascus, *The Orthodox Faith* 4, 11, in *Saint John of Damascus: Writings*, trans. Frederic H. Chase Jr. [New York: Fathers of the Church, 1958], 349–50)

By 1071, Seljuk Turks, a fierce Muslim group known as the Masters of Baghdad, were in control of Jerusalem. They advanced across Asia Minor, which had been a historic stronghold of Christians. Moreover, they established a new capital for the sultan at Nicaea, calling it Rûm, the Turkish word for Rome. With this religious and political threat of Muslims, Byzantine Christians at Nicaea and Constantinople appealed to Christians in the West for military aid to defend them against the Turks. Thus, while the Christian faith was expanding in Europe, it was losing ground in the homeland of the early church.

The Medieval Crusades

The word *crusade* comes from the Latin *cruce signati*, meaning "those signed by the cross."[98] The Crusades were a series of military campaigns from 1095

98. Thomas F. Madden, *The Concise History of the Crusades*, 3rd ed. (Lanham, MD: Rowman & Littlefield, 2014), 1.

to 1291, in which Christians in the West took up arms and made pilgrimages in the name of Christ to accomplish religious and political aims of the Roman pope and church in the West. The Crusaders, possessed by a passion for conquest and a zeal for Christian victory, identified themselves by sewing a red cross on one of their shoulders. Initially, they fought against Muslims in an effort to stop the advance of militant Islamic armies against Christians in the East.

In dealing with the Muslim presence in Spain, Christian theologians, as well as soldiers, engaged in the concept of holy war in reaction to the Muslim idea of *jihad*.[99] The Crusades began when Pope Urban II delivered a pivotal sermon at Clermont, France, calling on Christians to make the journey to Jerusalem to free the holy city from the Turks' control.[100] Urban declared, "From the confines of Jerusalem and from the city of Constantinople a horrible tale has gone forth. . . . An accursed race, a race utterly alienated from God . . . has invaded the lands of those Christians and depopulated them by the sword, plundering and fire. . . . Recall the greatness of Charlemagne. Start upon the road to the Holy Sepulcher, to tear that land from the wicked race and subject it to yourselves."[101]

Urban called on the "knights of Christ" to take up a war of liberation.[102] He made his appeal and the people responded, saying, "God wills it."[103] Urban replied, "It is the will of God. Let those words be your war cry when you unsheathe the sword. You are soldiers of the cross. Wear on your breasts or shoulders the blood-red sign of the Cross."[104] Soon, nearly forty thousand soldiers and civilians responded, ready to march while donning the red cross of the Christian Crusader.[105]

Even though Augustine of Hippo had applied the concept of holy war under the auspices of the state, the concept was new for the Christian church.[106] Now a war was conducted under the auspices of the kings of Europe at the will of the Roman pope. Whereas for Augustine the objective of just war was the vindication of justice and defending life and property, holy war was now for the faithful of the church to protect the faith of other Christians.

99. Madden, *Concise History of the Crusades*, 4.

100. Volz, *Medieval Church*, 82.

101. Robert G. Clouse, Richard V. Pierard, and Edwin M. Yamauchi, *Two Kingdoms: The Church and Culture through the Ages* (Chicago: Moody, 1993), 172.

102. Madden, *Concise History of the Crusades*, 7.

103. Bainton, *Christianity*, 165.

104. *HCC* 5:228–29.

105. Madden, *Concise History of the Crusades*, 11.

106. Bainton, *Christianity*, 165.

The Crusaders were not a highly organized army but rather a loosely organized throng of soldiers, clergy, and servants "heading in roughly the same direction for roughly the same purposes."[107] These "soldiers of St. Peter," as Urban referred to them, would not stop in their encounter with Seljuk Turks in Asia Minor but would forge ahead to liberate the holy land of Jesus and the twelve apostles.[108]

The culmination of the First Crusade was the fall of Jerusalem in 1099.[109] The Frankish Crusaders captured the holy city and established a Latin kingdom there, much to the disappointment of the Byzantine emperor, Alexios I Komnenos, who wanted the land added to his empire. Despite the apparent success of the Crusaders, one historian writes, "The scenes of carnage that followed belong to the many dark pages of Jerusalem's history and showed how, in the quality of mercy, the crusading knight was far below the ideal of Christian perfection. The streets were choked with the bodies of the slain. The Jews were burnt with their synagogues. The greatest slaughter was in the temple enclosure."[110]

In addition to the motive of just war, there was a motive of eternal salvation—not for the conquered Muslims but for the Crusaders. Among the first Crusaders who marched were those who had been promised that this pilgrimage would be a means of penance, which, in medieval theology of the Roman Church, had salvific merit in itself, in addition to the merit of Christ's death on the cross. The Crusaders had been told that if they fought against the Muslims and died, their sins would be forgiven. The abbot Guibert of Nogent wrote, "God invented the Crusades as a new way for the laity to atone for their sins, and to merit salvation."[111] Obviously, this was a very different message than the gospel of the New Testament (Gal. 1:6–7).

The Second Crusade (1147–1149) was led by the Holy Roman emperor Conrad III and King Louis VII of France. It was set into motion in Europe with news of the fall of Edessa to the Turks and Kurds, along with the enthusiastic eloquence of Bernard of Clairvaux, who was directed by the Roman pope.[112] The Third (1188–1192) and Fourth Crusades (1200–1204) were undertaken to regain Jerusalem lost to Saladin.[113] Swedes, Danes, and Frisians joined Welsh, English, French, and German pilgrims armed for battle. Even

107. Madden, *Concise History of the Crusades*, 10.
108. Madden, *Concise History of the Crusades*, 8.
109. Holland, *Dominion*, 233–34.
110. *HCC* 5:239.
111. *HCC* 5:217. Cf. Stark, *God's Battalions*, 107–8, 117.
112. *HCC* 5:252.
113. *HCC* 5:257.

Baldwin, the archbishop of Canterbury, accompanied an expedition. The siege and sack of Constantinople in 1204 marked the culmination of the Fourth Crusade. With this advance on Constantinople, the vision of the Crusades turned sharply, no longer with Christians liberating Christians from Muslims, but now with Crusader armies of the West looting and destroying parts of Constantinople, killing their fellow Christians in the East.

The Fifth Crusade began in 1217 as a result of Pope Innocent III's zeal for the reconquest of Palestine. Just two years earlier, an objective of the Fourth Lateran Council of the Roman Church was a new crusade, and "full indulgence was offered to the penitent contributing money" to help finance it.[114] In other words, by materially supporting the Crusaders, the donors were granted remission of temporal punishment in purgatory for their sins.

The Sixth and Seventh Crusades were initiated by Louis IX, the king of France. In 1245, the Council of Lyons established as one of its four objectives to bring "the relief of the holy places," and thirty-two thousand troops were given to this objective.

While there may have been good reasons of just war for Crusades, such as coming to the aid of fellow Christians to reclaim their land from the advance of Islamic warriors, after two hundred years there was no doubt that Christians in the West had provoked anger from Jews and Eastern Orthodox Christians as well as Muslims. At several levels, the manner in which Christians from the West carried out their mission as "soldiers of the cross" violated what it meant to be "God's chosen people, holy and dearly loved," clothed with "compassion, kindness, humility, gentleness and patience" (Col. 3:12). The Dutch theologian Desiderius Erasmus later said, "Truly, it is not meet to declare ourselves Christian men by killing very many but by saving very many, not if we send thousands of heathen people to hell, but if we make many infidels, Christian; not if we cruelly curse and excommunicate, but if we with devout prayers and with our hearts desire their health, and pray unto God, to send them better minds."[115]

Many of the Christians who engaged in the Crusades under the sign of the cross—while promised forgiveness of sins and eternal life by leaders of the church—conducted themselves as if they knew nothing of Christ and his cross.[116] In contrast to popes, rulers, and Crusaders engaging in holy wars, Francis of Assisi and his band of "lesser brothers" joined in the task of gospel witness.

114. *HCC* 5:278; Ferguson, *Church History*, 1:414–15.

115. *HCC* 5:289.

116. Volz, *Medieval Church*, 87.

Francis of Assisi and the Franciscan Friars

Francis of Assisi (1182–1226) was born the son of a wealthy clothing merchant of central Italy. At the age of nineteen, he sought to engage in the "glory of battle and outfitted himself as a knight to join the war with Perugia," the rival Italian city of Assisi.[117] After a sudden defeat, Francis was a prisoner of war for nearly a year in the neighboring city-state until his father raised the money to pay his ransom.

After Francis's release, he turned to the Bible for comfort and was challenged by the gospel, the values of Christian discipleship, and the teachings of the kingdom of God. Despite his Bible reading, he outfitted himself again as a knight but soon became dissatisfied with the material comforts of life. When he began to share his family's wealth with the poor people of Assisi, he frustrated his father. Then, at the age of twenty-seven, Francis believed that Jesus spoke to him as he read the following words:

> As you go, proclaim this message: "The kingdom of heaven has come near." Heal the sick, raise the dead, cleanse those who have leprosy, drive out demons. Freely you have received; freely give.
>
> Do not get any gold or silver or copper to take with you in your belts—no bag for the journey or extra shirt or sandals or a staff, for the worker is worth his keep. Whatever town or village you enter, search there for some worthy person and stay at their house until you leave. As you enter the home, give it your greeting. If the home is deserving, let your peace rest on it; if it is not, let your peace return to you. (Matt. 10:7–13)

Francis understood these words as God's call on his life to serve him as an evangelist.

The friction between Francis and his father came to a head when his father demanded that he repay all the money that he had squandered when showing generosity to the poor. In protest before the townspeople at the central piazza of Assisi, Francis stripped naked, renounced his inheritance, and handed his clothes to his father. The bishop of Assisi, who witnessed the dramatic act, immediately took his cloak and wrapped Francis with it. After this, Francis clothed himself during his years of ministry in a simple cloak.

117. Augustine Thompson, *Francis of Assisi: A New Biography* (Ithaca, NY: Cornell University Press, 2012), 3–11.

As Francis abandoned the luxuries of his former life, he traveled in Italy from village to village preaching the good news of God's kingdom.[118] Soon a group of disciples gathered around him. He sent them out two by two to preach the gospel. They referred to themselves as "lesser brothers" (*fraters minores*) and began to wander throughout Italy proclaiming the gospel, healing the sick, and feeding the poor.[119]

While Francis took vows as a monk, he did not seclude himself like those cloistered in a monastery. He and his band of friars practiced *mobilitas*, more like the long-distance traveling of the Celtic *peregrinati* than the *stabilitas* of the Benedictines and other orders.[120] Rather than establishing a long-term presence at a location, Francis and his friars traveled widely to towns, marketplaces, and universities in order to preach the gospel.[121]

In 1209, Francis wrote a simple rule for his followers. The rule was called the *Regula primitiva* (Primitive Rule) and required his brothers to "follow the teachings of [the] Lord Jesus Christ and to walk in his footsteps."[122] In the same year, Francis and his brothers walked to Rome to obtain the blessing of the pope for their order, which was called *Ordo Fratrum Minorum*, or Order of Lesser Brothers.[123] Pope Innocent III gave them his approval. In this meeting of pope and monks, the power and wealth of the papacy stood in stark contrast to the poverty and humility of Francis and his friars.[124]

In contrast to the Crusaders, Francis held a different approach toward Muslims. In 1219, he sailed across the Mediterranean with Crusaders on the Fifth Crusade.[125] Then, in dramatic fashion, he crossed the battle lines at Damietta, Egypt, in order to speak with the sultan by the name of Al-Malik al-Kamil, the nephew of Saladin, who had defeated the forces of the Third Crusade.

In the presence of the sultan, Francis spoke of Jesus Christ, knowing full well that any attempt to convert a Muslim, especially the sultan, was punishable by beheading. Despite the risk, al-Kamil proved to be a wise and

118. Ferguson, *Church History*, 1:476.

119. Lynch, *Medieval Church*, 229.

120. The members of the new orders were called not monks but brothers—in Italian *fratello*, or simply *fra*, and in English *friar*. Bainton, *Christianity*, 191, 193.

121. Ferguson, *Church History*, 1:481.

122. G. K. Chesterton, *St. Francis of Assisi* (New York: Image, 1924), 107–8.

123. Volz, *Medieval Church*, 135.

124. Bainton, *Christianity*, 193.

125. Paul Moses, *The Saint and the Sultan: The Crusades, Islam, and Francis of Assisi's Mission of Peace* (New York: Doubleday Religion, 2009), 62–64.

Figure 4.2. Encuentro con el Sultan (Meeting the Sultan), Saint Francis of Assisi Church, Apodaca, Nuevo León, Mexico. (Parroquia San Francisco de Asís, Apodaca, Estado de Nuevo León, México)

patient man. He was so impressed by Francis's courage and sincerity that he invited him to stay for a week of conversation. During the week, Francis spoke with other Muslims, too, about the gospel. Although none were converted to Christ, they were "converted to Francis" because of his genuine interest and love toward them.[126]

Following this experience in Egypt, Francis, along with others, wrote a longer rule known as the *Regula secunda* (Second Rule). In addition to vows of chastity and obedience, the rule required a vow of poverty that extended to the whole community of friars. Francis feared that his friars might follow after other monastic communities, such as the Benedictines or Cistercians, that had accumulated considerable wealth through their monasteries, living lavishly as a result. Instead, he insisted that his friars depend on God for their daily food, being like the birds of the air that depended on God to feed them (Matt. 6:26–34). The friars were directed to travel as pilgrims and strangers in the world, meeting people where they lived, whether in cities, villages, or remote lands, living simply and sharing the gospel at the level of the people.[127]

The longer rule also stipulated that the friars who were sent to evangelize Muslims (Saracens) were to conduct themselves in two ways. First, they were not to cause any disputes or strife but to "'be subject to every human creature for God's sake,' yet confessing themselves to be Christians."[128] Second, when they saw that the time was "pleasing to God," they were to witness to the

126. Moses, *Saint and the Sultan*, 145; John H. Smith, *Francis of Assisi* (New York: Scribner, 1972), 131.

127. Ferguson, *Church History*, 1:480.

128. Rule 16, Francis of Assisi, *The Writings of Saint Francis of Assisi*, trans. Paschal Robinson (Philadelphia: Dolphin, 1905), 49. Cf. Frank M. Rega, *St. Francis of Assisi and the Conversion of the Muslims* (Charlotte, NC: TAN, 2011), 89.

gospel of Jesus Christ so that the Muslims "may believe in Almighty God,—Father, Son, and Holy Spirit, the Creator of all, . . . Lord the Redeemer and Savior the Son, and that they should be baptized and be made Christians, because 'unless a man be born of water and the Holy Spirit, he cannot enter into the kingdom of God.'"[129]

Francis continued his work until his death. His last request was that he be stripped of his clothes and allowed to die naked as Jesus did. Francis and his friars combined the simple life of renunciation of the world with faithful evangelical witness.[130] They preached the gospel humbly and wore the cloak of materialism loosely.

Dominic and the Dominicans

In addition to Franciscans, the monastic order of Dominicans, named for the Spaniard Dominic (ca. 1170–1221), mobilized monks and nuns to evangelize nominal and heretical Christians in Europe.[131] His *Ordinis Praedicatorum*, or Order of Preachers, was active in education and in service to the broader society, preaching the gospel in the languages of the people for the salvation of their souls.[132] In 1217, Dominic sent seven of his followers to the university at Paris to establish a monastery with a focus on study and preaching.[133] He founded similar communities at the universities in Bologna in 1218 and Oxford in 1221. Like the Franciscans, Dominicans traveled in pairs or small bands with the goal of making disciples of Christ who were faithful to the Roman papacy.[134]

The earliest concentrated efforts to evangelize and instruct natives of the Americas were carried out by Franciscans, led by Pedro de Gante (ca. 1480–1572) and Vasco de Quiroga (1470–1565), and Dominicans, led by Bartolomé de Las Casas (1484–1566).[135] These monks followed in the path of a Christian layman named Christopher Columbus (1451–1506), who was sent by the Roman Catholic king and queen of Spain, Ferdinand and Isabella. As

129. Francis, *Writings of Saint Francis of Assisi*, 49.

130. Ferguson, *Church History*, 1:479.

131. Bainton, *Christianity*, 194–95.

132. Rudnick, *Speaking the Gospel*, 53.

133. Justo L. González, *A History of Christian Thought*, vol. 2, *From Augustine to the Eve of the Reformation* (Nashville: Abingdon, 2010), 230.

134. Volz, *Medieval Church*, 137; Tuttle, *Story of Evangelism*, 203.

135. Gérard Bouchard, *The Making of the Nations and Cultures of the New World: An Essay in Comparative History* (Montreal: McGill-Queens University Press, 2008), 158.

with other political advances of kings and emperors, their strategy of "Christianization" was built on Christendom's alliance of throne and church.

Cathedral Schools and Universities

During the early medieval period, monasteries were largely responsible for education.[136] Some of the well-educated monks were assigned to teach novice monks. If a monk or nun became an outstanding scholar, his or her fame spread. In turn, students from monastic houses in other areas would come to study with the renowned teacher. Often, young men and women from well-to-do families studied under the well-respected monastic tutors and then joined the regular clergy themselves, or took up secular employment.[137]

By the twelfth century, cathedral schools became the leading institutions of education. A cathedral with its bishop served as a center for several scholars who rented rooms to present their lectures, and students paid tuition per session to hear them. The chancellor taught liberal arts and theology to the more advanced students. As in monasteries, the instruction was generally theological and devotional.

From cathedral schools emerged universities, where education moved toward philosophical and academic theology.[138] A common method of teaching was the dialectical, based on Aristotle's method of philosophy. A question was presented and debated with answers from both sides, and then a conclusion was offered.

The first universities at Bologna in Italy, Paris in France, and Oxford in England led the way for scholasticism.[139] In every field of scholarly learning, the starting point was the texts or authorities written centuries earlier. In theology, the authorities were the Scriptures and writings of the church fathers. The colleges of a university resembled the groups of canons at a cathedral where the clergy lived together under a rule.[140] Universities were constructed with chapels for regular services. Biblical and theological texts were studied with a view to forming the whole life of the student in body, mind, and spirit.

136. Madigan, *Medieval Christianity*, 258–59.

137. Robert G. Clouse, Richard V. Pierard, and Edwin M. Yamauchi, *The Story of the Church* (Chicago: Moody, 2002), 111.

138. See Madigan, *Medieval Christianity*, 266–74.

139. Bainton, *Christianity*, 170–71.

140. Clouse, Pierard, and Yamauchi, *Story of the Church*, 112.

Raimundo Lulio

Raimundo Lulio, or Raymond Llull (ca. 1233–1315), from the island of Majorca, Spain, was considered a "worldly" man who wrote love poetry for women. At the age of thirty, he had a vision of Christ crucified, which led him to convert to faith and to respond to God's call to reach Muslims with the gospel.[141] On the advice of a Dominican friar, the young Lulio remained in Majorca for nine years while he studied Arabic and theology. To aid his studies, he purchased a Muslim slave, from whom he learned the Arabic language.[142] Moreover, Lulio read extensively in Arabic and Latin in order to learn Islamic and Christian theological and philosophical thought. Then he made provisions for his wife, Blanca, and his children and traveled on three occasions as a missionary to North Africa.

Lulio developed a strategy of evangelism that led him to persuade James II, king of Majorca, to establish a school there for Franciscans to study oriental languages.[143] Then Lulio traveled throughout Europe in an effort to interest kings as well as the pope to form schools to prepare missionaries to learn Arabic so that they could speak with the people of Tunisia and other North African countries about Jesus Christ. He believed that by studying languages and cultures, missionaries could significantly increase their effectiveness.

In 1305, Lulio completed a book titled *Great Art* (*Ars Magna*), in which he attempted to relate all forms of knowledge, including religious belief, to the manifestations of God's "Dignities" or attributes in the universe.[144] He took the monotheistic view common to Judaism, Christianity, and Islam as his starting point. Although the original purpose and inspiration of his *Great Art* was clearly the conversion of unbelievers to Christianity, he insisted that it was "'general' and 'universal,' an art of arts capable of discovering the truth about any subject, whether considered through evangelism, contemplation, or study."[145] Lulio also developed a theological reference guide by which students or readers could consider a question about the Christian faith, or

141. Mark D. Johnston, *The Evangelical Rhetoric of Ramon Llull: Lay Learning and Piety in the Christian West around 1300* (Oxford: Oxford University Press, 1996), 5–8.

142. Karen O'Dell Bullock, "Monastics on Mission," in *Discovering the Mission of God: Best Missional Practices for the 21st Century*, ed. Mike Barnett (Downers Grove, IL: IVP Academic, 2012), 242–43.

143. Régine Pernoud, *The Crusaders* (San Francisco: Ignatius, 2003), 345.

144. Johnston, *Evangelical Rhetoric of Ramon Llull*, 12–22.

145. Johnston, *Evangelical Rhetoric of Ramon Llull*, 17.

an argument against it, and turn to the index and corresponding pages to find the answer.

In 1311, after his reconnaissance mission to North Africa at the request of Pope Clement V, Lulio returned to Rome, where he suggested that, rather than through military force, the conquest of Muslims should be achieved by prayer and gospel witness.[146] In the same year, he achieved a major victory when the Council of Vienne approved his proposal that academic chairs of Hebrew, Arabic, and Chaldean be established at the universities of Bologna, Paris, Salamanca, and Oxford, as well as the Papal Court in Rome.[147]

Three years later, Lulio returned to North Africa, where he dialogued with Muslims and put his ideas into practice. He was saddened, however, when he did not make many new converts. In 1314, when he was in his eighties, he sailed a third time to North Africa. For a year he preached the gospel of Christ openly. Then, while in the city of Béjaïa, in present-day Algeria, he was stoned by an angry mob. Spanish merchants took him back to Majorca, but he soon died. Despite the personal challenges that he faced during his evangelistic work, Lulio believed that if God could convert Muslims to Christ, he could convert anyone in the world.[148]

Art and Architectural Evangelism

The meeting places of Christians and congregations, from caves and catacombs to basilicas in the early church, to gothic cathedrals and university chapels of the medieval period, utilized art and architecture to portray the gospel of Jesus Christ. For pagans who entered these spaces set apart for the worship of the triune God, paintings, adorned walls, and carved images were graphic aids to illustrate the gospel of Jesus's incarnation, crucifixion, resurrection, ascension, and glorious return.

The Chartres Cathedral of France, built between the years 1194 and 1220, for example, contains more than eight thousand images in various media.[149] The structure was "virtually a pictorial encyclopedia encased in a stone binding," portraying the drama of redemptive history from creation to final judgment.[150] The events of Christ's passion hold a prominent place

146. Scott W. Sunquist, *Understanding Christian Mission: Participation in Suffering and Glory* (Grand Rapids: Baker Academic, 2017), 3–4, 40.

147. Tomaž Mastnak, *Crusading Peace: Christendom, the Muslim World, and Western Political Order* (Berkeley: University of California Press, 2002), 216.

148. Rudnick, *Speaking the Gospel*, 71–72.

149. Bainton, *Christianity*, 185.

150. Bainton, *Christianity*, 185. Cf. Hill, *What Has Christianity Ever Done for Us?*, 75–76.

with episodes depicted on the walls in the stations of the cross that include Jesus's trial before Pilate, Christ receiving the cross, Christ stumbling and Simon of Cyrene being given the cross to carry, the crucifixion, the descent from the cross, and Christ's burial in the tomb.[151]

Christian art and images at times were not without controversy, however. The use of icons of Jesus, the twelve apostles, and other saints of the church was debated. Some Christian leaders opposed their use, while others such as John of Damascus favored them, arguing that because Christ became a man, and if man was made in the image of God, then an icon of Christ was a true image of God, not to be worshiped in itself but useful as an aid in the deeper reflection of God.[152]

In some cases, icons of Jesus and other portrayals of him were based on the tradition that artists used the face of the Mandylion of Edessa, later known as the Shroud of Turin, as a template.[153] The image of the crucified Christ was embedded into the fibers of the cloth itself and, because of multiple distinguishing marks, was accepted as the pattern for icons such as *The Christ Pantocrator* of St. Catherine's Monastery in Sinai, Egypt, dating from the mid-sixth century.[154] In this and other icons, the face of Christ is portrayed with a short beard, mustache, narrow face with long hair falling on the shoulders, and other distinguishable features. This image—believed to be that of Jesus Christ—appeared inside basilicas in the West, where the face was portrayed on crucifixes and statues, and inside domes in the East, where the face portrays Christ as the enthroned King, or Pantocrator, who rules over all creation.[155]

Whether icons of Jesus, paintings of parables, or walls adorned with the stations of the cross, Christian art and architecture have been used to

151. Bainton, *Christianity*, 185.

152. Tuttle, *Story of Evangelism*, 173. John of Damascus said, "I do not worship matter, but the Creator of matter, who for my sake became material and deigned to dwell in matter, who through matter effected my salvation." Georges Florovsky, *The Byzantine Fathers of the Sixth to Eighth Century* (Belmont, MA: Notable and Academic, 1987), 283.

153. A theory by a number of scholars, including Orthodox, Roman Catholic, and Protestant, is that the Mandylion of Edessa was taken to Constantinople and then, in 1204, carried west when the city was sacked by Crusaders during the Fourth Crusade. Gary R. Habermas, "The Shroud of Turin and Its Significance for Biblical Studies," *Journal of the Evangelical Theological Society*, 24, no. 1 (March 1981): 47–54; Mark Antonacci, *The Resurrection of the Shroud* (New York: Evans, 2000), 145–47.

154. John Galey, George Forsyth, and Kurt Weitzmann, *Sinai and the Monastery of St. Catherine* (London: Chatto & Windus, 1980), 92, 99.

155. Grant R. Jeffrey, *Jesus: The Great Debate* (Colorado Springs: Waterbrook, 1999), 152–54.

illustrate the gospel. For literate and illiterate people alike, multiple images portrayed the story of Jesus in ways that people could understand and easily repeat after hearing the story about them read from the Scriptures.

Discussion Questions

1. Power encounters like the one when Boniface cut down the sacred Oak of Donar are not typical today. Should Christians employ power encounters as a means of evangelism or play some role in seeing these occur? Or should these simply be left to God to perform?
2. Gregory the Great established the principle of evangelism that not all pagan temples, festivals, and practices should be eliminated from the lives of new believers. What are reasons for this principle? Cautions? Exceptions? What examples might we consider today?
3. Although Charlemagne wished for Saxons to convert to faith, his means were contrary to the way of Jesus. How can we be sure to evangelize without attempting to force conversion? How can we share the gospel without manipulating people? How do Christian ethics apply to evangelism? Do the ends *ever* justify the means?
4. If Francis of Assisi, Pope Urban II, John of Damascus, and Raimundo Lulio were in a room discussing the evangelization of Muslims, what would they say? Which one of them would most shape your approach today? Why?
5. Art was used as a tool for evangelism in the medieval era. Is art underutilized today? Underdeveloped? Why? What measures can local churches take to reclaim innovation in the arts in order to evangelize non-Christians?

5

Renaissance Evangelism

O Lord Jesus Christ, by Thy glorious resurrection, in which Thou didst appear alive and immortal to Thy disciples and faithful followers, by Thy forty days' abiding and sweet converse, in which by many infallible proofs, speaking of things pertaining to the Kingdom of God, Thou didst comfort them and assure them of Thine actual resurrection, removing all doubt from their hearts. We beseech Thee, O Lord, grant that we may be numbered among those who were fore-ordained by God to be witnesses of Thy resurrection, not only by word of mouth, but in reality of good works; for Thine honour and glory, who with the Father and the Holy Ghost livest and reignest ever one God, world without end. Amen.

—Ludolph of Saxony (ca. 1295–1378)[1]

The twelfth century brought notable achievements in philosophy, art, and architecture, as well as piety, monastic reforms, and theology. The pursuit of theology continued in the thirteenth century by Dominicans and Franciscans in their monastic schools, which were foundational for the earliest European universities and produced what became known as Scholasticism. By the fourteenth century, these endeavors, along with other forces, gave birth to the Renaissance, a cultural renewal in literature, politics, arts, and science.

1. J. Manning Potts, ed., *Prayers of the Middle Ages: Light from a Thousand Years* (Nashville: Upper Room, 1954), 74–75.

Scholasticism

Scholasticism, from the Latin *scholasticus*, meaning "devoted to learning," and from the Greek *schol* (school) and *scholastikos* (student), referred to the work of schoolmen in the late medieval period who studied Christian theology in an attempt to reconcile the thought of ancient philosophers like Aristotle with Christian thought and doctrine. This produced a method of learning in cathedral schools and medieval universities that emphasized dialectical reasoning in order to arrive at conclusions to questions, or resolutions to contradictions.

Anselm of Canterbury

The Italian philosopher of Christian theology who became known as the founder of Scholasticism was Anselm of Canterbury (ca. 1033–1109). He was born into nobility at Aosta, in a mountainous area of northern Italy, where as a boy he imagined God living in a palace high on a mountain. Anselm entered the Benedictine abbey of Bec in Normandy and followed in the footsteps of his abbot Lanfranc, who was appointed archbishop of Canterbury, a position that Anselm held later in life. In the meantime, finding himself at odds with King William Rufus on a range of ecclesiastical issues and church reforms, Anselm was exiled to Rome, where he wrote a book titled *Why God Became a Man* (*Cur Deus Homo*), in which he offered a rational explanation for Christ's incarnation in relation to his death on the cross.[2]

Completed in 1098, this treatise was the most coherent explanation in the West for the basis of Christian faith and the crux of the gospel itself, setting forth a logical proof for the satisfaction theory of Christ's atonement.[3] Anselm explained that sin is a serious matter because it is against God, who demands absolute moral honor. At the same time, God is concerned with human welfare. Only a human being ought to make satisfaction for sin but only God can provide the satisfaction.[4] Hence, the need for the God-man who is both God and human. Jesus Christ alone, by his death, provided willingly the offering or sacrifice to God. He offered himself as a man, but

2. Sally N. Vaughn, *Archbishop Anselm 1093–1109: Bec Missionary, Canterbury Primate, Patriarch of Another World* (New York: Routledge, 2016), 63–64.

3. Edward S. Prout, preface to Anselm, *Cur Deus Homo? Why God Became Man?*, trans. by Edward S. Prout (London: The Religious Tract Society, 1886), 19–20.

4. Everett Ferguson, *Church History*, vol. 1, *From Christ to Pre-Reformation* (Grand Rapids: Zondervan, 2005), 433–34.

what he did was of infinite worth because he was God. His death satisfied the moral honor and righteous demands of God.

Earlier than Anselm, the apostolic fathers were content to repeat phrases from the Scriptures that expressed their experience of redemption on the basis of Christ's death.[5] The church fathers of the second and third centuries were more speculative. While they held to the moral necessity of the death of Christ, it was Satan rather than God himself who figured more prominently into the scheme; the ransom to release sinners from bondage was paid to the devil.[6]

As for the satisfaction theory, Tertullian provided an initial statement.[7] Augustine of Hippo taught the vicarious sacrifice of Christ but did not expound the absolute moral necessity of a satisfaction for sin.[8] John of Damascus added to the doctrine, teaching that Christ's death was a vicarious sacrifice offered to God, not to the devil. Alcuin held a view that agreed substantially with Augustine.[9] However, Anselm presented the satisfaction theory in a more complete formulation.[10]

In the beginning of this treatise, Anselm asks the question "For what reason or necessity was God made man, and by His death, as we believe, restored life to the world?"[11] Following the pattern of medieval dialectic (from the Greek *dialogos*), Anselm poses the question and his friend Boso answers it, and in some cases the order is reversed.

Excerpts from *Why God Became a Man (Cur Deus Homo)* by Anselm

Anselm: Is sin, therefore, anything else than rendering to God what is His due?

Boso: What is it that is due which we owe to God?

Anselm: The entire will of a rational creature ought to be subject to the will of God.

5. Prout, preface, 6–7.

6. Carl E. Braaten, *Who Is Jesus? Disputed Questions and Answers* (Grand Rapids: Eerdmans, 2011), 98–99. Gustaf Aulén restated the ransom theory as Christ's victory over "sin, death, and the devil." *Christus Victor: An Historical Study of the Three Main Types of the Idea of the Atonement* (London: SPCK, 1953), 51.

7. Ferguson, *Church History*, 1:435.

8. Prout, preface, 9.

9. Prout, preface, 9–10.

10. Ferguson, *Church History*, 1:435.

11. Anselm, *Cur Deus Homo?*, 33.

Boso: Nothing can be truer.

Anselm: This is the debt which both angels and men owe to God. . . . This is the sole and entire honour which we owe to God, and which God requires from us. . . . The man who does not render to God this honour, which is His due, takes away from God what is His own, and dishonours God, and this is to sin. . . . Everyone who sins ought to render back to God the honour he has taken away and this is the satisfaction which every sinner ought to make to God. . . . What, therefore, will you pay to God for your sin?

Boso: If I owe to Him myself and all I can give, even when I do not sin, lest I should sin, I have nothing to render to Him in compensation for sin. . . .

Anselm: Thus, seriously do we sin whenever we knowingly, do anything, however slight, against the will of God. For, we are always in His sight, and he is always bidding us not to sin.

Boso: As I understand, we live in an exceedingly dangerous condition.

Anselm: It is clear that God requires satisfaction according to the amount of sin.

Boso: I cannot deny it.

Anselm: You do not, therefore, make satisfaction unless you return something greater than that for the sake of which you were under obligation not to have committed the sin. . . . Man, created in Paradise without sin, was, as it were, placed there for God, between God and the devil that he might overcome the devil by not consenting to his persuasives to sin, for the vindication and honour of God and for the confusion of the devil. . . . There is no one, therefore, who can make this satisfaction except God Himself.

Boso: That follows.

Anselm: But no one *ought* to make it except man; otherwise man does not make satisfaction.

Boso: Nothing seems more just than this.

Anselm: If, therefore, as is certain, it is needful that that heavenly state be perfected from among men, and this cannot be unless the above-mentioned satisfaction be made, which no one *can* make except man, it is necessary that one who is God-man should make it. . . .

Boso: In reply to which, you have shown by many and necessary arguments that the restoration of human nature ought not to remain unaccomplished, but yet could not be effected unless man paid to God what he owed for sin, and which debt was so great that though no one ought to pay for it who was not man, no one could pay for it who was not God, so that the same person must be both man and God. Whence it was necessary that God should take man into the unity of His person [in the incarnation], so that he who in his own nature ought to pay and could not, might be in a Person who could. In fine, you have shown that the man who also was God was to be taken out of a virgin, and from the Person of the Son of God, and how He could be taken without sin from the sinful mass. Moreover, you have most clearly proved that the life of this man was so exalted and so precious, that it may suffice to pay what is due for the sins of the whole world, and infinitely more.

(Anselm, *Cur Deus Homo? Why God Became Man?*, trans. Edward S. Prout [London: The Religious Tract Society, 1886], 63–64, 97, 100–101, 120, 164–65).

Anselm's satisfaction theory of the atonement became the dominant view during the late medieval period.[12]

Thomas Aquinas

The nature of evangelism during the medieval period consisted of persuading people to accept Christian baptism and then catechizing them in hopes that they would conform to the standards of Christian behavior. Baptism brought people into the church. It was taught that this rite was sacramental, conferring grace toward salvation.

The Dominican friar and theologian Thomas Aquinas (ca. 1225–1274) wrote several books; the most famous is a theological summary titled *Summa theologiae*. Aquinas followed the view of Peter Lombard (ca. 1100–1160), who taught that there were seven sacraments.[13] The sacraments had power to impart divine grace to those who received them, even if the priest

12. It continues to be the main view of the Roman Catholic Church and evangelical Protestants. Braaten, *Who Is Jesus?*, 99.

13. Brian Davies, *Thomas Aquinas's* Summa Theologiae: *A Guide and Commentary* (New York: Oxford University Press, 2014), 324.

lacked faith or charity.[14] The seven sacraments were baptism, confirmation, the Eucharist, penance, extreme unction (last rites), ordination, and marriage.[15] Lombard and Aquinas held that the sacraments, outward symbols, "contain and confer grace—*continere et conferre gratiam*."[16] The mode of this efficacy was *ex opera operato*—that is, by virtue inherent in the acts themselves. Aquinas distinguished between "the original cause of grace, which is God, and the instrumental cause, which is the sacrament."[17] Importantly, each of the seven sacraments was tied to the actions of priests of the Roman Church. *Summa theologiae*, though uncompleted at the time of Aquinas's death, defined the Roman Church's theology, largely from then to the present day.

In addition, Aquinas wrote *Summa contra gentiles*, an apologetic work for use by Dominican missionaries to win Muslims, Jews, Christian heretics, and pagans to orthodox Christian faith.[18] In the first three books, he drew from a body of shared knowledge—in the case of Jews, the shared acceptance of the Hebrew Bible (Old Testament), and in the case of Muslims, the shared monotheistic tradition and, at the time, an Aristotelian philosophy.[19] This apologetic treatise aided Dominican missionaries in Spain who sought to convert Jews and Muslims to Christianity.

Evangelistic Free Churches

During the twelfth and thirteenth centuries, there was a stark difference between those who emphasized salvation by receiving the church's sacraments and those who emphasized the apostolic gospel and living in obedience to the triune God. At a time when the broader population knew little of the Scriptures, lay movements of preachers sought to practice what ordained clergy neglected, or were not permitted to do. These lay preachers proclaimed the gospel in the language of the people, distributed portions

14. Justo L. González, *History of Christian Thought*, vol. 2, *From Augustine to the Eve of the Reformation* (Nashville: Abingdon, 2010), 279.

15. Thomas Aquinas, *The Summa Theologica, Part 2; no.* 2 (London: Washbourne, 1915), 108, 2, 4 (p. 308).

16. *HCC* 5:704.

17. *HCC* 5:705.

18. Brian Davies, *Thomas Aquinas's* Summa Contra Gentiles: *A Guide and Commentary* (New York: Oxford University Press, 2016), 10–12.

19. Etienne Gilson, *The Christian Philosophy of Saint Thomas Aquinas* (Notre Dame, IN: University of Notre Dame Press, 1994), 501–3.

of the Bible, taught the importance of Scripture memorization, and made disciples of Jesus who did the same.

Peter Waldo and the Waldenses

The Waldenses were an emerging free-church movement in Europe known for their bold witness to the gospel and life of discipleship. They were led by Waldo, or Vaudès (ca. 1140–1218), of Lyons, France, who began his career as a merchant from the burgeoning class of wealthy medieval merchants.[20] In 1175, he had a profound religious conversion and committed his life to proclaim the gospel while living in apostolic poverty, following Jesus's words literally: "If you want to be perfect, go, sell your possessions and give to the poor, and you will have treasure in heaven. Then come, follow me" (Matt. 19:21).[21]

Waldo obeyed the command, selling his possessions, making provisions for his wife and children, and giving the rest of his money to the poor. Freed from former concerns, he took Jesus's instructions as his standard. He traveled throughout the area where he preached repentance and taught the way of Jesus, meeting people in the streets, towns, and villages. He took nothing with him and received only alms that people gave him along the way.[22]

Because Waldo was not able to read the Latin Bible, he asked two priests to translate the New Testament into French, which formed the basis for his evangelism.[23] He memorized large portions of the Scriptures as well as writings of church fathers. With the Scriptures in hand and mind, he preached sermons that included long scriptural quotations from memory. Soon he attracted a band of followers who called themselves the "poor men of Lyons."[24] They imitated his apostolic poverty and devoted themselves to memorizing the Scriptures and lay preaching.

20. Roland H. Bainton, *Christianity* (Boston: Houghton Mifflin, 2000), 196.

21. Scott W. Sunquist, *Understanding Christian Mission: Participation in Suffering and Glory* (Grand Rapids: Baker Academic, 2017), 39.

22. Stark posits the principle: "Religious leaders have greater credibility when they receive low levels of material reward in return for their religious services," citing Waldo as an example. Rodney Stark, *The Rise of Christianity: How the Obscure, Marginal Jesus Movement Became the Dominant Religious Force in the Western World in a Few Centuries* (San Francisco: HarperSanFrancisco, 1997), 174.

23. Ronald Finucane, "The Waldensians," in *Handbook to the History of Christianity*, ed. Tim Dowley (Grand Rapids: Eerdmans, 1977), 315.

24. *HCC* 5:162.

The evangelistic strategy of Waldo and his followers was generally to go out two by two among the people.[25] At first, they presented their message on street corners and in market squares. Their evangelism was both simple and personal. With use of long quotations from the Bible, they made an appeal for listeners to follow the way of Jesus. In 1179, Waldo and one of his disciples traveled to Rome while the Third Lateran Council was in session. They requested papal recognition for their society of preachers and were welcomed by Pope Alexander III and the Roman Curia who assisted the pope.[26] Waldo and his disciple were asked to explain their beliefs before a panel of three clergy.[27] They discussed ideas about the universal priesthood, speaking the gospel in the common language, translating the Scriptures into French, and living the apostolic life of voluntary poverty. Although the pope viewed Waldo and the Poor Men with suspicion, they were granted limited authority to preach. Their ideas were soon condemned, however, and in 1184 they were excommunicated by the Council of Verona.

Nonetheless, they continued to preach the gospel, believing that their authority did not come from the pope or bishops but from Jesus Christ. Waldo said, "God commanded the apostles to 'preach the Gospel to all creation'" (Mark 16:15), and "We must obey God rather than men!" (Acts 5:29).[28] With these words from the lips of the apostle Peter, Waldo became known as "Peter" Waldo.

The Roman Church persecuted the Waldenses aggressively, even mounting an episcopal inquisition and threatening their punishment. These actions did not dissuade them, however. Several Waldenses traveled to isolated valleys in the Alps, and from there they preached the gospel in Italy, Germany, Bohemia, Spain, and the Netherlands.[29] The Waldensian leaders continued

25. Mendell Taylor, *Exploring Evangelism: History, Methods, Theology* (Kansas City, MO: Nazarene Publishing House, 1984), 83.

26. Bainton, *Christianity*, 196.

27. The chairman of the commission, Walter Map, severely criticized their Latin-to-French translation of the Bible as being unreliable, inaccurate, and inconsistent. M. Taylor, *Exploring Evangelism*, 84.

28. Kevin Madigan, *Medieval Christianity: A New History* (New Haven: Yale University Press, 2015), 193.

29. Robert G. Tuttle, *The Story of Evangelism: A History of the Witness to the Gospel* (Nashville: Abingdon, 2006), 206.

to live simple and austere lives, depended on the offerings of their followers, and evangelized as traveling preachers.[30]

Conventicles

A wave of persecution came against the Waldenses in 1211, in which some were burned at the stake in France and in Germany, and others martyred in northern Italy.[31] They carried out activities nevertheless, holding "conventicles" (from the Latin *conventiculum*, meaning "little gathering") in homes for worship, witness, and the care of souls.[32]

In subsequent decades—and even centuries—the Waldenses existed as an unauthorized, free-church movement, independent or "free" of the Roman Church. The Piedmont Valley of northern Italy remained their home base. They organized societies in various districts, and organized gatherings of congregations with two classes of followers: "Christ's paupers" (from the Latin *pauperes Christi*) composed of those who left secular life to evangelize, and "friends" (*amici*), those who remained in conventional occupations.[33] Conversion to Christian faith was followed by a time of testing, after which new converts were admitted to the congregation as "brothers" and "sisters."

The Waldenses emphasized the Bible as their rule of faith and translated it into other languages. They conducted worship services in the conventicles that included readings from the Bible, the Lord's Prayer, and sermons preached by men and women who were led by the Holy Spirit.[34] The leaders were called "the Seventy" and obeyed the gospel's instructions for their apostolic mission (Matt. 10:5–23).[35] The Waldenses rejected the Roman pope as the vicar of Christ on earth, masses and prayers for the dead, and indulgences as means of penance with merit for salvation. Instead, they stressed gospel simplicity, refused to take oaths, and taught that taking the life of another human being was morally wrong. Their beliefs were set forth later in the Waldensian Catechism.

30. Finucane, "Waldensians," 316.

31. Gunnar Westin, *The Free Church through the Ages*, trans. Virgil A. Olson (Nashville: Broadman, 1959), 28.

32. Joel Comiskey, *2000 Years of Small Groups: A History of Cell Ministry in the Church* (Morena Valley, CA: CCS, 2014), 62, 67–68, 103.

33. Westin, *Free Church through the Ages*, 28.

34. Sunquist, *Understanding Christian Mission*, 39.

35. A Waldensian Church still exists today in Europe, Uruguay, and North Carolina. John Mark Terry, *Evangelism: A Concise History* (Nashville: B&H, 2014), 59.

Waldensian Catechism

Question: If thou art asked, Who art thou?
Answer: *I am a creature of God, rational and mortal.*

For what end has God made you?
That I may know and serve him, and be saved by his grace.

On what rests thy salvation?
On three fundamental virtues, which are necessary to salvation.

Which are they?
Faith, Hope, and Love.

How do you prove this?
The Apostle writes: "Now abideth faith, hope, love, these three; but the greatest of these is love."

Which is the first fundamental virtue?
Faith; for the Apostle says: "It is impossible to please God without faith: for he that cometh to God must believe that he is, and that he is a rewarder of them that diligently seek him."

What is faith?
According to the Apostle, "faith is the substance of things hoped for, the evidence of things not seen."

How many kinds of faith are there?
Two kinds, a living faith and a dead faith.

What is living faith?
It is faith active in love as the Apostle testifies, that is "by keeping God's commandments." Living faith is to believe in God, that is, to love him and to keep his commandments.

What is dead faith?
According to St. James, faith which has no works is dead in itself; faith is idle without works. Or dead faith is to believe that God is, to believe about God, of God, but not to believe in God.

What is your faith?
The true catholic and apostolic faith.

Which is that?
It is the one which at the Council of the Apostles was divided into twelve articles.

(Waldensian Catechism, c. 1489. Philip Schaff, *The Creeds of Christendom: History of the Creeds*, vol. 1, part 2 [Eugene, OR: Wipf & Stock, 2007], 572–75)

In matters of Christian faith, the Waldenses were orthodox in their formulations, holding to the Apostles' Creed as a summary of the Christian gospel while emphasizing obedience to Jesus's ethical commands in the Sermon on the Mount. They influenced other reforming movements too, such as the Hussites and Taborites and, through them, the Moravian Brethren.

Criticisms within the Roman Church

During the late medieval period, the Roman Church became increasingly wealthy, powerful, and corrupt. Some of the popes lived openly with mistresses and fathered illegitimate sons and daughters.[36] Church officials bought and sold church positions—the scandal of simony—and many sought high positions solely to enrich themselves. Some parish priests held multiple positions, collecting multiple paychecks while neglecting their pastoral duties, or were absent from their posts altogether.[37] Therefore, the late medieval Roman Church faced criticisms increasingly from those within its ranks.

Francesco Petrarch

One critic was Francesco Petrarch (1304–1374), considered the "first Renaissance man."[38] He lived during the time of the Avignon papacy, a schism that

36. See E. R. Chamberlin, *The Bad Popes* (Stroud, UK: Sutton, 2003).

37. Justo L. González, *The Story of Christianity: The Early Church to the Present Day* (Peabody, MA: Prince, 1999), 1:337.

38. John D. Woodbridge and Frank A. James III, *Church History*, vol. 2, *From Pre-Reformation to the Present Day* (Grand Rapids: Zondervan, 2013), 79–81.

eventually led to three Roman popes at the same time. As a young cleric of the Roman Church, Petrarch struggled to justify his religious calling with his study of ancient classical writers, as well as his prolific writing in Italian and Latin. He grew up in Avignon, France, having observed firsthand the years of the papal "Babylonian captivity of the church" (1309–1377), when the papacy moved from Rome to Avignon.[39] In a statement critical of how the papacy had wandered from the simple mission of gospel proclamation, Petrarch said,

> Here reign the successors of the poor fishermen of Galilee; they have strangely forgotten their origin. I am astounded, as I recall their predecessors, to see these [papal] men loaded with gold and clad in purple, boasting of the spoils of princes and nations; to see luxurious palaces and heights crowned with fortifications, instead of a boat turned downwards for shelter. We no longer find the simple nets which were once used to gain frugal sustenance from the Lake of Galilee, with which, having labored all night and caught nothing, they took, at daybreak, a multitude of fishes, in the name of Jesus. One is stupefied nowadays to hear the lying tongues, and to see worthless parchments, turned by a leaden seal, into nets which are used, in Christ's name, but by the arts of Belial, to catch hordes of unwary Christians. These fish, too, are dressed and laid on the burning coals of anxiety before they fill the insatiable maw of their captors. Instead of holy solitude we find a criminal host and crowds of the most infamous satellites; instead of soberness, licentious banquets; instead of pious pilgrimages, preternatural and foul sloth; instead of the bare feet of the apostles, the snowy coursers of brigands fly past us, the horses decked in gold and fed on gold, soon to be shod with gold, if the Lord does not check this slavish luxury. In short, we seem to be among the kings of the Persians or Parthians, before whom we must fall down and worship, and who cannot be approached except presents be offered. O, ye unkempt and emaciated old men, is it for this you labored? Is it for this that you have sown the field of the Lord and watered it with your holy blood?[40]

39. Woodbridge and James, *Church History*, 2:32, 37–39. The Avignon papacy, which lasted seventy years, was described years later by Martin Luther as the "Babylonian captivity of the church." See Martin Luther and Erik H. Herrmann, *The Babylonian Captivity of the Church, 1520*, ed. Paul W. Robinson (Minneapolis: Fortress, 2016).

40. John A. Wagner, ed., *Documents of the Reformation* (Santa Barbara, CA: ABC-CLIO, 2019), 2.

The liturgy of worship services in the Roman Church was marked by multiple signs, gestures, striking of the breast, kneeling, kissing the altar, and kissing the missal.[41] It centered on the eucharistic mass as an offering of Christ.[42] The spirituality of the laypeople centered on acts of devotion such as prayers to the canonized saints, involvement in festivities for holy days, and devotion to the eucharistic host of the bread as the body of Christ. As Petrarch observed, the Roman Church had become a mere caricature of the church of Jesus and the apostles rather than devout followers who herald the good news.

John Wycliffe

In addition to the criticisms of Petrarch, the medieval Roman Church received criticisms from within its own ranks by the English priest John of Wycliffe (ca. 1324–1384).[43] He was born in the vicinity of Wycliffe in Yorkshire, in the diocese of Durham.[44] He attended Oxford University, and by 1365 he was head of Canterbury Hall, an experimental college for monastic and secular clergy.[45] Five years later he served as Oxford's leading philosopher and theologian, completing his doctorate in 1372.

During his studies, Wycliffe came under the sway of Augustinian theologian Thomas of Bradwardine, who taught justification by faith and warned against dependence on human merit through penance for salvation, as taught earlier by Aquinas and others.[46] Wycliffe came to hold that, according to Romans 8:30, God's grace alone brings justification and cannot be earned or merited.[47]

Wycliffe also developed his ideas about civil and religious government. When he spoke publicly at Oxford and London, he voiced the need for reform, preaching against the pope's secular sovereignty. Wycliffe maintained that the pope "has no more power in binding and loosing than any priest,

41. Robert E. Webber, *Ancient-Future Faith: Rethinking Evangelicalism for a Postmodern World* (Grand Rapids: Baker Books, 2000), 98.

42. Madigan, *Medieval Christianity*, 86–88.

43. Bainton, *Christianity*, 215.

44. Carl A. Volz, *The Medieval Church: From the Dawn of the Middle Ages to the Eve of the Reformation* (Nashville: Abingdon, 1997), 219–20.

45. A. N. S. Lane, "John Wyclif: 'Morning Star of the Reformation,'" in *Great Leaders of the Christian Church*, ed. John D. Woodbridge (Chicago: Moody, 1988), 174.

46. Westin, *Free Church through the Ages*, 31.

47. Westin, *Free Church through the Ages*, 33.

Figure 5.1. Wyclif Giving "The Poor Priests" His Translation of the Bible, ca. 1395, by William Frederick Yeames, 1835–1918. (The Picture Art Collection/Alamy Stock Photo)

and that the temporal lords may seize the possessions of the clergy if pressed by necessity."[48] With conviction, Wycliffe held that the pope, of all humans, was "most under obligation to obey the law of Christ" and that no Christian, including the Roman pope, "has the right to follow Peter, Paul or any of the saints except as they imitated Christ" (1 Cor. 11:1).[49] Wycliffe preached that "the true church consists only of the predestined and excludes the reprobate, who can be identified, even if they are popes, by behavior that is in glaring contradiction to that of the apostles."[50]

Wycliffe held that the Bible was inspired by God and that its authority was superior to that of popes and church councils.[51] In 1378, he expressed his views in a work titled *On the Truth of Holy Scripture* (*De veritate sacrae*

48. In one of his tracts, Wycliffe described the bishop of Rome as "the anti-Christ, the proud, worldly priest of Rome, and the most cursed of clippers of cut-purses." *HCC* 6:316.

49. It was Wycliffe's treatise *On the Church* (*De Ecclesia*) that later came to have tremendous significance in Bohemia. Westin, *Free Church through the Ages*, 32.

50. Bainton, *Christianity*, 215.

51. Westin, *Free Church through the Ages*, 32.

Scripturae), in which he contended that the Scriptures are the foundation of salvation, the basis of the church's teaching, and the guide for reform of church and state.[52] He taught that because the Bible is the inerrant statement of truth, it should be available to all Christians.[53] This view stood in contrast to the decision of the Council of Toulouse in 1227, which declared it unlawful for laypeople to read and interpret the Bible for themselves, a matter of great importance to many who preached the gospel.[54]

Pope Gregory IX pronounced Wycliffe a heretic, and in 1381, a series of condemnations were leveled against him. Fortunately, he was protected by John of Gaunt, son of the English king, who used his political power to give Wycliffe a voice and to keep him from punishment.

Wycliffe declared that the highest form of service was to preach the gospel "as Christ occupied himself most in that work."[55] He went so far as to say, "Yea, the preaching of the Word is a more precious occupation than the ministration of the sacraments." In reference to the Eucharist, he called the doctrine of transubstantiation—the view that the bread and wine are changed into the very substance of Jesus's body and blood—an innovation of "the recent church" (*novella ecclesia*).[56] Moreover, he considered papal indulgences useless, saying that God does not absolve sins for those who wish to reduce their time in purgatory on the basis of paying money.

Wycliffe's teachings about the priesthood of believers and the responsibility of every Christian to spread the knowledge of God's Word became foundational principles of his followers, known as Wycliffites or Lollards.[57] Wycliffe taught that all Englishmen needed to hear the gospel in the English language, and that laypeople and clergy alike should be equipped for this task.

John Wycliffe on the Gospel in the Mother-Tongue

Christians should labour day and night upon the text of Holy Scripture, especially upon the Gospel in their mother-tongue. And yet men will not suffer it that the laity should know the Gospel, and read it in their common life in humility and love. But pleasure-loving learned men of this world reply

52. Terry, *Evangelism*, 62.
53. O. C. Edwards, *A History of Preaching* (Nashville: Abingdon, 2004), 248, 250.
54. *HCC* 6:341.
55. *HCC* 6:329.
56. Westin, *Free Church through the Ages*, 33.
57. Volz, *Medieval Christianity*, 222.

and say, laymen may easily fall into error, and therefore they ought not to dispute upon questions of Christian faith. Alas! alas! what cruelty it is to rob a whole kingdom of bodily food because a few fools may be gluttonous, and may do themselves and others mischief by their immoderate use of such food! Quite as easily may a proud worldly priest fall into error contrary to the Gospel which is written in Latin, as a simple layman may err contrary to the Gospel which is written in English. When a child makes a slip in his first day's lesson, would there be any sense in making that a reason for never allowing children to come to lessons at all? Who then in this way of it would ever become a scholar? What sort of Antichrist is this who, to the sorrow of Christian men, is so bold as to prohibit the laity from learning this holy lesson which is so earnestly commanded by God? Every man is bound to learn it that he may be saved, but every layman who shall be saved is a very priest of God's own making, and every man is bound to be a very priest. . . .

Holy Scripture is the faultless, most true, most perfect, and most holy law of God, which it is the duty of every man to learn to know, to defend, and to observe, inasmuch as they are bound to serve the Lord in accordance with it, under the promise of an eternal reward. . . .

As the faith of the Church is contained in the Scriptures, the more these are known in an orthodox sense, the better. And since secular men should assuredly understand the faith, it should be taught them in whatever language is best known to them. Inasmuch, also, as the doctrines of our faith are more clearly and precisely expressed in the Scriptures than they may possibly be by priests, seeing, if one may venture so to speak, that many prelates are but too ignorant of Scripture, while others conceal parts of Scripture, and as the verbal instructions of priests have many other defects, the conclusion is abundantly plain, that believers should ascertain for themselves the matters of their faith, by having the Scriptures in a language which they fully understand.

Besides, it was by faith, as described by the apostle (Heb. ch. xi.), that the saints of old overcame kingdoms, and hastened to their own country. Why, then, should not the things of faith be disclosed to the people now, so that they may comprehend them more clearly? He, in consequence, who shall prevent this, or murmur against it, does his utmost to continue the people in a state of unbelief and condemnation. Hence, also, the laws made by prelates are not to be received as matters of faith, nor are we to confide in their public instructions, or in any of their words, but as they are founded on Holy Writ; for, according to the constant doctrine of Augustine, the Scriptures contain the whole of the truth; and this translation of them should therefore do at least this good viz. placing bishops and priests above suspicion as to the parts of it which they profess to explain. Other means also, as prelates, the pope, and friars, may prove defective; and to provide against this, Christ and His apostles evangelized the greater portion of the world by making known the Scriptures in a language which was familiar to the people. To this end, indeed, did the Holy Spirit endow them with the knowledge of all tongues. Why, therefore, should not the living disciples of Christ do as they did, opening the Scriptures to the people so clearly and plainly that they may verily understand them? (W. L. Watkinson, *John Wicklif* [London: T. Woolmer, 1884], 164–67)

As early as 1379, students and laymen began to enter the countryside as "poor priests" in order to proclaim the gospel of Jesus.[58] They visited with people wherever they went, along the roads and at the village greens. Like the Waldenses, they read or recited from memory large portions of the Scriptures and provided clear expositions so that listeners could understand their meaning. The Lollards wore long russet-colored robes and sandals, and like Franciscans, they were prohibited to ask for money but accepted whatever food and shelter were offered to them along the way.[59]

Eventually Wycliffe was driven from Oxford and retired to the rural pastorate at Lutterworth, where he and his associates, John Purvey and Nicholas of Hereford, translated the Bible from the Latin Vulgate into English, completing this task in 1382.[60] In this process, they coined the English word *evangelize*. Of the forty-three occurrences of the Latin word *evangelizare* in the Vulgate, Wycliffe and his associates transliterated the word as *evangelize* in thirty-six of them.[61]

58. Tuttle, *Story of Evangelism*, 234.

59. Edwards, *History of Preaching*, 254.

60. *HCC* 6:342. Wycliffe's translation of the New Testament was ready for distribution in 1382. The Old Testament was completed by Nicholas of Hereford in 1384. M. Taylor, *Exploring Evangelism*, 87. Wycliffe died before the translation was complete. John Purvey is considered responsible for the version of the Wycliffe Bible. Edwards, *History of Preaching*, 253.

61. In earlier translations, Wycliffe simply transliterated the Greek word *euangelizein* into the English text as *euangelisen*. In the second edition, published in 1388 after Wycliffe's death, thirty-three of the thirty-six uses of *evangelize* were changed to *preach*, except for Luke 1:19; 8:1; 16:16. David Barrett, *Evangelize! A Survey of the Concept* (Birmingham, AL: New Hope, 1987), 22.

As the number of Lollards grew, so too did their scrutiny and persecution by the Roman Church. Their main opponent was Thomas Arundel, who became archbishop of Canterbury in 1396. He not only authored the Constitutions of Arundel, which spoke against the views of the Lollards, but also used his ecclesiastical authority in an effort to stamp them out.

With the coming of King Henry IV of Lancaster, a strict policy was passed in 1401 that prohibited translating or owning a Bible and authorized the burning of heretics at the stake. A report regarding Wycliffe's English version stated, "This pestilent and wretched John Wycliffe, that son of the old serpent . . . endeavor[ing] by every means to attack the very faith and sacred doctrine of Holy Church, translated from Latin into English the Gospel, that Christ gave to the clergy and scholars of the Church. So that by his means it has become vulgar [from the Latin *vulgus*, meaning "of common people"] and more open to laymen and women who can read than it usually is to quite learned clergy of good intelligence. And so the pearl of the gospel is scattered and trodden underfoot by swine."[62]

The king's policy prohibited Lollards from preaching the gospel, holding conventicle meetings to study the Bible, and distributing books or portions of the Scriptures.[63] Only the Latin Vulgate was authorized.[64] Despite this prohibition, new Lollard congregations were planted by Wycliffe's followers.[65]

After Wycliffe's death, the Lollard movement continued their conventicle meetings and evangelistic activities. At the Council of Constance in 1415, forty-three years after his death, officials dug up Wycliffe's body, burned his bones, and threw his cremains into the Swift Brook. Anyone accused of holding views similar to Wycliffe was interrogated by bishops of the Roman Church. Yet Wycliffe's teachings spread. One chronicler observes, "They cast his ashes into the Swift, a brook running hard by. Thus this brook hath conveyed his ashes into the Avon, from there into the Severn, from there into the narrow seas, and then into the main ocean. And thus the ashes of Wycliffe, are the emblem of his doctrine, which is now dispersed the world over."[66]

62. Terence P. Noble, introduction to *Wycliffe's Bible: A Modern-Spelling Version of the 14th Century Middle English Translation*, trans. John Wycliffe and John Purvey (Vancouver, BC: Terence Noble, 2018), v–vi.

63. *HCC* 6:344, 351.

64. Westin, *Free Church through the Ages*, 34.

65. Edwards, *History of Preaching*, 253.

66. George Innis, *Wycliffe: The Morning Star* (Cincinnati: Jennings and Graham, 1907), 223–24.

The views of Wycliffe were carried from England to Bohemia, present-day Czech Republic.[67] Anne of Bohemia, the sister of King Wenceslas, married King Richard II of England, and, in turn, a number of Bohemian students followed her to England, where they attended Oxford University where Wycliffe taught. When they returned to Prague, they brought with them his teachings, as well as copies of his writings. Thus, in Bohemia, too, the medieval Roman Church soon received criticisms from within its own ranks.

Jan Hus

The chief proponent of Wycliffism in Bohemia was Jan Hus (ca. 1369–1415), and the second proponent was Jerome of Prague, a former student of Wycliffe's at Oxford.[68] Jan Hus was born to a Czech family at Husinec in southern Bohemia. As early as 1402, he was regarded as the chief defender of Wycliffe's views at the Charles University of Prague, where he served as professor and later as dean.

Also in 1402, Hus took on the role of the priest-presbyter at Bethlehem Chapel near the university. Like Wycliffe, he stressed the authority of the Scriptures and their application to daily life, encouraging his congregation and students to serve God and neighbor. To aid in this work, Hus made the exposition of the Scriptures a regular element of the worship services. With his preaching assignment, he studied the biblical nature and practices of the church.

During this time Hus developed convictions from the Scriptures about the church, defended the views of Wycliffe, and condemned what he saw as corrupt clergymen. In 1409, his sermons about church reform offended some of the German scholars at the university. They complained to the bishop of Prague, who was also a German. After hearing the complaints of his fellow countrymen, he ordered Hus to surrender his copies of Wycliffe's writings to be burned.

In 1410, Hus was excommunicated from the Roman Church and forced to leave the university. He left Prague altogether but continued to preach in the countryside, where he attracted followers as he preached in the Czech language. He wrote a letter to England about what was taking place in Bohemia, saying, "The people will hear nothing but the Scriptures, especially

67. *HCC* 6:358.
68. Bainton, *Christianity*, 216–17.

the gospels and epistles. And wherever, in town, village, house or castle, a preacher of the sacred truth appears, there the people flock together in crowds. Lo, I have but touched the tail of Anti-christ, and it has opened its mouth that it may swallow me up with my brothers. . . . Our Lord the king and his whole court, queen, barons, and common people are all for the word of Jesus Christ."[69]

Hus's scholarly study of the church culminated in his work titled *De ecclesia*, which he read at the national synod in 1413, held at the Bethlehem Chapel.[70] In this treatise he defended his views against the objections of Popes Alexander V and John XXIII and other critics. He said that "the Church can exist without cardinals and the pope and in fact for hundreds of years there were no cardinals."[71] As Hus broke from the accepted view of Western Christendom, he committed the grave offense of this period by denying the pope's infallibility.

In 1414, the Council of Constance ordered Hus to appear and explain his views. King Sigismund of Hungary and heir to the Bohemian crown, wanting to foster peace in his Christian kingdom, gave Hus a free-conduct pass to Constance in order to answer his critics in a public forum.[72] Upon his arrival, Hus thought he would be permitted to defend his views against any charges of heresy and regain his reputation in Bohemia. Despite an oath of protection granted by Sigismund, Hus was declared a heretic and burned at the stake. A witness described the final moments of his life: "When the executioners at once lit [the fire], the Master immediately began to sing in a loud voice, at first, 'Christ, Thou son of the living God, have mercy upon us,' and secondly, 'Christ, Thou son of the living God, have mercy upon me,' and in the third place, 'Thou, Who are born of Mary the Virgin.' And when he began to sing the third time, the wind blew the flame into his face."[73]

Hus's death galvanized his followers, who went on to found the Hussite church of Bohemia. They divided later into parties of Taborites and Calixtines and a third party, the Unitas Fratrum (United Brethren), also known as the Bohemian Brethren.[74] This latter group of Hussites, along with a remnant

69. Herbert B. Workman, *The Age of Huss* (London: Charles H. Kelly, 1902), 148, cited in David L. Larsen, *The Company of the Preachers: A History of Biblical Preaching from the Old Testament to the Modern Era* (Grand Rapids: Kregel, 1998), 1:148.

70. Woodbridge and James, *Church History*, 2:49.

71. *HCC* 6:369.

72. Woodbridge and James, *Church History*, 2:47.

73. Woodbridge and James, *Church History*, 2:50.

74. Bainton, *Christianity*, 219–20.

of German Waldenses, merged to join forces and eventually sent missionaries to preach the gospel in Europe, Turkey, Syria, Palestine, and Egypt.[75]

In the cases of the Hussites of Bohemia, the Lollards of England, and the Waldenses of France, they functioned as free dissenter movements, claiming an ecclesial identity separate from the church of the Holy Roman Empire. Each of these movements emphasized the authority of the Scriptures over popes and councils and stressed the communication of the gospel in the vernacular language.

Biblia Pauperum

Although the late medieval Roman Church faced criticisms increasingly from those within its ranks, this does not imply that all parish priests, bishops, and missionaries of the Roman Church were negligent in their roles. There were many who fulfilled their duties by setting godly examples for the people and presenting the gospel of Jesus Christ simply and clearly. For example, some missionary monks in northern Europe used the aids of *Biblia pauperum* to communicate the gospel of Jesus Christ.

Biblia pauperum, or in English "Paupers' Bible," were collections of graphic illustrations of the life of Christ and corresponding images of prophetic types from the Old Testament.[76] A single volume of *Biblia pauperum* commonly consisted of forty to fifty pages of scriptural images. The biblical illustrations told a story and sometimes contained brief texts. They were designed for the common people, especially useful for the vast number of illiterate people of the late medieval period.[77]

The historian H. N. Humphreys states that *Biblia pauperum* were "popular as a religious work for the instruction of the ignorant . . . ,—the work having been composed by St. Ansgarius [Ansgar], in the beginning of the ninth century."[78] Humphreys further explains:

75. *HCC* 6:391.

76. Pia Bengtsson Melin and Christina Sandquist Öberg, *Biblia pauperum (De fattigas Bibel): En rik inspirationskälla för senmedeltiden* (Stockholm: Kungliga Vitterhets Historie och Antikvitets Akademien, 2013), 12–14.

77. Ankete Heesen, "Within the Tradition of the Biblical Image," in *The World in a Box: The Story of an Eighteenth-Century Picture Encyclopedia* (Chicago: University of Chicago Press, 2002), 65.

78. Henry Noel Humphreys, *A History of the Art of Printing, from Its Invention to Its Wide-Spread Development in the Middle of the Sixteenth Century* (London: Quaritch, 1867), 38.

Figure 5.2. ***Biblia pauperum*****, sheet 25, Crucifixion, flanked by Abraham's sacrifice of Isaac and Moses lifting up the brass serpent, ca. 1465. Woodcut page from blockbook.** *(© The Trustees of the British Museum)*

It was while occupied in his missionary labours that he [Ansgar] is said to have composed the series of scriptural designs, briefly explained by passages from the Holy Scriptures, which afterwards became known as the Bible of the Poor,—"Biblia Pauperum." In an old copy of the xylographic "Biblia Pauperum" at Florence [Italy], there is an entry, in Latin, in writing in the 15th century, to the effect that the author of the book was St. Ansgar; and this view is further corroborated by several passages in mediæval chronicles to the effect that Saint Ansgarius wrote

> a book for the conversion of the pagans, entirely composed of signs,—the signs alluded to being no doubt the series of simple outline devices which were afterwards improved into those which served as the models of the first block-book.[79]

These scriptural designs of Ansgar were used later to create sculptures at the cathedral of Bremen and paintings in Hanover, Germany. Bremen became the seat of the combined Bremen and Hamburg archdiocese, where Ansgar served as bishop beginning in 848. Previously he traveled north to Scandinavia, where he witnessed the conversions of Danes and Swedes to Christ.[80]

Ansgar (801–865) was born in Picardy in the diocese of Amiens in northern France and educated at the abbey of Corbie, the product of Charlemagne's plan to evangelize the empire.[81] In 822, Ansgar was sent with a band of missionaries to found New Corbie abbey at Westphalia in Germany, and seven years later he was appointed as a missionary to Scandinavia. He traveled north knowing that he was risking his life to evangelize the Norsemen.[82]

Nevertheless, Ansgar and his assistant, Witmar, were received and saw people convert and baptized at the marketplace of Birka on Lake Mälaren, near modern-day Stockholm. The missionaries introduced bells into their worship services, which impressed the Nordic pagans who viewed them as instruments of magic. Ansgar and Witmar also started a hospital and worked to ransom captives, including some Christians who had been brought to Sweden from raids and held by Viking chieftains.[83] Ansgar purchased Scandinavian slave boys too. He took them with him in order to

79. Humphreys, *History of the Art of Printing*, 38.

80. Volz, *Medieval Christianity*, 43–44.

81. Rimbert, *Anskar: The Apostle of the North*, trans. Charles H. Robinson (London: Society for the Propagation of the Gospel in Foreign Parts, 1921), 9; Tuttle, *Story of Evangelism*, 200.

82. Ruth A. Tucker, *Parade of Faith: A Biographical History of the Christian Church* (Grand Rapids: Zondervan, 2015), 149.

83. Anders Winroth, *The Age of the Vikings* (Princeton, NJ: Princeton University Press, 2014), 201. When Ansgar arrived in Sweden, Christianity existed there in some form. The church at Kata Gård, a Viking-age farming estate in Varnhem, appears to have been founded by a lay lord. Maria Vretemark, "Aristocratic Farms and Private Churches: The Varnhem Case Study," in *The Buildings of Medieval Reykholt: The Wider Context*, ed. Guðrún Sveinbjarnardóttir and Bergur Þorgeirsson (Reykjavik: Snorrastofa and University of Iceland Press, 2017), 143–57. Cf. Madigan, *Medieval Christianity*, 81.

educate them so that they would return as missionaries who could speak the native language.[84]

During this period, Ansgar introduced *Biblia pauperum* for evangelistic and catechetical purposes. These illustrations were a simple and effective means to communicate the story of Jesus's life, death, and resurrection, and how he fulfilled Old Testament prophecies and biblical images that pointed to him. Each illustration had three scriptural images. The central figure came from an event in the Gospels and was accompanied by two images of Old Testament events that prefigured the central one. For example, the crucifixion of Jesus was associated with Abraham's call to sacrifice Isaac (Gen. 22) and Moses lifting up the serpent on a pole in the wilderness (Num. 21:4–9).[85] In a second example, the scene of Longinus, the "unnamed Roman soldier" (John 19:34) who speared Jesus when hanging dead on the cross, was accompanied by the image of God bringing forth Eve from the side of Adam (Gen. 2:21–22) and Moses striking the rock so that water flowed out (Num. 20:11). In a third example, the entombment of Christ (Matt. 27:59–60) was accompanied by the image of Joseph being let down into the well (Gen. 37:21–29) and Jonah being cast into the sea with the great fish (Jon. 1:11–17). In the case of *Biblia pauperum*, the gospel was explained within the larger redemptive story and had a formative impact on those who heard the message and could easily explain it to others.[86]

By the late medieval period and Renaissance, *Biblia pauperum* were used widely. Simple versions were affordable and used by regular and secular clergy alike. More opulent versions were expensive and available only to the wealthy. The early hand-copied manuscripts with Latin texts were produced in Bavaria and Austria. Some copies came from the school of the Dutch painter John van Eyck (ca. 1390–1441), who served John of Bavaria-Straubing of Holland.[87] Van Eyck painted secular and religious subjects that included altar pieces portraying images similar to *Biblia pauperum*. The collections of *Biblia pauperum* produced in block-book form came from Germany and the Netherlands, where both texts and images were created from a single

84. Winroth, *Age of the Vikings*, 110, 203.

85. Jean Philibert Berjeau, *Biblia pauperum: Reproduced in Facsimile, from One of the Copies in the British Museum; With an Historical and Bibliographical Introduction* (London: John Russell Smith, 1859), 33.

86. Bill Hull, *The Complete Book of Discipleship: On Being and Making Followers of Christ* (Colorado Springs: NavPress, 2014), 92.

87. Berjeau, *Biblia pauperum*, 7–19, 23.

woodcut for each page. The first edition produced by movable type was printed in German by Albert Pfister at Bamberg in 1462.[88]

Brethren of the Common Life

At the end of the medieval period, seeds of reform had been sown across Europe. On occasion, monastic communities turned from the austere life of the Rule of Benedict to economic luxury, spiritual lethargy, and obvious immorality. Such conditions spawned new monastic orders or Roman Catholic religious communities with renewed vision of the Christian life. Gerard Groote had such a vision.

Gerard Groote

Gerard Groote (1340–1384) was a Roman Catholic deacon from the Netherlands who founded the Brethren of the Common Life (*Fratres Vitae Communis*), a Roman Catholic, pietistic religious community.[89] Without taking up permanent vows, the Brethren joined together as a community, giving up worldly possessions in order to live simply in common houses, devoting themselves to divine services, preaching sermons, working productively, and eating meals in common as they read the Scriptures together.

Groote studied medicine, theology, and canon law at the University of Paris and at Prague.[90] While he was teaching philosophy and theology at the chapter school in his hometown of Deventer, he became concerned about the vanities of life, stripped himself of his possessions, and entered the practice of a devout life. He spent three years in meditation and prayer, and emerged with an apostolic zeal that attracted followers. Feeling constrained to preach, he went out as an evangelist, going from place to place calling people to repentance.

A follower of Groote named Florentius Radewyns asked him, "Master, why not put our efforts and earnings together, why not work and pray together under the guidance of our common Father?"[91] In response, Groote

88. Berjeau, *Biblia pauperum*, 14–20.

89. R. R. Post, *The Modern Devotion: Confrontation with Reformation and Humanism* (Leiden: Brill, 1968), 78.

90. Albert Hyma, *The Brethren of the Common Life* (Grand Rapids: Eerdmans, 1950), 16–17, 31.

91. Lewis W. Spitz, *The Renaissance and Reformation Movements* (St. Louis: Concordia, 1980), 41.

founded the Brethren of the Common Life. Unlike mendicant orders that lived off the alms of others, these brothers earned their living by the work of their hands. Groote also founded a community for women known as Sisters of the Common Life, located at Deventer. After Groote's death, Radewyns and other brothers became Augustinian canons and founded the Congregation of Windesheim. Several well-known people studied at schools of the Brethren of Common Life, including Thomas à Kempis, Martin Luther, and Desiderius Erasmus.[92]

Desiderius Erasmus

The Renaissance in the West brought renewed interest to the study of ancient texts. The revival of classical studies had begun with Latin literature because the early humanists—those who studied the humanities—read Latin, not Greek. However, in 1453, when Constantinople fell to the Turks, Byzantine Christians from the East fled west to Italy and brought their knowledge of classical Greek literature, texts, and the Scriptures with them, including the Septuagint and various copies of the Greek New Testament.[93]

At the time, Pope Nicholas V, who held the office from 1447 to 1455, was acquiring a book collection in addition to engaging in architectural projects. He employed agents to search for rare classical manuscripts and to hire humanities scholars to translate them into Latin for the Latin readers. His collection of thousands of rare manuscripts formed the basis of what became the Vatican Library in Rome.

The ideas of the Italian Renaissance soon spread to northern Europe. The chief proponent of the new learning of the humanities was the Dutchman Desiderius Erasmus (1469–1536), known as the "prince of humanists." Like many of his contemporaries, Erasmus believed that the study of authentic texts of Christian writings, combined with a study of Greek and Latin classics, would bring about a renewal of Christianity. His acquaintance with John Colet of England strengthened his resolve to seek the reconciliation of faith and reason, the Scriptures and literature, devotion and scholarship.

John Colet (1467–1519), dean of St. Paul's Cathedral in London, was a proponent of the study of the Greek language. He emphasized the need for reform of the Roman Church in England, stating that it had conformed to

92. Volz, *Medieval Christianity*, 179.

93. González, *Story of Christianity*, 1:366.

the world so much that its face was disfigured and filthy.[94] In a display of interest in the study of the Greek language, Colet presented a series of lectures at Oxford from the book of Romans using a historical-grammatical exegesis of the Greek text. In 1499, he inspired Erasmus also to study Greek.[95]

Erasmus was the son of a Roman priest, thus illegitimate.[96] He studied at the school of the Brethren of the Common Life in Deventer, became an Augustinian monk at Steyn in 1486, and was ordained as a priest in 1492. However, he enjoyed worldly comforts and decided not to pursue monastic life, receiving permission to leave the monastery. He spent the rest of his life as a scholar, traveling to various parts of Europe where he engaged in research, teaching, and writing. He began his study of the Scriptures at the University of Paris. At the University of Cambridge, he began to work on a critical edition of the Greek New Testament, which he completed in 1516.[97]

Using methods of textual criticism, Erasmus compared different Greek manuscripts and produced a composite edition based on what he considered was the most accurate reading of the text.[98] With this critical Greek edition of the New Testament, other scholars had a more accurate source to study and from which to translate the Scriptures into other languages. Erasmus also produced a Latin edition of the New Testament. Together, his Greek and Latin versions raised serious questions about the Latin Vulgate—the authorized version of the Roman Church—and its accuracy on matters of the Christian faith and teaching. Overall, Erasmus discovered nearly six hundred mistranslations in the Vulgate, mostly by Jerome, who had been commissioned in 382 to revise the Old Latin text of the four Gospels using the best Greek texts.[99]

94. Colet said, "As I am about to exhort you, reverend fathers, to endeavour to reform the condition of the Church; because nothing has so disfigured the face of the Church as the secular and worldly way of living on the part of the clergy, I know not how I can commence my discourse more fitly than with the Apostle Paul, in whose cathedral ye are now assembled. . . . If priests and bishops, the very lights, run in the dark way of the world, how dark must the lay-people be!" Frederic Seebohm, *The Oxford Reformers: John Colet, Erasmus, and Thomas More, Being a History of Their Fellow Work* (London: Longmans, Green, 1896), 233.

95. William R. Estep, *Renaissance and Reformation* (Grand Rapids: Eerdmans, 1986), 83.

96. González, *Story of Christianity*, 2:10.

97. Woodbridge and James, *Church History*, 2:98.

98. Alister E. McGrath, *The Intellectual Origins of the European Reformation* (Oxford: Blackwell, 2004), 121–36.

99. Larsen, *Company of Preachers*, 150.

Like several others, Erasmus became critical of the Roman Church from within its ranks.[100] As a student of the humanities, he drew on Aristotle's and Cicero's emphasis on *ēthos*, the importance of moral character that is necessary to win people over.[101] Erasmus's writings were sarcastic and satirical, especially as he wrote about the need for church reform. One of his books, with tongue in cheek, praised the church's folly as he illustrated abuses of doctrine and corrupt practices of the Roman Church, which eroded credibility and distorted people's understanding of the gospel.[102]

Erasmus's work titled *Handbook of the Christian Soldier* (*Enchiridion militis Christiani*) was an attempt to set forth what it meant to fight the good fight of Christian faith. He asked, "What point is there in your being showered with holy water if you do not wipe away the inward pollution of your heart? . . . You venerated the saints and delight in touching their relics, but you despise the best one they left behind, the example of a holy life."[103]

Erasmus pointed out that the greatest evil of his day was formalism, going through the motions of tradition without understanding their basis. He held that forms of religious life can either teach the soul how to worship God or quench the Spirit. He pleaded with his readers to be concerned with the meaning of religious devotion and to put their beliefs into practice rather than merely professing them:

> Do not tell me therefore that charity consists in being frequently in church, in prostrating oneself before signs of the saints, in burning tapers, in repeating such and such a number of prayers. God has no need for all of this. Paul defines love as to edify one's neighbor; to lead all to become members of the same body; to consider all one is in Christ; to rejoice in a brother's good fortune in the Lord just as you would concerning your own; to heal his hurt as you would try to heal your

100. Bainton, *Christianity*, 232–33.

101. Ross Dealy, *The Stoic Origins of Erasmus' Philosophy of Christ* (Toronto: University of Toronto Press, 2017), 19–25, 116–17, 126. Erasmus's study of Augustine's *On Christian Doctrine*, especially book 4, reinforced Cicero's rhetoric. Albert Rabil Jr., *Erasmus and the New Testament: The Mind of a Christian Humanist* (Lanham, MD: University Press of America, 1993), 22–24.

102. Alvin J. Schmidt, *How Christianity Changed the World* (Grand Rapids: Zondervan, 2009), 354–55. See Desiderius Erasmus, *The Praise of Folly and Other Writings* (New York: Norton, 1989).

103. Robert G. Clouse, Richard V. Pierard, and Edwin M. Yamauchi, *The Story of the Church* (Chicago: Moody, 2002), 149.

> own hurt, compassionately; to rebuke the erring; to teach the ignorant; to lift up the fallen; to console the downhearted; to help the toiler; to support the needy; in the highest degree to bring all your wealth, all your zeal, all your care to bear on this: that you may benefit as many as you possibly can in Christ.[104]

In his *Handbook of the Christian Soldier*, Erasmus argued from the Bible and Greek philosophy that everyone lives either according to the flesh or according to the Spirit. He hinted at the need for godly conversation, communication of the knowledge of Christ, and winning one's household to God, saying, "Let your study bring you to a clearer perception of Christ so that your love for him will increase and you will be able in turn to communicate this knowledge of him to others," and "Do not forget that your household must be won over to Christ."[105] In the final analysis, however, Erasmus did not articulate the gospel of Christ's life and work that provided justification by grace through faith, but called readers to subdue the flesh and to exercise the Spirit in the virtues.

Despite this, Erasmus prepared the way for a reformation of the church that recaptured the gospel that brings salvation. In his writings, he challenged the status quo by exhorting clergy to share the treasury of their knowledge with the laity. He also emphasized the need to pursue virtues and spiritual disciplines rather than institutional sacraments. He called for reformation that would be characterized by a return to the study of the Scriptures and writings of the church fathers. While he remained within the Roman Church, his teaching brought reform inside and outside the church. It has been said, "Erasmus laid the egg that Luther hatched."[106]

Discussion Questions

1. Athanasius stressed the incarnation of God in Jesus, and Anselm stressed that Christ's death on the cross satisfied the moral honor and

104. Desiderius Erasmus, *Christian Humanism and the Reformation: Selected Writings, with the Life of Erasmus by Beatus Rhenanus*, ed. John C. Olin (Gloucester, MA: Peter Smith, 1973), 8.

105. Desiderius Erasmus, *Handbook of the Militant Christian*, trans. John P. Dolan (Notre Dame, IN: Fides, 1962), 58–59, 100.

106. Desiderius Erasmus, *Colloquies*, trans. Craig R. Thompson (Toronto: University of Toronto Press, 1997), 1:420.

righteous demands of God. How do these emphases shape your understanding of the gospel?

2. While monastic orders in the West were sanctioned by the Roman papacy and remained loyal to the pope, Peter Waldo and his "poor men of Lyons" were excommunicated and functioned free from Rome. In what other ways were Waldenses different from monastic orders? What characteristics did they share with Christians of pre-Christendom?
3. John Wycliffe and Jan Hus emphasized that people must have the Scriptures in their own language. In Wycliffe's "Gospel in the Mother-Tongue," what do you consider to be his strongest point? Why? How do you practice putting the Scriptures into the common language of people?
4. Why were *Biblia pauperum* so popular in the centuries of the late medieval period and Renaissance? What do these scriptural illustrations tell us about sharing the gospel with common people today? What do you suppose would happen if you asked a non-Christian to explain the meaning of a medieval *Biblia pauperum* to you? If you explained the meaning to her or him?
5. The Renaissance emphasized a critical study of ancient authorities such as the Greek New Testament. Although some evangelists may become impatient with scholarly work like that of Erasmus, how important is it for evangelism, then and now? Why?

6

Reformation Evangelism

> Dear Lord, God and Father, convert them and defend us. Convert those who are still to become children and members of thy kingdom so that they with us and we with them may serve thee in thy kingdom in true faith and unfeigned love and that from thy kingdom which has begun, we may enter into thy eternal kingdom. Defend us against those who will not turn away their might and power from the destruction of thy kingdom so that when they are cast down from their thrones and humbled, they will have to cease from their efforts. Amen.
>
> —Martin Luther[1]

Reform is a prominent theme in the history of the church. A variety of reform movements appeared in the medieval period, mostly as new monastic orders with a vision for a more austere life in community and mission. However, in northern Germany and then Switzerland, reformers emerged within the ranks of the Roman Church with criticisms against its theology and pastoral care.[2] As the reformers uncovered the gospel in the New Testament, they concluded that the Roman Church had drifted from the teachings of Jesus and the apostles.

As mentioned previously, churchmen of the medieval church espoused a theology of salvation that depended on divine grace and human effort.

1. Martin Luther, *Luther's Works*, vol. 43, *Devotional Writings II*, trans. Carl J. Schindler, ed. Helmut T. Lehmann and Martin O. Dietrich (St. Louis: Concordia, 1968), 195–96.

2. Roland H. Bainton, *Christianity* (Boston: Houghton Mifflin, 2001), 232.

Salvation was viewed as the work of God through the sacrifice of Christ, but contributions by sinners through acts of penance were essential too, although the level of human contribution was debated.[3] Confessional manuals called penitentials, as well as catechisms, fostered an obsession with sin and made demands on sinners to "do penance" and redeem themselves, in part, by self-examination, self-punishment, and self-mortification.[4] Frequent interrogation at the confessional booth by priests was intended to make people aware of their sins prior to confession of their sins and absolution by the priest. However, this led some people to resent the religious system that provided little or no assurance of salvation.

Evangel and Evangelicals

With the Renaissance and its emphasis on returning "to the sources" (*ad fontes*), the reformers, still within the Roman Church, began to draw on the Scriptures as their authority along with the writings of church fathers like Augustine of Hippo.[5] They affirmed from their study that salvation is based wholly on the work of God in Jesus Christ and in no sense was based on human merit through penance or good works.[6] These reformers concluded that some teachings and practices of the Roman Church were contrary to the New Testament. In response, church and political authorities sought to suppress the reformers and their message of salvation by grace alone.

With a recovered evangel (*euangelium* in Latin), the reformers became known in German as *evangelisch*, meaning "evangelical," known by their eagerness to share the evangel with others.[7] The term "evangelical" had been used centuries earlier by Tertullian when he wrote in response to the heresies of Marcion, "The evangelical [*evangelicum*] Testament has apostles for its authors, to whom was assigned by the Lord Himself this office of publishing

3. Milton L. Rudnick, *Speaking the Gospel through the Ages: A History of Evangelism* (St. Louis: Concordia, 1984), 77.

4. The concept of "do penance" (in Latin *poenitentiam agite*) is the Vulgate's translation of the Greek word *metanoeite* (Mark 1:15). Erasmus preferred the Latin word *resipiscite*, meaning "come to your senses." Robert D. Sider, ed., *The New Testament Scholarship of Erasmus: An Introduction with Erasmus' Prefaces and Ancillary Writings* (Toronto: University of Toronto Press, 2019), 202–3.

5. Erwin W. Lutzer, *Rescuing the Gospel: The Story and Significance of the Reformation* (Grand Rapids: Baker Books, 2017), 49–50, 109–12.

6. Rudnick, *Speaking the Gospel*, 77.

7. Mark Hutchinson, *A Global Faith: Essays on Evangelicalism and Globalization* (Sydney: Sydney Centre for the Study of Australian Christianity, 1998), 156–57.

[announcing] the gospel [*evangelii*]."[8] Martin Luther used the term "evangelical" to reaffirm Paul's teaching of the evangel as the indispensable message of salvation, as well as to describe Jan Hus's view of salvation by faith in Christ.[9] In response to the reformers, Johannes Eck, Thomas More, and even Desiderius Erasmus denigrated those who emphasized salvation by grace, referring to them pejoratively as "evangelicals."[10] Thus, in the sixteenth century, *evangelisch* or "evangelical" became another word for "Protestant." The leaders of this movement, the Protestant Reformation, claimed they had recovered the evangel, long obscured by the medieval church.[11]

Martin Luther

The leading evangelical was Martin Luther (1483–1546) from Eisleben, Saxony, a German electorate in the Holy Roman Empire.[12] Luther had studied in Magdeburg under the supervision of the Brethren of the Common Life before attending the University of Erfurt, where he received the bachelor's degree in 1502. He continued his studies in a master's program at Erfurt, where he accessed every section of the library. He described one occasion when he discovered an old Latin Bible, the first copy of the Scriptures he had ever seen. He read and reread it with "inexpressible and never-ceasing delight, mingled with some astonishment."[13] Until this time, Luther merely imagined that the Roman Church's liturgy contained all of the Christian Scriptures.

In 1505, Luther completed the requirements for the master's degree. He then pursued the study of law according to his father's wishes. However, his legal studies came abruptly to an end when he was caught in a fierce thunderstorm. Fearing for his life, he pleaded with St. Anne, the patron saint of the miners of the town of Eisleben, crying out, "St. Anne, help me! I will

8. Tertullian, *Against Marcion* 4.2 (*ANF* 3:347).

9. John D. Woodbridge and Frank A. James III, *Church History*, vol. 2, *From Pre-Reformation to the Present Day* (Grand Rapids: Zondervan, 2013), 118.

10. David F. Wells and John D. Woodbridge, *The Evangelicals: What They Believe, Who They Are, Where They Are Changing* (Nashville: Abingdon, 1975), 21–36.

11. Woodbridge and James, *Church History*, 2:111. When Lutheran princes were defiant and issued a protestation against a move to reunify the empire as a Catholic nation, the term "Protestant" defined the evangelical movement, as well. Woodbridge and James, *Church History*, 2:137.

12. Bainton, *Christianity*, 237.

13. W. C. Martyn, *The Life and Times of Martin Luther* (New York: American Tract Society, 1866), 38, cited in Mendell Taylor, *Exploring Evangelism: History, Methods, Theology* (Kansas City, MO: Nazarene Publishing House, 1984), 137.

become a monk!"[14] When the storm subsided, Luther followed through with his vow to enter monastic life, hoping this would lead to his salvation.[15]

He joined the monastery of the Augustinians at Erfurt, where he devoted himself to the strict disciplines of study, prayer, and the sacraments, especially doing penance. He often wearied the priest with his long confessions of sin and punished himself with prolonged periods of prayer, fasting, and self-inflicted abuse.[16] Nothing seemed to break through the cloud of his spiritual darkness.

Luther's supervisor, Johannes von Staupitz, encouraged him to pursue his education, recognizing both his keen intellect and his need to end his excessive introspection. Therefore, Luther enrolled in Hebrew and Greek, giving himself entirely to the study of the Scriptures. He was ordained as a secular priest in 1507 and received an invitation to teach at the newly founded University of Wittenberg, where he would lecture on books of the Bible.[17] During this period, his eyes were opened to the message of the gospel that brings salvation by grace.

Along with another Augustinian monk, Luther was selected to travel to Rome, known as the Eternal City of the Saints, to present to the pope a dispute that had risen among Augustinians. He anticipated his visit to the western capital of Christendom, where he visited the holy places and sacred shrines. His initial impressions were to accept everything he saw, but soon he became critical.

The climax of his skepticism came when he climbed the *Scala Sancta*, the Roman relic of stairs that centuries earlier Jesus climbed when he entered the praetorium of Pontius Pilate in Jerusalem. In Luther's pilgrimage in Rome, he ascended each step on his hands and knees, repeating the Our Father (*Pater Noster*), kissing each step, as an act of penance to release his grandfather's soul from purgatory.[18] As he departed from the Eternal City,

14. Roland H. Bainton, *Here I Stand: A Life of Martin Luther* (Nashville: Abingdon-Cokesbury, 1950), 21.

15. Woodbridge and James, *Church History*, 2:108–9.

16. Luther was extremely conscious of his sin, seeing the human being as *incurvatus in se*, "turning in on oneself." Bainton, *Here I Stand*, 47.

17. Bainton, *Christianity*, 240.

18. The shallowness and superior mood of the city depressed Luther more than when he left Saxony, leading him to exclaim, "If there is a hell, Rome is standing on it." Kurt Aland, *A History of Christianity* (Philadelphia: Fortress, 1986), 2:38, cited in David L. Larsen, *The Company of the Preachers: A History of Biblical Preaching from the Old Testament to the Modern Era* (Grand Rapids: Kregel, 1998), 1:153.

he was discouraged and disillusioned by what he witnessed, including the corruption of the monks and priests.

When he returned to Saxony, he intensified his study of the Scriptures. He received a doctorate of theology in 1512, succeeded Staupitz as professor of Scripture, and began to minister as the priest of the university's Castle Church.[19] His study of the Psalms and the epistles to the Romans and Galatians, led him to conclude that God's perfect justice and loving grace come together in the cross of Christ.

While studying Psalm 22:1 in particular, Luther observed the same words that Jesus spoke on the cross, "My God, my God, why have you forsaken me?" (Matt. 27:46). He then asked, "Why should Christ have been so overwhelmed with desolation?"[20] The only logical conclusion was "that Christ took to himself the iniquity of us all. He who was without sin for our sakes became sin and so identified Himself with us as to participate in our alienation."[21] Luther wrote,

> Night and day I pondered until I saw the connection between the justice of God and the statement that "the just shall live by faith." Then I grasped that the justice of God is that righteousness by which through grace and sheer mercy God justifies us through faith. Thereupon I felt myself to be reborn and to have gone through open doors into paradise. The whole of Scripture took on a new meaning, and whereas before the "justice of God" had filled me with hate, now it became to me inexpressibly sweet in greater love. This passage of Paul became to me a gate of heaven.[22]

Luther's new understanding challenged the medieval notion of accumulating merit for salvation based, in part, on human merit.[23] He concluded that sinners are justified by faith alone. His transformation of mind and liberating experience of God's grace began to formulate his exegetical insights and theological views.[24]

In 1517, Luther reacted to the abuse of the sale of indulgences near Wittenberg by Johann Tetzel, an unscrupulous Dominican monk from Leipzig,

19. Woodbridge and James, *Church History*, 2:109.
20. M. Taylor, *Exploring Evangelism*, 143.
21. Bainton, *Here I Stand*, 62.
22. Bainton, *Here I Stand*, 65.
23. Timothy George, *Theology of the Reformers* (Nashville: Broadman, 1988), 71.
24. Larsen, *Company of Preachers*, 1:154.

Germany. The indulgences, according to the Roman Church, were available for purchase as a means of penance in order to reduce a person's time in purgatory, the place of temporary punishment for souls to be purged and prepared for heaven.[25] To make matters worse, the funds from the sales of these indulgences were used to finance construction of St. Peter's Basilica in Rome. In protest to the sale of indulgences, Luther posted his ninety-five theses for debate on the door of the Castle Church in Wittenberg, and respectfully sent a copy to his archbishop, Albert of Mainz, who in turn forwarded the copy to Pope Leo X.[26] In his sixty-second thesis, Luther said, "The true treasure of the church is the most holy gospel of the glory and grace of God."[27]

Luther came to understand that no human can accumulate sufficient merit from his or her own efforts but that salvation comes by God's grace, based on the merit of Christ's atoning death. His critique decried not simply the abuses of indulgences but the very idea itself.[28] His theses, written in Latin, were copied and distributed as a pamphlet in Basel and as placards in Leipzig and Nuremberg.[29] Then they were translated into German, and copies were sent across the country.

Tensions rose to the point that, in 1520, Pope Leo X issued a papal bull ordering Luther to recant under threat of excommunication. In the following year, he was summoned to appear before Emperor Charles V at the imperial Diet at Worms. Luther was issued a safe-conduct pass to attend the meeting, where the emperor signed the Edict of Worms that formally condemned his teachings.[30] The emperor permitted him to leave the city nevertheless. While Luther traveled, Frederick of Saxony, his ardent supporter, arranged to have him intercepted and taken to a secret location, Wartburg Castle near Eisenach. After a year at Wartburg, Luther returned to Wittenberg.

Luther stated publicly that the Scriptures alone were his authority.[31] At

25. Woodbridge and James, *Church History*, 2:112–14.

26. Justo L. González, *The Story of Christianity: The Early Church to the Present Day* (Peabody, MA: Prince, 1999), 2:20–23.

27. Jaroslav Pelikan, *The Christian Tradition: A History of the Development of Doctrine*, vol. 4, *Reformation of Church and Dogma* (Chicago: University of Chicago Press, 1990), 128.

28. Bainton, *Christianity*, 243. Cf. Woodbridge and James, *Church History*, 2:115: Luther "did not reject papal authority, the sacrament of penance, or the concept of indulgences. He did, however, stand firmly against exploitation of his congregants."

29. Lutzer, *Rescuing the Gospel*, 30.

30. Woodbridge and James, *Church History*, 2:126–27.

31. González says that, for Luther, "final authority rests neither in the church nor in the Bible, but in the gospel, in the message of Jesus Christ, who is the incarnate Word of God. Since Scripture gives a more trustworthy witness to the gospel than the pope's

Worms he had declared, "Unless I am convicted by Scripture and plain reason—I do not accept the authority of popes and councils, for they have contradicted each other—my conscience is captive to the Word of God. I cannot and will not recant anything, for to go against conscience is neither right nor safe. God help me. Amen."[32]

With the Scriptures as his authority, he made preaching the Bible the focus of worship at the Castle Church.[33] As with Waldo, Wycliffe, and Hus before him, Luther translated the Scriptures into the common language of the people. His German version was pivotal to the evangelical Reformation in Germany. When Luther had been intercepted and taken to Wartburg Castle, he began to translate the Bible from Greek and Hebrew into German. In 1522 he finished the New Testament, and in 1534 he finished the Old Testament.[34] His purpose for translating the Scriptures was twofold—namely, the evangelization of non-Christians and the edification of Christians.

Luther considered himself to be an evangelist and signed his letters with the words "by the grace of God, Evangelist at Wittenberg."[35] He was adamant that pastors preach the gospel; it was their divinely given vocation.[36] Yet he was just as concerned that laypeople engage in the evangelical work, saying, "Every Christian is also an evangelist, who should teach another and publish the glory and praise of God."[37] In several statements Luther emphasized the need to proclaim the gospel to pagans of Europe and elsewhere.[38]

It has been estimated that between the years 1522 and 1546, approximately ninety-five editions of Luther's New Testament were printed, totaling a minimum of 285,000 copies.[39] These editions were mass-produced using Gutenberg's newly developed movable-type printing press. In these editions

---

corrupt church, or even the best in Christian tradition, the Bible has authority over church, pope, and tradition." *Story of Christianity*, 2:31.

32. Bainton, *Here I Stand*, 185.

33. William R. Estep, *Renaissance and Reformation* (Grand Rapids: Eerdmans, 1986), 155.

34. Woodbridge and James, *Church History*, 2:129. Cf. Tom Holland, *Dominion: How the Christian Revolution Remade the World* (New York: Basic Books, 2019), 320–22.

35. Ewald M. Plass, *This Is Luther* (St. Louis: Concordia, 1948), 339, cited in M. Taylor, *Exploring Evangelism*, 155.

36. Michael Parsons, *Text and Task: Scripture and Mission* (Eugene, OR: Wipf & Stock, 2012), 74.

37. Martin Luther, *Luther's Works*, vol. 17, *Lectures on Isaiah Chapters 40–66*, trans. Herbert J. A. Bouman, ed. Hilton C. Oswald (St. Louis: Concordia, 1972), 13.

38. David J. Bosch, *Witness to the World: The Christian Mission in Theological Perspective* (Eugene, OR: Wipf & Stock, 2006), 121.

39. Plass, *This Is Luther*, 331, cited in M. Taylor, *Exploring Evangelism*, 149.

Figure 6.1. Law and Gospel, 1529, by Lucas Cranach the Elder, Herzogliches Museum, Gotha, Germany.

of the Scriptures, he included woodcut illustrations by Lucas Cranach the Elder (ca. 1472–1553).

One of the illustrations painted by Cranach in 1529 was titled "The Law and the Gospel." It illustrates visually Luther's understanding of the gospel.[40] In the illustration, two identical nude male figures appear on different sides of a tree. The left side of the tree is barren and dying, representing the law of Moses or Ten Commandments. The right side of the tree is living, representing the gospel of Jesus Christ that brings life. On the law side, Adam and Eve are eating the forbidden fruit, and the serpent is wrapped around the tree. Death and the devil pursue the male figure who is condemned by the law. On the gospel side, one of the four Evangelists is pointing to Jesus Christ on the cross, who crushes the serpent's head. Jesus is depicted as risen from the grave and ascending to heaven.

This illustration, along with its verbal explanation, constituted a simple presentation of the gospel. While the law condemns and brings death, the

40. Luther taught that God's revelation is "both a word of judgment and a word of grace. The two always come together." González, *Story of Christianity*, 2:32–33. Cf. Lutzer, *Rescuing the Gospel*, 49–51.

gospel promises forgiveness of sins through faith in Jesus Christ, who triumphs over death and the devil. In this illustration, the gospel is framed within God's redemptive story.[41] The illustration was an aid to explain the redemptive story and its themes of creation, fall, law, death, gospel, Jesus Christ, crucifixion, resurrection, and justification by grace through faith.

In 1520, Luther set out to write his small catechism as a resource to evangelize non-Christians and to build up Christians. In the design, he arranged his catechism differently from those of the Roman Church of the medieval period.[42] He began his catechism first with the Ten Commandments, second with the Apostles' Creed, and third with the Lord's Prayer. This followed the pattern that sinners are awakened to sin by the law, are redeemed by the gospel from sin and death, and express their faith in God through prayer.

Luther's Word about His Evangelical Catechism

It did not happen without God's special ordering that for the ordinary Christian, who cannot read the Scriptures, it is ordered that he learn and know the Ten Commandments, the Creed, and the Lord's Prayer. Certainly, in these three pieces is thoroughly and completely summarized all that is written in Scripture . . . , also all that is necessary for a Christian to know; [it is written] in such a short and easily to be grasped form that no one may complain or pretend it is too much or too difficult to remember what he needs for salvation. For man needs to know three things to be saved. First: he has to know what he should do and not do. Second: when he now sees that by his own strength he is unable to do what he should do and not do what he should not do, that [then] he knows from where he should take [and where] he should search and find [the strength] to do what he should do and not do what he should not do. Third: he has to know how he should search and get [that strength].

A sick person needs to know first what his sickness is, what he can or cannot do. Then he needs to know where the medicine is which could help him do or not do what a healthy person [can do or not do]. Third, he has to desire [the medicine], search and get it, or have it brought to him. In like manner, the commandments teach a person to recognize his sickness so that

41. Bonnie Noble, *Lucas Cranach the Elder: Art and Devotion of the German Reformation* (Lanham, MD: University Press of America, 2009), 27–49, 180.

42. Gottfried G. Krodel, "Luther's Work on the Catechism in the Context of Late Medieval Catechetical Literature," *Concordia Journal* 25, no. 4 (October 1999): 364–404.

> he sees and feels what he can and cannot do, and [thus] recognizes that he is a sinner and evil person. Then the Creed shows and teaches him, where to find the medicine [that is] grace, which will help him to become pious so that he obeys the commandments. And [the Creed] shows to him God and his mercy made manifest and offered in Christ. Third: the Lord's Prayer teaches him how to desire [that mercy], [and] get [it,] and appropriate it to himself, namely, through the . . . humble, and consoling prayer [of the Lord.] Then [mercy] will be given to him, and thus through the fulfillment of God's commandments he is saved. (Gottfried G. Krodel, "Luther's Work on the Catechism in the Context of Late Medieval Catechetical Literature," *Concordia Journal* 25, no. 4 [October 1999]: 374–75)

Luther's catechetical work provided information for his hearers to know and memorize. They were expected to rehearse the catechism about the law, gospel, and prayer on a daily basis. His reason for the ongoing practice of the catechism was that Christians are simultaneously righteous and sinful (*simul iustus et peccator*). Their reciting of the catechism reminded them of the gospel daily. By 1551, the small catechism included the following questions with the corresponding answers:

1. Do you believe that you are a sinner?
   Yes, I believe it; I am a sinner.

2. How did you obtain the knowledge thereof?
   From the Holy Decalogue or [Ten] Commandments; these I have not kept.

3. Do you feel sorrow on account of your sins?
   Yes, I feel sorrow for having sinned against God.

4. What have you deserved of God on account of your sins?
   His wrath and displeasure, temporal death, and eternal damnation. Romans 6:21 and 23.

5. But do you still hope to be saved?
   Yes, such is my hope.

6. Whence do you derive this hope and comfort?
From my blessed Lord and Saviour Jesus Christ.

7. Who is Christ?
The Son of God, true God and man.

8. Are there more Gods than one?
No, there is one God only, but there are three persons, Father, Son, and Holy Ghost.

9. What has Christ done for you that you find comfort in him?
He died for me, shedding his blood on the cross for me, for the forgiveness of my sins. Galatians 2:20; 2 Timothy 4:6–8.[43]

Luther spoke also of the Christian's attitude toward others, highlighting the connection between faith in God and love for neighbor. He claimed, "God has thus proceeded with us and given us all that is his, and has himself become our own, so that we may have through faith all things that are good and needful for us. What then are we to do? . . . While we live here, we should act in our neighbor's behalf, and should give ourselves to his welfare, as God hath given himself to us. Thus faith saves us, but love leads us to give to our neighbor whenever we have enough to give. That is, faith receives from God; love gives to our neighbor."[44]

In 1524, Luther produced a hymnbook with twenty-three hymns, having composed several himself, with the most famous being "A Mighty Fortress Is Our God."[45] Thus, he reformed not only theology but the church's music. In 1526, he wrote the German Mass (*Die Deutsche Messe*) so that people could worship in their own language. He considered music to be the handmaiden of Christian theology, calling it the "living voice of the gospel" (*viva voce evangelii*).[46]

43. Martin Luther, "Questions and Answers," in *Luther's Small Catechism; with Additions Including the Augsburg Confession* (Philadelphia: German Evangelical Ministerium of Pennsylvania, 1855), 23.

44. Martin Luther, *Commentary on Peter and Jude*, trans. John Nichols Lenker (Grand Rapids: Kregel, 1990), 109.

45. Bainton, *Christianity*, 345.

46. Alvin J. Schmidt, *How Christianity Changed the World* (Grand Rapids: Zondervan, 2009), 26. Within the Lutheran tradition, tunes and lyrics "helped to commend the Gospel stories" to those who sang them. Christopher Boyd Brown, *Singing the*

As Luther aged, he became more virulent in his arguments against other emerging Protestants, as well as Jews. His arguments against Jews were published in 1543 under the title *On the Jews and Their Lies*, which marked a dramatic shift from his pro-Jewish position twenty years earlier when he wrote the tract titled *Jesus Was Born a Jew*.[47] In the earlier work, Luther urged the German people to see Jews as God's chosen people "whom Christians should view in a cordial, even brotherly manner."[48] However, when his personal attempts to evangelize Jewish rabbis were met with failure, and he learned of rumors that rabbis had converted some Lutheran evangelicals to Judaism, his anger went out of control. He became indignant, seeing the Jewish people as those who consistently rejected the gospel and, for this reason, as worthy of condemnation. Sadly, his zeal for the gospel clouded his better judgment and hurt his evangelical witness.

Despite Luther's shortcomings, his impact was felt beyond Germany. Between the years 1520 and 1560, over sixteen thousand students attended the University of Wittenberg.[49] Nearly two-thirds came from outside northern Germany. Luther's arguments from the Scriptures convinced many to share the evangel of justification by grace. In turn, they carried the message of salvation to England, France, Poland, Sweden, Denmark, Norway, and the Balkans, where they influenced thousands of others.

Olavus Petri and Laurentius Petri

The brothers Olavus Petri (1493–1552) and Laurentius Petri (1499–1573), both students at Wittenberg under Luther, were main figures in the Reformation in Sweden.[50] Beginning in 1516, they studied under Luther and Philipp Melanchthon (1497–1560) at Wittenberg. While in Wittenberg, they heard Luther lecture on Hebrews and Galatians, and were firsthand witnesses of the controversy over the sale of indulgences with Johann Tetzel.[51]

When the Petri brothers returned to Sweden in 1518, they were convinced of Luther's understanding of the gospel, and like him, they preached against

---

Gospel: Lutheran Hymns and the Success of the Reformation (Cambridge, MA: Harvard University Press, 2005), 64.

47. Woodbridge and James, *Church History*, 2:144–45.

48. Woodbridge and James, *Church History*, 2:144–45.

49. Rudnick, *Speaking the Gospel*, 81; Bainton, *Christianity*, 252.

50. Carl Axel Aurelius, *Luther i Sverige: Svenska lutherbilder under tre sekler* (Skellefteå: Artos, 1994) 49–50.

51. Thorsten Prill, *Luther, Calvin, and the Mission of the Church: The Mission Theology and Practice of the Protestant Reformers* (Munich: GRIN, 2017), 36.

the selling of indulgences by those like Tetzel who had come to Sweden.[52] The Petri brothers then convinced Laurentius Andreae to the Lutheran view prior to his becoming chancellor of the Swedish kingdom. Under the protection of King Gustavus Vasa, Olavus and Laurentius Petri preached against other Roman Catholic practices such as pilgrimages to shrines and veneration of saints.

In 1527, Olavus Petri published *Answers to Twelve Questions* (*Svar på tolv spörsmål*), in which he insisted that the church's primary task was to preach the pure gospel.[53] With the permission of the king, his books and treatises were distributed throughout Sweden. Olavus also contributed to the translation of the New Testament into the Swedish language.

In 1529, a synod at Örebro banned Roman rituals and several Roman Church holidays. At Uppsala in 1536, a court ruled that worship services should be conducted in the Swedish language and that clerical marriage was permitted. In 1544, Sweden was proclaimed an *Evangelische* kingdom, and the king was to serve as the church's most prominent member.[54] With this Reformation in Sweden, it was decided that the entire Bible should be translated into the Swedish language. This was completed in 1541 with the publication of the Gustav Vasa Bible, furthering the Protestant Reformation.[55]

Katharina von Bora Luther

Katharina von Bora (1499–1552) of Saxon descent became the wife of Martin Luther. As a girl, she was sent by her parents to the school of the Benedictine order near Halle, Germany, in 1504.[56] Four years later, she entered the Cistercian convent of Nimbschen, where she studied Latin. In 1515, she took monastic vows to become a nun.

After several years in the convent, Katharina gained interest in the reforms led by Luther, while becoming dissatisfied with her life at the convent. Her monastic house was attached to the cloister church that had twelve altars and contained over three hundred relics, "which offered those who

52. Anders Kraal, "The Swedish Reformation Debates of 1527–28," *Lutheran Quarterly* 24, no. 4 (Winter 2010): 375–76.

53. Michael Roberts, *The Early Vasas: A History of Sweden, 1523–1611* (Cambridge: Cambridge University Press, 1986), 70.

54. Christopher Ocker, *Luther, Conflict, and Christendom: Reformation Europe and Christianity in the West* (Cambridge: Cambridge University Press, 2020), 212–13.

55. Roberts, *Early Vasas*, 70.

56. Ruth A. Tucker, *Katie Luther: First Lady of the Reformation* (Grand Rapids: Zondervan, 2017), 17.

venerated them many indulgences."[57] In 1523, conspiring with other nuns to leave the convent secretly, Katharina contacted Luther at Wittenberg and asked him for assistance.[58] She and eleven nuns fled Nimbschen, traveling in a covered wagon hauling fish barrels. The nuns found shelter at Wittenberg, where Katharina stayed with Lucas Cranach and his wife.[59]

In 1525 she married Luther, which at the time was scandalous. Because Luther was a priest, the marriage defied the Roman Church's teaching regarding celibacy of priests.[60] After the wedding, Martin spent time teaching, preaching, and writing, while Katharina ran the family business and raised their six children and four orphans. The family lived in the former monastery of Augustinian friars at Wittenberg, a building given to them as a wedding gift from John, the elector of Saxony.

Katharina turned the monastery into a dormitory and meeting place for resident students and visiting scholars. During times of widespread illness, she transformed the dormitory into a hospital and ministered to the sick alongside nurses.[61] Otherwise, she employed her entrepreneurial skills of planting a garden, raising cattle, and brewing beer—producing nearly nine thousand pints of ale per year. She invested any extra income into the estate by adding a fish pond and fruit orchard.[62]

As the Protestant Reformation moved across Europe, the Luthers' home served as the movement's epicenter. After dinner, Martin and house guests sat at the table to discuss theology and politics. The "table talks" were possible, of course, because of Katharina's work. She regularly joined discussions herself. Her knowledge of theology in the Latin language eventually earned her the honorary title "Katharina of Alexandria," named after the patron saint of the faculty of arts at the University of Wittenberg.[63] Katharina certainly played a vital role to promote the spread of the gospel. Her devotion

57. Martin Treu, "Katharina von Bora, the Woman at Luther's Side," *Lutheran Quarterly* 13 (1999): 159.

58. Ruth A. Tucker and Walter Liefeld, *Daughters of the Church: Women and Ministry from New Testament Times to the Present* (Grand Rapids: Zondervan, 1987), 180.

59. Heinz Schilling, *Martin Luther: Rebel in an Age of Upheaval*, trans. Rona Johnston (Oxford: Oxford University Press, 2017), 269.

60. Tucker, *Katie Luther*, 37.

61. Tucker, *Katie Luther*, 97–100.

62. Records show that the Luthers owned more cows and pigs than anyone else in Wittenberg. Andrew Curry, "How a Runaway Nun Helped an Outlaw Monk Change the World," *National Geographic*, October 20, 2017, https://www.nationalgeographic.com/news/2017/10/martin-luther-wife-protestant-reformation-500/.

63. Treu, "Katharina von Bora," 161.

to Christ remained steadfast, and she whispered on her deathbed, "I will stick to Christ as a burr [sticks] to cloth."[64]

Evangel and the Reformed (Calvinists)

In addition to the German *evangelische* movement associated with Luther, there came a stream of Protestants known as *reformiert*, meaning "reformed." Concurrent with the expansion of Lutheran evangelicalism, this movement began in German-speaking Switzerland, led by Huldrych Zwingli, but was shaped also by Martin Bucer, John Calvin, and others.

Huldrych Zwingli

Huldrych Zwingli (1484–1531) came to possess evangelical convictions through his study of the Greek New Testament and church fathers.[65] Like Luther, Zwingli accepted the supreme authority of the Bible and applied it to doctrine and practice. At Zurich in 1519, he announced that he would preach through the Gospel of Matthew rather than preach from selected texts of the liturgy for the year. One listener, after hearing Zwingli, said he felt as if he was "being pulled by the very hair on his head when he heard passages from the Word of God that had been neglected for over a thousand years."[66]

Whereas Luther saw the church's structure and liturgy as nonessential (*adiaphora*) and open to variety and freedom, Zwingli viewed the New Testament church as the pattern for every age. He sought to return the church to the practices of the first century, deconstructing the medieval Roman Church's tradition by removing images, dissolving monasteries, and eliminating nonessentials from church life.[67] He regarded the Christian church as the new Israel of God, the successor to the original chosen people. He held that the local society of people was a theocracy in which the church and state should submit to the will of God as set forth in the Scriptures—not merely in the New Testament but also the Old Testament.[68]

64. Roland H. Bainton, *Women of the Reformation in Germany and Italy* (Boston: Beacon, 1974), 42.

65. Geoffrey W. Bromiley, "Ulrich Zwingli: Third Man of the Reformation," in *Great Leaders of the Christian Church*, ed. John D. Woodbridge (Chicago: Moody, 1988), 198.

66. Bainton, *Christianity*, 259.

67. Bromiley, "Ulrich Zwingli," 198.

68. Bainton, *Christianity*, 261.

Heinrich Bullinger

After Zwingli's premature death, leadership in Zurich passed to Heinrich Bullinger (1504–1575), whose influence went beyond the city limits of Zurich.[69] Bullinger influenced the reform movement as he took part in writing three Reformed confessions. In 1536, he joined theologians from a number of Swiss Reformed cities to write the First Helvetic Confession. Martin Bucer and Wolfgang Capito, two of Strasbourg's reformers, adopted the confession in hopes that it would be a means of reaching agreement with the Lutherans.[70] In 1549, Bullinger and John Calvin coauthored the Zurich Agreement (*Consensus Tigurinus*), which became the basis for the Reformed view of the sacraments. Finally, in 1562 Bullinger drafted the Second Helvetic Confession, which became one of the most comprehensive statements adopted by the Reformed churches of France, Hungary, Poland, and Scotland.[71] This confession, published in 1566, made explicit statements about the gospel that they had recovered.

Excerpts from the Second Helvetic Confession, 1566

Jesus Christ Is the Only Savior of the World, and the True Awaited Messiah

For we teach and believe that this Jesus Christ our Lord is the unique and eternal Savior of the human race, and thus of the whole world, in whom by faith are saved all who before the law, under the law, and under the Gospel were saved, and however many will be saved at the end of the world. For the Lord himself says in the Gospel: "He who does not enter the sheepfold by the door but climbs in by another way, that man is a thief and a robber. . . . I am the door of the sheep" (John 10:1 and 7). And also in another place in the same Gospel he says: "Abraham saw my day and was glad" (ch. 7:56). The apostle Peter also says: "There is salvation in no one else, for there is no other name under heaven given among men by which we must be saved." We therefore believe that we will be saved through the grace of our Lord Jesus Christ, as our fathers were (Acts 4:12; 10:43; 15:11). For Paul also says: "All our fathers ate the same spiritual food, and all drank the same

69. Woodbridge and James, *Church History*, 2:157.

70. Rudolph W. Heinze, *Reform and Conflict: From the Medieval World to the Wars of Religion, A.D. 1350–1648* (Oxford: Monarch, 2006), 131.

71. Woodbridge and James, *Church History*, 2:157–58.

spiritual drink. For they drank from the spiritual Rock which followed them, and the Rock was Christ" (1 Cor. 10:3 f.). And thus we read that John says: "Christ was the Lamb which was slain from the foundation of the world" (Rev. 14:8), and John the Baptist testified that Christ is that "Lamb of God, who takes away the sin of the world" (John 1:29). Wherefore, we quite openly profess and preach that Jesus Christ is the sole Redeemer and Savior of the world, the King and High Priest, the true and awaited Messiah, that holy and blessed one whom all the types of the law and predictions of the prophets prefigured and promised; and that God appointed him beforehand and sent him to us, so that we are not now to look for any other. Now there only remains for all of us to give all glory to Christ, believe in him, rest in him alone, despising and rejecting all other aids in life. For however many seek salvation in any other than in Christ alone, have fallen from the grace of God and have rendered Christ null and void for themselves (Gal. 5:4). (Chap. XI)

What Is the Gospel Properly Speaking?

And although our fathers had the Gospel . . . in the writings of the prophets by which they attained salvation in Christ through faith, yet the Gospel is properly called glad and joyous news, in which, first by John the Baptist, then by Christ the Lord himself, and afterwards by the apostles and their successors, is preached to us in the world that God has now performed what he promised from the beginning of the world, and has sent, nay more, has given us his only Son and in him reconciliation with the Father, the remission of sins, all fulness and everlasting life. Therefore, the history delineated by the four Evangelists and explaining how these things were done or fulfilled by Christ, what things Christ taught and did, and that those who believe in him have all fulness, is rightly called the Gospel. The preaching and writings of the apostles, in which the apostles explain for us how the Son was given to us by the Father, and in him everything that has to do with life and salvation, is also rightly called evangelical doctrine, so that not even today, if sincerely preached, does it lose its illustrious title. (Chap. XIII)

The Teaching of the Gospel Is Not New, but Most Ancient Doctrine

And although the teaching of the Gospel, compared with the teaching of the Pharisees concerning the law, seemed to be a new doctrine when first preached by Christ (which Jeremiah also prophesied concerning the New

> Testament), yet actually it not only was and still is an old doctrine (even if today it is called new by the Papists when compared with the teaching now received among them), but is the most ancient of all in the world. For God predestinated from eternity to save the world through Christ, and he has disclosed to the world through the Gospel this his predestination and eternal counsel (2 Tim. 2:9 f.). Hence it is evident that the religion and teaching of the Gospel among all who ever were, are and will be, is the most ancient of all. Wherefore we assert that all who say that the religion and teaching of the Gospel is a faith which has recently arisen, being scarcely thirty years old, err disgracefully and speak shamefully of the eternal counsel of God. To them applies the saying of Isaiah the prophet: "Woe to those who call evil good and good evil, who put darkness for light and light for darkness, who put bitter for sweet and sweet for bitter!" (Isa. 5:20). (Chap. XIII)

Martin Bucer

The most influential reformer in the city of Strasbourg was Martin Bucer (1491–1551), who came from Schlettstadt in Alsace, which borders France and Germany.[72] The young Bucer began as a member of the Dominican order, but after meeting Luther at the Heidelberg disputation in 1518 and the Diet of Worms in 1521, he arranged to have his monastic vows annulled.[73] After reading Luther's commentary on Galatians, he described it as a "treasury full of the dogmas of pure theology."[74] In 1532, after marrying a former nun, Bucer helped establish the Reformed Church at Strasbourg, serving the parish of St. Aurelia.

In 1538, he published a work titled *Concerning the True Care of Souls*. While holding to central evangelical beliefs, he placed a strong emphasis on the transformation that faith in Christ brings to the life of a Christian, as well as the importance of the Christian disciplines and of church discipline administered by a congregation's elders.[75] In addition, Bucer devoted an entire chapter to evangelism titled "How the Lost Sheep Are to Be Sought," in which he argued for the importance of leading those who are estranged from God to faith in Jesus and into the fold of the sheep pen.[76]

72. Martin Bucer, *Concerning the True Care of Souls*, trans. Peter Beale, intro. David F. Wright (Carlisle, PA: Banner of Truth, 2009), ix.

73. Bainton, *Christianity*, 257; Bucer, *Concerning the True Care of Souls*, xi.

74. Bucer, *Concerning the True Care of Souls*, x.

75. Heinze, *Reform and Conflict*, 141.

76. Bucer, *Concerning the True Care of Souls*, 75–90.

Excerpts from "How the Lost Sheep Are to Be Sought" by Martin Bucer

The church of Christ is the assembly and fellowship of those who are gathered from the world and united in Christ our Lord through his Spirit and word, to be a body and members of one another, each having his office and work for the general good of the whole body and all its members. (1)

Those who exercise Christ's ministry in his church are to seek to bring all people to the knowledge of Christ. (76)

The lost sheep are all those whom God has elected to his kingdom but do not yet recognize Christ our Lord and are entire strangers to his church, whether they were baptized into the church as children or not. This alienation from the flock of Christ and going astray in the case of many comes from their getting so deeply involved in the affairs of the flesh that they have no respect for God and his kingdom; and when they are invited to the marriage-feast [Matt. 22:1–14] and the great supper of Christ [Luke 14:16–24], they say that they have other things to do; one has bought a field, another is trying out a new yoke of oxen, a third has taken a wife. In the case of many others they are hindered by false worship, as with the Jews, Turks, and the whole business of all the sects. (70–71)

True carers of souls and faithful ministers of Christ are not to miss anyone anywhere out with the word of salvation, but diligently to endeavour to seek out all those to whom they may have access in order to lead them to Christ our Lord. . . . [This] is the testimony and teaching . . . of all the prophecies and sermons concerning the kingdom of Christ which we have in the whole of Scripture. The Father has given authority to Christ our Lord over all flesh, he is to fulfil all things in heaven and on earth; every knee is to bow to him and every tongue honour and praise him. He is to rule until the end of the world, and all nations are to be his inheritance.

Sadly however, not all are chosen by God and there are many who despise the salvation which the Lord offers them: this is shown in the parable quoted above, where none of those who had been invited would get a taste of the Lord's banquet. But it is not the Lord's will to reveal to us the secrets of his election; rather he commands us to go out into all the world and preach his gospel to every creature. He says: *into all the world* and *to every creature* [Mark 16:15]. The fact that all people have been made by God and are God's creatures should therefore be reason enough for us to go to them, seeking with the utmost faithfulness to bring them to eternal life.

That is why the Lord has expressed it in general terms: *to every creature*. He does not want to be invited to his banquet only those who show themselves to be citizens and inhabitants of his city, but he tells his servant: Go *out into the streets and alleys and bring in the poor, the crippled, the blind and the lame. And again: Go out to the roads and country lanes and make them come in*. From this the Lord teaches us that his ministers are simply to endeavor to lead to his church and to the perfect fellowship of his salvation all those who wish to come, no matter how wretched and corrupted they may be—indeed, not only to lead but to urge and compel them. (77)

Compel them, the Lord says, *to come in*. [Luke 14:23] It is not that anyone can be compelled to come to Christ against his will, but that one should be so persistent with people that to the evil flesh it seems to be a compulsion and urgent pressing, because the Spirit in this way works against the flesh in order to lead people to Christ. (70–78)

All Christians, as they are all members and instruments of Christ, and it is Christ, not themselves, who is to live in their whole lives (each according to his calling and ability as Christ lives in each), are to serve the Lord above all and with the utmost diligence in order that all his lost sheep should be faithfully sought and led to him and brought into the fellowship of his church. Indeed, we pray for this before everything else: *Your kingdom come* [Matt. 6:10a]. (79–80) (Martin Bucer, *Concerning the True Care of Souls*, trans. Peter Beale, intro. David F. Wright [Carlisle, PA: Banner of Truth, 2009])

The Reformed Church of Strasbourg and its pastors, with Bucer as chief among them, worked to mentor the young John Calvin while he was exiled in the city between 1538 and 1541.[77] When Bucer's wife, Elizabeth, died from the plague, he married Wibrandis, the widow of his colleague Wolfgang Capito.[78]

As with other reformers, Bucer found himself within a state church, in which "the state" was the city of Strasbourg. With virtually the whole pop-

77. As a result, it may be better to describe "Calvin as Bucerian, than to determine anachronistically, whether, and to what extent, Bucer was a Calvinist." Bucer, *Concerning the True Care of Souls*, xiii.

78. Bucer, *Concerning the True Care of Souls*, x; Tuttle, *Story of Evangelism*, 238.

ulation of Strasburg baptized, his goal was to form a community of true Christians, those who knew Christ as Lord and obeyed his gospel. As with other Protestant Reformers, Bucer's ecclesiology lived with the tension between a church composed of baptized citizens, as with Augustine's *corpus permixtum* of wheat and tares, on one side, and a church composed of believers only, as with the *communio sanctorum* or community of saints, on the other.[79] Bucer spoke of this tension: "In our churches, where now everyone is baptized and is supposed to be a Christian, there is not the opportunity to practice discipline and penance that there was in the churches of the apostles and martyrs, when the congregations were small in number and those who wanted to be Christians were driven close together by persecution and were kept in humility and serenity. This is because no-one would profess the faith unless he was serious about it."[80] However, in contrast to Strasbourg's numerous Anabaptists who promoted credobaptism, Bucer maintained his insistence on the universality of paedobaptism for all citizens, accompanied by confirmation of faith at a later time.

When Emperor Charles V defeated the Lutheran princes militarily, he attempted to bring his own form of unity in 1548 with the Augsburg Interim, a temporary theological agreement between German Catholics and Protestants. Tensions grew with plans underway to implement the Interim at Strasbourg. In response, Bucer and his colleagues produced a memorandum on how to preserve their Reformed doctrine. Without the necessary support, however, Bucer was relieved of his position and fled Strasbourg as a refugee to England. After a brief period as the houseguest of Thomas Cranmer, Bucer was appointed Regius Professor of Divinity at the University of Cambridge, where he died. In his final two years, he wrote two books, lectured on the book of Ephesians, and helped serve the poor men and women of Cambridge.[81]

John Calvin

John Calvin (1509–1564), a French theologian and reformer who left the Roman Church at the age of twenty-four, provided Protestantism with an integrated doctrinal system in his *Institutes of the Christian Religion*.

Although France was Roman Catholic, those who were active in the evangelical Reformation began to speak out against it, distributing a pamphlet

79. Bucer, *Concerning the True Care of Souls*, xviii.
80. Bucer, *Concerning the True Care of Souls*, 144.
81. Bucer, *Concerning the True Care of Souls*, xii.

titled *True Articles Respecting the Horrible, Great and Insupportable Abuses of the Papal Mass*.[82] After a copy was nailed to the door of the royal palace, King Francis I had thirty-five Protestants burned at the stake, including Calvin's brother. The persecution that followed caused the reform movement to scatter, including Calvin, who fled to Metz and later to Basel and Strasbourg.

John Calvin was born at Noyon, France, where his father was a legal official for the bishop. He sent John to Paris University to prepare for the priesthood, but then redirected him to Orleans University to study law. While a student there, John developed friends who were reform-minded, following the theological leanings of Luther and Jacques Lefèvre d'Étaples (ca. 1455–1536), who translated the Bible into French. Calvin experienced a conversion to faith around the year 1533.[83]

As a refugee in Basel, Calvin released the first edition of the *Institutes of the Christian Religion*. The title page described the book as basic instruction on the teaching of salvation, and a book worth reading for all who aspired to godliness.[84] Calvin did not hesitate to appeal to peasants as well as potentates. He dedicated the work to King Francis I: "Let it be to your praise then, illustrious king, not to shut your ears or your heart to so righteous a cause, the more especially since it involves the defense of God's glory upon earth, the exaltation of divine truth, and the firm establishment of the Kingdom of Christ. Such a cause is worthy of your hearing, worthy of your consideration, worthy of your tribunal. . . . He is not a king, but a tyrant and a robber, who does not seek to promote the glory of his God."[85]

Calvin set out for Strasbourg but was invited to stay in Geneva, starting what ultimately became a mutually beneficial relationship with the city. He began to teach and preach, but by 1538 he was asked to leave because of theological conflicts. This led him to Strasbourg, where he translated Bucer's liturgy, served as pastor of a French-speaking congregation, revised his *Institutes*, and wrote a commentary on the book of Romans.[86] In 1540 he married Idellete of Buren, and a year later returned to Geneva.

Calvin worked out his pastoral theology in Geneva, where ministers performed their daily responsibilities of preaching, conducting worship services,

82. Henry M. Baird, *History of the Rise of the Huguenots of France* (Eugene, OR: Wipf & Stock, 2004), 1:164.

83. Woodbridge and James, *Church History*, 2:161.

84. James I. Packer, "John Calvin and Reformed Europe," in *Great Leaders of the Christian Church*, ed. John D. Woodbridge (Chicago: Moody, 1988), 211.

85. Paul Henry, *The Life and Times of John Calvin*, trans. Henry Stebbing (London: Whittaker, 1849), 1:55–56.

86. Woodbridge and James, *Church History*, 2:163.

exercising moral discipline, catechizing children and youth, administering the sacraments, and caring for people in need. Having removed the eucharistic altars from the Roman churches, the Genevan authorities redesigned the interiors to give priority to the regular preaching of the Scriptures.[87] With Geneva becoming a safe haven for Protestant refugees from other parts of Europe, the city served as a base to train pastors, evangelists, and missionaries.

For Calvin, the chief end of humans was not to be mystically united with God as the late medieval mystics taught, but to bow before God and his unfathomable character and to obey his unmistakable commands. In this respect, there was nothing that humans could do to earn salvation, because God, who stood outside time, decreed who would be saved and who would be damned. Calvin drew his theory of predestination more sharply than did Luther and Zwingli. This reformer taught that God punished some people according to what they deserved, and saved others according to his good pleasure in order to display his mercy and grace.[88] The center of his thought was the perfect and undivided sovereignty of God.

For Calvin, the grace of God through Christ was the only means of salvation—grace by divine election. However, this grace did not preclude efforts in evangelism but inspired a greater zeal to proclaim the gospel.[89] Calvin understood the very task of preaching the gospel as God's means to make people aware of their election and to enable them to hear the call of God's divine and saving grace. In regard to Christ's commission in Matthew 28:19, Jesus's words to make disciples of all nations, Calvin commented, "This is the point of the word 'go' (*exundi*): the boundaries of Judea were prescribed to the prophets under the law, but now the wall is pulled down and the Lord orders the ministers of the gospel to go far out to scatter the teaching of salvation throughout all the regions of the earth."[90] Calvin consistently pressed his congregation to share the gospel with others.[91]

87. Scott M. Manetsch, *Calvin's Company of Pastors: Pastoral Care and the Emerging Reformed Church, 1536–1609* (New York: Oxford University Press, 2013), 33.

88. See John Calvin, *Institutes of the Christian Religion*, trans. Ford Lewis Battles (Philadelphia: Westminster, 1960), 2:920–87.

89. This point was debated among Calvin's followers. M. Taylor, *Exploring Evangelism*, 179.

90. Timothy George, "The Challenge of Evangelism in the History of the Church," in *Evangelism in the Twenty-First Century*, ed. Thom Rainer (Wheaton, IL: Harold Shaw, 1989), 14.

91. Woodbridge and James, *Church History*, 2:175. Contra Tuttle, who says, "Both Calvin and Luther—like many of the reformers—apparently thought that the Great Commission was only for the Apostolic Church, and Protestant missions—by

The Protestants who came to Geneva for refuge returned to their homelands with Calvin's *Institutes* in hand and the recovered gospel on their lips. As a French-speaking city, Geneva naturally had connections with France. Between 1555 and 1562, Calvin and his colleagues sent eighty-eight evangelists there, resulting in over one hundred thousand Hugenots coming to faith in Jesus.[92] The Genevan consistory also sent missionaries to Italy, the Netherlands, Poland, Hungary, and the free imperial city-states in the Rhineland. In 1561 alone, Nicolas Calladon recorded that 151 missionaries were sent from Geneva to these places.[93]

In what was one of the most ambitious Protestant missionary efforts of the sixteenth century, Geneva sent missionaries Pierre Richier and William Chartier to South America, where they arrived in 1557 in what is now Rio de Janeiro.[94] These two missionaries, along with twelve laypeople, worked for a Genevan trading company while seeking to share the gospel with the native people.[95]

Calvin remained closely tied with many of the pastors, evangelists, and missionaries who were sent from Geneva, offering theological and practical counsel.[96] Again, he did not hesitate to appeal to potentates. He made a spiritual appeal to Edward VI, the youthful king of England, by sending him a copy of his *Commentary on Isaiah*, which he followed by dedicating to the monarch his *Commentary on the Catholic Epistles* and then the *Commentary on the Eighty-Seventh Psalm*.[97] Similarly, Calvin made a spiritual appeal to King Christian III of Denmark when he dedicated to him the French edition of his *Commentary of the Acts of the Apostles*.

As Luther initiated the Protestant Reformation and the German princes provided a political base for it to take root, the burgeoning Evangelical Lutheran (*Evangelisch-Lutherischen*) Church continued the paradigm of Chris-

---

and large—would not fully warm to the task until the eighteenth century." *Story of Evangelism*, 235.

92. Rudnick, *Speaking the Gospel*, 88–89.

93. Woodbridge and James, *Church History*, 2:176–77. Cf. Rudnick, who says, "From Geneva alone, more than two hundred preachers were sent between the years 1555 and 1570." *Speaking the Gospel*, 88–89.

94. Woodbridge and James, *Church History*, 2:178.

95. Bosch, *Witness to the World*, 122. Despite the fact that nothing came of their efforts, the commissioning of these missionaries showed Calvin's desire to take the gospel to all peoples.

96. Woodbridge and James, *Church History*, 2:177.

97. William S. Reid, *John Calvin: His Influence in the Western World* (Grand Rapids: Zondervan, 1982), 181–82.

tendom. Luther himself recognized that civil government was responsible to maintain the true faith but did not have the right to hinder the gospel.[98] The Reformed Church, following the teachings of Bucer and Calvin, also maintained an ecclesiology for a territorial state church.[99] The patterns of Constantine and Charlemagne remained but were fragmented to a smaller scale. Even the Roman Church, while still powerful, no longer possessed a monopoly on Europe's theology and ecclesial life.[100]

Evangel and the Anabaptists

During this period of the sixteenth century, the branch of Christians known as Anabaptists pursued even greater levels of reform and broke from the pattern of Christendom in hopes of returning to a pre-Constantinian form of the early church. Anabaptists held that God's church was wholly separate from the state or political authority. They followed the path of earlier dissenters—the Waldenses, Lollards, and Hussites.[101] In fact, Anabaptists rejected the Protestantism of the Lutherans and the Reformed churches, judging that they fell short of the ecclesial, theological, social, and moral reforms needed.[102]

The Anabaptists originated from Zwingli's circle of Reformed theology in Zurich. The name Anabaptist comes from the Greek words *ana* (again) and *baptizō* (baptism) and means "to baptize again." In their view, infant (paedo) baptism was not biblical but merely a "dipping in the Romish bath."[103] The true Christian baptism was believer (credo) baptism.

Conrad Grebel

An early leader of the Anabaptists was Conrad Grebel (ca. 1498–1526) of Zurich. He was educated in the humanities at Basel, Vienna, and Paris, and followed the view of Erasmus that emphasized freedom of the will. In 1521, Grebel returned to Zurich and joined Zwingli and others to study Greek and Hebrew. In the process, he converted to faith in the evangel.

98. Bainton, *Christianity*, 256.

99. Gunnar Westin, *The Free Church through the Ages* (Nashville: Broadman, 1959), 100.

100. Rudnick, *Speaking the Gospel*, 79.

101. Bainton, *Christianity*, 265.

102. Woodbridge and James, *Church History*, 2:188–89.

103. Roland H. Bainton, *The Reformation of the Sixteenth Century* (Boston: Beacon, 1985), 99.

Two years later, he began to doubt whether Zwingli was serious enough about the degree to which the church should reform. Grebel became impatient, especially when Zwingli accepted the decision that worship services in Zurich should be left in the hands of the city council and not with the leaders of the church. Grebel and others complained that the lifestyles of those who confessed the Reformed faith still fell below the New Testament standards, a point that neither Zwingli nor Luther denied, but both feared that church discipline would reduce the church to a handful of faithful disciples.[104]

Soon Grebel joined forces with Felix Mantz and George Blaurock, who also were disillusioned with the slow pace of reform at Zurich.[105] The three met to discuss the pattern of worship and governance of the church according to the pattern of the New Testament. They concluded that the early church was not supported from the tithes collected by the state, as done in Zurich, but from offerings by believers given freely.[106] Rather than wait for the city council to implement further reform, they organized separate conventicles of believers, as the Hussites had done, gathering faithful disciples to meet in homes.

The Anabaptists held that the church is not a sociopolitical but a spiritual body of believers in union with Christ marked by believer's baptism as a public act of Christian faith and discipleship. Therefore, they conducted baptisms in rivers and streams, practicing baptism by immersion rather than sprinkling.[107] Moreover, they held that anyone in the church who did not live as a Christian disciple according to the standards of the New Testament should be disciplined and, if necessary, excommunicated.

George Blaurock and Felix Mantz

The first congregation of Anabaptists was formed in 1525 by George Blaurock (ca. 1491–1529) at Zollikon near Zurich. Blaurock was a Swiss priest who broke ties with the Roman Church when he married in 1523. He was the first believer to be baptized by Conrad Grebel.[108] In turn, Blaurock baptized members of his congregation at Zollikon.[109]

104. Hans-Jürgen Goertz, *The Anabaptists*, trans. Trevor Johnson (London: Routledge, 1996), 8–12, 44.

105. Goertz, *Anabaptists*, 39–49, 70.

106. Bainton, *Christianity*, 263–66.

107. Woodbridge and James, *Church History*, 2:154.

108. González, *Story of Christianity*, 2:55.

109. Estep, *Anabaptist Story*, 14.

After Blaurock founded the congregation at Zollikon, he served as an itinerant evangelist, establishing congregations in the Tyrol region of the Austrian Alps. In 1527, he was captured, beaten with rods, and released. He continued to preach the gospel nevertheless, and two years later he was captured again. He was burned at the stake at Innsbruck at the hands of authorities of the Roman Church on the charge that he abandoned the office of a papist priest, taught the "new gospel" of the Anabaptists, and rejected the Roman Church's view of the Eucharist.

Felix Mantz (ca. 1498–1527) faced a similar martyrdom. He was the illegitimate son of a papist priest and studied Latin, Greek, and Hebrew before joining Grebel and Blaurock at Zurich. In addition to translating writings into the local language, he worked diligently as an evangelist and was arrested on several occasions between 1525 and 1527. When the city council determined that Anabaptist teachings were subversive to the state and heretical within the Roman Church, Mantz was drowned by authorities in a tributary of Lake Zurich.[110]

Michael Sattler

Persecution led to the dispersion of Anabaptists to other areas, including Germany where a new leader appeared. Michael Sattler (1490–1527), formerly a Benedictine monk from Freiburg in southern Germany, left his monastery during the Peasants' War of 1524–1525 when local peasants seized the abbey. Sattler came to Zurich, where he sat under the teaching of the Anabaptists, and in 1526 was rebaptized as a reborn believer in Christ. After carrying out an evangelistic ministry in the vicinity of Zurich, he moved to Strasbourg, where he met Bucer. In 1527, Sattler gathered with Swiss and German Anabaptists in the town of Schleitheim on the Swiss-German border and wrote an Anabaptist confession of faith known as the Schleitheim Articles.[111]

When returning from Schleitheim, Sattler and his wife were arrested and taken into custody.[112] The authorities discovered that he was carrying the confession of the Anabaptists. They took him to Rottenberg, where he, his wife, and nine others were brought to trial for violating the authorized teachings of the Roman Church. In addition, he was charged with promoting

110. Heinze, *Reform and Conflict*, 155.

111. Goertz, *Anabaptists*, 14.

112. Woodbridge and James, *Church History*, 2:192.

nonresistance toward the Turks. Sattler was sentenced to death, his tongue was cut out, and he died being pulled behind a wagon.[113] When his wife refused to recant her faith, she was drowned in the Neckar River, being mocked for her Anabaptist beliefs.

Balthasar Hubmaier

Balthasar Hubmaier (ca. 1480–1528) was born into a peasant family in Bavaria. Despite his family's poverty, he earned a master's degree from the University of Friedburg and a doctorate from the University of Ingolstadt.[114] He came to evangelical faith in 1524 after hearing a debate at Waldshut. He was baptized the following year on Easter Sunday, along with sixty others, and he himself went on to baptize nearly three hundred believers.[115]

When Waldshut was threatened by Archduke Ferdinand, brother of the emperor Charles V, Hubmaier fled to the Swiss territory of Schaffhausen. He wrote a book titled *About the Heretics and Those Who Burn Them*, appealing to the need for tolerance and religious freedom.[116] In 1525, he fled to Zurich to escape the Austrian army, but Zwingli had Hubmaier arrested. At the hands of city magistrates, he was tortured and forced to recant his Anabaptist views.[117] When Hubmaier was allowed to leave Zurich, he joined other Anabaptists going to Moravia, whose government provided religious toleration to dissenters. He settled in Nikolsburg, where he witnessed Count Leonhart von Lichtenstein convert to Christian faith. While at Nikolsburg, Hubmaier baptized as many as six thousand believers. He also wrote a treatise titled *On the Freedom of the Will*, in which he caricatured those in Nikolsburg who denied free will and blamed "all of their sin and evil on God," and who excused their sins by claiming, "It must be God's will that I be an adulterer and run after harlots."[118]

In 1527 the Archduke Ferdinand became ruler of Bohemia and Moravia, and Hubmaier was extradited and brought to trial at Vienna. The following

113. Heinze, *Reform and Conflict*, 144.

114. William R. Estep, *The Anabaptist Story: An Introduction to Sixteenth-Century Anabaptism* (Grand Rapids: Eerdmans, 1996), 77.

115. Heinze, *Reform and Conflict*, 159.

116. Westin, *Free Church through the Ages*, 67.

117. Hubmaier split with other Anabaptists in their opposition to the sword, considering war as a punishment for sin. Moreover, he sanctioned the taking of oaths. Westin, *Free Church through the Ages*, 103.

118. Heinze, *Reform and Conflict*, 161.

year, Emperor Charles V issued a mandate that all Anabaptists be subject to the death penalty. In Vienna, Hubmaier was tried for heresy, convicted, and taken to the public square where, refusing to recant, he was burned at the stake. Three days later, his wife was drowned as officials wrapped a rope around her neck tied to a large stone and plunged her headlong into the Danube River.[119]

Excerpts from Balthasar Hubmaier's Twelve Articles of Christian Belief, 1526

I believe and confess, my Lord Jesus Christ, that thou was conceived by the Holy Spirit, without any human seed, born from Mary, the pure and ever chaste virgin, that thou might bring again to me and all believing men, and might obtain from thy Heavenly Father the grace of the Holy Spirit, which was withdrawn from me by reason of my sin. I believe and trust that the Holy Spirit has come in me, and the power of the Most High God has, as with Mary, overshadowed my soul; that I may conceive the new man, and so in thy living, indestructible word and in the Spirit, be born again and see the kingdom of God. For thou, Son of the living God, didst become man, in order that through thee we might become children of God. (Art. III)

I believe also and confess a resurrection of the flesh, yea, even the body with which I am now surrounded, though if may be eaten by worms, drowned, frozen, or burned. Yea, and though my temporal honour, goods, body and life be taken from me, yet will I, at the day of the joyous resurrection of my flesh, first truly receive the true honour which avails before God, goods that pass not away, a body incapable of suffering, made clear and immortal, and eternal life. O my Mediator, Lord Jesus Christ, strengthen and hold me in thy faith! (Art. XI) (Henry C. Vedder, *Balthasar Hübmaier: The Leader of the Anabaptists*, trans. Howard Osgood [New York: Putnam and Sons, 1905], 130–37)

Despite persecution and martyrdom, the Anabaptists continued to increase. This dissenter movement won people to faith by sharing the gospel on roads and in homes, baptized converts and formed them as disciples,

119. Westin, *Free Church through the Ages*, 97.

and planted conventicles throughout Switzerland, in northern Germany, and down the Rhine to the Low Countries of Belgium, the Netherlands, and Luxembourg.[120]

The Anabaptist movement spread so broadly that the Roman and Lutheran churches feared that their own state-sponsored, authorized churches would be supplanted. Therefore, in 1529 at the Diet of Speyer, the Roman and Lutheran leaders agreed to subject Anabaptists to the death penalty. In turn, the Roman authorities burned Anabaptists, both men and women, at the stake, while Lutherans drowned them.[121] Luther was slow to give his consent, but by 1531 his fear of anarchy led him to concede to the death penalty for Anabaptists, not for heresy but for sedition.[122] Only the German prince Philip of Hesse refused to apply the death penalty to those of different or dissenting Christian views.

During this time of persecution, Anabaptists maintained their eschatological hope, believing that the second coming of Jesus was imminent. They described those who persecuted them as "heathen Christians" or "false brethren," while viewing themselves as true disciples who followed Jesus unto death.[123]

The Roman Catholic Church's Reformation

By the 1540s the Roman Catholic Church launched its own reform emphasizing spiritual leadership and formed new religious orders to meet the challenges of the Protestant Reformation. The Roman Catholic Church clarified its teachings at the Council of Trent, which met intermittently from 1545 to 1563. Although this council made strides toward practical and moral reforms for the papacy and the clergy, it rejected theological reforms proposed by the Protestant Reformers.[124] The practice of indulgences continued, but the Roman Catholic Church introduced reforms to prevent their abuse. The Council of Trent maintained that justification was by faith and human merit, not by faith alone.[125] The medieval system of the seven sacraments of Thomas Aquinas remained intact.

120. Bainton, *Christianity*, 265.

121. Heinze, *Reform and Conflict*, 157; González, *Story of Christianity*, 2:56–57.

122. Bainton, *Christianity*, 265.

123. Goertz, *Anabaptists*, 15.

124. Woodbridge and James, *Church History*, 2:212–13.

125. Leonardo De Chirico, "Not by Faith Alone? An Analysis of the Roman Catholic Doctrine from Trent to the Joint Declaration," in *The Doctrine on Which the Church*

Ignatius of Loyola

Among the new religious orders that worked for reform, the Jesuits stood above the others.[126] Ignatius of Loyola (ca. 1491–1556), the founder of the Jesuits—also known as the Society of Jesus—entered a monastery where he spent nearly a year in devotional practices, experienced mystical visions, and composed his work on spiritual warfare titled *The Spiritual Exercises*.[127] In addition to the three vows of regular clergy, Jesuits took a fourth vow of unconditional obedience to the Roman pope. Moreover, they followed the practice of *mobilitas*, traveling and ministering in public places rather than living within a cloister. In fact, the Jesuits were the first to use the Latin word *missio*, from *mittere*, meaning "to send," to speak of the strategic sending of special agents or missionaries of the church.[128]

Francis Xavier

Loyola returned to school, where he engaged in pastoral work among students. He was investigated several times, and twice imprisoned by the Inquisition for his unauthorized pastoral activity. During this time, he traveled from Spain to the University of Paris, where he gathered a band of students, including Francis Xavier (1506–1552), vowing to devote their lives to the Roman Catholic Church. In 1540, Pope Paul III approved the formation of the Jesuits as a monastic order and gave them an autocratic and military constitution.[129] The high standards of Jesuit scholarship and education made them valuable advocates of papal authority. In essence, they functioned as a new militia of the papacy, organized to recover Europe from the "heresy of Protestantism," and for the conversion of the indigenous peoples of the

---

Stands or Falls: Justification in Biblical, Theological, Historical, and Pastoral Perspective, ed. Matthew Barrett (Wheaton, IL: Crossway, 2019), 739–67.

126. Bainton, *Christianity*, 279.

127. George E. Ganss, ed., *Ignatius of Loyola: The Spiritual Exercises and Selected Works* (New York: Paulist, 1991), 12.

128. David J. Bosch, *Transforming Mission: Paradigm Shifts in Theology of Mission* (Maryknoll, NY: Orbis, 1991), 227–28; Dana L. Robert, *Christian Mission: How Christianity Became a World Religion* (Oxford: Wiley & Sons, 2009), 37–38; Craig Ott and Stephen J. Strauss, *Encountering Theology of Mission: Biblical Foundations, Historical Developments, and Contemporary Issues* (Grand Rapids: Baker Academic, 2010), xiv.

129. Woodbridge and James, *Church History*, 2:207–8.

Americas. Although noted for an emphasis on education, Loyola saw evangelism as their primary work.[130]

In 1541, obeying the command of Loyola, Xavier left on a day's notice for a decade of mission in India. Xavier had a remarkable career as a missionary, traveling throughout Asia. In 1545, he sailed for the east coast of India, and at Malacca he met Hachiro, a Japanese man who converted to faith in Christ. Four years later, he and Hachiro sailed for Japan, arriving there in 1549.[131] Xavier drew several thousand converts to the church until Buddhist monks expelled him from the country. He returned to India, where he built a college at Goa. Hoping to preach in China, he sailed for the county, but when he found the country closed to him, he died on an island off the coast.

Matteo Ricci and Michele Ruggieri

Later, Jesuit missionaries Matteo Ricci (1552–1610) and Michele Ruggieri (1543–1607) entered China as Confucian scholars, having the intent to study the teachings of the philosopher Confucius (551–479 CE). Not only did they identify with the Chinese people by wearing Chinese clothes, but they learned from the Chinese people, seeking to understand them, as they translated the gospel into the form of Confucian proverbs.[132] Ricci believed that theological and moral truth could be found in the ancient writings of the Chinese civilization, and that contextualizing the gospel to the Chinese way of thinking was an appropriate approach to his mission.[133]

In addition to the East, the major fields of expansion of the Jesuits included the New World, where they followed the Franciscans and Dominicans who followed the Spanish conquistadors.[134] The Jesuits took up activities in Paraguay in South America as well as Quebec in North America. French Jesuits explored the Mississippi River, mapped the upper lakes of the Midwest, and traced out the French territories in Louisiana and Canada.

130. Tuttle, *Story of Evangelism*, 236.

131. Tuttle, *Story of Evangelism*, 240.

132. Ralph R. Covell, *Confucius, the Buddha, and Christ: A History of the Gospel in Chinese* (Eugene, OR: Wipf & Stock, 1986), 43.

133. Covell, *Confucius, the Buddha, and Christ*, 47; Holland, *Dominion*, 348–50.

134. Mark A. Noll, *The Old Religion in a New World: The History of North American Christianity* (Grand Rapids: Eerdmans, 2020), 30, 41–43.

Evangel and the Reformed (Arminians)

As the pendulum swung from the Roman Catholic Church's position of salvation based on faith and works, some within the Reformed stream of Protestants moved to an extreme position of divine grace that emphasized divine sovereignty and election and allowed no room for human responsibility, even in the exercise of faith in the gospel. Among the Reformed to push back was a man named Arminius.

Jacobus Arminius

Jacobus Arminius (1560–1609) was a Dutch minister and theologian born in Oudewater in the Netherlands. His father died when he was an infant, and his mother and siblings were slaughtered by Spanish papists when Oudewater was destroyed in 1575. The young Arminius was adopted and attended school at Utrecht, taking up studies later at the universities of Leiden, Basel, and Geneva. The rector at Geneva was Theodore Beza, successor of John Calvin. Beza held unashamedly to the teaching that divine decrees willed the fall of humanity and determined the souls who would be saved, or lost.[135] At the time, Arminius stood in the mainstream of Reformed theology, affirming the Calvinist view of predestination, that those elected for salvation were chosen prior to Adam's fall in the garden.[136]

As a group of ministers thought about this subject, they concluded that such an arrangement made God responsible for the original sin of humankind. As this subject was discussed, an opposing group of ministers who sided with Beza thought that they should identify a person who could speak with authority on the subject. They concluded that no one was better prepared to defend the view of Calvin and Beza than Arminius, and he accepted the challenge.

Arminius decided to balance the arguments of both sides and then present a defense of his own view. To do justice to the opposing view, he made a careful study of the Scriptures and writings of the church fathers. The more he examined the sources, however, the more perplexed he became, especially regarding a defense of the absolute decree of predestination. Arminius real-

135. M. Taylor, *Exploring Evangelism*, 194.

136. John S. Knox, *Jacobus Arminius Stands His Ground: A Declaration against High Calvinism* (Eugene, OR: Wipf & Stock, 2018), 60–61.

ized that he was moving gradually toward the "very opinion which, at first sight, he had undertaken to impugn."[137] Soon his view became moderate with an understanding that predestination was based on foreknowledge. In other words, predestination meant God's foreknowledge of events, not his divine willing of those events.[138] To Arminius, the view of his mentor Beza appeared too harsh because it did not provide a place for the exercise of human choice in the matter of salvation.

After brief stays at the University of Padua, Rome, and Geneva, Arminius returned to the Netherlands. He was ordained in 1588 and served for fourteen years in pastoral ministry in Amsterdam, where he and other preachers circulated among the churches. In 1590, he married Lijsbet Real.

In 1591, Arminius prepared a series of expository sermons from the book of Romans. Criticisms were soon leveled against him, claiming that he said many things from the pulpit that were opposed to the Belgic Confession and the Heidelberg Catechism.[139] In his defense, he said that he wished not to make God the author of sin or do away with the freedom inherent in human will.[140] Arminius concluded that Beza's position, in effect, made God the author of sin, making God's love problematic. Arminius believed that divine grace was sufficient for the redemption of all humankind. However, this grace became efficient only on behalf of those who appropriated it by faith.[141] He presented his view, saying,

> Evangelical faith is an assent of the mind, produced by the Holy Spirit, through the Gospel, in sinners, who, through the law, know and acknowledge their sins, and are penitent on account of them: By which they are not only fully persuaded within themselves, that Jesus Christ has been constituted by God the author of salvation to those who obey Him, and that He is their own Saviour if they have believed in Him, and by which they also believe in Him as such, and through Him on God as the Benevolent Father in Him, to the salvation of believers and to the glory of Christ and God.[142]

137. Caspar Brandt, *The Life of James Arminius*, trans. John Guthrie (London: Word, 1854), 34, cited in M. Taylor, *Exploring Evangelism*, 194.

138. This was an *efficient* cause that guaranteed certain results, but not the *necessary* cause that determined the results. M. Taylor, *Exploring Evangelism*, 207.

139. Knox, *Jacob Arminius Stands His Ground*, 7–8, 32–33.

140. Knox, *Jacob Arminius Stands His Ground*, 23–24.

141. M. Taylor, *Exploring Evangelism*, 209.

142. James Arminius, *The Works of James Arminius*, trans. James Nichols and William Nichols (Grand Rapids: Baker, 1996), 2:400.

In 1603, Arminius was appointed as professor of theology, and in 1605 he became rector of the University of Leiden, holding that position until his death. The last years of his life were dominated by theological disputes in the Reformed Church, particularly with Franciscus Gomarus, his colleague at Leiden.

Remonstrants

After Arminius's death, forty-two ministers and two educators gave their support to his views. They gathered at the Hague in 1610, where they signed the Remonstrance, a theological statement written by Johannes Uyttenbogaert of Utrecht.[143] The statement contained five articles that were considered the irreducible minimums set forth by Arminius.[144] Those who signed it were referred to as Remonstrants.

Remonstrant Arminianism was then debated at the Synod of Dort (1618–1619) among clergymen of the Dutch Reformed Church. The synod included delegates from England, Germany, and Switzerland, as well as the Dutch church, all of whom were supporters of Gomarus. The views of Arminius were condemned, and Arminius's followers were expelled and forbidden politically to practice their faith.[145] In 1629, however, Arminius's works were published in Leiden under the title *Theological Works* (*Opera theologica*), and by 1630, the Remonstrant Brotherhood achieved legal toleration.

The views of Arminius became particularly important for the practice of evangelism in the Arminian stream of the Reformed Church and for numbers of evangelicals afterward, as shown in following chapters. Arminius taught that humans are sinners, that Christ died as the atoning sacrifice for sin, and that it is possible for "the last, the lost, and the least of mankind to be saved."[146]

143. Knox, *Jacob Arminius Stands His Ground*, 21–22, 84.

144. The five articles of the Remonstrance are (1) God chose to save through Jesus Christ all those who through grace would believe in him and persevere to the end; (2) Jesus Christ obtained forgiveness of sins sufficient for all; (3) fallen humanity can think or do nothing that is truly good by free will; (4) God's grace, which is not irresistible, is necessary for thinking or doing any good; (5) true believers are enabled by grace to persevere to the end, and it may be possible to lose this grace. Keith D. Stanglin and Thomas H. McCall, *Jacob Arminius: Theologian of Grace* (New York: Oxford University Press, 2013), 190.

145. Woodbridge and James, *Church History*, 2:257–58.

146. M. Taylor, *Exploring Evangelism*, 217.

Discussion Questions

1. With Luther, "justification by faith" became a central teaching for evangelicals. He taught that justification is based not on what humans do but entirely on what God has done in Christ, and thus sinners are justified by faith. If the Reformation was an uncovering of the gospel and, for Luther, a discovery of "justification by faith," does this suggest that "justification by faith" is the gospel? Central to the gospel? A benefit or result of the gospel?
2. Although church history lists the contributions of men, often their wives played substantial roles in promoting evangelism. What might Luther *not* have accomplished without Katharina? How did her ministries at Wittenberg contribute directly and indirectly to evangelism?
3. The Second Helvetic Confession addressed the criticism against Reformed Protestants that "the religion and teaching of the Gospel is a faith which has recently arisen, being scarcely thirty years old." How was this criticism addressed? How does the Second Helvetic Confession compare with your two-hundred-word summary of the gospel from chapter 1 (Acts 2:22–39; Rom. 1:2–5; 1 Cor. 15:1–6)? What are the differences?
4. What did Christian discipleship mean for Anabaptists? If they uncovered the gospel, what specifically did they uncover? How does Balthasar Hubmaier's *Twelve Articles of Christian Belief* compare death of the human body and the resurrection to come at Christ's return? Why was this important to Anabaptists?
5. The Reformation sparked a debate over God's sovereignty and human free will. Are there theologies that promote evangelism and evangelistic effectiveness, and others that stifle them? In "How the Lost Sheep Are to Be Sought," how did Martin Bucer handle divine election and the need to "diligently . . . endeavour to seek out all" the lost sheep of the village?

7

Pietist Evangelism

O Thou who art Love itself and who hast commanded us all to love Thee with whole heart and our neighbor as ourselves, let me learn to know this double duty and ever to practice it in deed and in truth so that I may become like Thee, showing active faith through love. Thou sweet Love! Give me Thy grace; let me experience a glut of love so that I truly love Thee and my neighbor with pure heart, good conscience, and unsullied faith, thus becoming Thy child, seized by everlasting love. Amen.

—Johann Arndt[1]

The original aim of Protestant Reformers was to reform the Roman Church to an evangelical theology. In this attempt, theological treatises were presented and disputes were held to convince the Roman Church that evangelical theology was indeed the teaching of Jesus and the apostles in the Scriptures. However, the theology of the Reformers was deemed heretical by the Roman Church, which refused to abandon the medieval theological system of the seven sacraments and church tradition.

The acceptance of evangelical theology by some magistrates and heads of state within territories of the Holy Roman Empire provided smaller geographical bases from which the Protestant Reformers could teach their evangelical views and establish Protestant churches. Within these geographical areas, evangelical views became authorized within the

1. John J. Stoudt, ed., *Devotions and Prayers of Johann Arndt* (Grand Rapids: Baker, 1958), 35.

principality or territory, and other views were considered unauthorized or dissenting.

This principle of the territorial church—*cuius regio, eius religio*, a Latin phrase meaning "whose realm, his religion"—became a reality in 1555 with the Peace of Augsburg.[2] This agreement allowed princes of the Holy Roman Empire to determine the religious confession of their subjects, either Roman Catholic or Evangelical Lutheran. This agreement was extended with the Peace of Westphalia in 1648 to include Reformed territories.[3] The principle was furthered by the practice of monarchical absolutism, which not only mandated uniformity of belief among peoples of a territory or principality but allowed a head of state to exercise a dominant role over the territorial church. The principle of Constantine's "one God, one emperor, one empire, one church" became "one God, one king, one nation, one church." In this arrangement, clergy in the evangelical Protestant territories came under control of the respective political or civil authorities.

In pursuit of evangelical theology, Reformation theologians produced writings that centered particularly on the doctrine of salvation as well as matters of ecclesiology. In order to do this, they relied heavily on medieval logicians for themes but based their arguments on the Bible as their final authority.[4] While the original writings were directed toward the Roman Church, the Reformers' inability to present a unified evangelical theology led to intramural disputes among themselves. Eventually, evangelical Protestant theology drifted toward "Protestant scholasticism," a technical and logical approach to theological systems in which the parts were defined in propositional forms.[5] The intent was to provide a technical theology for the church and academy with the goal of orthodoxy, or right teaching. At times, the emphasis of Protestant scholasticism led to debates about theological minutiae, trivial details that had little or no relevance to the proclamation of the gospel and the care of souls.

2. Ole Peter Grell and Bob Scribner, *Tolerance and Intolerance in the European Reformation* (Cambridge: Cambridge University Press, 1996), 7, 27, 36.

3. Roland H. Bainton, *Christianity* (Boston: Houghton Mifflin, 2001), 291; Tom Holland, *Dominion: How the Christian Revolution Remade the World* (New York: Basic Books, 2019), 369–70.

4. Justo L. González, *The Story of Christianity: The Early Church to the Present Day* (Peabody, MA: Prince, 1999), 2:175–76.

5. C. Scott Dixon, *The Church in the Early Modern Age* (London: Tauris, 2016), 161.

Pietistic Pursuit of Living Faith

In response, some evangelicals began to refer to Protestant scholasticism as "dead orthodoxy" void of "living faith."[6] They held that Christianity had been reduced to a system of premises and conclusions and church-sanctioned doctrines. While they caricatured Protestant scholasticism as the spinning of theological theories, they promoted the study of the Scriptures with the goals of edifying Christians, loving neighbors, proclaiming the gospel, and living the way of Jesus and the apostles.[7]

Evangelical Lutherans who promoted this pious life were soon labeled "Pietists." This stream of Lutherans saw themselves as the true heirs of Luther, embodying his orthodox theology and evangelical spirit. They emphasized personal conviction of sin, repentance, and the need for conversion to faith.

Johann Arndt

Johann Arndt (1555–1621), a Lutheran pastor, raised awareness of this matter by distinguishing between nominal or false Christians and devout or true Christians—a perennial challenge within Christendom.[8] Arndt was born at Ballenstedt, in Anhalt, Germany. He studied at Wittenberg under Luther's colleague Philipp Melanchthon and at Reformed universities in Switzerland. In 1583, he accepted a pastorate at Badenborn but was forced to leave after seven years because he irritated Duke John George, a Calvinist.[9] Arndt established a church at Quedlinburg, Germany, serving there for nine years before moving to Brunswick.

Arndt wrote several devotional books that were read widely. These books were compiled into a single volume titled *True Christianity* (*Wahres Christentum*). In this collected work, he presented basic Christian doctrines that drew on the evangelical teachings of Luther and Melanchthon and empha-

6. Roger E. Olson and Christian T. Collins Winn, *Reclaiming Pietism: Retrieving an Evangelical Tradition* (Grand Rapids: Eerdmans, 2015), 25–26, 51–52.

7. Olson and Collins Winn, *Reclaiming Pietism*, 26–27, 79–80.

8. Bosch notes that a structural link between church and state meant that every person in a given territory would at least be regarded as a Christian. David J. Bosch, *Transforming Mission: Paradigm Shifts in Theology of Mission* (Maryknoll, NY: Orbis, 1991), 254.

9. Olson and Collins Winn, *Reclaiming Pietism*, 25–26.

sized living faith that drew on the devotional writings of Thomas á Kempis and Johannes Tauler.[10] Arndt did not reject theological scholarship per se but rejected the purely intellectual pursuit of it at the expense of following the way of Jesus. He promoted orthodoxy *and* orthopraxy. In the foreword he wrote, "Dear Christian reader, that the holy Gospel is subjected, in our time, to a great and shameful abuse is fully proved by the impenitent life of the ungodly who praise Christ and his word with their mouths and yet lead an unchristian life that is like that of persons who dwell in heathendom, not in the Christian world. Such ungodly conduct gave me cause to write this book to show simple readers wherein true Christianity consists, namely, in the exhibition of a true, living faith, active in genuine godliness and fruits of righteousness."[11]

In his explanation of true Christianity, Arndt dealt first with the triune God and his image in humankind, saying, "The Holy Trinity has placed [his] image in man so that in the whole life and walk of man, pure divine holiness, righteousness, and goodness ought to appear and shine forth."[12] He then described the fall of Adam as turning from God to himself, and thus he "robbed God of the honour in that he [Adam] himself wished to be God."[13]

In addition to Luther's emphasis on justification by faith that dealt with the Christian's right standing before God, Arndt emphasized regeneration, the "new birth into a living hope" (1 Pet. 1:3).[14] He held that Christians should read and study the Scriptures so that they might live as Jesus's disciples, arguing that the Scriptures are "living and active" and "must bring forth spiritual fruit" in the daily life of the Christian.[15]

Arndt described regeneration as the second of two births. The first is "the carnal, sinful, damnable, and accursed birth that comes from Adam."[16] The second is "the spiritual, holy, blessed, gracious, new birth that comes out of Christ, by which the seed of God and the heavenly, godly man is perpetuated in a spiritual manner." Arndt emphasized that "Christ . . . must live in you, and renew the image of God in you."[17]

10. Johann Arndt, *True Christianity*, trans. Peter Erb (New York: Paulist, 1979), 25.
11. Arndt, *True Christianity*, 21.
12. Arndt, *True Christianity*, 29.
13. Arndt, *True Christianity*, 33.
14. Cf. John 1:12–13; 3:3–8; Titus 3:5; 1 Pet. 1:23.
15. Arndt, *True Christianity*, 49.
16. Arndt, *True Christianity*, 37.
17. Arndt, *True Christianity*, 39.

He posited that the prerequisite for the new birth is repentance: "A man must deny himself; that is, break his own self-will; give himself completely to God's will; not love himself but hold himself as the most unworthy, miserable man; deny all that he has; that is, reject the work and its honor and glory; consider his own wisdom and power as nothing; not depend on himself or on any creature but only and simply on God."[18] Without such repentance no one could be a disciple of Jesus. Along with repentance was the need for "true faith," which he described as "the deep assent and unhesitating trust in God's grace promised in Christ and in the forgiveness of sins and eternal life."[19]

In *True Christianity*, Arndt sought to awaken nominal Christians to the need to be born again and to live as disciples of Jesus. He said, "In a word, he who does not live here in time with Christ will not live with him there in eternity. Christ will not live in that person there, in whom he has not lived here. . . . Note with whom you have most conformed and unified your life here, with Christ or with the Devil. With whomever you have done so you will remain united after death in eternity."[20] In the centuries to follow, *True Christianity* was translated into several European languages and read widely in homes, awakening the readers to their personal need for Jesus Christ as Lord and Savior.

Philip Jacob Spener

Arndt's ideas were received heartily by Philip Spener, who wrote the preface to Arndt's *True Christianity*.[21] Philip Jacob Spener (1635–1705) was born in Rappoltsweiler, a town of Germany in the province of Alsace-Lorraine. At age sixteen, he enrolled at the University of Strasbourg, where he read Arndt's writings.[22] After his education at Strasbourg, he traveled to Switzerland, visiting Basel and Geneva.

When Spener returned to Germany in 1661, he was assigned to become an itinerant preacher in Strasbourg. Three years later, he passed his theological examination for the doctor of theology degree and on the same day

18. Arndt, *True Christianity*, 42.
19. Arndt, *True Christianity*, 45.
20. Arndt, *True Christianity*, 76.
21. Heiko A. Oberman, preface to Arndt, *True Christianity*, xiii.
22. John D. Woodbridge and Frank A. James III, *Church History*, vol. 2, *From Pre-Reformation to the Present Day* (Grand Rapids: Zondervan, 2013), 263.

married Susanna Erhardt. In the following year, he was called to become senior minister of the evangelical Lutheran church at Frankfurt am Main.

In his ministerial role Spener observed that many people in his local area, or more specifically the parish church, confessed the evangelical Lutheran faith but were far from living the Christian life. This observation led him to hold private gatherings or conventicles for their spiritual nurture. These meetings, called *collegia pietatis*, "schools of piety," were held throughout the city and attended by women and men interested in reading and studying the Bible, praying, and singing hymns.[23]

In 1675, Spener published a book that contained his criticisms of the evangelical Lutheran church and proposals for its reform. The book was titled *Pia Desideria*, meaning "Pious Desires," with the subtitle *For a God-Pleasing Reform of the True Evangelical Church*.[24] In this book, Spener commented on the prevailing moral laxity of clergy and laity, and affirmed the possibility of a second evangelical reformation, saying, "When one looks at the everyday life of those among us who are called Lutherans (but who do not deserve this name, for they do not understand dear Luther's teaching about living faith), does one not find grave offense—indeed, such offenses as are everywhere prevalent? . . . We must confess that drunkenness is to be counted among such sins . . . among persons of the ecclesiastical and political estates."[25]

Given the conditions that he observed, Spener offered six proposals for the church's reform. They were (1) to give more time to the public reading of the Scriptures and to their private study in order to more fully understand their meaning; (2) to reform the pastoral office as well as emphasize the priesthood of believers; (3) to cultivate spiritual life by loving one's neighbor and not simply accumulating knowledge; (4) to engage constructively in relationships with unbelievers as well as heretics, and to conduct theological disputations in a true spirit of love, not with the goal of winning the argument, but to benefit others; (5) to develop a curriculum for theological education that nurtures personal piety in addition to the study of books; and (6) to encourage preaching that edifies listeners and emphasizes the importance of living faith and bearing fruit.[26]

23. Nicholas Hope, *German and Scandinavian Protestantism, 1700–1918* (New York: Oxford University Press, 1995), 131; González, *Story of Christianity*, 2:205–6.

24. Carter Lindberg, ed., *The Pietist Theologians: An Introduction to Theology in the Seventeenth and Eighteenth Centuries* (Hoboken, NJ: Wiley, 2005), 7–8.

25. Philipp Jacob Spener, *Pia Desideria*, trans. Theodore G. Tappert (Philadelphia: Fortress, 1989), 58.

26. Robert G. Clouse, Richard V. Pierard, and Edwin M. Yamauchi, *The Story of the Church* (Chicago: Moody, 2002), 212.

Spener viewed reading, meditating on, and discussing the Scriptures as the chief means for church reform.[27] His concept of *ecclesiolae in ecclesia*, meaning "a little church within the church," promoted the regular use of conventicles.[28] While he valued the practice of the Anabaptists' use of conventicles to read and study the Scriptures, he and other Lutheran Pietists did not advocate separation from the territorial churches. Rather, they hoped for Pietist conventicles to reform their Lutheran parish congregations from within.

In 1686, Spener received a call to Dresden to serve as the chief court preacher of Saxony. He assumed this role with optimism but soon met criticism from those who opposed his Pietist message and practices. Tensions ended in 1690, when he accepted the invitation to Berlin to work as provost and counselor to the consistory, a role for the diocese. Nonetheless, he met critics there also. The faculty at the University of Wittenberg wrote a pamphlet titled *Christian Lutheran Views in Clear, Candid Teachings, According to the Word of God, and the Lutheran Church-Books, Especially the Augsburg Confession, and the Unrighteous Opposing Views of the Works of Dr. Spener.* The pamphlet listed no fewer than 283 errors in Spener's writings.[29] Despite the criticisms, Spener secured an important position for another Lutheran Pietist—namely, August Hermann Francke.

August Hermann Francke

August Hermann Francke (1663–1727) was born in Lübeck, Germany, where he was raised by devout Christian parents.[30] At sixteen, he enrolled at the University of Erfurt but then transferred to Kiel, where Spener's supporter, Christian Kortholt, influenced him greatly. In 1684, Francke entered the University of Leipzig and became associated with a group of Christians who shared the same desire to know the Bible better, and together they formed a campus society for Bible study and its application to daily life.[31]

Before long, Francke became aware of his need for a deeper relationship with Christ. While preparing a lesson on the topic of faith, he experienced conversion, later recalling, "In great fear I knelt before God on Saturday night and called out to the One whom I yet neither knew nor believed, for rescue

27. Spener, *Pia Desideria*, 91.

28. Lindberg, *Pietist Theologians*, 8.

29. Mendell Taylor, *Exploring Evangelism: History, Methods, Theology* (Kansas City, MO: Nazarene Publishing House, 1984), 226.

30. Olson and Collins Winn, *Reclaiming Pietism*, 51–52.

31. Woodbridge and James, *Church History*, 2:262.

from such a miserable state. . . . While I was still on my knees, He [God] suddenly heard me. Then, just as if one were to turn over one's hand, my doubts were all gone. My heart was sealed to the grace of God in Christ Jesus."[32]

Following this experience, Franke's conversion became paradigmatic for others within his Pietist circle. They viewed conversion as a crisis moment or datable event that was preceded by an "agonizing conviction of sin . . . to which one can point for confirmation."[33] From that moment, Francke led others to a similar encounter with the grace of God. With promptings by the Holy Spirit, he sought to glorify Christ by "winning souls in every place and by every means possible."[34]

In 1688, he launched a full-time ministry to university students. Under this work at Leipzig, students were enthusiastic to read the Scriptures, and in so doing, they experienced a spiritual revival that spread to others. As this Pietist awakening gained a large following, opposition came from university administrators, who suspended the meetings. At the same time, a friend who served as a pastor in Erfurt asked Francke to come and assist him there.

Francke traveled to Erfurt, where he carried out an extensive evangelistic ministry in homes. Whenever he was invited to dinner, before they ate, he offered to lead his hosts in a brief Bible study.[35] Despite his work in the parish, Francke soon realized that he preferred ministry with university students.

With Spener's recommendation, Francke became professor of Greek and Oriental languages at the new University of Halle, founded in 1694.[36] While there, he reoriented the theological faculty toward evangelical pietism by establishing conventicles at the university. Similar to Arndt and Spener, he said, "Not everyone who calls himself a Christian is a Christian. For a Christian has his name from the Lord Jesus Christ and means as much as one who belongs to Christ, is his faithful disciple, believes in his name from the heart in unfeigned love, even in affliction, imitates him, and is gifted and anointed to that end with his Spirit through whom he is willingly led and controlled."[37]

32. Paulus Scharpff, *History of Evangelism: Three Hundred Years of Evangelism in Germany, Great Britain, and the United States of America* (Grand Rapids: Eerdmans, 1966), 29.

33. Woodbridge and James, *Church History*, 2:262.

34. Scharpff, *History of Evangelism*, 29.

35. Scharpff, *History of Evangelism*, 30.

36. Woodbridge and James, *Church History*, 2:262.

37. August Hermann Francke, *Verlegung des Wäysen-Hauses* (Halle, 1709), I, cited

As for Francke's philosophy of theological education, his objective was to employ "the science of theology," which he posited could "be understood only by means of a lively faith" and in "connection with other means of grace to awaken and advance the Christian life."[38] Moreover, he sought "to establish [students] in the faith and to increase their ability to lead their congregations to Jesus Christ."[39] To accomplish these educational goals, Francke not only taught theology in the classroom but lived it before his students by inviting them to join him in his various ministries in Halle.

They began in the neighborhood of Glaucha, known for its deplorable conditions and economic blight.[40] This part of Halle contained a row of "degrading beer huts and dance houses" that people frequented for entertainment. Francke considered Glaucha to be a "den of iniquity" but also a mission field in which to test the transforming power of the gospel.[41] In this neighborhood, he and his students preached the gospel and engaged in discussions in the street and in homes, generally on Saturday nights and Sunday afternoons. His approach was never to preach a message without including the gospel of repentance and forgiveness so that if any hearer heard him once, she could receive salvation. The discussions were based on passages of the Bible or sections of Arndt's *True Christianity*.[42] For a time, Francke distributed bread to the poor every Thursday and invited those who received it to join him for a fifteen-minute gospel message.

Francke and his students met with those who converted to Christ, catechizing them "from house to house," and organizing prayer meetings in homes.[43] Eventually he and his band of student-disciples established a home for Christian single women. Francke purchased a building for the home that had been used previously as a tavern. All of these ministry experiences were spiritually formative, not merely for the newly converted, but for Francke's theology students who put their theology into practice, a demonstration of living faith.

---

in Gary R. Sattler, *God's Glory, Neighbor's Good: A Brief Introduction to the Life and Writings of August Hermann Francke* (Chicago: Covenant, 1982), 243.

38. A. Tholuck, *August Hermann Francke* (New York: Barton, n.d.), 464, cited in M. Taylor, *Exploring Evangelism*, 230.

39. Tholuck, *August Hermann Francke*, 464, cited in M. Taylor, *Exploring Evangelism*, 230.

40. Sattler, *God's Glory, Neighbor's Good*, 38.

41. M. Taylor, *Exploring Evangelism*, 231.

42. Scharpff, *History of Evangelism*, 30.

43. M. Taylor, *Exploring Evangelism*, 231.

Francke's experience in the slums of Halle made him aware of the need to provide education to neglected children who did not have opportunities to attend school. After he solicited funds, he started a "citizen's school" for children gathered from the streets. He purchased school supplies and initially used his own study for the classroom.[44] When he discovered that children came from homes that undermined much of what he taught, he began a ministry that furnished living quarters for the students in addition to their education.

In 1693, he purchased a house large enough for twelve students to live in. He added another house the following year. In 1698, he launched out by faith and built a larger facility called the Orphan House, and a year later, he formed the Orphan Latin School to prepare students for advanced studies.[45] In 1709, he established a school for sons of nobility and added a catechetical school associated with the university. His theological students worked with children of the Orphan House, allowing them again the chance to practice newly acquired pastoral skills in the catechizing of children. He also developed a program to train area ministers who lacked proficiency in Greek and Hebrew.

Beginning in 1717, despite his other responsibilities, Francke launched an evangelism tour for seven months, holding meetings in cities in central and southern Germany. He preached in churches and homes, and visited numerous public institutions, schools, and orphanages.[46] Records indicate that by 1727 there were 400 students in the Latin School, 1,724 students in the citizens' schools for boys and girls, and 132 residents in the Orphan House. The home for single women in Glaucha had eight residents, and a home that he purchased for widows had six.[47]

In regard to publishing and distributing books, Francke established the Orphan House Book Establishment, which printed and distributed inexpensive Bibles. Editions of the Scriptures were not limited to German. Testaments and Bibles were printed in Bohemian, Estonian, and Polish.[48]

Despite his work, Francke and his conventicles were criticized for their biblical revivalism and social activism. Even though he was dismissed by the established Lutheran Church for his pietistic views, he received favor with

44. M. Taylor, *Exploring Evangelism*, 231.

45. Sattler, *God's Glory, Neighbor's Good*, 59–62.

46. Scharpff, *History of Evangelism*, 30–31.

47. Tholuck, *August Hermann Francke*, 467–68, cited in M. Taylor, *Exploring Evangelism*, 232.

48. Sattler, *God's Glory, Neighbor's Good*, 84–89.

King Frederick William I of Prussia, who initiated legislation for similar educational and charitable institutions in his realm.

Pietist Missions

The Pietist impulse that combined conversion to faith with love of neighbor soon spilled over in eagerness to proclaim the gospel to other peoples.[49] Earlier, the Protestant Reformation of Luther, Zwingli, and Calvin was busy with recovering the gospel of salvation by grace through faith and with other church reforms within the Holy Roman Empire. Any cross-cultural missionary efforts were curtailed when Luther, in particular, advocated the dissolution of monasteries and promoted the marriage of monks and nuns. The unintended consequence of this was effectively to eliminate from the ranks of evangelicals what up until this time had been the major force of evangelism to other peoples.

Ziegenbalg and Plütschau

Therefore, a step in the direction of overseas mission by Protestants, since the time when Geneva sent missionaries to Rio de Janeiro, was taken by Frederick IV of Denmark when he appealed to Francke to send two missionaries to India. The Danish crown would provide the necessary funding and Halle would provide the personnel.

Two students from Halle, Bartholomew Ziegenbalg and Heinrich Plütschau, volunteered.[50] They set sail and arrived at the Trancquebar Colony in India in 1706.[51] The two students went despite criticisms by some of their Lutheran professors who held that "the church had already been planted everywhere; that the office of apostle had vanished; that God's grace no longer worked as powerfully as it did in the beginning; that those who were still pagans were under a curse; [and] that God, if he wished to convert them, would do so without human effort."[52]

49. Bosch, *Transforming Mission*, 252.

50. Dana L. Robert, *Christian Mission: How Christianity Became a World Religion* (Malden, MA: Wiley-Blackwell, 2009), 42; Sattler, *God's Glory, Neighbor's Good*, 78.

51. Richard V. Pierard, "German Pietism as a Major Factor in the Beginning of Modern Protestant Missions," in *The Pietist Impulse in Christianity*, ed. Christian T. Collins Winn et al. (Eugene, OR: Pickwick, 2011), 287–88.

52. Bosch, *Transforming Mission*, 253.

In the work at Trancquebar, which became known as the Danish-Halle Mission, Francke's influence was evident. Before the arrival of Ziegenbalg and Plütschau, schools were open to Brahmins only, the highest Hindu caste, and then for boys only. However, the two Halle missionaries founded schools for other castes and for girls.[53]

Francke's impact was felt in England too. The archbishop of Canterbury accepted two students from Halle to establish a Halle-type school in London. Moreover, several English students traveled to Halle for study. Published reports of Ziegenbalg and Plütschau soon caught the attention of Protestants across Europe.[54] Francke's influence stretched across Germany to Poland and the Balkans, to Bohemia and Moravia, to Austria and Hungary, and to Finland and Sweden.

Pietism in Sweden

During the last years of Charles XI's reign, pietism entered Sweden through the writings of Arndt, Spener, and Francke. After reading these works, some Swedish clergy sought to incorporate pietism into church life.[55] In 1693, Swedish students traveled to study at the University of Halle two years after Francke's arrival there, and returned to Sweden with his form of pietism along with books on the subject.[56]

Halle's pietism came to Sweden also when prisoners of war, who had been held captive during the Great Northern War between Sweden's Charles XII and Russia's Peter the Great, returned to Sweden beginning in 1722.[57] The soldiers had been held in internment camps in Siberia, where they came under pietistic influences from German prisoners of war as well as pietistic literature sent to them at Franke's initiative.

In Sweden, the Charles XII Bible, a revised version of the Vasa Bible, was published in 1703. During this time, a royal ordinance provided for the general instruction of children to read and learn Luther's catechism.[58]

53. Bosch, *Transforming Mission*, 254.

54. Scharpff, *History of Evangelism*, 31.

55. Hope, *German and Scandinavian Protestantism*, 373, 377, 472.

56. F. Ernest Stoeffler, *German Pietism during the Eighteenth Century* (Leiden: Brill, 1973), 7.

57. Woodbridge and James, *Church History*, 2:467.

58. Sune Fahlgren, "När slutade läsarna att läsa? Historiska och ecklesiologiska perspektiv på bibebruk," in *Läsarna i distraktionernas tid: Bibel, kyrka and den digitala revolutionen*, ed. Joel Halldorf (Stockholm: Samfundet Pro fide et Christianismo, 2014), 129.

It was determined that every child should be able to read the Bible, catechism, hymnbook, and *postilla*, a collection of Lutheran sermons.[59] The parish priest was responsible to examine every Swedish household, testing the competency of each family member according to Luther's catechism.

Reader Movement and Conventicles

The Charles XII Bible was the first common Bible in the Swedish language and important to the emerging "reader movement."[60] People soon gathered in homes to read the Bible, writings of Luther and Arndt, and other devotional literature.[61] As Pietism grew in popularity, some clergy sought to suppress the movement, claiming the principle of the territorial church. Therefore, in 1726, the Conventicle Law (*Konventikelplakatet*) was enacted to prohibit all unauthorized conventicles or use of a home for purposes other than normal domestic use.[62] The law extended to all religious meetings that were without a Lutheran clergyman present. Only worship services at the state church and family devotions in homes were permitted.

Among the cases that prompted the Conventicle Law was the Sicklagård conventicle in 1723. Lieutenant colonel P. Cedarparre explained that he, along with several friends, went to Nacka, near Stockholm, to visit the parish church. Afterward his friends came to a house at Sicklagård to stay overnight. Cedarparre recalled,

> When we arrived there, the lady of the house departed, leaving the cottage to us. The dinner was prepared and we ate. During the meal, we recalled what we had heard during the high mass at the church and the evening songs. Then we listened to a sermon [at the cottage] and began to praise God by singing the following hymns from the Swedish Hymnbook (*Svenska Psalmboken*): numbers 86, 87, 92, 95, 107, 108, 111, 140, and others, as I can sufficiently remember. And then we sang one or two numbers from the *Songs of Moses and the Lamb* (*Mose och Lamb-*

59. Fahlgren, "När slutade läsarna att läsa?," 129.

60. Fahlgren, "När slutade läsarna att läsa?," 126.

61. Oloph Bexell, "Kyrkligheter i Svenska kyrkan. Behandlar den kristna fromhetens olika uttrycksformer och innebörden av beteckningar som högkyrklighet, lågkyrklighet, ungkyrklighet, folkkyrka, frikyrka," in *Kyrkans liv: Introduktion till kyrkovetenskapen*, ed. Stephan Borgehammar (Stockholm: Verbum, 1988), 125.

62. Kjell O. Lejon, *Diocesis Lincopensis: Historik över Linköpings stift* (Skellefteå, Sweden: Norma, 2005), 372.

sens Wisor) at the request of a student named Hasselquist. After this, everyone joined in singing "God's Promise and Praise," worshiping so powerfully that by the grace of the Almighty we were awakened with a deep joy. Then we sang number 191 from the Swedish Hymnbook that "God alone is worthy." I must confess that we were not used to singing until 1:00 a.m.[63]

Figure 7.1. **Pietist conventicle, *Fanatikerne*, by Adolph Tidemand, 1866, National Museum, Oslo.** *(Photo: Hans Thorwid, National Museum, Stockholm)*

The devotion of the Pietists who continued to meet in conventicles stood in contrast to the formality of the parish churches. In some cases, parish clergy felt threatened by such conventicles, which appeared to circumvent their priestly role, triggering political developments that led to the Conventicle Law.[64] When Pietists were discovered for violating the law, they were punished by fines, imprisonment, or banishment. Although the edict did not prevent all religious meetings outside the state church, it discouraged

63. Erland Sundström, "De gick på möten," in *På stugmötenas tid: Till 100-årsminnet av konventikëlplakatëts upphävande 1858*, ed. Hilding Pleijel (Stockholm: Fosterlands-Stiftelsen, 1958), 52.

64. Sundström, "De gick på möten," 53.

them.[65] As the pietistic movement attracted followers, a subsequent Conventicle Act of 1735 made restrictions even more severe.

Herrnhut Pietism

With Moravia and Bohemia under the control of the Roman Catholic Church according to the Peace of Westphalia, the Moravians, followers of Jan Hus, came under intense persecution. Fleeing Moravia, they found refuge to the west, in Saxony, Germany. In 1722, they were welcomed by Count Nikolaus von Zinzendorf and built a community known as Herrnhut on his German estate.

Nikolaus von Zinzendorf

Zinzendorf (1700–1760) was born in Dresden, Germany, the son of a cabinet minister. The family knew Spener, who had served as a sponsor at Zinzendorf's infant baptism.[66] When Zinzendorf was ten years old, he began studies at Francke's school in Halle. While a student there, he and his classmates enjoyed eating meals with their beloved professor.[67]

Soon after Zinzendorf arrived at the school, he participated in his first communion service. He later testified of his conversion to faith, saying, "As the time came for me to go to communion, I experienced an unusual stirring in my soul and promised my Saviour to be eternally true and to follow him. . . . Twenty years later it is as fresh to me as if it had happened today. I have not lost which I found there then."[68]

While at Halle, Zinzendorf experienced the Pietist impulse of small gatherings for prayer and testimony—the *ecclesiola in ecclesiae*. Moreover, in 1715, he was impressed by the words of Ziegenbalg when he returned to Halle from India and spoke about the Christian's responsibility to take the gospel to the world. Ziegenbalg had even brought with him recently baptized Malays from Malabar. These visitors prompted Zinzendorf and his friends, George von Sohlethal, Anton von Sallbaum, and Frederick von Watteville, to

65. David M. Gustafson, "Swedish Pietism and American Revivalism: Kindred Spirits in the Evangelical Free Tradition," in Collins Winn et al., *Pietist Impulse in Christianity*, 200.

66. Woodbridge and James, *Church History*, 2:458.

67. M. Taylor, *Exploring Evangelism*, 238.

68. M. Taylor, *Exploring Evangelism*, 238.

form a "Compact for the Conversion of Pagans," in which they promised to take the gospel to those who had never heard it.[69] Reflecting on his years at Halle, Zinzendorf wrote, "The daily meetings in professor Francke's house, the edifying accounts concerning the kingdom of Christ, the conversation with witnesses of the truth in distant regions, the acquaintances with several missionaries, . . . the cheerfulness of that man of God in the work of the Lord, together with the various heavy trials attending it, increased my zeal for the cause of the Lord in a powerful manner, and laid the foundation of the knowledge of such things as tend either to the furtherance or hindrance of true Christianity."[70]

In 1716, Zinzendorf took up legal studies at the University of Wittenberg, after which he became a court lawyer and legal counselor at Dresden. Following Zinzendorf's marriage in 1722 to Countess Erdmuthe Dorothea von Reuss, he relocated to the German estate in Saxony where he welcomed the Moravian refugees.[71] After five years of service to the state, he devoted himself fully to the leadership of the Herrnhut community.

Leonhard Dober

Zinzendorf encouraged the Moravians at Herrnhut to maintain the discipline of the Unitas Fratrum, leading them in 1727 to establish a new society by the same name. This happened shortly after a communion service during the "Moravian Pentecost," when "a powerful work of the Holy Spirit surged through the congregation."[72] Zinzendorf then cast the vision to take the gospel to the peoples of the world. The first missionary, Leonhard Dober, responded to God's call after hearing Zinzendorf tell of a former slave named Anthony Ulrich from the island of St. Thomas, a Danish sugar colony in the West Indies.[73] Then Ulrich visited Herrnhut personally and explained that the slaves on St. Thomas were worked so severely that "unless those who went to preach to them would consent to become slaves themselves, and la-

69. M. Taylor, *Exploring Evangelism*, 239.

70. John R. Weinlick, *Count Zinzendorf* (Nashville: Abingdon, 1956), 29, cited in M. Taylor, *Exploring Evangelism*, 239.

71. Douglas H. Shantz, *An Introduction to German Pietism: Protestant Renewal at the Dawn of Modern Europe* (Baltimore: Johns Hopkins University Press, 2013), 256.

72. Woodbridge and James, *Church History*, 2:458.

73. Jon N. Hinkson, "Missions among Puritans and Pietists," in *The Great Commission: Evangelicals and the History of World Missions*, ed. Martin I. Klauber and Scott M. Manetsch (Nashville: B&H Academic, 2008), 39.

bour with the negroes in the plantations, they would have little opportunity of communicating divine instruction to them."[74]

In response to Ulrich's words, Dober and Christian David sailed to the island of St. Thomas in 1732.[75] After David departed, Dober lived among the slaves, shared the gospel with them, provided medical treatment to those who suffered malaria, and received care from them when he himself was stricken by the disease. The "first fruit" of the mission was an orphan boy named Obie, whom Dober adopted when he returned to Herrnhut.

Anna Nitschmann

Among the leaders at Herrnhut was Anna Nitschmann (1715–1760), who was only fourteen years old when elected to become chief eldress of the community.[76] Years earlier, her father and brother had been among those jailed in Moravia before fleeing to Herrnhut in 1725.[77] Two years later, Anna was among those deeply affected by the Moravian Pentecost. In response, she dedicated herself to Christian service and started by organizing the young women of Herrnhut to serve God and others. Her work soon caught the attention of the community's leaders, who nominated her chief eldress. In that role, she led eighteen "single sisters" to devote themselves to Christ and mission work around the world, providing a stream of female missionaries in the decades to follow.

In 1736, Nitschmann became part of the "Pilgrim congregation" that carried out evangelism in several countries and in the American colonies, where she helped to found the towns of Bethlehem and Nazareth, Pennsylvania. In addition to American colonists, the Pilgrim congregation ministered to indigenous peoples. Her songwriting led her to produce more than thirty hymns published in the Moravian's German hymnal. She refused offers of marriage twice, but a year after Zinzendorf's wife died, he asked her to

74. Bonnie Barton, *The Bow in the Cloud; or, The Negro's Memorial: A Collection of Original Contributions in Prose and Verse, Illustrative of the Evils of Slavery and Commemorative of Its Abolition in the British Colonies* (London: Jackson and Walford, 1834), 5–6.

75. Shantz, *Introduction to German Pietism*, 238.

76. Fred van Lieburg, *Pietism, Revivalism and Modernity, 1650–1850* (Newcastle, UK: Cambridge Scholars, 2008), 52.

77. A. Kenneth Curtis and Dan Graves, *Great Women in Christian History* (Worcester, PA: Christian History Institute, 2007), 127.

marry him and she accepted.[78] To the early Moravians, Anna Nitschmann was known as *Selige Juengerin*, the "Blessed Female Disciple."[79]

Rebecca Freundlich Protten

Rebecca Freundlich Protten (1718–1780) was born a slave on the Caribbean island of Antigua, the daughter of an African mother and European father.[80] When about six years old, she was kidnapped from Antigua and sold to a plantation owner by the name of Lucas van Beverhout on the island of St. Thomas.[81] She worked for the Beverhout family as a house servant and learned from them—members of the Dutch Reformed Church—the gospel of Jesus Christ and subsequently converted to faith. At twelve years of age, shortly after Lucas van Beverhout's death, the family set her free.[82]

In 1736, when additional Moravian missionaries arrived at St. Thomas, following Dober, Rebecca met Friedrich Martin, who noted in his diary, "I spoke with a mulatto woman who is very accomplished in the teachings of God. Her name is Rebecca."[83] The Moravian missionaries taught her how to read and write, and involved her in evangelism to the slaves. Despite the hostile environment of the slave masters, which included violence toward the slaves and verbal abuse toward the missionaries, Rebecca and the Moravian missionaries walked "daily along rugged roads through the hills in the sultry evenings after the slaves had returned from the fields" in order to converse with them about Jesus.[84] For Rebecca, her evangelistic ministry "took her to the slave quarters deep in the island's plantation heartland, where she proclaimed salvation to the domestic servants, cane boilers, weavers, and cotton pickers whose bodies and spirits were strip-mined every day by slavery."[85] Despite the challenges, she shared the gospel with hundreds of

78. W. R. Ward, *The Protestant Evangelical Awakening* (Cambridge: Cambridge University Press, 1992), 122.

79. Curtis and Graves, *Great Women in Christian History*, 129.

80. Jon F. Sensbach, *Rebecca's Revival: Creating Black Christianity in the Atlantic World* (Cambridge, MA: Harvard University Press, 2005), 30.

81. Sensbach, *Rebecca's Revival*, 31–32.

82. Sensbach, *Rebecca's Revival*, 25–26, 41–45.

83. Malcolm McCall, *Aspects of Modern Church History, 1517–2017: From an African Perspective* (Bloomington, IN: Westbow, 2018), 54. Cf. Sensbach, *Rebecca's Revival*, 45–46, 52–53.

84. Sensbach, *Rebecca's Revival*, 3.

85. Sensbach, *Rebecca's Revival*, 3.

slaves and, along with the Moravian missionaries, saw hundreds of slaves convert to faith in Christ.[86]

In addition to evangelism, Rebecca taught at the church "at the end of a rugged road through the hills of St. Thomas known to the enslaved as 'The Path.'"[87] In 1738, she and the Moravian missionary Matthäus Freundlich were united in marriage.[88] A few weeks later, Rebecca was named a deaconess of the Moravian community.

In 1742, Rebecca and Matthäus set sail for Germany with their daughter, Anna Maria, because of her husband's failing health. Sadly, he died just after arriving in Germany. Rebecca remained at Herrnhut, where two years later her daughter also died. Despite the grief, Rebecca became a respected member of the community and assumed leadership in the women's ministry.

In 1746, she married Christian Protten, similarly noted for his heritage of an African mother and European father.[89] Eventually, Rebecca and Christian moved to Christiansborg on Africa's Gold Coast in modern-day Ghana and, with the blessing of the Moravian community, taught African children at the Christiansborg Castle School. The children not only learned how to read and write but also learned the gospel of Jesus Christ.[90]

Moravian Mission Advance

During the early decades of the Moravian mission, nearly 225 missionaries from Herrnhut entered twenty-eight territories.[91] In addition to St. Thomas and Pennsylvania, the Herrnhut community sent female and male missionaries to Africa, Russia, Algeria, Greenland, the Georgia Colony, Demark, Norway, and Sweden. Many of the people to whom they ministered in turn sent missionaries to other parts of the world. For example, a Moravian congregation in England sent two hundred missionaries during this same time.

In 1736, Zinzendorf traveled to supervise the new societies built on the model at Herrnhut. He journeyed to Switzerland, Holland, England, West Indies, America, Russia, and Sweden. He advised the missionaries, "You

86. Woodbridge and James, *Church History*, 2:459.

87. David Hempton, *The Church in the Long Eighteenth Century* (New York: Tauris, 2011), 85.

88. Sensbach, *Rebecca's Revival*, 102–5.

89. Sensbach, *Rebecca's Revival*, 162.

90. Sensbach, *Rebecca's Revival*, 217–18.

91. Bosch, *Transforming Mission*, 255.

must live among the people as one of them. Earn your keep, for you are there to serve. Do not expect to convert masses of people all at once. Remember, the Lord already knows those whose hearts He has prepared to believe."[92] Like Leonhard Dober, Anna Nitschmann, and Rebecca Protten, the Moravian missionaries identified with the people to whom they were sent, and proclaimed the gospel in word and deed.[93]

The Moravians did not follow the pattern of other Protestant missionaries tied to colonial projects. Generally the colony-sponsored missionaries served primarily the spiritual needs of colonists and secondarily ministered to native peoples as time and resources allowed. In contrast, the Herrnhut community sent missionaries to work primarily with native peoples without provincial motives.[94] Zinzendorf advocated that the missionaries gather new believers into "pilgrim houses" and not form a territorial or national church.[95] In some instances, when the missionaries entered regions with authorized state churches, they sought simply to establish Moravian conventicles.

Moravian Missionaries in Sweden

The Swedish nobleman Carl Henrik Grundelstierna was associated with Zinzendorf and the Moravian Brethren at Herrnhut from the time when Unitas Fratrum was chartered. From the beginning, the society directed missionary attention to Sweden. In 1729, Grundelstierna returned to Sweden to prepare the soil.[96]

In most cases, missionaries needed legal permission to enter the country. In 1735, Zinzendorf visited Sweden and his reputation had preceded him.[97] When the Swedish government suspected him of weakening the national church, he was ordered to be deported. However, he had already left the country before the news reached him. He replied later in several letters to government officials that he had no intention of creating divisions but wanted only to encourage Christians in prayer and mission.

92. Gustafson, *Gospel Witness*, 89.

93. Bosch, *Transforming Mission*, 255.

94. Bosch, *Transforming Mission*, 253–54.

95. Douglas A. Sweeney, introduction to Klauber and Manetsch, *Great Commission*, 4.

96. Hilding Pleijel, *Svenska kyrkans historia*, vol. 5, *Karolinsk kyrkofromhet, pietism och herrnhutism, 1680–1772* (Stockholm: Svenska Kyrkan, 1935), 377.

97. Earle E. Cairns, *Endless Line of Splendor: Revivals and Their Leaders from the Great Awakening to the Present* (Eugene, OR: Wipf & Stock, 2015), 38.

Despite any concerns from Swedish authorities, Moravian-trained workers set out to minister in Sweden.[98] These included Swedish clergymen Arvid Gradin and Thore Odhelius.[99] Arvid Gradin (1704–1757), the son of a Swedish priest from Dalarna, became an associate professor at Uppsala University in 1736. Two years later he moved to Germany, where he joined the Unitas Fratrum and was ordained by them. Five years later he returned to Sweden, accompanied by Martin Dober, brother of Leonhard Dober, in order to visit with the Church of Sweden's archbishop, Johannes Steuchius. The Moravian churchmen explained that they did not intend to create divisions but wanted to work within the Lutheran Church of Sweden.[100] After discussions and presenting writings to the archbishop about the Unitas Fratrum, they were permitted to begin work. They were considered Lutheran because they held to the Augsburg Confession and promoted unity among Lutheran brethren.

The Swedish priest Thore Odhelius (1705–1777) had visited Reval, present-day Tallinn in Estonia, where he met the Moravian leader Christian David.[101] Odhelius was so impressed by him that he returned to Sweden as a leading proponent of Herrnhut pietism. Odhelius cooperated with Otto Reinhold Strömfelt, a baron in Stockholm, to found a Moravian church. In fact, the whole Strömfelt family played a role in providing refuge and employment to Moravian missionaries who entered Sweden. Hedvig Strömfelt, a daughter of the baron, was also a hymn writer who composed several songs for the Moravian songbooks, *Songs of Zion* (*Sions Sånger*) and *New Songs of Zion* (*Sions Nya Sånger*).[102] She and her sisters carried out evangelistic ministries to Stockholm's upper class.

Moravian missionaries led meetings also in the provinces of Västergötland, Skåne, and Norrland.[103] Since the Conventicle Law of Sweden was not always enforced, Moravian missionaries gathered people into conventicles

98. Gustafson, "Swedish Pietism and American Revivalism," 200. Zinzendorf expressed his views in sermons, hymns, and correspondence, emphasizing "heart religion" over rational precision. Peter Vogt, "Nicholas Ludwig von Zinzendorf (1700–1760)," in Lindberg, *Pietist Theologians*, 210, 213.

99. H. Wilbert Norton, *European Background and History of Evangelical Free Church Foreign Missions, 1887–1955* (Moline, IL: Christian Service Foundation, 1964), 26.

100. Bainton, *Christianity*, 332.

101. Van Lieburg, *Pietism, Revivalism and Modernity*, 195.

102. Van Lieburg, *Pietism, Revivalism and Modernity*, 203.

103. Frederick Hale, *Trans-Atlantic Conservative Protestantism in the Evangelical Free and Mission Covenant Traditions* (New York: Arno, 1979), 16.

and were even allowed to have devotional rooms and worship services.[104] They spread the gospel through tracts as well as conventicle meetings that included spontaneous prayer, testimonies, and laypeople preaching the gospel.

The reader movement in Sweden soon became a folk revival.[105] By 1761, the term "readers" was used in a religious sense for those who gathered in Pietist conventicles of the Herrnhut movement.[106] In the province of Småland, Maria Pettersdotter reported events of a conventicle meeting:

> In the village, during my childhood, there were a couple of God-fearing men who were spiritual leaders. One was named Måns of Ringsborg in Tolg parish, and the other was Jonas of Skogen in Örs parish. These men held spiritual gatherings in their homes. Many such meetings were held in my home too. Måns of Ringsborg had the custom of sitting at a table in the cottage. The rest of the participants at the meeting sat on blocks of wood and rough-sawn boards. Måns always read a section from the Bible and then explained the passage in his own words for those who were present. But above all, those who gathered sang several songs. Jonas of Vasebro accompanied the songs with his violin but the accordion was also used to lead the singing.[107]

Pettersdotter explained that the parish priests did not attend the house meetings because they did not know about them. The laypeople who came also attended the worship services of the parish church. The home meetings with the "Bible expositions" were directed to those present, and the exhortation that followed encouraged the reading of the Scriptures. As many as thirty to forty people, including children, attended the meetings.

In northern Sweden, conventicles were conducted by laypeople who read from Luther's *postilla*. In one case, people from Westerbotten, along with their children, walked several miles to hear the reading of one of Luther's sermons.[108] In 1810, a young farmer named Olof Palmgren began meetings at Svartbyn in Norrbotten that used Luther's *postilla*. A participant reported,

104. Gunnar Westin, *De frikyrkliga samfundet i Sverige: Historia och trosåskådning i kortfattad översikt* (Stockholm: Svenska Missionsförbundet, 1934), 16.

105. Fahlgren, "När slutade läsarna att läsa?," 123.

106. Anders Jarlert, *Sveriges kyrkohistoria*, vol. 6, *Romantikens och liberalismens tid* (Stockholm: Verbum and Svenska Kyrkans Forskningsråd, 2001), 73.

107. Sundström, "De gick på möten," 55.

108. P. P. Waldenström, "The Independent Movement and the Swedish Church," in

"[After Olof Palmgren] read from Dr. Luther's *postilla*, he urged the people to comment on what was read, and [then he] explained the words and their meaning, which was slightly broader, and for some people difficult to understand. This reading and message brought great blessing, fruit and benefit, and led to a change of minds and lives of many of these boastful and wicked people who had been living in their scandalous vices and wicked ways."[109]

As Moravian missionaries knew from experience, conventicles contributed to both the evangelization of nonbelievers and the edification of believers. The readings at meetings led spontaneously to explanation. The discussion was directed outward as an appeal to conversion and became a way of leading seekers to experience God's saving grace.[110]

The parish Lutheran church was tied, at least indirectly, to conventicles. On one hand, the Lutheran parish churches provided doctrinal instruction and evangelical liturgy that reinforced Lutheran orthodoxy, counteracting excessive exaggerations and enthusiasm. On the other hand, the Pietist impulse of conventicles provided more fervent fellowship and participation in discussion of the gospel and Christian witness.

In some parts of the country, civil and ecclesial authorities used their legal powers against conventicle lawbreakers. In such cases, legal action by authorities added to the sometimes bitter conflict between the awakened Pietists and Lutheran clergy. In 1845, a peasant in Dalecarlia was fined for reading the Lord's Prayer and a sermon from Luther's *postilla* in his home while non-family members were present.[111] Because the meeting took place on Sunday, he was fined additionally for breach of the Sabbath. When he could not pay the fines, he was subject to jail time at Gävle, where he was given only bread and water.

It became increasingly difficult, however, to squash the Pietists by coercive methods. On one occasion, a man came to a governmental official and informed him of people gathering for an unauthorized religious meeting at a particular location. The official sent the constable but found the door locked. The constable knocked and demanded in the name of the law to be admitted. During the delay, the Bible-reading Pietists made changes to the appearance

---

M. W. Montgomery, *A Wind from the Holy Spirit in Sweden and Norway* (New York: American Home Missionary Society, 1884), 96.

109. John Holmgren, *Norrlandsläseriet: Studier till dess förhistoria och historia fram till år 1830* (Stockholm: Svenska Kyrkans Diakonistyrelse, 1948), 53.

110. Sundström, "De gick på möten," 54.

111. Waldenström, "Independent Movement," 96.

of the room so that when the constable entered, he did not find any of them occupied with reading the Scriptures. Instead, the table was filled with beer mugs, pipes, and playing cards, which made the constable exclaim with disappointment, "Why, here are no Pietists, but only good Lutherans."[112]

Readers' meetings could sometimes be held without advance notice or preparation.[113] In other instances, they were held on a regular basis. A readers' meeting in Småland met on Thursday evenings at Surahalla near a wire mill where men and their sons came to process metal wire. Among the hymns that they sang were some of those composed by Hedvig Strömfelt.[114] A participant named Malcolm Johansson recalled the meeting. After his introduction of the ten men who participated, along with their sons, he wrote,

> It became cramped in the little house. The young boys climbed up to the rafters in order to make space for the older ones. When we were all gathered and everyone had taken his place, Petter Svensson stood up and instead of a welcome speech, said, "It is funny that so many of us were able to come together. Now let us start by singing the hymn 'Jesus Let Me Pray in Your Name, in All that I Do.'" Johannes Mikaelsson with his high beautiful voice began the song and all the others came in and sang with such enthusiasm that I thought the roof was raised. After this, Petter asked God to bless what was to be read. Then he took out the Scriptures from a wooden case which he made to protect this common treasure. He read a paragraph from a chapter, then handed the book to another man who continued the reading to the end of the chapter. Then one of them thanked God for what he gave everyone through his Word. Then the meeting ended with a song, and all went back to pulling wire until 10 or 11 in the evening, when we finished the work for the day.[115]

The Conventicle Law caused unrest until 1858, when it was repealed. Two years later Sweden granted religious freedom to Christians beyond the authorized services of the Lutheran Church of Sweden.

112. Waldenström, "Independent Movement," 96.
113. Sundström, "De gick på möten," 56.
114. Sundström, "De gick på möten," 57.
115. Sundström, "De gick på möten," 58.

Peter Fjellstedt and C. O. Rosenius

Among the leaders of the evangelical revival between 1840 and the repeal of the Conventicle Law in 1858 were Peter Fjellstedt and C. O. Rosenius.[116] Fjellstedt (1802–1881) was influenced by the Moravians in Sweden but remained within Sweden's state church.[117] He was born in the province of Värmland, trained for Christian ministry at Lund University, and was ordained in 1828. Because the Moravians left a deep impression on him, especially on his desire for global missions, he enrolled in missionary training with the Basel Mission.[118]

In 1832, he sailed to Palayamkottai in Tamil Nadu, India, for his first missionary assignment. After three years, he returned to Sweden because of poor health. He went on another assignment to Turkey and Malta, but left the mission field again in 1840. After these experiences, he returned to his homeland in order to establish the Lund Missionary Society along with others, and later he founded a mission training school, the Fjellstedtska School, in Uppsala. Subsequently, the school sent hundreds of colporteurs to proclaim the gospel in Sweden, as well as missionaries to various part of the world. In 1858, Fjellstedt was awarded an honorary doctorate of theology by the University of Halle in Germany.

Carl Olof Rosenius (1816–1868), son of a pietistic parish pastor, was born in Nysätra in Västerbotten.[119] He converted to faith at the age of fifteen and, through friendly interactions with Herrnhuters, adopted a Lutheran-Herrnhut theology. In 1838, some of his writings were published in a collection titled *Letters on Spiritual Topics from So-called Readers, Particularly among Peasants in Norrland*.[120] These letters emphasized the atonement of Christ's saving work and the necessity of Christians to be separate from the

116. Oloph Bexell, *Sveriges kyrkohistoria*, vol. 7, *Folkväckelsens och kyrkoförnyelsens tid* (Stockholm: Verbum and Svenska kyrkan, 2003), 51.

117. Emmet F. Eklund, *Peter Fjellstedt: Missionary Mentor to Three Continents* (Rock Island, IL: Augustana Historical Society, 1983), 32–34.

118. Eric J. Sharpe, "Peter Fjellstedt," in *Biographical Dictionary of Christian Missions*, ed. Gerald H. Anderson (Grand Rapids: Eerdmans, 1999), 214.

119. Kjell O. Lejon, "Carl Olof Rosenius (1816–68): A Personal Portrait," trans. David M. Gustafson, *Swedish-American Historical Quarterly* 67, no. 3 (July 2016): 121.

120. C. O. Rosenius, *Bref i andeliga ämnen från så kallade läsare, särdeles bland allmogen i Norrland* (Falun, Sweden: Huldberg, 1849).

world. In doctrinal terms, Rosenius's writings reflected Luther's views, while more personal sections reflected themes of the Moravian songbooks.[121]

In 1838, Rosenius began his theological studies at the University of Uppsala but was forced to give up after a year of illness and financial struggles. In Stockholm he joined the English Methodist minister George Scott, traveling throughout the country. Scott and Rosenius promoted reform within the Church of Sweden that emphasized preaching the gospel, conversion, conventicles, and foreign missions. After Scott's death, Rosenius took over as editor of the movement's periodical, *Pietisten* (The Pietist), which further promoted the Pietist revival across Sweden.

Conventicles in Pietist Evangelism

Despite variations in regions in Sweden and different social applications at particular times, the Pietist conventicles were led by laypeople, both male and female.[122] Leadership was based more on the qualification of spiritual maturity than educational preparation. Those present were invited to listen, read, and offer observations, participating freely. In most instances, the songs that were sung spoke of life's struggles and the victory in Jesus.[123] In contrast to the parish church, where the Lutheran priest spoke high-church Swedish, people in conventicles spoke the local dialect.

The Pietists emphasized conversion to faith in Jesus, and conventicles fostered an environment for this to happen. Certainly, conventicles met the needs of believers for edification, but the informal and participatory process of reading the Scriptures and discussing writings such as Arndt's *True Christianity*, which distinguished nominal and true Christians, prompted those present to convert to faith in Christ. The Pietists invited family, neighbors, and coworkers to join the conventicles, despite some at first showing little interest or resisting the idea. In several ways, the conventicles that spread across Scandinavia, Germany, and other parts of Europe captured elements of the early church. As Moravian missionaries had hoped, conventicles fostered living faith and prompted global missionary efforts.[124]

121. Sven Lodin, *C. O. Rosenius: Hans liv och gärning* (Stockholm: Evangeliska fosterlands-stiftelsen, 1956), 55–57, 61.

122. Sundström, "De gick på möten," 50.

123. Sundström, "De gick på möten," 55–56.

124. Sundström, "De gick på möten," 51. The titles of "readers" and "pietists" soon included an additional name for this movement—namely, "Mission Friends," composed of men and women with a desire to carry the gospel to the ends of the earth.

Discussion Questions

1. Johann Arndt advocated orthodoxy (right teaching) and orthopraxy (right practice). Disappointed by nominal Christians, he hoped to awaken them to follow Jesus daily. What ideas do you have to awaken nominal or "false" Christians so that they believe in and follow after Jesus Christ? What ideas from Arndt's *True Christianity* might be helpful?
2. August Hermann Francke integrated theological education in the classroom with practical field experience in Glaucha. Why are both classroom instruction and practical experience important for students to learn and engage in evangelism? What happens when one or the other is missing? Does this apply equally to a local church? Do you need to equip others in evangelism, or do you need training yourself?
3. The advice of Anthony Ulrich to those considering evangelism to the slaves at St. Thomas was that unless they "consent to become slaves themselves, and labour with the negroes in the plantations, they would have little opportunity of communicating divine instruction to them." How does this apply to reaching people in your neighborhood? Unreached peoples across the globe?
4. Anna Nitschmann and Rebecca Freundlich Protten were empowered early in their Christian lives in leadership and evangelism. What qualified them for evangelistic ministry? What qualifies any Christian for evangelistic ministry? How did their work not fit the paradigm of colonial missionaries? How can churches empower women for evangelism and leadership today?
5. Firsthand accounts provide a view into Pietist conventicles of the eighteenth and nineteenth centuries. What stands out to you? What social dynamics made conventicles a conducive environment for the Holy Spirit to bring non-Christians to faith? How can church small groups pursue a more evangelistic edge?

8

Revival Evangelism

Help me, Lord, to remember that religion is not to be confined to the church, or closet, nor exercised only in prayer, but that everywhere I am in thy presence. So may my every word and action have a moral content.

—Susannah Wesley[1]

In England, the Roman Church was the authorized church until political events and a series of parliamentary laws were enacted that formed the "Anglican Church" (*Ecclesia Anglicana*), the Church of England. This action was preceded by thoughts of Reformation circulating in England. After Luther nailed his ninety-five theses to the door of the Castle Church in Wittenberg, Germany, a small group in England, mostly followers of Wycliffe's teachings, embraced the German reformer's writings and promoted them in conversations and literature. Additionally, some people became acquainted with Luther's teachings from their travels to Germany, while others learned of his writings from German merchants working in London.

By 1521, support for Luther took hold at the University of Cambridge, where a student sullied a copy of the edict by the Roman pope that condemned Luther. Already, reform-minded students at Cambridge met weekly at the White Horse Inn. They were led by Robert Barnes, who had studied with Luther at Wittenberg. They gathered to discuss the German reformer's views. At the same time, Luther's writings were being sold at Oxford.[2]

1. William P. McDonald, *Gracious Voices: Shouts and Whispers for God Seekers* (Nashville: Discipleship Resources, 1996), 90.

2. Milton L. Rudnick, *Speaking the Gospel through the Ages: A History of Evangelism* (St. Louis: Concordia, 1984), 89–90.

Growing interest in evangelical reform came also from the distribution of the new English version of the New Testament translated by William Tyndale. He had met Luther at Wittenberg in 1524 and agreed with some of his ideas for reform.[3] Tyndale's unauthorized version of the New Testament was printed on the European continent and smuggled into England. His choice of words in his English translation favored the evangelical point of view.

English Reformation

At this time the crown of England needed a male heir to the throne. In this regard, the Reformation became political, not simply theological. Because marriage was a sacrament of the Roman Church, marriage was subject to ecclesial authority. Moreover, royal marriages were affairs of state, and kings were expected to produce a male successor.

Under these circumstances, King Henry VIII (reigned 1509–1547) compelled the English clergy and Parliament to reject papal authority over England and to declare him head of the Church of England. The pope, Clement VII, had refused to grant Henry VIII and Catherine of Aragon an annulment of their marriage.[4] After several miscarriages, she gave birth to a daughter, Mary Tudor, but had no son. Therefore, Henry determined to marry his secret lover, Anne Boleyn, hoping she would give him a male heir. He thought that if he could not receive an annulment from the pope, he would ask his newly appointed archbishop of Canterbury, Thomas Cranmer, to do so.[5]

Thomas Cranmer (1489–1556) was born in Nottinghamshire, England. He attended Jesus College at the University of Cambridge, where, as a student of theology, he gleaned insights from the Renaissance with its emphasis on studying the Bible in the original languages. Moreover, Cranmer became acquainted with Luther's teachings on justification by faith and rejected papal claims, particularly the claim that the pope had ecclesial jurisdiction over all of Christendom. This view made Cranmer a favorable appointment by Henry.

Henry VIII proceeded to instruct Parliament to enact several laws. In 1533, Parliament passed a law that prohibited making appeals in a foreign

3. John D. Woodbridge and Frank A. James III, *Church History*, vol. 2, *From Pre-Reformation to the Present Day* (Grand Rapids: Zondervan, 2013), 221. Cf. Ralph S. Werrell, *The Roots of William Tyndale's Theology* (Cambridge: James Clarke, 2013), 34.

4. Peter Marshall, "Britain's Reformations," in *The Oxford Illustrated History of the Reformation*, ed. Peter Marshall (New York: Oxford University Press, 2015), 196.

5. Marshall, "Britain's Reformations," 196–97.

court. With this ruling, Cranmer annulled the marriage of Henry to Catherine. In 1534, Parliament passed the Act of Supremacy that declared the king of England to be head of the Church of England and made the church's governance episcopal under the archbishop of Canterbury and not papal with ties to Rome.[6]

In 1536, with the view that all properties of the church should be vested in the state, Henry's minister, Cardinal Thomas Wolsey, took over a number of monasteries for revenue to build colleges and to finance Henry's navy. Over a period of five years, every monastery in England was dissolved, with the state receiving the proceeds.

In 1539, Henry commissioned Bishop Miles Coverdale to produce an authorized English translation of the Bible, which, at many parts, followed the Tyndale version. Despite these royal acts, the Church of England did not become Protestant until after Henry's death. He remained committed to Roman Catholic sacramental theology while making some concessions to those who were sympathetic to Lutheran views.[7]

In an effort to have a son, Henry married four more wives, but only one, Jane Seymour, produced a male heir and the boy was named Edward.[8] He was sickly and showed little promise owing to a chronic illness. By the time Henry married his sixth wife, Catherine Parr, the king suffered from gout and likely would not have more children.

When Henry died, the sickly King Edward VI (reigned 1547–1553) received the crown. Since he was only nine years old, the affairs of state were carried out by a Council of Regency, with his uncle, Edward Seymour, as Protector. Although Edward's reign was short, evangelical leaders made considerable progress and the Protestant Reformation took hold in England.[9]

Puritans

The English Reformation moved first toward Luther's views, then toward those of Zwingli, and finally toward those of Calvin.[10] A significant change was Cranmer's translation of the liturgy into the English language that was published as the *Book of Common Prayer*. Added to these printed resources

6. Woodbridge and James, *Church History*, 2:224–25.
7. Rudnick, *Speaking the Gospel*, 89.
8. Woodbridge and James, *Church History*, 2:231–32.
9. Woodbridge and James, *Church History*, 2:232–34.
10. Roland H. Bainton, *Christianity* (Boston: Houghton Mifflin, 2000), 274.

were hundreds of clergy and theologians who came to England from the cities of Strasbourg, Zurich, and Geneva. Both Cranmer's invitation and pressure from Emperor Charles V—prior to the Peace of Augsburg—accelerated the migration of churchmen (such as Martin Bucer mentioned in chapter 6) to England, where they were granted refuge and, in some cases, were appointed to positions in universities.

After Edward's death in 1553, his half-sister, Mary Tudor, daughter of Catherine of Aragon, secured forces and by popular acclaim was crowned Queen Mary. In 1554, she married her cousin, Philip of Spain, son of Emperor Charles V. Because Mary was a staunch Roman Catholic, she purposed to bring England back into conformity with the Roman Catholic Church. During her rule, more than three hundred Protestants were burned at the stake, including Archbishop Cranmer in 1556. Thousands of English Protestants fled to the Reformed cities of Geneva, Zurich, and Strasbourg, where they formed refugee congregations. Some found sanctuary at Geneva, where Calvin directed ministries of the churches.

After the death of Queen Mary, known then as "Bloody Mary," the Marian exiles in Geneva, Zurich, and Strasbourg returned to England. They brought with them Calvin's Protestant views, having learned firsthand from the Reformed churches how to lead a Reformed society. The Marian exiles, of course, were critical of the Church of England and hoped to purge it of all Romanism.[11] Their aim to "purify" the Anglican Church earned them the title "Puritans."

The successor of Mary was Queen Elizabeth, daughter of Anne Boleyn. During Elizabeth's rule, she established a *via media*, or middle way, between Romanism and Calvinism.[12] To Puritans, her middle way was a halfway attempt at reform, which they considered insufficient. In addition to their anti-Romanism, they viewed the Scriptures as the only source of Christian doctrine and practice. Moreover, they promoted several reforms, including that churches adopt presbyterian and congregational forms of governance. In addition, Puritans stressed the importance of personal conversion to faith in Christ and expected all Christians to live devout and disciplined lives. Their hope was that every parish would have a pastor who would faithfully proclaim the Scriptures, administer the sacraments, and discipline immoral church members.

In 1575, when Queen Elizabeth learned of Puritan conventicles, she feared they would stir opposition, and ordered the archbishop to suppress them.[13]

11. Bainton, *Christianity*, 296.
12. Woodbridge and James, *Church History*, 2:238.
13. Woodbridge and James, *Church History*, 2:243–44.

The conventicles were based on those in Switzerland where ministers met weekly to discuss profitable questions. With the queen's act, Puritans came increasingly under pressure. Some decided to form free congregations—separate or free from the state church. For example, John Robinson (1572–1625) led a group of separatists that met at Scrooby Manor in York. They fled to the Netherlands to avoid persecution. In 1620, William Bradford (1589–1657) led a group of separatists to North America onboard the *Mayflower*.[14]

By 1643, when the reins of government in England passed to the Puritan-dominated Long Parliament, more than twenty thousand English migrated by ship to New England. Under leaders such as governor John Winthrop (1588–1649) and pastor John Cotton (1584–1652), the Calvinist stream of the Congregational church was established in North America.[15] In the American context, every colonist was required to make a public declaration of their experience of the work of God's grace.

For a brief period, Puritans in England spearheaded a political revolution. With the abolition of the episcopal system in the Church of England, the Westminster Assembly of Divines convened and, in 1647, adopted the Westminster Confession as a presbyterian statement of faith.[16] Between 1649 and 1659, a commonwealth government replaced the royal monarchy and introduced certain religious freedoms. However, the Puritans were overthrown and forced again to conform to the Church of England. Furthermore, King Charles II set the Acts of Conventicles into motion against all dissenters. This act forced out more than two thousand Puritan clergymen and imprisoned more than eight thousand dissenting Christians.

Puritan Evangelistic Literature

Nevertheless, a number of prominent Puritan theologians and preachers remained and produced substantial writings on the themes of doctrine and Christian living.[17] Richard Baxter (1615–1691) wrote *A Call to the Unconverted* and *The Saints' Everlasting Rest*.[18] John Owen (1616–1683), who served

14. Robert G. Clouse, Richard V. Pierard, and Edwin M. Yamauchi, *The Story of the Church* (Chicago: Moody, 2002), 207.

15. Woodbridge and James, *Church History*, 2:271.

16. Clouse, Pierard, and Yamauchi, *Story of the Church*, 207.

17. Bainton, *Christianity*, 312–14.

18. Paulus Scharpff, *History of Evangelism: Three Hundred Years of Evangelism in Germany, Great Britain, and the United States of America* (Grand Rapids: Eerdmans, 1966), 66.

as an academic administrator at the University of Oxford, wrote *The Divine Power of the Gospel* and *The Death of Death in the Death of Christ*.

John Bunyan (1628–1688), a Baptist, while in the Bedfordshire County prison for violations of the Conventicle Act of 1664, produced *Pilgrim's Progress* and *The Holy War*. His writings were another means for his evangelistic work. In *Pilgrim's Progress*, Bunyan's main character, named Christian, journeys from the City of Destruction to the Celestial City.[19] Along the way, he meets a number of descriptive characters, including Evangelist, who directs the main character toward a "shining light."

John Milton (1608–1674), an English poet and civil servant, is best-known for his epic poems *Paradise Lost* and *Paradise Regained*. The book *Paradise Lost* portrays death as the result of human sin and describes the realities of heaven and hell, the archangel Michael's announcement of the Messiah, the incarnation of God in Christ, and Jesus's resurrection and ascension to heaven.[20]

These Puritan authors captured in their writings the essential elements of Puritan theology, including the element that conversion to faith in Christ is the signal experience that gives meaning to life. Conversion unites faith with action, worship with work, rest with labor, and the love of God with love of neighbor.[21]

English Baptists

In addition to Puritans, other groups appeared in England such as the Baptists. They began as Puritan separatists who fled from England to the Netherlands during the persecution by King James.[22] In the Netherlands, they came into contact with Waterlander Mennonites, followers of the Anabaptist leader Menno Simons (1496–1561). The English separatist leaders John Smyth and Thomas Helwys were soon won over by the Mennonite Anabaptist principles.[23] They rejected infant (paedo) baptism and practiced believer (credo) baptism by immersion. Moreover, they advocated for the separation

19. Alvin J. Schmidt, *How Christianity Changed the World* (Grand Rapids: Zondervan, 2009), 360.

20. Schmidt, *How Christianity Changed the World*, 361.

21. Woodbridge and James, *Church History*, 2:281.

22. Anthony L. Chute, Nathan A. Finn, and Michael A. G. Haykin, *The Baptist Story: From English Sect to Global Movement* (Nashville: B&H Academic, 2015), 17.

23. Bainton, *Christianity*, 299–300.

of church and state, holding to the scriptural belief that Christ's church is a gathering of baptized believers, not tied to any political state or territory.

Since Helwys felt that to remain in the Netherlands would be in conflict with the Bible's command to bear witness before governors and kings (Matt. 10:18), in 1611 he returned to London, where he founded a new congregation based on Anabaptist principles.[24] This community soon adopted the simpler title "Baptist."[25]

In 1688, when William II ascended to the English throne, he instructed Parliament to pass the Act of Toleration, which granted freedom of faith and conscience.[26] This repealed the earlier Acts of Conventicles and allowed religious societies to hold private meetings for the study of the Scriptures.

Moravian-Herrnhut Missionaries in England

In 1735, ten of the Moravian Brethren of Unitas Fratrum from Herrnhut arrived in London under the care of August Spangenberg, who handled immigration details with English officials. Later that year, twenty-six more Moravians passed through London on their way as missionaries to England's Georgia Colony in North America. While in London, the Moravian missionaries came into contact with James Hutton, who was deeply impressed by their devotion to Christ and vision to share the gospel. Hutton's response was to found a new religious society in his home—the Fetter Lane Society.[27] Similar groups were soon established in London, such as the house of Moravian Brethren at Chelsea near the Thames, a Moravian chapel at Moorfields, and a Herrnhut settlement called Fulneck at Yorkshire. Wherever they went, the Moravians organized society meetings and conventicles that nurtured the spiritual life of Christians and led spiritually lost people to faith in Jesus.[28]

The Wesleys

At Epworth, England, the Anglican pastor Samuel Wesley hosted a conventicle meeting at his church. His wife, Susannah Wesley (1669–1742), was an

24. Chute, Finn, and Haykin, *Baptist Story*, 19.

25. Woodbridge and James, *Church History*, 2:401.

26. Bainton, *Christianity*, 314–15.

27. Howard A. Snyder, *The Radical Wesley and Patterns for Church Renewal* (Eugene, OR: Wipf & Stock, 1996), 26–27.

28. Scharpff, *History of Evangelism*, 71.

avid reader of August Hermann Francke's writings and promoted conventicles.[29] Among the nineteen children of Samuel and Susannah, the fifteenth was John and the sixteenth was Charles.[30] In 1709, the Wesleys' home caught fire, and John, who was only six years old, was narrowly rescued, like a "burning stick snatched from the fire" (Zech. 3:2).[31]

John Wesley referred to his mother as a "preacher of righteousness."[32] When Samuel Wesley was away for a winter, Susannah served as the spiritual leader of the home. Their family conventicle included children from the neighborhood and soon expanded when a boy asked if his parents could join. Within weeks, the Wesley conventicle grew from thirty to forty. Susannah said, "With those few neighbours that then came to me, I discoursed more freely and affectionately. I chose the best and most awakening sermons we have. . . . Since this our company increased every night; for I dare deny none that ask admittance. . . . Last Sunday I believe we had above two hundred. And yet many went away, for want of room to stand."[33] Like others, Susannah Wesley was compelled to preach the gospel and set an example for her children to follow.

In 1729, Charles Wesley (1707–1788), then a student at the University of Oxford, began a conventicle called the Holy Club. He began this group to foster holy living among fellow students by reading the Scriptures together, practicing Christian disciplines, and doing works of charity, particularly visiting prisoners. Soon this group was nicknamed "Methodists" because they adopted a method for spiritual life.[34] While Charles formed the group initially, John Wesley (1703–1791) directed it, and another student, George Whitefield, soon joined.[35] This group continued to meet until 1735, when John and Charles left for Georgia Colony in North America.

29. Scharpff, *History of Evangelism*, 65.

30. Bainton, *Christianity*, 337.

31. Woodbridge and James, *Church History*, 2:406.

32. Ruth A. Tucker and Walter Liefeld, *Daughters of the Church: Women and Ministry from New Testament Times to the Present* (Grand Rapids: Zondervan, 1987), 237.

33. John Wesley, *The Works of John Wesley* (Grand Rapids: Zondervan, 1958), 1:385–86, cited in Tucker and Liefeld, *Daughters of the Church*, 237–38.

34. Clouse, Pierard, and Yamauchi, *Story of the Church*, 237. "Later, John defined a 'Methodist' as 'one that lives according to the method laid down in the Bible.'" Woodbridge and James, *Church History*, 2:406.

35. Arnold A. Dallimore, *George Whitefield: God's Anointed Servant in the Great Revival of the Eighteenth Century* (Westchester, IL: Crossway, 2010), 14–15.

Wesleys and Moravian-Herrnhut Missionaries

John and Charles Wesley accepted the invitation from General Oglethorpe to go to Georgia as chaplains, planning to preach to the colonists as well as to American Indians. When they boarded the ship, they met the Moravian missionaries that had passed through London. During the three-month journey by sea, the Wesleys were impressed by the faith and humility of the Herrnhuters. On one occasion, a terrible storm caused nearly everyone aboard the ship to fear for their lives. Nonetheless, in the midst of the storm, the Moravians sang and praised God with no apparent fear of harm or death.

When the ship landed, the Moravian leader, August Spangenberg, asked John, "Do you know Jesus Christ?"[36] Wesley was taken aback and answered, "I know He is the Saviour of the world." Spangenberg replied, "True, but do you know that he has saved you?" Wesley responded, "I hope he has died to save me." Later, Wesley said that he feared the words he spoke were "vain words."[37]

While in Georgia, John Wesley was dismayed to find the American Indians "less noble" than he had imagined. Moreover, he had hoped to court a young woman who rejected his interest in a relationship and chose another man. As for Charles Wesley, he did not get along with the governor, General Oglethorpe. Disappointed and disillusioned, the Wesley brothers returned to England in 1737.

In the meantime, George Whitefield had begun to see large crowds of people attend his evangelistic meetings. His topics were the "new birth" and "justification by faith."[38] His messages piqued the interest of the English as he addressed their spiritual malaise and presented the gospel of Jesus Christ.

In London, Charles Wesley met with the Moravian missionary Peter Böhler (1712–1775). Charles had agreed to teach Böhler the English language, and Böhler hoped to teach Charles and John the message of salvation by grace. On one occasion, John accompanied Böhler to Oxford, where they discussed the topic of saving faith. Earlier, John Wesley had written in his journal, "I who went to America to convert others was never myself converted to God."[39]

36. Kenneth J. Collins, *John Wesley: A Theological Journey* (Nashville: Abingdon, 2003), 63.

37. Collins, *John Wesley*, 63.

38. Scharpff, *History of Evangelism*, 65.

39. J. E. Hutton, *History of the Moravian Church* (Whitefish, MT: Kessinger, 2004), 200.

Böhler's teaching about God's grace was instrumental to the Wesley brothers' conversion to personal faith in Christ. After three months, Böhler urged them to embrace the gospel.[40] Charles made a profession of saving faith on May 21, 1738. Two days later he wrote a hymn about his conversion. The next day, at a Moravian meeting on Aldersgate Street in London, John expressed his personal faith in Christ. When John said that he accepted Christ, the two brothers sang Charles's newly composed "conversion hymn."[41]

John Wesley's Journal, May 24, 1738

In the evening I went very unwillingly to a [Moravian] society in Aldersgate Street, where one was reading Luther's preface to the Epistle to the Romans. About a quarter before nine, while he was describing the change which God works in the heart through faith in Christ, I felt my heart strangely warmed. I felt I did trust in Christ, Christ alone, for salvation; and an assurance was given me that He had taken away my sins, even mine, and saved me from the law of sin and death.

I began to pray with all my might for those who had in a more especial manner despitefully used me and persecuted me. I then testified openly to all there what I now first felt in my heart. But it was not long before the enemy suggested, "This cannot be faith; for where is thy joy?" Then was I taught that peace and victory over sin are essential to faith in the Captain of our salvation; but that, as to the transports of joy that usually attend the beginning of it, especially in those who have mourned deeply, God sometimes giveth, sometimes withholdeth, them according to the counsels of His own will.

After my return home, I was much buffeted with temptations, but I cried out, and they fled away. They returned again and again. I as often lifted up my eyes, and He "sent me help from his holy place." And herein I found the difference between this and my former state chiefly consisted. I was striving, yea, fighting with all my might under the law, as well as under grace. But then I was sometimes, if not often, conquered; now, I was always conqueror.

Thursday, 25.—The moment I awakened, "Jesus, Master," was in my heart and in my mouth; and I found all my strength lay in keeping my eye fixed upon Him and my soul waiting on Him continually. Being again at St. Paul's in the afternoon, I could taste the good word of God in the anthem

40. Mendell Taylor, *Exploring Evangelism: History, Methods, Theology* (Kansas City, MO: Nazarene Publishing House, 1984), 251.

41. James Townsend, "The Forgotten Wesley," *Christian History* 10, no. 3 (1991): 6.

which began, "My song shall be always of the loving-kindness of the Lord: with my mouth will I ever be showing forth thy truth from one generation to another." Yet the enemy injected a fear, "If thou dost believe, why is there not a more sensible change? I answered (yet not I), "That I know not. But, this I know, I have 'now peace with God.' And I sin not today, and Jesus my Master has forbidden me to take thought for the morrow."

Wednesday, June 7.—I determined, if God should permit, to retire for a short time into Germany. I had fully proposed, before I left Georgia, so to do if it should please God to bring me back to Europe. And I now clearly saw the time was come. My weak mind could not bear to be thus sawn asunder. And I hoped the conversing with those holy men who were themselves living witnesses of the full power of faith, and yet able to bear with those that are weak, would be a means, under God, of so establishing my soul that I might go on from faith to faith, and from "strength to strength." (John Wesley, *The Journal of John Wesley*, ed. Percy Livingstone Parker [Chicago: Moody, 1951], 64–65)

Newly converted, John and Charles Wesley were prepared to launch a new ministry. While John had earned the master's degree at Oxford and lectured in Greek, in 1738 he traveled to Germany where he was joined by others, such as Arvid Gradin of Sweden, to learn from Zinzendorf at Herrnhut.[42]

After visiting Herrnhut, Wesley returned to Britain to reach his countrymen with the gospel. He began preaching in churches but soon agitated nominal Christians. In response to their spiritual condition, he exclaimed, "Oh, who will convert the English into honest heathens!"[43] John, like other evangelicals, saw himself as recovering a core doctrine of the gospel, justification by faith alone, a doctrine that had been neglected by clergy of the Church of England.[44] Wesley and others began to stress conversion to Christ, the authority of the Bible, and living out the gospel in works of mercy, which included doing good, visiting the sick and prisoners, feeding and clothing people, and earning, saving, and giving all one can.[45]

42. Snyder, *Radical Wesley*, 29; Tuttle, *Story of Evangelism*, 285.

43. *The Journal of the Reverend John Wesley* (New York: Mason and Lane, 1837), 1:546.

44. Woodbridge and James, *Church History*, 2:403.

45. Kenneth J. Collins, *The Theology of John Wesley: Holy Love and the Shape of Grace* (Nashville: Abingdon, 2007), 267–68.

Wesley's preaching eventually led the Church of England to ban him from the Anglican pulpits. Despite this measure, when he visited his home parish, he stood on his father's gravestone and preached to the crowd that had gathered there to hear him.

England's Evangelical Revival

As George Whitefield had begun to preach out-of-doors, he encouraged John Wesley to do the same. At Kingswood, Whitefield had seen hundreds of coal miners weep for joy as tears of repentance streamed down their coal-smudged faces.[46] Encouraged by this experience, he held subsequent open-air meetings in which more than two thousand people attended. Within weeks, attendance swelled to twenty thousand at a single event. When news spread of this unprecedented response, other cities in England invited Whitefield to preach. After visiting Gloucester, he entered London, where in the city's parks forty thousand people gathered to hear him speak.

When John Wesley suggested to Whitefield that he travel to America, Whitefield asked Wesley to continue his ministry of field preaching in England. Wesley accepted the invitation reluctantly, saying, "In the evening I reached Bristol and met Mr Whitefield there. I could scarce reconcile myself at first to this strange way of preaching in the fields, of which he set me an example on Sunday; having been all my life, till very lately, so tenacious of every point relating to decency and order, that I should have thought the saving of souls almost a sin, if it had not been done in a church."[47] Wesley followed Whitefield's example. Soon, preaching to large crowds became a normal method of evangelism in Britain as well as in the American colonies.

When John Wesley entered a new area to evangelize, he took his stance at a favorable spot, usually in the town center. Then he would "preach the law in the strictest of terms" or "preach a fifteen-minute sermon" on the topic of "death or hell," and only when his listeners were clearly under conviction of sin would he "bring out the medicine of the gospel."[48] His coworkers circulated among those who responded, signing them up to attend a Methodist meeting later that day. Actually, the Methodist meetings were the most effective means for conversion. It was calculated that 70 percent of those

46. Rudnick, *Speaking the Gospel*, 135–36.

47. *Journal of the Reverend John Wesley*, 126.

48. M. Taylor, *Exploring Evangelism*, 261. Cf. David M. Gustafson, *Gospel Witness: Evangelism in Word and Deed* (Grand Rapids: Eerdmans, 2019), 140–41.

Figure 8.1. John Wesley Preaching from a Market Cross by W. Hatherall, RA, 1909, Wesley's Chapel, London. *(Reproduced with the permission of The Trustees of Wesley's Chapel, City Road, London)*

who converted to Jesus Christ under John Wesley's ministry did so during these meetings, often speaking to a Methodist coworker one-on-one.[49]

Although John Wesley won the approval of segments of the public, he faced denunciations and hostility from others. In some cases, riots ensued in which he barely escaped with his life. To compound matters, Wesley engaged in open-air peaching despite his own struggles against the world, the flesh, and the devil.

Charles Wesley's Evangelism

Charles Wesley was equally effective at evangelistic preaching.[50] In his journal, he estimated that he preached to nearly 150,000 people between the years 1739 and 1743.[51] In 1738 alone, Charles preached to ten thousand people at Moorfields and twenty thousand at Kennington Common. He sought particularly to evangelize prisoners, many of whom were awaiting execution. One record reads, "Charles visited [criminals] in the condemned cell, spoke to them plainly and tenderly about the grace of God and the love of Jesus, and offered them there and then immediate pardon in the name of Jesus. Many of them passed into life in the death cell, and he would then ride in the death cart with them, to be parted from them only as the noose dropped under their chin—all the while singing or praying with them, or preaching to the morbid crowd."[52]

Through music, Charles called men and women to repentance and faith in Christ. For him, the gospel hymn was as much a means of evangelism as preaching. He often set hymns to popular melodies such as the "Scotch Ballad" or to Handel's march "Jericho," or to popular folk tunes.[53] An example of Charles's gospel hymns is "And Can It Be," which most likely was his "conversion hymn."

"And Can It Be" by Charles Wesley, 1738

And can it be that I should gain / An int'rest in the Savior's blood?
Died He for me, who caused His pain? / For me, who Him to death pursued?
Amazing love! how can it be / That Thou, my God, shouldst die for me?

49. Tuttle, *Story of Evangelism*, 285.
50. M. Taylor, *Exploring Evangelism*, 268.
51. Townsend, "Forgotten Wesley," 7.
52. M. Taylor, *Exploring Evangelism*, 269.
53. M. Taylor, *Exploring Evangelism*, 266.

He left His Father's throne above, / So free, so infinite His grace;
Emptied Himself of all but love, / And bled for Adam's helpless race:
'Tis mercy all, immense and free; / For, O my God, it found out me.

Long my imprisoned spirit lay / Fast bound in sin and nature's night;
Thine eye diffused a quickening ray, / I woke, the dungeon flamed with light;
My chains fell off, my heart was free, / I rose, went forth, and followed Thee.

No condemnation now I dread; / Jesus, and all in Him, is mine!
Alive in Him, my living Head, / And clothed in righteousness Divine,
Bold I approach the eternal throne, / And claim the crown, through Christ my own.

Charles continued his itinerant preaching until 1756, when poor health forced him to minister as a resident pastor.[54] From the time of his conversion until his death, he averaged writing one hymn every two days.

John Wesley's Disciple-Making Strategy

While Charles focused often on reaching prisoners, John and his disciples ministered to the working class, particularly to coal miners and factory workers, a segment of society often overlooked by the Church of England during the industrial revolution. In John's effort to reach this segment of society, he rode on horseback to hamlets and mines throughout the British Isles. He said, "Our call is, to save that which is lost. Now we cannot expect such to seek us; therefore, we should go and seek them."[55] His vision of ministry stood in contrast to the expectations of the priests of Christendom. In an often-quoted statement, Wesley said, "I look upon the world as my parish; thus far I mean,

54. Townsend, "Forgotten Wesley," 7.

55. William Peirce, *Ecclesiastical Principles and Polity of the Wesleyan Methodists* (London: Hamilton and Adams, 1854), 116, cited in M. Taylor, *Exploring Evangelism*, 261.

that in whatever part of it I am, I judge it meet, right, and my bounden duty, to declare unto all that are willing to hear, the glad tidings of salvation."[56]

John Wesley believed that his fellow preachers were "particularly called, by going into the highways and hedges" where there was no witness of the gospel.[57] He not only traveled to preach but invited lay preachers to travel circuits to serve Methodist societies, classes, and bands. All the while, Wesley maintained his own circuit, traveling around 250,000 miles and preaching forty thousand sermons.[58]

Prayer Emphasis

Wesley called his followers to be people of prayer. He found Madame Guyon's "Short and Easy Method of Prayer," written in 1665, to be especially helpful.[59] The Methodists emphasized persevering prayer and reliance on the empowerment of the Holy Spirit. During a meeting in London on New Year's morning in 1739, those who gathered experienced a "Methodist Pentecost." Wesley described the meeting: "Mr. Hall, Kinchin, Ingham, Whitefield, Hutchins, and my brother Charles, were present at our love-feast in Fetter-Lane, with about sixty of our brethren. About three in the morning, as we were continuing instant in prayer, the power of God came mightily upon us, insomuch that many cried out for exceeding joy, and many fell to the ground. As soon as we were recovered a little from that awe and amazement at the presence of his Majesty, we broke out with one voice, 'We praise thee, O God; we acknowledge thee to be the Lord.'"[60]

Wesley knew that dependence on the Holy Spirit and prayer were vital to evangelism. This was important to him personally as he faced not only public criticism but personal struggles such as his difficult marriage with Mary Vaizelle.[61] Wesley's commitment to evangelism brought challenges to his home life as he struggled to balance ministry and domestic responsibilities. In this regard, he delegated several ministry responsibilities to others and equipped them for the task.

56. Snyder, *Radical Wesley*, 92.

57. Peirce, *Ecclesiastical Principles*, 116, cited in M. Taylor, *Exploring Evangelism*, 261.

58. Tuttle, *Story of Evangelism*, 286.

59. Woodbridge and James, *Church History*, 2:408.

60. *Journal of the Reverend John Wesley*, 117. Scharpff notes that Wesley's friend, Pastor Ingham, later became one of the most powerful evangelists of the Brethren. Scharpff, *History of Evangelism*, 70.

61. Woodbridge and James, *Church History*, 2:410.

Equipping Laypeople

John Wesley's first lay preacher was Joseph Humphreys, who assisted him in preaching as early as 1738. However, the person who decided the matter of lay preachers was Thomas Maxwell, who came to faith under Wesley's preaching at Bristol. In 1739 Wesley wrote, "After a time, a young man, named Thomas Maxwell, . . . came and desired to help me as a son in the gospel. Soon after came a second, Thomas Richards; then a third, Thomas Westall. These severally desired to serve me as sons, and to labour when and where I would direct them."[62]

Wesley gave careful supervision to his lay preachers.[63] After he appointed them, they visited Wesleyan societies, traveling on a circuit. Some endured opposition, if not persecution, being assaulted with clubs and stones, and being run down by horses or overrun by cows that farmers drove into the field during open-air meetings.[64]

From the lay preachers' broad appeal to crowds, Wesley organized societies, classes, and bands. His strategy was meant to conserve the fruit of evangelism and to equip the newly converted Christians for effective witness themselves. In fact, Wesley had misgivings about "fugitive preachers" who simply delivered evangelistic messages and moved on without giving time and attention to the nurture and care of the new believers.[65] For him, preaching the gospel was an important means to making disciples, but disciples needed teaching, Christian formation, and accountability in order to live the Christian life.

Societies, Classes, and Bands

A Methodist society was similar to a congregation, although Wesley did not view them as churches. Instead, he insisted that they were a means to renew the Church of England. He expected societies to augment the work of parish churches, not replace them. The socities were generally composed of twenty-five to one hundred members.

62. J. Everett et al., *The Disputants, or the Arguments in Favour of the Newly Established Theological Institution among the Methodists* (London: Fisher, Fisher, and Jackson, 1835), 44.

63. Snyder, *Radical Wesley*, 35, 63.

64. M. Taylor, *Exploring Evangelism*, 261.

65. D. Michael Henderson, *John Wesley's Class Meeting: A Model for Making Disciples* (Anderson, IN: Francis Asbury, 1997), 114.

The primary function of a Methodist society meeting was instruction. Those attending the meetings, at the invitation of a friend or open-air event, were introduced to Wesleyan teaching.[66] This instruction addressed a variety of topics such as Bible reading, prayer, justifying grace, the call to a holy life, and service.

Every society was subdivided into classes where members were encouraged to support one another. Generally, each class was composed of twelve people, with men and women, and a leader. Whereas Methodist societies focused on instruction, the classes promoted the practice of Christian disciplines. In early years, classes were held in homes, schoolrooms, attics, and even coal bins—wherever there was room for twelve people to meet. Women played a significant role, with a number serving as class leaders, as well as evangelists and exhorters.[67]

The band was the smallest of the Methodist groups. Each band was composed of four members who sought to cultivate personal holiness and godly thinking. Because of the confidential nature of bands, men met with men, and women met with women. These intimate groups provided accountability for personal change. Members asked each other questions such as "Have you the witness of God's Spirit with your spirit that you are a child of God?" and "Has no sin, inward or outward, dominion over you?" and "Do you desire to be told of all your faults and that plain and home?"[68] Wesley advised, "Speak freely and plainly," and "Ask as many and as searching questions as may be, concerning their state, sins, and temptations."[69]

Wesley operated a printing office, a warehouse, and a bookshop. From the beginning of his ministry, he published sermons, poems, hymns, tracts, and other literature. His periodical, *The Arminian Magazine*, published English prose and poetry about the lives of Methodist preachers.[70] He excelled in letter-writing with evangelistic purpose. Moreover, he wrote to the British press about current political and religious matters, comparative religion, defense of the gospel, Methodist doctrine, and social issues.

Although Methodists eventually separated from the Church of England, there remained an evangelical wing within the Anglican Church that included John Newton of Olney, who composed the hymn "Amazing Grace,"

66. Henderson, *John Wesley's Class Meeting*, 83–126.
67. Woodbridge and James, *Church History*, 2:410.
68. Henderson, *John Wesley's Class Meeting*, 117.
69. Tuttle, *Story of Evangelism*, 296.
70. M. Taylor, *Exploring Evangelism*, 265.

and Henry Venn, a mission administrator and member of the Clapham Sect.[71] Another well-respected Clapham member was William Wilberforce (1759–1833), who worked to abolish slavery in the British Empire.

George Whitefield's Evangelistic Strategy

George Whitefield (1714–1770) was born in Gloucester at the Bell Inn, described as a "little Sodom."[72] The son of a saloon keeper, the young Whitefield went to Oxford University in 1732. Besides enjoying drama and card playing, he became intrigued with the Scriptures, poring over the Bible for hours at a time.

At Oxford, after coming to know the Methodists, Whitefield began to live "according to the rules" of the Holy Club and tried to find salvation by obeying them.[73] However, this pursuit changed during a long illness when his struggle was replaced by a newfound joy in Jesus Christ as his Savior.[74] Of all the members of the Holy Club at Oxford, Whitefield was the first to experience personal conversion to Christ. He soon made "salvation by faith" and "spiritual birth" the focus of his messages and set both the pattern and the pace for evangelism.[75]

In 1736, Whitefield was ordained as a deacon at Gloucester. He began preaching in London and Bristol, where he was referred to as the "boy preacher." For a few months he preached every Sunday at the Chapel of the Tower and every Tuesday at the Ludgate prison.[76] In 1737, he published his first sermon, "The New Nature and the Necessity of Our New Birth in Christ Jesus in Order for Salvation." In this sermon he said,

> The sum of the matter is this: Christianity includes morality, as grace does reason. But if we are only mere Moralists, if we are not inwardly wrought upon and changed by the powerful operations of the Holy Spirit and our moral actions proceed from a principle of a new nature, however we may call ourselves Christians, we shall be found naked at the great day and in the number of those who have neither Christ's righ-

71. Woodbridge and James, *Church History*, 2:580.

72. Stuart C. Henry, *George Whitefield: Wayfaring Witness* (New York: Abingdon, 1957), 17.

73. Scharpff, *History of Evangelism*, 74.

74. Dallimore, *George Whitefield*, 21–22.

75. Scharpff, *History of Evangelism*, 73–74; Dallimore, *George Whitefield*, 22–23.

76. M. Taylor, *Exploring Evangelism*, 272.

> teousness imputed to them for the justification in the sight of God, nor holiness wrought in their souls as the consequence of that, in order to make them meet for the enjoyment of God. . . . Thou must be informed, that nothing short of a thorough sound conversion will fit thee for the kingdom of heaven. It is not enough to turn from profaneness to civility. But thou must turn from civility to godliness. Not only some, but "all things must become new" in thy soul. It will profit thee but little to do many things, if yet some one thing thou lackest. In short, thou must not only be an almost, but altogether a new creature, or in vain thou boasteth that thou art a Christian.[77]

At John Wesley's invitation, Whitefield traveled to Georgia shortly after the Wesleys had returned from there. Whitefield went to America to preach and founded an orphanage modeled after that of Francke in Halle.[78] In 1738, Whitefield set sail for Georgia on the first of seven trips across the Atlantic.[79]

He soon returned to England for ordination as a priest and to raise funds for the orphanage. He also engaged in open-air preaching to coal miners, describing his experience this way: "Having no righteousness of their own to renounce, they were glad to hear of a Jesus who was a friend to publicans, and came not to call the righteous but sinners to repentance. The first discovery of their being affected was the sight of the white gutters made by their tears, which plentifully fell down their black cheeks as they came out of their coal pits."[80]

One observer noted that these sermons that were preached outside a church gave them a certain freshness. By bringing the gospel to the entrance of the coal mines, the message was freed from "the artificiality and intolerable stuffiness of a dead and dull ecclesiasticism, and made . . . again part of the vital experience of mankind."[81] Some people came to hear Whitefield out of curiosity. Others admired his voice, which could be heard by thousands.[82] As a former actor, it was said that he could pronounce the word *Mesopotamia* so as to "bring tears to one's eyes."[83]

77. Lee Gatiss, ed., *The Sermons of George Whitefield* (Wheaton, IL: Crossway, 2012), 2:284–85.

78. Woodbridge and James, *Church History*, 2:411.

79. Dallimore, *George Whitefield*, 34.

80. Woodbridge and James, *Church History*, 2:412.

81. A. D. Belden, *London Quarterly Review* (July 1954): 217, cited in M. Taylor, *Exploring Evangelism*, 276.

82. John Mark Terry, *Evangelism: A Concise History* (Nashville: B&H, 2014), 120.

83. Bainton, *Christianity*, 341.

Whitefield played a leading role in the Scottish revival and the formation of the Welsh Calvinistic Methodist Association. Although the name "Methodist" was applied to Whitefield's followers, there were theological differences between him as a Calvinist and John Wesley as an Arminian.

In 1740 in America, Whitefield traveled north to New England for a series of evangelistic meetings. The people were eager to hear him because they had read about his meetings in newspaper articles, as well as read his published sermons. In Philadelphia, his pulpit was placed on the second-floor balcony of the Court House. He was known to preach in a highly dramatic style. For example, he said, "Father Abraham, who's in Heaven? Episcopalians? No! Presbyterians? No! Are there Methodists there? No, no, and again I say no! Well, who *is* there? 'We haven't heard anything here about these people,' came Abraham's answer. 'Here we have only Christians, people who believe in Christ, people who have overcome by the blood of the Lamb and the Word of His testimony.' If that's the case . . . may God help us all to forget the names of these groups and to become Christians in truth."[84]

Benjamin Franklin attended one of Whitefield's meeting in Philadelphia and was impressed by his ability to deliver a message to such a large gathering of people. Franklin dismissed earlier reports that Whitefield preached to crowds of thousands in England, considering it an exaggeration. Therefore, when Franklin heard Whitefield at the Philadelphia courthouse, the skeptical colonist walked toward his shop on Market Street until he could not hear the sound of Whitefield's voice distinctly. Then he estimated his distance from Whitefield and calculated the area of a semicircle that pivoted on the evangelist. Allowing two square feet per person, he realized that more than thirty thousand people could hear Whitefield preach.[85]

Excerpt from *The Autobiography of Benjamin Franklin*

In 1739 arrived among us from Ireland the Reverend Mr. Whitefield, who had made himself remarkable there as an itinerant preacher. He was at first permitted to preach in some of our churches; but the clergy, taking a dislike to him, soon refused him their pulpits, and he was obliged to preach in the fields. The multitudes of all sects and denominations that attended his sermons were enormous, and it was matter of speculation to me, who was one of the number, to observe the extraordinary influence of his oratory

84. Scharpff, *History of Evangelism*, 59–60.
85. Dallimore, *George Whitefield*, 56.

on his hearers, and how much they admired and respected him, notwithstanding his common abuse of them, by assuring them they were naturally half beast and half devils. It was wonderful to see the change soon made in the manners of our inhabitants. From being thoughtless or indifferent about religion, it seemed as if all the world were growing religious, so that one could not walk thro' the town in an evening without hearing psalms sung in different families of every street. And it being found inconvenient to assemble in the open air, subject to its inclemencies, the building of a house to meet in was no sooner proposed, and persons appointed to receive contributions, but sufficient sums were soon received to procure the ground and erect the building, which was one hundred feet long and seventy broad, about the size of Westminster Hall; and the work was carried on with such spirit as to be finished in a much shorter time than could have been expected. . . .

Mr. Whitefield, in leaving us, went preaching all the way thro' the colonies to Georgia. The settlement of that province had lately been begun, but, instead of being made with hardy, industrious husbandmen, accustomed to labor, the only people fit for such an enterprise, it was with families of broken shopkeepers and other insolvent debtors, many of indolent and idle habits, taken out of the jails, who, being set down in the woods, unqualified for clearing land, and unable to endure the hardship of a new settlement, perished in numbers, leaving many helpless children unprovided for. The sight of their miserable situation inspired the benevolent heart of Mr. Whitefield with the idea of building an orphan-house there, in which they might be supported and educated. Returning northward, he preached up this charity, and made large collections, for his eloquence had a wonderful power over the hearts, and purses of his hearers, of which I myself was an instance.

I happened soon after to attend one of his sermons, in the course of which I perceived he intended to finish with a collection, and I silently resolved he should get nothing from me. I had in my pocket a handful of copper money, three or four silver dollars, and five pistoles in gold. As he proceeded I began to soften, and concluded to give the coppers. Another stroke of his oratory made me ashamed of that, and determined me to give the silver; and he finished so admirably, that I emptied my pocket wholly into the collector's dish, gold and all. (Benjamin Franklin and Louis P. Masur, *The Autobiography of Benjamin Franklin: With Related Documents* [Boston: Bedford/St. Martin's, Macmillan Learning, 2016], 49–50)

For more than a month, Whitefield preached nearly every day.[86] In New England, it was estimated that as many as fifty thousand new members were added to the churches. When he left Boston, he preached to twenty thousand people at his farewell service.[87] A parish farmer, Nathan Cole, heard him preach in the open air and said,

> When I saw Mr. Whitefield come upon the scaffold he looked almost angelic, a young slim, slender youth, before some thousands of people with a bold, undaunted countenance; it solemnized my mind and put me in a trembling fear before he began to preach for he looked as if he was clothed with the authority from the great God. Hearing him preach gave me a heart wound [so that] by God's blessing, my old foundation was broken up and I saw that my righteousness would not save me, then I was convinced of the doctrine of election and went right to quarreling with God about it because all that I could do would not save me.[88]

Not everyone had favorable impressions of him, however. Whitefield had a decided squint in one of his eyes, and some mocked him because of his infirmity. His critics were insulting and gave him the nickname "Dr. Squintum."[89] Far from becoming a handicap to his preaching, though, the squint was said to be a means of holding the attention of his listeners.

Whitefield was considered the "grand itinerant" as he preached to mass audiences in the American colonies and British Isles, leaving behind him a trail of faithful converts. Despite the three-month journey by sea, Whitefield's seven trips to America meant that he crossed the Atlantic Ocean thirteen times. He ministered in most of the colonies, preaching every day and often several times a day.[90] In contrast to Wesley, Whitefield did not

86. Mark A. Noll, *The Old Religion in a New World: The History of North American Christianity* (Grand Rapids: Eerdmans, 2001), 52.

87. Terry, *Evangelism*, 120.

88. Nathan Cole, "The Spiritual Travels of Nathan Cole," *William and Mary Quarterly* 33, no. 1 (January 1976): 3, cited in Woodbridge and James, *Church History*, 2:413.

89. M. Taylor, *Exploring Evangelism*, 276.

90. Whitefield's interests became both spiritual and political as he sought to advance the British Empire. Moreover, he changed from criticism of slavery to lobbying for its introduction in Georgia Colony. Peter Y. Choi, *George Whitefield: Evangelist for God and Empire* (Grand Rapids: Eerdmans, 2018), 16, 36, 41, 55, 98, 127–68. For an explanation of abolition movements in America, see Rodney Stark, *For the Glory of God: How Monotheism Led to Reformations, Science, Witch-Hunts, and the End of Slavery* (Princeton, NJ: Princeton University Press, 2003), 339–49.

establish any societies or classes but cooperated with Anglicans, Presbyterians, Congregationalists, and Baptists to welcome converts into their congregations.

American Colonies' Great Awakening

Before Whitefield arrived in North America, the Great Awakening had already begun. The influence of Francke and conventicles had reached Cotton Mather (1663–1728), a Puritan minister.[91] The Calvinist movement had touched the Dutch Reformed preacher Theodore J. Frelinghuysen (ca. 1691–1747) and the Presbyterian Gilbert Tennent (1703–1764).

Whitefield said of Frelinghuysen, "He is a worthy soldier of Jesus Christ and was the beginner of the great work which I trust the Lord is carrying on in these parts."[92] Frelinghuysen was born in Germany and educated in Holland. He absorbed pietistic teachings during his theological training and was ordained as a pastor in the Dutch Reformed Church. In 1719, church officials sent him to New Jersey to oversee four Dutch Reformed churches in the Raritan Valley.[93]

Frelinghuysen believed "presumptuous security" to be people's main problem.[94] By this he meant they had been baptized, catechized, and accepted as full members of the church, but did not understand the meaning of salvation. They knew that salvation came through faith, but they interpreted faith as agreement with correct doctrine, not with knowing Christ personally.[95] Therefore, Frelinghuysen challenged his listeners to repent and believe the gospel, or suffer the torments of hell. He declared that everyone had to experience the terror of lostness before they could know the joy of salvation through Christ's forgiveness.[96] Throughout the Raritan Valley, he engaged in evangelistic preaching and personal witnessing in the church members' homes.

Gilbert Tennent became pastor of the Presbyterian Church in New Brunswick, New Jersey Colony, in 1726. He was acquainted with Freling-

91. Richard F. Lovelace, *The American Pietism of Cotton Mather: Origins of American Evangelicalism* (Eugene, OR: Wipf & Stock, 1979), 32–39, 71.

92. Nathan Hatch, Mark Noll, and John D. Woodbridge, *The Gospel in America* (Grand Rapids: Zondervan, 1979), 28, cited in Terry, *Evangelism*, 115.

93. Tuttle, *Story of Evangelism*, 287, 298.

94. Terry, *Evangelism*, 116.

95. Terry, *Evangelism*, 115–16.

96. Terry, *Evangelism*, 116.

huysen and quickly realized they shared the same desire for revival. In 1740, Whitefield's and Tennent's preaching kindled a revival in Boston that spread as far south as Virginia during the next two years.

Jonathan Edwards

In 1734, Whitefield visited Northampton, Massachusetts Colony, where he met the pastor Jonathan Edwards (1703–1758).[97] Edwards had entered Yale College when he was twelve years old and graduated first in his class in 1720.[98] He remained at Yale for the next two years, completing a master's degree, and experiencing conversion to faith in Christ. He served briefly in two churches, taught at Yale, and in 1727 began to assist his grandfather, Solomon Stoddard, at the Northampton Congregational Church.[99] When his grandfather died two years later, Edwards succeeded him there as pastor. Edwards delivered a series of sermons on the topic of justification by faith—the topic of his master's thesis—which led to a revival in the church that began in 1734. In evidence of the revival, his listeners agonized over the questions of Christian faith and eternity.[100]

Edwards reported more than three hundred conversions in half a year and spoke about the spread of the revival to ten cities in Massachusetts and fifteen communities in Connecticut. Out of a total population of 300,000, between 25,000 and 50,000 people joined local churches.[101]

Through numerous writings, Edwards articulated his Calvinist position that marked him as Colonial America's greatest thinker and placed him alongside the first rank of Reformed theologians of Europe. His best-known sermon, "Sinners in the Hands of an Angry God," was a summons for "colonists to awake."[102] He preached that God is indeed perfectly just and has every reason to "drop rebellious men in the flames of hell as men have to fling a venomous spider into the fire."[103] It was only the hand of God that prevented sinners from falling into the flames at any moment. Edwards

97. Justo L. González, *The Story of Christianity: The Early Church to the Present Day* (Peabody, MA: Prince, 1999), 2:228–29.

98. Douglas A. Sweeney, *The American Evangelical Story* (Grand Rapids: Baker Academic, 2005), 45.

99. Sweeney, *American Evangelical Story*, 46.

100. Tuttle, *Story of Evangelism*, 300.

101. Scharpff, *History of Evangelism*, 60.

102. Bainton, *Christianity*, 343.

103. Bainton, *Christianity*, 343.

preached, "O sinner! Consider the fearful danger you are in. . . . It would be no wonder if some persons, that now sit here in some seats of this meeting-house in health, and in quiet, and secure, should be in hell before tomorrow morning."[104] Before the close of Edwards's sermon, it was reported "there was a great moaning and crying out through the whole house, the shrieks and crys were piercing and amazing."[105] Edwards's desire was to see many within the community of Northampton convert to Christ.

After his years there, in 1751 Edwards became a missionary to Native Americans at Stockbridge, Massachusetts.[106] His book titled *The Freedom of the Will*, published in 1754, was an attack on Arminianism, arguing that if human beings have the metaphysical power to choose or refuse Christ as they please, then they are able to hold God at a distance, to make him await their pleasure. In 1757, Edwards agreed somewhat reluctantly to be appointed as president of the College of New Jersey, later named Princeton University.

The Great Awakening in North America led soon to a division between "old lights" and "new lights." After Gilbert Tennent preached a sermon titled "The Danger of an Unconverted Ministry," he was opposed by "old lights" who closed their pulpits to all revivalist preachers.[107] This led "new lights," supportive of revival, to organize separate societies and churches where revival preachers were welcome. Many of these churches became Baptist.

Baptists in America

The English Baptist views of John Smyth and Thomas Helwys spread to America. Roger Williams (ca. 1603–1683), a separatist preacher and advocate for freedom of faith and conscience, was banned from the Puritan colony of Massachusetts as a dissenter. In response, he founded the colony of Rhode Island on the principle that government should not coerce religious practice or belief, making the town of Providence a haven of religious tolerance for those with different views, including those of Jews and Quakers.[108] In 1639, Williams established the Baptist Church of Providence. In 1644, he published a tract titled *The Bloudy Tenent of Persecution for Cause of Conscience between Truth and Peace*, which set out a biblical argument for the free exercise

104. Bainton, *Christianity*, 343.
105. Bainton, *Christianity*, 343.
106. Sweeney, *American Evangelical Story*, 86.
107. Sweeney, *American Evangelical Story*, 56–59.
108. Noll, *Old Religion in a New World*, 44; Tuttle, *Story of Evangelism*, 270.

of religion.[109] From Rhode Island Colony, Baptist churches began to spread and flourish in the middle and southern colonies.

These Baptist churches emphasized evangelism, and revival meetings were the most common method. While itinerant preaching, extemporaneous preaching, and spontaneous prayer had been used earlier, they now became commonplace within the Baptist congregations. The revivalist style, in contrast to liturgical forms of older established colonial churches, was well suited for the American frontier. The Baptist churches abandoned the practices and many of the attitudes of European clergy and Christendom.[110]

Shubal Stearns

A leading Baptist was Shubal Stearns (1706–1771), who was born in Boston to Puritan parents.[111] After hearing Whitefield preach and experiencing spiritual birth, Stearns was ordained as a Separate Congregational minister in 1746 and formed a congregation in Tolland in Massachusetts Colony. Shortly afterward, he became convinced by a Separate Baptist pastor named Waitstill Palmer that he should be baptized by immersion. Following this, Stearns was ordained as a Separate Baptist pastor.

In 1755, he resettled in central North Carolina Colony, where he organized the Sandy Creek Separate Baptist Church.[112] His "mesmerizing stare" along with his "holy whine" mimicked the preaching of Whitefield and equally attracted curious visitors. Nearly nine hundred new converts joined Stearns's church.

As the membership expanded, the Sandy Creek Association of Separate Baptists was organized in 1758.[113] Joseph Bree, Daniel Marshall, and other ministers accompanied Stearns as they trekked across the Piedmont—the plateau region between the Atlantic coastal plain and the Appalachian Mountains. Between 1755 and 1765, they carried the gospel message across North Carolina, as well as into southwestern Virginia and South Carolina.

109. Noll, *Old Religion in a New World*, 44; Roger Williams, *The Bloudy Tenent, of Persecution, for Cause of Conscience, Discussed, in a Conference betweene Truth and Peace, Who, in All Tender Affection, Present to the High Court of Parliament, (as the Result of Their Discourse) These, (amongst Other Passages) of Highest Consideration* (1644).

110. Noll, *Old Religion in a New World*, 54.

111. Sweeney, *American Evangelical Story*, 44.

112. Darius Salter, *American Evangelism: Its Theology and Practice* (Grand Rapids: Baker, 1996), 89.

113. David S. Dockery, *Southern Baptist Consensus and Renewal: A Biblical, Historical, and Theological Proposal* (Nashville: B&H, 2008), 109.

George Liele

In America, a few African slaves were exposed to the gospel and received Jesus Christ as Lord and Savior. They came to Christian faith voluntarily and spread the gospel to fellow slaves spontaneously. Without a doubt, slaveholders were harsh and abusive, but some sought to treat their slaves more humanely, and even encouraged them to attend revival services and evangelistic meetings. While contemporary views rightly view all slavery as unjust and inhumane, at the time in America's history, some slaveholders sincerely wanted their slaves to convert to Christ, even if they hoped that conversion would make them "better slaves" in productivity and character.[114]

The first freed slave who was licensed to preach the gospel was George Liele (ca. 1750–1828). He was born into slavery in Virginia and relocated to Georgia Colony.[115] When Liele was twenty-three years old, he came to faith under the preaching of Matthew Moore, brother of Mildred Moore Sharp, the wife of Liele's master.[116] Henry Sharp was a Baptist, and a British Loyalist, who encouraged Liele to preach the gospel to other slaves in the area of Savannah, Georgia.

In 1778, during the American War of Independence, Sharp set Liele free. Liele left Georgia along with British Loyalists, ensuring his freedom and not risking reenslavement. On a ship bound for Jamaica, he received the status of an indentured servant in order to pay passage for himself, his wife, and their four children. In Jamaica, Liele repaid the debt and gained permission to preach to slaves on the island. He supported himself and his family by farming and hauling freight with a wagon and a team of horses. He preached at the racecourse at Kingston, where the novelty of an itinerant, ex-slave preacher attracted considerable attention.[117] It was noted that his style was similar to that of Whitefield and was equally effective. Liele preached to thousands, baptized hundreds, and organized new believers into congregations governed by Jamaicans. At times he was harassed by white colonists

114. Thomas S. Kidd, "Do the Holy Scriptures Countenance Such Wild Disorder? Baptist Growth in the Eighteenth-Century American South," in *Baptists and Mission: Papers from the Fourth International Conference on Baptist Studies*, ed. Ian M. Randall and Anthony R. Cross (Eugene, OR: Wipf & Stock, 2008), 127.

115. Kidd, "Holy Scriptures," 128.

116. Noel Leo Erskine, *Plantation Church: How African American Religion Was Born in Caribbean Slavery* (New York: Oxford University Press, 2014), 85–86.

117. Erskine, *Plantation Church*, 88–89.

and government officials because he "agitated the slaves." In one instance, he was imprisoned for three years. By 1814, his efforts had produced nearly eight thousand Baptists in Jamaica.

David George and Andrew Bryan

In 1773, a slave named David George (ca. 1742–1810) converted to faith under George Liele in Savannah, Georgia. David George knew Liele from childhood and was impressed by his conversion to Christ. After George's conversion, he and his wife, along with eight others, were baptized in the Savannah River.[118] Soon David George began to exhort his fellow slaves in their faith, which led him to become pastor of the Silver Bluff Baptist Church, founded in 1775, in Silver Bluff, South Carolina Colony.[119]

When the British left Savannah, George traveled with them to Nova Scotia, Canada, where he worked to establish the first Baptist churches composed of freed slaves.[120] In 1793, he immigrated with a small number of freedmen to the west coast of Africa, where he founded Baptist churches in Sierra Leone.[121]

In 1782, Andrew Bryan (1737–1812) converted to Christ under the preaching of George Liele. Andrew Bryan was born into slavery and served as the coachman to Jonathan Bryan. The Bryan plantation, owned by slaveholders Jonathan Bryan and Hugh Bryan, became a center for slaveholders to evangelize slaves. Preachers such as George Liele, David George, and Andrew Bryan all engaged in gospel preaching there.

When George Liele and David George, along with other freedmen, left with the British Loyalists, Andrew Bryan continued to preach in the vicinity of Savannah.[122] With encouragement from his slaveholders, he built a meeting house for the congregation that included blacks and whites. Although Andrew Bryan brought hundreds of his fellow slaves to faith in Christ, some slaveholders opposed the idea that they should be baptized. Fearing slave uprisings and desertions, some slaveholders prohibited their slaves from hearing Bryan's sermons.[123] When Andrew Bryan was jailed for preaching but accused of plotting a rebellion, Jonathan Bryan and other plantation

118. Kidd, "Holy Scriptures," 127.

119. Erskine, *Plantation Church*, 85–86; Edward E. Andrews, *Native Apostles: Black and Indian Missionaries in the British Atlantic World* (Cambridge, MA: Harvard University Press, 2013), 225–27.

120. Noll, *Old Religion in a New World*, 56.

121. Erskine, *Plantation Church*, 86.

122. Erskine, *Plantation Church*, 87.

123. Kidd, "Holy Scriptures," 128.

Figure 8.2. Family Worship in a Plantation in South Carolina by Frank Vizetelly, *The Illustrated London News*, December 5, 1863. *(Courtesy of the South Caroliniana Library, University of South Carolina, Columbia, SC)*

owners protested his imprisonment. Upon his release, Andrew continued to preach the gospel on the plantation.[124]

With support from several prominent whites who cited the "positive effect of religion on slave discipline," Andrew Bryan was ordained, and his church was legally registered in 1788.[125] When Jonathan Bryan died, Andrew was allowed to purchase his freedom. In 1794, he raised enough money to erect a church building named the Ethiopian Church of Jesus Christ, today known as First African Baptist Church of Savannah.[126] By 1800, the congregation numbered seven hundred members.[127]

Methodists in America

As mentioned earlier, Methodists expanded under the leadership of John and Charles Wesley. In New York Colony, Phillip Embury (1729–1775)

124. Erskine, *Plantation Church*, 87–88.

125. Albert J. Raboteau, *Canaan Land: A Religious History of African Americans* (Oxford: Oxford University Press, 2001), 29–30, 135.

126. Noll, *Old Religion in a New World*, 56.

127. Noll, *Old Religion in a New World*, 57.

preached the gospel and worked to found the first Methodist society in North America.[128] By 1769, Methodists in New York built Wesley Chapel, known today as John Street Methodist Church.

With the coming of the American War of Independence, Francis Asbury was the single Methodist minister to remain in America.[129] Given the fact that John Wesley supported the Loyalists in the American Colonies, it was nearly impossible to keep the Methodist movement alive. However, after the American Revolution, Methodists in the new republic began to flourish. In 1784, John Wesley named Thomas Coke (1747–1814) and Francis Asbury (1745–1816) as co-superintendents of the Methodists in the United States.[130]

Francis Asbury

Similar to those in the British Isles, Methodist "circuit riders" in America rode on horseback and proclaimed the need for personal conversion to faith. They were known to arrive at frontier settlements and preach the gospel even before the settlers completed building their cabins. The circuit riders aimed their messages at the common people. They lived the apostolic life of incessant travel and poverty, founding churches in urban and rural areas, in the north and south, east and west. Their austere life sifted out those who were "weak of body" and "feeble in character."[131] Besides circuit riders, there were hundreds of class leaders, lay preachers, and exhorters who preached the gospel across the new republic.

Francis Asbury preached in courthouses, fields, public houses (pubs), tobacco houses, and public squares, riding an average of six thousand miles per year, preaching nearly every day and conducting Methodist meetings and conferences.[132] His preaching circuit took him from Georgia to Maine and west to Kentucky and Ohio. Under his leadership, the Methodist Church grew in the United States from 1,200 to 214,000 members, and he ordained 2,000 Methodist preachers.

128. Richard P. Heitzenrater, *Wesley and the People Called Methodists*, 2nd ed. (Nashville: Abingdon, 2013), 272.

129. Heitzenrater, *Wesley*, 317.

130. Heitzenrater, *Wesley*, 319–23; Tuttle, *Story of Evangelism*, 288.

131. Ivan Howard, "Controversies in Methodism over Methods of Education of Ministers up to 1865" (PhD diss., University of Iowa, 1965), 11, cited in Salter, *American Evangelism*, 91.

132. Salter, *American Evangelism*, 90.

Richard Allen

Richard Allen (1760–1831) founded the African Methodist Episcopal (AME) Church in 1816. He was born into slavery to the slaveholder Benjamin Chew, a merchant from Philadelphia. Allen was sold as a child along with his family to a farmer in Delaware, where he began to attend meetings at a local Methodist society and taught himself to read and write.[133] In 1780, when his master became convinced that slavery was morally wrong, he offered his slaves the opportunity to buy their freedom, and Allen accepted the offer.

Excerpt from *The Life, Experience and Gospel Labours of the Rt. Rev. Richard Allen*, 1833

I was born in the year of our Lord 1760, on February 14th, a slave to Benjamin Chew, of Philadelphia. My mother and father and four children of us were sold into Delaware State, near Dover, and I was a child and lived with him until I was upwards of twenty years of age, during which time I was awakened and brought to see myself poor, wretched and undone, and without the mercy of God must be lost. . . . My sins were a heavy burden. I was tempted to believe there was no mercy for me. I cried to the Lord both night and day. One night I thought hell would be my portion. I cried unto Him who delighteth to hear the prayers of a poor sinner; and all of a sudden my dungeon shook, my chains flew off, and glory to God, I cried. My soul was filled. I cried, enough for me—the Saviour died. Now my confidence was strengthened that the Lord, for Christ's sake, had heard my prayers, and pardoned all my sins. I was constrained to go from house to house, exhorting my old companions, and telling to all around what a dear Saviour I had found. I joined the Methodist society, and met in class at Benjamin Wells's, in the forest, Delaware State. John Gray was the class-leader. I met in his class for several years.

My master was an unconverted man, and all the family; but he was what the world called a good master. He was more like a father to his slaves than any thing else. He was a very tender, humane man. My mother and father lived with him for many years. He was brought into difficulty, not being able to pay for us; and mother having several children after he had bought us, he sold my mother and three children. My mother sought the

133. Noll, *Old Religion in a New World*, 114.

Lord and found favour with him, and became a very pious woman. There were three children of us remained with our old master. My oldest brother embraced religion, and my sister. Our neighbours, seeing that our master indulged us with the privilege of attending meeting once in two weeks, said that Stokeley's negroes would soon ruin him; and so my brother and myself held a council together that we would attend more faithfully to our master's business, so that it should not be said that religion made us worse servants, we would work night and day to get our crops forward, so that they should be disappointed. . . . So we always continued to keep our crops more forward than our neighbours; and we would attend public preaching once in two weeks, and class meeting once a week. At length our master said he was convinced that religion made slaves better and not worse, and often boasted of his slaves for their honesty and industry. Some time after I asked him if I might ask the preachers to come and preach at his house. He being old and infirm, my master and mistress cheerfully agreed for me to ask some of the Methodist preachers to come and preach at his house. . . . Preaching continued for some months; at length Freeborn Garrison preached from these words, "Thou art weighed in the balance, and art found wanting." In pointing out and weighing the different characters, and among the rest weighed the slave-holders, my master believed himself to be one of that number, and after that he could not be satisfied to hold slaves, believing it to be wrong. . . .

It was in the time of the old revolutionary war between Great Britain and the United States. The Methodists were the first people that brought glad tidings to the coloured people. I feel thankful that ever I heard a Methodist preach. We are beholden to the Methodists, under God, for the light of the Gospel we enjoy; for all other denominations preached so high-flown that we were not able to comprehend their doctrine. Sure am I that reading sermons will never prove so beneficial to the coloured people as spiritual or extempore preaching. I am well convinced that the Methodist has proved beneficial to thousands and ten times thousands. It is to be awfully feared that the simplicity of the Gospel that was among them fifty years ago, and that they conform more to the world and the fashions thereof, they would fare very little better than the people of the world. The discipline is altered considerably from what it was. We would ask for the good old way, and desire to walk therein. (Richard Allen, *The Life, Experience and Gospel Labours of the Rt. Rev. Richard Allen* [Philadelphia, 1833], 5–7, 19)

In 1784, Allen was approved to preach at the first conference of the Methodist Church in Baltimore, Maryland. He returned to Philadelphia, where he met and married his wife, Sarah. He became a preacher at Saint George's Methodist Episcopal Church, preaching as often as five times a day.[134] However, since the church was composed mostly of whites, he was restricted to the early morning services. Although it was typical for segregated seating to be designated as the "negro pew" or "African corner," St. George's Church required black parishioners to use chairs around the perimeter, rather than sit in the pews.

In 1787, while Allen and his friend, Absolom Jones, were kneeling to pray, a couple of white trustees forced them to their feet and demanded that they move out of the area reserved for whites. One of the trustees grabbed Jones and said, "You must get up—you must not kneel here."[135] Jones asked him to wait until the time of prayer was over, but the trustee retorted, "No, you must get up now, or I will call for aid and force you away."

In response to this incident, Allen and Jones left the church. In turn, they founded the Free African Society, an organization that assisted fugitive slaves and newly freed black migrants in Philadelphia.[136] In 1793, Allen bought a blacksmith shop and turned it into the Bethel Church for Negro Methodists. Six years later, he was ordained as a deacon by Francis Asbury. In 1816, when the African Methodist Episcopal Church formed separately, Allen served as the first bishop.

Richard Allen promoted preaching and singing the gospel.[137] In 1801, he published a hymnal titled *A Collection of Spiritual Songs and Hymns Selected from Various Authors*. This hymnbook contained fifty-four hymns without musical score. It included works by Isaac Watts, Charles Wesley, and John Newton, as well as texts written in the African American oral tradition. The songs employed call-and-response, as well as wandering refrains attached to the stanzas. The practice of wandering refrains was a form of improvisation, and many of the hymns became favorites at Methodist camp meetings.

Sunday School Movement

The Sunday school movement began in England as a means to reach delinquent children and youth with the gospel. Hannah Ball (1734–1792), a

134. Noll, *Old Religion in a New World*, 114.

135. Wayne E. Croft, *The Motif of Hope in African American Preaching during Slavery and the Post–Civil War Era* (Lanham, MD: Lexington, 2017), 35.

136. Noll, *Old Religion in a New World*, 114.

137. Noll, *Old Religion in a New World*, 116.

Methodist, organized a form of Sunday school in 1769, and a number of Anglicans conducted similar religious instruction as well. With encouragement from Sophia Cooke, also a Methodist, Robert Raikes Jr. (1735–1811), a Congregationalist newspaper editor, led the popular Sunday school movement that began in 1780.[138]

Raikes was the son of a newspaper proprietor and editor, and as a young man, he was moved by the plight of prisoners in Gloucester. When he became acquainted firsthand with the "great unwanted" multitude of children as a result of their parents' imprisonments, Raikes determined not to let his sympathy end without action. Therefore, he organized the first Sunday school in Sooty Alley, across the street from the city prison.[139]

For almost three years Raikes maintained this school without publicity. His goal was not simply to teach the children to read and write, but for them to believe in and to conduct themselves in a manner worthy of the gospel of Christ. The Sunday school's teachers, mostly women, taught the students about hygiene and discipline, as well as reading and writing, often with the Bible as their textbook.[140] Soon there were eight branch schools in Gloucester. Many impoverished parents sent their children to Sunday school to provide them with the best opportunity of education available. For children of the industrial revolution who worked six days a week, Sunday was the only time available to acquire life skills and hear stories of the Bible.

The success of Raikes's Sunday school soon caught the attention of John Wesley and other prominent Christian leaders who promoted the idea elsewhere. By 1785, a society formed in London to link Sunday schools there. Many of the Methodist and Baptist churches launched their own schools too, along with schools established by a number of factory owners. After Raikes's death, when a memorial to him was unveiled, it was estimated that a quarter million students were being taught weekly in Sunday schools.[141] Their lessons, taught mostly by laypeople, spoke of Jesus's life, death, and resurrection, and God's larger redemptive story.

138. M. Taylor, *Exploring Evangelism*, 284.

139. Michael J. Anthony and Warren S. Benson, *Exploring the History and Philosophy of Christian Education* (Eugene, OR: Wipf & Stock, 2011), 262.

140. Schmidt, *How Christianity Changed the World*, 184–85.

141. M. Taylor, *Exploring Evangelism*, 285.

Discussion Questions

1. The Marian exiles under "Bloody Mary" returned to England from Switzerland to shape the Puritans. The exiles persecuted by King James returned to England from the Netherlands to shape the Baptists. Why were refugees and displaced (diaspora) peoples, including Moravian Brethren from Moravia and Bohemia, so receptive to theological and spiritual renewal? Does this phenomenon happen today? What should be our response?
2. George Whitefield and the Wesley brothers experienced fruit from open-air evangelistic meetings. Should this be accepted as the work of the Holy Spirit and not reproducible in human terms? Might mass evangelism still work in some cultures and places? Might it be effective in the future?
3. John Wesley was deeply affected by the Moravian-Herrnhut community but also by his study of Anglican theology. What theological understandings formed his view of societies, classes, and bands? How did his mother, Susannah, shape his view of disciple-making?
4. For Charles Wesley, prisons were a fertile ground to proclaim the gospel. Why are so many Christians hesitant to share the good news in jails and prisons? Charles's hymns were an expression of his understanding of God's redemptive work in Christ. Why are hymns and spiritual songs such a powerful medium for the gospel? How can we use music today as part of our evangelism?
5. How should we think about Whitefield's ties to evangelism in the American colonies and to slavery for the economic stability of his orphanage in Georgia? How about John Wesley's success at disciple-making and his difficult marriage with Mary Vaizelle Wesley? What can we learn from these evangelists and their faults?

9

Frontier to Urban Evangelism

> Our Heavenly Father, we pray that thou wilt give us more and more of the compassion of Christ. We read from the very beginning that he was moved with compassion, as this good Samaritan, when he met this poor, wounded and dying man. O God, give us the spirit of the good Samaritan! . . . May we go to the homes of the poor drunkards; may we go to the homes and hearts of gamblers, the homes of the fallen, the despised and the outcast, and tell them of Christ and heaven. O Spirit of God! come down upon this assembly, and may the Church of God find out who their neighbors are. And, O God, we pray thee that they may be filled with the Spirit of Christ, and that they may go and tell others the story of the cross.
>
> —Dwight L. Moody[1]

Following the American Revolution, the new republic—the United States of America—was founded with the separation of church and state and with religious liberty. In 1791, the First Amendment to the Constitution stated, "Congress shall make no law respecting an establishment of religion, or prohibiting the free exercise thereof."[2] Without an established church of the state, religion moved from the realm of government. As original states

1. Dwight L. Moody, Ira D. Sankey, and L. T. Remlap, *The Gospel Awakening: Comprising the Sermons and Addresses, Prayer-Meeting Talks and Bible Readings of the Great Revival Meetings Conducted by Moody and Sankey* (St. Louis: Scammel, 1878), 721.

2. Mark A. Noll, *The Old Religion in a New World: The History of North American Christianity* (Grand Rapids: Eerdmans, 2001), 72.

and colonial churches disestablished from each other, the new republic was no longer characterized by a political Christendom with an alliance of state and church.

The new reality was religious pluralism that included Roman Catholics, Jews, Deists, and Protestants of various traditions.[3] While the new republic was not established as a Christian nation, the Judeo-Christian influence was prominent and shaped the nation's cultural Christendom. Since previously state-sponsored denominations could no longer rely on government for funding, they found it necessary to compete in America's "free market religious economy."[4]

In this setting, churches and denominations that were deliberate at evangelism flourished. In particular, the Methodists and Baptists grew ahead of others because of their strong appeals to settlers and immigrants arriving in the cities and the frontier. Revival meetings remained as the starting point of evangelism.

The churches and denominations that were formerly established colonial churches—Puritans in Massachusetts and Anglicans in Virginia, for example—and previously held a "religious monopoly," worked to maintain their members and assimilate new arrivals from the homeland.[5] In some cases, their clergymen accused the newer denominations of "sheep stealing." In some instances, when clergy found America's "competition for souls" unnerving, they simply returned to the homeland and the familiar pattern of the state church there. Clergy who remained in the United States warned their adherents of the "heresies" of the other denominations, and to steer clear of them. Their objective was to keep all their sheep. This fostered an attitude of sectarianism or prejudice against other denominations.

Overall, the religious free market of the new republic did not adversely affect religious vitality. Rather, the competition for souls promoted efficiency and effectiveness on the part of clergy and churches. The competitive environment, nevertheless, could be perceived as rivalry and disunity, especially as churches and denominations moved closer to one another, into the same states, cities, and towns.

3. Noll, *Old Religion in a New World*, 18–19.

4. Roger Finke and Rodney Stark, *The Churching of America, 1776–1990: Winners and Losers in Our Religious Economy* (New Brunswick, NJ: Rutgers University Press, 2006), 54–59.

5. Finke and Stark, *Churching of America*, 60.

Religious pluralism did not necessarily end with sectarian attitudes, however. Some Protestants sought voluntary cooperation, or evangelical ecumenism, in an effort to join forces in evangelism and demonstrate Christian unity.

Evangelism on the American Frontier

In 1783, with the Treaty of Paris, the Mississippi River was established as the western boundary of the United States, and the trickle of settlers between the Allegheny Mountains and the Mississippi became a broad stream. Although small cities sprang up, the vast majority of settlers were scattered in valleys and forests. Life was hard as they struggled to clear land for crops and to harvest game for meat. At first, churches and clergy were sparse, but despite the challenges, thousands of settlers came to faith in Jesus and formed local congregations.[6]

There were encounters with Indian tribes—sometimes peaceful and sometimes hostile because of the settlers' encroachment. Native peoples were driven repeatedly from their lands. While Roman Catholic and Protestant missionaries sought to evangelize the tribes, government policies were often at odds with the gospel of Jesus Christ, making it difficult, if not impossible, for missionaries to evangelize, despite their protests over injustices. In areas where Christian missions found success, white settlers worshiped alongside indigenous Americans as well as enslaved Africans.[7]

Presbyterian missionaries traveled to Mississippi with the hope of evangelizing native peoples there. They ministered also to slaves on plantations in the Natchez District. The result was that more slaves than native peoples became members of these mission churches. Yet both enslaved Africans and indigenous Americans enrolled in the mission schools, ministered independently among their communities, and exercised leadership in newly formed churches.

Frontier Baptists

Baptist farmer-preachers lived among the settlers, ministering bivocationally on the pattern they had done in the eastern states. The farmer-preachers had

6. Milton L. Rudnick, *Speaking the Gospel through the Ages: A History of Evangelism* (St. Louis: Concordia, 1984), 173.

7. Barbara Krauthamer, *Black Slaves, Indian Masters: Slavery, Emancipation, and Citizenship in the Native American South* (Chapel Hill: University of North Carolina Press, 2015), 55.

little or no theological education but possessed a deep conviction of God's call to preach the gospel. They cleared fields, pulled stumps, tilled ground, split timber, raised barns, planted crops, fed hogs, preached sermons, officiated weddings, and conducted funerals.[8] They identified closely with the people by living and working with them.

John Taylor (1752–1833) was a pioneer Baptist planter-preacher in Kentucky. He was born into an Anglican family in Virginia and converted to faith under the ministry of William Marshall, a Baptist.[9] Two years later, Taylor was convinced that he needed to be baptized as a believing Christian, even though he was baptized as an infant. After his second baptism he joined the ranks of the Baptists and preached on Virginia's frontier.

In 1783, Taylor and his family journeyed by boat and horseback to Kentucky, settling in Woodward County, where he cleared woods for a farm. He and other Baptists in the area founded the Clear Creek Baptist Church, where he served for nine years. In 1795, he moved with his family to Boone County, where he was the designated preacher of Bullittsburg Baptist Church, the first congregation in the region.[10] As a bivocational preacher, he acquired both land and slaves to work the land. At the time, Taylor owned seven slaves, who became members of the Bullittsburg church.

In the early 1800s, the church experienced a revival in which nearly a hundred people converted to faith and were baptized. Not long afterward, Taylor and his family moved to Gallatin County along the Ohio River, where he purchased nearly three thousand acres of land and entered the planter class, holding twenty slaves. He maintained his preaching tours every summer and helped plant seven more churches in Kentucky, western Virginia, North Carolina, and Tennessee.[11]

Taylor's daughter, Jane, married Jeconiah Singleton, a Baptist pioneer-preacher. He and Joseph Craig, also a preacher, migrated from Virginia to Kentucky in 1781, with what was known as the Travelling Church of nearly six hundred members.[12] Craig came to Gilbert's Creek, Kentucky, along with "his beloved slave," Peter Durrett.

8. Luther M. Dorr, *The Bivocational Pastor* (Nashville: Broadman, 1988), 24.

9. William W. Sweet, *The Story of Religion in America* (Grand Rapids: Baker, 1973), 216.

10. John Taylor, *Baptists on the American Frontier: A History of Ten Baptist Churches of Which the Author Has Been Alternately a Member*, 3rd ed. (Macon, GA: Mercer University Press, 1995), 261–310.

11. Ed Stetzer, *Planting Missional Churches* (Nashville: B&H Academic, 2006), 58–59.

12. Thomas S. Kidd and Barry Hankins, *Baptists in America: A History* (New York: Oxford University Press, 2019), 69.

Peter Durrett (ca. 1733–1823) became a Baptist slave-preacher. Durrett was born into slavery on a plantation in Virginia and, after converting to faith, became active as a Baptist exhorter. In 1781, when he learned that his wife's slaveholder was planning to migrate to Kentucky, he convinced his own master to broker an exchange that would allow him and his wife to stay together. With the request granted, Durrett and his wife migrated with their new common master, Joseph Craig.

Initially, Durrett and his wife were members of Craig's church near Lexington. However, they soon gathered together slaves, preached the gospel, and baptized fifty people. Although Durrett was never ordained to public ministry, he and his wife had founded the First African Church of Lexington, Kentucky, by the year 1790.[13] This was the first Baptist congregation of African slaves west of the Allegheny Mountains, and the third black congregation in the United States.[14] At Durrett's death, the congregation totaled nearly three hundred members.

The self-determining, self-supporting, and self-governing feature of Baptist churches allowed them to multiply easily. Moreover, the Baptists did not require extensive education, whether for the slave-preacher or the planter-preacher. A preaching pastor simply needed to demonstrate a divine call to ministry, the gift of preaching, and a basic knowledge of the Scriptures.

Camp Meetings on the Frontier

The distinctive means of evangelism through the Cumberland Gap of Kentucky and Tennessee was the camp meeting, a series of revival meetings that lasted for a week or ten days. Settlers of the region gathered from miles around and slept in covered wagons and tents on the revival campgrounds.[15] News of upcoming camp meetings spread by those who had attended earlier, and by traveling evangelists. Frontiersmen brought their families, neighbors, and friends with them to the meetings. Services were held daily, generally at 11:00 a.m., 3:00 p.m., and 7:00 p.m.

At night, the campground was illuminated by large campfires. Organizers built platforms for the preachers and plank seating for the hearers. A pen of

13. Kidd and Hankins, *Baptists in America*, 69, 106.

14. George Washington Ranck, *"The Travelling Church": An Account of the Baptist Exodus from Virginia to Kentucky in 1781 under the Leadership of Rev. Lewis Craig and Capt. William Ellis* (Louisville, 1910), 22.

15. John B. Boles, *The Great Revival: Beginnings of the Bible Belt* (Lexington: University Press of Kentucky, 1996), 87–110.

Figure 9.1. Camp Meeting, watercolor by J. Maze Burbank, ca. 1839, Old Dartmouth Historical Society–New Bedford Whaling Museum, New Bedford, Massachusetts. *(The Picture Art Collection/Alamy Stock Photo)*

rails for anxious souls was constructed near the preaching platform. The meetings were ecumenical, hosted by Presbyterian, Baptist, and Methodist preachers who cooperated despite their doctrinal differences.

Settlers were drawn to camp meetings for social and spiritual reasons. Some were drawn by curiosity, some were seeking salvation, others were looking for a spouse, and some came "seeking sin." Opportunities for drunkenness in the whiskey culture, and for sexual promiscuity, were equally present.[16] Thus, the organizers appointed camp police to monitor the mixed crowds, and boys were hired to keep stray dogs and wild animals from roaming the campgrounds.

The revival services consisted mostly of singing hymns and preaching. The messages emphasized personal salvation from the horrors of hell and the promise of heaven for those who turned to Christ.[17] In order to prepare for conversion, sinners were invited to lament their sins and to pray for the Holy Spirit to work in their souls.[18]

16. Earle E. Cairns, *An Endless Line of Splendor: Revivals and Their Leaders from the Great Awakening to the Present* (Eugene, OR: Wipf & Stock, 2015), 101.

17. Rudnick, *Speaking the Gospel*, 175.

18. Rudnick, *Speaking the Gospel*, 175.

James McGready and Barton Stone

At Daniel Boone's invitation, two Presbyterian preachers, James McGready and Barton Stone, came to the Cumberland Gap. James McGready (ca. 1758–1817) had experienced revival in North Carolina and again at Hampden-Sidney College in Virginia, and hoped to see a similar revival on the western frontier.[19] In 1796, he moved to southern Ohio and then to Logan County, Kentucky. Four years later, he welcomed a group of Presbyterians to the Red River Meetinghouse in order to take part in the Lord's Supper.[20] The "lukewarm Presbyterians" who heard his fiery sermons and prayer meetings were spiritually awakened.[21] One person commented about McGready, "His person was not prepossessing nor his appearance interesting, except his remarkable gravity, and small piercing eyes. His coarse, tremulous voice excited in me the idea of something unearthy. His gestures were the reverse of elegance. Everything appeared by him forgotten, but the salvation of souls."[22] It was said that when McGready preached, people started shouting, fainting, and falling to the ground.[23]

McGready joined with other preachers to hold camp meetings at Gasper River in Logan County, and the response was dramatic, especially among the youth. As news of revival spread throughout Kentucky, the demand for similar camp meetings increased.

In 1801, Barton Stone (1772–1844), along with Methodist, Presbyterian, and Baptist preachers, organized a camp meeting at Cane Ridge in Bourbon County, Kentucky. Over twelve thousand people attended, coming from Kentucky, Tennessee, and Ohio.[24] A Methodist preacher described the scene at Cane Ridge:

> The vast seas of human being seemed to be agitated as if by a storm. I counted seven ministers, all preaching at one time, some on stumps,

19. Cairns, *Endless Line of Splendor*, 100.

20. Paulus Scharpff, *History of Evangelism: Three Hundred Years of Evangelism in Germany, Great Britain, and the United States of America* (Grand Rapids: Eerdmans, 1966), 102.

21. Cairns, *Endless Line of Splendor*, 100.

22. Charles W. Ferguson, *Organizing to Beat the Devil* (New York: Doubleday, 1971), 123, in Darius Salter, *American Evangelism: Its Theology and Practice* (Grand Rapids: Baker, 1996), 88.

23. Salter, *American Evangelism*, 88–89.

24. John Mark Terry, *Evangelism: A Concise History* (Nashville: B&H, 2014), 135.

> others in wagons, and one was standing on a tree which had, in falling, lodged against another. . . . Some of the people were singing, others praying, some crying for mercy in the most piteous accents, while others were shouting most vociferously. While witnessing such scenes, a peculiarly-strange sensation, such as I had never felt before, came over me. My heart beat tumultuously, my knees trembled, my lips quivered, and I felt as though I must fall to the ground. A strange supernatural power seemed to pervade the entire mass of mind there collected. . . . I stepped up on to a log, where I could have a better view of the surging sea of humanity. . . . Immediately followed shrieks and shouts that rent the very heavens.[25]

Hundreds of such camp meetings were held. However, the large camp meetings were soon replaced by revival meetings held at local churches.[26] Nonetheless, gatherings in campgrounds around campfires with gospel messages continued as a vital means of evangelism.

Frontier Methodists

Methodists remained an evangelistic force on the American frontier as they lived according to the simple motto "Saved to save."[27] The Methodists divided regions into districts, and districts into circuits that spanned some five hundred square miles. To cover a circuit, a circuit rider traveled on horseback for four to six weeks. Each rider was supervised by a district overseer, or so-called presiding elder, who also traveled a circuit. The bishops had oversight of the presiding elders and also traveled widely as they supervised districts.

Methodist preachers were commonly young single men with little theological education but possessing a deep commitment to Christ. They journeyed on horseback but also traveled by canoe and on foot, preaching to all who would listen. Following Wesley's model in England, Methodists in America preached in town squares, school houses, barns, and open fields. Horace Bishop, a circuit rider, described his experience, saying, "I preached twenty-eight times a month. I never took breakfast and dinner at the same

25. Ferguson, *Organizing to Beat the Devil*, 136, cited in Salter, *American Evangelism*, 93–94.

26. Scharpff, *History of Evangelism*, 102.

27. Scharpff, *History of Evangelism*, 98–99.

place except on Friday, which was laundry day in the country. . . . My wardrobe was one end of my saddlebags; my bookcase the other end. . . . My 'study' was the shade of any tree on the way to my appointments, where there was grass for my horse. . . . I slept wherever it was convenient, on a sheepskin or my Mexican blanket, occasionally on a dirt or a puncheon floor."[28]

The listeners who converted to faith were invited to join a Methodist society or class, where they learned to practice the disciplines of the Christian life.[29] When circuit riders visited classes, they checked on the spiritual progress of the new converts. While resident pastors eventually took over, circuit riders served the Methodist meetings until a local congregation could be formed. Any young man, and occasionally a woman, who demonstrated evidence of conversion to Christ and had the potential to preach was invited by a Methodist preacher to deliver a trial sermon. If the young person was effective, he or she received an exhorter's license from the Quarterly Conference.[30]

Evangelism in America's Northeast

Methodists did not apply this strategy only on the American frontier, but also used it to reach people in the Northeast. They gained exhorters, who, during intervals between circuit rider's visits, could direct the spiritual life of a Methodist class. Sometimes hundreds of people attended weekday meetings where an exhorter brought a simple testimony of faith and exhorted the people from the Scriptures.[31] With time, the exhorter might become an itinerant preacher with his or her own circuit of Methodist classes to visit and oversee.

Jarena Lee

Jarena Lee (1783–1864) was the first African American woman to become a Methodist exhorter. She was born into a free family in Cape May, New Jersey.[32] At seven years of age, she worked as a domestic servant, and then as

28. Ross Phares, *Bible in Pocket, Gun in Hand* (Lincoln: University of Nebraska Press, 1964), 156, cited in Terry, *Evangelism*, 128.

29. Rudnick, *Speaking the Gospel*, 174.

30. Scharpff, *History of Evangelism*, 99.

31. Scharpff, *History of Evangelism*, 97.

32. Carla L. Peterson, *Doers of the Word: African American Women Speakers and Writers in the North, 1830–1880* (New York: Oxford University Press, 1995), 23, 73.

a teenager she moved to Philadelphia, where she continued the same work. In Philadelphia she visited Bethel Church, where she heard a message by Richard Allen. In response, she converted to faith and was filled with the Holy Spirit.

In 1811, Jarena married Joseph Lee, a pastor of a Methodist society at Snow Hill, just outside Philadelphia.[33] Then she became deathly ill and later recalled, "From this sickness I did not expect to recover, and there was but one thing which bound me to earth, and this was, that I had not as yet preached the gospel to the fallen sons and daughters of Adam's race, to the satisfaction of my mind. I wished to go from one end of the earth to the other, crying, Behold, behold the lamb! To this end I earnestly prayed the Lord to raise me up, if consistent with his will."[34]

After seven years of marriage, Joseph died, leaving Jarena and their two small children to fend for themselves. Despite her condition, she heard a voice telling her, "Go preach the Gospel! . . . Preach the Gospel; I will put words in your mouth."[35] On one occasion, when a preacher was unable to finish his message, Lee stepped in spontaneously and did so extraordinarily. As a result, Allen affirmed God's call on her life to proclaim Jesus's gospel publicly. In 1819, she was licensed as an exhorter of the African Methodist Episcopal Church.

Excerpt from *Religious Experience and Journal of Mrs. Jarena Lee; Giving an Account of Her Call to Preach the Gospel*, 1849

June 10th, 1824. Left Eastern Shore for a journey to Bath [Pennsylvania], and went around the circuit with brother J. B., the elder. In the Old Methodist Church, at Fory's Neck, I had the privilege of speaking to a large congregation, which was made the power of God unto salvation. Visited Lewistown, and had a blessed meeting in the Methodist Church. The tears of the penitent flowed sweetly, which always encourages me to persevere in proclaiming the glad tidings of a risen Saviour to my fellow beings. When the heart is thus melted into tenderness, I feel assured the Lord sanctions the feeble effort of His poor servant—it is a good omen to my mind that the mourner is not

33. Peterson, *Doers of the Word*, 73.

34. Jarena Lee, *Religious Experience and Journal of Mrs. Jarena Lee, Giving an Account of Her Call to Preach the Gospel* (Philadelphia, 1849), 14.

35. Ruth A. Tucker and Walter Liefeld, *Daughters of the Church: Women and Ministry from New Testament Times to the Present* (Grand Rapids: Zondervan, 1987), 260.

forsaken of God, and that he yet stands knocking at the door for admittance. Oh! that those who weep for an absent Jesus may be comforted by hearing Him say—"Thy sins, which were many, are all forgiven thee: go in peace and sin no more." Elder J. B. preached in Greensboro, where I attended, and had a quickening time. Some enmity had existed among the brethren, but the spirit of love got the ascendancy, and the lion became as the lamb. The gospel is the best remedy to subdue the evil passions of men that has ever been discovered. Dear Master, let Thy gospel spread to earth's remotest bounds. I have travelled, in four years, sixteen hundred miles and of that I walked two hundred and eleven miles, and preached the kingdom of God to the falling sons and daughters of Adam, counting it all joy for the sake of Jesus. Many times cast down but not forsaken; willing to suffer as well as love. I spoke at Harris's Mills, in a dwelling house, to a large concourse of people, from Paul's Epistle to the Ephesians. . . . I observed there were some present that never would meet me again. Mr. J. B., the elder, then requested me to lead the class. Much mourning, weeping and rejoicing. Four days afterwards, a man that sat under this sermon, (a shoemaker by occupation) fell dead from his bench without having any testimony of a hope in Christ. How dreadful to relate the wicked shall not live out half their days. . . . The effects of the gospel of Christ was no less than at other great seasons, but was wonderful—backsliders reclaimed and sinners converted—there was mourning, weeping, shouting and praising of God for what he had done. I preached several sermons, and was well treated by all circles of people. We had large congregations of well-behaved people; and feeling my work done in this part, I proceeded to Carlisle, Pa. There was a small body of members; I spoke and led class for them during the time I was there, which was ten days; felt my discharge of God, and took stage to Shippensburg. There was great success at this place; fifteen joined the Church; some of the most hardened sinners became serious and reformed. I was astonished at the wonderful operations of the Spirit, and the immense congregations. At the first sermon the house was crowded, and I had the good attention of the people. A man came into the house intoxicated, and offered to interrupt by speaking, but a gentleman put him out so quietly that it had no effect upon the meeting. When I contemplate the goodness of God to the human family, in putting them in a proper capacity of choosing the way of salvation, I feel sometimes almost lost, to think that God has called such a worm as I to spread the common Saviour's name. But said the Lord, "I will send by whom I will"—praise the Lord who willeth not the death of sinners—"as I live, saith the Lord, I have no pleasure in the death of the wicked, but that they turn and live." (Jarena Lee, *Religious Experience and Journal of Mrs. Jarena Lee, Giving an Account of Her Call to Preach the Gospel* [Philadelphia, 1849], 35–42)

In addition to opposition by church leaders, the task of caring for her children made her itinerant ministry quite challenging. At first her mother cared for the children, and later Allen and his wife, Sarah, took care of the girls. In addition to preaching, Lee was active as an abolitionist and joined the American Antislavery Society in 1839.[36] Her work as an itinerant preacher led her to New Jersey, Pennsylvania, New York, Ohio, Michigan, and Canada. In one year alone she traveled nearly 2,500 miles and preached 178 sermons.

Revival at Yale College

Following the American Revolution, churches in New England were confronted not only with a loss of members but also with the continued controversy over revivalism, as well as by a division over Unitarianism—the doctrine that denied the triune nature of God. However, between the years 1797 and 1801, a series of revivals spread from Connecticut to New Hampshire.

Students at Yale College under President Timothy Dwight (1752–1817) were stirred in their faith and desired to follow Christ. Several evangelistic and missionary organizations soon formed. Some printed and distributed Bibles; others supported Christian education, especially Sunday schools; and others dealt with social concerns such as temperance, the abolition of slavery, and assistance to the poor and homeless. Since most denominations did not accept these causes as integral to the church's mission, concerned Christians united their energies and resources to meet the needs.[37]

The distribution of gospel literature had been undertaken already by the London-based Religious Tract Society, founded in 1799. A well-known convert through this ministry was Hudson Taylor (1832–1905), missionary to China and founder of the China Inland Mission. In the United States, the New England Religious Tract Society was organized in 1814, and in 1823 the name was changed to the American Tract Society. This society employed

36. Peterson, *Doers of the Word*, 74.
37. Rudnick, *Speaking the Gospel*, 173.

over six hundred colporteurs who distributed literature, with at least one hundred working among German immigrants.[38]

The society distributed thousands of pieces of literature in various languages to newly arriving immigrants at Castle Garden, and then Ellis Island, in New York City.[39] An example of a tract from 1814, titled *The Warning Voice*, followed an outline that sounded a warning to the reader who

> First, is living in sin,
> Second, remains a stranger of God and Christ,
> Third, thus, makes God his or her enemy,
> Fourth, lives with the reality of death and judgment, and,
> Fifth, must see the Gospel of Jesus Christ as the only way of escape.[40]

Another development came in New York in 1826, when representatives of the Congregational, Presbyterian, and Reformed churches founded the American Home Missionary Society to coordinate efforts to spread the gospel and plant new churches in the United States, especially within immigrant communities.

In further regard to the spiritual awakening at Yale College, the revival took a new direction when Nathaniel Taylor (1786–1858), professor of theology at Yale Divinity School, began to integrate revival experiences with Calvinist theology. While maintaining Reformed doctrine, Taylor affirmed that humans were free, rational, and moral creatures, able to make their own decision for God.[41] As this view grew in popularity, revivals were seen increasingly as the work of gifted preachers who were able to persuade sinners to believe and be saved.

Charles Grandison Finney

Charles G. Finney (1792–1875) was trained as a lawyer and experienced a dramatic conversion in 1821 that redirected his energies to preaching. He claimed

38. Scharpff, *History of Evangelism*, 103.

39. "The Gospel in 30 Tongues," *New York Times*, February 24, 1907, https://www.nytimes.com/1907/02/24/archives/the-gospel-in-30-tongues-american-tract-society-disseminated-much.html.

40. "The Warning Voice," in *Tracts Published by the New England Tract Society*, vol. 1 (Andover, MA: Flagg and Gould, 1814), 77–84.

41. Rudnick, *Speaking the Gospel*, 172.

that he received "a retainer from the Lord Jesus Christ to plead His cause."[42] Finney studied theology under the supervision of a Presbyterian minister and was ordained in 1824, despite his lack of formal theological education. He began preaching in small towns in upstate New York but moved to larger towns such as Troy and Utica.[43] In 1830, he held evangelistic meetings in Rochester and New York, and then traveled to Boston and Philadelphia.[44]

In 1835, Finney became president of Oberlin College in Ohio, founded just two years earlier in America's midwestern frontier. In his new role, he developed his theology of revivalism and prepared hundreds of students for evangelism. Despite his demands as president of the college, he remained active as an evangelist, preaching six months of the year, and conducted two preaching tours to England.[45]

Finney's contribution to evangelism was mostly methodological. His "new measures" were adapted from the frontier camp meetings. These measures included "protracted meetings," meaning revival meetings were held morning, afternoon, and evening, as long as the Spirit led. Another measure was use of the "anxious bench," where the "anxious" were invited to sit and meet with workers for spiritual counsel.[46] As was his custom, Finney called those who decided to give themselves fully to Christ to take a "first step" and stand up for prayer as a way to testify publicly to their faith in Christ.[47] In addition, he provided immediate instruction for new converts, stressing the need for them to join and serve in a local church. Finally, he emphasized Christian stewardship and taught that God owned all their possessions and that they needed to manage them well.[48]

Finney promoted his campaigns on the pattern of politicians in an effort to create interest and expectancy.[49] Posters and handbills were distributed throughout the towns and cities where he held meetings. Teams of visitors went door-to-door to invite residents to come and hear him. Prayer meetings were organized weeks in advance to ensure cooperation among all the pastors and churches, and to ask for God's blessing on the event.

42. Noll, *Old Religion in a New World*, 96–97.

43. Charles E. Hambrick-Stowe, *Charles G. Finney and the Spirit of American Revivalism* (Grand Rapids: Eerdmans, 1996), 46.

44. Salter, *American Evangelism*, 95.

45. Scharpff, *History of Evangelism*, 95, 108.

46. Douglas A. Sweeney, *The American Evangelical Story* (Grand Rapids: Baker Academic, 2005), 69; Salter, *American Evangelism*, 96.

47. Scharpff, *History of Evangelism*, 109.

48. Scharpff, *History of Evangelism*, 110.

49. Rudnick, *Speaking the Gospel*, 181.

As president of Oberlin College, Finney promoted not only preaching of the gospel but also social reform.[50] The school admitted female and African American students at a time when almost all other colleges did not. Moreover, Oberlin became a central base for abolitionists and served as a "station on the underground railroad," providing safe houses for runaway slaves bound for Canada. In 1858, when a slave named John Price was captured and taken by a US marshal to nearby Wellington, Ohio, a group of faculty, students, townspeople, and former slaves at Oberlin helped rescue him. Because they broke the Fugitive Slave Law that required an escaped slave to be returned to his master, thirty-seven of those from Oberlin were charged, and twenty-one were taken to Cleveland for trial and kept in jail for eighty-four days.

While Southern evangelicals such as Thornton Stringfellow in his book titled *Scriptural and Statistical Views in Favor of Slavery*[51] argued from the Bible to justify slaveholding, Theodore Dwight Weld (1803–1895), a convert to Christ at one of Finney's meetings, published counterarguments in his books *The Bible against Slavery* and *American Slavery As It Is*.[52] In 1835, Finney gave his own response to slavery, saying,

> The fact is that slavery is, pre-eminently, the sin of the church. It is the very fact that ministers and professors of religion of different denominations hold slaves, which sanctifies the whole abomination, in the eyes of ungodly men. . . . It is the church that mainly supports this sin. Her united testimony upon this subject would settle the question. Let Christians of all denominations meekly but firmly come forth, and pronounce their verdict, let them clear their communions, and wash their hands of this thing, let them give forth and write on the head and front of this great abomination, SIN! and in three years, a public sentiment would be formed that would carry all before it, and there would not be a shackled slave, nor a bristling, cruel slave-driver in this land.[53]

50. Priscilla Pope-Levison, *Models of Evangelism* (Grand Rapids: Baker Academic, 2020), 121–22.

51. Thornton Stringfellow, *Scriptural and Statistical Views in Favor of Slavery* (Richmond, VA: J. W. Randolph, 1856).

52. Theodore Dwight Weld, *The Bible against Slavery* (New York: American Anti-Slavery Society, 1838); Weld, *American Slavery as It Is: Testimony of a Thousand Witnesses* (New York: American Anti-Slavery Society, 1839). See Alvin J. Schmidt, *How Christianity Changed the World* (Grand Rapids: Zondervan, 2009), 280–82; Ruth A. Tucker, *Parade of Faith: A Biographical History of the Christian Church* (Grand Rapids: Zondervan, 2015), 405.

53. Charles G. Finney, *Lectures on Revivals of Religion* (New York: Leavitt, Lord, 1835), 137–38. Cf. Noll, *Old Religion in a New World*, 107.

Figure 9.2. Oberlin rescuers at Cuyahoga County jail, 1859, T. J. Rice, photographer. *(Library of Congress Prints & Photographs Online Catalog, cph 3b20680)*

Through Finney and his colleagues, Asa Mahan and Thomas Upham, Oberlin remained a center for evangelism and abolition.[54] Furthermore, the school promoted the spiritual life of "walking in the Spirit in righteousness and holiness," and "being filled with the Holy Spirit."[55] Finney claimed himself to have experienced a special empowerment of the Spirit in his evangelistic meetings.

Despite being a Presbyterian, Finney rejected certain tenets of Calvinism and embraced Arminianism. He held that sinners needed to know of God's redemptive work in Christ and that they could remain candidates for eternal condemnation or choose God's forgiveness and eternal blessedness. Of course, Finney did not believe that the sinner could make this decision apart from the work of the Spirit, but the Spirit did not make the saving decision for the sinner.[56] The Spirit enabled the sinner to decide.

54. Salter, *American Evangelism*, 123.

55. Scharpff, *History of Evangelism*, 108. See Thomas C. Upham, *Principles of Interior or Hidden Life* (Boston: D. S. King, 1843); Upham, *The Life of Faith* (New York: Harper, 1852); Asa Mahan, *Baptism with the Holy Ghost* (Louisville: Pickett, 1870).

56. Sweeney, *American Evangelical Story*, 68.

Similarly, Finney believed that God puts resources, both divine and human, for revival at the disposal of the church and that evangelists could precipitate revival by utilizing them. The two divine resources or agencies were divine providence and the Holy Spirit. Providence arranged external factors in such a way as to bring sinners into contact with divine truth. The Holy Spirit gave power to this truth when applied to the sinner. The two human resources or agencies were the preacher and the sinner.[57] The preacher acted so that the sinner received the Word of truth personally. In his lecture titled "How to Preach the Gospel," Finney said that "preaching should be conversational. . . . It must be the language of common life."[58] He further explained that the sinner, influenced by the preacher and others, including the Holy Spirit, acts to submit to the truth, to obey, or to refuse, as the case may be. A revival, then, according to Finney, was a well-designed and well-executed event in which these agencies combined to effect the conversion of sinners.

Asahel Nettleton

Asahel Nettleton (1783–1844) was alarmed by Finney's "new measures."[59] Nettleton's theology and practice of evangelism was distinctly Calvinistic. He was converted to faith during the spiritual awakening in North Killingworth, Connecticut, after reading the sermons of Jonathan Edwards.[60] Following his conversion, Nettleton had "a strong desire to become a missionary to the heathen," and after attending nearby Yale College, he was ordained to the gospel ministry in 1811.[61]

During the first decade of his ministry, Nettleton led revivals in New England. He operated differently than other evangelists, however. His practice was to move into a community for several weeks or months in order to get a sense of the spiritual condition of the people. Sometimes he filled pulpits of other churches where no pastor was employed, allowing him to care for people of the town. As a matter of policy, Nettleton would never preach where he had not been invited. He had witnessed earlier the problems that often resulted when resident pastors felt they were competing with itinerant evan-

57. C. Finney, *Lectures on Revivals of Religion*, 65.

58. C. Finney, *Lectures on Revivals of Religion*, 76.

59. Hambrick-Stowe, *Charles G. Finney*, 63–72.

60. Bennet Tyler and Andrew A. Bonar, *Nettleton and His Labours* (Edinburgh: T&T Clark, 1854), 20–27.

61. Tyler and Bonar, *Nettleton and His Labours*, 34–35.

gelists. With greater attention to pastoral care, Nettleton developed a ministry of home visitation, personal counseling, inquiry meetings, and pastoral follow-up that added to the effectiveness of his evangelistic preaching.[62]

Nettleton was Finney's most vocal critic and led the New Lebanon Conference in 1827, in which he and Lyman Beecher (1775–1863) attempted to persuade Finney and his colleagues to change their methods.[63] Nettleton rejected the idea that a preacher caused revival, and he recoiled against those who looked to him or any preacher, rather than God, to awaken sinners. He believed that salvation was the work of God alone, and therefore rejected Finney's use of the altar call, believing that this was a denial of the doctrine of total depravity. Despite Nettleton's efforts, Finney's approach to evangelism remained popular among Congregationalists and Presbyterians.[64]

Frontier Evangelism Westward

During the nineteenth century, American settlement expanded westward with the purchase of the Louisiana Territory from France in 1803. The Homestead Act and building of railways provided both incentives and means for settlers to travel west. In 1848, the Treaty of Guadalupe Hidalgo, following the Mexican-American War, gave land to the United States that became its southwestern territory. As settlers journeyed westward, Baptists sent missionaries and Methodists commissioned circuit riders to reach them with the good news.

John Mason Peck

John Mason Peck (1789–1858) was an American Baptist missionary. He came to faith at a revival meeting at the Congregational Church in his hometown of Litchfield, Connecticut. He married Sallie Paine and, shortly after the birth of their first son, joined a Baptist church.[65] After meeting Lu-

62. David W. Kling, "Edwards in the Second Great Awakening: The New Divinity Contributions of Edward Dorr Griffin and Asahel Nettleton," in *After Jonathan Edwards: The Courses of the New England Theology*, ed. Oliver D. Crisp and Douglas A. Sweeney (New York: Oxford University Press, 2012), 133.

63. Sweeney, *American Evangelical Story*, 70.

64. Sweeney, *American Evangelical Story*, 70.

65. William H. Brackney, "John Mason Peck," in *Biographical Dictionary of Christian Missions*, ed. Gerald H. Anderson (Grand Rapids: Eerdmans, 1999), 524.

ther Rice (1783–1836), Peck became interested in mission work and traveled to Philadelphia for further study. While there he met James Welch, his future coworker.

With secured funding, Peck and Welch became Baptist missionaries to Missouri Territory in 1817. They began preaching the gospel, and in the following February, Peck baptized two converts in the frigid Mississippi River. Peck soon founded the United Society for the Spread of the Gospel, taking up itinerant evangelism, as well as establishing Bible societies and Sunday school associations in St. Louis and the surrounding area.

In 1822, Peck moved to O'Fallon, Illinois, just east of St. Louis, where he traveled a circuit to visit the societies and Sunday schools he had established. During this time, he helped establish the African Baptist Church of St. Louis, known today as First Baptist Church. Of the original 220 members, two hundred were slaves.[66] Peck ordained a young freedman named John Berry Meachum (1789–1854) as pastor. Peck was invited to preach sermons on various occasions in the region and seized every opportunity to share the gospel. On one particular occasion, the title of his sermon was "The Snares of Sin. A Discourse Delivered from the Gallows in Edwardsville, Illinois, February 12, 1824, at the Execution of Eliphalet Green, for the Murder of William Wright."[67]

Under Peck's leadership, the American Baptist Home Mission Society was organized in 1832. This society was directed toward reaching settlers, indigenous Americans, and slaves. Peck also helped establish the Illinois State Baptist Convention in 1834 and served as its first president. He published widely in the areas of agriculture, Illinois history, geography, and indigenous Americans.[68] In 1843, he founded the American Baptist Publication Society and published a weekly religious journal titled *Western Pioneer*. During his tenure, he contributed to planting nearly nine hundred Baptist churches, ordaining six hundred pastors, and seeing thirty-two thousand people convert to faith. In 1852, Harvard College awarded him an honorary degree.

66. Harriet C. Frazier, *Runaway and Freed Missouri Slaves and Those Who Helped Them, 1763–1865* (Jefferson, NC: McFarland, 2004), 66.

67. John Mason Peck, *The Snares of Sin: A Discourse Delivered from the Gallows in Edwardsville, Illinois, February 12, 1824, at the Execution of Eliphalet Green, for the Murder of William Wright* (Edwardsville, IL: Hooper Warren, 1824).

68. John Mason Peck, *A Guide for Emigrants, Containing Sketches of Illinois, Missouri, and Adjacent Parts* (Boston: Lincoln and Edmands, 1831).

Ambrosio González

Shortly after Mexico declared independence from Spain, Presbyterian missionaries such as Sumner Bacon began distributing Spanish Bibles in Mexico, supplied by the American Bible Society.[69] Missionaries described how difficult evangelistic work was in Mexico, and this was only complicated by the Mexican-American War. For Mexican people to convert to the Protestant view of salvation by faith meant that they had to accept the teachings of their political enemies who had taken their land by military conquest.

In 1850, the Missionary Society of the Methodist Church sent Enoch Nicholson, along with his family, from Independence, Missouri, to Santa Fe, New Mexico. Three years later, he met Ambrosio González (1816–1884), south of Santa Fe, in the village of Peralta. Upon their meeting, Nicholson gave González a Spanish-language Bible.[70] González later recounted,

> It was the first Bible of any kind I had ever seen. . . . The book was a charm to me. When the rest retired, I sat up and read the good book. I read nearly the whole book of Genesis. I then turned to the New Testament and read several chapters in Saint John. One chapter was the fourteenth—"Let not your heart be troubled, etc."—It was to me a new book. I read until the chickens were crowing for day. I laid down on a lounge in the same room and soon fell asleep. When I woke the sun was shining through the window into my face. The Sun of Righteousness was shining brightly in my soul. I have been a Christian and a Protestant ever since.[71]

In 1855, the Methodist Church sent Dallas Lore to Peralta to examine the religious situation. In the three years since González had become an evangelical, Lore observed that seven men and seven women had converted to faith

69. Juan Francisco Martínez, *Sea la Luz: The Making of Mexican Protestantism in the American Southwest, 1829–1900* (Denton: University of North Texas Press, 2006), 51.

70. Moíses Sandoval, *Fronteras: A History of the Latin American Church in the USA since 1513* (San Antonio: Mexican American Cultural Center, 1983), 298.

71. Thomas Harwood, *History of New Mexico Spanish and English Missions of the Methodist Episcopal Church from 1850 to 1910* (Albuquerque: El Abogado, 1908), 1:45–46, cited in Eric Rivera, "The First Mexican Protestant Loved the Bible," *Christianity Today*, February 18, 2019, https://www.christianitytoday.com/history/2019/february/first-mexican-protestant-bible.html.

in Christ also and were meeting with González at his home. Before leaving Peralta, Lore organized the group into a Methodist class and appointed González as the class leader. It was reported in 1871 that "the little band of 14 had increased to 42."[72] Many people around Peralta viewed González as their pastor as he traveled to nearby mountain villages sharing the gospel, baptizing children, and accompanying Methodist missionaries in the area.[73]

Urban Evangelism in Britain and America

With the growth of the industrial revolution, numbers of people continued to move from rural areas to the cities, where they found work in mills and factories. This demographic shift brought new challenges and opportunities for evangelism in the urban centers. For example, in response to the industrial revolution that led to rapid urbanization in Scotland, Thomas Chalmers (1780–1843) promoted "district visitation" as a means of evangelizing adults and enlisting children in Sunday school.[74]

David Nasmith

David Nasmith (1799–1839) of Glasgow, Scotland, helped found over sixty Christian societies. At age fifteen, he and his friends founded three youth societies that supported foreign missions, tract distribution, and Bible reading.

Nasmith began work in manufacturing but hoped to become a missionary, applying to go to Africa and the South Seas, but was rejected because of his lack of education. Then he turned his evangelistic zeal to Glasgow, where he devoted his time to evangelistic and charitable work that included visiting local prisons. He once spent an entire night in a cell with two men who were to be executed the following day.[75]

In 1821, Nasmith became secretary of the Religious Societies of Glasgow. He founded the Young Men's Society for Religious Improvement in 1824, and two years later founded the Glasgow City Mission, which took Chalmers's

72. Harwood, *History of New Mexico Spanish and English Missions*, 46; Martínez, *Sea la Luz*, 58.

73. *Annual Report: Methodist Episcopal Church, Board of Home Mission and Extension for the Year 1875* (January 1876), 38.

74. Bainton, *Christianity*, 371–72.

75. John Campbell, *Memoirs of David Nasmith: His Labours and Travels in Great Britain, France, the United States and Canada* (London: Snow, 1844), 57.

district visitation further by making the work interdenominational, enlisting participation from all evangelical churches.[76] In this strategy, Nasmith encouraged the unchurched to attend an evangelical church and recruited laypeople full-time rather than using volunteers to conduct the evangelistic work. He discovered that not only were paid workers more dependable, but since several came from the working class, they were well suited to minister to the city's poor.[77]

When Nasmith founded Glasgow City Mission, the society's objective was "to promote the spiritual welfare of the poor of this city, and its neighbourhood, by employing persons of approved piety, and . . . properly qualified to visit the poor in their houses."[78] At the society's first annual meeting, he challenged the missionaries: "You will convert the houses that [are] tenanted by men of the foulest passions, into churches of the Redeemer, where the Lord the Spirit will dwell and the God of Salvation will be loved and served. You will arrest the progress of vice and promote the interest of virtue. You will make our poor, our ignorant, our degraded population stand forth in all that freshness and fairness of moral and of spiritual excellence."[79]

Besides the Glasgow City Mission, Nasmith formed the Edinburgh City Mission in 1832 and the London City Mission in 1835.[80] With his vision for city missions, he toured Scotland, Ireland, the United States, Canada, and France, encouraging local church leaders to form city missions and other evangelistic societies.

In this period of denominational rivalry, even among evangelicals, the London City Mission was founded as an interdenominational organization. Nevertheless, it had a shaky start. While its committee was drawn from eight denominations, some people in the Church of England were suspicious, even hostile, toward the society.[81] Therefore, Nasmith remained as secretary for over a year to work through any suspicions.

Nasmith clearly possessed an ability to organize mission work. However, he was not interested simply in founding societies. On one occasion,

76. Ian J. Shaw, "Thomas Chalmers, David Nasmith, and the Origins of the City Mission Movement," *Evangelical Quarterly* 76, no. 1 (January 2004): 35–36.

77. Shaw, "Thomas Chalmers, David Nasmith," 41.

78. Delores T. Burger, *Practical Religion: David Nasmith and the City Mission Movement, 1799–2000* (Kansas City, MO: Association of Gospel Rescue Missions, 2000), 27.

79. Burger, *Practical Religion*, 28.

80. Irene Howat and John Nicholls, *Streets Paved with Gold: The Story of the London City Mission* (London: Christian Focus, 2003).

81. Shaw, "Thomas Chalmers, David Nasmith," 37.

he stated his conviction, saying, "Every church shall be a missionary body, and every member a missionary."[82] He called churches to awaken from their slumber and to evangelize their neighborhoods.

At the founding of the Manchester City Mission in 1837, Nasmith said, "If we expected the poor to flood to our churches, we were greatly mistaken, and if we wanted our places of worship to be crowded, we must carry the Gospel to the homes of the poor."[83] The object of the Manchester mission was "not to make people Protestants or Roman Catholics, Baptist, Episcopalians, Methodists or any other sect," but "to unite all denominations of Christians, and by one strong effort, to pluck sinners as brands from the burning."[84]

Besides founding city missions, Nasmith helped train Sunday school teachers in Britain and the United States. His work was taken up by George Williams and the YMCA.

Excerpts from John Campbell, *Memoirs of David Nasmith*, 1844

David [Nasmith] was the means of promoting inquiry into the spiritual condition of the city population on the part of many who had never previously thought a moment on the subject. The zeal of some sentimental people promised, at first, to take a practical turn. "Some of the Lord's people here [in Ireland]," says David, "are speaking of forming a mission church with a pastor, teachers and evangelists; whose object it shall be, not only to edify those who may be associated in church fellowship, but to go forth and preach the gospel and plant churches in the cities, towns, and villages of Ireland, considering that every church is a missionary body. If this is of the Lord, it will prosper; if not, may it come to nought. Christ Jesus to be the bond of union, and not Presbyterianism, Independency, or Episcopacy. A union of saints is exceedingly desirable into one church of Christ, and a striving together for the advancement of the glory of God, and not our own opinion." . . . David plainly states that his missions were merely an artificial substitute for the churches of Christ, which are the natural missionary societies, the proper instruments for diffusing the Gospel, both at home and abroad. In a letter, about the same time, written to Mrs. Connell, the valued

82. Scharpff, *History of Evangelism*, 94.
83. *Manchester Guardian*, May 3, 1837, in Burger, *Practical Religion*, 46.
84. *Manchester Guardian*, May 3, 1837, in Burger, *Practical Religion*, 46.

relative of Mrs. Nasmith, David reverts to this important principle. "I long," says he, "for the period, when the churches of Christ, instead of these voluntary associations, formed for this purpose, shall become missionary bodies. There is a considerable shaking in that respect, in this place, not amongst the churches, but amongst individuals, as to the duty of churches. A church was formed yesterday week, of which Mr. Pope is pastor, upon such a basis, I mean, upon Scripture principles; but the principle that every member is, in his or her sphere, to become a missionary. Stir up your Christian friends to think of this!" (188–89, 190–91)

"These societies are of two classes, the natural and the artificial; the former Christian Churches, and the latter voluntary associations of Christian men. In the order of nature, conventional movements are first, and absolutely necessary. There is no other means of operation in a district of country, or in a locality of a town or city, where churches do not exist, or do not exist in number and strength sufficient to act congregationally upon the population around them. But these are only temporary expedients, which must ultimately give place to measures based on other principles. In proportion as churches come to exist in numbers and means adequate to the work of evangelizing their vicinities, the necessity for artificial combinations will gradually subside, and may at length be safely dispensed with. In them the Spirit of God resides; through them, as the principal means, he will subdue the world, and complete the conquests of the Head of the Heathen. Every church, like the glorious gospel, of which it is the depository, may be likened unto fire and leaven, which operate by assimilating to themselves their kindred elements, when such elements are brought into contact. Churches ought, at all points, to act on surrounding unbelievers, and at once to absorb the faithful into their several fellowships; or, to change the figure, the armies of the cross, like other armies, require their advanced guards, their spies, and pioneers, such as missionaries, itinerants, and other classes of labourers; but the conquests of that cross are to be completed, its authority and government established, and its empire upheld, by its own organized masses, that is, by Gospel Churches." (449–50) (John Campbell, *Memoirs of David Nasmith: His Labours and Travels in Great Britain, France, the United States and Canada* [London: J. Snow, 1844])

George Williams and the YMCA

In 1836, George Williams (1821–1905), typical of thousands of young men drawn to cities by the industrial revolution, moved to London. Williams worked as a draper, selling textiles for clothing, and lived in a room provided by the manufacturer. A year after his arrival, he converted to faith while attending a service at a Congregational church. He was so influenced by the preacher Thomas Binney, known by Finney as London's "archbishop of Nonconformity," that Williams's life goal was to win others to Christ.

Thus, Williams invited coworkers to his room, where they read the Bible and prayed together, calling their gathering the Draper's Evangelical Union.[85] In 1844, it was renamed the Young Men's Christian Association (YMCA) and was established for "the improvement of the spiritual condition of the young men engaged in houses of business, by the formation of Bible classes, family and social prayer meetings, mutual improvement societies, or any other spiritual agency."[86] YMCAs soon opened in Australia, Belgium, Canada, France, Germany, the Netherlands, Switzerland, and the United States.

In 1855, ninety-nine leaders of YMCAs attended the Paris Conference, formed a world association, and agreed to the "Paris Basis." Its main principle stated, "The Young Men's Christian Associations seek to unite those young men who, regarding Jesus Christ as their God and Saviour, according to the Holy Scriptures, desire to be his disciples in their faith and in their life and to associate their efforts for the extension of His Kingdom amongst young men."[87]

The addition of athletics to the YMCA led to, among other things, the inventions of basketball by James Naismith and volleyball by William G. Morgan.[88] With the integration of sports, the YMCA promoted "muscular Christianity" that combined Christian faith, discipline, and athleticism.[89] In

85. Schmidt, *How Christianity Changed the World*, 141.

86. *The First Annual Report of the Young Men's Christian Association Read at the Third Half Yearly Meeting of Members and Friends Held at Radley's Hotel, Bridge Street, Blackfriars, on Thursday Evening, November 6th, 1845* (London: YMCA, 1845), 9.

87. "Paris Basis, 1855," YMCA International, https://www.ymca.int/about-us/ymca-history/paris-basis-1855/; Kjetil Fretheim, "Whose Kingdom? Which Context? Ecumenical and Contextual Theology in the World Alliance of YMCAs," *International Review of Mission* 97, nos. 584/585 (2008): 116–28.

88. Robert Crego, *Sports and Games of the 18th and 19th Centuries* (Westport, CT: Greenwood, 2003), 194–95, 206–7, 234.

89. Nick J. Watson and Andrew Park, "Sports and Christianity: Mapping the Field,"

many countries, the YMCA became a driving force for missions, evangelism, and ecumenical cooperation.[90]

Anthony Bowen and the YMCA

Anthony Bowen (1809–1871), born into slavery, purchased his freedom in 1830 for $425. When he redeemed his wife from slavery, the couple moved to the nation's capital. Through his friend W. C. Langdon, who had founded the YMCA in Washington, DC, Bowen became impressed with the organization's ideals but soon was disappointed to learn that African Americans were not allowed to join. Therefore, in 1853, he organized the Colored Young Men's Christian Association.[91]

Bowen remained committed to the advancement of African Americans in the social and educational areas of life, as well as conversion to the Christian faith. Given the policies of the YMCA in the nation's capital during his years as director, the Colored YMCA was restricted to meetings in rented spaces, donated rooms, and members' living rooms.

William and Catherine Booth and the Salvation Army

After beginning as a Methodist preacher in England, William Booth (1829–1912) abandoned the ambition to become a pulpit minister in favor of taking the gospel directly to spiritually lost people. He and his friend Will Sansom began as lay evangelists "to the sinners of Nottingham."[92] In 1849, Booth reluctantly moved to London, where he found work as a pawnbroker. Although he engaged in lay preaching in churches, he preferred evangelism in the streets and at Kennington Common. In 1851, he joined the Methodist Reform Church to become the preacher of Binfield Chapel in Clapham, and four years later, he married Catherine Mumford (1829–1890).[93] Although Booth was a prominent Methodist evangelist, he was unhappy that the denomination's annual conference continued to assign him to a pastoral

---

in *Sports and Christianity: Historical and Contemporary Perspectives*, ed. Nick J. Watson and Andrew Parker (New York: Routledge, 2013), 21–22.

90. Scharpff, *Histoy of Evangelism*, 94.

91. Nina Mjagkij, *Light in the Darkness: African Americans and the YMCA, 1852–1946* (Lexington: University Press of Kentucky, 1994), 17–18.

92. Roy Hattersley, *Blood and Fire: William and Catherine Booth and the Salvation Army* (London: Abacus, 1999), 23–25.

93. Scharpff, *History of Evangelism*, 90.

position. When the conference refused his request to engage in full-time evangelism, he resigned from his position.

William and Catherine Booth returned to the East End of London in 1865 and founded the organization that operated initially under the name Christian Mission and had over one thousand evangelists and volunteers. The name was later changed to the Salvation Army, and the organization continued to preach the gospel and serve the basic physical needs of people, offering them "soup, soap, and salvation."[94]

Before Catherine's marriage to William, she had read the writings of Finney and Wesley and sensed God's call on her life. Along with William, she held evangelistic meetings and saw prostitutes, gamblers, and drunkards convert to faith. In her book titled *Aggressive Christianity*, Catherine wrote, "Here is the principle laid down that you are to adapt your measures to the necessity of the people to whom you minister; you are to take the gospel to them in such modes and habits of thought and expressions and circumstances as will gain for it from them a hearing."[95]

Clearly, the Booths reacted against the clergy-oriented ecclesiology of Christendom that defined ministry narrowly. Even the Methodist churches that were originally evangelistic had by this time gravitated toward a clergy-oriented ecclesiology in which Christians were expected simply to attend worship services, listen to sermons, and tithe their incomes. In turn, the pastor was expected simply to care for and feed the people spiritually, mostly by preaching from the pulpit, but also by visiting in their homes or visiting the hospital. In contrast, the Booths advocated a mission-oriented ecclesiology in which the pastor equipped and mobilized people for gospel witness and service to the surrounding community.

William and Catherine Booth involved their sons and daughters in the work of the Salvation Army, with their daughter Evangeline Booth (1865–1950) leading the way. Evangeline was only fifteen years old when she began to hold evangelistic meetings in the streets of London. From 1904 to 1934, she served as commander of the Salvation Army in the United States.[96] When she visited the mining towns of the Yukon in western Canada, which were rife with drunkenness and prostitution, she set up medical clinics and

94. John D. Woodbridge and Frank A. James III, *Church History*, vol. 2, *From Pre-Reformation to the Present Day* (Grand Rapids: Zondervan, 2013), 603.

95. Catherine Booth, *Papers on Aggressive Christianity* (London: Salvationist, 1880), 52–53.

96. Ruth A. Tucker and Walter Liefeld, *Daughters of the Church: Women and Ministry from New Testament Times to the Present* (Grand Rapids: Zondervan, 1987), 371, 373.

soup kitchens. When she preached, she spoke with wide gestures, capturing the attention of the miners, with as many as twenty-five thousand attending a single meeting. The miners did not always come to her, however. On at least one occasion, she was lowered into a mine in a large ore bucket while she sang "Nearer, My God, to Thee."[97] She described her evangelistic meetings as a "tremendous 'battle for souls,'" and there were "seldom less than a hundred seekers at the penitent form."[98]

Dwight L. Moody

Dwight L. Moody (1837–1899) became a city missionary of the YMCA in Chicago before launching his itinerant ministry as an evangelist in the major cities of the United States and Britain. He was born in Northfield, Massachusetts, the sixth of nine children.[99] His father died when he was four years old, leaving his mother, Betsy, a couple acres of land with a small farmhouse and a mortgage. In Northfield, the young Dwight received the customary education of four years of school.[100] He attended the Congregational church with his mother.

At seventeen, he moved to Boston, where he began work at his uncle's shoe store. In addition to selling shoes, Moody attended a Sunday school class, being forced by his uncle to do so. Moody's greatest ambition at the time was to earn money. Nonetheless, as he listened to "the plain and loving sermons of the pastor and the personal instructions of his Sunday school teacher, his heart began to soften."[101] In 1856, he converted to faith in Christ.

In the same year, Moody packed his belongings, boarded a westbound train, and headed for Chicago, ambitious to earn money in America's western frontier. Shortly after his arrival, he landed a job selling boots. He transferred his church membership from Mount Vernon Church in Boston to Plymouth Congregational Church in Chicago.[102] In addition, he attended a newly developed Sunday school at First Methodist Church, and a prayer

97. Tucker, *Parade of Faith*, 441–43.

98. Tucker and Liefeld, *Daughters of the Church*, 372.

99. W. H. Daniels, *D. L. Moody and His Work* (Hartford, CT: American Publishing, 1875), 3.

100. Lyle W. Dorsett, *A Passion for Souls: The Life of D. L. Moody* (Chicago: Moody, 1997), 36.

101. Daniels, *D. L. Moody and His Work*, 21.

102. Dorsett, *Passion for Souls*, 59.

meeting at First Baptist Church, where he met "Mother" Phillips, who taught him to study the Bible and how to reach Chicago's children with the gospel.[103] He also met Emma Revell, his future wife, and John V. Farwell, his friend and longtime supporter.

Chicago YMCA

In 1857 and 1858, Chicago experienced the prayer-meeting revival that was sweeping America's urban and industrial centers. Similar to earlier spiritual awakenings, this revival emphasized lay preaching and interdenominational cooperation. At the same time, Moody became active as a volunteer with Chicago's YMCA. After reading George Müller's book *The Life of Trust*, he decided that if God could provide for Müller to feed, clothe, and house thousands of England's orphans, he could certainly provide for the children of Chicago's streets.[104] Therefore, Moody left his career in boot sales and entered full-time Christian work.

He began a Sunday school in a beer hall on North Market Street and soon became known as "Crazy Moody," enticing children to attend Sunday school with promises of pony rides and candy, or "missionary sugar."[105] The Sunday school soon had over six hundred children in attendance and was so popular that in 1860 President-elect Abraham Lincoln visited and addressed Moody's pupils.[106] Moody's Sunday school became a model for urban child evangelism.

As the Sunday school grew to a thousand students and three hundred adults, Moody solicited help from evangelical churches to form a new independent church. However, the Congregationalists were the only ones willing to assist.[107] Moody's emphasis on a gathered church of believers and his distaste for ecclesiastical hierarchies found sympathy with the Congregationalists, who helped him draft articles of faith and bylaws for this nonsectarian church. The Illinois Street Church organized services and classes, Bible studies, testimony meetings, praise and thanksgiving services, open-air

103. Timothy George, "Introduction: Remembering Mr Moody," in *Mr Moody and the Evangelical Tradition*, ed. Timothy George (London: T&T Clark, 2004), 2.

104. Dorsett, *Passion for Souls*, 86.

105. George, "Introduction," 2.

106. Bruce J. Evensen, *God's Man for the Gilded Age: D. L. Moody and the Rise of the Modern Mass Evangelism* (New York: Oxford University Press, 2003), 11, 16.

107. James F. Findlay Jr., *Dwight L. Moody: American Evangelist, 1837–1899* (Grand Rapids: Baker, 1969), 109.

meetings, and conventicle meetings in homes. From the beginning, it was an independent, evangelical church with "the most aggressive evangelism program in Chicago."[108]

Moody continued with the Chicago chapter of the YMCA that formed in 1858 during the prayer-meeting revival. In 1860, John Farwell became president, and in 1861, Moody became the YMCA librarian and city missionary.[109] In the same year, he was invited to address the third annual Illinois State Sunday School Convention because of the large number of people intrigued by his work with Chicago's children.

During the Civil War, the YMCA formed the U.S. Christian Commission, and Moody served as a volunteer chaplain to Union soldiers, ministering alongside men and women of every denomination. He went to the battlefront nine times to minister to soldiers, and to take supplies to the wounded after the battles of Shiloh, Murfreesboro, and Chattanooga. In many ways, this experience led him to favor "union work" and to oppose sectarianism.[110] At the end of the war, he entered Richmond with the troops of General Grant.

Evangelism and Social Action

In 1865, Moody became president of the Chicago YMCA and served in this role for four years. Through his efforts, the noon prayer meetings were attended by as many as a thousand people. As YMCA president, his vision was to reach Chicago with the gospel, and one means was to expand the association's work among German, Swedish, and Norwegian immigrants. In 1867, the YMCA launched its publication of *Heavenly Tidings*, a four-page digest with selections from various religious newspapers.[111] In that year, the YMCA distributed over forty-two thousand copies of foreign-language newspapers. YMCA workers often followed up tract and newspaper distribution with personal visits to share the gospel.

In 1867, Moody came into contact with Swedes of the Pietist tradition who had immigrated to Chicago. During this time, a Swede named J. G. Princell (1845–1915) was drawn into Moody's circle when he attended Moody's meet-

108. Dorsett, *Passion for Souls*, 123.

109. Dorsett, *Passion for Souls*, 83.

110. Dorsett, *Passion for Souls*, 116.

111. Emmett Dedmon, *Great Enterprises: 100 Years of the YMCA of Metropolitan Chicago* (New York: Rand McNally, 1957), 63.

ings and became active in the work of the YMCA. In 1868, Princell and two friends founded the Swedish YMCA in Chicago.[112]

Besides tract distribution, relief work was a major part of the YMCA's program. In 1867, the chairman of the relief committee reported that aid was given to nearly four thousand applicants, and most were recent immigrants. In addition, Moody saw that English classes were offered to immigrants. Explaining the relationship between relief work and the spiritual goals of the YMCA, he said, "Opportunities have been afforded for reaching a large number of people with the gospel of peace, otherwise almost unapproachable, simply because its forerunners were bread, coal, and clothing. The heart as naturally opens to such kindness as flowers to the sunshine; and when Christianity thus opens human hearts, its power with God and men is recognized and felt."[113]

Besides leading the YMCA, in 1867 Moody traveled to England, where he attended the Mildmay Conference in London. There he was drawn into the circle of William Pennefather (1816–1873), the conference organizer. He also met members of the Plymouth Brethren such as George Müller, founder of the children's home in Bristol.[114] Moody also arranged to meet London's famous preacher, C. H. Spurgeon, and George Williams of the YMCA.

Müller introduced Moody to other Plymouth Brethren. Moody was inspired by their emphases on conversion, biblical authority, lay preaching, and the imminent return of Christ.[115] The Plymouth Brethren sought the simplicity of the early church and rejected clerical vestments and ecclesiastical trappings, the "formalism" and "popery" associated with the Church of England.[116]

Moody was influenced particularly by Henry Moorhouse, a member of the Plymouth Brethren who came to visit him in Chicago in 1868. Moorhouse preached at the Illinois Street Church seven times from a single verse of Scripture, John 3:16, on the topic of God's love. Moody remarked, "I never knew up to that time that God loved us so much. . . . [Moorhouse] just beat that truth down into my heart, and I have never doubted it since. I used to preach that God was behind a sinner with a double-edged sword ready to

112. Ulf Beijbom, *Swedes in Chicago: A Demographic and Social Study of the 1846–1880 Immigration* (Stockholm: Läromedelsförlagen, 1971), 255. Princell remained a proponent of Moody and in 1897 became a founding professor of Chicago's Swedish Bible Institute, known today as Trinity Evangelical Divinity School.

113. Dedmon, *Great Enterprises*, 60.

114. D. W. Bebbington, "Moody as a Transatlantic Evangelical," in George, *Mr Moody*, 78.

115. Findlay, *Dwight L. Moody*, 125–26.

116. Dorsett, *Passion for Souls*, 136.

hew him down. I have got done with that. I preach now that God is behind him with love, and he is running away from the God of love."[117]

Although Moody lacked formal theological education, he acquired theological education from personal Bible study, sermons he heard or read, and discussions with Bible teachers and preachers like Pennefather, Müller, Spurgeon, and Moorhouse. He strove to acquire knowledge from those with more theological education. Yet he never abandoned his small-town simplicity. Moody was known for his quaint pronunciation, illustrated by Spurgeon's remark that "Moody was the only man who could say 'Mesopotamia' in two syllables!"[118] Moreover, Moody was never ordained and insisted on being called "Mr. Moody" rather than "Reverend Moody."[119]

In 1867, the Chicago YMCA dedicated Farwell Hall, named for its principal benefactor and Moody's coworker. The *Chicago Times* referred to this hall as a "modern Pantheon" where "Arminianism and Calvinism sit side by side."[120] Moody's emphasis on extending the kingdom of God and not promoting denominations was expressed strongly at the Illinois State Christian Convention in 1868 when he said, "I would like to know to what denomination the Saviour would belong. I tell you, my friends, these denominational names do not come from on high. They are devices of the evil one."[121]

In 1870, Moody teamed up with Ira D. Sankey (1840–1908), a musician of exceptional talent, who, accompanied by a harmonium, moved audiences deeply with his songs and led them in inspirational singing.

In 1871, the Great Chicago Fire swept away the north side of the city. The fire destroyed eighteen thousand buildings, leaving ninety thousand people homeless.[122] Many of Chicago's churches were destroyed, including the Illinois Street Church, as well as Farwell Hall. Moody and his friends quickly erected a temporary meeting place, the North Side Tabernacle, which served as a relief center to feed and clothe thousands who lost their homes.[123] It served also as a temporary church from which to preach the gospel. Despite its simple and unsophisticated character, the building provided a refuge for children and adults.

117. William R. Moody, *The Life of Dwight L. Moody* (Chicago: Revell, 1900), 139.

118. George, "Introduction," 2.

119. Dorsett, *Passion for Souls*, 116.

120. Dorsett, *Passion for Souls*, 68.

121. "Third Annual Illinois State Christian Convention," *Advance* 2, no. 62 (November 5, 1868): 2, cited in August J. Fry, *D. L. Moody: The Chicago Years 1865–1871* (Amsterdam: Free University Press, 1984), 37.

122. Ross Miller, *The Great Chicago Fire* (Urbana: University of Illinois Press, 1990), 18.

123. Myron Raymond Chartier, *The Social Views of Dwight L. Moody and Their Relation to the Workingman of 1860–1900* (Hays: Fort Hays Kansas State, 1969), 30, 73.

Moody and Sankey's Evangelistic Tours

Moody and Sankey became popular from their evangelistic tour in the British Isles from 1873 to 1875. Although the original sponsors of the preaching tour died before they arrived, the two Americans found opportunities to preach in England through the YMCA. After a rough start at York, they moved to Scotland, where, aided by publicity in R. C. Morgan's periodical *The Christian*, they began to attract larger audiences.[124] Their publicity and promotion methods were refined, and support from clergy in the areas increased.

Moody and Sankey traveled in Ireland for several months, including the predominately Roman Catholic areas. When they returned to England, well-known evangelical leaders were recruited to administrate the campaigns. Larger venues were needed to accommodate the crowds, and attention was given to acoustics and to the "inquirers' room" where the "anxious" were invited for personal counsel, prayer, and gospel witness. In preparation for the campaigns, prayer groups were formed, house-to-house canvassing was conducted, and handbills were distributed. Financing was secured by local leaders from local sources. It was estimated that the American duo attracted as many as three million listeners during this tour.[125] When Moody and Sankey returned to America in 1875, they were international heroes.

After a brief rest at his hometown in Massachusetts, Moody began a series of evangelistic campaigns in America's largest cities. Again, much of the groundwork was done by city missionaries and volunteers of the YMCA. The tour took Moody and Sankey to New York, Philadelphia, Chicago, and Boston, spending two to three months in each city.

Preparing Christian Workers and Evangelists

In connection to the evangelistic meetings, Moody conducted workshops in which he impressed lay volunteers and clergy with the responsibility to evangelize personally. He enlisted and trained hundreds of them as Christian workers for the after-meetings. He believed it was better to train ten laypeople than for him to do the work of ten people.

A Swedish-American drawn into his circle was Fredrik Franson (1852–1908). In the fall of 1876, Franson arrived in Chicago from Nebraska to join Moody's evangelism campaign. The young Franson took full advantage of the

124. Rudnick, *Speaking the Gospel*, 184.
125. Rudnick, *Speaking the Gospel*, 185.

opportunity and learned Moody's methods of evangelistic work.[126] Along with others, Franson became proficient in the methods of leading inquirers to faith. From this experience, Franson became known as "Moody's Swedish disciple" and was the first missionary sent out from Moody's church in Chicago.[127]

Moody's message was simple. Although he was not theologically sophisticated, he was steeped in the Scriptures and communicated clearly and winsomely. Each message in a series of meetings addressed a theme of the gospel.[128] He had a fondness for the book of Genesis, especially two texts, "Where art thou?" (3:9) and "Come thou and all thy house into the ark" (7:1). He preached the Ten Commandments (Exod. 20) and from Isaiah, particularly chapters 53 and 55 that prophesy about Christ. While he spoke of Jesus's birth, death, resurrection, and second coming, he emphasized the benefits of salvation to the believing sinner, preaching messages on the prodigal son (Luke 15), the thief on the cross (Luke 23), and the hope of heaven, but also about the inhabitants of hell. Moody believed that the gospel summons a response, and made strong appeals to listeners with messages such as "Tomorrow May Be Too Late," "Lost and Found," "Repentance," and "What Must I Do to Be Saved?" In his message titled "Christ Seeking Sinners," he argued for "sudden conversion," saying, "Answer me—when was Zaccheus converted? He was certainly in his sins when he went up into the tree; he was certainly converted when he came down. He must have been converted between the branch and the ground."[129] At a basic level, Moody's evangelistic messages were as entertaining as they were inspiring.

In addition to evangelistic preaching, Moody founded educational institutions to prepare future Christian workers. In Northfield, Massachusetts, he established separate schools for young men and women. In Chicago, he founded the Chicago Bible Institute to train "gapmen," a term for those who could fill the gap between trained clergy and laypeople. These students heard Bible lectures in the morning and spent afternoons and evenings engaged in evangelism in Chicago.[130]

In contrast to others who simply "cast out" the gospel, Moody emphasized "drawing in the net," inviting people to faith in Jesus Christ. He said that he

126. Josephine Princell, *Frederick Franson: World Missionary* (Chicago: Chicago-Bladet, 1909), 11–12.

127. Robert G. Flood, *The Story of Moody Church* (Chicago: Moody, 1985), 11.

128. Garth Rosell, ed., *Commending the Faith: The Preaching of D. L. Moody* (Peabody, MA: Hendrickson, 1999).

129. D. L. Moody, *Twelve Select Sermons* (Chicago: Revell, 1881), 49.

130. Rudnick, *Speaking the Gospel*, 186–87.

used "after-meetings" as means to "draw in the net," giving people who heard the gospel an opportunity to respond. When asked by a group of preachers why his meetings were fruitful and their meetings were not, Moody answered, "You all cast out the net well enough, but I also draw it in."[131]

Discussion Questions

1. Camp meetings held in the "whiskey culture" needed to employ camp police. While some folks came to hear biblical messages, others came to socialize, or even for sexual promiscuity. Why is evangelism socially "messy"? If the frontier of mission is where "faith meets no faith," how should we handle the messiness of evangelism?
2. According to the account from Jarena Lee's journal, what were her motivations for evangelism? How did her motivations sustain her despite the ups and downs of evangelistic ministry? Would you say your motivations are more self-centered or God-centered? How can you cultivate proper motivations?
3. Charles Finney preached the gospel with evangelistic zeal, but did he go too far with his "new measures" and emphasis on human agency? At what point does any evangelist stifle the Holy Spirit with their evangelistic methods?
4. Despite social and moral questions over chattel slavery, racism, and injustice, people such as Peter Durrett, Jarena Lee, Ambrosio González, and Anthony Bowen were used by God to reach others with the gospel. What made them effective?
5. David Nasmith founded over sixty mission societies. Did this imply that he had no regard for local churches? What role did he see local churches playing to reach their neighborhoods and cities with the gospel? How did he see mission societies in relation to local churches?

131. David M. Gustafson, *D. L. Moody and Swedes: Shaping Evangelical Identity among Swedish Mission Friends, 1867–1899* (Linköping, Sweden: Linköping University, 2008), 209.

10

Social Gospel versus Soul-Saving Evangelism

The Lord said to me, "Don't you know that while you are getting ready souls are perishing? Go now and I will be with you." I told him that I could not talk to the people; I did not know what to say, and they would not listen to me. Jesus said, "You can tell the people what the Lord has done for your soul; tell of the glory of God and the love of Jesus: tell sinners to repent and prepare for death and the judgement, and I will be with you." Still I made one excuse after another, and Jesus would answer, "Go, and I will be with you." . . . Then Jesus said again, "Go, and I will be with you." I cried, "Lord, I will go. Where shall I go?" And Jesus said, "Go here, go there, wherever souls are perishing."

—Mary Woodworth-Etter[1]

At the time when Dwight L. Moody was conducting his evangelistic campaigns, theological developments were polarizing Protestants into two streams. By the beginning of the twentieth century, two streams of Protestants—modernists and fundamentalists—emerged as each provided different responses to the intellectual and social challenges of the day, and each offered particular understandings of the gospel. The modernists posited a social gospel while the fundamentalists held to the soul-saving

1. Mary Woodworth-Etter, *Marvels and Miracles God Wrought in the Ministry for Forty-Five Years* (Indianapolis: self-published, 1922), 18.

gospel.[2] A third stream—moderates—sought to hold social and personal dimensions together.

Social Gospel

Some progressive theologians—also known as modernists or liberals—began to question the supernatural elements of the gospel such as the virgin birth and the efficacy of Christ's death to atone for human sin. The liberal views challenged basic tenets of the gospel, including the need for personal salvation from sin. Soon the liberal social gospel appeared, emphasizing "social salvation"—a social improvement of the human condition that would usher in the kingdom of God.[3] Such a view denied humanity's spiritually lost condition and the need for conversion to faith in Jesus. Those who held to the liberal view dismissed the need for Christians to witness to the death and resurrection of Christ. For them, Christianity was living by the Golden Rule—"Do to others what you would have them do to you" (Matt. 7:12).

Some Protestants, especially those who held to the view that Jesus's second coming was imminent, or would occur at any moment, viewed social reforms of the social gospel as futile.[4] They looked askance at social action, thinking that performing good deeds or working to improve society would associate them with liberal theology and the progressive agenda of the modernists.[5] Instead, they stressed verbal witness to the soul-saving gospel. They held that if any improvement came to society, it would be from the conversions of souls to Christ.

Theological liberalism was shaped by Friedrich Schleiermacher (1768–1834), a German theologian, known as the "father of modern theology."[6] He put forward new ways of looking at the Bible, God and creation, and church and society.[7] Although Schleiermacher was raised in an evangelical,

2. John D. Woodbridge and Frank A. James III, *Church History*, vol. 2, *From Pre-Reformation to the Present Day* (Grand Rapids: Zondervan, 2013), 796–98.

3. H. Richard Niebuhr, *The Kingdom of God in America* (Middleton, CT: Wesleyan University Press, 1988), 161–63.

4. Ronald J. Sider, *Good News and Good Works: A Theology for the Whole Gospel* (Grand Rapids: Baker, 1999), 35.

5. Harvey Conn, *Evangelism: Doing Justice and Preaching Grace* (Grand Rapids: Academie, 1982), 60–62.

6. Woodbridge and James, *Church History*, 2:543–47.

7. Gary J. Dorrien, *The Making of American Liberal Theology: Imagining Progressive Religion 1805–1900* (Louisville: Westminster John Knox, 2001), xix–xxii, 59–79.

pietistic tradition, he was influenced by Enlightenment thinking that had come to the University of Halle, and adopted a rationalist, critical approach to the Scriptures.[8] Moreover, he was influenced by Romanticism, which held that the core of Christianity was what a person "feels within," a religious consciousness.[9]

The view of Charles Darwin (1809–1882) regarding human evolution, which followed nineteenth-century ideas of an old earth, further shaped the progressive culture.[10] While theological modernists became convinced of Darwin's theory and integrated it with Christian faith, others reacted against it, viewing his theory as contrary to the Bible's teaching on the origin of humankind.[11] Seven clergy of the Church of England published essays that claimed the Bible was simply an ordinary book, an opinion based on German higher criticism. In response, other clergy signed a letter of protest, affirming their belief in the inspiration of the Scriptures. Despite the debate, Darwin's ideas came to influence society and the church.

Albrecht Ritschl (1822–1889), a German theologian, wrote a treatise in which he stated that Christianity was neither a set of doctrines nor subjective feelings, but ethics. In other words, social ethics are at the heart of the Christian message. Ritschl posited that Christianity pertains primarily to how people live and what they do in society, framing the idea for the social gospel.[12]

In the mind of Walter Rauschenbusch (1861–1918), a Baptist pastor and theologian from Rochester, New York, the social gospel emphasized social redemption by means of ethics, morality, and good works. He promoted "the fatherhood of God and the brotherhood of man."[13] He also doubted

8. Justo L. González, *The Story of Christianity: The Early Church to the Present Day* (Peabody, MA: Prince, 1999), 2:285.

9. Roland H. Bainton, *Christianity* (Boston: Houghton Mifflin, 2000), 381–82; González, *Story of Christianity*, 2:286.

10. Dorrien, *Making of American Liberal Theology*, xxiii–xxiv, 173–80. Nineteenth-century theories of geology posited a uniformitarian view of the earth's formation over millions of years, in contrast to the historical Christian view that the earth was young. See Terry Mortenson, *The Great Turning Point* (Green Forest, AR: New Leaf, 2004).

11. Woodbridge and James, *Church History*, 2:532–42; González, *Story of Christianity*, 2:283.

12. Albrecht Ritschl, *The Christian Doctrine of Justification and Reconciliation* (New York: Scribner, 1900).

13. Woodbridge and James, *Church History*, 2:554. See Walter Rauschenbusch, *A Theology for the Social Gospel* (New York: Abingdon, 1917).

the substitutionary atonement of Jesus, saying that this was "not taught by Jesus; it makes salvation dependent upon a trinitarian transaction that is remote from human experience; and it implies a concept of divine justice that is repugnant to human sensitivity."[14] The hallmark of Rauschenbusch's position was the "importance of living like Christ, not believing a prescribed doctrine about Christ."[15]

In essence, Rauschenbusch became aligned with the liberal religious thinkers who espoused what was called the "new theology." Although he turned from the traditional, orthodox view of the Scriptures, he claimed to remain a devout disciple of Jesus. In 1855, he wrote to a friend, saying, "I tell you I am just beginning to believe in the gospel of the Lord Jesus Christ, not exactly in the shape in which the average person proclaims it as the infallible truth of the Most High, but in a shape that suits my needs, that I have gradually constructed for myself in studying the person and teachings of Christ and which is still in rapid progress of construction."[16]

Rauschenbusch's doubts about inerrancy and the substitutionary atonement stemmed from reading proponents of higher criticism—the literary analysis of the Bible as a text created by human authors. A leading voice of higher criticism was Julius Wellhausen (1844–1918), a German biblical scholar who set forth his documentary hypothesis regarding sources of the Pentateuch, the first five books of the Bible. Wellhausen challenged the traditional understanding that Moses wrote the Pentateuch under inspiration of the Holy Spirit.

In 1907, Rauschenbusch wrote *Christianity and the Social Crisis*.[17] He felt that preachers had concentrated too long on personal salvation while ignoring the economic and social distress of their local communities. He encouraged Christians to answer the call of Christ to care for the poor, feed the hungry, and alleviate the pain of those who suffered. He hoped that the church would move beyond individualism, personal salvation, and the winning of souls to a broad restructuring of society based on a Christian social order.

14. Paul M. Minus, *Walter Rauschenbusch: American Reformer* (New York: Macmillan, 1988), 43.

15. Minus, *Walter Rauschenbusch*, 47.

16. Minus, *Walter Rauschenbusch*, 46.

17. See Walter Rauschenbusch, *Christianity and the Social Crisis* (New York: Macmillan, 1907).

Soul-Saving Gospel

As theological modernists denied and discredited basic tenets of the Christian faith, traditionalists held to Christianity's fundamental and historical teachings. In response to liberalizing tendencies, they upheld the gospel as described by the New Testament, church fathers, ancient creeds, and the Protestant Reformers. They held to the fundamentals of the Christian faith—namely, the inspiration of the Scriptures, the incarnation of Jesus, his atoning death on the cross, his bodily resurrection, and miracles. With the Nicene Creed they confessed, "For us and for our salvation he [Jesus Christ] came down from heaven, was incarnate of the Holy Spirit and the Virgin Mary and became truly human. For our sake he was crucified under Pontius Pilate; he suffered death and was buried. On the third day he rose again."

Beginning in 1910, a series of booklets was published under the title *The Fundamentals: A Testimony to the Truth*, edited by A. C. Dixon and, later, Reuben A. Torrey. The series contained ninety essays in twelve volumes, was financed by Lyman Stewart, and was published by the Bible Institute of Los Angeles, known later as Biola University. The booklets reaffirmed orthodox theology in contrast to modernist theology. The commitment to the Christian fundamentals earned this group of traditional Protestants the pejorative title "fundamentalists."[18] An article in *The Fundamentals* by John Timothy Stone (1868–1954), pastor of Fourth Presbyterian Church in Chicago, titled "Pastoral and Personal Evangelism, or Winning Men to Christ One by One," emphasized the need for personal soul-saving salvation.

Excerpts from John Timothy Stone, "Pastoral and Personal Evangelism, or Winning Men to Christ One by One," 1915

Even, at this time, two hundred years after his unparalleled ministry, we are reminded of George Whitefield, who preached at times to fully thirty thousand people in the open air, and won his thousands and tens of thousands. . . . The strong evangelists of our own generation verify before our very eyes God's honor placed on those to whom He gives such signal power. But our thought goes back to the great universal method our Lord Himself instituted, of reaching the individual by his fellow man. (25)

18. George M. Marsden, *Fundamentalism and American Culture* (New York: Oxford University Press, 2006), 3–5, 118–24, 188.

[A] necessary element in winning men to the Master is a knowledge and appropriate use of God's Word. . . . The worker who knows his Bible will constantly read it for strength and apply it in dealing with the unconverted. He will not argue with men, nor talk *about* God's Word, but he will explain *with* it, and repeatedly refer to it. An open Bible before and with an inquirer almost always means conversion and spiritual growth to follow. When dealing with your subject, ask if he has ever considered what the Bible says on the point under discussion.

For instance, a man tells you he does not take much stock in what you have been saying about the necessity of the Cross; it seems somewhat foolish to him. Do not be angry, but reply pleasantly that you do not blame him a bit, in fact, Paul himself writes, in his first letter to the Corinthians that men will feel exactly that way. Tell him you appreciate his frankness, and meanwhile pull your Testament from your pocket or take it from the table, and turn to the passage in First Corinthians, one, eighteen; or better still, hand him another copy of the Bible open to the place, and read from your own copy: "For the preaching of the Cross is to them that perish foolishness, but unto us which are saved it is the power of God." Then, before he is angered or troubled about that word "perish," ask him to notice in the same connection the twenty-first verse, just below: "For after that in the wisdom of God the world by wisdom knew not God, it pleased God *by the foolishness* of preaching to save them that believe." These passages will at least arrest his attention, and unconsciously interest him somewhat in reading the Bible himself. (28–29)

We do not estimate the place and power prayer has in winning others to Christ, prayer for others in intercession, and prayer with others as we take them individually into the very presence of God. . . . No matter what your method or lack of method may be, take those for whom you are working up to God in prayer. Pray for them by name; pray that you may approach them aright and appeal to them with Divine wisdom. Pray that you may be able to put yourself in their place, and be patient as well as wise with them. Pray that you may turn to the right Scripture, and use the appropriate illustrations, to help them. . . . Pray that just the favorable opening may come to you, and that you may be ready to use it. Pray most of all for the Holy Spirit's power with you. (33)

The method [of evangelism] is, after all, secondary, and if it becomes too set and orderly, it will be self-destructive, for as soon as one sees your method, the heart and mind are steeled against it, and there is little or no interest.

> When God's Spirit leads, we are responsive to all kinds of openings and ways. Instead of studying approach we simply advance as the plan opens before us. (36)
>
> The greatest advantage which the large meeting has is so interesting individuals in the truth that they will inquire from individuals who are ready to help them, as to the application of the truth they hear. A valuable series of meetings is only sure in interest and result as individuals invite, seek and lead others to be present, and then follow them by individual effort. The successful revivals of today must follow this method if permanent and large results are to be attained. God works through men, and individuals must reach other individuals. (38)
>
> The Church of Christ universal has an immense force in herself to face the work of winning others to Christ, but we have not used that force. The foreign missionary lands have appreciated this fact in the work they are doing, and in some places the condition of winning others has been imposed upon new members before they are accepted into full communion. For instance, before a new member is received into the Korean Church, the convert must not only confess his faith in Christ, but also lead another to Christ. What if our membership were really working for others individually, and were trained with that in view? What if we called the attention of our new members to this very obligation and expectation? (38–39)
>
> Now, there is no question that a pastor has his definite work of preaching . . . but it is also his work to shepherd his flock, and a shepherd cannot properly do that work without teaching his flock to follow him. He first must be an inviter and winner of men to Christ, and he must train his people to follow him. (39) (John Timothy Stone, "Pastoral and Personal Evangelism, or Winning Men to Christ One by One," in *The Fundamentals: A Testimony to the Truth*, vol. 12 [Chicago: Testimony, 1915], 24–44)

John Gresham Machen

In 1923, Presbyterian scholar John Gresham Machen (1881–1937) published a significant work titled *Christianity and Liberalism* in which he stated that the theological changes proposed by modernists changed the Christian faith so radically as to make it essentially a new religion and thus a heresy.[19] Other conservatives responded to modernist theology with populist counterattacks.

At the same time, eschatological views of the world's future shaped the left and right streams. Liberal Protestants embraced an optimistic view of the future called postmillennialism, which emphasized positive, "this-world" developments in society and human progress that would climax with Jesus's return. On the other hand, a number of Christians held a view called premillennialism, inspired by the teachings of John Nelson Darby and popularized by Moody. This pessimistic view of the future posited that humankind would become increasingly corrupt, and history would end at Christ's return with the destruction of the earth, making temporal reforms of little use or value.[20]

Conflict over the social gospel and the soul-saving gospel centered on northern Presbyterians and Baptists, while ripples were felt in other denominations too. However, moderates stood between these two camps. On one side, they held to orthodox views of theology, but on the other side they embodied a more charitable spirit that avoided the harsh polemics of some fundamentalists. Theologians like Reinhold Niebuhr, H. Richard Niebuhr, and Karl Barth held to historic tenets of Christianity with new understandings of certain teachings.[21] H. Richard Niebuhr criticized the liberal, social gospel, describing it in these words: "A God without wrath brought men without sin into a kingdom without judgment through the ministrations of a Christ without a cross."[22]

John R. Mott

An example of a moderate was John R. Mott (1865–1955), who served for decades as a leader with the YMCA and the World Student Christian Federation. In 1910, he presided at the World Missionary Conference in Edinburgh, which launched the modern ecumenical movement.[23] Mott had been influenced by Moody and his commitments to the gospel and nonsec-

19. Woodbridge and James, *Church History*, 2:559. See J. Gresham Machen, *Christianity and Liberalism* (London: Victory, 1923).

20. Mark A. Noll, *The Old Religion in a New World: The History of North American Christianity* (Grand Rapids: Eerdmans, 2001), 144–47.

21. Woodbridge and James, *Church History*, 2:559–61.

22. Niebuhr, *Kingdom of God in America*, 193.

23. Douglas A. Sweeney, *The American Evangelical Story* (Grand Rapids: Baker Academic 2005), 97.

tarianism. In 1948, Mott was part of the formation of the World Council of Churches (WCC), which sought to maintain unity between all Christians. In his work titled *The Pastor and Modern Missions: A Plea for Leadership in World Evangelization*, Mott said, "It is possible for the most obscure person in a church, with a heart right toward God, to exercise as much power for the evangelization of the world, as it is for those who stand in the most prominent positions."[24]

The International Missionary Conference (IMC)—the continuing expression of the World Missionary Conference in Edinburgh—was committed originally to evangelism through the cooperative efforts of churches and denominations. Until the merger of the WCC and the IMC in 1961, both organizations focused on the church and its struggle to carry out its mission. After the merger, however, the focus shifted to the struggle throughout the world for human flourishing, protection of human rights, and social reforms in response to injustices, racism, and poverty.[25] In a push to identify such human concerns as the mission of the church, some ecumenical leaders not only ignored gospel proclamation but began to reject it as part of the church's mission, following the earlier program of the social gospel.[26]

Members of the WCC increasingly contended that the task of churches was not so much to proclaim Christ as to convert the world—in other words, to combat all dehumanizing forces and institutions, and create an environment where people could attain their fullest human potential and exercise their human rights. To accomplish this, Christians were to unite with others who shared these goals, regardless of their religious commitments.

Against this backdrop, a stream of evangelists with fundamental convictions about the Scriptures and the events of Jesus's birth, death, and resurrection continued to proclaim the soul-saving gospel. They stood opposed to liberal theology and the liberal wings of the Protestant church and preached "the gospel of Jesus' blood and his righteousness."[27]

24. John R. Mott, *The Pastor and Modern Missions: A Plea for Leadership in World Evangelization* (New York: Student Volunteer Movement for Foreign Missions, 1904), 203.

25. Craig Ott and Stephen J. Strauss, *Encountering Theology of Mission: Biblical Foundations, Historical Developments, and Contemporary Issues* (Grand Rapids: Baker Academic, 2014), 130.

26. Milton L. Rudnick, *Speaking the Gospel through the Ages: A History of Evangelism* (St. Louis: Concordia, 1984), 211.

27. Soong-Chan Rah, "The Ongoing Scandal of the Evangelical Conscience and

Billy Sunday

The soul-saving evangelist Billy Sunday (1862–1935) was a former baseball player whose antics and street slang led to his form of mass evangelism with the character of a religious vaudeville.[28] He was born in a log cabin near Ames, Iowa. His father, who had volunteered for the Union Army, died of pneumonia just a month after Billy was born.[29] With this hardship, Billy's mother sent him and his older brother to the Soldiers' Orphan Home at Glenwood, Iowa, and then to the Annie Wittenmeyer Home in Davenport.[30]

At fourteen, Billy returned to Ames to live with his grandfather but soon left to enter the workforce. After graduating from high school, he went to a tryout for a baseball team at Marshalltown, Iowa.[31] His big break came in 1883, when the manager of the Chicago White Stockings (later White Sox) saw him play and was so impressed that he offered him a big-league contract. Sunday signed it and traveled to Chicago with just a dollar in his pocket.

Billy Sunday was not a "big hitter" at the plate but impressed fans with his acrobatic catches and gutsy base running. In 1890, he stole eighty-four bases and held the record of rounding the diamond in fourteen seconds.[32] However, his life as a baseball player soon came to an end. It all began on a Sunday afternoon when he was out for a good time with his teammates in Chicago after a few drinks. They walked down State Street near Van Buren Street, when they heard the sound of music. An evangelistic street meeting was in progress. Billy heard the gospel message and began to weep, telling his teammates, "I am through. I am going to Jesus Christ."[33]

With counsel and the prayers of Sarah Clarke of the Pacific Garden Mission, Billy came to faith in Christ. Immediately, he took interest in study-

---

Mind," in *CCDA Theological Journal, 2012*, ed. Chris Jehle, Soong-Chan Rah, and Brandon Wrencher (Eugene, OR: CCDA and Wipf & Stock, 2012), 22.

28. Margaret Lamberts Bendroth, *Fundamentalists in the City: Conflict and Division in Boston's Churches, 1885–1950* (Oxford: Oxford University Press, 2005), 141–43.

29. Mendell Taylor, *Exploring Evangelism: History, Methods, Theology* (Kansas City, MO: Nazarene Publishing House, 1984), 525.

30. Elijah P. Brown, *The Real Billy Sunday* (New York: Revell, 1914), 20, cited in M. Taylor, *Exploring Evangelism*, 526.

31. Roger A. Bruns, *Preacher Billy Sunday and Big-Time American Evangelism* (Urbana: University of Illinois, 2002), 36–37.

32. Lee Thomas, *The Billy Sunday Story* (Grand Rapids: Zondervan, 1961), 39, cited in M. Taylor, *Exploring Evangelism*, 527.

33. William T. Ellis, *Billy Sunday: The Man and His Message* (Philadelphia: John C. Winston, 1914), cited in M. Taylor, *Exploring Evangelism*, 527.

ing the Bible at the YMCA and joined Jefferson Park Presbyterian Church, where he met Nell Thompson, his future wife.

Still as a major-league player, Sunday was invited to speak at YMCA meetings. He aimed his message "straight at the young men in front of him" and gave them "the truth in plain earnest language."[34] After the main meetings, he took an active part in talking with inquirers about Christ.

The YMCA recognized the advantage of having Sunday on its staff, and in 1891 the organization offered him a position that would pay $83 a month, considerably less than his major-league contract of $500 a month.[35] Despite the difference, Sunday chose evangelism over baseball. His duties with the YMCA included securing speakers for the noon prayer meetings, fundraising, distributing literature, and preaching the gospel at street meetings. Through this experience, he witnessed the power of the gospel to transform lives.

Sunday worked closely with J. Wilbur Chapman (1859–1918), a leading evangelist of the YMCA. In 1894, Chapman persuaded him to become a member of his evangelistic team, working as an advance agent to arrange meetings.[36] In this position, Sunday organized local committees, sold books, and preached the gospel to overflow crowds. In 1896, he took over Chapman's work and launched his first evangelistic campaign. Sunday's meetings drew thousands in attendance. His voice could be heard by as many as twenty-five thousand people, especially with the aid of a sound board that looked like "an inverted sugar scoop" over the preaching platform.[37]

In 1910, Sunday partnered with song-leader Homer Rodeheaver (1880–1955). The strength of Sunday's meetings was the well-designed organization. Whenever he arrived in a new area, he familiarized himself with the leading persons and cultural forces of the community. *The New Republic* described his meetings, saying, "When [his] organization has delivered the crowd, Billy is ready to sweat for it and spit for it and war-whoop for it and dive for base before the devil can reach him."[38]

The first part of every service was the congregational singing led by Rodeheaver. After thirty minutes, the atmosphere was prepared for his solo, and then Sunday's gospel message. Sunday was known for his dramatization as he acted out stories and Bible vignettes.[39] As people listened, he would run, jump, and walk. He was known to hurl imaginary baseballs and hit imag-

34. M. Taylor, *Exploring Evangelism*, 528.
35. M. Taylor, *Exploring Evangelism*, 528.
36. M. Taylor, *Exploring Evangelism*, 528.
37. Ellis, *Billy Sunday*, 66, cited in M. Taylor, *Exploring Evangelism*, 530.
38. *The New Republic*, April 28, 1917, 370, cited in M. Taylor, *Exploring Evangelism*, 532.
39. Bendroth, *Fundamentalists in the City*, 142.

inary home runs, slide for home plate, and shout in umpire-like fashion, "You're out!" to announce God's judgment on the unconverted. Journalists marveled at Sunday's agility and energy. One reporter estimated that during a sermon, Sunday would travel at least a mile.

In preaching, Sunday condemned social practices such as wearing stylish jewelry, playing card games, cursing, attending the theater, and "the cardinal sins of smoking, drinking, and dancing."[40] As a soul-saving evangelist, he brought the bad news of condemnation before offering the good news of salvation in Jesus.

Sunday employed some questionable techniques too. When taking an offering, he would begin by asking, "How many of you will give a dollar?" Then he would say, "Stand up!" Immediately, the pianists would begin to play "The Star-Spangled Banner," which brought all patriotic Americans to their feet, reaching for dollar bills for the offering baskets.[41]

The key expression that Sunday used in his appeal for listeners to decide for Christ was "hit the sawdust trail." This phrase originated in his evangelism campaign in 1910, in the logging town of Bellingham, Washington, where he learned that lumberjacks used the phrase when out in the dense, dark woods. As they walked from one location to another, they scattered sawdust from gunny sacks to mark the return path to the logging road. When the work was done, they would say, "Now if I can only find that sawdust trail I'll be safe and get home."[42]

For Sunday, those who walked the "sawdust trail" (aisle) at his evangelistic meetings would "come home to Christ." With this invitation, as "trail hitters" came forward, Sunday shook their hands. Church historian Sydney Ahlstrom explains,

> The "altar call" was, of course, the climax and goal of the revival service. Professional evangelists had made the decision increasingly easier, so that by Sunday's time any "decent American" could painlessly respond. The burden was easy and the sawdust trail was wide. His invitation on the twelfth day of his New York campaign was typical. "Do you want God's blessing on you, your home, your church, your nation, on

40. William G. McLoughlin, *Billy Sunday Was His Real Name* (Chicago: University of Chicago Press, 1955), 132–33, cited in M. Taylor, *Exploring Evangelism*, 533.

41. M. Taylor, *Exploring Evangelism*, 533–34.

42. McLoughlin, *Billy Sunday Was His Real Name*, 97, cited in M. Taylor, *Exploring Evangelism*, 534.

> New York? If you do, raise your hands. . . . How many of you men and women will jump to your feet and come down and say, 'Bill, here's my hand for God, for home, my native land, to live and conquer for Christ'?" Then Rody and the choir began their musical accompaniment, and a sea of humanity surged forward—one out of every ten in that audience of twenty thousand.[43]

Each person who came forward was asked to complete a decision card and indicate their preference of church or denomination. The cards were then distributed to participating pastors who then visited the new converts during the following weeks.

House Visitation Evangelism

In 1913, pastors in Indianapolis, Indiana, decided not to invite Billy Sunday to their city and instead agreed to conduct a three-year, citywide visitation campaign. Volunteers from participating churches went door-to-door throughout the city. At the end of the project, the pastors announced that they added twenty thousand new members to local congregations.

Elmer T. Clark

In 1914, Elmer T. Clark (1886–1966) wrote a book titled *The New Evangelism*, in which he outlined a similar campaign in St. Louis, Missouri, by a federation of cooperating churches.[44] Rather than inviting an evangelist, Clark's plan was to conduct a "religious census" that followed the pattern of the federal government census, taken every ten years. Trained volunteers from churches went street-by-street to survey residents about their religious affiliation or interest. Those who wanted more information were asked to complete a card to indicate their preferred church or denomination. Afterward, every interested resident received a visit from the pastor of the church.[45]

For several reasons, pastors preferred the strategy of community visitation over the mass evangelism of Billy Sunday and others. The "religious census"

43. Sydney E. Ahlstrom, *A Religious History of the American People* (New Haven: Yale University Press, 1974), 206–7, cited in Salter, *American Evangelism*, 103.

44. Rudnick, *Speaking the Gospel*, 201. See Elmer T. Clark, *The New Evangelism* (Nashville: Smith & Lamar, 1915).

45. Paulus Scharpff, *History of Evangelism: Three Hundred Years of Evangelism in Germany, Great Britain, and the United States of America* (Grand Rapids: Eerdmans, 1966), 321.

strategy was a systematic way to contact every person or family in the vicinity, including those who would never attend an evangelistic meeting. Moreover, the strategy relied heavily on laypeople to visit homes in the community, giving a personal and local appeal. The subsequent visits by local pastors gave them the opportunity to present the gospel, answer questions, address needs of those interested, and extend a personal invitation to their church, reducing the decision-to-disciple gap often associated with mass evangelism. In St. Louis, the federation of cooperating churches claimed that ten thousand new members joined congregations as a result of the citywide campaign.[46]

Earl Kernahan

The Reverend A. Earl Kernahan (1888–1944) refined this approach further.[47] Like an advance person for an evangelist, Kernahan was available to federations of cooperating churches for a fee in order to organize a visitation campaign in the city.[48] Pastors recruited lay volunteers, and Kernahan provided instructions on visitation methods, led the singing of inspirational songs, delivered a motivational message, and sent volunteers out two by two to their assigned neighborhoods.[49] He gave each pair of volunteers a stack of "prospect cards" and instructed them to write the results of their initial visits on the cards.

When the volunteers returned a second time to the home of a "prospect," the resident was asked to join a church. If they agreed, they were asked to sign a "decision card," which specified a date when they would join. Kernahan collected the cards, reviewed them, and followed up difficult cases. Moreover, he provided ongoing support to the volunteers when they faced an obstacle. When the lay workers finished visiting all the prospects, the campaign was complete.

Kernahan opened an office in Washington, DC, as headquarters for the Directed Survey and Visitation Campaigns.[50] He hired a staff to assist in

46. John Mark Terry, *Evangelism: A Concise History* (Nashville: B&H, 2014), 185.

47. See Arthur Earl Kernahan, *Visitation Evangelism: Its Methods and Results* (New York: Revell, 1925); Kernahan, *Adventures in Visitation Evangelism* (New York: Revell, 1928); Kernahan, *Christian Citizenship and Visitation Evangelism* (New York: Revell, 1929).

48. Terry, *Evangelism*, 186.

49. See Arthur Earl Kernahan, *Great Sermons on Evangelism* (Nashville: Cokesbury, 1934).

50. Scharpff, *History of Evangelism*, 321. See Arthur Earl Kernahan, *The Directed Survey and Visitation Evangelism* (New York: Revell, 1930).

every phase, from the religious census to the follow-up of those who decided to join a church.

House visitation campaigns had a broader appeal to Protestant pastors whether they embraced the social gospel or the soul-saving gospel. These campaigns depended on churches that wanted to work together, and reinforced a notion of cultural Christendom where everyone was expected to belong to a church. In some cases, the emphasis became more about joining a church than conversion to Christ. As Paulus Scharpff observed, "Visitation evangelism, like any other method in evangelism, must constantly examine its theology and its motives lest it degenerate into a church membership drive that asks no commitment to Jesus Christ."[51]

Pentecostal Evangelists

Pentecostal churches in America began with a revival of charismatic phenomena and the doctrinal claim that speaking in tongues was the initial evidence of the baptism of the Holy Spirit. The Pentecostal movement set in motion spontaneous, Spirit-filled evangelism in which millions of people have come to faith in Christ.

The modern Pentecostal movement in America began with Charles F. Parham (1873–1929), who directed Bethel Bible College in Topeka, Kansas.[52] During a meeting that Parham led in 1900, a student named Agnes Oznam (1870–1937) began to speak in an unknown tongue that sounded like Chinese.[53] She shocked those present by speaking a language she had never learned. Parham also began to teach that Christ's atonement promised deliverance from disease and sickness, and that divine healing should be expected. He and his students interpreted the charismatic phenomena that they witnessed as signs of the last days before Christ's second coming. Such Pentecost-like phenomena gave a sense of urgency for evangelistic mission.

51. Scharpff, *History of Evangelism*, 322.

52. Woodbridge and James, *Church History*, 2:695. Cf. David M. Gustafson, "August Davis and the Free-Free: Pentecostal Phenomena among the Swedish Evangelical Free," *Pneuma* 37, no. 2 (2015): 201–23.

53. Edith L. Blumhofer, *Restoring the Faith: The Assemblies of God, Pentecostalism, and American Culture* (Urbana: University of Illinois Press, 1993), i, 2, 50–51, 66n59; Vinson Synan, *The Holiness-Pentecostal Tradition: Charismatic Movements in the Twentieth Century* (Grand Rapids: Eerdmans, 1997), 91. The name Oznam is often rendered Ozman.

William J. Seymour

William J. Seymour (1870–1922), the son of a slave and student of Parham, moved to Los Angeles, California, where he started a house church with others from Baptist and Wesleyan holiness churches.[54] Seymour himself had been a member of the African Methodist Episcopal Church. In 1906, his coworker, Jennie Evans Moore, and his landlord, Edward Lee, began speaking in tongues during a revival meeting, similar to Oznam in Topeka. The spiritual gifts of prophecy and healing manifested too. With a display of Pentecostal phenomena, attendance increased at the meetings, making it necessary for Seymour and his fledgling group to find a new meeting place. They rented an empty warehouse on Azusa Street in Los Angeles and founded the Apostolic Faith Mission.[55] Revival meetings were held regularly for the next ten years in which women and men, African Americans and Hispanics, poor and rich were touched by the soul-saving gospel of Jesus.

The magnetism of Pentecostalism came from an emphasis on demonstrations and experiences of divine power. The baptism of the Holy Spirit was evidenced by speaking in tongues, divine healing, prophesying, and casting out demons, actions that were attributed to the presence of God. By 1911, independent Pentecostal congregations were established in cities and Pentecostal denominations began to form. Although racially integrated in the early years, white clergy within the movement formed the Assemblies of God in 1914. The United Pentecostal Church that held to a "Jesus Only" (Oneness or Unitarian) view of God formed the same year. Despite criticisms from other denominations and dissensions within Pentecostalism, the movement grew rapidly, with congregations meeting in city storefronts, rented spaces in rural villages, and upper-story rooms in urban neighborhoods.

Mary Woodworth-Etter

Among the early Pentecostal evangelists was Mary B. Woodworth-Etter (1844–1924) from New Lisbon, Ohio. She was born as Maria Beulah Underwood. She testified to her new birth at the age of thirteen and immediately answered God's call to serve him, later writing, "Soon after I was converted I heard the voice of Jesus calling me to go out in the highways and hedges and

54. Cecil M. Robeck Jr., *The Azusa Street Mission and Revival: The Birth of the Global Pentecostal Movement* (Nashville: Nelson, 2006), 19–23, 43–47.

55. Woodbridge and James, *Church History*, 2:695.

gather in the lost sheep."[56] In 1863, Mary married Philo Horace Woodworth, whom she divorced for infidelity in 1891. They had six children, five of whom died young.[57] In 1902, she married Samuel Etter.

Mary Woodworth-Etter studied the Scriptures and began preaching a message that God willed for people to be healed. She soon discovered how healing and evangelism went hand in hand as thousands of listeners converted to faith in Christ.[58] At first she attended a Disciples of Christ congregation, but left to join the Quakers, who supported women preaching publicly. During a meeting, while praying for God's anointing, she was "baptized with the Holy Ghost, and fire, and power" and began to preach.[59]

Woodworth-Etter prayed for the sick, believing that those with sufficient faith would be healed. People who attended the meetings fell on the floor in trancelike states and reported ecstatic spiritual experiences. For a time, she affiliated with the Brethren in Christ and then with the Church of God but was dismissed from that body in 1904.[60]

As Woodworth-Etter preached throughout the United States, her reputation grew. In 1912, she joined the burgeoning Pentecostals and preached widely in their circles. In 1914, she was at the meeting that formed the Assemblies of God, and four years later she founded the Lakeview Temple of Indianapolis, Indiana.[61]

Carrie Judd Montgomery

A female evangelist to follow Woodworth-Etter was Carrie Judd Montgomery (1858–1946). In 1890, Montgomery opened the People's Mission in San Francisco and the Beulah Rescue Home in Oakland, sponsored by the Salvation Army.[62] In 1894, she worked with her husband, George, to found the Shalom Training Institute in Cazadero, California.[63]

56. Woodworth-Etter, *Marvels and Miracles*, 12.

57. Ruth A. Tucker and Walter Liefeld, *Daughters of the Church: Women and Ministry from New Testament Times to the Present* (Grand Rapids: Zondervan, 1987), 362–63.

58. Tucker and Liefeld, *Daughters of the Church*, 363.

59. Blumhofer, *Restoring the Faith*, 24.

60. Blumhofer, *Restoring the Faith*, 24.

61. Blumhofer, *Restoring the Faith*, 116–17.

62. James Robinson, *Divine Healing: The Holiness-Pentecostal Transition Years, 1890–1906; Theological Transposition in the Transatlantic World* (Eugene, OR: Pickwick, 2013), 130–31.

63. Jennifer A. Miskov, *Life on Wings: The Forgotten Life and Theology of Carrie Judd Montgomery* (Cleveland: CPT, 2012), 95–96.

When the Azusa Street revival in Los Angeles began with Seymour and others in 1906, Montgomery attended the meetings. Although she was hesitant at first, in 1908, at the age of fifty, she experienced "Spirit baptism."[64] Soon she integrated the teaching about Spirit baptism into her evangelistic meetings. With the trust of both soul-saving Protestants and tongues-speaking Pentecostals, she introduced Spirit baptism to the former without the fanaticism of the latter. Her friendships extended to people such as A. B. Simpson of the Christian and Missionary Alliance; Minnie Abrams, a missionary to India; Pandita Ramabai at the Mukti mission in India; and Elizabeth Baxter, an evangelist in England.[65]

Francisco Olazábal

Francisco Olazábal (1886–1937), known popularly as the "Mexican Billy Sunday," was born in El Verano, Sinaloa, Mexico.[66] His mother, Refugio Olazábal, converted to personal faith in Christ in 1898 and became a lay Methodist evangelist, taking her son with her throughout the Sierra Madres of northern Mexico.[67] At seventeen years of age, Francisco immigrated to San Francisco, California. With hopes of becoming a mariner and sailing the world, he was challenged by the evangelistic message of George and Carrie Judd Montgomery. Carrie gave him a gospel tract to read and invited him to their home to discuss it. Through their witness, Olazábal came to saving faith in Jesus.[68]

He returned to Mexico shortly afterward to attend the Wesleyan School of Theology at San Luis Potosi.[69] Following his studies he took up evangelistic ministry and served as pastor of a Spanish-speaking Methodist church in El Paso, Texas. After a brief time, he traveled to Chicago for additional studies at Moody Bible Institute.[70] When Reuben A. Torrey (1856–1928), a champion of personal evangelism, went to Los Angeles to open the Bible

64. Miskov, *Life on Wings*, 114–16; Robinson, *Divine Healing*, 132.

65. Miskov, *Life on Wings*, 294n35; Tucker and Liefield, *Daughters of the Church*, 288.

66. Gastón Espinosa, "God Made a Miracle in My Life: Latino Pentecostal Healing in the Borderlands," in *Religion and Healing in America*, ed. Linda L. Barnes and Susan S. Sered (New York: Oxford University Press, 2005), 125; Miskov, *Life on Wings*, 136.

67. Espinosa, "God Made a Miracle in My Life," 125; Miskov, *Life on Wings*, 135.

68. Allan Anderson, *Spreading Fires: The Missionary Nature of Early Pentecostalism* (London: SCM, 2007), 195.

69. Espinosa, "God Made a Miracle in My Life," 125–26.

70. A. Anderson, *Spreading Fires*, 195; Miskov, *Life on Wings*, 135–36.

Institute of Los Angeles (Biola), he asked Olazábal to go with him to minister to the growing Mexican population in the area.[71] Olazábal accepted the offer but after a short time parted ways because of different understandings of the person and work of the Holy Spirit.

Olazábal ministered not merely in Los Angeles but also in Pasadena, California, where he established a Methodist mission-church. After his marriage to Macrina Orasco, he served as a circuit preacher to two Spanish-speaking congregations in San Francisco and Sacramento.

In 1916, Olazábal met again with George and Carrie Judd Montgomery. In their meeting, he experienced Spirit baptism and witnessed the healing of his wife, who had suffered for some time from thrombophlebitis in her femoral vein.[72] In 1917, Olazábal received ministerial credentials with the Assemblies of God and began to "preach the full gospel" of salvation and healing.[73] He began evangelistic campaigns in Los Angeles and near El Paso along the US-Mexico border, leading people to faith and planting churches.

Olazábal, continuing his evangelistic and healing campaigns, "crisscrossed the Southwest, preaching and praying for thousands of Mexicans in migrant farm labor camps, factories, and inner-city barrios."[74] In 1923, he began the Interdenominational Mexican Council of Christian Churches (Pentecostal) and returned to Los Angeles, where he held meetings in the Watts neighborhood. During this time, evangelist Aimee Semple McPherson attended some of his meetings and preached at his church.[75] In turn, she invited him to join her on the platform at Angelus Temple, along with members of his congregation. Although she suggested that the International Mexican Council of Christian Churches join forces with her organization, the Four Square Gospel Church, the council's decision not to join forces infuriated her, which led her to expel them from her office.

Despite the setback, Olazábal benefited from his association with the popular evangelist, especially as he gained respect from Spanish-speaking Pentecostals. He held meetings in Chicago; Indian Harbor, Indiana; Modesto, Cal-

71. Gastón Espinosa, "Brown Moses: Francisco Olazabal and Mexican American Pentecostal Healing in the Borderlands," in *Mexican American Religions: Spirituality, Activism, and Culture*, ed. Gastón Espinosa and Mario T. Garcia (Durham, NC: Duke University Press, 2008), 269. For Torrey, see Reuben A. Torrey, *How to Bring Men to Christ* (Chicago: Revell, 1893).

72. Espinosa, "Brown Moses," 270–71.

73. Espinosa, "God Made a Miracle in My Life," 127.

74. Espinosa, "God Made a Miracle in My Life," 128.

75. Espinosa, "Brown Moses," 274.

Figure 10.1. Francisco Olazábal. *(Flower Pentecostal Heritage Center)*

ifornia; Houston and Laredo, Texas; Puerto Rico; and Mexico City.[76] His evangelistic and healing campaign in Chicago's Opera House drew thousands every night for weeks.

In 1931, his meetings in the "Spanish Harlem" of New York City attracted no less than 100,000 people. As a result, Olazábal organized the Bethel Temple in New York City, which by 1932 grew to over fifteen hundred members, with many from Puerto Rico.[77] Moreover, he proposed to the council to change the organization's name to the Latin American Council of Christian Churches. He traveled to Puerto Rico, where he held the first "Pentecostal, island-wide evangelistic healing and revival crusade," in which nearly twenty thousand people came to faith in Christ.[78] Among those to convert was Maria Teresa Sapia, whom Gastón Espinosa describes, saying, "She was a notorious gambler, gun woman, and rumrunner during Prohibition. Castigation by some as one of the 'worst' women in Puerto Rico was the least of her problems: asthma and other ailments had wasted her body to a scant seventy-five pounds. She turned to Olazábal for healing and redemption. At one of his services, she claimed that she was dramatically healed and converted. Immediately she gave up her former lifestyle and began to assist Olazábal at his crusades, becoming a key staff member."[79]

Olazábal ignited the Hispanic Pentecostal vision for evangelism and church planting. The Bethel Temple became a beachhead for sending evangelists and missionaries to Cuba, the Dominican Republic, Mexico, Chile, Argentina, Venezuela, Ecuador, and Spain. At the time of his death in a

76. A. Anderson, *Spreading Fires*, 195.
77. Espinosa, "God Made a Miracle in My Life," 129.
78. Espinosa, "Brown Moses," 281.
79. Espinosa, "God Made a Miracle in My Life," 130.

tragic car accident, he worked to establish 150 churches, preached to 250,000 people, and saw 50,000 converted to faith in Christ.[80] For Olazábal and Latin American Pentecostals, evangelism was their highest privilege and duty, and healing through the laying on of hands and manifestations of charismatic phenomena were integral to the witness to Jesus Christ.[81]

Pentecostal worship services were preceded often by street meetings in which members fanned out into the city, gathered crowds by singing and preaching, and then brought listeners to the services. Teams of lay evangelists explored nearby neighborhoods, shared the gospel there, and formed Bible study groups, which often became new congregations.[82] Because of the indigenous nature of Hispanic Pentecostal churches, they had freedom to experiment with forms of evangelism that were meaningful to the local culture. When an evangelistic work began, newly converted believers were prepared and given responsibility for evangelism, pastoral care, and growth of the church.

While Olazábal knew the benefits of theological education, he and other Pentecostals did not assume that people became evangelists and pastors by attending seminary. Rather, they were qualified for this work by demonstrating their ability to win people to Christ, to bring them into congregational life, and to keep their trust.

Sister Aimee Semple McPherson

Aimee Semple McPherson (1890–1944), already mentioned, was a Canadian American Pentecostal evangelist who used radio to broadcast her gospel messages from the Angelus Temple in the Echo Park neighborhood in Los Angeles. As a Pentecostal, she conducted evangelistic meetings and faith healings in which thousands of people were delivered from sickness and disease.

She was born Aimee Kennedy near Ingersoll, Ontario, and lived with her parents in a "gospel car," in which they traveled from town to town holding revival meetings.[83] As a teenager, she was introduced to Pentecostal teachings by the evangelist Robert Semple, whom she married.[84] They served

80. Miskov, *Life on Wings*, 137.

81. Espinosa, "Brown Moses," 277.

82. Rudnick, *Speaking the Gospel*, 221.

83. Daniel M. Epstein, *Sister Aimee: The Life of Aimee Semple McPherson* (Orlando: Harcourt Brace, 1993), 5–7.

84. Epstein, *Sister Aimee*, 40–41, 46–54.

as missionaries to China until 1910 when Robert died. Aimee returned to the United States and took up evangelistic work with her mother and the Salvation Army.

In New York City, Sister Aimee met Harold McPherson, and after they married, the couple traveled as Pentecostal evangelists in their gospel car, living off the meager love offerings they received at their meetings.[85] When Aimee became dissatisfied with Harold, the marriage ended in divorce.[86] She continued her soul-winning work of gospel preaching and divine healing alongside her mother, who managed the business affairs. Slowly the young evangelist began to attract crowds and media attention. In 1918, she decided to make Los Angeles her home base and launched a series of meetings that catapulted her to national fame. Pastors of several denominations supported her citywide campaigns.

Charles S. Price

One example is Charles S. Price (1887–1947), pastor of First Congregational Church of Lodi, California. In 1921, some of his parishioners attended Sister Aimee's services and reported the large numbers of conversions and miracles they saw. As a theological liberal, Price ventured skeptically into one of Sister Aimee's meetings in the San Francisco Bay area. His plan was to expose her as a fraud, believing that everything she promoted was psychological, not supernatural. Before he attended her meetings, he presumptuously had placed an advertisement in the local newspaper with his next sermon title, "Divine Healing Bubble Explodes."[87]

When Price arrived at the meeting, the large tent was packed with six thousand people. He found a seat in the section reserved for people with infirmities who desired healing. Before the meeting began, he was shocked when greeted by his longtime friend, Dr. William Towner, pastor of First Baptist Church of Oakland, who had helped sponsor the event. Towner told Price, "Charlie, this is real. This little woman is right. This is the real gospel. I have been baptized with the Holy Ghost. It's genuine, I tell you. It is what you need."[88]

85. Edith W. Blumhofer, *Aimee Semple McPherson: Everybody's Sister* (Grand Rapids: Eerdmans, 1993), 117–18.

86. Blumhofer, *Aimee Semple McPherson*, 128–30.

87. Charles H. Barfoot, *Aimee Semple McPherson and the Making of Modern Pentecostalism, 1890–1926* (London: Routledge, 2015), 296.

88. Barfoot, *Aimee Semple McPherson*, 296.

Although Price expected McPherson's message to be fanatical, he was surprised to hear a message that was biblical and compelling. Hundreds of listeners responded to her invitation to come forward to accept Christ. When Price returned in the evening, he took his place on the platform with other clergy and witnessed firsthand numerous healings, including that of a blind person who regained sight and a lame person who walked. When Sister Aimee invited sinners to raise their hands to accept Christ, Price raised his hand. He recalled, "The next night a masterful message came from the lips of the evangelist and my modernistic theology was punctured until it leaked like a sieve."[89] On the fourth night, when Price came forward for prayer, he was baptized in the Holy Spirit and spoke in tongues.

Price began to preach the Pentecostal doctrines in his congregation, and nearly five hundred members were baptized in the Holy Spirit. Moreover, he and his members began to hold evangelistic street meetings in nearby towns. Price eventually joined the pastoral staff of Angelus Temple and became a noted Pentecostal evangelist himself.[90]

Sister Aimee's Angelus Temple

In 1923, Sister Aimee dedicated her church at Echo Park. This massive structure was built for five thousand people at a cost of $1.5 million. In 1924, she launched one of the first religious broadcast programs when the Angelus Temple opened the radio station KFSG (Kall Four-Square Gospel).[91] In 1927, the church was dedicated as Church of the Foursquare Gospel, a new Pentecostal denomination.

Near Hollywood, Sister Aimee and Angelus Temple increasingly took on the image of a religious Tinseltown. Thousands of visitors flocked to the church to watch the spellbinding extravaganzas that included elaborate sets and inspiring music that all climaxed with a dramatic sermon by Aimee. Much of her appeal was based on the spectacular, which included Pentecostal phenomena, along with her beauty and aura of optimism. The well-advertised services offered her Pentecostal faithful a taste of Hollywood while shunning its vices.

In addition to the extravagant services, parades, and uniforms, the church maintained an ambitious program to feed the hungry of Los Angeles. Sister

89. Barfoot, *Aimee Semple McPherson*, 297.
90. Barfoot, *Aimee Semple McPherson*, 293–96.
91. Blumhofer, *Aimee Semple McPherson*, 268.

Aimee ministered in other cities too, such as Denver, Colorado, and Winnipeg, Canada, where she made midnight forays to the red-light districts, embracing prostitutes and assuring them that she loved them. In San Francisco, she entered a dive on the Barbary Coast, sat down at the piano, and began to sing softly "Jesus, Lover of My Soul." She would also "preach in a prize-fight arena, drop gospel tracts from an open cockpit while flying in an aeroplane, [and] speak from the rear decks of crowded Pullman cars like a politician."[92]

Despite all that Sister Aimee accomplished in her soul-saving ministry, newspapers followed a number of incidents and scandals. In 1926, she disappeared for several weeks, presumed to have drowned off the Ocean Park Beach in Santa Monica. When she reappeared at Douglas, Arizona, she claimed to have been kidnapped and escaped.[93] Nevertheless, evidence pointed to an extramarital affair and her concocting a cover-up. She was accused of a number of financial improprieties, including funneling money to her personal accounts and purchasing a large private villa. She was dogged by numerous lawsuits, with as many as forty-five legal actions pending at a time. She had serious disagreements with fellow clergy and family, causing the church to split. In 1931, she married Hollywood actor David Hutton, but after he was photographed with scantily clad women, she divorced him, claiming personal reasons.[94] She became increasingly secluded from others and estranged from her mother and daughter. In 1944, Sister Aimee addressed ten thousand people in the Oakland Auditorium in California.[95] The following day she died from an apparent overdose of prescription drugs and sleeping pills.[96] Her death was ruled accidental.

Despite the scandals that plagued her, at the time of her death, the Church of the Foursquare Gospel claimed some four hundred branch ministries and nearly two hundred missions abroad. The Echo Park Evangelistic and Missionary Training Institute that she founded in 1923, known today as Life Pacific University, has graduated more than three thousand evangelists and missionaries.

Clearly, Sister Aimee evoked excitement in Christians and non-Christians alike by the experiences that were perceived as evidences of God's power. People attended her gatherings because of reports of miraculous healings.

92. Barfoot, *Aimee Semple McPherson*, 220.
93. Epstein, *Sister Aimee*, 296–99.
94. Epstein, *Sister Aimee*, 362–64, 434.
95. Epstein, *Sister Aimee*, 437.
96. Epstein, *Sister Aimee*, 438.

Many came out of curiosity, while others came out of desperate need. Despite the motives, they heard the gospel and discovered God's love in Christ and power in the Holy Spirit.[97] The soul-saving and wonder-working power demonstrated in Sister Aimee did not preclude her from temptations. Although she was a vessel used by God, she was human and failed, bringing disrepute to the name of Christ and the church. Stepping into the spotlight brought her public acclaim and public scrutiny.

Evangelism and Social Action

Some Christians within the evangelical tradition held to holistic gospel witness and continued to address the spectrum of human needs, operating soup kitchens, hospitals, rescue missions, orphanages, and schools while preaching the gospel.

Sister Ellen Modin

Ellen Modin (1853–1941) not only avoided pitfalls of mass evangelists but also held to the social and personal dimensions of the gospel. She associated originally with American Congregationalists in a mission to rescue Swedish women who had "adopted Mormon teachings and practiced the religion of polygamy."[98] Many of these women had been promised a good life by a Swedish Mormon man back in the homeland. However, many were unprepared for and surprised and disillusioned by the polygamous aspects of the heretical cult.

Ellen Modin was born in Hälsingland, Sweden, and immigrated to America in 1881. She was a teacher who had completed studies at Bollnäs Teacher's School in Gävleborg. In America, as she read accounts of a Swedish evangelical mission in Utah, led by Fredrik Franson, her interest was piqued to join the work. Arriving in Utah, she spent mornings studying the books of Mormonism, comparing their teachings with the Bible. In the afternoons, she visited with Swedish Mormon women in their personal apartments in order to persuade them to leave Mormonism and to accept the gospel of Jesus. Three years later she was joined by Lottie Axelson and Mathilda Johnson of the Swedish Free Mission.

97. Rudnick, *Speaking the Gospel*, 223.

98. David M. Gustafson, "Ellen Modin: The Swedish Lady Missionary," *Pietisten* 28, no. 1 (Spring-Summer 2013): 12–13.

In 1891, Modin returned to Minnesota, where she founded the Women's Alliance Mission Home in St. Paul. She was encouraged in this work by Franson, who had founded the Scandinavian Alliance Mission, known today as TEAM. Modin took it upon herself to travel and raise funds for a school, the Scandinavian Mission Alliance Women's Bible Institute and Seminary, where she served as the instructor.[99] Over the next two decades, hundreds of women were prepared as evangelists and missionaries. Most traveled sharing testimonies, leading music, and preaching the gospel.[100] In many cases, these female evangelists worked with male itinerant preachers to establish Swedish Free churches. Typically, a series of meetings led by the female evangelists lasted for several weeks or months, until a small group of spiritually awakened people expressed interest in forming a congregation. Then itinerant preachers would begin to serve the new congregation until a permanent pastor, when feasible, could be found to take over the work.

In 1907, when Modin's school closed, the board transferred the assets to her newly founded Scandinavian Home of Shelter in Minneapolis, a ministry for women. This home provided a safe refuge for women and children, particularly for single, Swedish teenage girls who were pregnant. The girls came to stay at the home during their pregnancy, birth, and adoption of the children. Modin adopted a son herself and raised him on her own, having never married.

Modin published a monthly periodical titled *The Life Line*, which included reports from the evangelists that she trained to preach the gospel.[101] She was also an activist with the Southside Citizen's Committee, which worked to close down Minneapolis's red-light district. Her organization, the Scandinavian Home of Shelter, later became the Scandinavian Rescue Mission of Minneapolis.[102]

99. Frank T. Lindberg, *Looking Back Fifty Years over the Rise and Progress of the Swedish Evangelical Free Church of America* (Minneapolis: Franklin, 1935), 58–59.

100. David M. Gustafson and Gregory C. Strand, "Ordination and Women: A Case Study in the Historiography of the Evangelical Free Church of America," *Theofilos* 11, no. 2 (2019): 161–93.

101. David M. Gustafson, "Mary Johnson and Ida Anderson: 'Free-Free' Missionaries of the Scandinavian Mission Society U.S.A. to Natal, South Africa," *Pneuma* 39, nos. 1–2 (2017): 55–77.

102. Compare the evangelistic ministries of Emma Ray (1859–1930) of Seattle and Emma Whittemore (1850–1931) of New York City. Priscilla Pope-Levison, *Models of Evangelism* (Grand Rapids: Baker Academic, 2020), 55–56.

The Clarkes and the Pacific Garden Mission

The Pacific Garden Mission in Chicago was founded in 1877 by George and Sarah J. Clarke, mentioned above. In 1880, the mission moved to a building that was formerly the Pacific Beer Garden. Dwight L. Moody suggested the new name, saying, "Strike out the 'beer' and add 'mission.'"[103] From the beginning, this evangelistic ministry combined the message of the gospel that "Jesus saves" with social action, providing food and clothing to the exploited and homeless. Some people even referred to the mission as "Hobo Church."

The cofounder, George R. Clarke (1827–1892), had attained the rank of lieutenant colonel in the Civil War and then entered business and was successful. He married Sarah J. Dunn (1835–1918), who had sensed God's call on her life to a ministry of evangelism. She persuaded George to visit Chicago's slums filled with gambling halls, saloons, and brothels.[104] He agreed to do so but remained more interested in making money than ministering to people. Nonetheless, while on a business trip, he came under deep conviction by the Holy Spirit that people mattered to God more than money. In response, he dedicated himself to God's service and telegraphed Sarah about his change of heart.

At her suggestion, they opened the mission in a vacant storefront on South Clark Street, setting up wooden benches for forty people. As the former lieutenant colonel wept and struggled for words, Sarah tried to keep order among the noisy, drunken, lewd people who attended the meetings. With his lack of experience in gospel witness, some of George's friends considered him "one of the world's worst preachers."[105] Nevertheless, he became proficient at sharing the good news and saw firsthand the work of the Holy Spirit to change lives.

Sarah Clarke was not content simply to minister inside the mission. Twice a week she visited the county jail, going from cell to cell to share the gospel. Among the jail converts was John Callahan, a notorious gang member from the city's westside. Callahan's cell mate, Butch Lyon, mocked the

103. Carl F. H. Henry, *The Pacific Garden Mission: A Doorway to Heaven* (Grand Rapids: Zondervan, 1942), 28.

104. Sarah D. Clarke, *The Founding of Pacific Garden Mission: Over Thirty-Five Years Contributed to the Master's Service* (Chicago: Pacific Garden Mission, 1914), 17.

105. C. Henry, *Pacific Garden Mission*, 28.

"angel of mercy," Mrs. Clarke, while Callahan fell to the floor and prayed for Jesus to save his soul from sin. Butch Lyon "met death on the gallows," and John Callahan "was born again and became superintendent of the Hadley Rescue Hall in New York City."[106]

Mel Trotter

In 1897, Mel Trotter (1870–1940), an alcoholic who was planning to commit suicide, wandered into a meeting at the Pacific Garden Mission. For weeks at a time Trotter had been leaving home after periods of drunkenness. On one occasion, he discovered his two-year-old son dead. Believing he was responsible for the death, Trotter considered suicide. As he stood beside his son's coffin, he swore that he would never touch liquor again. However, just two hours later he was staggering drunk. He boarded a train for Chicago, and when he arrived, he sold his shoes to buy a bottle of booze.[107] Drunk, broke, and shoeless, he was "nudged inside" the Pacific Garden Mission.[108] There he met Harry Monroe, who led him to faith in Christ. As a changed person, Trotter took up his trade again as a barber and spent nights at the mission, playing guitar and singing. Later, he founded the City Rescue Mission in Grand Rapids, Michigan, and served as the director for forty years.

At the beginning of the twentieth century, with the division between the modernists and fundamentalists, the Pacific Garden Mission and other ministries like it preached the soul-saving gospel and engaged in social ministries to the homeless, prostitutes, gangsters, alcoholics, and gamblers. The evangelists in these settings kept their sermons simple, saying, for example, "Nobody was ever too bad for Jesus to save. Amen, glory! You aren't saved because you're good; if you were good, you wouldn't need to be saved. But Jesus died for your sins. He paid it all, glory to God! Make him your savior tonight. Come down this aisle for prayer. Come just as you are."[109]

Numbers of people stood regularly at the Pacific Garden Mission to testify how God had delivered them from their sins and transformed their lives. Such testimonies to the power of Christ have been used to invite others to believe in and follow after Christ. In 1950, the Pacific Garden Mission

106. C. Henry, *Pacific Garden Mission*, 30.

107. Leona Hertel, *Man with a Mission: Mel Trotter and His Legacy for the Rescue Mission Movement* (Grand Rapids: Kregel, 2000), 17.

108. C. Henry, *Pacific Garden Mission*, 46–49.

109. C. Henry, *Pacific Garden Mission*, 22.

launched its radio program titled *Unshackled*, which has reached thousands of listeners with stories of ruin and redemption.

Carl F. H. Henry

In 1942, theologian Carl F. H. Henry (1913–2003) wrote the book *The Pacific Garden Mission*. In 1947, he wrote *The Uneasy Conscience of Modern Fundamentalism*, which signaled the need for soul-saving Protestants to reclaim social action as a biblical mandate.[110] Henry said, "There is a growing awareness in Fundamentalist circles that, despite the orthodox insistence upon revelation and redemption, evangelical Christianity has become increasingly inarticulate about the social reference of the Gospel."[111]

Henry's concern was that evangelical Protestants who held to the fundamentals of Christian faith had departed from the tradition of their forebears—such as the sixteenth-century reformers Martin Luther and John Calvin—who held to a historical and supernatural view of the gospel and possessed a vigorous social interest in human needs and problems.[112] Henry held that those within the evangelical tradition had articulated not merely statements of doctrine but also the social implications of redemption. He wrote,

> Replying to the imprisoned forerunner's inquiry concerning the Christ, Jesus endorses a particular expectation about the Messiah which [John] the Baptist had doubtless gleaned from the Old Testament: "Go and show John again those things which ye do hear and see; the blind receive their sight, and the lame walk, the lepers are cleansed, and the deaf hear, the dead are raised up, and the poor have the gospel preached to them" (Matt. 11:4–5; Luke 7:22). In view of so central a passage, it is difficult to find room for a gospel cut loose entirely from non-spiritual needs. . . . There is no room here for a gospel that is indifferent to the needs of the total man nor of the global man.[113]

Henry led a movement of "new evangelicals" who sought engagement with the broader society and culture, rather than separation from it.[114] As

110. Woodbridge and James, *Church History*, 2:808.

111. Carl F. H. Henry, *The Uneasy Conscience of Modern Fundamentalism* (Grand Rapids: Eerdmans, 2003), 14.

112. C. Henry, *Uneasy Conscience*, 38–39.

113. C. Henry, *Uneasy Conscience*, 34–35.

114. C. Henry, *Uneasy Conscience*, x–xiii.

historian John D. Woodbridge says, "Dr. Henry was the 'Great Recoverer' of social justice and the gospel and the relationship between them."[115]

Sunday School Programs

In the first half of the twentieth century, local churches expanded Sunday school as their primary means of evangelism and attracting new members. The Sunday schools were not merely a means of education for children but a means for pastors and teachers to reach parents too. Soon, local congregations expanded their facilities for Sunday school, provided funding for curriculum, and offered classes before or after Sunday-morning worship services.

Arthur Flake (1862–1952) of the Southern Baptist Convention provided leadership beginning in 1920 for the development of the denomination's Sunday school.[116] Through his book titled *Building a Standard Sunday School*, he laid out a five-point formula for Sunday school growth.[117] His formula included developing a list of prospects to reach, beginning new classes rather than expanding existing ones, recruiting and training new teachers for new classes, providing expanded space for new classes, and asking teachers to visit the prospects.

Thousands of churches followed Flake's plan and experienced growth. In turn, the Southern Baptists made the Sunday school their primary means of evangelism.[118] In 1945, J. N. Barnette wrote, "During the past quarter of a century approximately 85 percent of all church members, either by baptism or letter, have come out of the Sunday school enrollment. . . . The Sunday school is formed and operated for the purpose of reaching the lost."[119]

Thus, Sunday school tied evangelism to the local church rather than a cooperative endeavor of several churches, as done earlier. It became a means of inviting and assimilating new people into a local church. This happened at a time when education in the United States was increasing, making Sunday

115. "Carl F. H. Henry," Carl F. H. Henry Center for Theological Understanding, https://henrycenter.tiu.edu/carl-f-h-henry/.

116. Terry, *Evangelism*, 181.

117. Arthur Flake, *Building a Standard Sunday School* (Nashville: Sunday School Board of the Southern Baptist Convention, 1934).

118. Terry, *Evangelism*, 182.

119. J. N. Barnette, *The Place of Sunday School in Evangelism* (Nashville: Convention, 1945), 24, 26, cited in Terry, *Evangelism*, 182.

school a highly contextual means to teach the Christian faith. The Sunday school was highly programmatic, and evangelism happened as teachers presented Bible stories. Songs such as "The B-I-B-L-E" and "Jesus Loves the Little Children" taught Christian principles and values.

Churches across the modernist-fundamentalist spectrum employed Sunday school. While the fundamentalists viewed it largely as a means to lead children and their parents to a saving knowledge of Christ, modernists viewed it as a means to teach Golden Rule Christianity and educate children to live as Good Samaritans. Moderates embraced both.

Parachurch Societies

The first half of the twentieth century witnessed a proliferation of parachurch ministries. Many of these were specialized toward youth. The rapid multiplication of parachurch organizations has been described as "religion gone free enterprise."[120]

Student Volunteer Movement

In 1888, the YMCA and Inter-Seminary Movement combined efforts at Northfield, Massachusetts, with Dwight Moody and John R. Mott, to establish the Student Volunteer Movement (SVM) for Foreign Missions.[121] The primary purpose of the SVM was to enlist college students to serve as overseas missionaries. Eventually, 175,000 college students signed a pledge to consider this calling, and 21,000 eventually served in overseas mission fields. The Student Volunteer Movement adopted the motto "The evangelization of the world in this generation."[122]

The SVM became so popular that, at some colleges, 50 percent of the student body participated in the organization. The SVM continued to grow until 1920 but then faced a precipitous decline. Among the reasons was that many students began to embrace the liberal view that questioned the Bible's divine inspiration and the gospel's trustworthiness. Students at quadrennial

120. Jerry E. White, *The Church and the Parachurch: An Uneasy Marriage* (Portland, OR: Multnomah, 1983), 36.

121. Norman E. Thomas, *Missions and Unity: Lessons from History, 1792–2010* (Eugene, OR: Cascade, 2010), 35–38.

122. N. Thomas, *Missions and Unity*, 38. See John R. Mott, *The Evangelization of the World in This Generation* (New York: Arno, 1972).

meetings in the 1920s and 1930s expressed "that they did not know what message should be taken, so why go [to the mission field]?"[123] Social action soon replaced verbal witness to the gospel as the movement's primary concern.[124] With an erosion of confidence in the truthfulness of Jesus's incarnation, substitutionary death, and bodily resurrection, there came little impulse to take his message to spiritually lost souls.[125]

InterVarsity Christian Fellowship

The SVM's movement away from fundamentals of the Christian faith was seen in its relationship with InterVarsity Christian Fellowship (IVCF). This evangelical student organization spread from England to Canada, and in 1934 Stacey Woods, director of Canadian Inter-Varsity, met with students at the University of Michigan to form the first IVCF chapter on a US campus.[126] In 1947, IVCF helped form the International Fellowship of Evangelical Students.

In contrast to IVCF, the Student Volunteer Movement's board reported in 1948 that many of its chapters overseas had weakened or discontinued. On the other hand, missionary education and recruitment were being carried on by IVCF. Although SVM sought a good relationship with IVCF, their missionary programs became rivals. Keith and Gladys Hunt observed that IVCF reacted against SVM's "humanitarian drift," its goal of institutional preservation, and theological differences. IVCF saw itself as "true to the Bible" and emphasized the call to holiness "almost to the exclusion of catholicity" or an ecumenical spirit.[127]

From the view of IVCF, liberal theology had caused not merely a revised understanding of the gospel but changed the very concept of mission from evangelization to social concerns. IVCF held that proclamation

123. Ralph Winter, "The Student Volunteers of 1886, Their Heirs, and the Year 2000," *International Journal of Frontier Missions* 2, no. 2 (April 1985): 168.

124. Keith Hunt and Gladys Hunt, *For Christ and the University: The Story of InterVarsity Christian Fellowship of the U.S.A., 1940–1990* (Downers Grove, IL: InterVarsity Press, 1992), 46–55.

125. David F. Wells, "Word and World: Biblical Authority and the Quandary of Modernity," in *Evangelical Affirmations*, ed. Kenneth S. Kantzer and Carl F. H. Henry (Grand Rapids: Zondervan, 1990), 171–72.

126. Hunt and Hunt, *For Christ and the University*, 67.

127. Hunt and Hunt, *For Christ and the University*, 137.

of the gospel was the chief purpose of the church's mission. In 1946, IVCF sponsored a student missions conference in Toronto, which two years later moved to the University of Illinois at Urbana and is known today as the Urbana conference. Today IVCF has 750 chapters on college campuses in the United States.[128]

Christian Business Men's Committee

Christian Business Men's Committee (CBMC) began in Chicago in 1930. Originally, its plan was to host a group of businessmen for six weeks. A. J. Leaman, a part-time pastor of a small church in Chicago, was devoted to the idea of "praying down a revival" in the city.[129] He believed that the most strategic approach would be to sponsor a prayer meeting at noon on a daily basis.[130] From the beginning, he emphasized prayer and testimonies by businessmen, but instead of the group meeting for six weeks, the prayer meetings continued.

Christian businessmen in other cities caught the vision of what could happen through "man-to-man" contact in order to win businessmen to faith in Christ. The multiplication of CBMCs led to a national meeting in Chicago in 1937.[131] The first chairman was C. B. Hedstrom, who described the organization, saying, "Everyone connected with them works gladly and willingly to give his time and money that the work of soul-saving might go on. This is the day when God calls men to launch out into the deep in a real effort to 'rescue the perishing, care for the dying, and snatch them in pity from sin and the grave.'"[132]

CBMC conducted activities such as breakfasts, luncheons, and banquets to reach businessmen with the gospel. Moreover, their aim was to evangelize "as God gives opportunity through open-air and jail meetings, service men's centers, county farms, rescue missions, etc."[133] By 1947 there were 162 CBMCs in full operation, most of them in the United States and

128. Terry, *Evangelism*, 175.

129. M. Taylor, *Exploring Evangelism*, 484.

130. David R. Enlow, *Men Aflame: The Story of CBMC* (Grand Rapids: Zondervan, 1962), 18.

131. M. Taylor, *Exploring Evangelism*, 485.

132. Enlow, *Men Aflame*, 29. "A Prince in Israel Has Fallen," *The Evangelical Beacon* 10, no. 14 (April 14, 1942).

133. Enlow, *Men Aflame*, 64.

Canada, and by 1960 the total number of committees reached the five hundred mark.[134]

Christian Business Men's Committee, Accountability Questions (Selected)

- Do I cherish in my heart a feeling of dislike or hatred for anyone?
- Am I studying my Bible daily?
- How long [has it been] since I had a direct answer to prayer?
- Do I estimate the things of time and eternity at their true value?
- Am I praying and [co-]working for anyone's salvation?
- Is there anything I cannot give up for Christ?
- How does my life look to those who are not Christians?
- Where am I making my greatest mistake?
- Am I honest with the Lord's money?
- Am I doing anything that I would condemn in others?

(David R. Enlow, *Men Aflame: The Story of CBMC* [Grand Rapids: Zondervan, 1962], 35)

Radio Evangelism

An evangelistic method unique to the first part of the twentieth century was Christian radio. The first public broadcast of a church service was in 1921, when station KDKA of Pittsburgh, Pennsylvania, broadcast an evening vesper service of Calvary Episcopal Church.[135]

Then, in 1922, the mayor of Chicago, William Thompson, erected a radio station on the roof of Chicago City Hall and invited the public to provide programming.[136] A local pastor-evangelist named Paul Rader (1879–1938), a former cowboy, football coach, and boxer who had served at Moody Church of Chicago and founded the Chicago Gospel Tabernacle in 1922, accepted the invitation. His program was the first to be broadcast nationwide.[137]

134. M. Taylor, *Exploring Evangelism*, 487.
135. Pope-Levison, *Models of Evangelism*, 165.
136. Terry, *Evangelism*, 199.
137. Jeffrey K. Hadden and Charles E. Swann, *Prime Time Preachers* (Reading, MA: Addison-Wesley, 1981), 73–75.

Moody Radio

By 1925, six hundred radio stations were on the air in the United States, and sixty-three were owned by churches and religious organizations.[138] Moody Bible Institute of Chicago was a pioneer with station WMBI. Most broadcasts included music, prayer, and a gospel message. In 1927, the station conducted a fifteen-minute Swedish service hosted by Gustav Edwards (1874–1948) to reach Scandinavian listeners in Chicago and nearby cities.[139]

World Radio Missionary Fellowship

World Radio Missionary Fellowship began in 1931 as radio station HCJB in Quito, Ecuador. This ministry was started by Clarence W. Jones (1900–1986), the son of a Salvation Army minister. After Jones graduated from Moody Bible Institute, he worked with Paul Rader at the Chicago Gospel Tabernacle, overseeing Rader's weekly radio station WJBT.[140] From this experience, Jones decided in 1928 to travel to South America to look for a suitable location for an evangelistic radio station that he hoped to establish. Despite initial difficulties to obtain a government permit, he finally received approval from the Congress of Ecuador to operate a station with the call letters HCJB.[141] The first program, in both English and Spanish, was broadcast on Christmas Day 1931.[142] The station was powered by a two-hundred-watt tabletop transmitter from a studio in Jones's living room in Quito.

Walter A. Maier

Another radio pioneer was Walter A. Maier (1893–1950), professor at Concordia Seminary in St. Louis. In 1930, Maier launched a thirty-six-program series

138. Hadden and Swann, *Prime Time Preachers*, 73–75.

139. David M. Gustafson, "Dr. Gustav Edwards, President and Dean of the Bible Institute and Seminary of the Swedish Evangelical Free Church, 1916–44," *Swedish-American Historical Quarterly* 69, no. 1 (January 2018): 44–45.

140. The call letters WJBT refer to "Where Jesus Blesses Thousands." Lois Neely, *Come Up to This Mountain* (Wheaton, IL: Tyndale, 1980), 31.

141. The call letters HCJB refer to "Heralding Christ Jesus' Blessings." Clarence W. Jones, *Radio: The New Missionary* (Chicago: Moody, 1946), 25–33.

142. Janet Benge and Geoff Benge, *Clarence Jones: Mr. Radio* (Seattle: YWAM, 2005), 160.

called *The Lutheran Hour* over a national network.[143] After the economic depression, the program resumed and expanded until, by the time of his death in 1950, it was broadcast on twelve hundred stations throughout the world.

Charles E. Fuller

After several years of working in business and agriculture, Charles E. Fuller (1887–1968) accepted Christ and attended the Bible Institute of Los Angeles (Biola). In 1925, he founded Calvary Baptist Church, and four years later started to broadcast the church's Sunday-evening services. In 1933, he left the pastorate to devote his full attention to the radio ministry, incorporated as the Gospel Broadcasting Association. Fuller's program, *The Old-Fashioned Revival Hour*, was broadcast nationally over the Mutual System in 1934, and internationally in 1941.[144]

Each broadcast began with the theme song "Heavenly Sunshine." Then Fuller gave a simple expository sermon. A choir sang familiar songs, and his wife, Grace, read letters from listeners. By 1939 *The Old-Fashioned Revival Hour* was carried on more stations in prime time than any other program of any type. By 1944, the popular media estimated Fuller's weekly audience at twenty million listeners.

In 1944, the National Association of Evangelicals (NAE) encouraged the formation of the National Religious Broadcasters (NRB). This organization promoted the establishment of evangelical radio stations and programs.[145]

Fulton J. Sheen

In 1930, Fulton J. Sheen (1895–1979) began a weekly NBC Sunday-night radio broadcast called *The Catholic Hour*.[146] Sheen's messages were prophetic as he referred to World War II as not only a political struggle but also a theological struggle, and described Hitler as "an example of the Anti-Christ."[147] Two

143. Rudnick, *Speaking the Gospel*, 208.

144. Earle E. Cairns, *An Endless Line of Splendor: Revivals and Their Leaders from the Great Awakening to the Present* (Eugene, OR: Wipf & Stock, 2015), 217–19.

145. Terry, *Evangelism*, 201.

146. Thomas C. Reeves, *America's Bishop: The Life and Times of Fulton J. Sheen* (San Francisco: Encounter, 2001), 80–81.

147. James Hennesey, *American Catholics: A History of the Roman Catholic Community in the United States* (New York: Oxford University Press, 1981), 280.

decades later, Sheen's broadcast reported a weekly audience of four million listeners. *Time* magazine described him in 1946 as "the golden-voiced Msgr. Fulton J. Sheen, U.S. Catholicism's famed proselytizer," and reported that he received three thousand to six thousand letters weekly from listeners.[148]

In 1952, Sheen conducted the first religious service to be broadcast on television.[149] His program, *Life Is Worth Living*, was broadcast live from the Adelphi Theater in New York City. After he received an Emmy Award for his broadcasts, he joked to the audience at the ceremony, saying, "I'd like to thank my writers—Matthew, Mark, Luke, and John."[150]

Discussion Questions

1. Billy Sunday became known for his antics and street slang that were characterized as a "religious vaudeville," and Sister Aimee and her ministry increasingly took on the image of a "religious Tinseltown." Can a medium become louder than its message? How can Christians communicate the gospel within their cultural context without overidentifying with it? Or does evangelistic drama have potential today? If so, how?
2. Neighborhood visitation became a means to reach every household of a city. Might this be a useful means of evangelism today, or has it become too identified with heretical religious groups? How might this model be modified? Prayer walks through the neighborhood, stopping to chat with those who appear open to visit?
3. Pentecostals of the twentieth century comprised a movement that emphasized the Holy Spirit, prayer, miracles, healing, and soul-saving evangelism. In what ways did this movement challenge liberal theology and the social gospel? Why? How did the emergence of female, African American, and Hispanic evangelists contribute to Pentecostalism's spontaneous and exponential growth?
4. Histories of the Student Volunteer Movement (SVM) and InterVarsity Christian Fellowship (IVCF) illustrate the shift and tension between theological liberalism of the social gospel and evangelical conservativism of the soul-saving gospel. What happens when the gospel of Jesus is no longer the driving force for missions? What lessons can be learned from SVM?

148. Reeves, *America's Bishop*, 181.
149. Reeves, *America's Bishop*, 223–24.
150. Reeves, *America's Bishop*, 240.

5. Ellen Modin and George and Sarah Clarke maintained commitments to soul-saving evangelism and social action. Which is more important—serving the poor and seeking justice for the oppressed, or sharing the gospel? How can we find a way to address both without overlooking either one?

11

Global Indigenous Evangelism

My prayer for those . . . who have not yet been saved is that they may seek and find Christ Jesus, our blessed Redeemer, for the salvation of their souls. "Our citizenship is in Heaven; from whence also we wait for the Saviour, the Lord Jesus Christ" (Phil. 3:20). "Unto Him that loved us, and washed us from our sins in His own Blood; and hath made us kings and priests unto God and His Father; to Him be glory and dominion for ever and ever. Amen" (Rev. 1:5, 6).

—Pandita Ramabai[1]

The evangelical revivals in Britain and the United States kindled the modern Protestant missionary movement. During the nineteenth and twentieth centuries, numbers of mission societies were founded to take the gospel to the world. Missionaries carried the gospel "'from Greenland's icy mountains to India's coral strands,' from the Ganges to the Limpopo, from the fiords to the jungles, from the [Inuit] Eskimos to the Zulus."[2]

While motivation for world evangelization grew out of these revivals, opportunities for Protestant missions grew out of colonial expansion by Western nations. Whereas Britain had been content earlier to trade in India, southern Asia, and Africa, now the British Empire sought to rule. Along with other European nations, Britain gained vast holdings on the African continent. Moreover, nations of the East, particularly China and Japan, opened their doors to Western trade and influence. The Pacific Islands and West Indies were taken over by Britain, France, and the United States.

1. Helen S. Dyer, *A Great Life in Indian Missions: Pandita Ramabai, Her Vision, Her Mission and Triumph of Faith* (London: Pickering and Inglis, 1923), 53–54.

2. Roland H. Bainton, *Christianity* (Boston: Houghton Mifflin, 2000), 349.

Until this time, Protestants had done little by way of mission work, compared to that of the Roman Catholic Church, whose work by monastic missionaries was far-reaching. Protestant missions had begun with Ziegenbalg, Plütschau, Dober, and others who entered regions of the world with the evangel. The Anglican Church joined the Protestant mission movement by forming the Society for Promoting Christian Knowledge (SPCK), which in 1709 assisted Ziegenbalg in publishing a translation of the Bible into Tamil.[3]

William Carey (1761–1834), more than any single person, ignited the flame of missionary zeal among Protestants. He was a Baptist cobbler-preacher who laid a historical and theological foundation in his treatise titled *An Enquiry into the Obligation of Christians to Use Means for the Conversion of the Heathens*.[4] This work, along with other efforts, led to the formation of the Baptist Missionary Society. Carey was the first missionary, arriving in India in 1793. He located at Serampore, where he practiced a strategy that promoted learning the culture and history of the native peoples, translating and distributing the Scriptures widely, preaching the gospel wherever possible, and planting indigenous churches.[5] Carey and his colleagues carried out this strategy with considerable success. Furthermore, they labored for social reforms that included the abolition of both temple prostitution and widow-burning.[6]

Other mission societies—both denominational and interdenominational—joined the Protestant missionary movement. During the last half of the nineteenth century and early decades of the twentieth century, Protestant missions surpassed those of the Roman Catholic Church.[7] The Protestant missionary movement gained momentum at the World Mission Conference in Edinburgh in 1910.[8] This gathering was attended by 1,215

3. Daniel Jeyaraj, "Mission Reports from South India and Their Impact on the Western Mind: The Tranquebar Mission of the Eighteenth Century," in *Converting Colonialism: Visions and Realities in Mission History, 1706–1914*, ed. Dana L. Robert (Grand Rapids: Eerdmans, 2008), 29–31.

4. Dana L. Robert, introduction to Robert, *Converting Colonialism*, 9.

5. Milton L. Rudnick, *Speaking the Gospel through the Ages: A History of Evangelism* (St. Louis: Concordia, 1984), 189.

6. Ellen Alexander and Beulah Wood, "India—Steps Forward on a Journey in India," in *Global Voices on Biblical Equality: Women and Men Serving Together in the Church*, ed. Aída Besançon Spencer, William David Spencer, and Mimi Haddad (Eugene, OR: Wipf & Stock, 2008), 22–23.

7. Rudnick, *Speaking the Gospel*, 188.

8. David A. Kerr and Kenneth R. Ross, "Introduction: The Edinburgh 1910 World

delegates of missionary societies working around the world. More than a thousand delegates came from Britain and America, and 170 from the rest of Europe. Fifteen delegates from Asia represented the non-Western nations, including a Chinese delegate named Cheng Ching Yi who spoke during one of the discussion sessions.[9]

Indigenous Evangelism

As a result of the Protestant missionary movement, peoples in Africa, Asia, and Latin America came to faith in Christ. Soon their forms of Christianity grew beyond that of earlier colonial forms.[10] As the gospel entered new contexts, Christian practices reflected the language, culture, and customs of the native peoples, in contrast to patterns and practices of Western, Christendom-oriented missionaries.[11]

Originally, it was customary for missionary societies to carry out their work through mission stations that functioned as refuges for both missionaries and new converts. When newly converted Christians were shunned or ostracized by their families, they could receive food, shelter, and emotional support at the stations. Sometimes new converts were employed by the mission's school, hospital, or general operation.

The strategy of the mission station was not without problems, however. In some instances, new converts were unnecessarily isolated from their family and friends. Moreover, mission stations tended to "Westernize" new converts according to the patterns and practices of Western Christendom.[12] In addition, new converts remained subordinate to missionaries, who in some

---

Missionary Conference: Its Eight Commissions in Historical Context and Their Continuing Significance," in *Edinburgh 2010: Mission Then and Now*, ed. David A. Kerr and Kenneth R. Ross (Eugene, OR: Wipf & Stock, 2010), 3–4.

9. Peter Tze Ming Ng, *Chinese Christianity: An Interplay between Global and Local Perspectives* (Boston: Brill, 2012), 67–89, 133–42. No Africans, Pacific Islanders, or Latin Americans attended because only missionary societies could send delegates, not the churches that resulted from their work. Kerr and Ross, *Edinburgh 2010*, ix.

10. Peggy Brock, Norman Etherington, Gareth Griffiths, and Jacqueline Van Gent, *Indigenous Evangelists and Questions of Authority in the British Empire 1750–1940* (Leiden: Brill, 2015), 4–6.

11. Lamin Sanneh, *Disciples of All Nations: Pillars of World Christianity* (New York: Oxford University Press, 2008), 94.

12. Jesse Ndwiga Kanyua Mugambi, *African Christian Theology: An Introduction* (Nairobi: East African Educational Publishers, 1994), 32, 48.

cases were reluctant to give up leadership or control of their ministries—the pattern of paternalism.[13]

In contrast, Henry Venn and Rufus Anderson proposed a "three-self" strategy.[14] They posited that missionaries should establish and cultivate churches that are self-governing, self-supporting, and self-propagating.[15] They advocated that the native converts should develop methods of evangelism rather than adopting those of the missionaries.

This strategy was applied by John Livingston Nevius (1829–1893), a missionary to Shandong, China, and then briefly to Korea. Nevius's version of the three-self strategy became known as the Nevius method.[16] In 1886, he published a book titled *The Planting and Development of Missionary Churches*, emphasizing that new converts should live in their neighborhoods and pursue their occupations, being witnesses to their coworkers and neighbors, and that churches should practice indigenous forms of gospel witness.[17]

In the early twentieth century, Roland Allen wrote two books that promoted these ideas: *Missionary Methods: St. Paul's or Ours?* and *The Spontaneous Expansion of the Church: And Causes That Hinder It.*[18] The missionary movement recognized that the gospel spreads most rapidly and develops most vigorously when new Christians assume responsibility for the church and evangelism.[19] New converts need the opportunity, authority, and responsibility to carry out Christ's commission of making disciples.

Indigenous Evangelists

The history of evangelism includes not merely missionaries who crossed geographical and cultural boundaries but also the indigenous people they

13. Kyo-Seong Ahn, "From Mission to Church and Beyond: The Metamorphosis of Post-Edinburgh Christianity," in Kerr and Ross, *Edinburgh 2010*, 76.

14. Brock et al., *Indigenous Evangelists*, 7, 23, 35.

15. Craig Ott and Stephen J. Strauss, *Encountering Theology of Mission: Biblical Foundations, Historical Developments, and Contemporary Issues* (Grand Rapids: Baker Academic, 2014), xxv, 115.

16. Wi Jo Kan, *Christ and Caesar in Modern Korea: A History of Christianity and Politics* (Albany: State University of New York Press, 1997), 30.

17. See J. L. Nevius, *The Planting and Development of Missionary Churches* (New York: Foreign Mission Library, 1899).

18. See Roland Allen, *Missionary Methods: St. Paul's or Ours?* (London: Scott, 1912), and Allen, *The Spontaneous Expansion of the Church: And Causes That Hinder It* (London: World Dominion, 1927).

19. Rudnick, *Speaking the Gospel*, 192.

reached. From the "first fruits" of their missionary work came indigenous evangelists whose cultures shaped their expressions of Christianity and evangelistic work. In some instances, missionaries sought to form converts along Western lines.[20] However, in the end, indigenous agency won over, and the indigenous evangelists adapted Western forms or developed new ones for their culture and context.[21] In a few cases, indigenous Christians experienced a "divine visitation" that prompted them to reach others with the gospel, having little or no influence from Western missionaries.[22]

Ko Tha Byu of Burma

The concept of indigenous evangelism received considerable attention in the nineteenth century with the rapid conversion of the Karens of Burma. Beginning in 1810, missionary efforts produced few converts among the Burmese, who were mostly Buddhist. However, in the 1830s, hundreds of illiterate and animist Karen people began to convert to Christ.[23] They came to faith in groups, as whole families and villages, through the witness of Ko Tha Byu (ca. 1778–1840).[24]

Tha Byu was born in the Karen village of U Twa. Early in life, he turned to crime and violence, engaging in robbery and even committing murder. After being sold as a slave to a Burmese Christian, he converted in 1828 after hearing the gospel explained by Adoniram Judson (1788–1850).[25] Tha Byu

20. Brock et al., *Indigenous Evangelists*, 4.

21. Brock et al., *Indigenous Evangelists*, 5.

22. An example of a divine visitation comes from Ezekiel Handinawangu Guti in 1960. He wrote, "This is the God of heaven whom I preached to you who showed himself to me at [Cottage] 593 so that I may walk in Him and preach his kingdom to you." Kudzai Biri, "Sacred Sites in an African Indigenous Church in Zimbabwe," in *Multiplying in the Spirit: African Initiated Churches in Zimbabwe*, ed. Ezra Chitando, Masiiwa Ragies Gunda, and Joachim Kügler (Bamberg, Germany: University of Bamberg Press, 2014), 68–69. See also J. Kwabena Asamoah-Gyadu, "Christ Must Increase: New Horizons in Mission and the Influence of the Spirit," *Transformation* 31, no. 4 (October 2014): 282–90.

23. Elizabeth Koepping, "India, Pakistan, Bangladesh, Burma/Myanmar," in *Christianities in Asia*, ed. Peter C. Phan (Malden, MA: Wiley-Blackwell, 2011), 25, 29, 32; Jay Riley Case, "From the Native Ministry to the Talented Tenth," in *The Foreign Missionary Enterprise at Home: Explorations in North American Cultural History*, ed. Daniel H. Bays and Grant Wacker (Tuscaloosa: University of Alabama Press, 2003), 62–69.

24. See Francis Mason, *Ko Tha Byu, the First Karen Christian: With Some Traditions of the Karen Race* (Rangoon, Burma: American Baptist Mission Press, 1928). *Ko* is a title applied to an elderly man.

25. San Crombie Po, *Burma and the Karens* (London: Elliot Stock, 1928), 1.

left his life of crime and began to accompany the Baptist missionary George Boardman (1801–1831). When baptized, he shared his testimony, and three men who heard him asked if he would be willing to come to their villages to tell his story to the people there. This response prompted him, Boardman, and two others to launch an evangelistic mission to the Karen people.

Their work continued with native preachers, who proved to be the most effective at evangelism. After twelve years, 1,270 Karens were baptized, despite the deaths of Tha Byu and Boardman, as well as persecution by the Burmese government.[26] The importance of indigenous evangelism became even greater when the government enacted a law that prohibited American missionaries from working in southern Burma. The national preachers continued to visit the villages, reinforcing the importance of indigenous evangelism. In 1845, the American Baptist Missionary Union stated, "Our main reliance here, as in every highly successful mission, must be upon the native evangelists and pastors God shall raise up and endow."[27]

By 1914, there were over forty-seven thousand Christians with nearly two hundred ordained pastors and over five hundred evangelists actively sharing the gospel.[28] The indigenous evangelists were largely responsible for turning Christianity from an alien faith to a lived faith among the Burmese.

Siu Yu Chi and Ng Shek Hing of Southeastern China

With the mission strategy of Venn, Anderson, and Nevius in China, the gospel spread through indigenous evangelists there too. When J. Hudson Taylor (1832–1905), founder of the China Inland Mission, appealed for a thousand missionaries to go to China, people like Hans Jensen von Qualen (1854–1918), a Danish immigrant to America, considered going there as a missionary.[29] While studying in Chicago in the 1880s, he met two Chinese men, Siu Yu Chi (1866–1946), known also as Eugene Sieux, and Ng Shek Hing (1857–1931), known as John Lee.[30]

26. Alan Neely, "George Dana Boardman," in *Biographical Dictionary of Christian Missions*, ed. Gerald H. Anderson (Grand Rapids: Eerdmans 1999), 71.

27. Case, "From the Native Ministry," 62.

28. Rudnick, *Speaking the Gospel*, 191.

29. Erik Sidenvall, *The Making of Manhood among Swedish Missionaries in China and Mongolia, c. 1890–c. 1914* (Leiden: Brill, 2009), 1. Sidenvall notes that Fredrik Franson promised to recruit two hundred of the one thousand missionaries from among Scandinavians in Norway, Denmark, Sweden, and the United States (30–31).

30. David M. Gustafson and Tan Chi Sing, "Chinese Pioneers of the Swedish Evangelical Free Mission: Siu Yu Chi and Ng Shek Hing," *Trinity Journal* 37 (2016): 3–4.

As von Qualen taught an English-language course for Chinese workers, the three men became friends. After Siu and Ng came to faith in Christ, they asked von Qualen to travel with them to China and work among the Chinese people. In 1887, von Qualen was commissioned as the first missionary of the Swedish Evangelical Free Mission, to Canton, modern-day Guangzhou. Siu arrived in China before von Qualen and later was ordained and supported as a missionary. In 1888, three more missionaries arrived in China, including Ng.

In Canton, the mission renovated a store for a chapel on Honam Island, and a decade later purchased a large boat to serve as a "floating chapel" to reach people living in junks on the Pearl River. After one successful evangelistic tour, the mission's boat was pelted with stones. Siu and Ng were jailed, "bound with chains because they preached the gospel from the boat."[31]

The first convert to faith through their ministry was an opium smoker named Law Iu Tong. Delivered from his opium habit, he applied his business skills and opened a shop that specialized in making glassware. The new venture provided a solution for other new converts who were expelled from their work guilds because of their newfound faith in Christ. Moreover, the glass shop welcomed artists to visit, read the Bible, and discuss the gospel. Law's glass shop witnessed seven artists convert to faith and become evangelists.

Another convert of Siu and Ng was Wong Yuet Ch'oh, also an opium addict, as well as a geomancer.[32] After reading Christian literature, Wong converted to faith, gave up his former work, and was delivered from his opium addiction. Soon, he took turns preaching the gospel at the noonday chapel meetings along with Siu, Ng, and von Qualen.[33]

In 1907, Siu accepted a call to Honolulu as a teacher, and later returned to Chicago where he took up missionary work with the Chinese Christian Union, which in 1915 became the Chinese Christian Union Church of Chicago.[34] In 1923, he returned to China, where he oversaw the Evangelical Free Mission churches, especially during the politically turbulent time when missionaries were being expelled from the country. Both Siu and Ng played

31. Gustafson and Tan, "Chinese Pioneers," 17. Compare similar accounts of persecution in Liao Yiwu, *God Is Red: The Secret Story of How Christianity Survived and Flourished in Communist China* (San Francisco: HarperOne, 2012).

32. Gustafson and Tan, "Chinese Pioneers," 15.

33. Ng Shek Hing (John Lee) served as a church planter of the South China Mission for more than four decades.

34. Gustafson and Tan, "Chinese Pioneers," 21.

important roles in planting churches, equipping evangelists, and directing the work of the Canton Bible Institute, known later as Evangel Seminary of Hong Kong.[35]

Dora Yu and China's Bible Women

Another important development in China was the role of Bible women. Before them, female missionaries from the West evangelized Chinese women but faced typical linguistic and cultural challenges. For this reason, during the second half of the nineteenth century, several missions began to recruit Chinese "Bible women" to share the gospel.[36] At first, Bible women were recruited from among employees of the missionary families, or from mothers or wives of Chinese male evangelists. Bible women began teaching other women and children, mostly in rural areas. As their numbers grew, their roles expanded to that of visiting the sick and providing basic medical care. In some cases, they led meetings with men and women.

Yu Cidu (1873–1931), also known as Dora Yu, was the daughter of a Presbyterian minister and became one of the most well-known Bible women of China.[37] She studied medicine at the Women's Medical School in Suzhou. In addition to medicine, Yu engaged in itinerant evangelism. In 1897, she accompanied Josephine Campbell to Korea, where Yu combined her practice of medicine and preaching the gospel.

Six years later, Yu returned to China and gave up medicine to devote herself fully to the work of evangelism. At one meeting, a woman named Lin Heping converted to Christ, and, at a subsequent meeting, her son, Ni Tuosheng, known also as Watchman Nee, came to faith in Christ. Both went on to become successful evangelists themselves.[38]

In 1910, Yu participated in the first conference of the National Evangelism Society held in Hankou, giving the keynote address on the topic of Bible women and female evangelists. She also decided to cut off financial support from the West. Moreover, in 1927, she appealed to Western societies to stop

35. Gustafson and Tan, "Chinese Pioneers," 26.

36. Mary Keng Mun Chung, *Chinese Women in Christian Ministry: An Intercultural Study* (New York: Lang, 2005), 116–17.

37. Mark A. Noll and Carolyn Nystrom, *Cloud of Witnesses: Christian Voices from Africa and Asia* (Downers Grove, IL: InterVarsity Press, 2011), 187–99.

38. Alexander Chow, "The Remarkable Story of China's 'Bible Women,'" *Christianity Today*, March 16, 2018, https://www.christianitytoday.com/history/2018/march/christian-china-bible-women.html.

sending missionaries to China, fearing that they would destroy the faith of Chinese Christians. In particular, she opposed the liberal theology of missionaries who denied Christ's incarnation, atoning death, and resurrection.[39] After forming a Bible study and prayer house, her work developed into the Jiangwan Bible School in Shanghai, which trained men and women for ministries in China.[40]

John Song of China

Song Shangjie, or John Song (Sung) (1901–1944), was also an indigenous evangelist in China, coming from the Hinghwa district of southeastern China.[41] His mother was a devout Buddhist until she converted to Christ the year before he was born.[42] His father became a Christ follower too.

Song was one of thousands in the Buddhist stronghold of Hinghwa to be converted during the so-called Hinghwa Pentecost.[43] A short while after his conversion to faith, he became known as Hinghwa's "little pastor" because he accompanied his father on preaching tours and even substituted for him when he was busy with other activities. As Song preached in the open air, his listeners came to faith in Jesus.

In 1919, after Song completed secondary school, he received a letter from a woman in the United States who offered him funding to attend Ohio Wesleyan University in Delaware, Ohio. He accepted the offer, and with financial support from Chinese pastors and friends, he purchased his ticket, arriving by steamship to America.[44] He began his studies in science, winning awards in physics and chemistry. In 1924, he earned a master's degree, and two years later the PhD in chemistry. Nevertheless, he could not forget how fulfilled he was years earlier when preaching the gospel. He sensed God calling him back to evangelism.

39. Noll and Nystrom, *Clouds of Witnesses*, 198.

40. Noll and Nystrom, *Clouds of Witnesses*, 194.

41. Daryl R. Ireland, *John Song: Modern Chinese Christianity and the Making of a New Man* (Waco: Baylor University Press, 2020), xi, xiii; Noll and Nystrom, *Cloud of Witnesses*, 214.

42. Ruth A. Tucker, *From Jerusalem to Irian Jaya: A Biographical History of Christian Missions* (Grand Rapids: Zondervan, 2004), 432–34.

43. Ruth Tucker, "Revival in the East: John Sung," in *More Than Conquerors: Portraits of Believers from All Walks of Life*, ed. John D. Woodbridge (Chicago: Moody, 1992), 156.

44. Ireland, *John Song*, 13.

With advice from a friend, he enrolled at Union Theological Seminary in New York City, where he was introduced to liberal theology. In his classes, he was taught that the Bible could not be trusted, that the biblical account of creation was a legend, and that the miracles of Jesus were myths perpetuated by his disillusioned disciples.[45] Song began to doubt the Scriptures and the gospel altogether. After a brief return to the religion of his ancestors—chanting Buddhist scriptures and studying Taoism—he felt like a "leaking, storm-driven ship without captain or compass."[46]

In his doubt and depression, he attended a series of evangelistic meetings at Calvary Baptist Church in New York, where he heard a message by Uldine Utley (1912–1995), a fifteen-year-old female evangelist.[47] Her message was simple but powerful and brought Song to conviction just as the Hinghwa Pentecost had done years earlier. He returned to following Christ.[48] In his spiritually awakened state, he fell asleep and dreamed that he was dead, lying in a coffin that was draped with his academic diplomas. He then awoke with a new desire to preach the gospel. When a total stranger handed him a globe free for the taking, he sensed it was a sign from God for him to bring the good news to the world.

In the meantime, while back at Union Theological Seminary, Song set aside his liberal textbooks to read the Bible. He prayed late into the nights, sang hymns in his room, and shared his testimony of faith as he walked through the halls of the seminary. With his sudden change of behavior, the school's administrators thought that his enthusiasm was a symptom of mental instability and had him committed to a psychiatric ward in a hospital, confined against his will for more than six months.[49] While in the hospital, he read the Scriptures from Genesis to Revelation nearly forty times, and shared the gospel with other patients. In 1927, Song returned to China to follow his call to serve as an evangelist.[50]

He began under the auspices of the Bethel Mission, traveling a circuit of more than thirty cities and speaking at nearly nine hundred meetings in a

45. Tucker, "Revival in the East," 157.

46. Tucker, "Revival in the East," 158.

47. Ireland, *John Song*, 147–48n25. Uldine Utley, from Durant, Oklahoma, converted to faith in 1921 under the preaching of Aimee Semple McPherson in Fresno, California. Within two years Utley was preaching, and at the age of fourteen, she preached to an audience of fourteen thousand people at Madison Square Garden. She was ordained by the Methodist Episcopal Church but suffered throughout her life with mental and emotional illness. Edith L. Blumhofer, *Aimee Semple McPherson: Everybody's Sister* (Grand Rapids: Eerdmans, 1993), 181–82.

48. Tucker, "Revival in the East," 158.

49. Tucker, "Revival in the East," 158.

50. Ireland, *John Song*, 29–31.

six-month period.[51] As he traveled from place to place, he discovered that his time in a theologically liberal seminary had prepared him for his work in China. After hearing a Western missionary applaud the teachings of the liberal churchman Harry Emerson Fosdick, as well as Mahatma Gandhi, Song responded by saying, "China does not need the teaching of Fosdick or Gandhi. The teaching of Confucius is far better than theirs. What the Chinese need is Jesus Christ and His Cross."[52]

In the years to follow, Song preached wherever he could get a hearing—in the open air, in village churches, or on university campuses. In 1934, he left the Bethel Mission and launched out on his own.[53] For the next eight years, he traveled throughout China, speaking to crowds of several thousand.[54] People came from miles around to hear him and to ask for prayer for healing. His itinerant ministry took him further to Formosa (Taiwan), the Philippines, Singapore, Malaysia, and Thailand, where thousands of listeners converted to Christ.[55]

Like Dora Yu, Song became critical of Western missionaries. Despite his criticisms, many of them observed his rapport with the Chinese people that they could never have. In addition to his own evangelism, he developed teams of evangelists to multiply his work. He recruited several evangelists who had come to faith under his ministry. In addition, thousands of lay Christians were mobilized to go to cities and villages to share the message of Jesus. They traveled within China and abroad, and saw hundreds of thousands commit their lives to Jesus Christ.[56] Song's ministry was further enlarged by the Bible conferences and training centers that he helped to establish. Although Song was known to have little time and patience for social graces and diplomacy, his single-minded commitment to Christ earned him respect as an evangelist around the globe.[57]

Excerpt from *The Diary of John Sung [Song]*

In the past, I viewed the work of the evangelistic bands as of paramount importance. Now, I think that praying is more important. The spiritual realm

51. Tucker, "Revival in the East," 159.
52. Tucker, "Revival in the East," 158. Also Ireland, *John Song*, 76.
53. Ireland, *John Song*, 94–95.
54. Tucker, *From Jerusalem to Irian Jaya*, 434.
55. Tucker, *From Jerusalem to Irian Jaya*, 434.
56. Tucker, "Revival in the East," 159.
57. Tucker, "Revival in the East," 156.

knows no bounds. When I pray in the Spirit, I sense that workers in the Last Days must have the following. . . .

Understand the whole Bible: One must not read the Bible with human wisdom, or analyze it with theological knowledge. One should digest the Bible so that the Word becomes our flesh and bones. . . .

Listen to the still, small voice while praying: One must receive revelation from above. One must break through the forces of darkness, and have close and direct communion with God. One must enter into the holy of holies with the Lord to take part in intercessory prayers, to receive power in the presence of the Lord to destroy all the wiles of the devil. Only when the self dies can there be any true gain.

Be truly and totally immersed in the Holy Spirit: One can run along the path of obedience if one's feet are totally immersed [in the Holy Spirit]. One can pray continuously if one's knees are totally immersed. One can bear testimony with boldness if one's waist is totally immersed. Miracles follow those whose hands are immersed in the Holy Spirit. One can bear witness that pierces through the heart of listeners if one's lips are totally immersed. One can take the Lord's heart as his own if one's heart is totally immersed. . . .

Have a heart that loves souls: He is tortured within when he sees an unsaved soul. His love for souls is extreme, even willing to give up his life for the sheep. He is willing to lose the world to save the soul. Paul . . . said: "Woe to me if I do not preach the Gospel." . . .

Hold high the Gospel of the Cross: Many people take the gospel lightly and think that it is rather basic and inconsequential, and build their Tower of Babel instead with philosophy, the rudiments of the world, tradition and the law. The gospel of the Cross is the great power of God, and only by lifting the Cross high can one draw the multitudes to the Lord.

Have a community for spiritual communion: Before the Ascension, the Lord instructed His disciples to wait in Jerusalem as a single body. There they received the outpouring of Living Water in the Upper Room. . . . In an age when truths are neglected, be a pillar of the church, stand upright, do not waver. No one advocated missionary work to faraway lands, and yet the church in Antioch established a missionary-sending agency. No one promoted pioneer evangelism or mission, and yet Philip went to the wilderness to win a soul. . . . No one mentioned social welfare, and yet they took care of widows and orphans. What they received in the Spirit could not be divorced from their fervent prayers in the Upper Room. . . .

Pray in vigilance and wait patiently for the coming of the Lord: Have faith, hope and joy when you face tribulations. Sing cheerfully at night, and be faithful even unto death! Pray to the Lord that He will raise up more workers. (Shangjie Song, *The Diary of John Sung: Extracts from His Journals and Notes*, trans. Thng Pheng Soon [Singapore: Armour, 2012], 388–90)

Toyohiko Kagawa of Japan

Toyohiko Kagawa (1888–1960) was an evangelist, author, and social worker who brought the gospel to millions of people in Japan and around the world. He was born in Kobe, Japan, to a philandering businessman and his concubine.[58] Orphaned early in life, Kagawa was sent away to school, where he studied under two American missionary teachers, Harry Myers and Charles Logan. They introduced him to the Scriptures, and in 1904, he converted to faith in Christ and was baptized at Tokushima Church. The cost of following Jesus was felt immediately when his extended family disowned him.[59]

Kagawa attended Meiji Gakuin Presbyterian College in Tokyo and, later, Kobe Theological Seminary. While a student at the seminary, he became troubled over the other students' preoccupation with Christian theology, specifically over doctrinal technicalities that did not lead to actions as taught by Jesus—for example, those in the parable of the Good Samaritan.[60] In 1914, Kagawa traveled to New Jersey, where he continued his theological studies at Princeton Theological Seminary. In addition, he took courses in the humanities and sciences. These years were formative for Kagawa, shaping him theologically as an evangelical. He believed that Jesus Christ is the only power to transform lives. However, he was also shaped socially and politically to become a Christian social reformer who championed social justice.

Kagawa returned to Japan, where, in 1918, he organized unions among factory workers and farmers. He was arrested twice during strikes because of his role with labor activism.[61] Moreover, in 1921, he launched a movement

58. Jessie M. Trout, *Kagawa, Japanese Prophet: His Witness in Life and Word* (New York: Association Press, 1960), 8.

59. Trout, *Kagawa, Japanese Prophet*, 10–11.

60. William Axling, *Kagawa* (New York: Harper, 1946), 28–41.

61. Trout, *Kagawa, Japanese Prophet*, 19.

called the Friends of Jesus, a "poor men of Lyons" type of band that practiced spiritual disciplines, compassion for the poor, and evangelical witness to the gospel.[62] On one hand, he believed that only through repentance and faith can someone do a "right-about-face and be born again."[63] On the other hand, such a "right-about-face" and new birth must lead the person to love his neighbor (Mark 12:31). Kagawa held that evangelism "means the conversion of people from worldliness to Christlike godliness."[64]

In order to improve living conditions, Kagawa chose to live in the slums, where he could advocate change from within. Furthermore, he believed that God had called him to serve the poor by engaging in "full-rounded emancipation," which sought to redeem the physical, economic, social, psychological, and spiritual conditions of people.[65] He put his faith into practice in 1923 when he organized relief work following the Great Kanto Earthquake. He said, "I read in a book that a man called Christ went about doing good. It is very disconcerting to me that I am so easily satisfied with just going about."[66]

In addition, Kagawa founded the Anti-War League and in 1941 visited the United States in an attempt to prevent war between the nations. Despite the war, he dedicated himself afterward to reconciling Japanese tradition and democratic ideals.

Despite his activities, Kagawa identified as an evangelist. Between the years 1920 and 1940, one and a half million people heard him preach, with an estimated twenty-five thousand coming to faith in Christ.[67] As an indigenous evangelist, he never doubted that God wanted the spiritually lost to be made whole physically, economically, socially, psychologically, and spiritually.

Sadhu Sundar Singh of India

In India, Sundar Singh (1889–ca. 1929) was born into a landowning Sikh family in the village of Rampur in northern Punjab.[68] His mother took him

62. Mark R. Mullins, "Japan," in Phan, *Christianities in Asia*, 205; Darren T. Duerksen and William A. Dyrness, *Seeking Church: Emerging Witnesses to the Kingdom, Missiological Engagements* (Downers Grove, IL: IVP Academic, 2019), 90.

63. Tuttle, *Story of Evangelism*, 359.

64. John Stott, *Christian Mission in the Modern World* (Downers Grove, IL: InterVarsity Press, 2008), 61.

65. Tuttle, *Story of Evangelism*, 360.

66. Donald R. Heiges, *The Christians Calling* (Philadelphia: Muhlenberg, 1958), 19.

67. Tuttle, *Story of Evangelism*, 360.

68. Noll and Nystrom, *Cloud of Witnesses*, 157–58.

regularly to learn from a *sadhu*, an ascetic holy man. She also sent her son to Ewing Christian High School in Ludhiana, where he learned English. When his mother suddenly died, Sundar, just fourteen years old, fell into a depression with fits of anger. In an act of defiance against Christians, he obtained a copy of the New Testament and burned it page by page for others to watch. He considered ending his life by lying on railway tracks, but before he could carry out his plan, he had a vision of Jesus Christ. Singh later wrote,

> At about 4:30 [in the morning] I saw something strange. There was a glow in the room. At first I thought there was a fire in the house, but looking through the door and windows, I could see no cause for the light. Then the thought came to me: perhaps this was an answer from God. . . . Then I saw a figure in the light, strange but somehow familiar at once. It was neither Siva nor Krishna nor any of the other Indian incarnations I had expected. Then I heard a voice speaking to me in Urdu, "Sundar, how long will you mock me? I have come to save you because you have prayed to find the way of truth. Why then don't you accept it?" It was then I saw the marks of blood on his hands and feet and knew that it was Jesus, the one proclaimed by the Christians. In amazement I fell at his feet.[69]

Singh was then converted to Christ but soon met his first test as a disciple when his father pleaded for him not to follow Christ.[70] When Sundar refused, his father gave him a farewell banquet and summarily disowned him. In addition, Sundar's brother tried to poison him. Therefore, he sought the aid of Christians nearby, and they offered him shelter and economic support. He continued on the path of discipleship, and in 1906, he was baptized by an Anglican missionary at the parish church in Simla in the Himalayan foothills.[71]

Singh worked briefly at the Christian Leprosarium at Sabathu, near Simla, where he ministered to lepers. Then he decided to set out on a journey—at seventeen years of age. He wore a saffron robe and turban, typical attire of a Hindu sadhu. Singh said, "I want no home, no possessions. Like Him I will belong to the road, sharing the suffering of my people, eating with those who will give me shelter, and telling all men of the love of God."[72]

69. Noll and Nystrom, *Cloud of Witnesses*, 158–59.

70. Cyril Davey, "Apostle with the Bleeding Feet: Sadhu Sundar Singh," in Woodbridge, *More Than Conquerors*, 148.

71. Noll and Nystrom, *Cloud of Witnesses*, 159.

72. Davey, "Apostle with the Bleeding Feet," 148.

Singh's decision to identify as a Christian sadhu stemmed from his thought that Indian people would listen to him more readily if he lived according to Indian culture and customs.

As he traveled northward through the Punjab, he crossed the Banihal Pass to Kashmir, and then returned back through the Muslim territories of Afghanistan and Baluchistan.[73] His saffron robe gave him little protection from the weather, and his feet became bloodied from rocks, earning him the title "the apostle of the bleeding feet."[74] He suffered stoning along the way because of his Christian message and was arrested on different occasions.

In 1908, he crossed the frontier of Tibet, a closed Buddhist region where missionaries had failed to penetrate with the gospel. Since the day of his baptism, Singh dreamed of going to Tibet, and at nineteen he entered the country for the first time. Seeing Tibet, he was appalled by the filth of the people and their living conditions. His own practice was to bathe in cold water, but even the idea angered local Tibetans, who believed that holy men never wash.[75]

Singh continued his journey to Mumbai (Bombay), where he planned to board a ship to Palestine in order to visit the holy land of Jesus, but he was refused permission to travel there. His journey to that point was not in vain, however. On his return northward, he was reminded of a principle when he saw what happened with a man of the Brahmin caste after he collapsed in a hot, crowded carriage.[76] The Brahmin refused a cup of water when it was offered to him because it was not from his own drinking vessel. After his own cup was filled, he drank and was soon refreshed back to health. In that moment, Singh was struck further by the thought that the people of India would not accept the gospel if it were offered in a "Western cup."[77] Thus, he continued in his effort to shape an Indian Christian identity for Indian Christians, rather than adopt forms that were not indigenous.

His thinking on this matter was further confirmed in 1909, when he began theological studies at St. John's Divinity College, an Anglican school in Lahore.[78] He was troubled by the way the gospel was presented in his

73. Davey, "Apostle with the Bleeding Feet," 149.

74. See Alfred Zahir, *The Apostle of the Bleeding Feet: An Account of the Devoted Life and Work of Sadhu Sunder Singh, the Faqir Evangelist of North India* (Sikandra-Agra, India: CMS Mission, 1919).

75. Davey, "Apostle with the Bleeding Feet," 149.

76. Davey, "Apostle with the Bleeding Feet," 150.

77. A. Scott Moreau, *Contextualization in World Missions: Mapping and Assessing Evangelical Models* (Grand Rapids: Kregel, 2012), 107.

78. Noll and Nystrom, *Cloud of Witnesses*, 160.

courses, concluding that much of the material taught was irrelevant to the needs and questions of the Indian people. Moreover, the rector requested that he remove his sadhu robe and wear Anglican clerical clothing. Additionally, the rector asked him to abide by Anglican worship and not preach outside the local parish without permission. With his deep sense of God's call on his life, Singh decided it was best to leave the college and travel back to Tibet. He left wearing his saffron robe.

Singh's evangelistic messages came from his early morning devotions, especially from his meditation from the Gospels. People often said of him, "He not only looks like Jesus; he talks like Jesus must have talked."[79] While people converted after hearing Singh's messages, the results of his evangelism remained largely unknown because of the lack of records. Moreover, Tibetan Buddhists to whom he spoke were threatened by death if they converted to Christianity.

In 1918, Singh made a tour of South India and Ceylon, and the following year he was invited to Malaya, Burma, Japan, and China. For years he hoped to visit Britain. The opportunity came when his father, Dher Singh, who had disowned him earlier, came to tell him that he had converted to Christ.[80] As a gift, he paid his son's fare to Britain. In 1920, Singh visited the United States and Australia, and then two years later visited Europe.[81] After all his travels, he became disillusioned with the materialism of Western societies.

In 1929, against the advice of others, Singh chose to make a trek to Tibet. Local villagers said that he reached Kalka, a small town below Simla, but he was never seen again.[82] The details of his death remained a mystery, while the details of his life were clear: he lived to make known "the Christ of the Indian road."[83]

Pandita Ramabai of India

The evangelist Pandita Ramabai (1858–1922) was born with the name Rama Dongre to a high-caste, Brahmin family.[84] Her father was a Sanskrit scholar,

79. Anand Amaladass, ed., *Indian Christian Thinkers* (Chennai, India: Satya Nilayam 2006), 1:214.

80. Davey, "Apostle with the Bleeding Feet," 151.

81. Noll and Nystrom, *Cloud of Witnesses*, 164.

82. Noll and Nystrom, *Cloud of Witnesses*, 166.

83. Davey, "Apostle with the Bleeding Feet," 151.

84. Meera Kosambi, *Pandita Ramabai: Life and Landmark Writings* (London: Routledge, 2016), 7.

always searching for the truth. Pandita learned Sanskrit as a child and memorized thousands of Hindu sayings and stories. At age sixteen, she became an orphan. With few resources, she and her brother, Srinivas, traveled around India, reciting Sanskrit scriptures. Later, she recalled, "I cannot describe all the sufferings of this terrible time. My brother and I survived and wandered about, still visiting sacred places, bathing in rivers, and worshiping the gods and goddesses in order to get our desire. . . . After years of fruitless service we began to lose our faith in them."[85]

Ramabai and her brother settled in Kolkata (Calcutta), where she was invited to lecture as a Sanskrit scholar. While there, she learned about Jesus Christ for the first time. She began to study the Bible while also reading the Vedas, the most sacred writings of Hindu literature.[86] Soon she became known throughout India for her outspoken views, including some that were contrary to Hindu teachings, such as her views about the status of women in Hindu society, particularly the distress placed on widows.[87]

Ramabai's concern for widows heightened after she herself became a widow just nineteen months after her marriage to a Bengali lawyer who died of cholera. When her brother, Srinivas, died, she was left alone with her infant daughter, Manoramabai.

Despite these losses, Ramabai continued to travel and lecture, forming chapters of a society that she founded, the Arya Women's Society, which served the needs of oppressed women.[88] For a brief time, she joined the reformist monotheistic movements of Brahmo Samaj of Bengal and Prarthana Samaj of Maharashtra.[89] Then she met a Baptist missionary and learned that salvation in Jesus Christ is offered freely as the gift of God, not something earned by pilgrimages or other devout acts. The missionary also addressed her misconception that Christians must live like Europeans, eat their foods, and wear their clothes.

In 1883, when Ramabai had difficulty raising funds for her organization, she traveled to England, taking her daughter with her. In the town of Wantage, they stayed at the convent of Anglican sisters. Although vowing before she left India that nothing would induce her to embrace Christianity, she found herself drawn

85. Dyer, *Great Life in Indian Missions*, 24.

86. Kosambi, *Pandita Ramabai*, 268.

87. Tucker and Liefeld, *Daughters of the Church*, 344.

88. Tucker and Liefeld, *Daughters of the Church*, 344.

89. A. Kenneth Curtis and Dan Graves, *Great Women in Christian History* (Worcester, PA: Christian History Institute, 2007), 95.

to Christ and the New Testament.[90] Sister Geraldine and other nuns taught her about Jesus, and in response she confessed faith in him and was baptized.

When news of her baptism reached India, many women were outraged, hearing that India's female social reformer had betrayed her people and culture.[91] For Ramabai, however, her decision to accept Christ was not a betrayal of her culture. Ironically, her insistence on this point created friction between her and the sisters of the Wantage convent. In fact, Ramabai resisted the idea of joining the Church of England.[92] She considered herself to be a Christian woman and resented efforts by the Anglican sisters to make her conform to their lifestyle. She later wrote to Sister Geraldine, saying,

> I am, it is true, a member of the Church of Christ, but I am not bound to accept every word that falls down from the lips of priests or bishops. . . . I have just with great efforts freed myself from the yoke of the Indian priestly tribe, so I am not at present willing to place myself under another similar yoke by accepting everything which comes from the priests as authorized command of the Most High. . . . How would an Englishwoman like [it if she were] called proud and prejudiced if she were to go and live among the Hindus for a time but not think it necessary to alter her customs when they were not hurtful or necessary to her neighbors?[93]

In 1886, Ramabai sailed across the Atlantic to the United States, where she studied educational methods and spoke to Christians about the needs of Indian women. She also published an important book titled *The High-Caste Hindu Woman*.[94] She returned to India, where, in 1889, she opened a school on a farm that she had inherited from her extended family, and purchased an adjacent property from a liquor dealer. The school was named Mukti, meaning "salvation."[95] To help the women become self-supporting, Ramabai taught them arts and crafts to sell, and together they cultivated the farm's orchard.

90. Kosambi, *Pandita Ramabai*, 84.

91. Kosambi, *Pandita Ramabai*, 86.

92. Tucker and Liefeld, *Daughters of the Church*, 345.

93. Shamsundar Manohar Adhav, *Pandita Ramabai* (Madras, India: Christian Literature Society, 1979), 131, cited in Tucker and Liefeld, *Daughters of the Church*, 345.

94. See Ramabai Sarasvati, *The High-Caste Hindu Woman* (Philadelphia: Rodgers, 1887).

95. Edith L. Blumhofer, "Pandita Ramabai and U.S. Support for Foreign Missions," in Bays and Wacker, *Foreign Missionary Enterprise at Home*, 165.

At first, Ramabai made the Bible available to the students of the school and did not pressure the Hindu girls to become Christians.[96] She did not want them to perceive Christianity as alien to Indian culture and the Hindu writings. In fact, she was critical of missionary schools that showed little respect for Indian customs.[97] In the beginning, her approach was successful, but as some of the Hindu girls read the Bible and observed Ramabai's life, they converted to Christ and were baptized. Some of the Hindu families complained that she was proselytizing students and betraying Indian culture. As a result, some parents removed their daughters from the school. Thus, by 1898, Ramabai came to the conclusion that she could not straddle the two religious systems. She decided that the school would be Christian and introduce the gospel and Christian teachings to all the students.[98]

In the years that followed, the school's enrollment grew considerably, especially during the famine of 1900, when physical and social needs of girl brides and child widows multiplied.[99] During this time, the Mukti mission fed thousands of girls and young women who would have otherwise starved. A spiritual breakthrough came when over one thousand of them professed faith in Christ.[100]

When Ramabai heard about the Welsh revival in 1904, she prayed that revival would come to the Mukti mission as well, and that God would demonstrate his power and presence through signs and wonders. She wrote, "I was led by the Lord to start a special prayer circle at the beginning of 1905. There were about seventy of us who met together each morning and prayed for the true conversion of all the Indian Christians, including ourselves, and for special outpouring of the Holy Spirit. . . . In six months from the time we began to pray in this manner, the Lord graciously sent a glorious Holy Ghost Revival among us, and also in many schools and churches in this country."[101]

Soon, as many as 550 girls and young women gathered daily at Mukti. On June 29, 1905, when the Holy Spirit came upon them, they wept, confessed sins, and spoke in tongues. They testified to a "holy burning inside them that was almost unbearable."[102] They spent hours a day praying for people

96. Curtis and Graves, *Great Women in Christian History*, 97.

97. Tucker and Liefeld, *Daughters of the Church*, 346.

98. Curtis and Graves, *Great Women in Christian History*, 97.

99. Kosambi, *Pandita Ramabai*, 152.

100. Tucker and Liefeld, *Daughters of the Church*, 346.

101. Adhav, *Pandita Ramabai*, 19, cited in Tucker and Liefeld, *Daughters of the Church*, 347.

102. Curtis and Graves, *Great Women in Christian History*, 98.

whom they had never met. Many of the girls and women of Mukti committed themselves to serving Christ, and in the years that followed, dozens went out with the gospel to the surrounding regions.

Figure 11.1. **Pandita Ramabai.** *(Chronicle/Alamy Stock Photo)*

Desiring for all of India to know the reality of God's saving grace, Ramabai prayed for 100,000 Christians to go and share the gospel with others.[103] In the meantime, she was asked to provide food and shelter for twenty-five thousand female orphans. She viewed this as the first installment of God's answer to her prayer. In 1907, she wrote, "Dear brother and sister, . . . may you realise your responsibility to give the gospel of Jesus Christ to my people in this land, and pray for them, that they may each and all be cleansed from their filthiness, and from all their idols, that they may find the true way of salvation."[104]

William Wadé Harris of West Africa

In Africa, William Wadé Harris (ca. 1865–1929) was an indigenous evangelist who led a mass movement to Christianity.[105] He inspired a form of African Christianity that changed the religious life of the southern Ivory Coast and contributed to the growth of Protestant and Roman Catholic churches as well as the establishment of Africa's Harrist Church.

Harris was born at Half Graway to a family of the Grebo tribe that lived five miles east of Cape Palmas in southeastern Liberia.[106] His father was a spiritist associated with traditional sacrifices, witchdoctors, and fetishes,

103. Curtis and Graves, *Great Women in Christian History*, 98.

104. Dyer, *Great Life in Indian Missions*, 53–54.

105. Tite Tiénou, "The Great Commission in Africa," in *The Great Commission: Evangelicals and the History of World Missions*, ed. Martin I. Klauber and Scott M. Manetsch (Nashville: B&H, 2008), 169.

106. Noll and Nystrom, *Cloud of Witnesses*, 66.

while his mother was a Christian.[107] When Harris was twelve years old, he learned to read and write Grebo and English from attending school at the Methodist Episcopal Mission. As a teenager, he came to faith in Christ and was baptized by the missionary Jesse Lowrie.

In 1910, Harris was jailed for treason because of his alleged coup d'état that sought to replace the Liberian government, led by descendants of the original African American settlers, with a government tied to Britain.[108] While imprisoned, he experienced a vision in which the angel Gabriel appeared to him and told him to preach as a prophet of the last days, to call people to destroy their fetishes, and to baptize all who received his message of repentance and faith in Jesus Christ. The angel Gabriel also instructed him to set aside his Western clothes in favor of a white robe.

When Harris was released from prison in 1913, he left Liberia and began his preaching tour, wearing the white robe and turban but no shoes. His religious meetings were noisy, beginning with the clatter of calabashes—rattles made from gourds—in order to attract the people's attention.[109] As he and those who accompanied him sang and danced, Harris invited his hearers to repent of their sins and come to God.

He carried a small cross and baptismal bowl wherever he went. For those who repented, he baptized them in the name of the triune God, sprinkling them with water from the bowl.[110] His practice of baptizing people immediately after their conversion grew out of their need to leave the "old spiritual powers."[111] In addition, he asked the new converts to bring their fetishes and idols to him in order to burn them publicly.[112]

Harris healed the sick by holding a Bible in front of their faces and crying out to God to make them well. His impact was dramatic as thousands of listeners responded to his messages.[113] He encouraged them to join churches, whether Protestant or Roman Catholic. If there were no churches in the area, he selected a group of "twelve apostles" from among the newly converted—

107. Elizabeth Isichei, *A History of Christianity in Africa: From Antiquity to the Present* (Grand Rapids: Eerdmans, 1995), 284–86.

108. Kwame Bediako, *Jesus and the Gospel in Africa: History and Experience* (Maryknoll, NY: Orbis, 2004), 85–86.

109. David A. Shank, "The Legacy of William Wadé Harris," *International Bulletin of Missionary Research* 10, no. 4 (October 1986): 170.

110. Noll and Nystrom, *Cloud of Witnesses*, 77.

111. Shank, "Legacy of William Wadé Harris," 176.

112. Noll and Nystrom, *Cloud of Witnesses*, 75.

113. Bediako, *Jesus and the Gospel in Africa*, 85.

generally former witchdoctors—to lead the new Christian community.[114] He instructed them to erect a church building and to "wait for a white man with a Bible" to come and explain the meaning of their conversion more fully.[115]

New converts were impressed by Harris's Christ-centered messages and the spiritual power that accompanied his preaching.[116] Healings were reported, as well as stories of colonial administrators who died unexpectedly when they interfered with his ministry. Similarly, death came to newly baptized converts who did not burn their fetishes.[117] Some even claimed that Harris raised people from the dead.

When he had extended time in one place, Harris taught the converts to recite the Ten Commandments, the Apostles' Creed, and the Lord's Prayer.[118] When crowds grew large and local officials encouraged him to move on, he left some new converts with a staff and water bowl, assigning them the task of continuing his work. It is estimated that hundreds of evangelists known as "water people" proclaimed the gospel while carrying crosses, clattering calabashes, and sprinkling their converts with water from bowls.[119]

In response to the large number of converts, Protestant and Roman Catholic churches of the Ivory and Gold Coasts were overwhelmed by the thousands of people who came to them as the direct result of Harris's preaching.[120] While many missionaries were critical of him over his indigenous theology and toleration of polygamy, most rejoiced at the spiritual harvest that his movement reaped in areas where their work earlier had been meager.[121]

In 1924, when a Protestant missionary arrived from Europe, to his surprise he encountered thousands of Harrist Christians. Immediately they asked about the "white man with a Bible" for whom Harris had told them to wait.[122] When additional missionaries from Europe arrived, they explained the meaning of Christian conversion more fully.

114. Shank, "Legacy of William Wadé Harris," 172.

115. Noll and Nystrom, *Cloud of Witnesses*, 77.

116. Mark A. Noll, *Turning Points: Decisive Moments in the History of Christianity* (Grand Rapids: Baker Academic, 2012), 280.

117. Shank, "Legacy of William Wadé Harris," 172.

118. Shank, "Legacy of William Wadé Harris," 172.

119. Noll and Nystrom, *Cloud of Witnesses*, 75.

120. Ogbu Uke Kalu, *African Christianity: An African Story* (Trenton, NJ: Africa World, 2007), 285.

121. Shank, "Legacy of William Wadé Harris," 174.

122. Allan Anderson, *African Reformation: African Initiated Christianity in the 20th Century* (Trenton, NJ: Africa World, 2001), 73.

Despite the benefits of these missionaries, disputes followed when they undermined the work of Harris's disciples, or attacked the African social conventions such as polygamy. In the end, Harris and his followers drafted a "last will and testament" that declared their intent to remain independent of European missionaries. John Ahui succeeded Harris and continued the work by founding the Harrist Church of the Ivory Coast.

Harris's ministry demonstrated the gospel taking root in indigenous soil.[123] His theology was contextual as it addressed questions about spiritism as well as the political situation of colonialism.[124] Harrist churches were uniquely African and preserved indigenous social structures as well as the conceptual and ritual elements of the culture.

Arthur Wellington Clah of the Pacific Northwest Territory

Arthur Wellington Clah (1831–1916) was a Tsimshian of the Pacific Northwest coast of British Columbia, Canada. He was born at a settlement called Laghco, where the Hudson's Bay Company established a trading post in 1834. As a young man, in 1857, Clah met the Anglican missionary William Duncan at Fort Simpson (Lax Kw'alaams).[125]

Clah is the anglicized version of his hereditary Tsimshian name, Ła'ax. He also went by the name T'amks from his leadership of the matrilineal house-group of the Gispaxlo'ots, one of the Nine Tribes of Lax Kw'alaams. In addition, he took the English name Arthur Wellington. He married Dorcas Datacks of the Laxgibuu, of the Nisga'a Nation.

When missionary William Duncan arrived at Port Simpson, Clah taught him the Tsimshian language, and Duncan taught Clah to read and write English, with both using the Chinook Jargon in the meantime.[126] Clah soon became a mediator for Duncan and the Tsimshian people.

Four years after meeting Duncan, Clah came to faith in Christ. Having learned to write English, he kept a diary for nearly fifty years, chronicling his experiences, including his work of evangelism. Clah's writings reflected the voice of a Tsimshian who had acquired English as a second language. He described his conversion, writing,

123. Noll, *Turning Points*, 281; Philip Jenkins, *The Next Christendom: The Coming of Global Christianity* (New York: Oxford University Press, 2011), 63–64, 70.

124. A. Anderson, *African Reformation*, 211–12.

125. Brock et al., *Indigenous Evangelists*, 195–203.

126. Peggy Brock, *The Many Voyages of Arthur Wellington Clah: A Tsimshian Man on the Pacific Northwest Coast* (Vancouver, BC: UBC Press, 2014), 157.

Figure 11.2. Arthur Wellington Clah, Victoria, BC, 1889. Royal British Columbia Museum, Victoria, BC, Canada. *(Image J-04841 courtesy of the Royal BC Museum)*

About three years ago I heard about God; then I travelled about five hundred miles to find Jesus. Another year I went North again, and when I came back I found just what I wished. It was as when the snow comes down from heaven; I saw a track and did not know what it was—now I find it was Jesus. I say now to all my friends, "Come." If I am in a great storm I know it cannot hurt me. And now I do thank God that he has sent the Missionary [Duncan], and I thank the good people of Canada for their help. I pray much that I may see the house of God put up. Long ago I was blind, and now God has opened my eyes. I hope all the good people of Canada will still pray for us, for we are very dark.[127]

After his conversion, Clah began to share the gospel with his people and neighboring groups.[128] He worked closely with Duncan and on one occasion intervened to save his life. When Clah's tribal chief, Ligeex, ordered Duncan at knifepoint to stop tolling the church bell on the day of his daughter's initiation into a Tsimshian secret society, Clah stepped in and calmed the situation. Later, Duncan led Ligeex to Christ.

In 1862, when Duncan moved to Metlakatla, Clah remained near Fort Simpson, along the Nass River. When the Methodist missionary Thomas Crosby arrived, Clah benefited from his ministry too. However, Clah chose to practice the Christian faith along the lines of Tsimshian culture, rather than that of Duncan and Crosby.[129] In one instance Clah said, "News come up yesterday to say Duncan laugh at me because I teach the people in tents. . . . Some news [of this] said to me if I got license alright I can preach [to] the people. Now I think [this is] his [Duncan's] little mistake [because] God gave the license in our hearts."[130]

Clah desired to proclaim the gospel to those seeking God. On one occasion he wrote, "Church bell in evening George Pemberton came in my house [to] ask if I preach [to] the [Christian] friends. I don't want to preach amongs[t] our Christianity [Christians] I want [to] preach [to] all pline [blind] friends [to] some stranger amongs[t] us who [were] not interested [in] words of god [but now] they wanted to be Christian. Some time I help the [these] friends everyw[h]ere where I travel round preach them sometimes in the Name of our lord Jesus Christ some I teach them how to prayer and song."[131]

Clah did not receive missionary funding but combined his evangelism with his daily work of hunting, fishing, mining, and trading. This took him along trails and rivers that connected villages.[132] If a house or tent were available, he would preach there, and if not, he would meet the people in

127. Susan Neylan, *The Heavens Are Changing: Nineteenth-Century Protestant Missions and Tsimshian Christianity* (Montreal: McGill-Queen's University Press, 2003), 162–63.

128. Neylan, *Heavens Are Changing*, 174.

129. Peggy Brock, "Two Indigenous Evangelists: Moses Tjalkabota and Arthur Wellington Clah," *Journal of Religious History* 27, no. 3 (October 2003): 354.

130. Clah Diary, January 18, 1874, 140/5, cited in Brock, "Two Indigenous Evangelists," 354.

131. Brock, "Two Indigenous Evangelists," 354n29.

132. Brock, "Two Indigenous Evangelists," 355.

the open air. During the winter months when he was not traveling, Clah focused on those of his own village. Even when he was on prospecting trips, or provided transportation to nonindigenous people, he shared the gospel with them.[133]

Clah based his messages on the Bible but combined Christian and Tsimshian images. For example, he took the biblical concept of light and darkness and spoke of the Tsimshian view that the Raven brought light into the world that he took from the Chief of Heaven.[134] While Clah received teaching and encouragement from missionaries, he resisted their forms of Christianity, preferring to communicate the gospel and his messages from the Scriptures in ways that were meaningful to the Tsimshian people.

Juan Varetto of Argentina

Protestant missionary work in Argentina began in 1818, when James Thompson arrived in Buenos Aires, serving with the British and Foreign Bible Society. In 1904, Henry Strachan, a Canadian Baptist, and his wife, Susanna, arrived under the auspices of Regions Beyond Missionary Union (RBMU) and founded a Baptist church in Tandil, Argentina.[135]

In 1916, the Congress on Christian Work in Latin America met in Panama. Soon, the Strachans envisioned a strategy for continent-wide evangelism. In 1918, they chose San José, Costa Rica, as a center for an interdenominational evangelistic effort. Beginning in 1920, Strachan and Juan Varetto of Argentina launched an evangelism campaign that marked a new approach to evangelism.[136] Many of the evangelical Protestant churches began to preach and teach in the public areas of their neighborhoods, giving Christians increased confidence to overcome the timidity and inferiority that had characterized their churches earlier.

In 1921, Strachan and Varetto, along with others, formed the Latin American Evangelization Campaign (LAEC), which became known as the Latin American Mission (LAM). Since education was crucial to equip pastors and evangelists, they opened the Costa Rican Bible Institute in 1923, and Varetto was asked to lead the evangelistic preaching for all of South America.[137]

133. Brock, "Two Indigenous Evangelists," 356.

134. Brock, "Two Indigenous Evangelists," 356.

135. Justice Anderson, *An Evangelical Saga: Baptists and Their Precursors in Latin America* (Longwood, FL: Xulon, 2005), 190.

136. J. Edwin Orr, *Evangelical Awakenings in Latin America* (Minneapolis: Bethany Fellowship, 1978), 78, 93.

137. J. Anderson, *Evangelical Saga*, 192.

Juan Crisóstomo Varetto (1879–1953) was born in Argentina of Italian descent. In 1894, he converted to Christ through the ministry of Methodist pastor John F. Thomson. Varetto began as a Methodist colporteur and evangelist, but then joined the Baptists, becoming the first native Argentine ordained as a Baptist pastor. His ministry as a preacher, evangelist, and author made him a recognized leader among Protestants across Latin America.[138] In 1927, he spent four months in Guatemala, where he preached in the major cities, and two years later he launched an evangelistic radio program that was broadcast from Argentina.[139]

Varetto and Strachan worked with several missions and churches to hold evangelistic campaigns in Argentina, Peru, Brazil, and Bolivia.[140] Their strategy was not limited to large gatherings alone. As Varetto had done earlier, he encouraged local churches to take the gospel outside the walls of their buildings and hold evangelistic meetings in public areas, including city plazas and vacant lots. Some churches purchased tents to hold meetings in nearby neighborhoods or villages where they hoped to plant new congregations. A North American Baptist missionary commented, "Pastor Varetto keeps up an almost continuous campaign of tent services. He has found the tent to be a splendid method of reaching the people who probably would never be enticed to enter one of our usual preaching halls. We trust it may prove to be, at least, one solution to the ever-present problem—how to reach the *peladas* [rural] people."[141]

By 1930, Varetto and his team had planted fifty-five Baptist churches with over 3,300 members.[142] He expected all Christians to take an active role in the church's evangelism, whether by open-air preaching, helping with tent meetings, participating in home visits, distributing tracts, or assisting in charitable works in the neighborhoods. Moreover, he emphasized the importance of evangelism as a way of daily living, saying, "[We] Christians must confess Christ in every place where we find ourselves. We must talk about Him in factory workshops, offices, and wherever we find immortal

138. J. Daniel Salinas, *Taking Up the Mantle: Latin American Evangelical Theology in the 20th Century* (Carlisle, UK: Langham Global Library, 2017), 46.

139. J. Anderson, *Evangelical Saga*, 410.

140. J. Anderson, *Evangelical Saga*, 425.

141. María Eugenia Cornou, "Worship as a Formative Practice: The Worship Practices of Methodists, Baptists, and Free Brethren in Emerging Protestantism in Argentina, 1867–1930" (PhD diss., Vrije Universiteit Amsterdam, 2016), 139–40.

142. Cornou, "Worship as a Formative Practice," 139–40.

souls; we must bear witness of our faith among our relatives, among our friends, and even among our enemies."[143]

Varetto practiced what he preached, making several preaching tours in Latin America and Spain. In his evangelistic preaching, he was known for his "good measure of humor and popular elements" that made him "an early successful attempt of Argentinization of the message of the gospel" that came to distinguish a new generation of native evangelists.[144] Among them was his daughter, Agustina Varetto, and his son-in-law, Santiago Canclini.[145] Juan Varetto's leadership in evangelistic events in city plazas, tent meetings, and stadiums left an impact on Latin America. (Another Argentine, Luis Palau, discussed in chapter 12, would have a similar impact around the world.) Varetto's meetings captured the attention of people who were otherwise oblivious to the gospel.

Kenneth Strachan, son of Henry Strachan, built on the foundational work of his father and Varetto. He developed a comprehensive strategy of "saturation evangelism" that was called Evangelism-in-Depth (EID).[146] This strategy aimed to mobilize all Christians and all churches to use all methods of evangelization for a year, in a concerted effort. The strategy proved effective, especially in countries where evangelical Protestants were a minority, such as Guatemala, Nicaragua, Bolivia, and Venezuela.[147]

In this strategy, the coordination of resources and methods allowed churches to mobilize Christians in a sustained effort to reach their village or city.[148] Training was provided for laypeople and clergy to learn various methods of evangelism. Moreover, projects to benefit the village or neighborhoods were promoted to foster goodwill and public confidence toward the churches.[149]

143. Cornou, "Worship as a Formative Practice," 218.

144. Cornou, "Worship as a Formative Practice," 145–46.

145. Santiago Canclini (1900–1977) was converted through the ministry of Varetto and later became the first Argentine president of the Baptist Seminary. Cornou, "Worship as a Formative Practice," 58–60.

146. Mortimer Arias, "Contextual Evangelization in Latin America: Between Accommodation and Confrontation," *Occasional Bulletin of Missionary Research* 2, no. 1 (January 1978): 23.

147. Arias, "Contextual Evangelization," 23.

148. Rudnick, *Speaking the Gospel*, 203–4.

149. Arias, "Contextual Evangelization," 23.

Elka of the Wai Wai of the Amazon

A final example of indigenous evangelism is Elka of the Wai Wai. In 1948, two brothers, Robert and Neil Hawkins, entered an area of the Amazon rainforest.[150] They were missionaries with the Unevangelized Fields Mission (UFM), today CrossWorld. They came to the Wai Wai of the Amerindian forest people of Guyana and Brazil, bearing the gospel and gifts of fish hooks, knives, and steel axes.

Elka (ca. 1925–1995), the chief of the Wai Wai, greeted them but, like others, was not happy to see them for fear that they were murderers who had come for revenge.[151] Years earlier, white missionaries had come to the same area, and after greeting them, the Wai Wai poisoned their drinks and bludgeoned them to death. But seeing the kindness of the Hawkins brothers, the Wai Wai were pleasantly surprised by them.

The missionaries told them of the Creator God who made the trees, rocks, and sun, and about the Creator's Son named Chisusu who came to his creation to take away the badness of people, including that of the Wai Wai. Elka thought about the missionaries' message, knowing that he, too, was bad. In addition, he knew how the Wai Wai disguised their hate with smiles, how they had killed with deception, and how the men would steal or trade wives.

When Robert Hawkins and his wife, Florine, lived among the Wai Wai, they explained more fully the message of "God's Paper" as they translated the words of the New Testament into the Wai Wai language.[152] At first, Elka laughed at their attempts to speak God's Paper in Wai Wai words, but soon he became intrigued by their efforts and even assisted them in speaking about the Creator, helping them to use the Wai Wai words more precisely.

Elka and others began to attend the weekly meetings hosted by the missionaries, hearing messages and singing songs about God's Paper. A missionary nurse, Florence Reidle, arrived too, and the Wai Wai were glad to receive her help, accepting both her "pills and shiny needle."[153]

One day, Elka helped the missionaries translate 1 John 4:18, which says, "There is no fear in love. But perfect love drives out fear, because fear has to

150. Ruth Tucker, *From Jerusalem to Irian Jaya: A Biographical History of Christian Missions* (Grand Rapids: Zondervan, 2004), 435.

151. See Homer E. Dowdy, *Christ's Witchdoctor* (Gresham, OR: Vision House, 1994), and Dowdy, *Christ's Jungle* (Gresham, OR: Vision House, 1995).

152. Tucker, *From Jerusalem to Irian Jaya*, 435.

153. Roy Elliot Oakley, "Opening the Waiwai Ewto: Indigenous Social and Spatial Relations in Guyana" (PhD diss., University of Edinburgh, 2019), 174.

do with punishment. The one who fears is not made perfect in love." Elka was intrigued by the words because he had lived his life in fear of Kworokyam, the great spirit.

Decades earlier, Elka had watched a witchdoctor named Mafolio call on Kworokyam to heal a sick person.[154] Kworokyam was considered by the Wai Wai to be the sum of all spirits in the world. Kworokyam was mostly evil and caused illness, but he could be petitioned to bring cures. Elka learned to petition Kworokyam and had become a witchdoctor himself, revered for his healing abilities as well his wisdom and leadership. For this reason, the people had made him their chief.

As Elka helped to translate the words "There is no fear in love," he pondered the love of God who sent his Son, Jesus. He knew that he needed to decide whether he would live according to Kworokyam or according to Jesus. When Elka shared his dilemma with his wife, Ahmori, and his friends, they warned him that Kworokyam would become angry if he followed Jesus. Elka struggled with his decision until he had a dream and heard the words "Let go of your sins. Say to Jesus, 'Come in.' If you do, he will come in."[155] Early the next morning, Elka went to an open field and prayed. He looked up to the sky and said, "Father, I want to know you, so make yourself known to me forever." Elka confessed his sins to God and asked him to remove his old person with its badness, saying, "Fix me to be like Jesus."[156]

As Elka grew in his Christian faith, he acknowledged his need to give up witchcraft. At a community celebration, he handed his basket of charms to the missionary and told the people that he had decided to trust in God rather than charms and Kworokyam.[157] The Wai Wai people were convinced that he would die immediately, or at least within a few days.

Though the villagers disapproved at the time, Elka's conversion to Christ proved to be a turning point for the Wai Wai people. Others, after their own hesitation, began to take the same step of faith that he had done, with most of them following en masse.[158] They began to learn forgiveness, patience, mercy, honesty, and other characteristics of Christ followers. The mission-

154. Elka's father died shortly after his birth. Therefore, he was sold to an uncle for one otter skin and five feathered arrows. At fifteen years of age, he underwent the stinging ants test with belts of stinging ants wrapped around his legs. Dowdy, *Christ's Witchdoctor*, 14.

155. Dowdy, *Christ's Witchdoctor*, 121.

156. Dowdy, *Christ's Witchdoctor*, 122.

157. Jack Voelkel, "Elka of the Wai Wai," *Urbana Articles*, June 15, 2015, https://urbana.org/blog/elka-wai-wai.

158. Oakley, "Opening the Waiwai Ewto," 49–50.

aries encouraged the Wai Wai to select spiritual elders and to apply the principles they learned from the Scriptures. The missionaries did not set rules about clothing, marriage, polygamy, or social structures. They were confident that God would show the Wai Wai how to live and when to make any necessary changes. When Robert Hawkins once lost his voice, the native elders began to lead the meetings on Sunday, including the singing and preaching. Elka volunteered to preach and did so with evidence of God's power.[159] The Wai Wai also led the Wednesday meetings, during which they taught from God's Paper. The men stopped wife-stealing and began to share domestic chores that they had not done before.

In 1956, the Wai Wai became burdened over their need to preach the gospel to other tribes.[160] In their sermons, they stressed how the people around them lived as they had before—fearful of evil spirits, suspicious of others, and killing with the club. Elka said, "Jesus came far. So let us go far, too. He died for us. We haven't yet died for him. Let us die for Jesus."[161] These words set their evangelistic efforts in motion, to reach out to those of the Amazon jungle, including the Waimiri-Atroari and Karafawyana peoples near the Rio Anauá and Rio Mapuera.[162]

Similar to Christians in other parts of the world, the Wai Wai took seriously Jesus's commission to make disciples of all nations. Like others, their ministry showed what happens when the gospel is planted in indigenous soil. While they received both teaching and encouragement from missionaries, the Wai Wai communicated the gospel in ways that were uniquely meaningful to Amerindian forest people of the Amazon.

Discussion Questions

1. Some Christians experience a "divine visitation" in which an angel or Jesus Christ himself appears to them. How do you explain such experiences from the Scriptures? How would you discern if a divine visitation was authentic or not?
2. After reading this chapter, what advice would you give to missionaries who engage with people from a very different culture? What should the missionaries attempt? What should they avoid?

159. Tucker, *From Jerusalem to Irian Jaya*, 437.

160. Oakley, "Opening the Waiwai Ewto," 49–50.

161. Dowdy, *Christ's Witchdoctor*, 232.

162. Oakley, "Opening the Waiwai Ewto," 177, 181; Tucker, *From Jerusalem to Irian Jaya*, 437.

3. In his diary, John Song offers advice for evangelism. What advice resonates most with you now, and why? How will practicing this piece of advice make you more fruitful in sharing the gospel with others?
4. Rather than a local church practicing a single method of evangelism, Varetto and Strachan applied several at once. Are there combinations of evangelism that complement each other and create a synergy in which the sum of the whole is greater than the parts? Is it possible to use too many methods at once? What do you think is the best rule of thumb?
5. What groups of people in your own neighborhood, city, or country are without the gospel of Jesus Christ? How might you and others from your church begin to share the gospel with them? Thinking like missionaries to an unreached people, what steps would you take to establish an indigenous church among this group?

12

Personal to Holistic Evangelism

> Sovereign God, we acknowledge that You are the head of Your body, the church. Forgive us for our selfish motives and our often pious religious spirit. Open our eyes to the physical, spiritual, and mental "lostness" of those around us. Once again we offer You our souls and bodies as living sacrifices to live and work to Your praise and glory. Please teach us to pray, teach us to listen, teach us to obey You individually and corporately. Send more labourers into Your world to be effective Christ-like witnesses for You—with Your love, passion and concern for all we encounter. Send your Holy Spirit afresh upon us and upon Your whole Church that we might be the "Kingdom People"—one in our heart, vision, and call. Amen.
>
> —**Christian Association of Nigeria**[1]

In 1952, the conference of the International Missionary Council at Willingen, Germany, called for "an increasing flow of Christian laymen and women who go out across the world in business, industry, and government; and who do so with deep conviction that God calls them to witness for him in all of life."[2] Two years later, the World Council of Churches (WCC)

1. David Claydon, ed., *A New Vision, a New Heart, a Renewed Call: Lausanne Occasional Papers from the 2004 Forum of World Evangelization* (Pasadena, CA: William Carey Library, 2005), 2:13.

2. David A. Kerr and Kenneth R. Ross, *Edinburgh 2010: Mission Then and Now* (Eugene, OR: Wipf & Stock, Regnum, 2009), 162.

at Evanston, Illinois, described laypeople as "the spearhead of the Church in the world," saying that "the true twentieth century evangelist is the instructed and witnessing layman."[3]

In the following decade, a number of statements of the Roman Catholic Church emphasized the conversion of non-Christians by preaching the gospel and planting churches throughout the world. The Vatican II meetings from 1962 to 1965 stressed that the missionary task belongs to the laity as well as the clergy.[4] Indeed, the whole church was called to proclaim the kingdom of Christ among all peoples and, in this way, was to become a means to bring salvation to the world. Evangelical Protestants, too, emphasized the importance of personal soul-winning and equipped Christians to share the gospel with family and friends at school, work, and neighborhood.[5]

There came also an effort to define the term *evangelism*, which stemmed, in part, from earlier debates of the social gospel and soul-saving gospel. However, some who favored the soul-saving gospel opposed the term because of its tie with revival-oriented evangelists who were known to misuse resources and abuse authority and who lacked moral accountability. In some cases, soul-saving evangelists were easy to caricature. In the best-selling novel written in 1927 by Sinclair Lewis, the character named Elmer Gantry played the role of a traveling evangelist who loved whiskey, wealth, and women.[6] Lewis won a Nobel Prize for Literature, and Elmer Gantry became a synonym for displays of showmanship, arrogance, and hypocrisy.[7]

3. Alexander Craig Forsyth, "Apostolate of the Laity: A Re-discovery of Holistic Post-War Missiology in Scotland, with Reference to the Ministry of Tom Allan" (PhD diss., University of Edinburgh, 2014), 127.

4. See Paul VI, *Decree on the Mission Activity of the Church: Ad Gentes* (Boston: Daughters of St. Paul, 1965).

5. See Rebecca Manley Pippert, *Out of the Saltshaker and Into the World* (Downers Grove, IL: InterVarsity Press, 1979); Jim Petersen, *Evangelism as a Lifestyle* (Colorado Springs: NavPress, 1980); Joe Aldrich, *Lifestyle Evangelism* (Portland, OR: Multnomah, 1981).

6. See Sinclair Lewis, *Elmer Gantry: A Novel* (London: Jonathan Cape, 1927); George M. Marsden, *Fundamentalism and American Culture* (New York: Oxford University Press, 2006), 188.

7. Paulus Scharpff, *History of Evangelism: Three Hundred Years of Evangelism in Germany, Great Britain, and the United States of America* (Grand Rapids: Eerdmans, 1966), 318; Grant Wacker, *One Soul at a Time: The Story of Billy Graham* (Grand Rapids: Eerdmans, 2019), 28.

Rallies and Crusades

In response to such caricatures, a few Christian leaders concluded that large revival meetings were relics of the past and should not be used for evangelism. Others said that evangelistic campaigns simply needed reform. With this concern, at the end of the Second World War, a number of evangelical Protestants began to reach America's youth by holding youth rallies, but they also promoted the idea of individual Christians sharing the gospel personally.

Jack Wyrtzen of New York

Jack Wyrtzen (1913–1996), a former trombonist for a military band, and Harry Bollback (1925–2021), a veteran of the Marine Corps, began street-preaching in Long Island, New York. When crowds grew, they moved to a church in Brooklyn to conduct Sunday-night meetings, beginning with two hundred in attendance at the first service. Three months later, with six hundred attending, Charles J. Woodbridge (1902–1995) spoke, and fifty-five listeners responded to the gospel, trusting in Christ.[8]

In 1940, Wyrtzen began meetings on Saturday nights in New York's Times Square and then launched a radio program called *Word of Life Hour* on station WHN. Soon, a thousand students gathered weekly for youth meetings. Even more attended rallies that filled Madison Square Garden and Yankee Stadium. In addition, the Word of Life ministry purchased a campground at Schroon Lake, New York, for youth camp during the summers.[9] Wyrtzen advocated that every generation of Christians is responsible to reach their own generation with the good news.

Youth for Christ

Youth rallies were held in other cities too, including Chicago, Washington, DC, Detroit, Indianapolis, and St. Louis. In 1944, Torrey M. Johnson (1909–2002), pastor of Midwest Bible Church of Chicago, held a rally called

8. David Wyrtzen, "Words of Life: Jack Wyrtzen," in *More Than Conquerors: Portraits of Believers from All Walks of Life*, ed. John D. Woodbridge (Chicago: Moody, 1992), 171.

9. Harry Bollback, *The House That God Built: The Story of Jack Wyrtzen* (Schroon Lake, NY: Word of Life, 1998), 149.

"Chicagoland for Christ" with similar results to the meetings in New York. In 1945, several of the youth ministries of major cities became known collectively as Youth for Christ (YFC), and Johnson became the first president. YFC cast the vision to reach every town in North America with the gospel. By 1950, it was an international movement, and its first full-time evangelist was Billy Graham.[10]

Billy Graham of North Carolina

Billy Graham (1918–2018) was born on a farm in the mountains near Charlotte, North Carolina. He attended worship and Sunday school at a Presbyterian church, and his parents welcomed visiting evangelists to their home. Despite these Christian influences, Graham's interests in high school were baseball, drama, and girls.[11]

When he was sixteen years old, an evangelist named Mordecai Ham came to Charlotte for a four-week, citywide campaign. Ham's tent meetings reached all types of people, including Graham and his friends, Grady Wilson and his brother, T. W. Wilson.[12] In response to the evangelist's invitation, Billy went forward during a meeting to accept Christ as Lord and Savior. He said, "When my decision for Christ was made, I walked slowly down and knelt in prayer. I opened my heart and knew for the first time the sweetness and joy of God, of truly being born of God."[13]

Following the campaign, another evangelist named Jimmie Johnson came to Charlotte. Johnson invited Graham and the Wilson brothers to join him at an evangelistic service held at a local jail. After the meeting started, the evangelist called on Graham—without advance notice—to share his testimony of faith. Graham stood to his feet and said, "I was a sinner and a no good! I didn't care anything about God, the Bible or people. Jesus changed my life. He gave me peace and joy! He can give you peace and joy. He will forgive your sins as He forgave mine, if you will only let Him into your heart. Jesus died so He could take your sins on His shoulders."[14] This was Graham's first experience sharing his Christian faith publicly.

10. Billy Graham, *Just as I Am: The Autobiography of Billy Graham* (San Francisco: HarperSanFrancisco, 1997), 92–97.

11. Mendell Taylor, *Exploring Evangelism: History, Methods, Theology* (Kansas City, MO: Nazarene Publishing House, 1984), 541.

12. Graham, *Just as I Am*, 21–34.

13. Roger A. Bruns, *Billy Graham: A Biography* (Westport, CT: Greenwood, 2004), 9.

14. M. Taylor, *Exploring Evangelism*, 543.

Following this meeting, he received an invitation to conduct a revival meeting at a small Baptist church near Palatka, Florida. When the converts from the meeting expressed their desire to be baptized by immersion, Graham joined them in the baptism rite.

After graduating from high school and with encouragement from his parents, he enrolled at Bob Jones College in Greenville, South Carolina, but after a semester transferred to Florida Bible Institute in Tampa. He joined a local Baptist church and was ordained as a Southern Baptist pastor. After completing the program in Florida, Graham enrolled at Wheaton College near Chicago, graduating with the BA in anthropology in 1943.[15] During this time, he met Ruth Bell, and the couple married two months after graduation.[16]

Graham accepted the role of pastor at a Baptist church in Western Springs, Illinois, and worked closely with Torrey Johnson to conduct a Sunday-night radio program broadcast over the Moody radio station, WMBI.[17] When Johnson's activities with YFC demanded more time, he asked Graham to take over the program. Graham invited George Beverly Shea to assist with the music.[18]

In January 1945, Johnson asked Graham to become a full-time employee of YFC. Before the year was over, Graham had spoken "in almost every state in the union at Youth for Christ rallies and ran up the impressive total of seven thousand conversions."[19] Moreover, he traveled throughout Canada and the British Isles, organizing YFC groups while holding evangelistic youth rallies.

At a rally in Asheville, North Carolina, he met Cliff Barrows (1923–2016), who ably led the singing at the last minute when the announced leader failed to show up. Graham then asked Barrows to join his team and "sing the gospel" while Graham preached it.[20] In 1947, Graham was asked to become president of Northwestern Schools in Minnesota.[21] He accepted the position on the condition that he could continue as an evangelist with YFC.

15. Scharpff, *History of Evangelism*, 327; Graham, *Just as I Am*, 39–60, 62–68.

16. Graham, *Just as I Am*, 71–80.

17. Wacker, *One Soul at a Time*, 20–22; Graham, *Just as I Am*, 86–87.

18. Wacker, *One Soul at a Time*, 22–24; Graham, *Just as I Am*, 85–86.

19. William G. McLoughlin Jr., *Billy Graham: Revivalist in a Secular Age* (New York: Ronald, 1960), 40.

20. See Cliff Barrows, *Singing Evangelism* (Winona Lake, IN: Rodeheaver, Hall-Mack, 1950).

21. Graham, *Just as I Am*, 112–22.

In the midst of his commitments, he began to have doubts about the authority of the Bible. His struggles persisted until August 1949, when he was invited to Forest Home, a Christian campground in the mountains of Southern California, and took daily hikes for exercise and prayer.[22] During a hike, he experienced an encounter with God that resulted in his taking all of Scripture by faith in the same way he received salvation by faith. From that point on, he proclaimed the gospel boldly because it is rooted in the Bible's authority.

Graham's Los Angeles Crusade

Some weeks later, Graham's meetings in Los Angeles catapulted him to national attention.[23] His team set up a large tent that seated six thousand people. At the end of the third week, attendance reached the 100,000 mark, and the number of conversions totaled more than fifteen hundred. With this response, the campaign was extended to five and then to nine weeks.[24] A total of 350,000 people came to his evangelistic meetings. A significant factor for the large attendance was the conversion of well-known personalities, including Stewart Hamblen, a local television personality; Louis Zamperini, a former Olympic track star and war hero; and Jim Vaus, a member of the mafia.[25]

During the meetings, the newspaper tycoon William Randolph Hearst sent a note to his editors saying, "Puff Graham."[26] With this cue, Graham's evangelist campaign was splashed across the headlines of several California newspapers. Following Los Angeles, Graham held evangelistic crusades in major cities, from San Francisco in the West to Boston in the East, from Chicago in the North to New Orleans in the South. His crusades ranged from ten days to six weeks, with crowds filling the largest auditoriums or

22. Wacker, *One Soul at a Time*, 32–34.

23. Wacker, *One Soul at a Time*, 35–39; Graham, *Just as I Am*, 143–58.

24. Scharpff, *History of Evangelism*, 328.

25. After his conversion, Zamperini returned to Sugamo Prison in Tokyo, Japan, where he shared the gospel with his former captors during the Second World War. As a result, some converted to Christ. Steve Chawkins and Keith Thursby, "Louis Zamperini Dies at 97; Olympic Track Star and WWII Hero," *Los Angeles Times*, July 3, 2014. Later, Graham helped Zamperini launch his work as an evangelist. Heath W. Carter and Laura Porter, *Turning Points in the History of American Evangelicalism* (Grand Rapids: Eerdmans, 2017), 240.

26. Grant Wacker, *America's Pastor: Billy Graham and the Shaping of a Nation* (Cambridge, MA: Belknap Press of Harvard University Press, 2014), 73–90.

stadiums available. Graham then traveled abroad, where he held hundreds of meetings in major cities, attaining international recognition. In addition, he spoke on radio and television programs and published several books. His support staff far exceeded those of Moody and Sunday, but, like them, he held meetings only at the invitation of local pastors and sponsors.

Criticisms and Changes

Graham's evangelistic crusades were not without criticism, however.[27] Some people took issue with his willingness to cooperate with a spectrum of churches from fundamentalist to liberal. Some fundamentalists accused him of doctrinal compromise, despite his convictions regarding the gospel, the Scriptures, and salvation by grace through faith. Reformed clergy took aim at his "decision theology," which they concluded was entirely the work of the sinner.[28] Liberals criticized him for an oversimplified approach to Christian faith without regard for the social applications of the gospel.[29] Sacramentalists questioned his lack of reference to the sacraments, which they held as essential forms of the gospel. Others were critical of his meetings, which they claimed were more effective at generating enthusiasm among Christians than converting skeptics.

In response to another criticism—namely, that only a few active disciples emerged from the large numbers of those who came forward at a crusade—Graham recognized the challenge and turned to his friend Dawson Trotman, asking him to develop follow-up materials for all who professed faith in Christ.[30] Trotman prepared a six-week Bible study for new Christians.

In response to a criticism over social justice, Graham preached that a relationship with Jesus Christ touches every area of life, including race and racism. Graham refused to conduct meetings where admission or seating arrangements were based on the color of one's skin.[31] Just weeks after the civil rights march from Selma to Montgomery, Alabama, Graham and his team came to Montgomery to hold an eight-day crusade at the Crampton Bowl Stadium. Despite several white pastors refusing to participate, the thousand-

27. Wacker, *One Soul at a Time*, 104–18.

28. Milton L. Rudnick, *Speaking the Gospel through the Ages: A History of Evangelism* (St. Louis: Concordia, 1984), 201–3.

29. Scharpff, *History of Evangelism*, 325.

30. Robert F. Ramey, "Pathfinder in Evangelism: Billy Graham," in Woodbridge, *More Than Conquerors*, 168.

31. Graham, *Just as I Am*, 162–64; Scharpff, *History of Evangelism*, 325.

member choir was composed of four hundred African Americans.[32] Graham said that he and Martin Luther King Jr. (1929–1968) spoke about the use of nonviolent demonstrations to end racial segregation. King urged Graham to keep preaching the gospel to integrated audiences and supporting civil rights by his example, saying, "You stay in the stadiums, Billy, because you will have far more impact on the white establishment there than you would if you marched in the streets."[33]

Graham was also aware of criticisms against evangelists over finances. In 1950, in Atlanta, Georgia, after eight thousand people responded to his invitation to trust in Christ, he received his percentage of the love offering. When the meeting closed, the newspaper *Atlanta Constitution* ran two photos side by side, one of Graham in the pulpit exhorting the crowd, and the other of the head usher carrying a bag with the love offering that totaled $16,000. The implication to the readers was unmistakable.[34]

While Graham discussed finances earlier with his team, they decided that he would receive a fixed salary and remove the possibility of having financial motives tied to evangelism.[35] His initial salary from the newly formed Billy Graham Evangelistic Association (BGEA) was $15,000 a year plus travel expenses. All offerings received went directly to the BGEA, which was governed by a board.

The Modesto Manifesto from *Just As I Am* by Billy Graham

One afternoon during the Modesto [California] meetings, I called the team together. . . . Then I asked them to go to their rooms for an hour and list all the problems they could think of that evangelists and evangelism encountered. When they returned, the lists were remarkably similar, and in a short amount of time, we made a series of resolutions or commitment among ourselves that would guide us in our future evangelistic work. In reality, it was more of an informal understanding among ourselves—a shared commitment to do all we could do to uphold the Bible's standard of absolute integrity and purity for evangelists.

32. Wacker, *America's Pastor*, 127; Scharpff, *History of Evangelism*, 326.

33. Michael G. Long, *The Legacy of Billy Graham: Critical Reflections on America's Greatest Evangelist* (Louisville: Westminster John Knox, 2008), 151. Cf. Wacker, *America's Pastor*, 125–34.

34. Harold H. Martin, "A Vivid Portrait of the Famous Revivalist, Billy Graham," *Saturday Evening Post*, April 13, 1963, 22, cited in M. Taylor, *Exploring Evangelism*, 562.

35. Wacker, *America's Pastor*, 15–16; M. Taylor, *Exploring Evangelism*, 552.

> The first point on our combined list was money. Nearly all evangelists at that time—including us—were supported by love offerings taken at the meetings. The temptation to wring as much money as possible out of an audience, often with strong emotional appeals, was too great for some evangelists. In addition, there was little or no accountability for finances. It was a system that was easy to abuse—and led to the charge that evangelists were in it only for the money. I had been drawing a salary from YFC (Youth for Christ) and turning all offerings from YFC meetings over to YFC committees, but my new independent efforts in citywide campaigns required separate finances. . . .
>
> The second item on the list was the danger of sexual immorality. We all knew of evangelists who had fallen into immorality while separated from their families by travel. We pledged among ourselves to avoid any situation that would have even the appearance of compromise or suspicion. From that day on, I did not travel, meet or eat alone with a woman other than my wife. We determined that the Apostle Paul's mandate to the young pastor Timothy would be ours as well: "Flee . . . youthful lusts" (2 Tim. 1:22, KJV).
>
> Our third concern was the tendency of many evangelists to carry on their work apart from the local church, even to criticize local pastors and churches openly and scathingly. We were convinced, however, that this was not only counterproductive but also wrong from the Bible's standpoint. We determined to cooperate with all who would cooperate with us in the public proclamation of the Gospel, and to avoid an antichurch or anticlergy attitude.
>
> The fourth and final issue was publicity. The tendency among some evangelists was to exaggerate their successes or to claim higher attendance numbers than they really had. This likewise discredited evangelism and brought the whole enterprise under suspicion. It often made the press so suspicious of evangelists that they refused to take notice of their work. In Modesto we committed ourselves to integrity in our publicity and our reporting. (Billy Graham, *Just As I Am: The Autobiography of Billy Graham* (San Francisco: HarperCollins, 1997), 128–29)

BGEA Crusades

Preparation for Graham's crusades began generally two years in advance as his staff directed local leaders to promote the crusade, enlist prayer and financial support, arrange for the large choir, train counselors, and advertise the meetings.[36] The climax of each meeting was the moment of decision, when listeners were invited to respond to the gospel and come forward to express their decision for Christ.[37] Often tens of thousands of people made decisions and came to stand in front of the platform, where they met with trained lay Christian workers who forwarded their names for follow-up with the six-week Bible study.[38]

Some people attended Graham's meetings out of curiosity to hear what the "celebrity evangelist" would say.[39] Since the crusades continued for several weeks, seekers had multiple opportunities to hear various themes of the gospel, including personal sin, God's love, Jesus's sacrifice on the cross, new birth, and heaven and hell.[40] Hearing multiple messages week after week had a persuasive impact on the listeners.

Graham's crusades were catalytic events that rallied thousands of Christians in a coordinated effort to invite their non-Christian friends, family, and coworkers to hear the celebrity evangelist. The crusades were also a catalyst to equip thousands of Christians in personal evangelism and new believer follow-up. Typically, the advance team trained ten thousand to twenty thousand Christian laypeople before Graham arrived in town, hosting a six-night course on personal evangelism.[41] In some instances, spiritual seekers became Christians before hearing Graham preach. The invitation to the crusade by a friend and the evangelism training that the Christian received led to conversations about Jesus Christ that resulted in the friend's conversion to faith. Graham's crusades were simply the "rally point" for Christians to engage in evangelism for themselves.

Graham's Worldwide Evangelism

In addition to maintaining a humble attitude, Graham willingly submitted to the Modesto Manifesto—a compact that dealt with money received from offerings, reporting attendances accurately, and never being alone with a woman other than one's wife.[42] In his self-effacing manner, he credited God for everything that happened through his ministry. In total, he preached the gospel to an estimated 215 million people who attended one of his more

36. M. Taylor, *Exploring Evangelism*, 556.
37. Wacker, *America's Pastor*, 55–56, 63–66.
38. Wacker, *America's Pastor*, 143, 151.
39. Wacker, *America's Pastor*, 13, 29, 68, 78.
40. Wacker, *America's Pastor*, 33–35, 41–43, 49–51, 54.
41. M. Taylor, *Exploring Evangelism*, 554.
42. Wacker, *One Soul at a Time*, 27–29; Wacker, *America's Pastor*, 10–11, 56, 304.

than four hundred meetings, simulcasts, and evangelistic crusades in 185 countries and territories.[43]

Beyond evangelistic crusades and films, Graham and Carl F. H. Henry organized the World Congress on Evangelism, held in Berlin, Germany, in 1966.[44] Following this event, in 1974, Graham led the committee of the International Congress on World Evangelization in Lausanne, Switzerland.[45] The Lausanne Congress produced the Lausanne Covenant, a statement of the church's orthodox beliefs and commitment to evangelism. In part, the Lausanne Covenant states, "We believe the gospel is God's good news for the whole world, and we are determined, by his grace, to obey Christ's commission to proclaim it to all mankind and to make disciples of every nation. We desire, therefore, to affirm our faith and our resolve, and to make public our covenant."[46] At Lausanne, nearly 2,700 leaders and evangelists attended from 150 countries for the purpose of strengthening the global church for world evangelization.[47]

Luis Palau of Argentina

Another evangelist who held similar crusades and stressed the importance of personal evangelism was Luis Palau (1934–2021). At twelve years of age, Palau devoted his life to Jesus Christ. Four years later, he heard a radio broadcast by Billy Graham that inspired him to preach as well.[48] Palau was born in Maschwitz, Buenos Aires, Argentina. When his father died, the financial hardship on his mother and siblings forced him to leave a British boarding school and work at a bank in Córdoba.

After hearing Ray Stedman, a visiting pastor from California, preach at a theater in Buenos Aires, Palau spoke with him and Stedman encouraged

43. "Billy Graham, 1918–2018: Official Obituary," February 21, 2018, https://memorial.billygraham.org/official-obituary/.

44. Graham, *Just as I Am*, 562–67; Wacker, *One Soul at a Time*, 188–89.

45. Wacker, *America's Pastor*, 18, 38–39; Graham, *Just as I Am*, 567–73.

46. John Stott, *The Lausanne Covenant: Complete Text with Study Guide* (Peabody, MA: Hendrickson, 2012), 11.

47. Opoku Onyinah, "A Pentecostal Perspective on the Lausanne Movement," in *The Lausanne Movement: A Range of Perspectives*, ed. Margunn Serigstad Dahle, Lars Dahle, and Knud Jørgensen (Eugene, OR: Wipf & Stock, 2014), 419–25.

48. Ruth Tucker, *From Jerusalem to Irian Jaya: A Biographical History of Christian Missions* (Grand Rapids: Zondervan, 2004), 423. See Luis Palau, *The Luis Palau Story: An Autobiography* (London: Pickering, 1981). For Palau's relationship with Graham, see Graham, *Just as I Am*, 438; Wacker, *America's Pastor*, 79–80.

him to come to Palo Alto, California, for a summer internship with him at Peninsula Bible Church.[49] Following the internship, Palau enrolled at Multnomah School of the Bible in Portland, Oregon.

Despite his dedication to his studies, Palau was tempted to give up the Christian life, having become weary of trying to live the Christian faith in his own strength. Renewal came, however, when he heard a chapel message by Major Ian Thomas (1914–2007) of the Torchbearers in England. After the message, Palau went to his room, knelt by his bed, and with tears in his eyes prayed in his native Spanish, "Lord, now I understand! The whole thing is 'not I, but Christ in me'" (Gal. 2:20).[50]

Following graduation from Multnomah, Palau and his wife, Patricia, served as missionaries in Mexico and Colombia for eight years, and then returned to Oregon. He began working for Billy Graham as a Spanish translator, and in 1970, Graham provided seed money for him to launch his own evangelistic ministry.[51] Palau began in Mexico City, where his evangelistic crusade drew 106,000 people with 6,670 making decisions for Christ. With invitations from other places, he saw crowds pack stadiums and arenas in countries as diverse as Guatemala and Hungary, Brazil and India, Indonesia and Costa Rica, Peru and Romania, and Singapore and the Soviet Union.

In addition to preaching the gospel in person, Palau hosted three daily radio programs, including an English program carried by nine hundred stations in twenty-three countries, and two Spanish programs carried by 880 stations in twenty-five countries. After a conversation with a former Chinese government official at Beijing, he published a book titled *A Friendly Dialogue between an Atheist and a Christian*.[52]

Palau saw the value of large crusades. The large meetings could sway public opinion in whole cities toward Christ and the gospel. The momentum of the meetings often emboldened Christians in their personal witness.

Despite his commitments to public and personal evangelism, Palau saw the need to organize evangelical leaders to address social concerns of the broader community.[53] For example, in Portland, Oregon, he worked along-

49. Mark S. Mitchell, *Portrait of Integrity: The Life of Ray C. Stedman* (Grand Rapids: Discovery, 2004), 113.

50. Ramey, "Pathfinder in Evangelism," 183.

51. Nancy Haught, "In Portland: Evangelist Palau Drew Inspiration, Help from Graham," *The Oregonian*, June 24, 2005, A13.

52. See Luis Palau and Zhao Qizheng, *A Friendly Dialogue between an Atheist and a Christian* (Grand Rapids: Zondervan, 2009).

53. Ramey, "Pathfinder in Evangelism," 185.

side officials and pastors to address the city's homeless challenges through an initiative called the Season of Service.[54] While Palau held unwaveringly to the need for the verbal proclamation of the gospel, he supported the value of building goodwill with the city in order to establish a platform from which to share the good news.

Reinhard Bonnke of Germany

While Graham and Palau held crusades around the world, the German Pentecostal evangelist Reinhard Bonnke (1940–2019) preached to large crowds in Africa. Born in Königsberg, Germany, Bonnke grew up during the Second World War. During the evacuation of East Prussia, his family relocated to Denmark.[55] At the age of nine, he converted to Christ, and the following year he experienced Spirit baptism. Moreover, he sensed God's call to go as a missionary to Africa.

To prepare for this work, Bonnke studied at the Bible College of Wales in Swansea. After graduation, he worked as a pastor in Germany and led a series of evangelistic meetings at Rendsburg that led to other invitations in Germany.

In 1967, he began his work in Africa, preaching in Lesotho in southern Africa, and then around the continent. Yet he became frustrated with the slow progress and his meager results. Then he began to have recurring dreams in which he saw a map of Africa and heard God saying, "Africa shall be saved."[56] This led him to change his strategy from a small-scale missionary approach to large-scale evangelism. By faith, he rented a stadium at Gaborone, Botswana, and began to hold meetings with one hundred people in attendance, but soon the stadium meetings grew to thousands.

In 1974, Bonnke founded Christ for All Nations (CFAN), based originally in Johannesburg, South Africa, and relocated later to Frankfurt, Germany. In 1984, he ordered a tent that could accommodate thirty-four thousand people, but when it was destroyed by a sudden windstorm, he and his team

54. Tom Krattenmaker, *The Evangelicals You Don't Know: Introducing the Next Generation of Christians* (Lanham, MD: Rowman & Littlefield, 2013), 27–31.

55. Reinhard Bonnke, *Living a Life of Fire* (Jupiter, FL: Harvester, 2019); Colin Whittaker, *Reinhard Bonnke: A Passion for the Gospel* (Eastbourne, UK: Kingsway, 2005).

56. Ezekiel Ajani, "Reinhard Bonnke's Crusades in Nigeria: Cultural Adaptation or Evangelical Renewal," in *Creativity and Change in Nigerian Christianity*, ed. David O. Ogungbile and Akintunde E. Akinade (Lagos, Nigeria: Malthouse, 2010), 111.

held the campaign in the open air with an estimated 100,000 people in attendance and thousands converted to Christ, both blacks and whites.[57]

In 2000, Bonnke hosted a major crusade at Lagos, Nigeria. In the middle of Africa with little medical care, he preached about salvation and healing. His marketing tagline, "Come and Receive Your Miracle," drew an estimated 1.6 million people in a single night.[58] In conjunction with the major crusades, he led Fire Conferences to instruct and inspire Christians in personal evangelism, giving every participant a copy of his book *Evangelism by Fire*.[59]

Like other mass evangelists, Bonnke faced criticisms. It was reported that CFAN did not disclose financial reports and inflated attendance numbers, and few converts assimilated into local churches.[60] However, Bonnke's campaigns were known to promote unity among churches and Christians.

Parachurch Disciple-Making

Besides mass meetings like those of Bonnke, Palau, and Graham that required large venues and organizational and marketing expertise, other Christian leaders focused their efforts on equipping laypeople for personal witness. While laypeople often considered themselves less polished than celebrity evangelists and lacked confidence initially, their witness to the gospel could be nurtured and personalized to reach family, friends, neighbors, and coworkers. Even Graham, as mentioned above, turned to Dawson Trotman for help to train Christians for personal evangelism and new believer follow-up. Besides Trotman, people like Bill Bright focused on equipping laypeople. However, all of these men—Graham, Trotman, and Bright—were profoundly influenced by a woman, Henrietta Mears.

Henrietta Mears

Henrietta C. Mears (1890–1963) was born into a Baptist family in Fargo, North Dakota.[61] She graduated from the University of Minnesota and, after a decade

57. Tuttle, *Story of Evangelism*, 398.

58. Tuttle, *Story of Evangelism*, 412.

59. Ajani, "Reinhard Bonnke's Crusades in Nigeria," 118. See Reinhard Bonnke, *Evangelism by Fire* (Lake Mary, FL: Charisma House, 2011).

60. Ajani, "Reinhard Bonnke's Crusades in Nigeria," 110, 117, 120–23, 125–30.

61. Earl O. Roe, *Dream Big: The Henrietta Mears Story* (Ventura, CA: Gospel Light, 2012), 58–59.

of teaching, took a sabbatical that included a trip to California. In Los Angeles she met leaders of Hollywood Presbyterian Church who offered her the role of director of Christian education, which she began in 1928. Within two years, the church's Sunday school had grown to an average of 4,200 people per week.

In 1933, Mears founded Gospel Light Publications that produced Sunday school materials for children across the country. In 1937, she founded the Forest Home, the Christian camp where Graham came to his conviction about the authority of the Bible. In 1953, she wrote the widely read book *What the Bible Is All About.*[62] Her influence was felt not merely through gospel teaching and literature; she also mentored young leaders such as those mentioned.[63]

At Hollywood Presbyterian Church, as well as at Forest Home, Mears taught the Scriptures and spoke into the lives of young adults. In these settings, she personally led seekers to faith in Christ while those she mentored watched her in action as she shared the gospel clearly and compellingly. Graham, Trotman, and Bright were drawn into her circle, in which she inspired them to do great things for God and challenged them to pursue their particular ministries of evangelism and discipleship.[64] For this reason, Mears has been described as the "mother" of modern evangelicalism.[65]

Dawson Trotman and the Navigators

Dawson E. Trotman (1906–1956) founded the Navigators ministry in 1933. This ministry did not end with "getting people saved" but rather focused on "making disciples" who would obey everything that Jesus commanded (Matt. 28:19). As Trotman worked in Los Angeles, he benefited from the basic discipleship principles that he had learned.[66] In turn, he taught the same principles, applying the apostle Paul's words spoken to his disciple Timothy, "And the things you have heard me say in the presence of many wit-

62. See Henrietta C. Mears, *What the Bible Is All About* (Ventura, CA: Regal, 1953).

63. Graham, *Just as I Am*, 137–38, 145–46.

64. Helen Kooiman Hosier, *100 Christian Women Who Changed the Twentieth Century* (Grand Rapids: Baker, 2000), 170–75.

65. Arlin C. Migliazzo, *Mother of Modern Evangelicalism: The Life and Legacy of Henrietta Mears* (Grand Rapids: Eerdmans, 2020). Cf. Wendy Murray Zoba, "The Grandmother of Us All," *Christianity Today*, September 16, 1996, https://www.christianitytoday.com/ct/1996/september16/6ta044.html.

66. Ken Albert, Susan Fletcher, and Doug Hankins, eds., *Dawson Trotman: In His Own Words* (Colorado Springs: NavPress, 2014), 43.

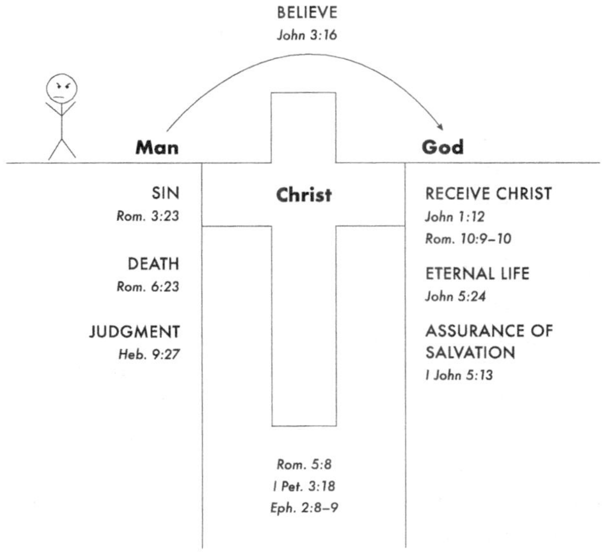

Figure 12.1. "Bridge of Life" as taught by Dawson Trotman and The Navigators. *(David M. Gustafson)*

nesses entrust to reliable people who will also be qualified to teach others" (2 Tim. 2:2).

Trotman practiced these principles with sailors in the US Navy, beginning with Les Spencer. They spent hours together studying the Bible, praying, and memorizing Scripture verses, and Spencer's life was transformed. When he was asked by a shipmate about the reason for his changed life, Spencer brought him to Trotman and said, "Teach him what you taught me." Trotman responded, "You teach him!"[67]

In order to equip sailors for evangelism, Trotman developed a simple illustration called the "Bridge of Life" that a Christian could sketch on a piece of paper.[68] The illustration combined Scripture verses and showed that the only way for sinful humans to be reconciled to God was through

67. Lorne Sanny, *The Pathfinder: A Condensed Story of Dawson E. Trotman* (Colorado Springs: Discipleship Library [reprinted from *Crusade* magazine, London], n.d.), 13.

68. For Trotman's view of evangelism, see Ken Albert, Susan Fletcher, and Doug Hankins, eds., *Dawson Trotman: In His Own Words* (Colorado Springs: NavPress, 2014), 164–73.

Jesus Christ—the bridge between humankind and God. After Trotman introduced this illustration, over a hundred men on the USS *West Virginia* began to share the gospel. Trotman intended this method of gospel witness to be reproducible, allowing laymen to learn and teach it quickly, and new Christians to replicate it easily. By the end of the Second World War, thousands of sailors around the world had learned to share the Bridge of Life, along with the Navigators' principle of spiritual reproduction.

Tragically, Trotman drowned just after saving a girl from drowning. While at the Word of Life campground at Schroon Lake, he and the girl were thrown into the water when their boat hit a sharp wave.[69] Trotman used all his strength to keep the girl above water until another swimmer reached her. Although she was safe, Trotman was too fatigued to swim and drowned before anyone could reach him. His friend Billy Graham spoke at the funeral.

The Navigators soon grew beyond the military to establish ministries on university campuses and with businessmen and women in every occupation. In 1949, the ministry's first overseas missionary traveled to China, and other missionaries soon followed to other countries. The Navigators' facility in Glen Eyrie, Colorado, for decades has provided various programs for Christian growth and training for students and laypeople in evangelistic witness.

Bill Bright and Cru

William R. "Bill" Bright (1921–2003) began his ministry with college students. Bright was born in Coweta, Oklahoma, and studied economics at Northeastern State University in Tahlequah, Oklahoma. As a young man, he moved to Los Angeles, where he founded a company called Bright's California Confections. He attended First Presbyterian Church of Hollywood, where he dedicated his life to Christ under the ministry of Mears.[70]

Bright continued theological studies at Fuller Theological Seminary but soon sensed God's call to reach college students with the gospel at nearby UCLA.[71] He sold his candy business, withdrew from his theological program, and rented a house in Los Angeles near the university. In 1951, he founded Campus Crusade for Christ, known today as Cru. The first board

69. Mark Senter, "Daws: Dawson Trotman," in Woodbridge, *More Than Conquerors*, 168.

70. Senter, "Daws," 168.

71. Richard Quebedeaux, *I Found It: The Story of Bill Bright and Campus Crusade* (San Francisco: Harper & Row, 1979), 16–18.

of directors consisted of Mears, Graham, Trotman, and J. Edwin Orr, a professor at Fuller.[72]

After a few months, more than 250 students, including Olympic champion Rafer Lewis Johnson, had professed faith in Jesus Christ.[73] A year later, Bright expanded the ministry to other campuses on the West Coast, and by 1960 there were 109 staff ministering on forty campuses in fifteen states, as well as in South Korea and Pakistan.

To prepare students and staff to share the gospel, Bright developed a twenty-minute gospel presentation called "God's Plan for Your Life." The presentation, which contained the "four spiritual laws," was memorized and shared with nonbelievers using illustrations drawn on a napkin and asking questions. This presentation was first published in tract form in 1965 as *Have You Heard of the Four Spiritual Laws?* and was commonly referred to as the Four Spiritual Laws.[74] Since then over a billion copies have been published in numerous formats and languages.

Using this evangelistic tool, the ministry trained Christian students to share the gospel in dormitories, fraternities, and sororities and with sports teams. Leadership training classes prepared students to lead Bible studies and to make disciples who would do the same. By following the motto "win, build, send," the vision of Cru was to win students to Christ, build them in the Christian faith, and send them to do the same with others.

By the year 1971, a two-day conference called the Lay Institute for Evangelism was organized to equip laypeople for this same purpose. The popular use of the Four Spiritual Laws by students and laypeople, in part, defined evangelism and the gospel for many churches and Christians during the twentieth century. This tool was intended for a Christian to engage in a conversation about the gospel with a non-Christian by presenting the themes of God's love, humankind's sin, Jesus Christ, and faith, with corresponding Scripture texts to be read. While the Four Spiritual Laws provided a means for spiritual conversations, Bright emphasized that ultimately evangelism was "taking the initiative to share Christ in the power of the Holy Spirit and leaving the results to God."[75] The Four Spiritual Laws presentation was a tool to help this happen.

72. Quebedeaux, *I Found It*, 16–18.

73. John G. Turner, *Bill Bright and Campus Crusade for Christ: The Renewal of Evangelicalism in Postwar America* (Chapel Hill: University of North Carolina Press, 2008), 59.

74. Turner, *Bill Bright*, 99–103.

75. Bill Bright, *Witnessing without Fear: How to Share Your Faith with Confidence* (Orlando: NewLife, 2003), 71.

In 1972, Campus Crusade hosted Explo '72 in Dallas, Texas, with the goal of gathering eighty thousand high school and college students for training in personal evangelism, and casting the vision for them to take the gospel to the world.[76] The week of events included training sessions, door-to-door evangelism, and nightly meetings at the Cotton Bowl Stadium, which featured musicians such as Larry Norman and Johnny Cash, well-known speakers such as Billy Graham, and personal testimonies of Christian faith by professional athletes.[77]

In 1976, the ministry launched the largest evangelistic campaign in American history, called Here's Life America, which reached ten million homes in the United States and Canada, with participation by fourteen thousand churches.[78] A highly visible media campaign with television, radio, and billboards generated interest, which was followed by laypeople calling through their local telephone directories to ask if they could present the Four Spiritual Laws over the telephone. Those who agreed and prayed to accept Jesus Christ were visited by trained Christians of the community, given follow-up materials, and encouraged to join a Bible study in their neighborhood.[79] An estimated eighty-seven thousand decisions were recorded of people believing the gospel for the first time.

Over the years, Cru has demonstrated creativity in its evangelistic methods. Ministries such as Athletes in Action, apologist Josh McDowell, and illusionist André Kole provided large evangelistic events to reach college students. The "Jesus Film," led by Paul Eschelman and based on the Gospel of Luke, has been translated into 1,834 languages.[80] Since its release in 1979, Cru has partnered with hundreds of organizations and denominations so that the film has been viewed by audiences totaling 8.1 billion, with an estimated 572 million indicating decisions to believe in Christ.

76. Patrick G. McLeod, "An Historical and Theological Analysis of Campus Crusade for Christ's Evangelistic Practice in Two American University Contexts" (PhD diss., Boston University, 2009), 31.

77. Turner, *Bill Bright*, 139–46.

78. Turner, *Bill Bright*, 158–75.

79. Terry, *Evangelism*, 189–90.

80. Turner, *Bill Bright*, 182–84; "Official Jesus Film Project Ministry Statistics," January 22, 2020, https://www.jesusfilm.org/about/learn-more/statistics.html.

Joon Gon Kim and Korea Cru

Cru was established in South Korea under the leadership of Joon Gon Kim (1925–2009) from Chi-do Island.[81] After the Second World War, Korea was divided when Communists gained control of the northern state. In 1950, Kim was studying to become a Presbyterian minister when North Korean soldiers invaded South Korea and began murdering civilians who disagreed with Communist ideology. Kim and his family fled to his father's house at Chi-do Island.

At the hands of Communists, Kim's father and wife were brutally killed before his very eyes. He was beaten with a club several times, and once was nearly thrown from a cliff to the sea, when his life was spared. In the midst of these trials, he experienced fellowship with Jesus in extraordinary ways. Kim emerged not fearing men but fearing only God and responded to God's call on his life to reach Communists with the gospel.

With the fear of Communists gone, he took his daughter with him to visit the home of a Communist man. Shocked by Kim's boldness, the man invited him in. Kim reported, "As I spoke to him of salvation through Christ, he wept over his sins. We prayed together, and this man later became a faithful witness among the Communists."[82] When United Nations troops retook Chi-do Island, Kim asked them to spare the lives of the Communists who had killed his family. This merciful act enabled him later to serve as a pastor in the area where he led several of the former Communists to Christ.

In 1953, when hostilities ended, Kim began to preach at youth meetings in an effort to reach college students. He soon realized that he needed better preparation, and so he traveled to Southern California to enroll at Fuller Theological Seminary, founded by Charles Fuller. There he met Cru staff, who arranged for him to meet Bill Bright.[83] Kim said, "I saw that Campus Crusade's simple, basic message was the key that God could use to open the hearts of men. They talked of Jesus Christ, the new birth, the Holy Spirit, prayer, and Scripture."[84]

Bright convinced Kim to join the staff and return to Korea to begin Campus Crusade's first overseas ministry. He returned in 1958 and, shortly

81. Bill Bright, "Heart and Seoul: Joon Gon Kim," in Woodbridge, *More Than Conquerors*, 187.

82. Bright, "Heart and Seoul," 188.

83. Turner, *Bill Bright*, 94–95.

84. Bright, "Heart and Seoul," 188.

after his arrival, met with forty college professors, whom he trained to reach students with the gospel.

In 1960, Kim climbed a mountain, accompanied by two hundred Christian students, for a day of prayer and fasting, asking God to evangelize Korea. Kim said, "There is no shortcut for evangelism apart from prayer."[85] Although he started his ministry by evangelizing students, he organized two large training conferences that shaped the course of the Korean church.[86] In 1974, over 323,000 delegates attended Explo '74 with evening meetings open to the public reaching attendances of over one million people every night for five nights. In 1980, the campaign Here's Life South Korea drew an estimated ten million. The participants of this campaign shared the gospel with people in their neighborhoods and saw 1.3 million respond to receive Christ. Pastors of the eight largest churches in South Korea attributed the numerical growth of their congregations to the evangelism training the churches received from Kim's ministry.

Televangelism

In the second half of the twentieth century, the number of Christian radio and television programs increased exponentially. By 1980, there were 1,450 Christian radio and television stations throughout the world with audiences of 292 million.[87] In addition, there were 834 million who heard or viewed Christian broadcasts over stations with general audiences.

Oral Roberts of Oklahoma

The "televangelist" Oral Roberts (1918–2009) of Pontotoc County, Oklahoma, began his life in poverty and nearly died of tuberculosis. After high school, he studied at Oklahoma Baptist University and Phillips University. Ordained first as a Pentecostal Holiness preacher at age eighteen, he pastored small churches at the start of his ministry.[88]

When Roberts was twenty-nine, he picked up his Bible, which fell open to the verse "I wish above all things that thou mayest prosper and be in health, even as thy soul prospereth" (3 John 2 KJV). The next day, he pur-

85. Bright, "Heart and Seoul," 190.
86. Turner, *Bill Bright*, 151–53.
87. Rudnick, *Speaking the Gospel*, 207–8.
88. Terry, *Evangelism*, 203.

chased a Buick automobile and announced that God had called him to heal the sick. He began traveling as a faith-healing evangelist with a tent that could hold three thousand people seated in folding chairs.

In 1947, Roberts launched into radio, and in 1954, he entered television. As a pioneer Pentecostal televangelist, he soon attracted a wide viewership. His messages taught listeners to expect miracles, and his emphasis on "seed-faith" further laid the foundation for what became known as the prosperity gospel—the promise of financial wealth and physical health to all Christians.[89]

In time, Roberts's ministry was criticized for financial problems; lawsuits; excesses of clothing, jewelry, and residences; and his self-professed ultimatums from God to raise money or die. Despite a checkered history, Roberts conducted over three hundred crusades on six continents and laid his hands on more than two million people for their healing.

In 1963, he founded Oral Roberts University in Tulsa, Oklahoma, in what he described as direct obedience to God's command. The school has graduated notable alumni such as Kenneth Copeland, Billy Joe Daugherty, Ted Haggard, Richard Roberts, and Joel Osteen. Despite the overwhelming challenges of establishing a charismatic liberal arts university, Roberts never lost sight of the importance of ministering the gospel to the whole person in spirit, mind, and body.

As Christian television broadcasting grew in popularity, other preachers entered the limelight, hosting TV talk shows and televising their worship services in order to expand their reach into homes around the globe. For example, in 1961, Pat Robertson launched into broadcasting by founding the Christian Broadcasting Network (CBN).[90]

Scandals and Exploitations

In 1974, Jim Bakker introduced the PTL Club to a station in Charlotte, North Carolina. Bakker's popularity climbed until he faced financial and sex scandals.[91] Hush money was paid to a church secretary for an alleged rape leading to his resignation from PTL. As an ordained clergyman, he was de-

89. Simon Coleman, *The Globalisation of Charismatic Christianity: Spreading the Gospel of Prosperity* (Cambridge: Cambridge University Press, 2000), 41. See Oral Roberts, *A Daily Guide to Miracles and Successful Living through Seed-Faith* (Grand Rapids: Revell, 1975), 228–31.

90. Ben Armstrong, *The Electric Church* (Nashville: Nelson, 1979), 101–2.

91. Jim Bakker, *I Was Wrong: The Untold Story of the Shocking Journey from PTL Power to Prison and Beyond* (Nashville: Nelson, 1997), 512.

frocked by the Assemblies of God. Investigations for misusing funds brought about his conviction and imprisonment, and the strain of it all resulted in his divorce from his wife and cohost, Tammy Faye Bakker (1942–2007).[92]

Robert Schuller (1926–2015) of the mainline Reformed Church in America launched his program *Hour of Power* from Garden Grove, California, while the Southern Baptist preacher Jerry Falwell (1933–2007) televised his worship services from Lynchburg, Virginia. In 1971, Falwell raised millions of dollars to launch Liberty University.

Televangelists spent a considerable amount of time during their programs appealing for money to cover the costs of airtime.[93] In addition, they raised funds to build schools, medical facilities, and, for Bakker, a theme park called Heritage USA that eventually went bankrupt and remained in disrepair. In most cases, more Christians tuned into the television programs than non-Christians.[94] Televangelists spoke more often about what God was doing on their programs than addressing specific needs and questions of non-Christian viewers. Nevertheless, by virtue of the programs' broad reach, a small percentage of non-Christians tuned in and heard testimonies of changed lives, lyrics of gospel songs, and messages of God's love, forgiveness, and miracles through Jesus Christ.[95]

The majority of televangelists followed in the footsteps of Aimee Semple McPherson, coming from Pentecostal churches; these include Oral Roberts, Rex Humbard, Jimmy Swaggart, Jim Bakker, James Robison, Paul Crouch, Robert Tilton, and Kenneth Copeland. They have emphasized the validity of experiencing God's supernatural healing power. A few have recognized that this aspect of their ministry is susceptible to fanaticism, extremism, and exploitation.

Televangelists have been susceptible to justifying their vices, expending funds for personal use, and rationalizing marital divorce, claiming the words of the psalmist, "Do not touch my anointed ones; do my prophets no harm" (Ps. 105:15). Without forms of biblical accountability, an authentic ministry can turn quickly to scandals and thereby dishonor the witness of Christ. The misuse of funds solicited for world evangelization only to be used to support

92. John Wigger, *PTL: The Rise and Fall of Jim and Tammy Faye Bakker's Evangelical Empire* (New York: Oxford University Press, 2017), 151–53. Cf. Elmer J. Theissen, *The Ethics of Evangelism* (Milton Keynes, UK: Authentic, 2014), 191.

93. Rudnick, *Speaking the Gospel*, 209.

94. Terry, *Evangelism*, 208.

95. Jeffrey K. Hadden and Charles E. Swann, *Prime Time Preachers: The Rising Power of Televangelism* (Reading, MA: Addison-Wesley, 1981), 51.

the lavish lifestyles of the evangelists and their families has disillusioned many donors and damaged the church's testimony to the gospel. While this susceptibility and temptation holds true for every Christian, the heightened visibility to the broader public requires moral safeguards such as those advocated by Billy Graham in the Modesto Manifesto.

Charismatic Movement

While televangelists were preaching messages on the airwaves, California real estate developer and dairyman Demos Shakarian (1913–1993), in 1951, founded the Full Gospel Business Men's Fellowship International, which moved Pentecostalism closer to the mainstream.[96] Shakarian used his organizational skills to facilitate evangelistic campaigns, working closely with people like Charles S. Price and Oral Roberts. Moreover, the Pentecostal evangelist David Wilkerson (1931–2011), known for his book *The Cross and the Switchblade*, founded an addiction recovery program called Teen Challenge that reached thousands of addicts, as well as gang members like Nicky Cruz, with the gospel.[97]

With influences like Shakarian, Roberts, and Wilkerson who held interdenominational meetings, the Pentecostalist practice of the gifts (*charismata*) of the Holy Spirit became more widely accepted. Soon a burgeoning charismatic movement spread to mainline churches in which pastors and laypeople adopted Pentecostal notions of spiritual gifts.[98] This renewal movement resulted in charismatic Catholics, Episcopalians, Lutherans, and Methodists. Many, however, kept a distance from Pentecostalism for theological and social reasons. Needless to say, the charismatic movement of the late 1960s and 1970s awakened people to God's presence and power, often leading to their conversion to faith in Christ.

96. Earle E. Cairns, *Christianity through the Ages: A History of the Christian Church* (Grand Rapids: Zondervan, 1996), 492–93. See Val Fotherby, *The Awakening Giant: The Miraculous Story of the Full Gospel Business Men's Fellowship International* (London: Marshall Pickering, 2000).

97. Gastón Espinosa, *Latino Pentecostals in America: Faith and Politics in Action* (Cambridge, MA: Harvard University Press, 2014), 341.

98. Rudnick, *Speaking the Gospel*, 220.

Jesus Movement

The "Jesus movement" was concurrent with the charismatic movement but composed of converts from the American counterculture of hippies.[99] The Jesus movement began on America's West Coast and spread across the country, and then to Europe and Central America. Among the early leaders of the loosely connected movement were Duane Pederson, Jack Sparks, Lonnie Frisbee, Chuck Smith, and Arthur Blessitt.[100] Frisbee served as an evangelist during the growth of the Calvary Chapel of Costa Mesa, California, along with Smith, who welcomed hippies coming to faith in Jesus.[101]

Arthur Blessitt quit his studies at Golden Gate Baptist Theological Seminary to reach hippies with the gospel.[102] He began at Griffith Park in Los Angeles and, in 1968, opened a coffeehouse called His Place located next to a topless dance club in Hollywood. Blessitt soon was known as the "minister of Sunset Strip."[103] After his inspiration to build a twelve-foot wooden cross, he began to make "cross walks" in the area, and then carried the cross from Los Angeles to Washington, DC, sharing the gospel with all who spoke with him.[104]

The Jesus movement sought a return to the life of the early church, and so "Jesus people" also "devoted themselves to the apostles' teaching and to fellowship, to the breaking of bread and to prayer" (Acts 2:42). They believed in "wonders and signs" (Acts 2:43). Another distinguishing element of many was the practice of communal living in which "all the believers were together and had everything in common" (Acts 2:44). Moreover, Jesus people engaged in evangelism, appealing often to Jesus's imminent return as described in Hal Lindsey's best-selling book *The Late Great Planet Earth*.[105]

99. Larry Eskridge, *God's Forever Family: The Jesus People Movement in America* (New York: Oxford University Press, 2018), 1, 12.

100. Ronald M. Enroth, Edward E. Ericson, and C. Breckinridge Peters, *The Jesus People: Old-Time Religion in the Age of Aquarius* (Grand Rapids: Eerdmans, 1972), 79, 86, 107–9, 155; Eskridge, *God's Forever Family*, 2, 3, 33, 38, 55–57, 95–96.

101. Eskridge, *God's Forever Family*, 8, 68–72.

102. Richard A. Bustraan, *The Jesus People Movement: A Story of Spiritual Revolution among the Hippies* (Eugene, OR: Pickwick, 2014), 39, 44, 49.

103. Arthur Blessitt, *Give Me a "J"! It's All about Jesus* (Denver: Legacy, 2006), viii.

104. Blessitt has continued his cross-walking for a total of 41,550 miles. "Evangelism in Every Book of the Bible," Arthur Blessitt website, https://www.blessitt.com/evangelism-in-every-book-of-the-bible/.

105. Eskridge, *God's Forever Family*, 25–32, 76, 163, 297. See Hal Lindsey, *The Late Great Planet Earth* (Grand Rapids: Zondervan, 1970).

Jesus Music

The music of the Jesus movement was extremely influential, forming a genre later called contemporary Christian music. "Jesus music" featured guitars,

Figure 12.2. **Jesus People concert, ca. 1970.** *(From the Duane Pederson Jesus People International and Hollywood Free Paper Collection; photo made available by Fuller Theological Seminary, Pasadena, California, www.fuller.edu)*

drums, and tambourines, emerging initially from rock street musicians who converted to Christ. Leading musicians of the Jesus movement were Barry McGuire, Randy Stonehill, Nancy Honeytree, Keith Green, and Larry Norman. Chuck Smith of Calvary Chapel developed a place for musicians to write and play their music and, in 1971, founded the first Christian rock label, Maranatha! Music, which featured the song "Seek Ye First," written and performed by Karen Lafferty.[106]

As Jesus people musicians formed Christian bands, they traveled across the country to play at coffeehouses and youth meetings, often with little or no advance invitation from the hosts.[107] As bands set up and began to play, teen-

106. Eskridge, *God's Forever Family*, 218–19.
107. Eskridge, *God's Forever Family*, 3–5, 166–67.

agers and young adults flocked to hear them. When seating capacity reached a maximum, people sat in aisles and on windowsills to hear and join in the singing. The evangelistic impact of the bands came from the song lyrics, testimonies from band members, and discussions afterward about what it meant to be born again (John 3:1–8). As teens and young adults converted to Christ, they shared the gospel with family and friends, inviting them to subsequent youth meetings, coffeehouses, and Christian concerts. Some of the Christians were prompted to reach out to the homeless, prostitutes, and drug addicts.

John Wimber and Power Evangelism

John Wimber (1934–1997) was a native of Kirksville, Missouri, who grew up with no religious beliefs.[108] He was a talented musician and at fifteen years of age played semiprofessionally at a venue in Orange, California. In 1963, Wimber converted to faith and enrolled immediately at Azusa Pacific College to study the Bible. After graduation he accepted a position at Yorba Linda Friends Church and, within a few years, was leading several Bible studies.

He was introduced to charismatic teachings about the gifts of the Spirit but was discouraged by some at his church from practicing them.[109] Therefore, he formed a house church that associated briefly with Calvary Chapel and, in 1977, joined the burgeoning group of churches called Vineyard Christian Fellowship. He began teaching from the Scriptures about signs and wonders such as healing, prophecy, and speaking in tongues, and, in 1980, was joined at his church by Lonnie Frisbee.[110]

Wimber promoted "power evangelism," which he described as "a presentation of the gospel that is rational but that also transcends the rational (though it is in no way 'irrational' or anti-rational). The explanation of the gospel—the clear proclamation of the finished work of Christ on the cross—comes with a demonstration of God's power through signs and wonders."[111] Wimber believed that signs and wonders were proof of Jesus's messiahship,

108. Donald E. Miller, *Reinventing American Protestantism: Christianity in the New Millennium* (Berkeley: University of California Press, 2007), 46–47.

109. Miller, *Reinventing American Protestantism*, 48–49.

110. Andy Park, Cindy Rethmeier, and Lester Ruth, *Worshiping with the Anaheim Vineyard: The Emergence of Contemporary Worship* (Grand Rapids: Eerdmans, 2017), 40.

111. John Wimber and Kevin Springer, *Power Evangelism* (Bloomington, MN: Chosen, 2009), 77.

evidences of the kingdom of God.[112] He argued that if the early church functioned in this way, then Jesus intended such evidences to be part of the disciples' witness throughout history. Wimber was critical, however, of Pentecostal and charismatic faith healers who appeared to normalize God's supernatural power, or manipulated people for material gain.

Wimber taught the importance of the priesthood of believers, emphasizing that clergy and laypeople are called equally to proclaim the gospel and to pray for the sick to be healed.[113] These activities were not limited to special services but could happen in the streets and neighborhoods by all Christians. He emphasized practical ministries to the poor as well, insisting that "kingdom ministry" must be directed to the dispossessed.[114] Thus, his congregation, Vineyard Christian Fellowship of Anaheim, served a million meals every year and operated a food bank to feed homeless people. Moreover, Wimber promoted church planting as the best means of evangelism. With his initial vision, the Association of Vineyard Churches has planted 2,400 churches worldwide.

Church-Based Evangelism Training

Lay evangelism training was introduced not merely by parachurch ministries but also by pastors and denominational leaders. The Home Mission Board of the Southern Baptist Convention sponsored Lay Evangelism Schools.[115] In order to prepare members for evangelism, laypeople were trained to share their testimonies and to explain the gospel using a tract titled *How to Have a Meaningful Life*, similar to the booklet *Have You Heard of the Four Spiritual Laws?* The Lutheran Church Missouri Synod developed Dialog Evangelism and Witness Workshops led by W. Leroy Biesenthal (1924–2015).[116] As an

112. Rich Nathan and Ken Wilson, *Empowered Evangelicals: Bringing Together the Best of the Evangelical and Charismatic Worlds* (Boise: Ampelon, 2009), 21–22, 34–35.

113. John Wimber, *Everyone Gets to Play: John Wimber's Writings and Teachings on Life Together in Christ* (Boise: Ampelon, 2008), 122–28.

114. Don Williams, "Theological Perspectives and Reflections on the Vineyard Christian Fellowship," in *Church, Identity, and Change: Theology and Denominational Structures in Unsettled Times*, ed. David A. Roozen and James R. Nieman (Grand Rapids: Eerdmans, 2005), 172. Wimber was influenced theologically by George Eldon Ladd's writings. Wimber and Springer, *Power Evangelism*, 12. See George Eldon Ladd, *Jesus and the Kingdom: The Eschatology of Biblical Realism* (Waco: Word, 1964), and Ladd, *The Gospel of the Kingdom* (Grand Rapids: Eerdmans, 1981).

115. Terry, *Evangelism*, 188.

116. Rudnick, *Speaking the Gospel*, 207.

evangelist, Biesenthal not only enjoyed sharing the gospel personally with others but equipped thousands of Lutherans to do the same, fulfilling the role of an evangelist to equip God's people for works of service (Eph. 4:11–12).

D. James Kennedy and Evangelism Explosion

D. James Kennedy (1930–2007), the pastor of Coral Ridge Presbyterian Church in Fort Lauderdale, Florida, developed a lay evangelism course called Evangelism Explosion. Kennedy had converted to faith in Christ after hearing a radio message by Donald Grey Barnhouse.

In 1959, when Kennedy arrived to begin as pastor of the Presbyterian church in Fort Lauderdale, forty-five people were meeting at an elementary school. As he began to offer teaching on evangelism, he noticed that fear kept them from sharing the gospel. However, when he took the people with him and modeled how to share the gospel using a basic outline and involving them in the conversation, their confidence increased and personal evangelism "took off like a rocket."[117]

In 1967, Kennedy formally launched the Evangelism Explosion ministry. An essential feature of his method was to ask people two diagnostic questions. The first was "Have you come to the place in your spiritual life where you know for certain that if you were to die today you would go to heaven?"[118] The second question was "Suppose you were to die today and stand before God and He were to ask you, 'Why should I let you into my heaven?' what would you say?"[119] If a person's answer to these questions was uncertain or depended on their own good works, the Christian would present the gospel around the themes of grace, humanity, God, Christ, and faith. This was followed by an invitation to join in a prayer of commitment to Christ. The training lasted for sixteen weeks and included memorization of the gospel outline and evangelism experiences with a trained Christian who led the way.

In 1978, Kennedy began a weekly television program called the *Coral Ridge Hour* that reached a weekly audience of three million viewers in two hundred countries.[120] More than broadcasting expository sermons, however,

117. Terry, *Evangelism*, 193.

118. D. James Kennedy, *Evangelism Explosion: Equipping Churches for Friendship, Evangelism, Discipleship, and Healthy Growth* (Wheaton, IL: Tyndale, 1996), 26.

119. Kennedy, *Evangelism Explosion*, 27.

120. J. Gordon Melton, Phillip C. Lucas, and Jon R. Stone, *Prime-Time Religion: An Encyclopedia of Religious Broadcasting* (Phoenix: Oryx, 1997), 172–73.

Kennedy employed Christian apologetics as he explained that Christianity had support from history and science. His messages formed the basis of his books titled *Why I Believe*, *Skeptics Answered*, and *Solving Bible Mysteries*. In *Skeptics Answered* he said, "Christianity has answers that are not only satisfying for the soul but also satisfying for the mind."[121] In 2001, he produced a one-hour television program titled *Who Is This Jesus?* that aired on CBS affiliates with actor Dean Jones, and he produced a follow-up program for Easter titled *Who Is This Jesus: Is He Risen?*

In 1979, Kennedy earned the PhD in education from New York University, writing his dissertation on the subject of equipping a congregation for evangelism.[122] He argued that pastors must be educated and equipped for spiritual conversations, and that they are responsible to equip the people of their congregation to do the same by modeling personal evangelism to them.[123]

Awana Clubs International

In 1941, the children's program of the North Side Gospel Center in Chicago began to lay the foundation for Awana, an organization whose name stands for "Approved Workmen Are Not Ashamed" (2 Tim. 2:15).[124] This ministry was designed to share the gospel with neighborhood children and form them for a life of following Christ. The club format emphasized activities and games, devotional messages, lessons and assignments, and Scripture memory.

This ministry began when pastors Lance Latham (1894–1985) and Art Rorheim (1918–2018) developed the weekly meetings. Soon other churches became interested, and so, in 1950, Awana Clubs was founded as a nondenominational ministry. Laypeople led groups of children with the goal of leading them to faith in Christ using, for example, an illustration called "The Gospel Wheel" and devotionals that illustrated the gospel with colors: black for sin, red for Jesus's blood, white for a cleansed heart, green for Christian

121. D. James Kennedy, *Skeptics Answered: Handling Tough Questions about the Christian Faith* (Sisters, OR: Multnomah, 1997), 13.

122. D. James Kennedy, "The Genesis, Development, and Expansion of Evangelism Explosion International, 1960–1976" (PhD diss., New York University, 1979).

123. Kennedy, *Evangelism Explosion*, 2–7.

124. Randall H. Balmer, *The Encyclopedia of Evangelicalism* (Louisville: Westminster John Knox, 2002), 45–46.

growth, and gold for the promise of heaven. Some assignments required that the children invite and bring a friend to a club meeting.

In 2019, Awana, as the global leader in child evangelism and discipleship, worked with 61,000 churches in 122 countries, reaching 4.8 million children every week.[125] Awana has published resources and offered training for adults to engage actively in evangelism with children and their families.

Church Growth Movement

In the second half of the twentieth century, the church growth movement emerged from the research of Donald A. McGavran (1897–1990), who was convinced that God desired for the gospel to be proclaimed so that spiritually lost people would be found and live as responsible members of the church.[126]

McGavran was born in Damoh, India, to missionary parents, and graduated from Yale Divinity School in 1922. Through the influence of John R. Mott and the Student Volunteer Movement (SVM), he went as a missionary to India in 1923, working primarily as an educator with the United Christian Missionary Society of the Christian Church, Disciples of Christ. After serving two terms in India, he traveled to New York to study at Columbia University, where he earned the PhD in 1935.[127] As a missiologist, McGavran held that social sciences aid our understanding of how people act and interact with each other, and that this knowledge is helpful in the task of evangelism.

McGavran observed that people come to faith in Christ and into church membership through interpersonal relationships. He observed that new converts function as "bridges of God" to reach whole networks of people.[128]

125. *Awana Annual Ministry Report 2019* (Streamwood, IL: Awana Clubs International, 2020), 15.

126. Donald A. McGavran, *Understanding Church Growth*, 3rd ed., rev. and ed. C. Peter Wagner (Grand Rapids: Eerdmans, 1990), 24; Priscilla Pope-Levison, *Models of Evangelism* (Grand Rapids: Baker Academic, 2020), 97–99.

127. Donald Anderson McGavran, "Education and the Beliefs of Popular Hinduism: A Study of the Beliefs of Secondary School Boys in Central Provinces, India, in Regard to Nineteen Major Beliefs of Popular Hinduism" (PhD diss., Columbia University, New York, 1935).

128. Donald A. McGavran, *Bridges of God: A Study in the Strategy of Missions* (Eugene, OR: Wipf & Stock, 2005), 21–23.

Moreover, he described a social phenomenon that he called the homogeneous unit principle (HUP), which posited that people become Christians more easily "without crossing racial, linguistic or class barriers."[129] In other words, these barriers make it exceedingly difficult, if not impossible, for non-Christians to accept the gospel, or for them to attend and join a local church. To many, Christianity and Christian churches appear culturally alien. Thus, to reach non-Christians with the gospel, the evangelist must not only present the gospel clearly for them to understand but also engage in forms of evangelism and church life that belong to their linguistic and cultural group so that they can understand and "feel at home in it."[130]

Decision-to-Disciple Gap

McGavran held strongly to the need for personal conversion to Christ but was concerned about methods of evangelism that did not produce tangible results—namely, baptized disciples who become responsible members of local churches. In this regard, he challenged the theological and methodological assumptions of several mass evangelists and parachurch organizations whose objective was merely to register decisions for Christ. Similarly, Win Arn (1923–2006) noted that for many popular forms of evangelism, there was a "decision to disciple gap" that needed to be addressed.[131] George Peters (1907–1988) of Dallas Theological Seminary was concerned equally that not all evangelism resulted in church growth, noting there was a discrepancy between professions of faith and church membership.[132]

After serving as a missionary in India, McGavran taught at Fuller Theological Seminary along with his protégé, C. Peter Wagner (1930–2016). Wagner and others such as John Wimber (1934–1997) and Carl F. George applied the principles of McGavran to the American context. The church growth movement subsequently grew in popularity, particularly among independent, evangelical, and charismatic churches. While intrigued by McGavran's understanding that God desired for the gospel to be proclaimed so that spiri-

129. McGavran, *Understanding Church Growth*, 176–78.

130. Rudnick, *Speaking the Gospel*, 199.

131. Win Arn, "A Church Growth Look at 'Here's Life,'" *Church Growth America*, January–February 1977, 4–7; Win Arn and Charles Arn, *The Master Plan for Making Disciples* (Pasadena, CA: Church Growth, 1982), 7.

132. Terry, *Evangelism*, 192.

tually lost people would be found, some pastors who applied these principles soon saw their congregations grow to become megachurches.

Denominational leaders learned about church growth as well, and implemented the principles in congregations under their care. Small group ministries in churches organized people by affinities of life phase and felt needs, applying the HUP. Social ministries, especially those that addressed felt needs like addiction and grief, were viewed as means of evangelism. In many cases, the goal to grow churches numerically turned churches inward. Spiritual gift assessments of laypeople were used mostly for programs within the local church with little attention given to using them for service to the broader neighborhood or community. Moreover, the goal to grow churches numerically often led to Christian nominalism, increased attendance without a commitment to Christian discipleship or living a devout life.[133]

Church Planting

Wimber's vision for church planting as the best means of evangelism promoted the church planting movement. Throughout church history, the founding of new congregations among non-Christians was consistently an effective means of making new Christians. Wimber and Wagner recognized that church planting required Christians to reach out to those around them with the gospel and to assimilate them into the church. New churches could begin with a "target group" in mind—applying McGavran's understanding of the HUP—and engage in forms of evangelism and congregational life from that linguistic and cultural group so that they would "feel at home."

In South Barrington, Illinois, Bill Hybels began Willow Creek Community Church in a movie theater with the goal of reaching the target profile of "unchurched Harry and Mary."[134] The target group was made to feel comfortable in "seeker services" with upbeat music and a message that addressed their questions, needs, and concerns. Rick Warren of Saddleback Church in the Saddleback Valley of Orange County, California, pioneered a "seeker-

133. The Reveal Study of Willow Creek discovered that many people were stalled in their spiritual lives. Greg L. Hawkins, Cally Parkinson, Eric Arnson, and Bill Hybels, *Reveal: Where Are You?* (Barrington, IL: Willow Creek Resources, 2007), 58.

134. Lynne Hybels and Bill Hybels, *Rediscovering Church: The Story and Vision of Willow Creek Community Church* (Grand Rapids: Zondervan, 1995), 57–60. See Lee Strobel, *Inside the Mind of Unchurched Harry and Mary: How to Reach Friends and Family Who Avoid God and the Church* (Grand Rapids: Zondervan, 2010).

friendly church" that targeted "Saddleback Sam," a research composite of the unchurched yuppie in the surrounding areas whose preferences shaped the style of the worship services and ministries.[135] While Hybels and Warren were tremendously gifted as evangelists who grew megachurches, their application of the HUP to people of a certain racial, ethnic, and economic class produced largely homogeneous congregations.

Cell Churches

The church growth movement pointed to churches outside America as well.[136] In 1958, David Yonggi Cho (1936–2021) founded Yoido Full Gospel Church in Seoul, South Korea. Ten years later, when plagued by ill health, Cho collapsed during a baptismal service.[137] Following this health crisis, he decentralized the congregation by reorganizing the members into cell groups of ten to thirty people with each group led by a lay cell leader. Every cell would meet on a weekday for worship and Bible study in the home of the cell leader and gather for a Sunday celebration service to worship corporately. Everyone within each cell was encouraged to invite friends and family members to the cell meetings to learn about Jesus Christ.[138]

The emphases on evangelism, multiplication of cell groups, and spiritual accountability led Cho's church to become the largest congregation in the world.[139] However, Cho explained that prayer was the key to conversion and cell multiplication, and the church held prayer vigils regularly at the Osanri prayer mountain.[140] Cho also established the International Theological Institute for theological and evangelistic training, and the Elim Welfare Village for the elderly, homeless, and unemployed.

135. Charles L. Chaney, *Church Planting at the End of the Twentieth Century* (Carol Stream, IL: Tyndale, 1993), 121.

136. C. Peter Wagner, *Your Church Can Grow: Seven Vital Signs of a Healthy Church* (Ventura, CA: Regal, 1993), 103–4.

137. Young-hoon Lee, "The Life and Ministry of David Yonggi Cho and the Yoido Full Gospel Church," in *David Yonggi Cho: A Close Look at His Theology and Ministry*, ed. Wonsuk Ma, William W. Menzies, and Hyeon-sung Bae (Baguio City, Philippines: Asian Pacific Theological Seminary, 2004), 7.

138. David Yonggi Cho and David Hostetler, *Successful Home Cell Groups* (Alachua, FL: Bridge-Logos, 1981), 55–69; Joel Comiskey, *2000 Years of Small Groups: A History of Cell Ministry in the Church* (Morena Valley, CA: CCS, 2014), 221–48.

139. Wagner, *Your Church Can Grow*, 103.

140. See Paul Yong-gi Cho, *Prayer: Key to Revival* (Nashville: Nelson, 1987).

Another cell-based church, Misión Carismática Internacional (MCI), led by Cesar and Claudia Castellanos of Bogotá, Colombia, began in 1983. This church was established on the principle that every Christian should make disciples, with the goal for each Christian to make twelve disciples.[141] Through this strategy that raises the expectation of disciple-making, MCI has become one of the largest churches in South America with more than 200,000 members and more than 45,000 cell groups.

Holistic Evangelism

Several events began to shape a new awareness of the need for evangelical Protestants to address social concerns in addition to personal salvation. This did not imply abandoning a commitment to the gospel but embracing the gospel mandate more fully. The Great Commission to "make disciples of all nations" was not simply a mandate to announce the gospel but required teaching disciples to obey everything that Jesus commanded (Matt. 28:19). This included the formation of Christians who apply, for example, Jesus's teachings of the Sermon on the Mount (Matt. 5–7) that address social concerns.[142]

When it became apparent to Tom Skinner (1942–1994) that social concern was excluded from the agenda of the National Association of Evangelicals that formed in 1942, he founded the National Black Evangelical Association (NBEA) in 1954.[143] Then he wrote a book titled *Black and Free* about his life as a gang leader in Harlem, and how, after his conversion to faith, leaving his gang was not without consequences. Despite threats, he became an evangelist, conducting meetings in the United States, Guyana, Bermuda, Barbados, and Jamaica.

In 1970, Skinner spoke at InterVarsity's Urbana conference about the need for racial reconciliation, and six years later published *How Black Is the Gospel?*[144] In this book he described his hope for reconciliation between blacks and whites, urbanites and suburbanites, and advocates of the social gospel and soul-saving gospel. As a leader of NBEA, Skinner saw

141. Comiskey, *2000 Years of Small Groups*, 254–57.

142. David J. Bosch says, "It is inadmissible to lift these words [Matt. 28:19] out of Matthew's gospel, as it were, allow them a life of their own, and understand them without any reference to the context in which they first appeared." *Transforming Mission: Paradigm Shifts in Theology of Mission* (Maryknoll, NY: Orbis, 2011), 58.

143. James Earl Massey, "The Unrepeatable Tom Skinner," *Christianity Today*, September 12, 1994, 11.

144. See Tom Skinner, *How Black Is the Gospel?* (Philadelphia: Holman, 1976).

the importance of calling evangelical organizations to engage in the social concerns of hunger, poverty, and racism. While some people urged him to disengage from white evangelicals, he refused to do so, insisting that the consciousness-raising process should happen with all believers in Christ.

In 1973, a group of evangelical Protestants drafted a document titled the "Chicago Declaration of Evangelical Social Concern."[145] This became the founding document for Evangelicals for Social Action (ESA), which organized the following year. With support from Carl F. H. Henry, Ron Sider, Jim Wallis, and John Perkins, the ESA sought to bring evangelism and social action together.[146]

In 1974, the Lausanne Congress under the leadership of Billy Graham, as mentioned above, and John R. W. Stott (1921–2011) discussed evangelism and its connection with social concern with others such as C. René Padilla (1932–2021) and Samuel Escobar.[147] After much discussion, the Lausanne Covenant reflected their thinking: "We express penitence both for our neglect and for having sometimes regarded evangelism and social concern as mutually exclusive. Although reconciliation with other people is not reconciliation with God, nor is social action evangelism, nor is political liberation salvation, nevertheless we affirm that evangelism and socio-political involvement are both part of our Christian duty. For both are necessary expressions of our doctrines of God and Man, our love for our neighbour and our obedience to Jesus Christ."[148]

While the debate about the relationship between verbal proclamation and social action continued, many began to think in terms of the integration of the two. Leaders such as John Perkins, who founded the Christian Community Development Association, provided both a model and resources for churches and Christian leaders.[149]

145. Brantley W. Gasaway, *Progressive Evangelicals and the Pursuit of Social Justice* (Chapel Hill: University of North Carolina Press, 2014), 8–10, 23–25.

146. Priscilla Pope-Levison, *Models of Evangelism* (Grand Rapids: Baker Academic, 2020), 122–23. While many acknowledged the need for social involvement, they continued to place priority on the verbal proclamation of the gospel. Rudnick, *Speaking the Gospel*, 212.

147. Daniel Salinas, *Latin American Evangelical Theology in the 1970's: The Golden Decade* (Leiden: Brill, 2009), 26.

148. John R. W. Stott and Lausanne Committee for World Evangelization, *The Lausanne Covenant: Complete Text with Study Guide* (Peabody, MA: Hendrickson, 2009), 28.

149. John M. Perkins, *With Justice for All: A Strategy for Community Development* (Grand Rapids: Baker, 1982), 16–33.

Urban ministers like Consuella York (1923–1995), a Baptist preacher in Chicago, demonstrated what it meant to preach Christ in Christ's way. She visited Cook County Jail weekly for forty-three years, "bringing the Christian message of love and redemption to inmates and correctional officers alike."[150] Known affectionately as Mother York, she considered the inmates as part of her congregation, Christ Way Missionary Baptist Church.

In 1970, Bob Pierce (1914–1978) founded Samaritan's Purse with the vision "to meet emergency needs in crisis areas through existing evangelical mission agencies and national churches."[151] Franklin Graham, son of Billy Graham, met Pierce in 1973, and they made several trips together to visit mission partners and relief projects in Asia. In 1979, Franklin became president of the organization following Pierce's death.

As the organization grew, Samaritan's Purse not only funded mission partners but developed its own international relief projects. Known mostly for Operation Christmas Child, designed to spread the gospel to children around the world, Samaritan's Purse formed Disaster Relief to respond to emergency situations worldwide, and World Medical Mission to provide medical care to countries in crisis. Samaritan's Purse has actively recruited and deployed thousands of Christians in relief work in the United States following disasters such as Hurricane Katrina in 2005, floods in Colorado in 2013, and the COVID-19 outbreak in New York City in 2020. Samaritan's Purse has represented the shift among evangelical Protestants toward a holistic gospel that embodies good news for the whole person.[152]

Discussion Questions

1. How does the Modesto Manifesto of Graham's evangelism team compare with the monastic vows of Pachomius and Benedict, for example, from earlier centuries? What does this say about the need for community and accountability to live the Christian life? How might you benefit from following the guidelines of the Modesto Manifesto?

150. "Remembering Consuella York, the 'Jail Preacher,'" From the Vault, Wheaton College, February 3, 2020, https://fromthevault.wheaton.edu/2020/02/03/the-jail-preacher-remembering-reverend-consuella-york/.

151. Franklin Graham and Jeanette W. Lockerbie, *Bob Pierce: This One Thing I Do* (Nashville: Word, 1983), 77.

152. Cf. Hwa Yung, "Strategic Issues in Missions—an Asian Perspective," in *The Study of Evangelism: Exploring a Missional Practice of the Church*, ed. Paul W. Chilcote and Laceye C. Warner (Grand Rapids: Eerdmans, 2008), 379.

2. Joon Gon Kim established a church among his former enemies. Who are your enemies today, and how can you share the gospel with them? If you were to plant a church among them, what steps would you take?
3. Awana is described as an evangelism and discipleship ministry to children. How does it compare to earlier practices of catechizing children as a means to lead them to faith in Christ? Why is it important to form children for a life of discipleship? What role do you envision adult leaders taking in the formation of the children?
4. D. James Kennedy advocated that pastors should see themselves primarily as equippers of the laity and model evangelism to them. How does his description challenge your previous perceptions of pastoral ministry? If God is leading you to pastoral ministry, how do you envision modeling evangelism for people in your congregation apart from preaching sermons?
5. Why do some people consider church planting the best form of evangelism? What elements of church planting make it effective in evangelism? How might these same elements become part of any church's ecclesial life?

Epilogue

Evangelism in the Twenty-First Century

Throughout the past twenty centuries, untold numbers of Christians, including laypeople, evangelists, and prophets as well as missionaries and pastors, have proclaimed the gospel with a view toward making disciples of Jesus Christ. Now in the twenty-first century, the church around the world faces new challenges and opportunities in this task.

While the popularity of the church growth movement of McGavran and Wagner was increasing, critics in Europe began to view it as the product of American pragmatism, based more on techniques than theological substance. The homogeneous unit principle as a means to grow homogeneous megachurches (and not simply a sociological principle to understand how to reach non-Christians) was challenged by critics in Europe and America as a denial of the unity of believers and a compromise of Christian ethics.[1] Critics argued that in Christ, Jews and gentiles were made one because he "destroyed the barrier, the dividing wall of hostility" (Eph. 2:14).

Moreover, critics viewed the church growth movement, with its goal of incorporating people into the church, as a product of late cultural Christendom.[2] While the movement's aim was conversion and the addition of members, little attention was paid to mission, witness, and service to the broader community in which the churches were located. Churches appeared ecclesiocentric and self-serving.[3] The local church was the end or aim, rather

1. Lesslie Newbigin, *The Open Secret: An Introduction to the Theology of Mission* (Grand Rapids: Eerdmans, 1995), 126–27, 140, 145. See Bruce W. Fong, *Racial Equality in the Church: A Critique of the Homogeneous Unit Principle in Light of a Practical Theology Perspective* (Lanham, MD: University Press of America, 1996), and Robert K. Hudnut, *Church Growth Is Not the Point* (New York: Harper & Row, 1975).

2. Donald A. McGavran, *Understanding Church Growth*, 3rd ed., rev. and ed. C. Peter Wagner (Grand Rapids: Eerdmans, 1990), 24.

3. Mark Scandrette, *Practicing the Way of Jesus: Life Together in the Kingdom of Love* (Downers Grove, IL: InterVarsity Press, 2011), 14.

than equally a means or instrument of God's mission to the neighborhood and wider area.[4]

Missional Church Movement

Proponents of the "missional church" argued that the church does not exist for itself but is rooted in and exists for God's mission to the world. God calls and sends his church to live as witnesses and servants in neighborhoods, villages, and cities.[5] The church exists to worship the triune God and build up Christian disciples who in turn engage in works of service and compassion outside themselves, and proclaim the gospel both individually and collectively.[6] The writings of Lesslie Newbigin especially provided the principal inspiration for the missional church movement.

After serving thirty-five years in India, Anglican bishop Lesslie Newbigin (1909–1998) retired to Birmingham, England. In his native country, he noticed how it had become more irreligious than when he left for the mission field. The cultural Christendom that had dominated Europe had eroded. Christian beliefs and ethics that had been the norm were replaced by secular thought and action, leading him to ask, "Can the West be converted?"[7] Although Europe had once been central to Western Christendom, it was again a mission field.

Newbigin was a native of Newcastle upon Tyne, England, and attended Queens' College at the University of Cambridge, where he converted to faith in Christ. Later he trained for ministry at Cambridge's Westminster College and, in 1936, was ordained by the Presbytery of Edinburgh to serve as a missionary with the Madras Mission in India.[8]

In 1947, the fledgling Church of South India, which began at the initiative of several Protestant churches, appointed Newbigin to become one of their

4. Although writing from a church growth perspective, Charles Van Engen developed a missional model of the local church that drew on the church's mark of apostolicity. See *God's Missionary People: Rethinking the Purpose of the Local Church* (Grand Rapids: Baker Academic, 1991), 78–79.

5. Darrell L. Guder, ed., *Missional Church: A Vision for the Sending of the Church in North America* (Grand Rapids: Eerdmans, 2009), 4–5.

6. Mark C. Powers, *Going Full Circle: Worship That Moves Us to Discipleship and Missions* (Eugene, OR: Resource Publications, 2013), 19–20.

7. Lesslie Newbigin, "Can the West Be Converted?," *International Bulletin of Mission Research* 11, no. 1 (January 1, 1987): 2–7.

8. Lesslie Newbigin, *Unfinished Agenda: An Updated Autobiography* (Eugene, OR: Wipf & Stock, 2009), 1–35.

first bishops.[9] In addition to this role, he served as general secretary of the International Missionary Council, overseeing its merger with the World Council of Churches, in which he played an active part. In 1974, he and his wife, Helen, returned to England, where he lectured on mission at Selly Oak Colleges. During these years, he wrote three important works: *The Open Secret*, *Foolishness to the Greeks*, and *The Gospel in a Pluralist Society*.[10] These and other writings profoundly shaped the missional church movement of the twenty-first century.

Newbigin observed that many churches viewed mission merely as a financial commitment to support overseas missionaries and had little or no mission of their own to their neighborhoods or cities.[11] In order to re-evangelize the West, he proposed that local churches see themselves as communities sent by God or as mission centers to reach their neighborhoods, and for Christians to see themselves as local missionaries.

This missional movement was directed mainly toward the church in the West, which faced the challenges of postmodernism, pluralism, and post-Christendom. Newbigin noted that Western culture had become "far more resistant to the gospel than the pre-Christian paganism with which cross-cultural missions have been familiar."[12] Spurred by his vision and writings, other scholars and practitioners, such as David Bosch, Darryl Guder, Paul Weston, Mike Breen, and Alan Hirsch, added to the thinking and application of missional church principles.

Fulfilling the Great Commission

While the West became more resistant, the Global South's receptivity to the gospel led it to become Christianity's new epicenter.[13] Currently, 67 percent of all Christians live in the Global South. Most church planting is carried out by missionaries who come from countries in this part of the world, in-

9. Paul Weston, ed., *Lesslie Newbigin: Missionary Theologian; A Reader* (London: SPCK, 2006), 8.

10. Lesslie Newbigin, *Foolishness to the Greeks: Gospel and Western Culture* (Grand Rapids: Eerdmans, 1986); Newbigin, *The Gospel in a Pluralist Society* (Grand Rapids: Eerdmans, 1989).

11. Michael W. Goheen, "'As the Father Has Sent Me, I Am Sending You': J. E. Lesslie Newbigin's Missionary Ecclesiology" (doctoral diss., Utrecht University, 2000), 199.

12. Newbigin, *Foolishness to the Greeks*, 20.

13. Philip Jenkins, *The Next Christendom: The Coming of Global Christianity* (New York: Oxford University Press, 2011), 1.

cluding Brazil, India, the Philippines, and Mexico. In China, India, and most nations of sub-Saharan Africa, for example, church planting is done almost entirely by nationals who understand the local languages and cultures and can communicate with the people most effectively.

With technological advances in telecommunication and transportation, the world has become a global village. People have migrated for reasons of education and employment, bringing new opportunities for evangelism, both in the gospel's telling and in its hearing. The movement of people to Western nations has brought a stream of Christians from nations more recently impacted by the gospel.[14] In some cases, "reverse mission" has occurred in which Christians from Asia, Latin America, and Africa send missionaries to Europe and North America.[15] Moreover, thousands have sought refuge or asylum in the West, leaving their homelands to escape the ravages of war and economic blight.[16] These diaspora peoples have provided increased opportunities for Christians and churches to reach out with the good news.

In other parts of the world, there remain unreached peoples who have no knowledge of the gospel and no churches within their reach. In 2000, the Billy Graham Evangelistic Association hosted Amsterdam 2000 with over ten thousand evangelists and ministry leaders participating.[17] Three-quarters of those in attendance came from the Majority World, including, for example, 495 from India and 249 from Ghana.[18]

A significant portion of this conference was for leaders to consider how to bring the gospel to every unreached people. For several days, representatives of mission organizations and denominations held meetings at seventy-five tables to discuss how to complete this task. With a vision toward coordination and cooperation, Paul Eshleman asked leaders to adopt the remaining unengaged, unreached people groups, which were estimated to

14. Jenkins, *Next Christendom*, 120–31.

15. S. Hun Kim, "Migrant Workers and 'Reverse Mission' in the West," in *Korean Diaspora and Christian Mission*, ed. S. Hun Kim and Wonsuk Ma (Eugene, OR: Wipf & Stock, 2011), 146–47.

16. See Sam George and Miriam Adeney, *Refugee Diaspora: Missions Amid the Greatest Humanitarian Crisis of the World* (Pasadena, CA: William Carey Library, 2018); cf. Sam George, ed., *Diaspora Christianities: Global Scattering and Gathering of South Asian Christians* (Philadelphia: Fortress, 2019).

17. J. I. Packer and Thomas C. Oden, *One Faith: The Evangelical Consensus* (Downers Grove, IL: InterVarsity Press, 2004), 196–97.

18. Ted Olsen, "Amsterdam 2000 Called the Most Multinational Event Ever," *Christianity Today*, August 2, 2000, https://www.christianitytoday.com/ct/2000/julyweb-only/32.od.html.

be 232. After a stream of leaders came forward to report which groups they would adopt, there were ninety-one groups left. Those at table 71 decided to "take the rest." To do this, however, they invited additional organizations to join them, forming the Table 71 Partnership.[19]

Since Amsterdam 2000, more denominations and Christian organizations have joined the effort to fulfill the Great Commission, including leaders who gather for call2all conferences around the world. In addition, hundreds of leaders gather annually at the Amplify conference in Wheaton to prepare leaders and laypeople for the task of sharing the good news with all people. Moreover, the Lausanne Movement hosts gatherings, forums, and consultations to prepare leaders to take the gospel to every man, woman, and child of the world. In 2010, the Cape Town Congress of the Lausanne Movement was the most representative gathering of Christians from around the world.[20]

Challenges and Opportunities

The church of the twenty-first century faces challenges such as articulating and defending the gospel. While Christianity's epicenter has shifted southward and eastward, discerning Christians in the Global South express their concern over the popularity of the "prosperity gospel" that promises every Christian "health and wealth."[21] This syncretistic message that fuses victory in Jesus with the "American dream" of health, wealth, and prosperity distorts the apostolic message of the New Testament. The so-called prosperity gospel is *not* the gospel.[22] As Athanasius stood for the biblical gospel in the fourth century, so the church must do so today.

The church today must contend with numerous competing ideas. There remains the teaching that salvation comes by "works righteousness," which

19. Following the Amsterdam 2000 meeting, it was determined that the number of unreached people groups had been underestimated. In 2021, Finishing the Task reported that there remain 111 unengaged, unreached people groups (UUPGs) plus 35 deaf UUPGs for a total of 146. "The UUPG List," Finishing the Task, https://www.finishingthetask.com/about-finishing-the-task/people-group-list/.

20. Allen L. Yeh, *Polycentric Missiology: Twenty-First-Century Mission from Everyone to Everywhere* (Downers Grove, IL: IVP Academic, 2016), 127–53.

21. David W. Jones and Russell S. Woodbridge, *Health, Wealth, and Happiness: How the Prosperity Gospel Overshadows the Gospel of Christ* (Grand Rapids: Kregel, 2017), 39–67.

22. Costi W. Hinn, *God, Greed, and the (Prosperity) Gospel: How Truth Overwhelms a Life Built on Lies* (Grand Rapids: Zondervan, 2019), 149–77.

fuses human merit and divine merit, typical of the medieval church. Another popular idea is the so-called moralistic therapeutic deism, which promises heaven to those who are nice and fair to others.[23] The religious vacuum left by post-Christian liberalism has been filled with postmodern ideas and ideologies that offer visions of human reconciliation, liberation from oppression, and eschatological hope apart from the person and work of Christ.[24] A form of American folk religion asserts that loved ones die only to become "our angels" and look down from heaven on us, but at times come so near that "we can feel them."[25] Of course, all such notions are *not* the gospel of Jesus and the apostles (2 Cor. 11:4). Unless the church is faithful to present the biblical gospel framed within God's redemptive story, we will not be faithful to the task of evangelism (Acts 20:29–30; Gal. 1:8–9).[26]

Thus, the church's challenge in the twenty-first century is to define and communicate the gospel clearly. For this to happen, evangelism must be biblically grounded and understood clearly by listeners.[27] This raises the need for the serious study of evangelism. Rather than following trends or adopting an approach in which "the latest is the greatest," evangelism must be informed and thoughtful. In many cases, the lack of serious study in the past has weakened, if not damaged, the church's witness (Phil. 1:27; 2 Pet. 2:2).

To aid in the study of evangelism, a number of theological seminaries and divinity schools during the twentieth century established courses and programs that moved beyond training students in evangelistic methods to the study of evangelism that integrated biblical studies and knowledge from other disciplines, such as communication theory, intercultural studies, evangelism history, and Christian ethics. In 1973, the Academy for Evangelism in Theological Education (AETE) formed as a society to support this

23. Christian Smith and Melinda Lundquist Denton, *Soul Searching: The Religious and Spiritual Lives of American Teenagers* (New York: Oxford University Press, 2005), 162–71.

24. Voddie T. Baucham Jr., *Fault Lines: The Social Justice Movement and Evangelicalism's Looming Catastrophe* (Washington, DC: Salem, 2021), 42, 81.

25. Roger E. Olson, *Questions to All Your Answers: The Journey from Folk Religion to Examined Faith* (Grand Rapids: Zondervan, 2009), 14–16.

26. Contemporary discussions among evangelicals are between a gospel of salvation and a gospel of the kingdom. For example, see Matthew Bates, "Good News? Are T4G/TGC Leaders Starting to Change Their Gospel?," *Jesus Creed: A Blog by Scot McKnight*, April 20, 2020, https://www.christianitytoday.com/scot-mcknight/2020/april/good-news-are-t4g-tgc-leaders-starting-to-change-their-gosp.html.

27. David M. Gustafson, *Gospel Witness: Evangelism in Word and Deed* (Grand Rapids: Eerdmans, 2019), 37–57.

work.[28] Those in the field have sought to engage in teaching, research, and publication that serves churches, denominations, pastors, missionaries, and evangelists around the world, and to learn from them. The importance of the study of evangelism should continue in the twenty-first century.

A number of models and methods will also be effective at reaching spiritually lost people.[29] As seen in the New Testament and church history, there has not been a single form of gospel witness but multiple forms. Theologian Helmut Thielicke insightfully said, "The Gospel must be preached afresh and told in new ways to every generation, since every generation has its own unique questions. This is why the Gospel must be constantly forwarded to a new address because the recipient is repeatedly changing his place of residence."[30] This is true not only of every generation but also of people of different cultural contexts.

Moreover, this idea can be widened to engage multiple forms and methods of evangelism in a single context. In New York City, for example, Timothy Keller advocates ministries of compassion and justice, equipping laypeople to communicate the gospel, and for pastors to preach gospel-centered messages that address questions and assumptions of non-Christians.[31] Ajith Fernando of Sri Lanka advocates that Christians devote themselves to serving marginalized groups of society, such as the homeless and the aged, but not neglect proclaiming the gospel proactively to people of other religions in order to win them to Christ.[32] Nicky Gumbel in London advocates the use of small group discussions that follow a common meal and brief message on

28. The first president of AETE was George E. Sweazey, followed by Robert E. Coleman and Lewis A. Drummond. "Past Presidents of the Academy," AETE, https://aete.online/officers-committees/. See also Charles Yrigoyen, *T&T Clark Companion to Methodism* (London: Bloomsbury, 2014), 234, and Mark Teasdale, "The State of Evangelism in Theological Education in 2019," *Witness: Journal of the Academy for Evangelism in Theological Education* 33 (2019): 1.

29. See Ryan K. Bolger, ed., *The Gospel after Christendom: New Voices, New Cultures, New Expressions* (Grand Rapids: Baker Academic, 2014).

30. Helmut Thielicke, *How Modern Should Theology Be?* (London: Fontana, 1970), 10, cited in Peter Kuzmic, "Europe," in *Toward the Twenty-First Century in Christian Mission: Essays in Honor of Gerald H. Anderson*, ed. James M. Phillips and Robert T. Coote (Grand Rapids: Eerdmans, 1993), 160.

31. Timothy Keller, *Center Church: Doing Balanced Gospel-Centered Ministry in Your City* (Grand Rapids: Zondervan, 2012), 17–20, 38, 47, 277–89. See Timothy Keller, *Reason for God: Belief in an Age of Skepticism* (New York: Penguin Books, 2008).

32. Ajith Fernando, "Holistic Mission and Priority of Evangelism," 2007, https://ajithfernando.com/holistic-mission-and-priority-of-evangelism/.

a doctrinal theme of Christianity.[33] Ben Kwashi of Nigeria holds large evangelistic meetings and emphasizes the importance of personal evangelism to friends and neighbors.[34] Ying Kai of Taiwan trains Christians to share their testimonies of faith and to plant house churches.[35] Yesu Darbar in North India forms fellowships along Indian social patterns and also establishes schools to reach Indian villages with the gospel. In several of these examples, the gospel is embodied as well as spoken, and evangelists apply multiple methods that complement each other.

As the early Christians practiced word and deed ministries, this should continue in the twenty-first century. The early church proclaimed the gospel and displayed acts of kindness toward believers and pagans. Early Christians reinforced the message of Jesus by sponsoring hospitals and schools and offering hospitality to travelers. Christ's love was demonstrated by caring for the sick, teaching the uneducated, visiting prisoners, and feeding the hungry. The church of the twenty-first century will be wise to continue these practices.

In addition to models and methods of previous centuries, the church in the twenty-first century should continue to utilize new technologies for gospel communication. A number of apps, for example, have been developed for gospel presentations on smart phones and tablets. The Big Story by James Choung is now available for download, as well as the gospel presentations Two Ways to Live and Life in 6 Words.

While apps can be used on handheld devices, there remains a need for printed Bibles and booklets. As the four Gospels of the New Testament have been used for evangelism since the first century, one-on-one and small group studies that gather people to read and study a Gospel will remain an effective form of Christian witness. Many non-Christians have never read one of the four Gospels, but when invited by a Christian to do so, they respond positively. Small group studies composed of Christians, spiritual seekers, and skeptics provide a safe context to ask questions and explore the person of Jesus. This model gives nonbelieving people the opportunity to reflect on the Scriptures and to observe the life of Christ followers. Studying

33. Nicky Gumbel, *Questions of Life: An Opportunity to Explore the Meaning of Life* (Colorado Springs: Cook, 2003).

34. Benjamin A. Kwashi, *Evangelism and Mission: Biblical and Strategic Insights for the Church Today* (Bukuru, Nigeria: Africa Christian Textbooks, 2018), 111–23.

35. See Steve Smith and Ying Kai, *T4T: A Discipleship Re-revolution* (Monument, CO: WIGTake, 2011).

a Gospel week after week gives the time that is often necessary for an individual, family, or group of people collectively to convert to faith.

In order for Christians to engage in evangelism and lead small groups for seekers, they must be equipped and encouraged by their church and ministry leaders. Jesus formed relationships with his disciples, demonstrated how to announce the gospel of the kingdom, and sent them to do the same. In the twenty-first century, pastors, evangelists, and church leaders should model evangelism also, preparing laypeople for the task. The greatest challenge will be for pastors to be equippers, not merely expositors.[36]

A number of organizations that have specialized in training Christians for evangelism should continue this work. Nicky Gumble and the Alpha Course have mobilized thousands of Christians, as have Mary Schaller with Q Place, and Ying Kai with T4T. These ministries emphasize the equipping of Christians in ways that are transferable and reproducible. In addition, Christians must be challenged to live on mission, approaching daily life with a missional, gospel-sharing perspective (John 20:21–22; Acts 11:19–21). In 2019, the Barna Group released findings in their study titled *What Non-Christians Want from Faith Conversations*.[37] The study found that nonbelievers are open to exploring the person of Jesus but look for conversation partners who will listen to their questions and thoughts without rushing to judgment against them. Therefore, it will be important for Christians to self-identify as Christ followers and seize opportunities to talk with others about Christ in ways that foster healthy conversation rather than stifle it.

As Christians are missional—sent to reach others with the good news—we will cross boundaries in our neighborhoods and communities, encountering people of different ethnic, racial, and socioeconomic backgrounds. The more that we are missional, the more we will encounter people different from us. As we share the gospel and bring them into our fellowship, our congregations will reflect increasingly those within our local contexts. The more diverse our congregations become ethnically, racially, and socioeconomically, the greater will be our collective witness to the reconciling power of the gospel.

Although churches should be missional to their neighborhoods and cities, there remains the need to send missionaries to other regions of the

36. Michael J. Breen and David M. Gustafson, *Missional Disciple-Making* (Greenville, SC: 3DM, 2019); Michael W. Goheen, "Pastoral Theology in a Missional Mode," *Journal of Biblical and Theological Studies* 3, no. 1 (2018): 118–38.

37. Barna Group, *Reviving Evangelism: Current Realities That Demand a New Vision for Sharing Faith* (Ventura, CA: Barna Group, 2018).

world. Some missionaries will go as specialists to prepare nationals for evangelism, to teach in theological education, and to employ their knowledge and skills in places not overtly open to Christian missionaries.[38]

In the decades to come, we must be reminded continually that the triune God goes before us and will manifest his creative power and manifold ministries. We trust that God's supernatural work will continue to be a sign of his reign on earth. We trust that he will lead people to faith and will use us in this process. However, he may also choose to use miracles and divine visitations, as seen in church history and in parts of the world today. In these instances, we may simply observe and discern the activity of God. Of course, all evangelism is ultimately dependent on God at work (John 6:44; 1 Cor. 2:4).

May God by his grace make us more like all known and anonymous evangelists since the day of Pentecost who have loved Christ and by the power of the Spirit faithfully proclaimed the gospel of his incarnation, crucifixion, and resurrection. May we labor with one another in this task, knowing that "this gospel of the kingdom will be preached in the whole world as a testimony to all nations, and then the end will come" (Matt. 24:14).

Discussion Questions

1. As you consider all the people described in this history of evangelism (besides Jesus), who stood out the most to you, and why? What did you learn about evangelism from this person?
2. How might you expand your gospel witness beyond your past and present activity? What historical method(s) might inform you to do this?

38. Glenn D. Deckert, *Working Abroad with Purpose: The Way of a Tent-Maker* (Eugene, OR: Wipf & Stock, 2019).

Selected Bibliography

Abraham, William J. *The Logic of Evangelism*. Grand Rapids: Eerdmans, 1989.

Ajani, Ezekiel. "Reinhard Bonnke's Crusades in Nigeria: Cultural Adaptation or Evangelical Renewal." In *Creativity and Change in Nigerian Christianity*, edited by David O. Ogungbile and Akintunde E. Akinade, 109–30. Lagos, Nigeria: Malthouse, 2010.

Albert, Ken, Susan Fletcher, and Doug Hankins, eds. *Dawson Trotman: In His Own Words*. Colorado Springs: NavPress, 2014.

Allen, Roland. *Missionary Methods: St. Paul's or Ours?* London: Scott, 1912.

———. *The Spontaneous Expansion of the Church: And Causes That Hinder It*. London: World Dominion, 1927.

Amaladass, Anand, ed. *Indian Christian Thinkers*. 3 vols. Chennai, India: Satya Nilayam, 2006.

Anderson, Allan. *African Reformation: African Initiated Christianity in the 20th Century*. Trenton, NJ: Africa World, 2001.

———. *Spreading Fires: The Missionary Nature of Early Pentecostalism*. London: SCM, 2007.

Anderson, Gerald H., ed. *Biographical Dictionary of Christian Missions*. Grand Rapids: Eerdmans, 1999.

Anderson, Justice. *An Evangelical Saga: Baptists and Their Precursors in Latin America*. Longwood, FL: Xulon, 2005.

Andrews, Edward E. *Native Apostles: Black and Indian Missionaries in the British Atlantic World*. Cambridge, MA: Harvard University Press, 2013.

Anselm. *Cur Deus Homo? Why God Became Man?* Translated by Edward S. Prout. London: Religious Tract Society, 1886.

Anthony, Michael J., and Warren S. Benson. *Exploring the History and Philosophy of Christian Education*. Eugene, OR: Wipf & Stock, 2011.

Antonacci, Mark. *The Resurrection of the Shroud*. New York: Evans, 2000.

Arbuckle, Gerald A. *Earthing the Gospel*. Eugene, OR: Wipf & Stock, 2001.

Arias, Mortimer. *Announcing the Reign of God: Evangelization and the Subversive Memory of Jesus*. Eugene, OR: Wipf & Stock, 2001.

———. "Contextual Evangelization in Latin America: Between Accommodation and Confrontation." *Occasional Bulletin of Missionary Research* 2, no. 1 (January 1978): 19–28.

Arminius, James. *The Works of James Arminius*. 3 vols. Translated by James Nichols and William Nichols. Grand Rapids: Baker, 1986.

Armstrong, Ben. *The Electric Church*. Nashville: Nelson, 1979.

Arndt, Johann. *True Christianity*. Translated by Peter Erb. New York: Paulist, 1979.

Augustine. *Confessions*. Translated by Vernon J. Bourke. New York: Fathers of the Church, 1953.

Aurelius, Carl Axel. *Luther i Sverige: Svenska lutherbilder under tre sekler*. Skellefteå, Sweden: Artos, 1994.

Axling, William. *Kagawa*. New York: Harper, 1946.

Bainton, Roland H. *Christianity*. Boston: Houghton Mifflin, 2001.

———. *Here I Stand: A Life of Martin Luther*. Nashville: Abingdon-Cokesbury, 1950.

———. *The Reformation of the Sixteenth Century*. Boston: Beacon, 1985.

———. *Women of the Reformation in Germany and Italy*. Boston: Beacon, 1974.

Baird, Henry M. *History of the Rise of the Huguenots of France*. 2 vols. New York: Scribner, 1879. Reprint, Eugene, OR: Wipf & Stock, 2004.

Balmer, Josephine. *Classical Women Poets*. Newcastle upon Tyne, UK: Bloodaxe, 1996.

Balmer, Randall H. *The Encyclopedia of Evangelicalism*. Louisville: Westminster John Knox, 2002.

Bandas, Rudolph G. *Contents and Methods of Catechization: For the Use of Lay Teachers of Religion, Sisters, Seminarians, and Priests*. Eugene, OR: Wipf & Stock, 2009.

Banks, Robert J. *Paul's Idea of Community: Spirit and Culture in Early House Churches*. Grand Rapids: Baker Academic, 2020.

Banks, Robert, and Julia Banks. *The Church Comes Home*. Peabody, MA: Hendrickson, 1998.

Barfoot, Charles H. *Aimee Semple McPherson and the Making of Modern Pentecostalism, 1890–1926*. London: Routledge, 2015.

Barna Group. *Reviving Evangelism: Current Realities That Demand a New Vision for Sharing Faith*. Ventura, CA: Barna Group, 2018.

Barnes, Linda L., and Susan S. Sered, eds. *Religion and Healing in America*. New York: Oxford University Press, 2005.

Barnett, Mike, ed. *Discovering the Mission of God: Best Missional Practices for the 21st Century*. Downers Grove, IL: IVP Academic, 2012.

Barrett, David. *Evangelize! A Survey of the Concept*. Birmingham, AL: New Hope, 1987.

Barrows, Cliff. *Singing Evangelism*. Winona Lake, IN: Rodeheaver, Hall-Mack, 1950.

Bediako, Kwame. *Jesus and the Gospel in Africa: History and Experience*. Maryknoll, NY: Orbis, 2004.

Bendroth, Margaret Lamberts. *Fundamentalists in the City: Conflict and Division in Boston's Churches, 1885–1950*. Oxford: Oxford University Press, 2005.

Berjeau, Jean Philibert. *Biblia Pauperum: Reproduced in Facsimile, from One of the Copies in the British Museum; With an Historical and Bibliographical Introduction*. London: John Russell Smith, 1859.

Bettenson, Henry, and Chris Maunder, eds. *Documents of the Christian Church*. New York: Oxford University Press, 2011.

Bexell, Oloph. *Sveriges kyrkohistoria*. Vol. 7, *Folkväckelsens och kyrkoförnyelsens tid*. Stockholm: Verbum and Svenska Kyrkan, 2003.

Blumhofer, Edith W. *Aimee Semple McPherson: Everybody's Sister*. Grand Rapids: Eerdmans, 1993.

———. *Restoring the Faith: The Assemblies of God, Pentecostalism, and American Culture*. Urbana: University of Illinois Press, 1993.

Boice, James Montgomery. *Foundations of the Christian Faith: A Comprehensive and Readable Overview of Christian Beliefs*. Downers Grove, IL: InterVarsity Press, 1986.

Boles, John B. *The Great Revival: Beginnings of the Bible Belt*. Lexington: University Press of Kentucky, 1996.

Bollback, Harry. *The House That God Built: The Story of Jack Wyrtzen*. Schroon Lake, NY: Word of Life, 1998.

Bonnke, Reinhard. *Evangelism by Fire*. Lake Mary, FL: Charisma House, 2011.

Booth, Catherine. *Papers on Aggressive Christianity*. London: Salvationist, 1880.

Borgehammar, Stephan, ed. *Kyrkans liv: Introduktion till kyrkovetenskapen*. Stockholm: Verbum, 1988.

Bosch, David J. *Transforming Mission: Paradigm Shifts in Theology of Mission*. Maryknoll, NY: Orbis, 2011.

———. *Witness to the World: The Christian Mission in Theological Perspective*. Eugene, OR: Wipf & Stock, 2006.

Braaten, Carl E. *Who Is Jesus? Disputed Questions and Answers*. Grand Rapids: Eerdmans, 2011.

Bradley, James E., and Richard A. Muller. *Church History: An Introduction to Research, Reference Works and Methods*. Grand Rapids: Eerdmans, 1995.

Bradshaw, Paul F., Maxwell E. Johnson, and L. Edward Phillips. *The Apostolic Tradition: A Commentary*. Minneapolis: Fortress, 2002.

Breen, Michael J., and David M. Gustafson. *Missional Disciple-Making*. Greenville, SC: 3DM, 2019.

Bright, Bill. *Witnessing without Fear: How to Share Your Faith with Confidence*. Orlando: NewLife, 2003.

Brock, Peggy. *The Many Voyages of Arthur Wellington Clah: A Tsimshian Man on the Pacific Northwest Coast*. Vancouver, BC: UBC Press, 2014.

———. "Two Indigenous Evangelists: Moses Tjalkabota and Arthur Wellington Clah." *Journal of Religious History* 27, no. 3 (October 2003): 348–66.

Brock, Peggy, Norman Etherington, Gareth Griffiths, and Jacqueline Van Gent. *Indigenous Evangelists and Questions of Authority in the British Empire 1750–1940*. Leiden: Brill, 2015.

Brown, Christopher Boyd. *Singing the Gospel: Lutheran Hymns and the Success of the Reformation*. Cambridge, MA: Harvard University Press, 2005.

Bruce, F. F. *Jesus and Christian Origins outside the New Testament*. Grand Rapids: Eerdmans, 1974.

Bruns, Roger A. *Billy Graham: A Biography*. Westport, CT: Greenwood, 2004.

———. *Preacher Billy Sunday and Big-Time American Evangelism*. Urbana: University of Illinois, 2002.

Bucer, Martin. *Concerning the True Care of Souls*. Translated by Peter Beale. With an introduction by David F. Wright. Carlisle, PA: Banner of Truth, 2009.

Burger, Delores T. *Practical Religion: David Nasmith and the City Mission Movement, 1799–2000*. Kansas City, MO: Association of Gospel Rescue Missions, 2000.

Bustraan, Richard A. *The Jesus People Movement: A Story of Spiritual Revolution among the Hippies*. Eugene, OR: Pickwick, 2014.

Cairns, Earle E. *Christianity through the Ages: A History of the Christian Church*. Grand Rapids: Zondervan, 1996.

———. *An Endless Line of Splendor: Revivals and Their Leaders from the Great Awakening to the Present*. Eugene: OR: Wipf & Stock, 2015.

Calvin, John. *Institutes of the Christian Religion*. Translated by Ford Lewis Battles. 2 vols. Philadelphia: Westminster, 1960.

Campbell, John. *Memoirs of David Nasmith: His Labours and Travels in Great Britain, France, the United States and Canada*. London: Snow, 1844.

Carter, Heath W., and Laura Porter. *Turning Points in the History of American Evangelicalism*. Grand Rapids: Eerdmans, 2017.

Chadwick, Henry. *The Early Church*. London: Penguin, 1993.

Chaney, Charles L. *Church Planting at the End of the Twentieth Century*. Carol Stream, IL: Tyndale, 1993.

Chartier, Myron Raymond. *The Social Views of Dwight L. Moody and Their Relation to the Workingman of 1860–1900*. Hays: Fort Hays Kansas State, 1969.

Chilcote, Paul W., and Laceye C. Warner, eds. *The Study of Evangelism: Exploring a Missional Practice of the Church*. Grand Rapids: Eerdmans, 2008.

Choi, Peter Y. *George Whitefield: Evangelist for God and Empire*. Grand Rapids: Eerdmans, 2018.

Chung, Mary Keng Mun. *Chinese Women in Christian Ministry: An Intercultural Study*. New York: Lang, 2005.

Chute, Anthony L., Nathan A. Finn, and Michael A. G. Haykin. *The Baptist Story: From English Sect to Global Movement*. Nashville: B&H Academic, 2015.

Clark, Elmer T. *The New Evangelism*. Nashville: Smith & Lamar, 1915.

Clarke, Sarah D. *The Founding of Pacific Garden Mission: Over Thirty-Five Years Contributed to the Master's Service*. Chicago: Pacific Garden Mission, 1914.

Clouse, Robert G., Richard V. Pierard, and Edwin M. Yamauchi. *The Story of the Church*. Chicago: Moody, 2002.

———. *Two Kingdoms: The Church and Culture through the Ages*. Chicago: Moody, 1993.

Cohick, Lynn. "Melito of Sardis's 'Peri Pascha' and Its 'Israel.'" *Harvard Theological Review* 91, no. 4 (October 1998): 351–72.

Coleman, Simon. *The Globalisation of Charismatic Christianity: Spreading the Gospel of Prosperity*. Cambridge: Cambridge University Press, 2000.

Collins, Kenneth J. *John Wesley: A Theological Journey*. Nashville: Abingdon, 2003.

———. *The Theology of John Wesley: Holy Love and the Shape of Grace*. Nashville: Abingdon, 2007.

Collins Winn, Christian T., G. William Carlson, Christopher Gehrz, and Eric Holst, eds. *The Pietist Impulse in Christianity*. Eugene, OR: Pickwick, 2011.

Comiskey, Joel. *2000 Years of Small Groups: A History of Cell Ministry in the Church*. Morena Valley, CA: CCS, 2014.

Conn, Harvey. *Evangelism: Doing Justice and Preaching Grace*. Grand Rapids: Academie, 1982.

Cornou, María Eugenia. "Worship as a Formative Practice: The Worship Practices of Methodists, Baptists, and Free Brethren in Emerging Protestantism in Argentina, 1867–1930." PhD diss., Vrije Universiteit, Amsterdam, 2016.

Covell, Ralph R. *Confucius, the Buddha, and Christ: A History of the Gospel in Chinese*. Eugene, OR: Wipf & Stock, 1986.

Crisp, Oliver D., and Douglas A. Sweeney. *After Jonathan Edwards: The Courses of the New England Theology*. New York: Oxford University Press, 2012.

Cullhed, Sigrid Schottenius. *Proba the Prophet.* Mnemosyne, Supplements 378. Leiden: Brill, 2015.

Curtis, A. Kenneth, and Dan Graves. *Great Women in Christian History*. Worcester, PA: Christian History Institute, 2007.

Cyprian. *St. Cyprian: Letters 1–81*. The Fathers of the Church 51. Translated by Rose Bernard Donna. Washington, DC: Catholic University of America, 1964, 2010.

Dahle, Lars, Margunn Serigstad, and Knud Jorgensen, eds. *The Lausanne Movement: A Range of Perspectives*. Eugene, OR: Wipf & Stock, 2014.

Dallimore, Arnold A. *George Whitefield: God's Anointed Servant in the Great Revival of the Eighteenth Century*. Westchester, IL: Crossway, 2010.

Daniels, W. H. *D. L. Moody and His Work*. Hartford, CT: American Publishing, 1875.

Davies, Brian. *Thomas Aquinas's Summa Contra Gentiles: A Guide and Commentary*. New York: Oxford University Press, 2016.

———. *Thomas Aquinas's Summa Theologiae: A Guide and Commentary*. New York: Oxford University Press, 2014.

De Chirico, Leonardo. "Not by Faith Alone? An Analysis of the Roman Catholic Doctrine from Trent to the Joint Declaration." In *The Doctrine on Which the Church Stands or Falls: Justification in Biblical, Theological, Historical, and Pastoral Perspective*, edited by Matthew Barrett, 739–67. Wheaton, IL: Crossway, 2019.

Dedmon, Emmett. *Great Enterprises: 100 years of the YMCA of Metropolitan Chicago*. New York: Rand McNally, 1957.

DeYoung, Kevin, and Greg Gilbert. *What Is the Mission of the Church? Making Sense of Social Justice, Shalom, and the Great Commission*. Wheaton, IL: Crossway, 2011.

Dickson, John. *The Best Kept Secret of Christian Mission*. Grand Rapids: Zondervan, 2010.

Dix, Gregory, and Henry Chadwick, eds. *The Treatise on the Apostolic Tradition of St. Hippolytus of Rome, Bishop and Martyr*. London: Curzon, 1992.

Dixon, C. Scott. *The Church in the Early Modern Age*. London: Tauris, 2016.

Dockery, David S. *Southern Baptist Consensus and Renewal: A Biblical, Historical, and Theological Proposal.* Nashville: B&H, 2008.

Dorr, Luther M. *The Bivocational Pastor.* Nashville: Broadman, 1988.

Dorrien, Gary J. *The Making of American Liberal Theology: Imagining Progressive Religion 1805–1900.* Louisville: Westminster John Knox, 2001.

Dorsett, Lyle W. *A Passion for Souls: The Life of D. L. Moody.* Chicago: Moody, 1997.

Dowdy, Homer E. *Christ's Witchdoctor.* Gresham, OR: Vision House, 1994.

Dowley, Tim, ed. *Eerdmans' Handbook to the History of Christianity.* Grand Rapids: Eerdmans, 1977.

———, ed. *Introduction to the History of Christianity.* Minneapolis: Fortress, 2002.

Duckett, Eleanor Shipley. *Alcuin, Friend of Charlemagne: His World and His Work.* New York: Macmillan, 1951.

Duerksen, Darren T., and William A. Dyrness. *Seeking Church: Emerging Witnesses to the Kingdom, Missiological Engagements.* Downers Grove, IL: IVP Academic, 2019.

Dyer, Helen S. *A Great Life in Indian Missions: Pandita Ramabai, Her Vision, Her Mission and Triumph of Faith.* London: Pickering and Inglis, 1923.

Edwards, O. C. *A History of Preaching.* Nashville: Abingdon, 2004.

Eklund, Emmet F. *Peter Fjellstedt: Missionary Mentor to Three Continents.* Rock Island, IL: Augustana Historical Society, 1983.

Elwell, Walter A., ed. *Evangelical Dictionary of Theology.* 2nd ed. Grand Rapids: Baker Academic, 2001.

Enlow, David R. *Men Aflame: The Story of CBMC.* Grand Rapids: Zondervan, 1962.

Enroth, Ronald M., Edward E. Ericson, and C. Breckinridge Peters. *The Jesus People: Old-Time Religion in the Age of Aquarius.* Grand Rapids: Eerdmans, 1972.

Epstein, Daniel M. *Sister Aimee: The Life of Aimee Semple McPherson.* Orlando: Harcourt Brace, 1993.

Erasmus, Desiderius. *The Praise of Folly and Other Writings.* New York: Norton, 1989.

Erickson, Millard J. *Christian Theology.* 3 vols. Grand Rapids: Baker, 1983–1985.

Erskine, Noel Leo. *Plantation Church: How African American Religion Was Born in Caribbean Slavery.* New York: Oxford University Press, 2014.

Eskridge, Larry. *God's Forever Family: The Jesus People Movement in America.* New York: Oxford University Press, 2018.

Espinosa, Gastón. "Brown Moses: Francisco Olazabal and Mexican American

Pentecostal Healing in the Borderlands." In *Mexican American Religions: Spirituality, Activism, and Culture*, edited by Gastón Espinosa and Mario T. Garcia, 263–94. Durham, NC: Duke University Press, 2008.

———. *Latino Pentecostals in America: Faith and Politics in Action*. Cambridge, MA: Harvard University Press, 2014.

Estep, William R. *The Anabaptist Story: An Introduction to Sixteenth-Century Anabaptism*. Grand Rapids: Eerdmans, 1996.

———. *Renaissance and Reformation*. Grand Rapids: Eerdmans, 1986.

Evensen, Bruce J. *God's Man for the Gilded Age: D. L. Moody and the Rise of the Modern Mass Evangelism*. New York: Oxford University Press, 2003.

Feinberg, John S., ed. *Continuity and Discontinuity: Perspectives on the Relationship Between the Old and New Testaments*. Westchester, IL: Crossway, 1988.

Ferguson, Everett. *Church History*. Vol. 1, *From Christ to Pre-Reformation*. Grand Rapids: Zondervan, 2005.

———. "Women in the Post-Apostolic Church." In *Essays on Women in Earliest Christianity*, edited by Carroll D. Osburn, 1:493–513. Joplin, MO: College Press, 1993. Reprint, Wipf & Stock, 2007.

Findlay, James F., Jr. *Dwight L. Moody: American Evangelist, 1837–1899*. Grand Rapids: Baker, 1969.

Finke, Roger, and Rodney Stark. *The Churching of America, 1776–1990: Winners and Losers in Our Religious Economy*. New Brunswick, NJ: Rutgers University Press, 2006.

Finney, Charles G. *Lectures on Revivals of Religion*. New York: Leavitt, Lord, 1835.

Finney, John. *Recovering the Past: Celtic and Roman Mission*. London: Darton, Longman & Todd, 2011.

Florovsky, Georges. *The Byzantine Fathers of the Sixth to Eighth Century*. Belmont, MA: Notable and Academic, 1987.

Fluegge, Glenn K. "The Dual Nature of Evangelism in the Early Church." *Concordia Journal* 42, no. 4 (2016): 305–21.

Fong, Bruce W. *Racial Equality in the Church: A Critique of the Homogeneous Unit Principle in Light of a Practical Theology Perspective*. Lanham, MD: University Press of America, 1996.

Forsyth, Alexander Craig. "Apostolate of the Laity: A Re-discovery of Holistic Post-War Missiology in Scotland, with Reference to the Ministry of Tom Allan." PhD Diss., University of Edinburgh, 2014.

Fotherby, Val. *The Awakening Giant: The Miraculous Story of the Full Gos-*

pel Business Men's Fellowship International. London: Marshall Pickering, 2000.

Freeman, Phillip. *St. Patrick of Ireland*. New York: Simon & Schuster, 2004.

Fretheim, Kjetil. "Whose Kingdom? Which Context? Ecumenical and Contextual Theology in the World Alliance of YMCAs." *International Review of Mission* 97 (2008): 116–28.

Ganss, George E., ed. *Ignatius of Loyola: The Spiritual Exercises and Selected Works*. New York: Paulist, 1991.

Gasaway, Brantley W. *Progressive Evangelicals and the Pursuit of Social Justice*. Chapel Hill: University of North Carolina, 2014.

Gatiss, Lee, ed. *The Sermons of George Whitefield*. 2 vols. Wheaton, IL: Crossway, 2012.

Gehring, Roger W. *House Church and Mission: The Importance of Household Structures in Early Christianity*. Peabody, MA: Hendrickson, 2004.

George, Timothy. "The Challenge of Evangelism in the History of the Church." In *Evangelism in the Twenty-First Century*, edited by Thom Rainer, 9–21. Wheaton, IL: Shaw, 1989.

———. *Theology of the Reformers*. Nashville: Broadman, 1988.

———, ed. *Mr Moody and the Evangelical Tradition*. London: T&T Clark, 2004.

Glassé, Cyril. *The Concise Encyclopaedia of Islam*. London: Stacey, 2008.

Goertz, Hans-Jürgen. *The Anabaptists*. Translated by Trevor Johnson. London: Routledge, 1996.

Goheen, Michael W. *The Church and Its Vocation: Lesslie Newbigin's Missionary Ecclesiology*. Grand Rapids: Baker Academic, 2018.

———. *A Light to the Nations: The Missional Church and the Biblical Story*. Grand Rapids: Baker Academic, 2011.

———. "Pastoral Theology in a Missional Mode." *Journal of Biblical and Theological Studies* 3, no. 1 (2018): 118–38.

González, Justo L. *History of Christian Thought*. Vol. 2, *From Augustine to the Eve of the Reformation*. Nashville: Abingdon, 2010.

———. *The Story of Christianity: The Early Church to the Present Day*. 2 vols. Peabody, MA: Prince, 1999.

Graham, Billy. *Just as I Am: The Autobiography of Billy Graham*. San Francisco: HarperSanFrancisco, 1997.

Green, Bernard. *Christianity in Ancient Rome: The First Three Centuries*. London: T&T Clark, 2010.

Green, Michael. *Evangelism in the Early Church*. Grand Rapids: Eerdmans, 1970.

Greer, Rowan A. *The Fear of Freedom: A Study of Miracles in the Roman Imperial Church*. University Park, PA: Penn State University Press, 1990.

Grell, Ole Peter, and Bob Scribner. *Tolerance and Intolerance in the European Reformation*. Cambridge: Cambridge University Press, 1996.

Guder, Darrell L. *Called to Witness: Doing Missional Theology*. Grand Rapids: Eerdmans, 2015.

Gundry, Robert H. *A Survey of the New Testament*. Grand Rapids: Zondervan, 2003.

Gustafson, David M. "August Davis and the Free-Free: Pentecostal Phenomena among the Swedish Evangelical Free." *Pneuma* 37, no. 2 (2015): 201–23.

———. "Church Growth by Conversion: Creating Strategies That Observe the Principles of Evangelism." DMin Diss., Fuller Theological Seminary, 1995.

———. "Creating and Critiquing Evangelism Strategies." *Journal of the Academy for Evangelism in Theological Education* 12 (1996–1997): 69–76.

———. *D. L. Moody and Swedes: Shaping Evangelical Identity among Swedish Mission Friends, 1867–1899*. Linköping, Sweden: Linköping University, 2008.

———. *Gospel Witness: Evangelism in Word and Deed*. Grand Rapids: Eerdmans, 2019.

———. "Mary Johnson and Ida Anderson: 'Free-Free' Missionaries of the Scandinavian Mission Society U.S.A. to Natal, South Africa." *Pneuma* 39, nos. 1–2 (2017): 55–77.

———. "Missionality of Apostolicity." *Theofilos* 9, no. 1 (2017): 83–104.

———. "Swedish Pietism and American Revivalism: Kindred Spirits in the Evangelical Free Tradition." In *The Pietist Impulse in Christianity*, edited by Christian T. Collin Winn, G. William Carlson, Christopher Gehrz, and Eric Holst, 199–214. Eugene, OR: Pickwick, 2011.

Gustafson, David M., and Tan Chi Sing. "Chinese Pioneers of the Swedish Evangelical Free Mission: Siu Yu Chi and Ng Shek Hing." *Trinity Journal* 37 (2016): 3–29.

Gustafson, David M., and Gregory C. Strand. "Ordination and Women: A Case Study in the Historiography of the Evangelical Free Church of America." *Theofilos* 11, no. 2 (2019): 161–93.

Habermas, Gary R. "The Shroud of Turin and Its Significance for Biblical Studies." *Journal of the Evangelical Theological Society* 24, no. 1 (March 1981): 47–54.

Hadden, Jeffrey K., and Charles E. Swann. *Prime Time Preachers: The Rising Power of Televangelism*. Reading, MA: Addison-Wesley, 1981.

Hale, Frederick. *Trans-Atlantic Conservative Protestantism in the Evangelical Free and Mission Covenant Traditions*. New York: Arno, 1979.

Halldorf, Joel, ed. *Läsarna i distraktionernas tid: Bibel, kyrka and den digitala revolutionen*. Stockholm: Samfundet Pro fide et Christianismo, 2014.

Hambrick-Stowe, Charles E. *Charles G. Finney and the Spirit of American Revivalism*. Grand Rapids: Eerdmans, 1996.

Harnack, Adolf von. *The Expansion of Christianity in the First Three Centuries*. Translated and edited by James Moffatt. 2 vols. London: Williams and Norgate, 1904–1905. Reprint, Eugene, OR: Wipf & Stock, 1998.

Hatch, Nathan, Mark Noll, and John D. Woodbridge. *The Gospel in America*. Grand Rapids: Zondervan, 1979.

Hattersley, Roy. *Blood and Fire: William and Catherine Booth and the Salvation Army*. London: Abacus, 1999.

Hawkins, Greg L., Cally Parkinson, Eric Arnson, and Bill Hybels. *Reveal: Where Are You?* Barrington, IL: Willow Creek Resources, 2007.

Hayward, Douglas. "Contextualizing the Gospel among the Saxons: An Example from the Ninth Century of the Cultural Adaptation of the Gospel as Found in *The Heliand*." *Missiology* 22, no. 4 (October 1994): 439–53.

Heinze, Rudolph W. *Reform and Conflict: From the Medieval World to the Wars of Religion, A.D. 1350–1648*. Oxford: Monarch, 2006.

Heitzenrater, Richard P. *Wesley and the People Called Methodists*. 2nd ed. Nashville: Abingdon, 2013.

Henderson, D. Michael. *John Wesley's Class Meeting: A Model for Making Disciples*. Anderson, IN: Francis Asbury, 1997.

Hennesey, James. *American Catholics*. Oxford: Oxford University Press, 1981.

Henry, Carl F. H. *The Pacific Garden Mission: A Doorway to Heaven*. Grand Rapids: Zondervan, 1942.

———. *The Uneasy Conscience of Modern Fundamentalism*. Grand Rapids: Eerdmans, 2003.

Henry, Stuart C. *George Whitefield: Wayfaring Witness*. New York: Abingdon, 1957.

Hertel, Leona. *Man with a Mission: Mel Trotter and His Legacy for the Rescue Mission Movement*. Grand Rapids: Kregel, 2000.

Hill, Jonathan. *What Has Christianity Ever Done for Us? How It Shaped the Modern World*. Downers Grove, IL: InterVarsity Press, 2005.

Holland, Tom. *Dominion: How the Christian Revolution Remade the World*. New York: Basic Books, 2019.

Holmgren, John. *Norrlandsläseriet: Studier till dess förhistoria och historia fram till år 1830*. Stockholm: Svenska Kyrkans Diakonistyrelse, 1948.

Hope, Nicholas. *German and Scandinavian Protestantism, 1700–1918*. New York: Oxford University Press, 1995.

Hosier, Helen Kooiman. *100 Christian Women Who Changed the Twentieth Century*. Grand Rapids: Baker, 2000.

Howat, Irene, and John Nicholls. *Streets Paved with Gold: The Story of the London City Mission*. London: Christian Focus, 2003.

Hull, Bill. *The Complete Book of Discipleship: On Being and Making Followers of Christ*. Colorado Springs: NavPress, 2014.

Hunt, Keith, and Gladys Hunt. *For Christ and the University: The Story of InterVarsity Christian Fellowship of the U.S.A., 1940–1990*. Downers Grove, IL: InterVarsity Press, 1992.

Hunter, George G., III. *The Celtic Way of Evangelism: How Christianity Can Reach the West Again*. Nashville: Abingdon, 2000.

Hutchinson, Mark. *A Global Faith: Essays on Evangelicalism and Globalization*. Sydney: Sydney Centre for the Study of Australian Christianity, 1998.

Hutton, J. E. *History of the Moravian Church*. Whitefish, MT: Kessinger, 2004.

Hybels, Lynne, and Bill Hybels. *Rediscovering Church: The Story and Vision of Willow Creek Community Church*. Grand Rapids: Zondervan, 1995.

Hyma, Albert. *The Brethren of the Common Life*. Grand Rapids: Eerdmans, 1950.

Isichei, Elizabeth. *A History of Christianity in Africa: From Antiquity to the Present*. Grand Rapids: Eerdmans, 1995.

Jarlert, Anders. *Sveriges kyrkohistoria*. Vol. 6, *Romantikens och liberalismens tid*. Stockholm: Verbum and Svenska Kyrkans Forskningsråd, 2001.

Jeffrey, Grant R. *Jesus: The Great Debate*. Colorado Springs: Waterbrook, 1999.

Jenkins, Philip. *The Next Christendom: The Coming of Global Christianity*. New York: Oxford University Press, 2011.

Johnston, Mark D. *The Evangelical Rhetoric of Ramon Llull: Lay Learning and Piety in the Christian West around 1300*. Oxford: Oxford University Press, 1996.

Jones, David W., and Russell S. Woodbridge. *Health, Wealth, and Happiness: How the Prosperity Gospel Overshadows the Gospel of Christ*. Grand Rapids: Kregel, 2017.

Julian, Helen. *Francis and Clare: A Gospel Story*. Ijamsville, MD: Word Among Us, 2005.

Kaiser, Walter C., Jr. "The Identity and Mission of the 'Servant of the Lord.'" In *The Gospel according to Isaiah 53: Encountering the Suffering Servant in Jewish and Christian Theology*, edited by Darrell L. Bock and Mitch Glaser, 87–107. Grand Rapids: Kregel Academic, 2012.

———. *Mission in the Old Testament: Israel as a Light to the Nations*. 2nd ed. Grand Rapids: Baker Academic, 2012.

Kalu, Ogbu Uke. *African Christianity: An African Story*. Trenton, NJ: Africa World, 2007.

Kan, Wi Jo. *Christ and Caesar in Modern Korea: A History of Christianity and Politics*. Albany: State University of New York Press, 1997.

Kane, J. Herbert. *A Global View of Missions*. Grand Rapids: Baker, 1975.

———. *Understanding Christian Missions*. Grand Rapids: Baker, 1987.

Kelly, J. N. D. *Early Christian Creeds*. Oxfordshire, UK: Taylor & Francis, 2017.

Kennedy, D. James. *Evangelism Explosion: Equipping Churches for Friendship, Evangelism, Discipleship, and Healthy Growth*. Wheaton, IL: Tyndale House, 1996.

———. "The Genesis, Development, and Expansion of Evangelism Explosion International, 1960–1976." PhD diss., New York University, 1979.

Kernahan, Arthur Earl. *Visitation Evangelism: Its Methods and Results*. New York: Revell, 1925.

Kerr, David A., and Kenneth R. Ross, eds. *Edinburgh 2010: Mission Then and Now*. Eugene, OR: Wipf & Stock, 2010.

Kidd, Thomas S., and Barry Hankins. *Baptists in America: A History*. New York: Oxford University Press, 2019.

Kim, S. Hun, and Wonsuk Ma, eds. *Korean Diaspora and Christian Mission*. Eugene, OR: Wipf & Stock, 2011.

Klauber, Martin I., and Scott M. Manetsch. *The Great Commission: Evangelicals and the History of World Missions*. Nashville: B&H, 2008.

Knox, John S. *Jacobus Arminius Stands His Ground: A Declaration against High Calvinism*. Eugene, OR: Wipf & Stock, 2018.

Kofsky, Arieh. *Eusebius of Caesarea against Paganism*. Boston: Brill Academic, 2002.

Kosambi, Meera. *Pandita Ramabai: Life and Landmark Writings*. London: Routledge, 2016.

Kraal, Anders. "The Swedish Reformation Debates of 1527–28." *Lutheran Quarterly* 24, no. 4 (Winter 2010): 373–93.

Krattenmaker, Tom. *The Evangelicals You Don't Know: Introducing the Next Generation of Christians*. Lanham, MD: Rowman & Littlefield, 2013.

Krauthamer, Barbara. *Black Slaves, Indian Masters: Slavery, Emancipation, and Citizenship in the Native American South*. Chapel Hill: University of North Carolina Press, 2015.

Kreider, Alan, and Eleanor Kreider. *Worship and Mission after Christendom*. Scottdale, PA: Herald, 2011.

Krodel, Gottfried G. "Luther's Work on the Catechism in the Context of Late Medieval Catechetical Literature." *Concordia Journal* 25, no. 4 (October 1999): 364–404.

Kwashi, Benjamin A. *Evangelism and Mission: Biblical and Strategic Insights for the Church Today*. Bukuru, Nigeria: Africa Christian Textbooks, 2018.

Ladd, George Eldon. *The Gospel of the Kingdom*. Grand Rapids: Eerdmans, 1981.

———. *Jesus and the Kingdom: The Eschatology of Biblical Realism*. Waco: Word, 1964.

Lampe, Peter. *Christians in Rome in the First Two Centuries: From Paul to Valentinus*. London: Continuum, 2006.

Larsen, David L. *The Company of the Preachers: A History of Biblical Preaching from the Old Testament to the Modern Era*. 2 vols. Grand Rapids: Kregel, 1998.

Law, Timothy M. *When God Spoke Greek: The Septuagint and the Making of the Christian Bible*. New York: Oxford University Press, 2013.

Lee, Jarena. *Religious Experience and Journal of Mrs. Jarena Lee, Giving an Account of Her Call to Preach the Gospel*. Philadelphia, 1849.

Leithart, Peter J. *Defending Constantine: The Twilight of an Empire and the Dawn of Christendom*. Downers Grove, IL: IVP Academic, 2010.

Lejon, Kjell O. "Carl Olof Rosenius (1816–68): A Personal Portrait." Translated by David M. Gustafson. *Swedish-American Historical Quarterly* 67, no. 3 (July 2016): 121–42.

———. *Diocesis Lincopensis: Historik över Linköpings stift*. Skellefteå, Sweden: Norma, 2005.

Lieburg, Fred van. *Pietism, Revivalism and Modernity, 1650–1850*. Newcastle, UK: Cambridge Scholars, 2008.

Liefeld, Walter L. "Women and Evangelism in the Early Church." *Missiology* 15, no. 3 (July 1987): 291–98.

Lindberg, Carter. *The European Reformations*. Cambridge, MA: Blackwell, 1996.

———, ed. *The Pietist Theologians: An Introduction to Theology in the Seventeenth and Eighteenth Centuries*. Hoboken, NJ: Wiley, 2005.

Litfin, Bryan M. *After Acts: Exploring the Lives and Legends of the Apostles*. Chicago: Moody, 2015.

———. *Early Christian Martyr Stories: An Evangelical Introduction with New Translations*. Grand Rapids: Baker Academic, 2014.

Lodin, Sven. *C. O. Rosenius: Hans liv och gärning*. Stockholm: Evangeliska fosterlands-stiftelsen, 1956.

Logan, F. Donald. *A History of the Church in the Middle Ages*. London: Routledge, 2002.

Long, Michael G. *The Legacy of Billy Graham: Critical Reflections on America's Greatest Evangelist*. Louisville: Westminster John Knox, 2008.

Lovelace, Richard F. *The American Pietism of Cotton Mather: Origins of American Evangelicalism*. Eugene, OR: Wipf & Stock, 1979.

Luther, Martin. *Commentary on Peter and Jude*. Translated by John Nichols Lenker. Grand Rapids: Kregel, 1990.

Lutzer, Erwin W. *Rescuing the Gospel: The Story and Significance of the Reformation*. Grand Rapids: Baker Books, 2017.

Lynch, Joseph. *The Medieval Church: A Brief History*. London: Routledge, 2014.

Ma, Wonsuk, William W. Menzies, and Hyeon-sung Bae, eds. *David Yonggi Cho: A Close Look at His Theology and Ministry*. Baguio City, Philippines: Asian Pacific Theological Seminary, 2004.

Machen, J. Gresham. *Christianity and Liberalism*. London: Victory, 1923.

MacMullen, Ramsey. *Christianizing the Roman Empire A.D. 100–400*. New Haven: Yale University Press, 1984.

Madden, Thomas F. *The Concise History of the Crusades*. 3rd ed. Lanham, MD: Rowman & Littlefield, 2014.

Madigan, Kevin. *Medieval Christianity: A New History*. New Haven: Yale University Press, 2015.

Male, David, and Paul Weston. *The Word's Out: Principles and Strategies for Effective Evangelism Today*. Abingdon, UK: Bible Reading Fellowship, 2019.

Manetsch, Scott M. *Calvin's Company of Pastors: Pastoral Care and the Emerging Reformed Church, 1536–1609*. New York: Oxford University Press, 2013.

Marsden, George M. *Fundamentalism and American Culture*. New York: Oxford University Press, 2006.

Marshall, Peter, ed. *The Oxford Illustrated History of the Reformation*. New York: Oxford University Press, 2015.

Martin, Ralph P., and Carl N. Toney. *New Testament Foundations: An Introduction for Students*. Eugene, OR: Cascade, 2018.

Martínez, Juan Francisco. *Sea la Luz: The Making of Mexican Protestantism in the American Southwest, 1829–1900*. Denton: University of North Texas Press, 2006.

Mason, Francis. *Ko Tha Byu, the First Karen Christian: With Some Traditions of the Karen Race*. Rangoon, Burma: American Baptist Mission Press, 1928.

Mastnak, Tomaž. *Crusading Peace: Christendom, the Muslim World, and Western Political Order*. Berkeley: University of California Press, 2002.

McDermott, Gerald R., and Harold A. Netland. *A Trinitarian Theology of Religions: An Evangelical Proposal*. New York: Oxford University Press, 2014.

McGrath, Alister E. *The Intellectual Origins of the European Reformation*. Oxford: Blackwell, 2004.

McKnight, Scot. *The King Jesus Gospel: The Original Good News*. Grand Rapids: Zondervan, 2016.

McLeod, Patrick G. "An Historical and Theological Analysis of Campus Crusade for Christ's Evangelistic Practice in Two American University Contexts." PhD diss., Boston University, 2009.

McLoughlin, William G., Jr. *Billy Graham: Revivalist in a Secular Age*. New York: Ronald, 1960.

Melin, Pia Bengtsson, and Christina Sandquist Öberg. *Biblia pauperum (De fattigas Bibel): En rik inspirationskälla för senmedeltiden*. Stockholm: Kungliga Vitterhets Historie och Antikvitets Akademien, 2013.

Melton, J. Gordon, Phillip C. Lucas, and Jon R. Stone. *Prime-Time Religion: An Encyclopedia of Religious Broadcasting*. Phoenix: Oryx, 1997.

Migliazzo, Arlin C. *Mother of Modern Evangelicalism: The Life and Legacy of Henrietta Mears*. Grand Rapids: Eerdmans, 2020.

Miller, Donald E. *Reinventing American Protestantism: Christianity in the New Millennium*. Berkeley: University of California Press, 2007.

Minus, Paul M. *Walter Rauschenbusch: American Reformer*. New York: Macmillan, 1988.

Miskov, Jennifer A. *Life on Wings: The Forgotten Life and Theology of Carrie Judd Montgomery*. Cleveland: CPT, 2012.

Mjagkij, Nina. *Light in the Darkness: African Americans and the YMCA, 1852–1946*. Lexington: University Press of Kentucky, 1994.

Modin, Ellen. *Eko från flydda dagar: Några teckningar öfver flydda erfarenheter från verksamheten bland Mormonerna i Utah*. Minneapolis: self-published, 1906.

Moffett, Samuel H. *A History of Christianity in Asia*. Maryknoll, NY: Orbis, 1998.

Montgomery, M. W. *A Wind from the Holy Spirit in Sweden and Norway*. New York: American Home Missionary Society, 1884.

Moody, Dwight L., Ira D. Sankey, and L. T. Remlap. *The Gospel Awakening: Comprising the Sermons and Addresses, Prayer-Meeting Talks and Bible Readings of the Great Revival Meetings Conducted by Moody and Sankey*. St. Louis: Scammel, 1878.

Moody, William R. *The Life of Dwight L. Moody*. Chicago: Revell, 1900.

Moreau, A. Scott. *Contextualization in World Missions: Mapping and Assessing Evangelical Models*. Grand Rapids: Kregel, 2012.

———, ed. *Evangelical Dictionary of World Missions*. Grand Rapids: Baker Books, 2000.

Moses, Paul. *The Saint and the Sultan: The Crusades, Islam, and Francis of Assisi's Mission of Peace*. New York: Doubleday Religion, 2009.

Mott, John R. *The Evangelization of the World in This Generation*. New York: Arno, 1972.

———. *The Pastor and Modern Missions: A Plea for Leadership in World Evangelization*. New York: Student Volunteer Movement for Foreign Missions, 1904.

Mugambi, Jesse Ndwiga Kanyua. *African Christian Theology: An Introduction*. Nairobi: East African Educational Publishers, 1994.

Murphy, G. Ronald. *The Heliand: The Saxon Gospel; A Translation and Commentary*. New York: Oxford University Press, 1992.

Nathan, Rich, and Ken Wilson. *Empowered Evangelicals: Bringing Together the Best of the Evangelical and Charismatic Worlds*. Boise, ID: Ampelon, 2009.

Neill, Stephen. *A History of Christian Missions*. London: Penguin, 1986.

Nevius, J. L. *The Planting and Development of Missionary Churches*. New York: Foreign Mission Library, 1899.

Newbigin, Lesslie. "Can the West Be Converted?" *International Bulletin of Mission Research* 11, no. 1 (January 1, 1987): 2–7.

———. *Foolishness to the Greeks: The Gospel and Western Culture*. Grand Rapids: Eerdmans, 1986.

———. *Unfinished Agenda: An Updated Autobiography*. Eugene, OR: Wipf & Stock, 2009.

Neylan, Susan. *The Heavens Are Changing: Nineteenth-Century Protestant Missions and Tsimshian Christianity*. Montreal: McGill-Queen's University Press, 2003.

Ng, Peter Tze Ming. *Chinese Christianity: An Interplay between Global and Local Perspectives*. Boston: Brill, 2012.

Niebuhr, H. Richard. *The Kingdom of God in America*. Middleton, CT: Wesleyan University Press, 1988.

Noble, Bonnie. *Lucas Cranach the Elder: Art and Devotion of the German Reformation*. Lanham, MD: University Press of America, 2009.

Noll, Mark A. *The Old Religion in a New World: The History of North American Christianity*. Grand Rapids: Eerdmans, 2001.

———. *Turning Points: Decisive Moments in the History of Christianity*. Grand Rapids: Baker Academic, 2012.

Noll, Mark A., and Carolyn Nystrom. *Cloud of Witnesses: Christian Voices from Africa and Asia*. Downers Grove, IL: InterVarsity Press, 2011.

Norton, H. Wilbert. *European Background and History of Evangelical Free Church Foreign Missions, 1887–1955*. Moline, IL: Christian Service Foundation, 1964.

Oakley, Roy Elliot. "Opening the Waiwai Ewto: Indigenous Social and Spatial Relations in Guyana." PhD diss., University of Edinburgh, 2019.

Ocker, Christopher. *Luther, Conflict, and Christendom: Reformation Europe and Christianity in the West*. Cambridge: Cambridge University Press, 2020.

Oden, Thomas C. *How Africa Shaped the Christian Mind: Rediscovering the African Seedbed of Western Christianity*. Downers Grove, IL: InterVarsity Press, 2010.

O'Loughlin, Thomas. *Discovering Saint Patrick*. London: Darton, Longman & Todd, 2005.

Olson, Roger E. *Questions to All Your Answers: The Journey from Folk Religion to Examined Faith*. Grand Rapids: Zondervan, 2009.

Olson, Roger E., and Christian T. Collins Winn. *Reclaiming Pietism: Retrieving an Evangelical Tradition*. Grand Rapids: Eerdmans, 2015.

Orr, J. Edwin. *Evangelical Awakenings in Latin America*. Minneapolis: Bethany Fellowship, 1978.

Ott, Craig, and Stephen J. Strauss. *Encountering Theology of Mission: Biblical Foundations, Historical Developments, and Contemporary Issues*. Grand Rapids: Baker Academic, 2010.

Packer, J. I. *Evangelism and the Sovereignty of God*. Downers Grove, IL: InterVarsity Press, 1975.

Packer, J. I., and Thomas C. Oden. *One Faith: The Evangelical Consensus*. Downers Grove, IL: InterVarsity Press, 2004.

Palau, Luis. *The Luis Palau Story: An Autobiography*. London: Pickering, 1981.

Park, Andy, Cindy Rethmeier, and Lester Ruth. *Worshiping with the Anaheim Vineyard: The Emergence of Contemporary Worship*. Grand Rapids: Eerdmans, 2017.

Parsons, Michael. *Text and Task: Scripture and Mission*. Eugene, OR: Wipf & Stock, 2012.

Patrick. *The Works of St. Patrick, St. Secundinus Hymn on St. Patrick*. Edited and translated by Ludwig Bieler. New York: Paulist, 1953.

Paul VI. *Decree on the Mission Activity of the Church: Ad Gentes*. Boston: Daughters of St. Paul, 1965.

Pernoud, Régine. *The Crusaders*. San Francisco: Ignatius, 2003.

Peters, Paul. "The Fruits of Luther's Mission-Mindedness." *Wisconsin Lutheran*

Quarterly 67, no. 1 (January 1970): 41–59; 67, no. 4 (October 1970): 253–76; 68, no. 1 (January 1971): 31–58; 68, no. 4 (October 1971): 237–60.

———. "Luther's Practical Mission-Mindedness." *Wisconsin Lutheran Quarterly* 66, no. 2 (April 1969): 103–22.

Peterson, Carla L. *Doers of the Word: African American Women Speakers and Writers in the North, 1830–1880*. New York: Oxford University Press, 1995.

Phan, Peter C., ed. *Christianities in Asia*. Malden, MA: Wiley-Blackwell, 2011.

Phillips, James M., and Robert T. Coote, eds. *Toward the Twenty-First Century in Christian Mission: Essays in Honor of Gerald H. Anderson*. Grand Rapids: Eerdmans 1993.

Pleijel, Hilding, ed. *På stugmötenas tid: Till 100-årsminnet av konventikëlplakatëts upphävande 1858*. Stockholm: Fosterlands-Stiftelsen, 1958.

Po, San Crombie. *Burma and the Karens*. London: Elliot Stock, 1928.

Pope-Levison, Priscilla. *Models of Evangelism*. Grand Rapids: Baker Academic, 2020.

Prill, Thorsten. *Luther, Calvin, and the Mission of the Church: The Mission Theology and Practice of the Protestant Reformers*. Munich: GRIN, 2017.

Princell, Josephine. *Frederick Franson: World Missionary*. Chicago: Chicago-Bladet, 1909.

Quebedeaux, Richard. *I Found It: The Story of Bill Bright and Campus Crusade*. San Francisco: Harper & Row, 1979.

Raboteau, Albert J. *Canaan Land: A Religious History of African Americans*. Oxford: Oxford University Press, 2001.

Rah, Soong-Chan. "The Ongoing Scandal of the Evangelical Conscience and Mind." In *CCDA Theological Journal, 2012*, edited by Chris Jehle, Soong-Chan Rah, and Brandon Wrencher, 17–27. Eugene, OR: CCDA and Wipf & Stock, 2012.

Ranck, George Washington. *"The Travelling Church": An Account of the Baptist Exodus from Virginia to Kentucky in 1781 under the Leadership of Rev. Lewis Craig and Capt. William Ellis*. Louisville: Ranck, 1910.

Randall, Ian M., and Anthony R. Cross, eds. *Baptists and Mission: Papers from the Fourth International Conference on Baptist Studies*. Eugene, OR: Wipf & Stock, 2008.

Rauschenbusch, Walter. *Christianity and the Social Crisis*. New York: Macmillan, 1907.

———. *A Theology for the Social Gospel*. New York: Abingdon, 1917.

Reeves, Thomas C. *America's Bishop: The Life and Times of Fulton J. Sheen*. San Francisco: Encounter, 2001.

Rega, Frank M. *St. Francis of Assisi and the Conversion of the Muslims*. Charlotte, NC: TAN, 2011.

Reid, William S. *John Calvin: His Influence in the Western World*. Grand Rapids: Zondervan, 1982.

Riddle, John M. *A History of the Middle Ages, 300–1500*. Lanham, MD: Rowman & Littlefield, 2016.

Rimbert. *Anskar: The Apostle of the North*. Translated by Charles H. Robinson. London: Society for the Propagation of the Gospel in Foreign Parts, 1921.

Ritschl, Albrecht. *The Christian Doctrine of Justification and Reconciliation*. New York: Scribner, 1900.

Robeck, Cecil M. *The Azusa Street Mission and Revival: The Birth of the Global Pentecostal Movement*. Nashville: Nelson, 2006.

Robert, Dana L. *Christian Mission: How Christianity Became a World Religion*. Malden, MA: Wiley-Blackwell, 2009.

———, ed. *Converting Colonialism: Visions and Realities in Mission History, 1706–1914*. Grand Rapids: Eerdmans, 2008.

Roberts, Alexander, James Donaldson, and A. C. Coxe, eds. *The Ante-Nicene Fathers*. 10 vols. Buffalo: Christian Literature, 1885–1887.

Roberts, Michael. *The Early Vasas: A History of Sweden, 1523–1611*. Cambridge: Cambridge University Press, 1986.

Robinson, James. *Divine Healing: The Holiness-Pentecostal Transition Years, 1890–1906: Theological Transposition in the Transatlantic World*. Eugene, OR: Pickwick, 2013.

Roe, Earl O. *Dream Big: The Henrietta Mears Story*. Ventura, CA: Gospel Light, 2012.

Rosenius, C. O. *Bref i andeliga ämnen från så kallade läsare, särdeles bland allmogen i Norrland*. Falun, Sweden: Huldberg, 1849.

Rousseau, Philip. *Basil of Caesarea*. Berkeley: University of California Press, 2008.

Rudnick, Milton L. *Speaking the Gospel through the Ages: A History of Evangelism*. St. Louis: Concordia, 1984.

Salinas, J. Daniel. *Latin American Evangelical Theology in the 1970's: The Golden Decade*. Leiden: Brill 2009.

———. *Taking Up the Mantle: Latin American Evangelical Theology in the 20th Century*. Carlisle, UK: Langham Global Library, 2017.

Salter, Darius. *American Evangelism: Its Theology and Practice*. Grand Rapids: Baker, 1996.

Sandoval, Moíses. *Fronteras: A History of the Latin American Church in the USA Since 1513*. San Antonio: Mexican American Cultural Center, 1983.

Sanneh, Lamin. *Disciples of All Nations: Pillars of World Christianity*. New York: Oxford University Press, 2008.

Sattler, Gary R. *God's Glory, Neighbor's Good: A Brief Introduction to the Life and Writings of August Hermann Francke*. Chicago: Covenant, 1982.

Sawyer, John F. A. *The Fifth Gospel: Isaiah in the History of Christianity*. New York: Cambridge University Press, 1996.

Schaff, Philip. *The Creeds of Christendom*. Vol. 1, *History of the Creeds*. Eugene, OR: Wipf & Stock, 2007.

———, ed. *The Nicene and Post-Nicene Fathers*, Series 1. 14 vols. 1886–1889. Reprint, Peabody, MA: Hendrickson, 1994.

Schaff, Philip, and David S. Schaff. *History of the Christian Church*. 8 vols. New York: Charles Scribner's Sons, 1882–1910.

Schaff, Philip, and Henry Wace, eds. *The Nicene and Post-Nicene Fathers*, Series 2. 14 vols. 1890–1900. Reprint, Peabody, MA: Hendrickson, 1994.

Scharpff, Paulus. *History of Evangelism: Three Hundred Years of Evangelism in Germany, Great Britain, and the United States of America*. Grand Rapids: Eerdmans, 1966.

Schilling, Heinz. *Martin Luther: Rebel in an Age of Upheaval*. Translated by Rona Johnston. Oxford: Oxford University Press, 2017.

Schmidt, Alvin J. *How Christianity Changed the World*. Grand Rapids: Zondervan, 2009.

Scudieri, Robert J. *The Apostolic Church: One, Holy, Catholic and Missionary*. St. Louis: Mission Nation, 2016.

Shank, David A. "The Legacy of William Wadé Harris." *International Bulletin of Missionary Research* 10, no. 4 (October 1986): 170–76.

Shantz, Douglas H. *An Introduction to German Pietism: Protestant Renewal at the Dawn of Modern Europe*. Baltimore: Johns Hopkins University Press, 2013.

Shaw, Ian J. "Thomas Chalmers, David Nasmith, and the Origins of the City Mission Movement." *The Evangelical Quarterly* 76, no. 1 (Jan 2004): 31–46.

Sheridan, Mark. "Early Egyptian Monasticism: Ideals and Reality, or: The Shaping of the Monastic Ideal." *Journal for the Canadian Society of Coptic Studies* 7 (2015): 9–24.

Sidenvall, Erik. *The Making of Manhood among Swedish Missionaries in China and Mongolia, c. 1890–c. 1914*. Leiden: Brill, 2009.

Sider, Robert D., ed. *The New Testament Scholarship of Erasmus: An Introduc-*

tion with Erasmus' Prefaces and Ancillary Writings. Toronto: University of Toronto Press, 2019.

Sider, Ronald J. *Good News and Good Works: A Theology for the Whole Gospel*. Grand Rapids: Baker, 1999.

Skinner, Tom. *How Black Is the Gospel?* Philadelphia: Holman, 1976.

Smither, Edward L. *Mission in the Early Church: Themes and Reflections*. Eugene, OR: Cascade, 2014.

———, ed. *Rethinking Constantine: History, Theology, and Legacy*. Eugene, OR: Pickwick, 2014.

Snyder, Howard A. *The Radical Wesley and Patterns for Church Renewal*. Eugene, OR: Wipf & Stock, 1996.

Song, Shangjie. *The Diary of John Sung: Extracts from His Journals and Notes*. Translated by Pheng Soon Thng. Singapore: Armour, 2012.

Spencer, Aída Besançon, William David Spencer, and Mimi Haddad, eds. *Global Voices on Biblical Equality: Women and Men Serving Together in the Church*. Eugene, OR: Wipf & Stock, 2008.

Spener, Philipp Jacob. *Pia Desideria*. Translated by Theodore G. Tappert. Philadelphia: Fortress, 1989.

Spitz, Lewis W. *The Renaissance and Reformation Movements*. St. Louis: Concordia, 1980.

Stanglin, Keith D., and Thomas H. McCall. *Jacob Arminius: Theologian of Grace*. New York: Oxford University Press, 2013.

Stark, Rodney. *For the Glory of God: How Monotheism Led to Reformations, Science, Witch-Hunts, and the End of Slavery*. Princeton, NJ: Princeton University Press, 2003.

———. *God's Battalions: The Case for the Crusades*. New York: HarperOne, 2009.

———. *The Rise of Christianity: How the Obscure, Marginal Jesus Movement Became the Dominant Religious Force in the Western World in a Few Centuries*. San Francisco: HarperSanFrancisco, 1997.

———. *The Triumph of Christianity*. New York: HarperOne, 2011.

Stetzer, Ed. *Planting Missional Churches*. Nashville: B&H Academic, 2006.

Stoeffler, F. Ernest. *German Pietism during the Eighteenth Century*. Leiden: Brill, 1973.

Stone, John Timothy. "Pastoral and Personal Evangelism, or Winning Men to Christ One by One." In *The Fundamentals: A Testimony to the Truth*, 12:24–44. Chicago: Testimony, 1915.

Stott, John R. W. *Christian Mission in the Modern World*. Downers Grove, IL: InterVarsity Press, 2008.

———, ed. *Making Christ Known: Historic Mission Documents from the Lausanne Movement, 1974–1989*. Grand Rapids: Eerdmans, 1997.

Stott, John R. W., and Lausanne Committee for World Evangelization. *The Lausanne Covenant: Complete Text with Study Guide*. Peabody, MA: Hendrickson, 2009.

Sunquist, Scott W. *Understanding Christian Mission: Participation in Suffering and Glory*. Grand Rapids: Baker Academic, 2017.

Sweeney, Douglas A. *The American Evangelical Story*. Grand Rapids: Baker Academic, 2005.

Synan, Vinson. *The Holiness-Pentecostal Tradition: Charismatic Movements in the Twentieth Century*. Grand Rapids: Eerdmans, 1997.

Tabbernee, William, ed. *Early Christianity in Contexts: An Exploration across Cultures and Continents*. Grand Rapids: Baker Academic, 2014.

Taylor, John. *Baptists on the American Frontier: A History of Ten Baptist Churches of Which the Author Has Been Alternately a Member*. 3rd ed. Macon, GA: Mercer University Press, 1995.

Taylor, Mendell. *Exploring Evangelism: History, Methods, Theology*. Kansas City, MO: Nazarene Publishing House, 1984.

Teasdale, Mark. "The State of Evangelism in Theological Education in 2019." *Witness: Journal of the Academy for Evangelism in Theological Education* 33 (2019): 1–22.

Tejirian, Eleanor H., and Reeva Spector Simon. *Conflict, Conquest, and Conversion: Two Thousand Years of Christian Missions*. New York: Columbia University Press, 2014.

Terry, John Mark. *Evangelism: A Concise History*. Nashville: B&H, 2014.

Theissen, Elmer J. *The Ethics of Evangelism*. Milton Keynes, UK: Authentic, 2014.

Thomas, David R. *Syrian Christians under Islam: The First Thousand Years*. Leiden: Brill, 2001.

Thomas, Norman E. *Missions and Unity: Lessons from History, 1792–2010*. Eugene, OR: Cascade, 2010.

Thompson, Augustine. *Francis of Assisi: A New Biography*. Ithaca, NY: Cornell University Press, 2012.

Tiénou, Tite. "The Great Commission in Africa." In *The Great Commission: Evangelicals and the History of World Missions*, edited by Martin I. Klauber and Scott M. Manetsch, 164–75. Nashville: B&H, 2008.

Treu, Martin. "Katharina von Bora, the Woman at Luther's Side." *Lutheran Quarterly* 13, no. 2 (Summer 1999): 156–78.

Trout, Jessie M. *Kagawa, Japanese Prophet: His Witness in Life and Word*. New York: Association Press, 1960.

Tucker, Ruth A. *From Jerusalem to Irian Jaya: A Biographical History of Christian Missions*. Grand Rapids: Zondervan, 2004.

———. *Katie Luther: First Lady of the Reformation*. Grand Rapids: Zondervan, 2017.

———. *Parade of Faith: A Biographical History of the Christian Church*. Grand Rapids: Zondervan, 2015.

Tucker, Ruth A., and Walter Liefeld. *Daughters of the Church: Women and Ministry from New Testament Times to the Present*. Grand Rapids: Zondervan, 1987.

Turner, John G. *Bill Bright and Campus Crusade for Christ: The Renewal of Evangelicalism in Postwar America*. Chapel Hill: University of North Carolina Press, 2008.

Tuttle, Robert G. *The Story of Evangelism: A History of the Witness to the Gospel*. Nashville: Abingdon, 2006.

Tyler, Bennet, and Andrew A. Bonar. *Nettleton and His Labours*. Edinburgh: T&T Clark, 1854.

Vanhoozer, Kevin J. "Scripture and Hermeneutics." In *The Oxford Handbook of Evangelical Theology*, edited by Gerald R. McDermott, 35–51. New York: Oxford University Press, 2013.

Vaughn, Sally N. *Archbishop Anselm 1093–1109: Bec Missionary, Canterbury Primate, Patriarch of Another World*. New York: Routledge, 2016.

Vedder, Henry C. *Balthasar Hübmaier: The Leader of the Anabaptists*. Translated by Howard Osgood. New York: Putnam and Sons, 1905.

Volz, Carl A. *The Medieval Church: From the Dawn of the Middle Ages to the Eve of the Reformation*. Nashville: Abingdon, 1997.

Vretemark, Maria. "Aristocratic Farms and Private Churches: The Varnhem Case Study." In *The Buildings of Medieval Reykholt: The Wider Context*, edited by Guðrún Sveinbjarnardóttir and Bergur Þorgeirsson, 143–57. Reykjavik: Snorrastofa and University of Iceland Press, 2017.

Wacker, Grant, and Daniel H. Bays. *The Foreign Missionary Enterprise at Home: Explorations in North American Cultural History*. Tuscaloosa: University of Alabama Press, 2003.

Wacker, Grant. *America's Pastor: Billy Graham and the Shaping of a Nation*. Cambridge, MA: Belknap Press of Harvard University Press, 2014.

———. *One Soul at a Time: The Story of Billy Graham*. Grand Rapids: Eerdmans, 2019.

Wagner, John A., ed. *Documents of the Reformation*. Santa Barbara, CA: ABC-CLIO, 2019.

Wainwright, Geoffrey, and Karen B. Westerfield Tucker. *The Oxford History of Christian Worship*. New York: Oxford University Press, 2005.

Ward, W. R. *The Protestant Evangelical Awakening*. Cambridge: Cambridge University Press, 1992.

Watson, Nick J., and Andrew Parker, eds. *Sports and Christianity: Historical and Contemporary Perspectives*. New York: Routledge, 2013.

Webber, Robert E. *Ancient-Future Evangelism: Making Your Church a Faith-Forming Community*. Grand Rapids: Baker Books, 2003.

———. *Ancient-Future Faith: Rethinking Evangelicalism for a Postmodern World*. Grand Rapids: Baker Books, 2000.

Wedderburn, A. J. M. *The Reasons for Romans*. New York: T&T Clark International, 2004.

Weinrich, William C. "Evangelism in the Early Church." *Concordia Theological Quarterly* 45, nos. 1–2 (January–April 1981): 61–75.

Wells, David F. "Word and World: Biblical Authority and the Quandary of Modernity." In *Evangelical Affirmations*, edited by Kenneth S. Kantzer and Carl F. H. Henry, 153–75. Grand Rapids: Zondervan, 1990.

Wells, David F., and John D. Woodbridge. *The Evangelicals: What They Believe, Who They Are, Where They Are Changing*. Nashville: Abingdon, 1975.

Werrell, Ralph S. *The Roots of William Tyndale's Theology*. Cambridge: James Clarke, 2013.

Wesley, John. *The Journal of John Wesley*. With an introduction by Hugh Price Hughes. Appreciation of the journal by Augustine Birrell. Edited by Percy Livingstone Parker. Chicago: Moody, 1951.

Westin, Gunnar. *De frikyrkliga samfundet i Sverige: Historia och trosåskådning i kortfattad översikt*. Stockholm: Svenska Missionsförbundet, 1934.

———. *The Free Church through the Ages*. Translated by Virgil A. Olson. Nashville: Broadman, 1959.

White, Jerry E. *The Church and the Parachurch: An Uneasy Marriage*. Portland, OR: Multnomah, 1983.

Whittaker, Colin. *Reinhard Bonnke: A Passion for the Gospel*. Eastbourne, UK: Kingsway, 2005.

Wigger, John. *PTL: The Rise and Fall of Jim and Tammy Faye Bakker's Evangelical Empire*. New York: Oxford University Press, 2017.

Wild-Wood, Emma. "African Evangelists: The Case of Apolo Kivebulaya." In *Communities of Faith in Africa and the African Diaspora: In Honor of Dr. Tite Tiénou, with Additional Essays on World Christianity*, edited by Casely B. Essamuah and David K. Ngaruiya, 181–98. Eugene, OR: Pickwick, 2013.

Wimber, John, and Kevin Springer. *Power Evangelism*. Bloomington, MN: Chosen, 2009.

Winter, Ralph. "The Student Volunteers of 1886, Their Heirs, and the Year 2000." *International Journal of Frontier Missions* 2, no. 2 (April 1985): 151–80.

Wood, A. Skevington. *The Inextinguishable Blaze: Spiritual Renewal and Advance in the Eighteenth Century*. Eugene, OR: Wipf & Stock, 2006.

Woodbridge, John D., ed. *Great Leaders of the Christian Church*. Chicago: Moody, 1988.

———, ed. *More Than Conquerors: Portraits of Believers from All Walks of Life*. Chicago: Moody, 1992.

Woodbridge, John D., and Frank A. James III. *Church History*. Vol. 2, *From Pre-Reformation to the Present Day*. Grand Rapids: Zondervan, 2013.

Woodworth-Etter, Maria. *Marvels and Miracles God Wrought in the Ministry for Forty-Five Years*. Indianapolis: self-published, 1922.

Yeh, Allen L. *Polycentric Missiology: Twenty First Century Mission from Everyone to Everywhere*. Downers Grove, IL: IVP Academic, 2016.

Yiwu, Liao. *God Is Red: The Secret Story of How Christianity Survived and Flourished in Communist China*. San Francisco: HarperOne, 2012.

Yohannan, K. P. *Revolution in World Missions*. Carrollton, TX: Gospel for Asia, 2004.

Zahir, Alfred. *The Apostle of the Bleeding Feet: An Account of the Devoted Life and Work of Sadhu Sunder Singh, the Faqir Evangelist of North India*. Sikandra-Agra, India: CMS Mission, 1919.

Index